CARTOGRAPHIES OF VIOLENCE:
JAPANESE CANADIAN WOMEN, MEMORY,
AND THE SUBJECTS OF THE INTERNMENT

In 1942, the federal government expelled more than 22,000 Japanese Canadians from their homes in British Columbia. From 1942 to 1949, they were dispossessed, sent to incarceration sites, and dispersed across Canada. Over 4,000 were deported to Japan. *Cartographies of Violence* analyses the effects of these processes for some Japanese Canadian women. Using critical race, feminist, anti-colonial, and cultural geographic theory, Mona Oikawa deconstructs prevalent images, stereotypes, and language used to describe the 'Internment' in ways that mask its inherent violence.

Through interviews with women survivors and their daughters, Oikawa analyses recurring themes of racism and resistance, as well as the struggle to communicate what happened. She argues that the Internment is best understood as violence perpetrated by the Canadian government and its citizens against Japanese Canadians. Disturbing and provocative, *Cartographies of Violence* explores women's memories in order to map the effects of forced displacements, incarcerations, and the separations of family, friends, and communities.

MONA OIKAWA is an associate professor in the Department of Equity Studies at York University.

STUDIES IN GENDER AND HISTORY

General Editors: Franca Iacovetta and Karen Dubinsky

MONA OIKAWA

Cartographies of Violence

Japanese Canadian Women,
Memory, and the Subjects of the
Internment

UNIVERSITY OF TORONTO PRESS
Toronto Buffalo London

© University of Toronto Press 2012
Toronto Buffalo London
www.utppublishing.com
Printed in Canada

ISBN 978-0-8020-9901-3 (cloth)
ISBN 978-0-8020-9601-2 (paper)

Printed on acid-free, 100% post-consumer recycled paper with
vegetable-based inks.

Library and Archives Canada Cataloguing in Publication

Oikawa, Mona, 1955–
Cartographies of violence : Japanese Canadian women, memory, and the subjects of
the internment / Mona Oikawa.

(Studies in gender and history)
Includes bibliographical references and index.
ISBN 978-0-8020-9901-3 (bound). – ISBN 978-0-8020-9601-2 (pbk.)

1. Japanese Canadians – Evacuation and relocation, 1942–1945.   2. Japanese
Canadian women – Social conditions – 20th century.   3. Japanese Canadian women –
Interviews.   I. Title.   II. Series: Studies in gender and history

FC106.J3O39 2012   971'.004956   C2011-902651-1

Parts of chapters 4, 5, and 10 were published as M. Oikawa, 'Cartographies of
Violence: Women, Memory, and the Subjects of the "Internment,"' *Canadian Journal of
Law and Society* 15 (2000): 39–69. Reprinted by permission of *Canadian Journal of Law
and Society*, © University of Toronto Press Incorporated 2000.

This book has been published with the help of a grant from the Canadian Federation
for the Humanities and Social Sciences, through the Awards to Scholarly Publications Program, using funds provided by the Social Sciences and Humanities
Research Council of Canada.

University of Toronto Press acknowledges the financial assistance to its publishing
program of the Canada Council for the Arts and the Ontario Arts Council.

   Canada Council   Conseil des Arts   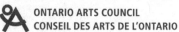 ONTARIO ARTS COUNCIL
for the Arts   du Canada   CONSEIL DES ARTS DE L'ONTARIO

University of Toronto Press acknowledges the financial support of the Government
of Canada through the Canada Book Fund for its publishing activities.

In memory of my parents,
Ernest Yoshio Oikawa and Sally Saeko Eguchi Oikawa

Contents

Illustrations follow page 172

Preface

> Thus memory weighs heavily in what I write, in how I begin and in what I find to be significant.
>
> Toni Morrison, 'The Site of Memory'[1]

The twenty-second of September 2008 marked the twentieth anniversary of the negotiated redress settlement between the Canadian federal government of Prime Minister Brian Mulroney and the National Association of Japanese Canadians (NAJC)[2] to acknowledge that the Internment[3] of Japanese Canadians did occur in the 1940s and that it was 'unjust.'[4] I drafted and wrote this book in the post-redress period and completed it in the twenty-second anniversary year of redress. In doing so, I was drawn to reflect upon how my desire to write about the Internment was fortified through my participation in the redress movement between 1985 and 1988. The research and writing of this book have also been inspired by conversations with, and critical and artistic productions of Japanese Canadians and our allies that preceded and followed the redress settlement. Most importantly, I have learned a great deal from the women who agreed to be interviewed for this book and from the Japanese Canadian individuals and communities with which I have had the pleasure of working.

While I commemorate the achievements of the redress movement and the efforts of Japanese Canadians to rebuild a sense of community and create spaces for remembrance and hopeful activism, I believe that more work must be done to represent the Internment in ways that remember those who were interned and to critically address its ongoing legacy in our families and communities. Despite the acknowledgment

of the occurrence of the Internment by a past federal government, I believe that the effects of the Internment have not be adequately enumerated and addressed, especially the ways in which it shaped Japanese
Canadians across generations and in relation to them notions of the
Canadian nation and Canadian citizens. While the Internment, when
remembered, is cast as past history belonging to Japanese Canadians,
the ways in which the Internment is connected to and is part of the
histories of all Canadians, through differently located complicities and
the hegemonies of racialization and citizenship that it helped to secure,
have largely been forgotten. Hence, the forgetting of these effects is also
constitutive of the subjects forgotten as well as those who forget. This
conclusion is informed by the interviews I conducted for this book; the
conversations I have had with people who were interned and their family members; the Japanese Canadian community organizations I have
worked with at both national and local levels in Toronto, Vancouver,
and Winnipeg; as well as by the years I have devoted to researching the
subject of the 'Internment.'

'How did the policies enacted by the Canadian federal government in
the 1940s and implemented by bureaucrats and Canadian citizens affect
Japanese Canadians[5] and, in particular, Japanese Canadian women?'
and 'How do they remember this experience?' were questions that propelled me to write this book. While (mis)representations of survivors[6]
proliferate, how do they, in their embodied selves, actually remember
the Internment in the scattered destinations to which they were sent?

I am conscious, however, that this book constitutes but a partial response to these questions. Its content is informed by my own experience as a child of families who experienced these policies and I thus feel
it is crucial that I name this at the outset. My need to understand how
this history has affected my own life led me to examine how it is remembered across generations of women. When I began to think about
interviewing women who had been forcibly moved from the West
Coast, I would often approach women of my own Sansei[7] generation
with my questions about what they knew of our parents' histories and
how they understood these histories. Inspired through these conversations, I decided to interview both mothers and daughters in my attempt
to understand how we remember this historical legacy.

I realized early on in this work that my own experience differed from
what was represented in some of the literature and depictions of this
history. In contrast to the many images I was presented of 'silent' Nisei
parents through popular discourse, I never considered my parents to

be silent about their histories of exclusion.[8] I was aware at a very early age that my mother had been forced to leave her childhood home in Chemainus, British Columbia. This knowledge came to me through our shared ritual of pouring over her photographs stored in a cardboard suitcase, photos from 'camp,' a word etched in my memory, always associated with a mixture of emotions from her recollections of herself as a young woman – grief from loss, joy from friendship, deep regret for the termination of her schooling, fear for the unknown future. All of these conversations were overlaid with a pain that was palpable, and yet I remember wanting to be with her in sharing the contents of this container of memory, wanting to know her younger self.

I also knew at a very young age that my father had fought in the Second World War as part of the Allied forces. But military service usually so revered in Canada as a symbol of citizenship and patriotism seemed incongruent with *his* experience, which was never acknowledged during our annual Remembrance Day memorials in public school.[9] I never saw anyone of Dad's likeness shown in the photographs of veterans at our school ceremonies or in the crowds at the cenotaph in Ottawa on the evening news. Slowly over time my father began to fill in the gaps in my understanding. I learned that his mother spent years in Tashme, a 'camp' different from Slocan, the camp to which my mother had been sent with her mother, while he was forced to move to a road camp in Ontario. Dad subsequently voluntarily enlisted in the British Army (because the Canadian Army would not accept him as a Canadian recruit)[10] after being moved to work in Toronto. I grew up aware of my father's anger at racism and his comparisons of the history of the Internment to other atrocities perpetrated globally.

And while Canada forgot my father's role in its national military narrative taught to me in my childhood years, the public performance of acceptable memory impelled my mother to outfit me with a poppy at the appropriate time each November. I now think that my mother knew that I would be subjected by exclusionary processes, as she was aware of her own subjection in this country and thus her provision of the visible mnemonic symbol. Mother, however, in her struggle to make ends meet, saved poppies in her sewing cabinet, and it was from this stash that she withdrew my perennial poppy. I became conscious each year of my well-worn poppy and that I had not put money into the veteran's box. Despite my mother's efforts, the interweaving of class, racialization, gender, and nationalism underlined my non-belonging and constructed me outside of the Canadian nation. I now see my mother's

actions as wise in knowing when to articulate the symbols of the Canadian nation and at the same time how to negotiate the practices of
exclusion (including her construction as not Canadian or not the wife
of a Canadian veteran by white veterans selling poppies) that occurred
during these moments of public displays of citizenship. The knowledge
imparted to me by my parents has thus led to a dissonance: Whenever
I hear Japanese Canadians described as silent in relation to the Internment, I hear *them* in those moments when they each articulated and remembered their histories, histories never acknowledged nor taught to
me in public school and undergraduate courses in university. I learned
that their utterances of the words 'evacuation,' 'camp,' 'ghost town,'
'Hastings Park,' 'horse stall,' 'sugar beets,' 'Slocan,' 'Tashme,' 'road
camp' formed part of an encoded lexicon expressing great loss, humili-
ation, separation, and acknowledgment of the suffering they and others
had endured. I also learned that each had their own relationship to a
word, something that I now determine as having to do with the spatialization of the incarcerations and dispersal, the racialized, gendered,
and classed constitution of space, and the language used to describe
these spaces. Hence my mother's more frequent articulation of the
word 'Slocan,' as a result of her incarceration there, exacted a nuanced
difference from my father's pronunciation of the word; my father, on
the other hand, spoke vividly of having to leave his employment in
Vancouver, his loss of personal belongings and the home he had just
purchased with his brothers for his mother, his forced movement with
other men to a road camp in Ontario, and how he was separated from
his mother who was sent to Tashme. These words, made through a historically and geographically specific racial violence, continue to inflect
these meanings for me – a handed-down traumatic lexicon – and I am
reminded of their other resonances when I hear them repeated even in
their benign or benevolent everyday usage.

The disjunction between my experience and the discourses that
claim to represent my parents' histories has led me to ask questions
regarding the homogenization of the subjectivities of those who survived this historical violence and the ways in which representations
of the Internment serve to reinscribe hegemonic notions of Japanese
Canadians, white[11] Canadians, and the nation of Canada. I continue
to live these disjunctive moments when my knowledge meets with the
forgetting of this history by non-Japanese Canadians in the different
social spaces in which I live. While some might argue that the Internment has been 'acknowledged' by the Canadian state and is thus re-

membered, it is *what* is remembered and *what* is forgotten that are of interest to me in this project. My work suggests that in order to promote an image of Canada as a benevolent country, national violence[12] must be forgotten, and I examine various sites in which this forgetting is actively produced.

In this book, I am attempting to address some of the questions raised by the spectre of the Internment that has affected my life in so many ways and has been a part of my consciousness from a very young age. Though these cursory self-identifiers are partial signifiers of a shifting subjectivity, they briefly historicize my interpellation as a 'Japanese Canadian woman.' I would hope that my work will in some way challenge the homogenizing portrayals of Japanese Canadians and the Internment, calling attention to the ways in which domination is made and reinscribed, and how women remember and contest these hegemonic practices.

In 1985 I commemorated the completion of my master's thesis[13] with the writing of a poem for my grandmother, Shizu Eguchi. It was entitled 'For Shizu.'[14] This poem, filled with despair and a sense of prevailing loss, was for me the only means to express how I felt after years of researching and writing about the mass expulsion and forced dispersal of Japanese Canadians in the 1940s.

Due to the destruction of connections to a Japanese culture enacted on my family, one of the many consequences of the Canadian government's actions, my grandmother was unable to read this poem because it was written in English and I was unable to write in Japanese, the language that my grandmother was able to read. It was only in 1996, when I finally mustered the courage to ask the editor of a community newspaper to translate it for me, that my grandmother was finally able to read what I had written for her over ten years earlier.[15]

There is no redemption in this telling, no narrative of facile closure. Let me just say that the Internment's shadow loomed between us as I visited with my grandmother until the year of her death at the age of ninety-eight, and it has followed me through this journey in contemplating its meaning for me and all the women I had the honour to interview in the completion of this project. My need to translate my poem for my grandmother hinged in part on a desire to repair the chasms forged between us, divisions that were effects of the Internment and other forms of social violence. I now realize the enormity and impossibility of that task and question deeply the liberal insistence on language and speech as a remedy for 'historical trauma.'[16]

This book is similar to my poem 'For Shizu,' in that it has been kept over time, written and rewritten, always in the process of becoming, yet incomplete in the articulation that lies before you. Never could it convey the complexity of the memories inspiring its creation or the lived experiences of those who entrusted me with their re-memberings.[17] My attempts to 'translate' my poem for my grandmother reflect in many ways the untranslatability of history and the impossibility of representing the totality of the Internment and its lived effects on generations of women and men. With this awareness of the fissures in my work, I offer it in the hope that the questions I raise will provide openings, challenges, and possibilities.

Acknowledgments

This book has been written over years and through moves to different cities. I would like to acknowledge the following people who have been a part of the process of creating it.

First, I would like to thank the twenty-one women whose interviews informed my research and analysis. They shared with me the gift of their words, analyses, and memories, and I am truly grateful for this gift.

This book began with research conducted for my doctoral dissertation. I wish to thank Sherene Razack for her supervision, inspiring scholarship, and support of my project. As a master's degree student, I was encouraged by Ruth Roach Pierson to conduct research at the National Archives of Canada, a resource that has been critical to many of my projects. Her suggestion for the book's cover art and her supportive words in the last months of completing the manuscript are truly appreciated. I am grateful for Ruth's participation on my dissertation committee, as well as the involvement of Kari Dehli, Franca Iacovetta, and Dana Takagi.

Franca Iacovetta encouraged me to submit my manuscript to the Studies in Gender and History Series of the University of Toronto Press and her early advice was invaluable. I wish to thank her and Karen Dubinsky for including my book in this important series.

I would especially like to thank Kirsten Emiko McAllister for her understanding of the importance of critical work on the 'Internment,' and her supportive listening to the challenges I encountered while completing the book. Her unflagging encouragement throughout the years has helped me to persist in bringing the book to publication.

I wish to thank my brothers Edward Oikawa and Michael Oikawa for their support and their interest in my work. Conversations I have had with them have confirmed for me that there is a need in some 'children of the Internment' to understand its ongoing effects in our lives.

For the support they have extended to me and for sharing their knowledge with me since I first met them during the redress movement, I would like to thank Toshi Oikawa and Nobu Oikawa. I would also like to thank the following people with whom I have discussed the book project at different moments in its production: Bonita Lawrence, Natasha Williams, Grace Eiko Thomson, Roy Miki, Enakshi Dua, Leslie Komori, Hijin Park, Sheryl Nestel, Pat O'Riley, Tania Das Gupta, Peter Cole, Barbara Heron, and Sheila Cavanagh.

I would like to thank my research assistants Abetha Mahalingam and especially Tod Duncan for his meticulous work. I would also like to acknowledge Stephan Dobson's assistance in editing the manuscript in its early stages.

For their care, I would like to thank Trudy Chernin, Maureen Dwight, Paul Jaconello, Nancy McKinnon, Tim Hideaki Tanaka, and Charles Tator.

At the University of Toronto Press, I had the pleasure of working with Acquisitions Editors Jill McConkey and Len Husband. I would like to thank Wayne Herrington for his assistance throughout the editorial and production processes, and Mary Newberry for the indexing of the book. For the time they devoted to reading my manuscript and their constructive comments, I would like to thank the three anonymous readers.

I would like to recognize the Japanese Canadian National Museum for permission to publish photographs from its collection and the individuals who donated these precious photographs to the museum. I would also like to thank the National Association of Japanese Canadians and Arthur Miki for permission to publish the maps.

For his artistic work and the art that graces the book cover, I would like to acknowledge the contribution of the late Kazuo Nakamura. I am grateful to the Art Gallery of Ontario for permission to use his painting.

Earlier versions of sections of the book were previously published in *Canadian Journal of Law and Society* 15, no. 2 (December 2000): 39–69; Sherene H. Razack, ed., *Race, Space and the Law: Unmapping a White Settler Society* (Toronto: Between the Lines, 2002), 72–98; and Rick Riewe and Jill Oakes, eds., *Aboriginal Connections to Race, Environment and Traditions* (Winnipeg: Aboriginal Issues Press, University of Manitoba, 2006), 17–26.

The doctoral research from which this book was developed was funded in part by a Social Sciences and Humanities Research Council Doctoral Fellowship. The National Association of Japanese Canadians Endowment Fund and the Japanese-Mennonite Scholarship also assisted in funding my doctoral research. I would like to acknowledge funding received from the Margaret Laurence Endowment Fund through a Post-Doctoral Fellowship held in the Women's Studies Program at the University of Manitoba, and in addition to the Endowment Fund committee members, I would like to thank Janice Ristock for this support of my research. Additional funding was obtained from the University of Ottawa and York University. A grant from the Canadian Federation for the Humanities and Social Sciences, through the Awards to Scholarly Publications Program, using funds provided by the Social Sciences and Humanities Research Council assisted in the publication of this book. All funding is thoroughly appreciated.

I have often thought of my late parents, Ernest Yoshio Oikawa and Sally Saeko Eguchi Oikawa, while researching and writing this book. It is to their memory that I dedicate it.

Map 1
Japanese Canadians in Internment Camps in British Columbia

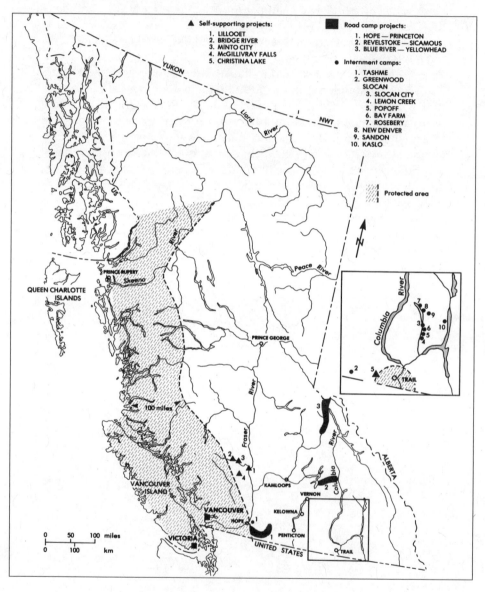

▲ Self-supporting projects:
1. LILLOOET
2. BRIDGE RIVER
3. MINTO CITY
4. McGILLIVRAY FALLS
5. CHRISTINA LAKE

■ Road camp projects:
1. HOPE — PRINCETON
2. REVELSTOKE — SICAMOUS
3. BLUE RIVER — YELLOWHEAD

● Internment camps:
1. TASHME
2. GREENWOOD
SLOCAN
3. SLOCAN CITY
4. LEMON CREEK
5. POPOFF
6. BAY FARM
7. ROSEBERY
8. NEW DENVER
9. SANDON
10. KASLO

Protected area

Map 2

Distribution of Japanese Canadian Population after the Mass Uprooting from the 100-mile Coastal Zone (as of 31 October 1942)

Road construction camps:	945*
Blue River - Yellowhead	258
Revelstoke - Sicamous	346
Hope - Princeton	296
Schreiber	32
Black Spur	13
Sugar beet farms:	3,991
Alberta	2,588
Manitoba	1,053
Ontario (males only)	350
Camps in BC	12,029
Greenwood	1,177
Slocan Valley	4,814
Sandon	933
Kaslo	964
Tashme	2,636
New Denver	1,505
Self-supporting sites	1,161
Special permits to approved employment	1,359
Repatriated to Japan	42
Uprooted prior to March 1942	579
Interned in prisoner of war camps in Ontario	699
In detention in Vancouver	111
Hastings Park hospital	105
TOTAL	**21,460****

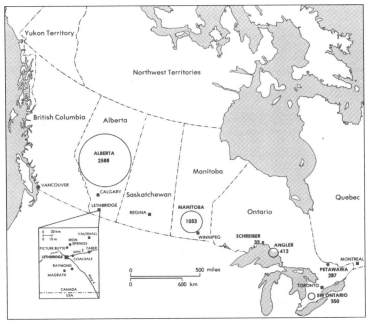

*Between March and June 1942, a total of 2,161 Japanese Canadians were placed in road construction camps.

**92 persons, representing Japanese Canadians married to non-Japanese Canadians and their children, were issued permits April 11, 1942, exempting them from uprooting orders.

Sources: Canada, BC Security Commission, *Removal of Japanese from Protected Areas* (October 31, 1942); Ken Adachi, *The Enemy That Never Was.*

CARTOGRAPHIES OF VIOLENCE:
JAPANESE CANADIAN WOMEN, MEMORY,
AND THE SUBJECTS OF THE INTERNMENT

Introduction

In 1942, after Canada's declaration of war on Japan, the Canadian federal government under Liberal Prime Minister W.L. Mackenzie King used the War Measures Act[1] to forcibly remove from their homes over 22,000 people of Japanese ancestry living within a 100-mile radius of the Canadian West Coast who had committed no crime.[2] Many were incarcerated in various sites in British Columbia: detention camps in the BC interior, road camps, and 'self-support' camps. Other women, men, and children were sent to work on farms in Alberta, Manitoba, and Ontario. Some men were sent to road camps and prisoner-of-war (POW) camps in Ontario and Alberta. Seventy-five per cent of those forcibly displaced were Canadian citizens. In the United States, over 120,000 Japanese Americans were expelled from the West Coast and incarcerated in ten internment camps.[3]

With as little as twenty-four hours' notice to move, Japanese Canadians hurriedly sold possessions or gave them to neighbours for safekeeping; with strict baggage limits placed upon them, they were unable to take much with them, and their property and other possessions left behind were held by the Custodian of Enemy Property. Authorized by the federal cabinet, the Custodian sold all of the chattels and property without the consent of the owners. The government then required that the little money acquired through these sales be used by the recipients to pay for the expenses of their upkeep in each site. Thus the money acquired from the sale of possessions and property was used to pay for the incarcerations.[4] From February 1945 to August 1945, the federal government required all Japanese Canadians to sign a 'repatriation survey,' indicating that they would move east of the Rocky Mountains (i.e., out of the province of British Columbia) or be deported to Japan.[5] Most people were required to make this decision under conditions of incarceration and destitution. Between 31 May 1946 and 24 December 1946, after the war with Japan was over, 3,964 people were deported to Japan, of whom 66 per cent were Canadian citizens.[6] On 1 January 1947, only 6,776 Japanese Canadians remained in British Columbia; over 11,000 people had been forcibly dispersed east of the province's border.[7] It was not until 1 April 1949 that the last of the federal restrictions imposed upon Japanese Canadians were removed and they were allowed to live within the 100-mile BC coastal area.[8] It was also on this date that Japanese Canadians were given the right to vote.

Little is known about the lives of Japanese Canadians during the period of the 1950s to the 1970s and descriptive histories and social analyses are needed to better understand the impact of the Internment on the lives of those interned. As Grace Eiko Thomson writes, '[T]he years following internment and dispersal were spent in re-establishing homes and jobs, in survival mode.'[9] When the centennial of Japanese Canadians living in Canada was celebrated in 1977, people gathered to remember the past, including the years of incarceration and dispersal. As Arthur Miki states, 'The next ten years heralded much community discussion and political activity as many Japanese Canadian organizations advocated for compensation for the violation of civil rights and other damages such as loss of property and income, disruption of families and education, and the psychological and emotional upheaval resulting from the wartime experience.'[10] After organizing on local and national levels, on 22 September 1988, the National Association of Japanese Canadians signed a redress agreement with the Federal Government of Canada. The agreement included an official acknowledgment, delivered in the House of Commons by Conservative Prime Minister Brian Mulroney, that the Government of Canada 'wrongfully incarcerated, seized the property, and disenfranchised thousands of citizens of Japanese ancestry.'[11]

The linear history outlined above, though incomplete, may be familiar to some readers. As Kirsten Emiko McAllister suggests, there is a need for the writing of narratives of internment that challenge such a 'repetition of linear history.'[12] In her view, '*the* history of Japanese Canadians' rendered 'heterogeneous experiences into linear trajectories' and 'entraps us ... exerts fixity, making anything diverging from it a threat.'[13]

Ken Adachi and Ann Sunahara have examined the use of the War Measures Act and the causes of the expulsion of Japanese Canadians from British Columbia. Sunahara is credited as the first researcher to view previously restricted government documents written in the 1940s regarding the practices of the federal government in relation to Japanese Canadians.[14] From this research she concluded that the federal cabinet's decision to expel Japanese Canadians was based not on 'national security' but on a 'politics of racism,' bolstered by the characterization of those expelled as of the 'Japanese race.' This racial characterization disregarded their citizenship and constituted them as enemies to Canada. As Sunahara states, 'The [government] documents demonstrate that each order-in-council under the War Measures Act that affected Japanese Canadians – uprooting, confinement, dispossession, deportation and dispersal – was motivated by political considerations rooted in racist traditions accepted, and indeed encouraged, by persons within the government of the day.'[15] She adds that 'at no point in the entire seven years of their exile were Japanese Canadians ever a threat to national security' and reveals that the decision to expel them was 'strongly opposed by the most senior officers of the Royal Canadian Mounted Police and the military, and by the entire Far Eastern Division of the Department of External Affairs.'[16] Sunahara suggests as well that economic motives were critical to the decision to expel and dispossess Japanese Canadians. Their flourishing farms, fishing boats, and other commercial ventures were confiscated by the Custodian of Enemy Property with little remuneration given to their owners.

The work of Sunahara and Adachi cleared a path for analyses of the Internment and its effects. Their research and analyses were employed and augmented by Japanese Canadian activists and writers who used their work during the redress movement to develop a 'language of redress'[17] and build collective action to protest the lack of formal acknowledgment by any federal government for the injustices endured. *Cartographies of Violence* builds on and is indebted to the work of Adachi and Sunahara. It is part of an area of scholarship and cultural production that Annette Kuhn and Kirsten Emiko McAllister call 'memory projects,' representations that 'rework ... the traumatic experiences of past generations: experiences that continue to haunt the present.'[18] While Adachi and Sunahara focused on the causes of the Internment, I concentrate on some of its effects through an analysis of memories of women who were expelled from the coast and of their daughters. I seek, therefore, to contribute to a critical analysis of some of the effects experienced by those subjected by the Internment and the non-interned generation that followed, which are aspects that have received little attention in the Canadian Internment literature.

Specifically, the book presents an analysis of memories of the Internment articulated by eleven survivors and ten of their daughters, interviewed between 1992 and 1996, and to a lesser extent representations of
this history written by scholars and government officials. The purpose
of this examination is to illuminate what the Internment produced for
the women interviewed and to consider what the implications of the
Internment are for all Canadians. The book, however, does not claim to
represent all women who were interned, nor all daughters of parents
who were interned. I argue that the people who were interned and
their experiences of the Internment can never be exhaustively represented or known. Rather than trying to record the details of women's
experiences of the Internment, the book focuses on and analyses recurring themes suggested by the women's interviews. It examines what
women re-member of the expulsion, displacements, dispossession, incarcerations, forced labour, and the separation of families, friends, and
communities. In addition to the major theme of tracing some of the
effects of the Internment, the book examines the actualization of racialization processes and racism in the lives of the women interviewed
both during and after the Internment. Other themes are the violence
of the Internment process, the interlocking of race, gender, and class
in the processes of the Internment, the spatial production of racialized
identities, the transmission of the Internment history from mothers to
daughters, and the racialized and gendered construction of Japanese
Canadian women. These multiple thematic subjects of the Internment
are examined in this book.

A question that underlies this work is, How are we each connected to
the history of the Internment? While my connections appear quite clear
and I describe some of them, non-Japanese Canadians may think they
are not connected to the Internment, especially those who were not
alive in the 1940s, did not live in BC, did not know Japanese Canadians,
and so on. The reasons are numerous. I am asking readers to see how
they are connected to the Internment and to understand the processes
that enable us to forget how we are connected to the histories of others.

Race and the Subjects of the 'Internment'

Although the biological notion of 'race' and racial difference has been
thoroughly disproved,[19] the word race is still applied to bodies, and
still draws upon mythical racial categories, that have been constructed
through histories of colonialism and racism, and the hegemonies of a

white social order. By using the term racialization, I underscore that applying notions of race to groups and individuals is a social process of producing racial difference in relation to whiteness and assigning inferiority to those racialized in relation to the superiority of those deemed to be white.[20] Hence while 'race' as a biological concept is a fiction, 'race' in its application in the past and present has real and deleterious consequences.

Often the Internment history is written as though only a few politicians used power to expel Japanese Canadians from the coastal area. While I agree that power was exerted by the federal cabinet and certain BC politicians who wanted to rid the province of Japanese Canadians, I understand power to be more complicated than this contained, top-down version. This version of power does not address how a national project, such as the Internment, could be accomplished if only a few people wielded power over Japanese Canadians. This understanding of power does not account for the participation of numbers of people in the Internment process, nor the positions of those who watched over 22,000 people leave their homes and move from place to place. While Sunahara uncovered that the leadership of the military and the RCMP opposed the expulsion, this leadership and its staff were critical to the enactment of the plans they initially opposed and the RCMP held responsibility for policing Japanese Canadians on regional and national levels, policing that continued years after the end of the war. Theoretical tools are required to address how power produced the subjects of the internment, both Japanese Canadians who through the Internment were constituted as 'peripheral *subjects* as a result of the effects of power,'[21] and those subjects who exerted power over them through processes of expelling, dispossessing, incarcerating, policing, dispersing, forced labour, and other forms of contact.

I use the work of Michel Foucault to understand that power circulates through people; people are themselves products and sources of power. As Foucault states, 'Power is exercised through networks, and individuals do not simply circulate in those networks; they are in a position to both submit to and exercise this power.'[22] Such a theory of power asks us to see how we are each implicated in processes of domination and subordination. Following Foucault, I understand power to be exercised through discourses and 'it is in discourse that power and knowledge are joined together.'[23] Discourse is not only language, but also the rules that govern their practice, what can be said and what cannot be said. Some of the discourses of race and racism have been examined in the Internment literature, for example, the notion of Japanese Canadians as of the same biological 'race' of the enemy promulgated by the federal government, which it used to justify the expulsion and incarcerations. However, understanding that Japanese Canadians were constituted as a race is only a partial picture of how discourses of race functioned in the 1940s. For example, while some people are constituted as the 'racists' in narratives of the Internment, it is suggested that some who participated in the processes of the Internment were not racist. Such a dichotomy renders some white people as 'innocent'[24] of the harms done to Japanese Canadians. Discourses of race position everyone in relation to them, and while white people may not think of themselves as racist, they still participate in the rules and practices that sustain a racial social order and from which they benefit. Racial discourses also produce knowledge and shape what is known about the Internment and how we come to know or not know about it. For example, while the social construction of race and racism in relation to Japanese Canadians has been analysed in the literature, the production of whiteness in relation to them, during and after the Internment, has itself been less analysed.[25] The power that is embedded in the privilege of whiteness continues in the lack of analysis of how racial discourses are relational and how they procure power for and bring benefit to differently socially located white subjects through the racialization of Japanese Canadians. An example of how knowledge is produced by and how it sustains racial discourse is the prominent focus on what is constructed as the 'silent' female survivor of the Internment. The trope of the silent Japanese Canadian female survivor, as I argue in chapter 2, is shaped through raced and gendered notions of Japanese Canadian women, enabling the circulation and reproduction of racialized and gendered notions of them while the silence of white participants in and white witnesses to the Internment goes unremarked, reproducing the unmarking of the power of whiteness. Hence whiteness is discursively unmarked and normalized through some of the Internment narratives themselves. Therefore, in representing the racialization of Japanese Canadians in the past, we may reproduce the rules that produce white domination in the present. Discourses of the Internment themselves, as McAllister suggests above, may fix what can and cannot be said about it. In examining some of the processes of racialization and their effects as reported by Japanese Canadian women, I argue that the Internment played and plays a critical role in making and reproducing a racial social order in Canada.

Modernist thinking promotes the notion of a person as fixed and unitary. Critics of this analysis of the subject, including postmodern thinkers, argue that subjects do not come ready made with innate or 'essential' qualities, rather they are 'constituted and self-constituting within particular discursive formations.'[26] Hence subjects are produced through discourses of power. While I focus my discourse analysis on the testimonies of Japanese Canadian women and the processes of their production as gendered, racialized, and classed subjects, I wish to signal that their construction is relational to the construction of those who authorized and organized the practices of the Internment, those with whom they have interacted 'after' the Internment, and those who continue to produce knowledge about them, engagements that construct both individual and national identities.

The racialization of Japanese Canadians as an enemy 'race' served to normalize the identity of a Canadian citizen as white. The web of power authorized through the War Measures Act enabled the making of white bourgeois subjects who were deemed lawful and the subordination of Japanese Canadian subjects who were without the protection of the law. While it is ultimately white bourgeois subjects who held the most political power in Canada and who enacted the Orders-in-Council[27] that determined the fate of Japanese Canadians in the 1940s, white citizens of both genders, different class backgrounds, and ethnicities served in implementing the orders and in policing Japanese Canadians and also benefited from their expulsion. Through the expulsion, incarceration, and dispersal, the Mackenzie King government created a network of surveillance, policing, and control simultaneous to the production of sites to which Japanese Canadians were sent. White working-class and ethnicized people were differently situated socially from white anglo-bourgeois subjects in the web of power, yet the Internment allowed them various entry points into the national racial project of expulsion, discipline, and control of Japanese Canadians. Hence their participation may have had a role in shifting some of their social positions and in supporting the racial exclusion that the Internment secured. Importantly, whiteness itself was reinforced through the carving out of spaces of entitlement for white citizens in relation to the sites of exclusion inhabited by Japanese Canadians, something from which all citizens constructed as white benefited. It is these and other 'effects of the power of ... discourse[s]'[28] mobilized in relation to the Internment that I analyse in relation to some of its numerous subjects.

The draconian use of the War Measures Act against Japanese Canadians in the 1940s is sometimes deemed uncharacteristic of Canada as a liberal democracy. However, Ian McKay argues that the 'internment and subsequent disenfranchisement of Japanese Canadians by the Liberal government in the 1940s ... [are] indications of underlying organic tensions within the liberal project itself.'[29] Sunahara also points out the contradiction that 'Canada imposed repressive policies on a racial minority while ostensibly fighting for justice and equality for all.'[30]

In this regard, I am interested in how violence can be instituted and masked using a discourse of liberalism. As Saidiya Hartman argues, '[T]he universality or unencumbered individuality of liberalism relies on tacit exclusions and norms that preclude substantive equality ... Abstract universality presumes particular forms of embodiment and excludes or marginalizes others.'[31] Liberal notions, such as 'freedom' and 'humanity,' were used in relation to the subjects of the Internment and as I argue, their moments of articulation were instances of relational subject constitution, that of the Japanese Canadian subject denied the rights of liberalism (though this denial was masked through the use of these very concepts) and the subject entitled to these rights.

As Sunera Thobani argues, the modernist notion of the subject as a 'stable, conscious, unified, and enduring figure, whose actions are shaped primarily by reason' is foundational to the creation of the mythology of the Canadian 'national' subject who is deserving of rights and the benefits of citizenship. [32] This national subject's qualities and 'humanity' are presented as naturally embodied in certain Canadians who are then deemed deserving of the rights that they accrue. As Thobani argues, 'In the case of Canada, the historical exaltation of the national subject has ennobled this subject's humanity and sanctioned the elevation of its rights over and above that of the Aboriginal and the immigrant.'[33] In my critique of the symbolic liberal subject, I concentrate on these features: the notion that he[34] is an autonomous, rational, humane individual and that this symbolic Canadian subject was formed in relation to Japanese Canadians during the 1940s and materialized through the subjecthood claimed by some of the enactors of and the administrators and witnesses to the Internment process.

Wendy Brown explains how autonomy is accomplished for the liberal subject: 'political membership in the liberal state involves abstracting from one's social being, it involves abstracting not only from the contingent productions of one's life circumstances but from the *identificatory* processes constitutive of one's social construction and position.'[35]

Hence the liberal autonomous subject cannot be tethered by history and therefore must forget his historical attachments to and dependence upon the exclusion of others. He must forget that his autonomy and freedom are secured through the non-freedom of others. He must forget that his identity is relational to the identities of others and the processes of domination that produce it. The forgetting of the history of the Internment and its effects, therefore, produces the subjects forgotten and the forgetting subjects. In contrast, the women interviewed for this book indicated that their subjecthoods were historically forged and their histories interconnected with those of other Japanese Canadians. In this book I am most interested in how Japanese Canadian women re-member the Internment. Their memories contest a forgetting of their selves and the effects of the Internment, a forgetting that I argue was instrumental in producing notions of the liberal subject 'without' history and a white subject disengaged from a history of racial violence. As Ernest Renan argues in his oft-cited quote, 'Forgetting, I would even go so far as to say historical error, is a crucial factor in the creation of a nation ...'[36] While some might argue that the Internment is remembered by non-Japanese Canadians, in this book I ask questions about what is remembered and what this remembrance procures for Japanese Canadians, other Canadian citizens, and for the Canadian nation. I also point to examples of 'highly organized and strategic'[37] forgetting of the many subjects and effects of the Internment. It is these processes of remembering and forgetting that position us and that continue to construct us in relation to the Internment and its multiple subjects.

Space, Interlocking Analysis, and the Subjects of the Internment

As is illustrated through the literature, Canadian law was used to authorize the expulsion, the incarcerations, and the dispersal that ensued. The enactors of the War Measures Act and Orders-in-Council and their administrators established who went where. Audrey Kobayashi has analysed the use of Canadian law to produce the racial and spatial exclusion of Japanese Canadians.[38] In addition, Kirsten Emiko McAllister has examined social and geographical aspects of the New Denver incarceration site, particularly in its contemporary use as a commemorative location of the Nikkei Internment Memorial Centre.[39] While the extant literature on the Internment describes this and other BC interior camps, and other sites of incarceration, for example, the sugar beet farms, the prisoner-of-war camps, 'self-support' camps, and the road camps,[40]

little work exists that analyses the sites and their connection to the production of the identities of the people interned.

While over 22,000 Japanese Canadians were removed from the
coastal area and were cast as one 'race,' women's experiences were not
identical to men's or even each other's. The federal government and
its administrators used discourses of race, gender, class, ability, nationality, and others in determining who went where. Each discourse affected and enabled the other and their interlocking insinuated power
relations in a complex way producing hierarchies of relational subjects
in relational places. Discourses of power produced different subject positions[41] for each person, imposed and assumed, positions from which
they experienced the Internment and from which they remember it. I
use a feminist interlocking analysis[42] to examine some of the discourses
producing the sites of the Internment and produced through them in
order to see the people whose identities were made through these discourses and spaces and who were greatly affected by them.

Caroline Knowles defines the concept of space as a 'general category
from which places are made in more specific terms.'[43] Place, on the
other hand, as Doreen Massey points out, has an identity, which is a
product of social interactions.[44] Cultural geographers ask us to see the
connections between places and the identities of the people who inhabit them. For example, Edward Soja argues that space is not 'fixed,
dead, undialectical'[45] but has a critical and interactive relationship to
the people who inhabit a given place and to the places and people
seemingly exterior to it. Forcibly moving 22,000 people across municipal, provincial, and national boundaries was a profoundly spatialized
and deliberate orchestration. While it is clear that the places of incarceration were 'material'[46] in their geography and topography, and I
use this term to denote these aspects, I also understand the 'spatial'
to be socially constructed.[47] Such an analysis is particularly useful to
understanding the complex spatial construction of the Internment in
relation to the identities of the people who were incarcerated. As Radhika Mohanram argues, 'racial difference is also spatial difference';[48]
places are used to make racial and other identities stick to the bodies
inhabiting them. Racialized spaces are established as inferior to white
bourgeois spaces as part of the production of differing entitlements to
power. Space, therefore, serves to make relational identities.

Richard Phillips uses the term 'unmap' to describe the project of
'denaturalis[ing] geography,' in order 'to undermine world views that
rest upon it.'[49] I use the concept of 'unmapping' in order to render vis-

ible the material and symbolic connections between the places in which Japanese Canadians were incarcerated and the making of the nation of Canada. Canada was founded through the expulsion of Indigenous peoples by European settlers from their territories. The violence of colonialism, including the confiscation of land, was thus foundational to the making of a white Canadian settler nation. Those who had the power to expel also had the power to map and to name. In banishing Indigenous peoples from cities and the centres of political power to reserves, white settlers constituted Indigenous spaces as uncivilized or 'degenerate'[50] in relation to their own communities, which were deemed civilized and respectable. This relational spatial and social construction was used by white settlers to justify the colonial project and the continuing domination over the land and those indigenous to it, rendering Indigenous peoples marginal to a national narrative of progress. Japanese Canadians were expelled from the restricted BC coastal area in the 1940s and their spaces of incarceration were used to further racialize them as foreign to Canada and to mark them as potentially disloyal and dangerous, thus requiring their distance from white populations whose spatial security was considered sacrosanct. I propose to pay attention to the production of the spaces of the Internment, asking what the forced movement of over 22,000 people and the places in which they were incarcerated enabled both in the past and the present, and the role the Internment has played in the reproduction of a racial social order and a white settler nation-state.

By using the term cartography I underline that the mapping of the Internment physically and socially expelled Japanese Canadians from the nation as well as the rights of citizenship. As Kathleen Kirby argues, cartography is used as the 'measure between human and non-human, civilized and savage' and 'reinforce[s] the lines drawn between European white subjects and Others.'[51] I underline that the material and the social were mapped out for Japanese Canadians: the specific delineation of the 100-mile restricted coastal area from which Japanese Canadians were forced to move and the numerous spaces of incarceration and dispersal, including those in which they currently live.

I consider Japanese Canadians to have been incarcerated in the places of the Internment. I use Foucault's concept of the 'carceral'[52] to describe the spaces in which Japanese Canadians were subjected to practices of punishment, constraint, surveillance, coercion, supervision, and moral regulation. I also describe these processes as racial and 'national' violence done to over 22,000 persons, individual in their application and effects and national in their source, scope, and effects. As Nicholas Blomley argues, expulsion itself is violence and 'violence has a geography.'[53] However, maps can also be used to forget violence through the erasure of the people whose lives are mapped by them; the very places and place names may also obscure their real purpose; in addition, the erasure of the places on subsequent maps or evidence of their past purposes if the names are retained can be used to forget those who were incarcerated in them.

The women interviewed, however, re-member the places of the Internment and the effects of their dis-placements. Their testimonies unmap the relational construction of the places of the Internment and the relational identities of people incarcerated therein. The noun 'cartography' is pluralized to emphasize the numerous social and material geographies lived by each person, heterogeneous by virtue of the different sites of incarceration and dispersal, and the subjects interpellated through relational spatial segregations and social divisions. As I will show, survivors' memories are themselves affected by the places of the Internment. The places of their mothers' incarcerations are also critical to their daughters' efforts to re-member the Internment and understand its effects in their own lives. Unmistakably articulated through the twenty-one interviews were the long-term effects of the Internment upon survivors and subsequent generations, effects that underlined the systematic exclusions of white racial domination over time and space. Importantly, the notion of cartographies of violence illuminates that the mapping of the Internment and the making of the subjects of the Internment is relational to the mapping of Canada and the making of the nation and its citizens, based in part upon systematic racial, gendered, classed, and other exclusions. Tracing the specific geographies of the Internment uncovers both the scale of the violence perpetrated on Japanese Canadians and the microprocesses of power required to accomplish it.

Women's memories also reveal histories of struggles against racism in Canada and various forms of resistance as part of these struggles. Foucault reminds us that '[w]here there is power, there is resistance ... this resistance is never in a position of exteriority in relation to power.'[54] Unmapping itself, as Richard Phillips argues, is a form of resistance to 'mapped world views.'[55] While I problematize the notion of 'resistance' as it is written in some of the narratives of the Internment, I am also aware that the concept of resistance, although often used to convey the idea that people contest domination, can in its instantiations reinforce

the hegemonies of power that they wish to contest.[56] I am cognizant
as well of the dangers in representing women's memories, knowing
that they run the risk of 're-codification, re-colonisation,'[57] given the
hegemonies that continue to construct them as subjects, and the racialized, gendered, and classed ways in which Japanese Canadian women
are read.

Overview of the Book

In chapter 1, I illustrate how the violence inherent to a process that
subjugated Japanese Canadians was minimized and forgotten through
representations authored by the federal government and its administrators. In this chapter, I raise questions about historical and political
representations of the Internment that continue to produce a forgetting
of the harms of the Internment through liberal narratives and static, homogenizing characterizations of Japanese Canadians. In chapters 1 and
2, I argue that the Internment was and is productive of both Japanese
Canadian and white subjects and illustrate moments of this relational
construction. As I contend in chapter 1 and throughout the book, the Internment helped to secure the notion of a liberal white Canadian subject
– autonomous, rational, and humane – in relation to Japanese Canadians. In chapter 2, I take a closer look at some of the tropes operationalized in representations of the Internment that produce the gendered,
racialized Japanese Canadian female survivor. In particular, the image
of the 'silent' female survivor is examined for its raced and gendered
significations. Here, I also ask questions about the subjects remembered
(and what is remembered about them) and the subjects forgotten.

Chapter 3 discusses the method of interviewing and raises methodological issues related to recounting and witnessing Internment testimonies. In this chapter, I present my concept of 'memory of community'[58]
(later applied in chapter 7) to explain how the memories of the Internment reported by women were informed by their connections to others
interned. This concept derives from women's narratives that are replete
with descriptions of the wrenching apart of families, friends, and communities. Hence their representations of their histories are constructed
in relation to the histories of other people and communities interned.

Chapter 4 begins an analysis of the spatialization of the Internment.
The spatial methodology used in chapters 4 through 9 was inspired by
each woman's vivid description of the places to which they were moved
and the places from which they were excluded. I examine some of the

ways in which women describe the effects of the initial implementation of the War Measures Act authorizing the increasing limitation of spaces in which Japanese Canadians were allowed to exist prior to their expulsion and begin a relational analysis of some of the incarceration sites.

In chapters 5 and 6, I examine how the interlocking discourses of race, gender, class, sexuality, and ability produced carceral spaces and the relational subjects interned therein and how they were used to socially and spatially divide families and communities. In these chapters, I illustrate how the carceral places themselves affect memory and how the processes that created them are, as a result, difficult to describe.

In chapter 7, I re-member some of the people lost during the Internment and conclude my discussion of the internment years by asking questions about representations of the family and the subject in interpretations of women's testimonies. The discussion of what the Internment produced for daughters is the focus of chapters 8 and 9. Chapter 8 examines the transmission of memories of the Internment from mothers to daughters and analyses some of the effects of the Internment as reported by the daughters. As did their mothers, the daughters each mentioned places of incarceration; the daughters tried to imagine and represent to themselves and me where their mothers had lived before their expulsion and where they had lived during the years of incarceration. The daughters' descriptions, in chapters 8 and 9, of where and how they learned about the Internment and where they were able and not able to learn about this history, underline the importance of place and ongoing processes of racial exclusion in memory and knowledge production. Chapter 9 illustrates how women use 'subjugated knowledges'[59] in order to contest the forgetting of the Internment. The daughters' descriptions of their experiences of racism as connected to the history of the Internment signals some of the ongoing processes of racial construction and exclusion in Canada.

Re-membering the places of the Internment and the people who were forced into them, as these women do, reveals part of the ideological and spatial framework through which Canada was made and the simultaneous implementation of the enactment and forgetting of national violence that have been essential to the project of Canadian nation-building and the making of citizens. The women interviewed verbally unmap the nation, revealing how their identities as racial Others were imposed and reinforced through spatial exclusions, rendering visible how Canada is built and rebuilt through struggles over entitlement to place and citizenship. Their memories contest the fixed and immutable atlas version of Canada and a narrative of Canadian history writ large as harmonious progress. Their dispersed presence across the country begs us to engage with how histories of violence are procured and then deliberately forgotten through the mapping of Canada and hegemonic ideologies of forgetting. Their memories of racism and their lived geographies of racial exclusion, including the very production of the separated places in which they currently live, enable us to see how the racial social order was historically and geographically produced in Canada, and hence how it produced Canada. This book, therefore, is also about how the Internment was critical in making the Canadian nation, a material and discursive process through which subjects were and are made with consequences that affect all those who constitute themselves as citizens of Canada.

While I am cognizant of the fact that I write after the redress settlement of 1988, I argue that despite the formal 'acknowledgment' by a Canadian government, the violence of the Internment (its complex construction and effects), its numerous subjects, and its role as formative in making the Canadian nation and its citizens have not been sufficiently analytically addressed. This book is an attempt to re-member the Japanese Canadian subjects of the Internment and contribute to a critical analysis of the Internment and its effects.

Naming the Internment against the Forgetting of the Internment

When I was a child, I grew up separated from a community of Japanese Canadians, and my home (and the homes of my extended family) was the only place in which I could hear the namings of the Internment. In contrast to my parents' numerous and repeated descriptions of the different places they had inhabited in the 1940s and their conditions, using explicit language and various codes of the Internment and their different analyses of their experiences, when I stepped outside of this familial space, I was confronted by a hostile forgetting of my parents' profound knowledge of their Canadian history. The authorized version of Canada's history taught to me at school and through the media excluded our history as Japanese Canadians and importantly the history of the Internment. Inevitably, I learned where and when this history could be articulated and witnessed occasions when my parents' understandings of an exclusionary nation were vigorously contested and dismissed. In later years, I too underwent many challenges to the counterhegemonic discourses inherited from my family.

As a researcher, I have pieced together the ways in which this national collective forgetting of the formative and far-reaching implications of the Internment was produced and its enduring consequences masked. Weeding through government reports and documents in the attempt to see beyond the screens of obfuscation and self-aggrandizement, I have used the wisdom my parents imparted to me. I have also been bolstered by community members whose questioning of this obfuscation have contributed to my own ability to name. The forgetting of the Internment has been continually contested by Japanese Canadians through the non-public burden of personal memories, their representations in familial and communal sites, and through political organizing such as that witnessed throughout the redress struggle. Yet we are continually negotiating the effects of the Internment in our attempts to name it. For example, the inadequacy of language to describe the events, due to the linguistic masking of the deeds while they were done, leads one to ask: What do we call this significant historical inheritance? Do we call it 'Internment'? Why do some researchers still call it 'evacuation'? And if researchers have difficulty negotiating the language of the Internment and its obfuscating effects, how do survivors negotiate the minefields of linguistic masking and their children's attempts to countername it?

I therefore approached my research as an inheritor of the perpetrators' euphemistic language, the collective forgetting of violence perpetrated against many subordinated groups in Canada, and the memory of the Internment passed down to me from my family. I know that I would not have been able to attempt to name some of the effects of the Internment without activists, cultural workers, and scholars whose past and concurrent work sustains and challenges my own.

1 The Forgetting Subjects and the Subjects Forgotten

That Canada should desire to restrict immigration from the Orient is regarded as natural, that Canada should remain a white man's country is believed to be not only desirable for economic and social reasons, but highly necessary on political and national grounds

William Lyon Mackenzie King,
Report on Mission to England (1908)[1]

The stopping of Oriental immigration entirely is urgently necessary, but that in itself will not suffice, since it leaves us with our present large Oriental population and their prolific birth rate. Our Government feels that the Dominion Government should go further, and by deportation or other legitimate means, seek to bring about the reduction and final elimination of this menace to the well being of the white population of this Province.

British Columbia Premier John Oliver (1927),
quoted in W. Peter Ward, *White Canada Forever* [2]

The success of the Government's re-establishment program will be determined in the final analysis by its long-term effects on the Japanese Canadian minority group in particular, and on Canadian unity in general.

Canada, Department of Labour,
*Report of the Department of Labour on the
Re-Establishment of the Japanese in Canada: 1944–1946* [3]

In response to the government of Canada's Department of Labour's reference in 1947 to the 'effects on the Japanese Canadian minority group' as cited above, this book emphasizes that the effects of the federal government's actions were long term and that they cannot be construed as a success story for Japanese Canadians or other racialized groups despite the ways in which the story was and is represented by the government or scholars. The acts of removing over 22,000 people from their homes in a matter of months had profound consequences for those removed. The term 'Internment' is insufficient to describe these processes in that it gives a broad and sweeping sense of one monolithic action engendered by the federal government, when in fact over 22,000 people underwent innumerable acts of violation. Although the expulsion of Japanese Canadians from their homes and the destruction of their communities have been depicted as an 'evacuation' and a past (and finished) event, these actions inflicted physical, social, and psychological injuries on them and, additionally, on the following generations. Indeed, the word 'violence' itself does not do justice to what was done to Japanese Canadians in the 1940s and the ways in which expulsion, dispossession, incarceration, and dispersal shaped their lives in subsequent years, but its use in this book is an attempt to counter the obfuscating euphemisms coined by the government of the time and that are still in currency today.

Tellingly, the Department of Labour situated the Internment in relation to 'its long-term effects on Canadian unity in general.' The success imagined by the Department of Labour was one of unifying Canada through the Internment and dispersal of Japanese Canadians. Clearly, this project was not only one of nationalism but also of racism. This book elucidates some of the ways in which the prediction about the production of Canada was accomplished and how it affected Japanese Canadians. Since dominant notions of nationhood and citizenship must be continually re-imagined and re-made, the role of the Internment in materializing the national imaginary and in sustaining domination must be analysed – that is, who was excluded from Canada and who was included. Processes of racial subjugation were re-enacted and reaffirmed. White settler citizenship and the entitlement to inhabiting Canada, violently achieved through the confiscation of land from Indigenous peoples and their relegation to reserves and spaces marginal to the Canadian nation, were both reiterated through the expulsion of Japanese Canadian from the coastal areas.

Kirsten Emiko McAllister enumerates many of the deleterious acts and events of the Internment and argues that these were 'violent events'[4] and thus evidence that it was political violence. Political violence is defined by McAllister as 'structured by domination' and 'systematically deployed acts taken against a particular group which damage or destroy their capacity to operate as a social collective.'[5] I concur with McAllister that the Internment was composed of 'violent events' and was political violence; in my work I emphasize the relationship of the 1940s destruction of Japanese Canadian communities and the destruction of their sense of themselves to the construction of the Canadian nation and its ideal of the subject-citizen. Hence, I use the term 'national violence' to include the physical acts of destroying communities, families, and subjecthoods simultaneous to the production of the nation of Canada.[6] This concept underlines not only the role of the Canadian government under the Liberal prime minister Mackenzie King but also the participation of Canadian citizens – the latter in their support of the implementation of and benefiting from the expulsion, dispossession, incarceration, and dispersal. This violence includes particularized mobilizations of violence such as epistemic violence, the production of knowledge about Japanese Canadians as racial Others inferior to white Canadians, and the simultaneous forgetting of histories of subordination that is required by the epistemologies that normalize racial, gendered, and classed hierarchies. I use the term 'racial violence' to stress that 'violence is inherent in racist expression'[7] and that constituting the Other as enemy is to 'engage him or her in relations of power.'[8] Naming some of the effects of these violent processes in the making of the nation of Canada through the Internment is the goal of the writing that follows. In examining the critical role of the Internment in making the Canadian nation, we may better understand how '[v]iolence itself both reflects and accelerates the experience of society as an incomplete project, as something to be made.'[9]

David Goldberg insists that the 'violence of power and the power of violence' are central to 'defining exclusions and inclusion.'[10] In addition, Allen Feldman warns us that we may not grasp how violence is mobilized locally if we 'simply study power at the "center"... from the perspective of formal political rationalities.'[11] We must, therefore, investigate how power is mobilized between people and not theorize power as 'external to its effects.'[12] Power, therefore, circulates in different ways and through differently socially located people who 'act as the vehicle for transmitting a wider power,'[13] and, as will be illustrated throughout this book, the entitlement of dominant subjects to occupy the nation as its rightful citizens is remade through the discursive and material expulsion of racialized Others. In this book I attend to how this national violence affected twenty-one Japanese Canadian women and how they remember its effects. While the Internment shaped Japanese Canadians, it was also constitutive of white people who participated in its far-reaching processes. Part of this process, as I argue in this chapter, entailed obfuscating and forgetting its effects and harms, that is mnemonic processes that produced both the subjects forgetting and the subjects forgotten. This chapter discusses some of the ways in which the harms of the Internment were obfuscated by those who participated in it. I also use examples from historical texts to illustrate how the obfuscation continues into the present.

Forgetting the Deed While Doing It

According to the 1941 Canadian census, at that time there were 22,096 people of Japanese ancestry living in British Columbia, most residing in the coastal areas of the province. The census lists 9,670 in the 'Japanese' category as female and 12,426 as male.[14] Fewer than 900 lived outside the province of British Columbia.[15] In a report dated 31 October 1942, the lengths to which the British Columbia Security Commission (BCSC)[16] – the federally appointed citizen body who administered the Internment between March 1942 and February 1943 – went to banish Japanese Canadians from the coastal area were statistically itemized. Every person's whereabouts was accounted for: 579 were allowed to leave the restricted area prior to March 1942 and were 'spread across Canada but under RCMP supervision'; 19,867 were moved to various incarceration sites; approximately 225 remained in Hastings Park, slated for impending expulsion; and a 'few Japanese families where the husband [was] a Japanese and the wife [was] a white woman and vice versa and their children' remained in the restricted area.[17] The report elaborated upon those remaining in Hastings Park who awaited removal. They included 105 patients suffering from tuberculosis. It mentioned that approximately 100 'difficult cases' remained in Vancouver and had been turned over to the RCMP, and twenty-five people were still in the 'protected' area of the Kootenays but would be removed in the next ten days.[18] By 1 January 1947, only 6,776 Japanese Canadians remained in British Columbia; 13,782 had been moved to other parts of Canada and 3,964 had been deported to Japan.[19]

The disappearance of over 22,000 people from their West Coast communities and their reappearances in various sites of incarceration and dispersal required tremendous structural and legal manoeuvring. Ann Sunahara has described the legislative processes of the Mackenzie King government and the role of some of the key governmental decision-makers in implementing the expulsion.[20] The rapid removals were initiated by the politicians who used the War Measures Act to expel Japanese Canadians, but also involved the participation of many citizens across the country. While some academic attention has been given to Japanese Canadians' memories of the Internment, little work has been done to show how the Internment was described and, simultaneously, actively forgotten by white people who participated in it and who witnessed its execution. How is this forgetting of a history belonging to Canada, through which notions of Canada were reaffirmed, accomplished? How did white participants describe their actions in expelling Japanese Canadians and in witnessing their expulsions and incarcerations? In tracing some of the discourses used by the architects, implementers, and narrators of the Internment, I examine how these actions were and are described and how their import was minimized. What are some of the mechanisms at work in an ongoing forgetting of the destruction of communities, of the expulsion, incarceration, and dispersal of over 22,000 people, and the appropriation and vandalizing of their property? While much more research is needed to answer these questions, this chapter focuses on various discourses used during and after the Internment that not only produced the subjects of the Internment but also the interning subjects and those who write about these subjects. Hence what is highlighted throughout this chapter is how the events of the Internment were (mis-) named and the effects of their (mis-) naming.

Language of Forgetting

Language marks social relations, and each term coined to describe/obfuscate the Internment must be seen as being 'attached to a history of colonialism'[21] and being a part of a rhetoric constructing notions of Canadian nationhood and citizenship. At the same time, by using euphemisms, governments disallow the linguistic mapping of violence in their practices and their connections to historical precedents and antecedents. One way in which collective forgetting of the violence of the Internment was accomplished was through the language used by the federal government and its administrators. Three reports issued by the federal government, *Removal of Japanese from Protected Areas: Report of the British Columbia Security Commission*, *Report of the Department of Labour on the Administration of Japanese Affairs in Canada, 1942–1944*, and

Report of the Department of Labour on the Re-establishment of the Japanese in Canada, 1944–1946, are illustrative of its discourses and especially of the euphemisms used within its discourses.[22] Some may dismiss these reports as mere propaganda for the government's actions during the period 1941 to 1946. However, these reports provide evidence of how the state inculcated a discursive framework for a national collective memory of the Internment through particular descriptions – explanations and justifications – of what it did and by creating a language in which what was done was obfuscated. This encoded language was circulated through intragovernmental documents and then through notices posted in the various incarceration sites.

The language in these documents is important because of its critical role in making the actions of the 1940s comprehensible to others. Since the language obliterates the harm done to Japanese Canadians, the continuing use of these government discourses limits our ability to appropriately name these actions and their consequences for over 22,000 people. For example, spatial euphemisms such as 'interior housing centres,' 'self-support communities,' 'road camps,' 'sugar beet projects,' and 'domestic service placements' were used to describe the different places to which Japanese Canadians were forced to move after their expulsions from the British Columbia coastal areas. These words conjure up images of hierarchical work and living arrangements but not the notion of incarceration. Therefore, to countername these spaces in the present as carceral[23] more clearly brings into view the fact that people were moved against their will. Similarly, the processes of expulsion, incarceration, dispersal, and deportation were euphemistically named *evacuation, relocation, resettlement,* and *repatriation.* Connoting a sense of voluntary movement on the part of Japanese Canadians and benevolence on the part of the government, these descriptors mask the power and the force that produce these processes and that are produced through them.

Strict control was maintained over the lexicon of the Internment invented by politicians and government employees. For example, in 1944, F. Charpentier, Chief Censor of the Directorate of Censorship with the Canadian Department of National War Services, wrote to the editor of the Anglican weekly, *The Canadian Churchman,* to inform him that the term 'internment camp' should be replaced by 'the word "settlement"… in any future publicity on this subject.'[24] This control over a collective discourse on the Internment can also be seen in federal Department of

Labour correspondence three years after the end of the Pacific war. In 1948, E.C. Anderson, the manager of a financial institution, wrote to the government as part of a reference check for a man whom he described as having been employed at the Tashme 'Concentration Camp.'[25] Cleo V. Booth responded to the letter by stating, '[T]he Tashme Centre was not a Concentration Camp, but *merely* a Re-location Centre.'[26]

The written expression of Japanese Canadians in the 1940s was also affected by the 'censorship and the control and suppression of publications … and means of communication'[27] authorized by the War Measures Act. The following is an extract from instructions given to Japanese Canadians by the Canadian Postal Censor in Vancouver:

> Write in English. If in Japanese, it should be confined to essential news and information, avoiding inconsequential gossip … Do not slow up the Censor's reading by using unusual symbols … Do not enclose in envelopes addressed to Occidentals correspondence to be passed on to Japanese nationals. This places upon the Occidental the duty of reporting your action to government authorities.[28]

The orders from the Censor clearly authorized 'Occidentals' to betray the contents of personal correspondence and the correspondents themselves if they deemed it appropriate. In this way, the government extended the powers of policing to white people in receipt of letters from Japanese Canadians.

From these examples, I do not wish to impute that the linguistic obfuscation of the harm done to Japanese Canadians was always necessarily deliberate. On the contrary, the most revealing aspect of the actions of some of the white participants in the Internment is that they actually believed that their actions – that is, forcibly moving, detaining, and profiting from the expulsion of over 22,000 people who had committed no crime – were not wrong, rather, were even laudatory and commendable; some even believed that they were demonstrating moral character through their deeds. How does one feel good about oneself and publicly proclaim one's goodness while asserting one's dominance over others? In addition to the use of euphemisms, there were other means through which participants and witnesses masked the violence of the Internment and secured their morality. In the next section I examine two related liberal concepts used during the Internment, 'freedom' and 'humanity.'

The Participating and Witnessing Subjects

Ann Sunahara makes this distinction between two groups of participating subjects: 'The difference between racists and liberals in that period lay primarily in the fact that racists believed non-white minorities could never assimilate, while liberals believed they could and should.'[29] Although, I agree that there were those who took either position, I would suggest that the line between the two groups delineated was not always that clear. As David Goldberg states,

> Liberalism plays a foundational part in this process of normalizing and naturalizing racial dynamics and racist exclusions. As modernity's definitive doctrine of self and society, of morality and politics, liberalism serves to legitimate ideologically and to rationalize politico-economically prevailing sets of racialized conditions and racist exclusions.[30]

Racial assumptions informed the practices of both those who advocated for the expulsion of all Japanese Canadians from Canada and those who advocated for their dispersal. There was no organized protest of the mass expulsion from their homes by any non-Japanese Canadian group and, as Sunahara documents, those she describes as 'liberals' actively supported the dispersal of Japanese Canadians 'east of the Rockies.' Nevertheless, I would agree that a liberal discourse was significant to the operationalization of the processes of the Internment. This discourse aided in the forgetting of the violence of the Internment, including that of the assimilation process itself, and in producing the liberal subjects who participated in this national project. It is to a few examples of these liberal discourses that I now turn.

The actions of the architects of the Internment and the implementers of government policy drew accolades from various sectors of the government and citizenry. In 1944 the federal Department of Labour congratulated the BCSC for a job well done. In the *Report of the Department of Labour on the Administration of Japanese Affairs in Canada, 1942–1944*, it stated: 'That this difficult task was done efficiently, economically and quietly in the course of 8 or 10 months is a real tribute to the members and officials of the B.C.S.C.'[31]

Although he was not an administrator of government policies, sociologist Forrest E. La Violette held a unique and privileged vantage point from which to witness and write about the Internment. Funded by the federal government, La Violette was given access to the incarceration sites to conduct research.[32] In 1948 he also commended the government's actions in his description of the 'acquisition of a housing and general housing area' as a slow process compared to a speedier process that would have required it to be done in a 'Hitler fashion.'[33] His comments minimize the government's actions – for example, the fact that many people were notified by officials that they had to leave their homes within twenty-four hours – and reflect his high regard for the decency and humanity of those who implemented government policy. La Violette furthers this estimation by comparing the Canadian experience of the Internment to the American, concluding: 'There seems to be less display of force' in Canada.[34] The 1942 BCSC report, *Removal of Japanese from Protected Areas: Report of the British Columbia Security Commission*, claimed that the Internment (or what it called the 'transplanting of the great aggregation of the Japanese') was not carried out 'without regard to the diverse needs of the people concerned, but at all times [paid] scrupulous attention to the dictates of *civilized humanity*.'[35] That same year, A. MacNamara, deputy minister of labour, wrote to G. Pearson, minister of labour for the province of British Columbia: 'The evacuation resolved itself largely into the problem of getting 22,000 persons out of an area and settled elsewhere as quickly and *humanely* as possible.'[36] With the 'humane' treatment of Japanese Canadians and his own humanity underscored in this missive (and the effects of this quick expulsion forgotten), MacNamara could then focus upon how the work affected his own person, which is apparent in his comment, 'I need hardly say that the work is full of headaches.'[37]

As is evident from government correspondence on the institution of the expulsion policy, humanitarian consideration for Japanese Canadians was not behind the decision to use abandoned mining towns, called 'ghost towns,' in the BC interior. That the government's administration of the Internment was driven in part by economic motive – to be cost efficient – is clear from various government documents and secondary sources, where government officials compared their options to those of U.S. administrators who planned to incarcerate Japanese Americans in buildings built for that purpose. For example, in 1942, R.H. Webb, lieutenant-colonel of National Defence, argued that the camp system in the BC interior (or what he called the 'family system'), that would use existing abandoned buildings in Greenwood, Slocan, New Denver, Sandon, and Kaslo, would be 'the best and most economic' plan. If people prepared their own meals, he added, the government would have fewer expenses: 'Central Halls, Central Kitchens will call for wages ... Family life will eliminate wages ... The family will be encouraged to use initiative, work for themselves, and, consequently, live better and *more freely*, and incidentally, cut down the cost of feeding them by what they produce themselves.'[38]

Austin Taylor, chairman of the BCSC, concurred with Webb's position, acknowledging that the sites chosen were in desolate areas and the buildings in disrepair. In a letter to Associate Deputy Minister of Labour A. MacNamara, Taylor describes the site of Sandon as 'practically uninhabited. It is probably eighteen years since the houses were occupied ... However, we believe this is an excellent opportunity to utilize space at a minimum cost.'[39] Add to these comments Sunahara's stunning revelation that those expelled had to use the proceeds from the sale of their confiscated properties to pay for living expenses in their sites of incarceration and it is apparent that the Canadian government attempted to minimize its own costs with little concern for those incarcerated.[40]

The quotes from Webb, La Violette, and MacNamara above illustrate how three white men, two participants and a witness in the Internment process, construct themselves through their own forgetting of Japanese Canadians. Webb's use of the concept of a 'free' subject is paradoxical to say the least given the context of expulsion; nevertheless, it illustrates how incarceration was masked through spatial confinement that was different from a common-sense notion of prison. This masking was furthered through the use of the euphemisms noted above.

The use of the concept of freedom in relation to Japanese Canadians within such a setting invokes the image of a liberal autonomous subject whose invention in this moment elides the material effects of confinement upon freedom and is perhaps most revelatory of the moves that dominant subjects make to uphold their own separation and hence autonomy from the deleterious acts in which they are engaged. This reveals instances where the liberal concepts of 'freedom' and 'humanity' are made in relation to Japanese Canadians and where their use simultaneously masks and incorporates the carceral into their meanings.[41] I would argue that this process of masking and incorporation is occurring through euphemisms used to describe the sites to which Japanese Canadians were sent. If we call them something other than 'carceral' or incarceration, then we can say that Japanese Canadians lived 'more freely' and, even more importantly, we can see ourselves as 'humane' through this representation. Moreover, the use of the concepts of 'freedom' and 'humanity' in this context suggests that they may have different meanings (and thus differing limits), depending on the subjects to whom they are applied. This raises the question as to whether these practices would be described as 'freedom' and 'humane' if applied to those who authorized or administered them.

The concept of freedom is imported into the discourse of choice and phraseology that maintains that Japanese Canadians chose or volunteered to move to their sites of exile. For example, after forcing Japanese Canadians to decide whether they would move out of British Columbia or be deported to Japan through the repatriation survey in 1945, the Department of Labour described the process in this way: 'The evacuees have been free to make their own choice voluntarily.'[42] Thus the constraints upon choice and the processes of coercion are all erased through the discourse of choice: in this case, the context of destitution, dispossession, the illegality of returning to the coastal area, facing the unknown future and probability of racism in moving east of BC, and the offer of $200 to each adult and $50 to each child for those who agreed to move to Japan as opposed to the $35 to each adult ($60 to a married couple) and $12 to each child offered to those who moved east of BC.[43] These discourses – of freedom and choice – however, are critical to the making of the liberal mythology that Canadians live in a free country where everyone has freedom of choice.

Mary Louise Fellows and Sherene Razack have theorized the concept of 'respectability' to illustrate how white bourgeois subjects come to know themselves in relation to subordinate Others. They argue that 'respectability' is attained relationally: one can only be 'respectable' in relation to people who are deemed 'degenerate' Others. Thus 'respectability is a claim for membership in the dominant group; attaining it, even one aspect of it, requires the subordination of Others.'[44] This construction is apparent in the language used in 1936 when the appeals of Japanese Canadians for the right to vote were rejected and they were described as 'savages and degenerates.'[45]

The federal government's tribute to its employees' efficiency demonstrates the self-making of dominant white subjects, re-enfigured as the epitome of the bourgeois subject whose 'efficiency, economy, and quietude' re-confirm their rationality, frugality, and composure through meeting the challenge of the difficult 'problem.' In the face of the violence of the Internment, or perhaps *because* of the enormous implications of that violence, white participants attempted to secure their 'respectability' through marking the boundaries between themselves and Japanese Canadians and through a forgetting of how those boundaries were inscribed. Representation of their actions through euphemistic language created not only a lexicon of misnaming but also a methodology for exclusionary and violent practices that rendered them supposedly benign or even benevolent. These representational practices simultaneously fashioned as the heroes of a national story those in various positions of power. Geographical space, the 100-mile radius of the restricted coastal area, was used to mark the physical divide between a constructed whiteness and a Japaneseness. Incarceration sites across the country further enforced geographical markings of racialized spaces in relation to the white space of the Canadian nation. The discursive production of the government necessarily supported the material in marking the boundaries between respectable spaces and degenerate ones and between respectable subjects and those deemed degenerate, the latter marked as deserving of expulsion and incarceration.

Meyda Yeğenoğlu has argued that a notion of the 'Other' is critical to the formation of the autonomous 'Western' subject. White dominant subjects come to know themselves through their racialization of subordinate Others. Yet this dependence upon the inferiorized Other must be repressed or forgotten in order to preserve the 'very condition of the autonomy and universality of the subject.'[46] While the expulsion of Japanese Canadians from the West Coast was constitutive of the formation of a white nation and the domination of white citizens, this interdependent relationship and its inherent violence must be forgotten (or never known, which amounts to the same thing) by white citizens in order to protect their respectability and autonomy. As the sites of incarceration were readily imagined and materialized, the harms done to Japanese Canadians were repressed by their architects in order to create the image of a humane and respectable citizenry and nation. As people were demonized as racial aliens, they were also narrated as having choices and freedom so as to obfuscate the material constraints imposed upon *their* autonomy. While the white subject created the Others' differences, he simultaneously denied how he was also made through the differences he imposed on others. Hence, the liberal Canadian subject's reproduction of self as respectable and as autonomous necessitated forgetting the expulsion of Japanese Canadians as violence and its innumerable damaging effects.

The BCSC reported that 'the transplanting ... did not create an exodus of refugees, uncared for and uncontrolled.'[47] As Michel Foucault argues, the claim to humane technologies of punishment and imprisonment is a hallmark of the modernist period and reflective of the 'moral claims of humanism.'[48] As he underlines, '"Humanity" is the respectable name given to this economy [of punishment] and to its meticulous calculations.'[49] Hence the displacement of over 22,000 people (most of whom were Canadian citizens) resulted in their new constitution as refugees without place who must necessarily be controlled by the relationally constituted humane and caring white subjects.

Even while purporting to be humane, however, the BCSC also emphasized that its administration of its policies were 'scrupulously attentive.'[50] In one of its reports, it stated, 'A strict observation is kept on the movements of Japanese [sic] throughout the various schemes by the establishment of road blocks at the necessary places, as it is not deemed desirable that the Japanese [sic] shall be permitted to wander at will throughout the country.'[51] As legislators, public servants, and other white participants carved out racialized and carceral spaces in relation to their own entitlement to move and live freely in Canada, so too did they simultaneously procure an image of Canada and themselves as fair, rational, and moral through their use of a discourse of humanity.

The concept of humanity is used as well in narrating the Canadian nation as a 'humane' country, linking it to La Violette's assertions concerning the relative slowness of the expulsion and his comparison to the Internment in the United States. The discourse that Canada is a more 'humane' place than the United States is part of the construction of the Canadian self as more 'respectable' than other nations' citizens. In narrating the Canadian self as more respectable than the Nazi or American self through discourses distancing Canadian state actions from those of Germany or the United States, the metanarrative of respectability is maintained, thus producing the representation of the Internment in Canada as something other than force, incarceration, or violence.[52] Typically, in this construction of the humane Canadian nation and, by extension, its humane citizens, our attention is diverted to other national contexts and the harm done to people through colonialism, racism, male domination, and other systems of domination in Canada is minimized.[53] These examples demonstrate moments in the historical formation of the identities of a white bourgeois Canadian citizen and of Canada, characteristics of which have resonances today.[54]

In the case of the Internment, that which was often claimed by the government and its administrators to be humane and civilized treatment obfuscates the ways in which incarceration was extended throughout the social body of the nation through numerous spatial displacements, engaging white participants who were granted powers of surveillance, control, and discipline. The bureaucratization of control, on a large scale, stemmed from federal departments and their ministers to the individuals who worked in fine detail monitoring every action and communication of those interned. The activities of Japanese Canadians were reported on by agencies such as the RCMP and the Regional Placement Offices.[55] Another way in which all white Canadians could participate in the Internment process was through a discourse of social regulation – the notion of 'assimilating' Japanese Canadians.

On 4 August 1944, Prime Minister Mackenzie King outlined government policy on the fate of Japanese Canadians.[56] In his address to Parliament, he stated that 'no person of Japanese race born in Canada has been charged with any act of sabotage or disloyalty during the years of war.' Yet, in a contradictory comment, he managed to cast doubt upon their proven loyalty by stating that 'those who have shown disloyalty to Canada during the war should not have the privilege of remaining in Canada.'[57] Through this statement, King set in motion the process for creating disloyalty, which would take place in the form of the government's repatriation survey of 1945.[58]

Prime Minister King advocated that all of the provinces share BC's 'problem' and accept Japanese Canadians who had been moved to other provinces. King presented his policy in this way:

> There is little doubt that, with co-operation on the part of the provinces, it can be made possible to settle the Japanese more or less evenly throughout Canada. They will have to settle in such a way that they must be able to pursue the settled lives to which they are entitled, and that they do not present themselves as an unassimilable bloc or colony which might again give rise to distrust, fear and dislike. It is the fact of concentration that has given rise to the problem. The sound policy and the best policy for the Japanese Canadians themselves is to distribute their numbers as widely as possible throughout the country where they will not create feelings of racial hostility.[59]

Through this policy address, King admits that 'feelings of racial hostility' were central to his government's policies regarding Japanese Canadians. He constructs them racially as an 'unassimilable bloc or colony' and a threat to 'the people of British Columbia and the interests of the country as a whole.'[60] Moreover, he holds Japanese Canadians responsible for the racism directed at them. He attributes the hostility they faced in British Columbia to their living in communities. In this way, King marks the spatial terrain as clearly one where Japanese Canadians lived outside of the imagined Dominion in a degenerate 'colony,' and it is imputed that this spatial separation was one for which Japanese Canadians were solely responsible. The discursive construction of the reasons for expulsion as originating outside of Canada are also found in a BCSC report naming Japanese Canadians as the 'victims of the cruel action of their race,' 'their native countrymen,' who had attacked Pearl Harbor.[61] Constructing Japanese Canadians as outside of the nation, as we shall see in chapter 4, disentitled them from the rights of citizenship. It also conveniently turned attention away from what was being done within Canada to Japanese Canadians and how the Internment was not only demonstrative of white imaginings of exterior territories but was also about imagining their nation.

Thus King's policy statement associated dispersal with assimilation. The term 'assimilation' is another term of obfuscation that epitomizes Anglo-whiteness as the criterion for citizenship. When applied to Japanese Canadians, the process of 'assimilation' meant destruction of their communities, separation of friends and families, dispossession, and the demonization of their selves, their use of the Japanese language, and their connections to relatives in Japan. In other words, what was an inherently violent process became normalized through the rhetoric of Prime Minister King, government officials, and all who advocated for the dispersal policy. In soliciting the 'cooperation' of all the Canadian provinces to share what was constituted as BC's 'problem,' King also delegated the powers of surveillance and control of Japanese Canadians to all Canadian citizens, as we saw above in the case of their written correspondence. Through the promulgation of the discourse of 'assimilation,' presented as the end goal of separating Japanese Canadians from each other, King's address amounted to advocating that, in Foucault's words, 'all citizens … participate in the punishment of the social enemy.'[62] In this way, assimilation was presented as a national project, one where all white citizens could participate in the policing of Japanese Canadians. The concept of assimilation therefore normalized the unmarked white Canadian citizen in relation to the racialization of Japanese Canadians. The assumption was that racialized Others must aspire to be and must be forced to act like white anglo-Canadians. Hence, the ideal of a white citizenry was re-made through Prime Minister King's address and the Internment itself.

Heeding the Call to Canadianize the Racialized Other

There was no organized opposition by white Canadians to the government's policy of expulsion and internment in the 1940s.[63] Throughout their incarceration and dispersal, it was Japanese Canadians themselves who organized to individually and collectively voice their protests of government policies. While the Co-operative Committee on Japanese Canadians, a Toronto-based coalition of predominantly white citizens did protest the deportation orders issued by the government subsequent to the repatriation survey, they also supported the dispersal policies.

Some may argue, as does Sunahara, that there were white people who assisted Japanese Canadians during their years of incarceration. Nonetheless, this assistance, sometimes construed as solely humanitarian, was critical in implementing the policies initiated by the government because it helped to sustain certain discourses, including that the Internment and dispersal were 'humane.' In other words, if 'good' people were in these sites (for example, Christian missionaries and ministers), then the experience for Japanese Canadians could not have been so bad. While more research is needed to analyse the subject formation of these Internment participants, I would argue that these 'helpers' were participating in knowing who *they* were through what Barbara Heron calls 'colonial continuities.' She explains 'colonial continuities' as 'deeply racialized, interrelated constructs of thought [that] have circulated from the era of empire and today remain integral to the discursive production of bourgeois identity.'[64] The encounters between Japanese Canadians and white Christians were further instances in the production of the identity of the humane Canadian, this time one who saved the racialized Other, a reiterated subjectivity that has been historically claimed by colonizers who have defended their actions in relation to Indigenous and other colonized peoples.[65]

The Christian churches actively supported and participated in the dispersal process.[66] This encounter between Christian individuals and Japanese Canadians drew on a history of colonialism in which missionaries promulgated the superiority of Western culture and produced knowledge about the people in their charge. In Canada, the involvement of Christian denominations has been witnessed in their participation in colonial processes of subjugating Indigenous peoples, the institutionalization of churches in Indigenous communities, and the separation of families through the residential school system.[67] Regardless of their individual opinions on the Internment, the very presence of Christian workers in the sites of incarceration lent credibility to the processes of the Internment. The Christian churches' roles of teaching and ministering were not benign or solely humane acts but existed within structures of power that sought to discipline, control, and identify Japanese Canadians as different and inferior; what follows are some examples of how missionaries and others who considered themselves 'experts' on the 'Orient' participated in the Internment.

Neither kindergartens nor high schools were funded by any level of government in the BC interior camps. As a result, the federal government allowed Christian churches to establish kindergartens and high schools staffed by white teachers with Japanese Canadians as 'voluntary' assistants.[68] Catholic schools were staffed by nuns and priests.[69] Frank Moritsugu and his co-authors describe the church workers in this way:

> These voluntary arrivals were mostly church workers from the United, Anglican and Roman Catholic Churches. Some were bilingual missionaries returned from Japan, sent home just before the outbreak of the Pacific war. Others had been among the few *hakujin* working within the larger Japanese communities on the Coast as religious missionaries or kindergarten teachers. Later these church people were joined in the detention camps by a handful of men also linked to churches. They were conscientious objectors to the war ...[70]

La Violette makes clear the assimilationist intent of their objectives: 'It was hoped by all of the church workers to counter the influence of the Buddhist Church and its close association with Japanese culture and life of the Old Country.'[71] That the presence of the Christian churches and their missionaries in the sites of incarceration furthered the notion of the cultural difference of Japanese Canadians is evident through this description of their mission. Few white Christians would have been unaware of the function of their churches in non-Christian countries. By engaging returned missionaries from Japan to be the ministers of Japanese Canadians, the churches reinforced the idea that those incarcerated were Japanese foreigners living in Canada when most were born in Canada. Intranational carceral spaces became racialized as 'Japanese' space and their association with the enemy nation was materialized not only by their designation as separate sites for those expelled from the West Coast but also by placing therein missionaries who had worked in Japan. Thus the work of ministering to the Japanese in Japan and the transfer of this work to a Canadian context consolidated the construction of the people incarcerated in Canada as Japanese, 'foreign,' and outside of the definition of Canadian citizen.

As these missionaries, government administrators, and witnesses to the Internment participated in constructing notions of Japanese Canadians, they also engaged in constituting themselves through these practices.[72] Part of this constitution of self was the role of the expert on 'the Japanese.' Thus La Violette was described by the author of the preface to his book as 'acquainted with the Orient.'[73] At least one government administrator, G.E. Trueman, had worked in Japan prior to becoming the Placement Officer for the BCSC in southern Ontario in August 1942.[74]

Cleo V. Booth, Director of Education and Women's Projects for the Japanese Division of the Department of Labour,[75] had 'worked at the Japanese consulate in Vancouver'[76] and was cited above in relation to promoting certain euphemistic discourses of the Internment. Many of the senior positions in the Internment administration were held by men, yet Booth and other female staff were also engaged in the expulsion, internment, and dispersal of Japanese Canadians.[77] Historically, white middle-class women have held a tenuous position in relation to the masculine ideals of bourgeois subjecthood because of their positions of gender subordination and their susceptibility to being deemed 'degenerate' through processes of misogyny and male domination. The Internment, however, provided them with an opportunity to join in the national racial project of the incarceration and dispersal of Japanese Canadians and thus bolster their own identities as white Canadian citizens.

As Heron argues, colonial continuities that structure the encounter between white bourgeois subjects and racialized subjects position the former as the 'knower' and 'to know in this context was (and is) to control. A key aspect of these undertakings was to Christianize.'[78] Whether selected by others or self-selected to participate in the Internment process, the staff noted above were presupposed to know those who were incarcerated due to their work in Japan or on the 'Orient.' This 'Orientalist'[79] knowledge formation reinscribed Western claims of entitlement to know and civilize the 'Oriental' Other, practices which were historically forged through colonial and imperial conquest. It also presumed that the Other was in need of 'civilizing,' or 'Westernizing – two colonial concepts often captured by the term 'Canadianizing' that was used during the Internment. This claim to knowledge of the 'Oriental' benefited these participants materially because it secured jobs for them and it bolstered their own sense of selves as knowers who were in control of the tasks and the people at hand. The discourse of humanity and its concrete construction through the use of Christian church personnel who produced knowledge about Japanese Canadians and dispensed it through their work could indicate another means of forgetting the harms of the Internment, buried as they are under the conflicting images of the sites of incarceration and the white Christians ministering, teaching, and researching there. Moreover, narratives of positive encounters with white Christians by Japanese Canadians may be misread by their witnesses as survivors' acceptance of the Internment. Emotional bonds that formed in such bounded, carceral sites were complex, where power – including the power of whiteness – was imbalanced and coercive, and where Japanese Canadians were captive to an overriding Christian ideology presented as one of the means through which they could demonstrate assimilation and loyalty to Canada, characteristics they needed if they were to be allowed to stay in Canada.

Using Space to Forget Expulsion, Incarceration, and Dispersal

I explore the spatial configurations of expulsion, incarceration, and dispersal further in chapters 4 through 9. Here, I would like to give examples of how the names given to various sites used to incarcerate Japanese Canadians mark places while simultaneously masking their carceral function. This is the case for Tashme, named by combining the first two letters of the last names of the chairman and two commissioners for the BCSC: Taylor, Shirras, and Mead.[80] One might question the notoriety gleaned from having a detention camp named after oneself, yet it is the symbolism here that is of importance. Tashme was the only interior detention camp constructed solely for the incarceration of Japanese Canadians: that is, the site and the buildings established upon it were created specifically for the purpose of incarceration. Despite the highly racialized nature of this site (or perhaps *because* of its racial significance), white men deemed it important to etch upon it their permanent mark of ownership. In the tradition of the colonizers whose names litter the places of their 'discovered' nation, Tashme bears the permanent signature of its administrators and to this day remains on maps of British Columbia. This naming is also a remarkable signifier of white homosocial bonding, a melding together of patrimonial nomenclatures in the collective forging of violence. Yet their discursive legacy is, on the one hand, a bold mark of entitlement to the ownership of the nation while, on the other hand, their proprietary relationship is obfuscated by a discursive masking, in this case through combining the initials of three names.

As most of the buildings, shacks, latrines, and other evidence of the Internment have been razed from the sites of incarceration, the names of the camps and the towns to which people were sent take on enormous significance for survivors and their families. This razing of the land-scape became clear to me during a tour of the BC interior camp sites in 1992. At the Lemon Creek site, people scoured the terrain for latrine holes in order to reconstruct the position of shacks in relation to the land now empty of buildings.[81] At the Popoff site, we were met by a vacant field and quickly gathered around the one woman on the tour who had been incarcerated there. She vividly pointed out where the buildings had been and made references to the Popoffs, the Russian-Canadian family who owned the land and after whom the site was named.

Joseph Fry has described the Neys 'hostel,' the site in northern Ontario through which people were dispersed to other destinations, as 'covered with mature red pine and campsites for park visitors.' Neys was used as a prisoner-of-war camp for captured enemy combatants sent from Germany prior to its usage in confining and dispersing Japanese Canadians. Pine trees have been planted for park visitors, and Fry states that 'it has been suggested they have helped to veil the last vestiges of the internment at Neys.' He adds, 'The names of the local features including Prisoner Cove and Detention Island provide the only lasting hint of what occurred at Neys between the years of 1941 and 1947.'[82]

Representing the Internment: Nation and Forgetting

In 1964, at the opening of the Japanese Canadian Cultural Centre in Toronto, Prime Minister Lester Pearson described the Internment with this statement: 'That action by the Canadian government of the day – though taken under the strains and fears and pressures and irrationalities of war – was a black mark against Canada's traditional fairness and devotion to the principles of human rights.'[83] Over twenty years later, in 1988, Prime Minister Brian Mulroney's certificate of 'Acknowledgment' to the recipients of the negotiated redress settlement included this statement: 'The acknowledgment of these injustices serves notice to all Canadians that the excesses of the past are condemned and that the principles of justice and equality in Canada are reaffirmed.'[84] As is apparent in these quotations, when Canadian heads of government (and few they have been) have publicly acknowledged the Internment as having occurred in Canada, the admission is often accompanied by a recuperation of liberal notions of Canada as a just and fair country; the reification of Canada as a nation committed to 'fairness' and 'justice' remains unchallenged.

The Internment, contrary to this laudatory representation, must be considered not as antithetical to the liberal democratic development of Canada but rather as an integral component of the paradigmatic making of Canadian nationhood and citizenship. As Ian McKay argues, the categorization of historical injustices as past 'mistakes' requires an analysis of the 'socio-cultural structures, the non-accidental and general reasons for such phenomena.'[85] In contrast to the narration of racial violence, including the Internment, as a mistake of the past, this narration itself should be viewed as part of a process of constructing notions of Canada and its citizens.

This section addresses questions regarding how the story of the Internment is told: What language is used to describe the Internment? What are the major narrative tropes and what subjects are produced through this narration? How does liberal discourse structure the story of the Internment so as to produce particular memories of these events, while also instilling a forgetting of the harms experienced by Japanese Canadians and the role of the perpetrators and beneficiaries of the Internment? How does the imprint of liberalism provide a template for the Internment story, a predictable narrative structure that produces a certain image of Canada and its citizens? This section emphasizes the constructedness of history and argues that liberal constructions of the Internment serve to limit our understanding of its multiple subjects in relation to nation, citizenship, and social domination. As McKay suggests, historical representation must be critiqued for its inattention to the historical production of liberalism in Canada in the past and especially for the notion of the individual it presumes, reproduces, and even promotes.[86]

Writing the History of the Internment

In the 1970s, Ken Adachi struggled with the problem of language in confronting the euphemisms coined by the federal government to describe the acts committed against Japanese Canadians in the 1940s and the places of their incarcerations. He thoughtfully described the challenge of how to describe the BC interior camps in this way:

> [T]hese camps came to be labelled by government administrators as 'interior housing centres,' 'relocation centres' or 'interior settlements.' But these almost reassuring descriptive terms ... were simply euphemisms for what many Nisei and others preferred to call 'internment' or 'concentration camps'... To call them 'concentration camps,' however, after the pattern of Dachau or Treblinka or even the ten camps in the United States, or to label them 'prison camps' after the pattern of prisoner-of-war camps in Europe or Asia would be a gross exaggeration ... what all the official euphemisms glossed over was the inescapable fact that the evacuees were being held involuntarily.[87]

Adachi's analysis suggests that one cannot easily adopt words connected to other historically specific atrocities to describe the processes of expelling, incarcerating, and dispersing Japanese Canadians. However, Adachi did not have access to government records, like those above, which illustrate why Japanese Canadians were moved to the sites chosen. Moreover, his struggle to name the Internment for what it was is connected to the specificities of place and reflects how the design of the Internment in Canada and the sites chosen mask the carceral. Roger Daniels, in fact, has argued for the application of the term 'concentration camp' to describe the sites of detention for Japanese Canadians and Americans, explaining that the use of this term began at the end of the nineteenth century when people were incarcerated because of their 'race or ethnicity.'[88] Interestingly, while Franklin D. Roosevelt used the term 'concentration camp' to describe the camps in the United States[89] and the Canadian government used the same term to describe the places where Ukrainian Canadians were interned between 1914 and 1920,[90] Canadian officials (as mentioned above) strictly prohibited the use of this term in relation to the places in which Japanese Canadians were incarcerated.

Drawing on the governmental discourses of the Internment, the misnaming of the events of the Internment continues in the present. Some writers still utilize euphemistic language, such as 'evacuation' and 'relocation,' in their representations of the Internment. Even though Raymond Okamura and others had been critical of euphemistic government terminology in the 1980s,[91] in 1991 Patricia Roy, J.L. Granatstein, Masako Iino, and Hiroko Takamura continued to use the term 'evacuation.' In response, scholar Audrey Kobayashi argued that these historians *chose* to use this term and that this 'euphemism should have been put to rest here.'[92] Such usage by historians is not an innocent reflection of the past but serves to recreate a more humane image of Canada.

Clearly some scholars are critical of the practices obfuscated by these misnomers and these critiques are addressed in the literature, especially regarding the use of the term 'repatriation.'[93] It is difficult to devise terminology that successfully describes the magnitude of these actions, as well as the complexity of and connections between the social relations producing the multiple acts and sites of incarceration, enforced labour, dispersal, and the expulsion of Japanese nationals and Japanese Canadian citizens to Japan. In my work, I have also fallen prey to the need to encapsulate some of these actions with the inadequate and problematic term 'Internment.' In attempting to devise a counterlanguage (and counterpractices), however, we may encounter other problems of missignification. The debate over which terms we should continue to use and which we should discard is emblematic of the difficulties in naming domination in a country where national violence occurring within it must be linguistically contained and minimized.

The Internment story takes two major narrative trajectories when it enters a Canadian master narrative. The first is that it was a result of the Japanese military's bombing of Pearl Harbor and Japan's position as an enemy nation during the Second World War. The second is the Internment occurred a long time ago and is a sad episode in Canada's mainly spotless past. The depiction of the Internment and anti-Japanese legislation as solely a wartime event, however, is inaccurate. Exclusionary legislation against Asians living in British Columbia was enacted from the time of their immigration to Canada, and Orders-in-Council were executed against Japanese Canadians both during and after the war.[94] The war in the Pacific served as a rationale for enacting increasingly restrictive and punitive legislation, including the use of the War Measures Act against Japanese Canadians.[95]

Periodization emphasizes that the Internment (when it is acknowledged) is a corollary to the epic narrative of the Second World War, and the fallacious notion of the Internment as military necessity or solely reducible to military causes continues to be bolstered through this semantic association.[96] Time and space become mythologized and distantiated as a way to produce an innocent notion of Canada. The story, neatly contained within the military history of the Second World War, is as follows: 'The Internment was due to the actions of Japan. The Japanese in Japan are therefore responsible for what occurred in Canada.' Sporting these spatial and temporal blinders inhibits us from seeing how and where the Internment actually occurred and to whom it happened, who benefited from it, and, more importantly, how the Internment variously affected Canadians of Japanese ancestry living within Canada during the war and up until the present day.

When past/present historicist temporality presents the Internment as an unusual blip on the Canadian horizon of progress and tolerance, it 'creates a sense of distance between the past and present that tends to deny the presence of the past.'[97] Relegating racial violence to the past facilitates the process of forgetting the devastation of its long-term effects. This narrative construction of the Internment and, more generally, racism as something of the past serves three functions: it obfuscates the long-term material and social effects for those whose dominance (of white supremacy and class position) was reinforced through it and those who were subordinated by it; it mitigates against claiming that racial violence continues to be part of making Canada and Canadian citizens; and it serves to divide Indigenous peoples and people of colour from each other.

Ann Sunahara for one adopts this 'past history' position in the prefatory remarks to The Politics of Racism: 'What is past is past ... my intention is to tell frankly what the record shows about an unhappy event in Canadian history, an event inconsistent with the public image most Canadians hold of their society.'[98] Sunahara's emphasis in both the preface and conclusion to her book on this history as being an 'unhappy event' of the past demarcates the Internment as a single episode rather than a continuing process.[99] Nevertheless, her comment also clearly identifies the mythology of an innocent national identity, untarnished by connected histories of racial domination and violence. The notion that the Internment is incongruent with the usual actions of the Canadian state is an oft-repeated qualifier.[100] So, even in the rare moments where racially motivated injustices are acknowledged, they are used to further a particular notion of Canada as a 'just' and 'tolerant' nation.

Using the tool of periodization, histories of colonial and racial violence are told as of the past and as unrelated to each other. This paradigmatic construction serves to isolate victims of colonial and racial violences from each other and obscures the interconnected relations of domination, including colonialism and nationalism, structured through processes of settler nation building. Thus the notion of Canada and its citizens as non-racist and committed to equality is maintained, thereby inhibiting a more complicated articulation of 'racial formation'[101] in Canada and the systematic upholding of whiteness and colonialism as criteria for citizenship. As such, what must be further explored is the continual recuperation of Canadian humanity or benevolence simultaneous to its processes of subjection.

Muting the Implications of Racism and Racial Violence

In some of the historical literature, there is an emphasis on the fear and attitudes of British Columbians following the bombing of Pearl Harbor as a logical explanation for the Internment. For example, La Violette states that 'knowing as we do the attitudes of British Columbians ... demands for their evacuation [were] the logical outcome.'[102] Roy and her co-authors explain the Internment in this way: 'In short, the Canadian government acted largely out of ignorance and in response to public fear.'[103] Roger Daniels echoes this analysis in his 1991 afterword to the second edition of Adachi's *The Enemy That Never Was*: '[T]heir west coast communities were destroyed by a frightened and vindictive government.'[104] The emphasis on the 'fear' of the dominant group masks the social processes that produced the decision to expel Japanese Canadians and protects those who benefited from this decision. David O'Brien and Stephen Fugita critique this oft-cited justification or explanation for the Internment in the United States in this response:

> [T]he most damaging evidence with respect to any case that one might try to make that the incarceration was simply a hysterical reaction to Pearl Harbor and not motivated by racism and self-interest is the fact that with the exception of about one thousand individuals, persons of Japanese ancestry in Hawaii were not sent to camps.[105]

Importantly, the focus on the rationale of 'fear' obscures the social relations of racialization, racism, and economics that produced the Internment. For example, in Canada, Japanese Canadian property was either stolen or purchased at nominal cost after individuals and families were forced to move from their respective homes. In Hawai'i, the U.S. settler state in which Pearl Harbor is located, the removal of 157,905 Japanese Americans, 37 per cent of the state's population in 1940, 'would perhaps have caused a collapse of the local economy.'[106]

Sunahara attributes the 'abuse of Japanese Canadians' to various 'villains,' including British Columbia Member of Parliament Ian Mackenzie, Vancouver Alderman Halford Wilson, Member of Parliament Humphrey Mitchell, and the federal cabinet.[107] She asserts that it was an 'ill-informed majority ... [that] wreak[ed] havoc on a blameless minority.'[108] Without question it is important to name those who used their power to enact the decisions to destroy Japanese Canadian communities in British Columbia, and this is a major contribution of both Sunahara's and Adachi's work. To their credit, both authors name race and racism as part of the ideological construction of the legitimization for the Internment, as compared to Roy and co-authors who focus their work on the concerns of 'fearful' white people.

The individualization of racism, however, is the hallmark of a liberal discourse where the 'rational' individual is presented as demonstrating 'irrational' fears or errors in judgment. Julian Henriques points out that this process of situating racism in attitudes ultimately vindicates the use of power to subordinate and those who benefit from domination by rationalizing racism as exceptional individual events.[109] It can also ultimately exonerate racist action by originating the cause of racism in the perceived 'difference' of the racialized, as was the case in Prime Minister King's 1944 statement, thus holding them responsible for exhibiting 'different' physical characteristics or demonstrating a 'different' culture.

Focusing on racism as resulting from ignorance also suggests that it is through education that racial exclusion will not reoccur. As Goldberg argues, this solution to racism is infused with the belief that rationality attained through learning will overcome errors in judgment.[110] Hence, the complex social relations structuring systems of domination and the benefits reaped from these multiple exclusions are forgotten; the profound psychological, social, and material benefits of having power through whiteness remain unacknowledged. Relegating the responsibility for the Internment to the actions of a few 'villains' also obscures who has benefited from this violence. In combination with the past–present binary and the claim that reforms will lead to equality, this construction of racism relegates it to a 'singular' wrong or mistake on the part of individuals in the past.

When there is actual acknowledgment that the Internment may have harmed Japanese Canadians, the liberal paradigm is drawn upon to propose that people can heal from this 'unhappy' past. The healing metaphor in its liberal sense connotes an individualized solution and in psychologized forms often, not surprisingly, emphasizes using speech as a way to heal. What actually constitutes 'healing' from violence that is difficult to name? How and why are survivors pathologized for the use of an inherited governmental 'evacuation' discourse and a lack of a language to describe heterogeneous experiences of incarceration and displacement? Is healing equivalent to 'forgetting' à la national amnesia? I will return to some of these questions in chapter 3.

The Subjects Produced through Historical Depictions of the Internment

The Historian as Rational, Objective Subject

Despite claims of objectivity on the part of some academics, power is always embedded in the relationship between the historian and the subject being researched. The positivist determination of history as an objective science obscures the ways in which knowledge itself is a product of relations of power. The discourse of objective knowledge production can mask how we are implicated in the histories about which we write, thereby allowing us to avoid being accountable to the communities about which we write. Writers of history are not only reconstructing narratives and subjects of 'the past' but also are engaging in narrating the nation and citizenship. This section outlines some of the ways in which historians not only produce a liberal historical narrative but also produce the self as rational through their claims of objectivity.

In his 1948 preface, H.F. Angus praised La Violette's *The Canadian Japanese and World War II* for not 'pass[ing] judgment on the wartime policy of the Canadian government.'[111] The claim to objectivity of academic writing in this instance reflects a positivist discourse establishing sociology and psychology as objective sciences. The editors of the series that includes Adachi's *The Enemy That Never Was* were also careful to point out that their 'histories are to be objective, analytical, and readable.'[112]

Patricia Roy and her co-authors' statements in 1990 are reminiscent of H.F. Angus' laudatory remarks on the accomplishment of objectivity in academic production. They preface their book *Mutual Hostages: Canadians and Japanese during the Second World War* with this definition of the historian's 'traditional task': 'to set out what happened and to try to determine the reasons.' They add, 'We have sought to explain, not to condone or condemn.'[113] The authors claim to be writing a more complex history than Sunahara's *The Politics of Racism*, in which she explicitly condemned the Canadian government's actions:

> In recent years, some Japanese Canadians have published their own accounts. Joy Kogawa's powerful and popular novel *Obasan* has had great emotional impact ... We wrote this book with the intention of examining the events of the war years as dispassionately as possible and trying to explain them in the context of their times. Fingers can easily be pointed at historical actors, blame can readily be affixed on politicians and generals, but that would do little to help today's Canadians and Japanese understand the wartime actions of their compatriots and governments.[114]

Thus the authors of *Mutual Hostages* claim to be 'dispassionate' in contrast to the 'emotional' accounts authored by Japanese Canadians. The authors' appeal that they are establishing reason(s) for the Internment is another flag of liberalism that, in this case, legitimizes certain discourses and subject positions as authoritative, relegating 'insiders' to the realm of native informants whose emotional, embodied accounts (or ability to engender emotion in others) are cause for exclusion from the stuff of 'real' history.[115] Therefore, the knowledge of those who were interned and affected by the Internment, such as that of Kogawa, and through her family connections Ann Sunahara, is constituted as outside of knowledge. By implication Japanese Canadians are found to be lacking historical legitimacy by virtue of their passionate condemnation of the events of the 1940s; whereas these four historians act as gatekeepers to the boundaries of what they consider to be knowledge and historical writing and perform themselves as rational, objective knowledge producers in the liberal paradigm.[116] Their claim to objectivity is illustrative of Sherene Razack's contention that 'the unbiased liberal subject achieves definition through comparison to the racialized subject.'[117] What the statements of Roy and her co-authors obfuscate are their own social locations in relation to the Internment and the social construction of historical texts. As Audrey Kobayashi states in her review of their book, 'The facts do not "speak for themselves," they are constructed ... Historians *do* make value judgements and to deny doing so is uncritical and can be dangerous.'[118]

It is important to underline that, through their prefatory remarks, Roy and her co-authors are responding to the challenges posed by Japanese Canadians who have developed 'representational spaces'[119] for the representation of *their* histories of the Internment, including through organizing for redress. Thus, racialized subjects also represent and remake themselves in sites of knowledge production. In fact, Roy and her co-authors credit the redress campaign with keeping this 'emotional subject ... in the public conscience,'[120] reiterating the subject as one of emotion and not one of harm or social injustice. It is interesting to note how these historians' consciousness of the impact Japanese Canadians and the redress movement have had on the public understanding of the Internment informed their combined effort to write *Mutual Hostages*.

Japanese Canadian Subjects

Who are the subjects reconstructed by liberal historical narratives? What identities are possible within these liberal narratives in which racism and the Internment are relegated to the past and 'healing' is the responsibility of Japanese Canadian survivors? The reconstruction of the Internment through a liberal historical framework not only produces a narrative of nation and its citizens but also characterizes racialized subjects as homogeneous. In contrast to the white 'individual,' racialized subjects are often viewed as all the same; their complex and sometimes contradictory subject positions are not considered. This framework therefore essentializes racial difference while reifying a white Canadian identity.

Citizen Versus Alien/Loyal Versus Disloyal

Portraying Japanese Canadians as an undifferentiated group of people does not allow for an understanding of their heterogeneous subject positions. Even among writers who condemn the actions of the government, there exists a discourse in the arguments for its indefensibility that seeks to minimize 'difference' between white Canadians and Japanese Canadians in the 1940s. This occurs in references attesting to the 'Canadian' comportment, attitudes, or citizenship of many who were incarcerated. This kind of argumentation is problematic in that it obfuscates the historical construction of 'difference' and further marginalizes those whose differences (i.e., by virtue of class, place of birth, language, religion) distance them from the definition of 'Canadian.' The binary construction of the 'Japanese' subject as opposed to the 'Canadianized' subject contributes to the reification of a fixed notion of Canadian identity. It reinscribes the boundaries of acceptable identifiers of Canadian citizenship while consolidating notions about 'outsiders.'

This construction is most noticeable when differentiations are made between the Issei and Nisei generations. In both the Canadian and American literature the concept of culture is used to assign certain characteristics to each generational cohort. These generalizations draw upon fixed notions of Japanese culture, often from the Meiji period, to explain what is denoted as Issei difference. These cultural explanations always operate in relation to what is presented as a Western or Canadian definition of culture, which is, of course, in binary fashion presented as progress. Lisa Lowe refers to generational comparisons as the 'privatized familial opposition,' a paradigm used to 'displace social difference.'[121] The tendency in the literature (and among Japanese Canadians) to generalize characteristics from and to each generation and to speak of the Issei, the Nisei, and the Sansei as undifferentiated groups contributes to a monolithic and contained construction of all Japanese Canadians, when, in fact, most autobiographical data illustrate heterogeneity across generations.

The Japanese–Canadian binary is, in part, a response to the spectre of the disloyal Japanese alien, an image mobilized by the federal government in the 1940s. In order to prove that Japanese Canadians were loyal, some historians argue that they, especially the Nisei, were Canadianized and were 'taught that things British and Canadian were right.'[122] Responding to the mythologized theory of the Japanese enemy in Canada's midst by creating an essentialized notion of Japanese people and Japanese culture contrasted to a Canadian identity, however, furthers categories of racial difference. We must therefore ask what constitutes loyalty, whose loyalty is questioned, and how racialized and cultural differences are used to determine loyalty; we must examine how nationhood excludes certain people from the definition of citizenship.

In the 1940s, the government created the figure of the disloyal citizen of Japanese ancestry, a haunting presence reiterated in Prime Minister King's speech in 1944; this spectre, based upon an Orientalist construction of racial difference, is central to the ways in which the Internment history is written and underpins the historical construction of racialized people in Canada. 'Disloyalty' and its adjunct – disentitlement from Canadian citizenship – continue to haunt historians of the Internment. Despite government documents revealed by Sunahara and others that demonstrate that the government's actions were based upon racism and economic opportunism and that no Japanese Canadians were ever legally charged with acts of treason or disloyalty, critical historical writing on the Internment is still being asked to prove that the Internment was wrong and the search for its justification continues by those unwilling to admit its role in securing white and economic domination. For example, the response of Roy and her co-authors to Sunahara's work is to argue that they 'uncovered' a 'mixture of loyalties' on the part of Japanese Canadians in the 1940s.[123] This 'mixture,' however, is presented as proof that the actions of the government were justified. As Yuji Ichioka suggests, '[M]ultiple and often conflicting loyalties ... [shift] over time and with changing circumstances,' and these 'complex, ambivalent sentiments and attitudes' must be viewed in relation to the subjects' subordinated social positions or 'marginality.'[124] Roy and her co-authors' focus on 'accepting the complexity of motivation ... [and] understanding the context and attitudes of a half century ago'[125] privileges the 'context and attitudes' of white Canadians and disallows an understanding of how immigrants and racialized citizens negotiate and struggle with exclusionary practices past and present. Rather than 'exploring how difference is established, how it operates, how and in what ways it constitutes subjects who see and act in the world,' these authors use the uninterrogated experiences of Japanese Canadians as 'evidence for the fact of difference.'[126] They vindicate the Canadian government by stating that, although Canada was committed to 'freedom and democracy,' 'few in Canada before the war had viewed the Japanese Canadians as full citizens.'[127] Thus they consider that their differential treatment from the stated principles of Canadian citizenship was understandable. Audrey Kobayashi cogently points out that while these 'authors go into the fine details of what the Canadian government did because they assumed Japanese Canadians were not *real* Canadians, they fail to address the belief itself.'[128]

The titular syllogism of *Mutual Hostages* feeds upon the notion of white people as citizens – the racialized viewed as non-citizens binary. The authors' argument that both 'wartime Canada and Japan looked on the Japanese [*sic*] and Canadians under their control as mutual hostages'[129] renders equivalent the relationship of Canadian prisoners taken by Japan to that of Japanese Canadians incarcerated by the Canadian government. What this false equivalency fails to recognize is that most Japanese Canadians were incarcerated by their own country of citizenship while Canadians incarcerated in Japan were not citizens of Japan. The fact that these authors fail to convincingly substantiate this thesis in their book is secondary to the way in which their argument demonstrates how *they* have accepted the assumptions that premise this thesis. While they argue that the Canadian government did not regard Japanese Canadians as citizens and thus disallowed them the rights of citizenship, their own arguments and language continue this disentitle- ment. For example, their conclusion that '[w]ar forced both Canada and Japan into the hostage business ... [and that] it was the Japanese [*sic*] in Canada and the Canadians in Japan ... who paid the price as mutual hostages,'[130] relegates them to the status of foreigner in Canada.

Passive, Silent Subjects, and Model Minority Subjects

There are three figures of Japanese Canadians that predominate in both the historical literature and in popular culture: the silent, passive subject of the Internment; the post-Internment silent survivor; and the model minority. In 1948, La Violette reported that the 'Japanese looked upon the whole evacuation as a gross violation of their rights' and conse- quently made demands and complaints 'to administrators in each proj- ect, to various officials in Ottawa and to the Spanish Consulate.'[131] This must be contrasted with Adachi's 1976 account that describes Japanese Canadians as a 'relatively docile, co-operative group of victims.'[132] The earlier depiction of protesting Japanese Canadians appears to have been forgotten in the consolidation of an image of Japanese Canadi- ans as 'docile' and 'cooperative.' This representation also illustrates how Japanese Canadians are complicit in the processes of forgetting, although they do so from differently situated social locations.

The construction of Issei and Nisei subjects of the Internment as docile victims translates into the predominantly current representa- tion that insists on their silence and unwillingness to speak about their Internment experiences. The prevailing image of the silent Japanese Canadian will be further problematized in chapter 2, but I would em- phasize here that the possibilities for speech for racialized peoples are limited within a liberal framework wherein the ability to speak and be heard is clearly connected to power. That the silence of survivors of the Internment is often associated, at least in part, with what is perceived as their 'cultural/racial difference' further signals that the notion of speech is pinned to relations of power. Culturalization and racialization serve to 'Other' the survivors of the Internment. With an insistence on individual healing and disclosure as a way of dealing with the trauma of oppression, the pathologization of survivors is a frequent outcome.

The recurring use of the term *shikata ga nai* to describe the attitude of people who were incarcerated is also a part of this Othering narrative. Adachi 'translates' the term as 'it can't be helped,' part of what he constitutes as a system of 'traditional values' imparted to the Nisei by the Issei generation. Used within the context of describing the Nisei as 'compliant' and 'accepting' of the 'outrage of the evacuation,'[133] this essentializing description serves to homogenize the identities of the incarcerated subjects and erases the different ways in which they negotiated the actions to which they were subjected. Moreover, the 'translation' of this term into the dominant language of English may never convey the meanings held by those who uttered it. Rather than thinking we know the meaning of the term and thus know the subjects who used it, we might examine the social relations that produce unified figures of Japanese Canadians as accepting of their expulsion, the circumstances that produced the loss of the practice of a language, and hence a term whose meanings are lost in translation.

May was one of two women I interviewed who used the term *shikata ga nai* in describing how one might deal with the legacy of the Internment. Her use of the term conveyed to me the pain incurred through loss and the understanding that the losses are irretrievable. This explanation of how she has coped with the losses sustained through the Internment arose when I asked her about the possessions her mother had left with friends in Vancouver. Taking a job as a domestic worker, leaving behind her mother and sister in the Slocan camp, supporting her family with her wages, and going to school in a community where she knew no one did not avail her with the time nor energy needed to track down her family's possessions. She explained, 'I learned that was one of the things you learn to do to survive was to let things go ... So it was a way of dealing with the pain. You know, Japanese say, "*shikata ga nai.*"'[134] This is not capitulation or the fixity conveyed through the term 'silence' or passivity; it is a complex negotiation of dealing with great loss and its effects while trying to survive them.

It is also important to note that the tendency to pathologize Japanese Canadians occurs both when they do not speak *and* when they speak. Despite La Violette's reports of the numerous ways in which Japanese Canadians protested the government's actions while they were incarcerated, he concludes by minimizing their forms of resistance and questioning *their* moral character in statements like 'the Japanese were exceedingly hostile towards the government, it became a game for them to make demands, as well as to try to deceive government officials.'[135]

Against the image of the pathologized survivor is drawn the success story of the model minority. Sunahara offers this characterization of Japanese Canadians and their social context: '[I]ndividuals have prospered, discrimination has diminished considerably, and Japanese Canadians have earned a reputation as a model minority.'[136] Despite the fact that Adachi criticized the term 'model minority' for giving 'credence to the notion that racism can be overcome – thus salving the white conscience,' by describing the Nisei as 'neat, well-dressed, efficient,' he does not undermine the homogenizing effects of the label.[137]

The specific application of the model minority label to Japanese Americans gained currency in the 1960s and continues to the present day.[138] Although the use of the term model minority appears to be more endemic to the United States than to Canada, the fact that both Adachi and Sunahara use it in their descriptions of Japanese Canadians necessitates critical engagement with it. As Donald Nakanishi explains, this reductive label 'portrayed Japanese Americans as having faced seemingly insurmountable racial and economic barriers in the past ... but as now exhibiting high aggregate-level indicators of group socio-economic and educational attainment.'[139] The model minority paradigm reinforces the liberal redemptive narrative of individualism and ahistorical merit-based achievement. In her analysis of how the Canadian educational system uses the concept of the model minority in its non-differentiation of Asian students, Kyo Maclear argues that the model results in the denial of social difference and the creation of prescriptive hierarchies for students of colour. The deployment of the concept of model minority, she argues, 'amounts to a form of social control,' thereby disallowing the notion that students are 'complex, diverse, and communicating subjects.'[140]

The term 'blessing in disguise' feeds the image of the model minority subject overcoming adversity. Both Adachi and Sunahara use this term in describing how 'most' or 'many' Nisei interpret the consequences of the Internment.[141] Sunahara squarely situates the origins of this phrase within the apologist position that attributes the improvement in the socio-economic status of Japanese Canadians to their expulsion from the West Coast. However, her use of this phrase to describe Nisei as 'swallow[ing] the blessing-in-disguise argument without question'[142] again constructs them as largely homogeneous.

The notion of a model minority is mobilized through the past–present binary in redemptive narratives emphasizing that Japanese Canadians benefited from their expulsion and incarcerations during the

1940s.[143] In addition to rendering invisible those who benefited from dispossessing and expelling Japanese Canadians, class and other social differences among Japanese Canadians and the differently lived effects of the Internment are erased. In fact, it is the social and psychological effects – for example, the ruptures and irreparable destruction of families and communities (through the material annihilation of communities and their particular geographic and social histories), the historical denigration or objectification of the body and cultural practices[144] that, along with racism and the material exclusions of labour-force stratification, underpin the present of Japanese Canadians.

Research is needed to analyse the process of class formation for Japanese Canadians, both survivors of the Internment and their children. I would argue that geographic separation and the forced assimilation policies of the federal government were critical to producing class privilege for some Japanese Canadians who were forced to be autonomous from 'their' racialized group, through speaking English or French only, or both, excelling in education or institutions of the dominant culture, and using their middle-class status in an attempt to demonstrate their 'loyalty to the nation.'[145] It was also necessary for some of us to be allowed to succeed according to the hegemonic standard of middle-class Canadian culture and be visible in our success in order to redeem the nation for the Internment. Little attention, however, has been given to those who did not acquire a middle-class position after their dispersal in Canada and after returning from Japan in the post-war period. The homogenizing construction of Japanese Canadians as a middle-class 'model minority' forgets those who do not conform to this model.[146] The prominence of middle-class Japanese Canadians who are seen as representatives of survivors of the Internment or representative of a 'Japanese Canadian' (like myself) render invisible the complex social processes (including processes of gender, racialization, ableism, nationalism, and international economics and politics) that shaped the class positions of Japanese Canadians and those of their families.

Thus the notion that all Japanese Canadians are currently financially and socially secure disallows recognition of the differences in class among survivors and their descendants. Of the former group, few acquired positions of power in government, for example.[147] People of Japanese ancestry who immigrated after the Internment and who did not come from families who were incarcerated are also differently located in relation to this history.[148] The lack of representation of the social differences among ourselves as Japanese Canadians and our different relationships to the Internment, something to which I will return in chapters 2, 8, and 10, contributes to the notion of a monolithic Japanese Canadian community.

The images of the passive, silent subject and the model minority subject obscure the relations of power that underpin their construction and the ways in which complex subjects are formed within this nexus of power and in relation to other differently, socially located subjects. They foreclose engagement with contradictory positioning. As Elena Tajima Creef points out, homogeneous constructions 'permit little or no room for more complex voices, criticisms, or reflections.'[149]

Conclusion

The liberal construction of the Internment as a past historical event masks its long-term effects on the lives of those who were incarcerated and the lives of subsequent generations. In its construction as being solely about Japanese Canadians and the fearful politicians and citizens, it erases questions of complicities in a project that was national and racial. History represented as a march of progress can be used to simultaneously minimize the harms committed in the past and those of the present, as the past and the future are always the measure against which present harms are compared. In such scenarios, like the text of the redress agreement, for example, where the Internment has been acknowledged by a federal government, its construction as a past mistake is used to consolidate the notion of the nation as one where equality is the rule.

The construction of history through a liberal temporal discourse minimizes the violence of the Internment. The forgetting of that violence is, in fact, a continual process of remembering in ways that exonerates those who inhabit the present and negates complicity in the processes of domination – white supremacy, patriarchy, economic exploitation, nationalism, heteronormativity, able-bodiedness, et cetera – upon which present privilege is founded. The Japanese Canadian subjects produced through liberal historical reconstructions are limited in that they are unable to demonstrate contradictory and contesting subjectivities. Euphemistic language such as 'evacuation,' and other terms used in relation to each site as part of the normative discourse of Internment, is itself a mechanism of control through which we come to know the Internment, and the subjects of the Internment come to know themselves, which in turn affects the ways in which they re-member that history.

However, the surviving generations of the Internment are the always potentially contradictory memory-bearers challenging a nation's selective amnesia.

This chapter ends with a question that it in part attempts to address: 'How has an enormous collective "silence" on the part of white people who witnessed and benefited from the Internment been forgotten?' As Evelyn, one of the women I interviewed, astutely pointed out to me when we were discussing white people's claim to 'ignorance' of the Internment, 'It was interesting that people didn't know about it. The children were there one day and they were gone the next. Where did they go?'[150]

In this chapter, I have argued that a collective forgetting of the violence of the Internment was produced simultaneously to producing the Internment. Not only have most of the sites of incarceration been forgotten by physical and discursive maskings but, as Evelyn suggests, so have the very people who inhabited them and the processes through which they suddenly disappeared and then appeared in other places. They have been forgotten through the *silence* of most of the white witnesses to, and participants in, the Internment. The forgetting of the Internment by white participants and witnesses, therefore, was both an individual and collective endeavour.

The processes of the Internment produced the subjects interned and the subjects involved in its implementation. Those who represent the Internment through historical, literary, and other cultural texts also make themselves in relation to the Internment and Japanese Canadians while writing about them. In this way, the Internment continues to produce relational subjects. Rather than focusing our attention upon the white witnesses to the Internment who have grown 'silent' since the 1940s, however, those representing the Internment have drawn our attention towards what they construe as the 'silent' Japanese Canadian female subject, something I discuss further in the next chapter.

2 The Silencing Continues: 'Speaking for' Japanese Canadian Subjects of the Internment

Our words may be therein destabilized; they are not silent.

Audrey Kobayashi, 'Birds of Passage or Squawking Ducks'[1]

Where is the subjectivity of Japanese Canadians in this document? The last word is written in the rhetoric of dominant language ... Japanese Canadians are still *spoken for*.

Roy Miki, 'Asiancy'[2]

As a researcher and daughter of families who were incarcerated, dispossessed, forced to labour in road camps and on farms, and separated from family members during the 1940s, I follow with concern the depiction of the subjects of the Internment through academic texts and other media. Given the continuing, pervasive characterization of Japanese Canadians as generationally unified and homogeneous, the ways in which racial homogeneity is secured through the tropes of silence and speech is a still necessary discussion. Even after the redress settlement of 1988, during which Japanese Canadians individually and collectively spoke against a hegemonic Canadian collective silence on the Internment and the erasure of knowledge of the Internment, the recurring images of the silent Japanese Canadian Internment survivor are evidence of a persistent homogenizing racialization and gendering of the subjects of the Internment.

My goal in this chapter is to ask questions about the recurring construction of the silent Japanese Canadian Internment survivor in various texts and media and our responsibility in reproducing this predominant image. I draw attention to some of the texts through which the image of the female Internment survivor is constructed, through the figures of Issei and Nisei women, tracing its genealogy from some of the critical reception to the novel *Obasan*, the use of Muriel Kitagawa in public discourses produced through a newspaper and a museum exhibit, and lastly the reception to Linda Ohama's film *Obāchan's Garden*. My argument is that while the critical literature on Japanese Canadian cultural production burgeons, the entrenchment and use of the trope of silence communicates racialized and gendered significations despite their complex analytical contexts. Some of the tropes that operate in the construction of the subjects of the Internment are still repeated, yet they are rarely interrogated. What also is lacking in these critiques is an examination of how women are often used as exemplary examples of the 'silent survivor' and that these very visible racialized and gendered usages of silent women variously affect the visibility of Japanese Canadian men. In addition, the gendered and racialized construction of the silent Internment survivor serves to exceptionalize the speaking Japanese Canadian subject. More importantly, the ongoing scholarly and cultural production that professes to represent Japanese Canadians continues to produce the subjects of the Internment and a collective cultural memory of them through the 'power-effects'[3] of discourse, a discourse that homogenizes and silences those subjected by it. The effects of the silence–speech binary therefore render most interned Japanese Canadians as silent and 'still spoken for,'[4] while simultaneously producing notions of the normative subject and Canada.

In what follows, I attend to what Lisa Lowe has called the importance of 'collectively forged images' and her argument that 'the question of aesthetic representation is always also a debate about political representation.'[5] Images of Japanese Canadians are constructed ones and are not windows to the authentic Japanese Canadian self. Moreover, no subject can ever be entirely accurately represented due to what Laura Hyun Yi Kang calls the 'always already ideologically saturated discursive field that in some ways anticipates the "self" and re-constructs it.'[6]

The Binary of the Passive, Silent Orientalized Female Subject and the Speaking Canadianized Female Subject

What are some of the meanings attached to the images of Asian woman? As Kang suggests, the binary relationship between the Western subject and what is construed as the Asian subject is one that is markedly gendered, wherein the 'Asian female has been a recurring figure of silence, passivity, sexual mystery, exotic inscrutability in this tradition of myth-making and identification.'[7] Images of women who were interned situate Japanese Canadian women in relation to the polarized, fixed binary of the speaking 'Canadianized' or westernized woman and the silent 'Japanese' woman.

Rather than attempt to represent the 'real' Japanese Canadian woman, this chapter draws attention to the representation of Japanese Canadian women, in particular through the binary construction of the silent Internment survivor and the speaking Canadianized subject. While I argue that both sides of the binary reinforce the Western liberal male subject, further work is needed to understand how Japanese Canadian women are constructed in relation to notions of white femininity. While I pay less attention to images of Japanese Canadian men in this chapter, it must be remembered that the racialized gendering of the Asian Canadian woman also enables particular constructions of the Asian Canadian man, and while males are not exempted from the mark of silence, it is frequently the woman who is called upon in various representations to carry the trope of silence to its foregone conclusion. Through this gendered hierarchy of visibility, the binary is also used to maintain the heterosexual construction of the Asian female as 'available'[8] to a hegemonic Western masculinity.

Reproducing the Silence–Speech Binary through Readings of Obasan

The theme of 'silence' and 'speech' resonates through diverse historical, autobiographical, literary, artistic, psychological, and sociopolitical production, a theme that is brought into the foreground in titles such as *Stone Voices*, *Shedding Silence*, and *Too Long Silent*. And, indeed, much has been written about Joy Kogawa's use of silence in *Obasan*.[9] Published in 1981, *Obasan* was the first Canadian novel about the Internment written by a Japanese Canadian author.[10] It appeared in the same year as Ann Sunahara's *The Politics of Racism*, and both of these groundbreaking publications launched historiographical and literary challenges to a white-dominated Canadian historical narrative. Through her novel, Kogawa articulates a history theretofore barely documented. From the canonical standpoint of Canadian literature, her contribution ruptured a silence of the imaginary and, in light of this fact alone, it must be regarded as a pivotal text. This moment of rupture is described by Roy Miki as an 'inaugural crisis,' one in which the writer expresses 'the urgency to speak back to the barrier of a denied personal and communal past.'[11]

Kogawa utilized the papers of Muriel Tsukiye Kitagawa in her characterization of one of the book's protagonists, Aunt Emily, and she acknowledges her seminal role in the novel's preface. It must be emphasized, however, that *Obasan* is a work of fiction, and it is the translation of fictional characters as emblematic of real and transparent selves that obscures the spectatorial selves imagining and reiterating homogeneous enfigurations of Internment survivors. Kogawa's book is one of the major literary representational sources for the construction of the trope of the silent survivor not only through its use of metaphors of silence in the book but importantly as a vehicle from which its characters are appropriated and through which critics construct their own representations of Japanese Canadians. Rather than analyse Kogawa's own representations here, I turn to some examples from North American literary criticism as an important source of the production and communication of this trope.

In the novel, the narrator, Naomi, remembers her experiences of expulsion from Vancouver, her family's incarceration in the Slocan camp, and labouring on an Alberta sugar beet farm. The death of her uncle evokes memories of her family's life prior to, during, and after these events as they gather to mourn in the small Alberta town to which they were sent after their incarceration in Slocan. It is during her engagements with the past and her conversations with surviving family members and their friend, who is a Christian minister, that she comes to know the answer to a lifelong question: What was her mother's fate after she left them to accompany her own mother to Japan before the war? As Naomi struggles to remember and to know, she confronts the complex ways in which memory is revelatory, both through remembering and forgetting.

The theme of silence in *Obasan* is constituted through the various characters' different relationships to the traumatic histories of the Internment, the nuclear bombing of Hiroshima and Nagasaki, and child sexual abuse. Although Aunt Aya's (Obasan's) 'silence' is highlighted in the novel – in particular her resistance to speaking about the disappearance of Naomi's mother – there are many silences that circulate in this story, including that of Naomi's experience of sexual assault as a child, a violence she has not disclosed to anyone.

Kogawa does set up a certain binary tension between the central characters of Aunt Aya and Aunt Emily. Separated from other family members, Aunt Aya and Uncle Isamu raised Naomi and her brother Stephen during the Internment years. Naomi's Aunt Emily, after being forced to leave her Vancouver home, was able to move to Toronto. In the novel, Naomi reflects on the differences between the aunts, Aya who has not told her much about the Internment period and Emily who has described the injustice of the Internment. She states, 'How different my two aunts are. One lives in sound, the other in stone.'[12] The complexities of speech and silence, however, are elaborated upon in the following sentence, 'Obasan's language remains deeply underground but Aunt Emily, BA, MA, is a word warrior.[13] Kogawa is providing a social context for speech here: Aunt Aya has a language, one that is underground, and Aunt Emily is situated as an 'educated' woman, thereby granting her some possibilities for speaking denied to Aya. Her first language, therefore, and that of all of the Issei, is Japanese, which was forced in many ways to go 'underground' both during the Internment and after the dispersal given the ways in which it was used symbolically to signify difference and disloyalty.

Some of the reception to the novel in the United States repeats uncritically the trope of the silent Japanese Canadian. U.S.-based scholar Shirley Geok-Lin Lim makes an intrinsic connection between silence and submission when she describes Naomi's lack of knowledge about the whereabouts of her mother: '[H]er relatives seek to protect her through their silent submission. Her mystification ... derives from her Japanese American [sic] community's silent submission to Canadian racism.'[14] In addition to misidentifying Naomi as American, Lim's totalizing comment (similar to that of Ken Adachi's quote in chapter 1) ignores not only acts of resistance to racism in the novel itself but also feeds a discourse of racialization in the simplistic critique of Japanese Canadians for not protesting their expulsion and incarceration. The reduction of the complex lived processes of displacement and incarceration to such generalizations negates the various ways in which the subjects of the Internment negotiated relations of power imposed upon them and also how their options were limited as a result of these processes. Moreover, such analyses fail to interrogate what constitutes resistance and how notions of the liberal, masculine subject – the self-actualized, speaking man – inform ideas of what resistance is. For example, the men known as the Nisei Mass Evacuation group, who protested the separation of families in 1942 and were sent to prisoner-of-war camps in northern Ontario, are constructed in some Internment narratives authored by Japanese Canadians as the resisters of the expulsion,[15] whereas the resistance and protest of women, other than Muriel Kitagawa (as described below), are rarely acknowledged.

What is also forgotten in such representations of the 'submission' of Japanese Canadians is the fact that there were no organized protests by non-Japanese Canadians to the expulsion, incarceration, and dispossession. In fact, the policy of forced dispersal was actively supported by white Christian church groups (as we saw in the previous chapter) and women's and other organizations.

Other U.S.-based critics, however, render a more complex reading of Japanese Canadians in the novel. For example, King-Kok Cheung's analysis of *Obasan* attempts to break out of the binary of the valuing of speech over silence. Her critique is aimed most directly at Anglo-American feminists' valorization of speech (in the 'liberatory' discourse of 'coming to voice') and 'revisionist Asian American male critics who refute stereotypes by renouncing silence entirely.'[16] Her work emphasizes that the 'mostly critical or patronizing'[17] attitudes towards the silence of Asian Americans rely upon Orientalist conceptualizations of the Asian subject. She also draws attention to the effects of trauma on memory and the ability to articulate memories.

Nevertheless her emphasis on the 'positive cultural and aesthetic manifestations of reticence'[18] reinforces difference based as it is on her aestheticization of behaviour explained by fixed notions of Japanese culture. While what is represented as the silence of Japanese Canadians is often explained through interpretations of their different culture – for example using concepts such as *enryo* and *gaman*[19] – the search for its origin in Japan or Japanese culture ignores other geographies of this silence. It is interesting how fixed notions of culture that are used to explain Issei behaviour, in particular, are also used in historical accounts and in popular discourses to explain the actions of the Nisei during and after the Internment.[20] To imagine behaviours as explicable through and reducible to national origins outside of Canada conveniently dislocates a discussion of how silence and speech for Japanese Canadians have been mediated through processes of incarceration and forced geographic and social displacement, and the violence of these processes. Rey Chow's statement that '[d]isplacement constitutes identity, but as such it is the identity of the ever-shifting'[21] challenges the idea that diasporic identities are determined by and are hence derivative or watered-down versions of one cultural and national origin and recognizes that the continual physical and symbolic displacements of

Japanese Canadians must involve massive destabilizations of identity. Thus we must interrogate the raced and gendered use of 'Japanese culture' as explanatory of behaviour and ask questions about how immigrant origins are imagined and socially produced *within* Canada (and the United States) and how they are variously mobilized to secure a dominant notion of the nation.

As Cheung points out, *Obasan* actually disrupts the unified notion of the 'silent' Issei woman through the character of Naomi's grandmother. It is she who unlocks a door of unknowing for Naomi and provides her with information about her mother's absence. Through a missive, her Issei grandmother communicates with her, disclosing the details of her mother's injuries and eventual death in the bombing of Nagasaki. This testimonial act complicates our understanding of communication about traumatic events; various modalities that are utilized to convey histories of violence to family members are not vocalized speech but neither are they silence.

Making Generational and Racial Differences through the Speech–Silence Binary

A Canadian critic, Frank Davey, quotes from Naomi's grandmother's letter in *Obasan*, which discloses the details of her mother's death, 'For the burden of these words, forgive me.' Davey concludes that this quote is demonstrative of 'an Issei text, *yasashi* in tone, and framed by apology.'[22] Davey's description of *yasashi*, in his view a concept embodied by Aya, is 'modesty, unassuming kindness, and self-effacement.'[23] In this way, he draws attention to his perception of gendered, racial difference in the writing of the letter rather than focusing upon how it serves to disrupt notions of a monolithic Issei generation. This unity not only of individual identity but also of an entire generation is necessary to Davey's formulation that the characters in *Obasan* represent 'three generations of immigrant experience.'[24]

While Davey draws attention to how, despite its title, the novel is not affiliated with any one generation, his description of the three generations as 'immigrants' reinforces the notion of their tenuous relationship to Canada. In addition, Davey suggests that two of the generations are characterized in this way: the Issei are 'inclined towards silence and forgetting, as hoping not for full participation in their new country, but merely to be harassed as little as possible';[25] the Nisei are 'eager to participate in Canadian society, angry and indignant about their wartime treatment, and naively trusting that protest and appeals to law will bring redress.'[26]

Audrey Kobayashi argues that '[t]he myth of generational difference is synonymous with the myth of the Issei as "other," with their foreign ways and unassailable silences.'[27] Within a Western liberal context, Aunt Aya is thus read as the 'Oriental' Issei and Aunt Emily is understood as the 'Canadianized' Nisei who uses the dominant language to fight for equality. The culturalization of Aya's 'silence' and its categorization as passivity or apathy obscure and reproduce the notion that, within the context of Canada, people who do not speak English (or French in Quebec) are not considered to be full citizens or political subjects. What is brought to the forefront in analysing Aya's silence is the equation between her 'not speaking' and passivity or submission at the neglect of analysing silence in relation to the trauma induced through violence. This construction of subjects of the Internment as passive and not resisting is also part of an Orientalist construction of Japanese Canadians and a reinforcement of the white subject as the active, self-actualized agent. The interpretation of the Issei as not wanting 'full' citizenship and the 'naivety' of the Nisei situate these generations as somehow underdeveloped, not nearing the sophistication of 'real' citizens. This infantilization of Japanese Canadians speaks to what Kang refers to as a nationalist discourse that marginalizes racialized citizens with 'the promise of achieving subjecthood and maturity in time.'[28] It fits as well within a narrative that is described by Kirsten Emiko McAllister and Scott Toguri McFarlane as a 'mythologized Japanese Canadian history,' representing Japanese Canadians as 'childlike and passive.'[29]

Based on his reading of the two Sansei characters in Obasan as 'dissimilar' and unconnected to the Sansei generation, a generation he describes as being 'vulnerable to assimilation,' Davey concludes that the Sansei generation is not represented in the novel.[30] He fails to interrogate what he views as dissimilarity as a potential problematic for his own homogenization of the Issei and Nisei generations. Also disturbing in his and many other representations of the generations are the fixed and distinct characteristics that are used to separate them. How geography, history, and social domination have produced connected yet heterogeneous subjects within and between the generations is therefore not analysed. Inevitably, what is constructed through this homogenization of generational categories is a notion of racial Others who are determined by their cultural origins and relationships with one another. A more complex analysis of social differences within and between the generations would include an understanding that their identities are forged through processes of immigration, racial and gendered racial violence, the exclusionary practices of citizenship and nation-building, and differential resistance to these processes.

In Kogawa's descriptions of the generations in her book, the boundaries are less clear than critics impute them to be; for example, Naomi's uncle, although born in Japan, straddles the generations of Issei and Nisei because he was brought to Canada as a child. In Davey's and other readings of *Obasan*, however, the generations are clearly seen as discretely separate and the subjects are identified by and analysed through a preconceived and prescriptive notion of generational position.

The Speaking Female Japanese Canadian Subject

Using a white Western-informed analysis of female subjection as constructed through the oppositional binary of woman–man, some critics construct an opposition between Japanese Canadian men and Japanese Canadian women. Hence the racialized woman is often called into view in relation to what is deemed patriarchal in the racialized man. When the Japanese woman is constructed as progressing towards the model of the white liberal subject, the Japanese man must thereby be shown as more patriarchal than the white Canadian male.

Davey argues in his essay on *Obasan* that the 'speaking' characters in the novel (who according to him are Grandmother Sato, Naomi, and Aunt Emily) 'break with the Japanese woman's confinement to silence or unprovocative discourse.'[31] It must be emphasized that the generalized construction of 'Japanese' women as confined to silence is Davey's, not Kogawa's, and the figures of the speaking exception and the silent rule are simultaneously produced by the critic here. Moreover, the speaking woman is portrayed as breaking her connections to her Japanese 'confinement,' a liberation accorded through speech.

As Wendy Brown suggests, the analysis that speech is liberatory is part of a feminist discourse that reinscribes a liberal subject with a core essential truth. As she states, '[T]ruth-telling about our desires or experiences is construed as deliverance from the power that silences and represses them (rather than as itself a site and effect of regulatory power).'[32] Therefore, by focusing on what we construct as 'silent' Japanese Canadians and their liberation through speech, we ignore the regulatory power that is invested in these constructions, including the judgment of silence as 'confinement' and speech as 'breaking confinement,' and our evaluation of what they say and don't say.

By concluding that *Obasan* is a 'feminist novel' within the context of Japanese culture, Davey remakes himself as knower of what constitutes feminism in Japan and dislocates the relations of male domination to a national space different from that inhabited by white Canadian men. In this way he invokes a particular white Western-informed notion of feminism whereby the racialized woman requires rescue by white civilization from the uncivilized racialized man.[33] Davey's appropriation of *Obasan* for use in a white Western feminist discourse is interwoven through an Orientalist and heterosexist discourse that casts aspersion upon Japanese Canadian men, which is evident in his comment that Naomi and Emily are 'single because of an apparent lack of worthy men.'[34] While Davey does not specify that it is Japanese Canadian men who are unworthy, his prefatory remarks about Japanese patriarchy and the breaking away from this repression by the novel's three 'speaking' characters suggest that he is referring to men who share this cultural history. In addition, Davey does not mention that it was actually a white man whom Naomi had dated and with whom she had felt the mark of 'difference.'

Davey also emphasizes how 'their inherited Japanese culture is one of male privilege.'[35] The binary of the patriarchal Japanese man and the oppressed Japanese woman can serve to construct the concomitant notions of Japan as a backward and patriarchal nation in contrast to the progressive nation of Canada. The patriarchal Japanese (Canadian) man is thus used to produce the progressive white Western man whose very masculinity depends upon emasculating and feminizing the racialized man. What also is obscured in this depiction of Japanese men as patriarchal in a context where the hegemony of white Anglo-Canadian men is ignored are the ways in which white Canadian men (politicians, administrators, employers, etc.) during the Internment implemented gendered practices that sustained male domination.

If the causes of Japanese Canadian women's subordination are only examined as originating from Japanese culture, one may fail to look at how the gendering process inculcated through the mechanisms of the Canadian state contributes to the construction of Aya's silence and how her silence is judged against a liberal notion of an autonomous speaking/resisting subject. Given the gendered segregation of the incarcerations – many women were sent to detention camps and many of their

male partners, brothers, and sons were sent to road or POW camps –
women such as Aya held sole responsibility for the care of children,
the elderly, and people with disabilities. Such gendered responsibility
for the survival of one's dependents would necessarily constrain one's
ability to speak critically. The threat of further family disruption and
separation would have weighed heavily on those who were caregiv-
ers. Also neglected in the binary examination of differences between
Aya and Emily are the different spatial contours of their expulsions
and displacements. Aya was forced to move with children to the Slocan
camp; Emily, also forcibly moved from her home, was eventually given
a permit to move to Toronto, but without dependents. Although still
subjected to government restrictions in Toronto, Emily inhabited a different social space from that of Aya, one in which she was able to write
and speak more critically.

The images of Japanese Canadians rendered by writer Joy Kogawa
in her novel *Obasan* are representations of one extended family. With
the exception of Aunt Emily, most of the attention in the book is focused on the Issei characters of the aunt and uncle, and the Sansei narrator Naomi. In the acclaimed novel *The Electrical Field*,[36] Sansei author
Kerri Sakamoto chose to write from the position of a Nisei narrator.
Sakamoto's and Kogawa's decisions to narrate novels from subject positions generationally different from their own are important authorial
underpinnings. Given that these are both works of fiction, it cannot
be expected from these authors that they are portraying real people;
their characters are mediated by the authors' own different social locations as well as the processes of editorial review and publication. The
reception to these novels and other cultural production that general-
izes characteristics found in their fictionalized characters to all Japanese
Canadians or that assumes that a Japanese Canadian author must be
conveying real representations of Japanese Canadians might therefore
be viewed as part of a homogenizing process of racialization.

Muriel Kitagawa: Using the Speaking Subject to Produce Silent Internment Subjects

As was stated above, Kogawa made use of the papers of Muriel Tsukiye
Kitagawa in her creation of the character of Aunt Emily in *Obasan*.[37] A
journalist by profession, Kitagawa lived in Vancouver with her husband and two children when Canada entered the war against Japan.

While the federal government began its process of expelling 22,000 Japanese Canadians from the British Columbia coast, Kitagawa, who was pregnant with twins, was one of few people granted the authorization to move with her family to Toronto in 1942.

Kitagawa's extant papers, deposited at the Library and Archives Canada, include letters she wrote to her brother, Wesley Fujiwara, who was a medical student at the University of Toronto. The letters document her perceptions of the expulsion, incarceration, and dispossession of her friends and family, and are a complex representation of her relationship to the nation and Canadian citizenship. In this section I draw attention to how Kitagawa has been used to signify an exceptional speaking subject and produce the silencing of other differently located Japanese Canadians.

Kitagawa's letters and journalistic accounts, rare textual archives written in the 1940s, have been used to construct the gendered speaking 'Canadianized' subject of the Internment. Kitagawa is much less known than the fictionalized character of Aunt Emily in *Obasan* who is based on her. Through *Obasan* and its resounding impact, Aunt Emily has taken on a metonymic presence larger than the 'real' woman on whom she is based.[38] Yet Kitagawa has also become a critical figure in how the Internment is renarrated at moments of national engagement with this history, and her important reappearances in these instances illustrate how Japanese Canadian visibility is also marked by discourses of nation.

On the occasion of the signing of the redress agreement with the Canadian government, Gerry Weiner, then Minister of State for Multiculturalism, issued a press release in which he asks rhetorically: 'Why *did* [Japanese Canadians] remain loyal to this country?' In answer he quotes Aunt Emily: '*Is* this my own, my native land? ... Yes. It is. For better or worse, *I Am Canadian*.'[39] Although Weiner attributes the words to Kogawa's protagonist, those familiar with Kitagawa's writings will identify them as being from her essay 'This Is My Own.'[40] Weiner uses Aunt Emily's/Kitagawa's words as the authentic screen – 'Only someone who is Japanese Canadian can explain ...' – for his subsequent redemption of the Canadian nation. He reasserts through a liberal discourse of progress how Canadians have 'grown' and 'acquired new wisdom and compassion' in the years after the Internment.[41]

A week after the Canadian Race Relations Foundation (CRRF) office – established as part of the redress settlement – was finally opened in Toronto, the *Toronto Star* devoted approximately a third of a page to the announcement of its establishment.[42] According to the *Toronto Star*, 'the most moving part' of the Foundation's inauguration was a reading from *This Is My Own* (although note that the *Toronto Star* misnames the book as *Letters to Wes*). The newspaper announces the Foundation's opening by renarrating in a few sentences the Internment story; but most of the text is quoted from Kitagawa's work. This includes an excerpt from Kitagawa's devastating descriptions of Hastings Park, the first site of incarceration for 8,000 people, and the reaction of her children and friends to the 'Nazi-fashion[ed]' 'hell' of BC.[43] Kitagawa's words, both here and in the original texts, are complex, critical, and revelatory of her struggle to define self and citizenship in the face of actions that daily demeaned the self and that called into question the terms of Canadian citizenship. Interestingly, the *Toronto Star*'s last quotation from Kitagawa are her phrases, similar to those used by Weiner to portray Kitagawa as loyal to the nation, 'This is my own, my native land! ... God! God! were my soul "so dead" I could not thus agonize for the land betrayed!'[44] Kitagawa thus presented evokes the image of the loyal citizen who despite the Internment remains committed to Canada. Hers is an unmistakably gendered and heterosexual discourse, where devotion to children, husband, and family are used by the newspaper in the service of narrating a 'gentler,' 'more compassionate,' feminized image of nation.

In a review of *This Is My Own*, American scholar Gordon Hirabayashi recommended that it be given to 'new Canadians' with their 'citizenship certificate.'[45] He stated, 'It is a most appropriate introduction to Canada and her character, its weakness when citizens waver, its strength when citizens give commitment to the principles for which she stands.'[46] Hirabayashi's recommendation has an even more complex significance when we consider that *he* challenged the U.S. government in May 1942 by refusing to honour the curfew law and the orders to move from the coast. Hirabayashi pursued this challenge to the U.S. Supreme Court where the charges of violating the curfew order and failing to report for expulsion were upheld.[47] Hirabayashi's statement, written in 1942, explaining why he refused the orders, resonates with what he describes of Kitagawa's struggle and its relationship to nation: 'I consider it my duty to maintain the democratic standards for which this nation lives.'[48]

A more recent example of the use of Kitagawa by an institution funded by the Canadian federal government is found in a section entitled *Forced Relocation. Un Déplacement Forcé* at the Canadian War Museum in Ottawa.[49] Kitagawa once again appears as a spokesperson for all

Japanese Canadians in the text that accompanies a photograph of her at a typewriter.[50] Part of the text in the accompanying signage reads, 'Journalist Tsukiye Muriel Kitagawa vividly evoked the despair and bitterness experienced by the Japanese-Canadian community in a series of wartime letters to her brother in Toronto.'[51] The choice of nouns is interesting: 'despair' and 'bitterness' suggest resignation and even pathology, nouns that mask the sheer outrage and sharp critique articulated in her letters and essays. Clearly this portrait also serves to homogenize the different political and emotive reactions of those who comprised the 'Japanese-Canadian community.'

Some might argue that these appearances of Kitagawa in state discourses describing the Internment are evidence of remembering the atrocities committed against Japanese Canadians in the 1940s. I would suggest that the ways in which Kitagawa is used to narrate this history in these governmental acknowledgments is evidence of the forgetting of the extent of the harm and how it was so frequently contested and not only by Kitagawa. They commodify as well a particular Japanese Canadian subjectivity that reifies nation and the liberal subject as its citizen. Re-presented as a loyal, assimilated citizen, Kitagawa's scathing criticism of the actions taken by the government and Canadian citizens in the 1940s may be overshadowed. Her resistance in naming these atrocities is used in a way that attests to the inherent goodness of the always ever redeemable Canadian nation. In the unique attention given to her as a loyal critic, *she* is regarded as unique in the community for which she is designated spokesperson. In this way, Kitagawa is reconstituted as the autonomous, liberal subject who is allowed to speak freely in Canada and who uniquely resisted injustice while her community largely remained silent. What is forgotten in these re-presentations and uses of Kitagawa are her profound analyses of the actions taken against Japanese Canadians and how her analysis was informed through her observations of the effects of the expulsion on her community and her connections to it. Her speech was also constituted through her position as a writer who, though expelled from Vancouver, was moved to Toronto, a place different from those occupied by most incarcerated Japanese Canadians. Hence what is reproduced through these images is the myth, as articulated by Lim above, that most Japanese Canadians did not contest nor resist their incarcerations. The construction of Kitagawa as autonomous and isolated is heightened through these governmental and media representations of her while the lesser known (to non-Japanese Canadians) Nisei Mass Evacuation Group who resisted the order to move from the coast and protested the separation of fam-

ily members, the Japanese Canadians who organized to fight the sale
of their possessions without their permission in 1943,[52] and the Nisei
Mass Evacuation Women's Group (see chapter 4), and thus the historical importance of collective organizing by Japanese Canadians against
the violations instituted by the federal government before and during
the 1940s receive less public memorialization and acknowledgment.

The mobilization of gender is also critical in these uses of Kitagawa
as she is clearly a feminized symbol of loyalty. While Japanese Canadian men who served for Canada during the First and Second World
Wars are sometimes used to conjure up similar images of loyal citizens
(an approbative militaristic symbolism from which Japanese Canadian
women were excluded), they appear less frequently in public nationalist discourses than their counterparts in the United States.

Ironically, at the Canadian War Museum, whose purpose is to provide
a 'superb panorama of Canadian military history,'[53] there is no representation of the Japanese Canadian men who fought in the Canadian
military during the Second World War in the exhibit on the Internment.
There is only a photograph of a Japanese Canadian veteran Matsumi
Mitsui – dressed in civilian clothes – who served in the Canadian Ex-
pedition Forces of the First World War.[54] The 'speaking,' 'despairing,'
and 'bitter' Japanese Canadian woman is featured at the bottom of a
vertical arrangement of three photographs, Joy Kogawa's image is on
the top and Mitsui's is in the middle. Museum attendees do not, therefore, have to grapple with any portraits of Japanese Canadian men who
volunteered to fight for Canada during the Second World War while
their families were incarcerated and dispersed across Canada.[55] In effect, Kitagawa is once again exceptionalized – this time by a Canadian
institution of commemoration – as one of few Canadian racialized figures in the museum. The larger panorama of Canadian military history
is definitively painted as being made up of a largely white masculine
corps, despite the number of racialized men who served in its ranks.[56]
The exceptionalized images of two racialized Canadian Nisei women
(Kitagawa and Kogawa) who are strategically placed across from another exhibit entitled *Protecting Canada's West Coast* and a mannequin
dressed in the uniform of the Japanese army portrayed as the threat to
Canada's security isolates them from racialized Canadian men, including Japanese Canadian Nisei men. This representation may also serve
to divide other racialized groups from Japanese Canadians and even
Nisei veterans from Kitagawa and Kogawa as they view the women's
presence in relation to their absence.

Although Kitagawa can be used to mobilize the claims of the racialized to the rights of Canadian citizenship, her presence in the museum underscores how her exceptionalism can be used and received with ambivalence. Cast as one of few racialized Canadians in the entire museum and placed in close proximity to the Japanese male enemy, Kitagawa can actually be viewed as part of the section depicting the threat to a vulnerable Canada and her expulsion from the west coast thus linked to its protection rather than the racism instigated by Canadians. The dominant figures of white Canadians surrounding them are staged as those who are threatened and the white military ultimately as Canada's protectors and heroes. Kitagawa, despite her speech, is therefore visually and spatially dominated by the opposing Japanese male figure and the overwhelmingly white and masculine Canadian military; the lack of portraits of Japanese Canadian men who served in the Canadian military in the Second World War erases and silences these men, conveniently securing the white masculinity of the museum's military representation. Despite her sometimes use by the Canadian state and media as a figure who experienced injustice and committed herself to Canadian citizenship, this citizenship can be called into question or received as marginally so because of her gendered and racialized subject positions. Moreover, she is again exceptionalized and used to produce and homogenize a silent Japanese Canadian majority. As these examples illustrate, the representation of the silent and speaking subjects of the Internment are also always deeply associated with the construction of the Canadian nation and citizenship.

Finally, it must be noted that Muriel Kitagawa died in 1974, before the publication of *Obasan* and before the National Association of Japanese Canadians began its concerted national struggle for redress.[57] Her words have therefore been mediated by others, including Kogawa, government officials, the media, and the Canadian War Museum. Paradoxically, the speaking subject herself has been spoken for through the political, social, and cultural use of her original writings, and she has not been present to witness this use of her work and her self, nor to speak back to it.

Obāchan's Garden:[58] Using the Silent Subject to Present Ourselves as Knowledgeable Subjects

Director Linda Ohama's film *Obāchan's Garden* focuses on her grandmother, Asayo Murakami, whose life is recreated through interviews, archival research, and fictionalized reconstructions. While the Internment plays a significant role in the narrative of the film, the focal point becomes Murakami's revelation that she had a previous marriage when she was a young woman in Japan. In addition, she reveals that her first husband left her and took their two daughters; she had not seen them since. Clearly, Ohama's speaking, intelligent, and witty protagonist cannot be reduced to a 'silent' Japanese Canadian woman. However, some of the reception to the film repeats the silence trope even against the visual and auditory evidence in the film. For example, Deborah L. Begoray writes, 'The information about the Japanese relocation and internment contained in this film, while explored in novels and history textbooks, is not often related by members of the Japanese [sic] community.'[59] While Rocio G. Davis states that the purpose of her analysis of Ohama's film is to analyse '[t]he complexity of the Japanese Canadian experience'[60] and 'to consider the ways this experience has been represented and articulated,'[61] she describes 'the older generation' as having 'suppressed many memories.'[62] Despite the recognition of Murakami in the film, these examples of how she was received indicate that, once again, a speaking Japanese Canadian woman is exceptionalized and used to produce silent Japanese Canadians.

How do the authors of these texts know that the history of the Internment is 'not often related' or that their memories have been 'suppressed'? This depiction of the Issei is reminiscent of Davey's comment, cited above, that they are 'inclined towards silence and forgetting.' Whatever the source for their construction of their own authoritative voices, the repetitions of this uninterrogated, stock description of the 'older generation' are themselves productive of the ongoing power of these reiterations and their effects as they render invisible the memories and representations of other Japanese Canadians and, in particular, those of the Issei generation. Thus most Japanese Canadians who were interned are frozen as silent figures across time; these simplified calcifications do not acknowledge their complex articulations of self at different moments of their expulsion, incarceration, forced labour, dispersal, deportation, and in the years that followed, up until the present time. Critics of the cultural production of Japanese Canadians thus produce themselves as knowledgeable about interned Japanese Canadians; their truths are enhanced while the truths articulated by most Japanese Canadian survivors past and present and their historical lack of access to public means of self-representation are not acknowledged. It would seem that while critics position themselves as knowledgeable about

Japanese Canadians, such generalizations actually demonstrate a lack of knowledge of them and *their* social and representational spaces. The reiterated trope of the silent survivor should therefore be reappraised, given the gaps in our abilities to portray their speech and complex identities, including those of the Issei, whose first – and, for some, only – language was/is Japanese. What we know of the Issei and Nisei from novels such as *Obasan* and *The Electrical Field* must be problematized to account for what can never be known about them by the authors and readers.

As many non-interned children, like myself, did not learn the Japanese language, we have not been able to read texts written in Japanese, including diaries, histories, and literature authored by the Issei. Audrey Kobayashi, however, used her Japanese-language skills to make visible to an English-speaking audience some of the poetry clubs and poems produced by the Issei before, during, and after the Internment. For example, she demonstrates that in contrast to the totalizing notion that the Issei suppressed their memories, the Suhoken Kukai (Strong Friends Poetry Circle) wrote in the preface to their book that they 'cannot forget the days of anxiety on being forcibly removed to road camps and ghost towns.'[63]

The Speaking Subjects: Children of Survivors

While much has been written about survivors' behaviour as demonstrations of *shikata ga nai*, silence, and so on, little attention has been paid to how their children have been part of this social construction of their parent(s) and do so from very specific subject positions. For social and material reasons (for example, class, education, access to funding, among others), most representational work on the Internment has been authored either by Japanese Canadians who were not incarcerated or by non-Japanese Canadians, and not by survivors themselves. As Audrey Kobayashi states in her analysis of the myth of generational differences and the characteristics attributed to each generation, 'it is necessary to understand how the myths have been constructed and reconstructed within community discourse, as well as within the broader social discourse that has defined all Japanese Canadians as other.'[64] Kobayashi therefore suggests that, Japanese Canadians, as well as others, have been responsible for mythologizing generational characteristics, including that of the silent Issei Internment survivor.

All of us engaged in the production of images of Japanese Canadians are participating in the construction of Japanese Canadian subjects and our image of others is necessarily tied to the image we wish to present of ourselves. This relational process renders children of survivors the speaking subjects when they represent their parent(s) as being silent about their experiences of expulsion and incarceration. Literary and artistic work by Sansei and Yonsei artists testify to their interpretations of this history's effects upon their generations and their need to bear witness to this legacy. In addition to Linda Ohama's *Obāchan's Garden*, filmic examples include Michael Fukushima's *Minoru: Memory of Exile*, an animated exploration of his father's deportation from Canada, and Midi Onodera's examination of her relationship to her grandmother in *Displaced View*.[65] Another powerful Canadian example is Haruko Okano's monograph entitled *Come Spring: Journey of a Sansei*. Through poetry, prose, and visual art, Okano describes her 'deep longing for a sense of physical and emotional history.'[66] A notable American film, *History and Memory: For Akiko and Takashige*, explores Rea Tajiri's relationship to her mother's incarceration at the Poston internment camp through images of her own visit to the camp site.[67] Her reconstructions of familial memories, juxtaposed with clips from films depicting the Second World War raise important questions about representation and memory.

Stan Yogi examines memory and Sansei Americans' poetic representations of the Internment. He uses poet Janice Mirikitani's work to make a case for the Sansei as the speaking subject when he states that 'the daughter has taken on the role of parent because she has the strength to confront the past that the mother cannot acknowledge.'[68] As previously discussed, Asian North Americans have been constructed by dominant subjects as less developed and less deserving of the rights of citizenship. Yogi's characterization of Mirikitani contributes to a discourse of infantilization of the Nisei mother. The different social conditions that enable the Sansei artist to speak and be published are not addressed in this essay. Yogi also furthers the liberal notion of speech as healing. His statement that '[s]peaking frees memory, even tragic memory, and transforms pain and denial into strength and power'[69] confers on the act of speaking alone, a transformative resolution to the legacy of the Internment.

Yogi's line of argument, that Sansei have an 'incomplete sense of themselves' due to the 'absence of personal narratives and family stories about the war years,'[70] replicates a predominant construction of children of survivors: Sansei lack a sense of self and their history because their parents were silent regarding their experiences of the Internment. The singularization of the 'silence' of our parents as the origin of destabilization obscures the complex configurations of oppression and the traumatic effects of the Internment. While many Japanese Canadians may have difficulty speaking about their experiences of the Internment, to situate them as the source of these difficulties is to obscure and forget the power relations that produced the Internment itself. In problematizing the representation of Japanese Canadians and the trope of silence reiterated through the narratives of the Internment, we can perhaps ask more complex questions about its subjects and representation and the spectatorial selves revealed through the focus upon the silence of Japanese Canadians. Does what we interpret as *their* silence become an opportunity to reinvoke dominance, presenting 'the occasion for *our* speech'?[71] Could the yearning for a 'complete' sense of self be critically examined by asking who the complete subject is and if this complete subject, this sense of a whole or unified self, is the liberal subject whose wholeness depends upon the incompletion of others through their subordination and the forgetting of this interdependent subject constitution? And is this the subject we really want to be? If not, can we creatively situate our incomplete selves as the place from which we might imagine a 'new kind of subject'?[72]

Conclusion

The Orientalist construction of the subjects of the Internment assists the liberal discourse in its quest for closure, a forgetting that is integral to the minimization of the effects of colonial and national violence. By focusing on Japanese Canadians' 'silence' in the aftermath of the Internment, attention is diverted from the actions of the perpetrators and beneficiaries of this violence. An Orientalist interpretation of silence also attempts to translate Japanese Canadian subjects as members of a unidimensional knowable group whose 'racial' and 'cultural' characteristics are always measured against those of unmarked dominant subjects. Such a deflection from an analysis of the systems of domination as they impinge upon the possibilities for resistance and speech conveniently limits the understanding of the complex effects on memory formation of oppression and the trauma resulting from the Internment.

The use of and reception to the cultural production by Japanese Canadians cited above render images of Japanese Canadian women highly visible: the mapping of their silence and speech as mutually exclusive is integral to the continuing racialization and gendering of the subjects of the Internment. In the case of the examples from the critical response to the novel *Obasan*, silence is indicative of submission and racial difference and is particularly assigned to most members of the Issei generation; speech is the mark of aspiring to sameness with the white Canadian subject, which is in theory, part of the gift of 'freedom' to be gained if proved to be loyal to the nation. Continually presented as silent figures, the Issei are the homogeneous extras lost in the crowd, providing the scenery for the real action waged and speech mobilized by non-Japanese Canadians, members of the Sansei, and to a lesser extent Nisei generations. Their construction as silent conveniently erases questions about the limits of the English language and the eradication of Japanese as a publicly practised language in Canada for most of the Nisei in the post-war period and its non-acquisition for most of the Sansei and subsequent generations. The inattention to the processes that produced the disappearing of the Japanese language also normalizes that loss rather than illuminating the violence of that process.

In the use of writer Muriel Kitagawa's work by the Canadian government, its politicians, and representatives as promulgated through newspapers and the Canadian War Museum, the exceptional speaking subject of the Internment is drawn against a silenced Japanese Canadian majority. The racialized and gendered figure of Kitagawa is thus mobilized to redeem the Canadian nation through her selection as a spokesperson whom they allow to speak, especially as she proclaims her commitment to Canada despite her own expulsion from British Columbia. Kitagawa's phrases used in politicians' speeches and museum exhibits are removed from the context of their longer texts and from the author herself. She did not live long enough to see the representations of herself by others; thus, she was unable to speak to or critique them.

The exceptionalized speaking subject used to produce a majority of silent Internment survivors persists in some of the reception to Linda Ohama's film *Obāchan's Garden*. Despite the vibrant, vocal figure of Asayo Murakami, who is the only Issei interviewed in Ohama's film, the absent other Issei are reconstructed by some critics as not speaking or even as repressing their memories. The relational process of remembering the Internment renders us as the speaking subjects when we represent the Issei and Nisei as silent about their experiences of expulsion and incarceration. My goal in this chapter has been to question this continuing static representation on the part of critics who imagine Japanese

Canadian survivors as being homogeneous backgrounds to their own texts even against the evidence of the representations critiqued.

Rather than questioning the accountability of the representer of the subjects of the Internment for the power inherent in processes of cultural production and critique distantiated from their subjects (processes that have been historically, for the most part, inaccessible to survivors), our representations speak for them and construct ourselves as knowers of the truth. In simplifying the complex processes and histories of the Internment in the representation of Japanese Canadians as silent, the accountability for this representation is not addressed. Hence the power inherent in the production of a liberal epistemology that disallows articulations of knowledges of national violence and the processes of representation and commodification that import speech and 'silence' into an enhancement of witnessing selves as knowers of truth are both obscured. As well, the erasure of the regulatory processes of making others speak for our benefit or rendering them silent obfuscates the redemptive benefits we glean from controlling the interpretation of survivors' speech and silence and from producing ourselves not only as materially and symbolically innocent but also as unimplicated in the power that produces these representations.

This obfuscation of power relations is perhaps most evident in the discourses that insist on verbal disclosure as a sign of healing or progress towards resolution. What constitutes healing from the innumerable losses and pain of the Internment? Is the desire for their speech also a desire for the non-interned to heal our feelings of culpability and complicity (if they are healed, we do not have to feel badly or responsible) or to stabilize the feelings of incertitude that accompany the witnessing of the histories of the Internment – or, indeed, both? How do representations of silent and homogeneous Japanese Canadians reproduce raced and gendered domination while ignoring the risks or costs of speech for Japanese Canadians?

In her seminal essay 'Can the Subaltern Speak?' Gayatri Spivak suggests we interrogate the gaze of Othering promoted through academic studies of the subaltern.[73] The 'object' of our investigations should thus consider the 'masculine-imperialist ideological formation'[74] informing monolithic constructions of racialized women and how hegemonic ideologies influence our constructions of ourselves as critics and representers. In this way we can commit ourselves to situating the discussion of speech differently in relation to the subject(s) of domination. While I seek to uncover some of the 'mechanics' of the constitution of 'silence' in relation to the Internment and heed Spivak's recommendation that *'measuring* silences'[75] may help us undermine hegemonic ideological formations, it is not towards the 'silence' of Japanese Canadians that I ultimately turn my questioning gaze.

At a lecture on photographic images of the American internment camps presented by Japanese American photographer Masumi Hayashi,[76] a young white woman approached my friend and me, the only Japanese Canadians in the room. She told us that her mother had been a friend of a Japanese Canadian girl in British Columbia and the friend and her family had suddenly moved. Her mother had asked her own mother why her friend had to leave and was told: 'You must never talk about that.' The entire family was told never to talk about their neighbours' sudden departure. Silences are thus multiply constructed. How this particular family and all those who witnessed the disappearance of their neighbours constructed their forgetting and their silence reveals their relationships to domination and nation.

Most of the Issei who were incarcerated have passed on, and the Nisei are now viewed as the 'older generation.' In contrast to the federal government's 1940s policy of racializing Japanese Canadians as a unified and undifferentiated group, it would be hoped that we remember those who were interned as people whose communications about their histories were and are varied. Denied, for the most part, the public means to articulate *their* analyses and memories, their control over the process of communicating their experiences may well be in their own selection of witnesses to whom *they* decide(d) to speak.

3 Method, Memory, and the Subjects of the Internment

It was quite a traumatic experience, I think, for a family to just up and move. You know, with your belongings.

– S., interview[1]

As was discussed in the last chapter, images of women interned have been constructed in different texts and in the reception to those texts. However, there has been little analysis of how gender functioned in the processes of the Internment or in making the subjects interned. While some authors have described gender oppression, particularly as experienced by Issei women in the pre-Second World War period,[2] little critical attention has been paid to how the Internment was a gendering process for Japanese Canadians. In this book, I examine survivor's memories of the Internment in order to contribute to a social analysis of their gendered experiences of the Internment. In conceptualizing the book as one that analyses some of the effects of the Internment, I also decided to interview the daughters of the women who were interned and to analyse how cross-generational memories of the Internment were transmitted between them. This decision was inspired by conversations with female friends whose parent or parents had been interned and by the extant cultural and scholarly production of non-interned 'daughters of the Internment.'[3] Despite the wealth of representations of the Internment authored by non-interned children of the Internment (see chapters 2 and 9), there is little analysis in the literature of the actual processes of conveying the history of the Internment to these children.[4] The ubiquitous construction of Japanese Canadians as being 'silent' about their Internment histories also propelled me to investigate how some daughters actually learned about this history.

Lisa Lowe describes the privatization and feminization of relations between Asian mothers and daughters as 'the trope of the mother–daughter relationship' and argues that this trope promotes the notion of the generational dyad as the sole source of cultural transmission and difference.[5] While I investigate how mothers have transmitted knowledge of the Internment to their daughters, I argue that familial knowledge production on the Internment cannot be separated from relations of power that construct gender, race, class, and other discourses of social difference in Canada.

The Women Interviewed

Multiple qualitative methods were used in the research conducted for this book. Archival research and interviews were the primary methods used in generating the material that follows. My research was further enhanced by my twenty-five year history of working in Japanese Canadian communities in different geographical areas of Canada. In this chapter, I focus on the method of interviewing used to generate the testimonies analysed in the remainder of the book. A purposive strategy[6] was used to find the twenty-one women I interviewed. This strategy required that I find Japanese-Canadian women who had daughters and who had been expelled from the British Columbia coast. Both mothers and their daughters had to be willing to be interviewed to participate in the project.

The women interviewed were located through word of mouth and through contacts with people in different Canadian cities and towns.[7] Eleven lived through the West Coast expulsion; ten are daughters of the women expelled. Most of the interviews were conducted between 1994 and 1996.[8] I did not know most of the women before the interview process.[9] Mothers and their daughters were interviewed as close in time as was possible, but sometimes the geographical distance between them hampered the fulfilment of this goal. The mothers and daughters lived in three different geographical regions of Canada. Not all of the mothers lived in the same region as their daughters. All of the women were interviewed individually, except for Ann, whose daughter was present with her consent. The qualitative method of semi-structured, in-depth interviews used in this project allowed for the exploration of 'topic[s] in detail' and 'in constructing theory.'[10] In writing this book, I have used only the information for which women have given their permission.[11]

The women interviewed are presented below in their family relationships, with grandmother or mother noted first, and daughter or
granddaughter last. I was able to interview the paternal and maternal grandmothers of one woman, Kyo. Kyo's paternal grandmother
is Ann, Mayumi's mother. Her maternal grandmother is Aya, Louise's
mother. Their ages at the time of the interview are noted in brackets.
Pseudonyms are used for each woman. Some selected the pseudonym
themselves; others requested I select one for them. The women are as
follows: Ann (82), Mayumi (42); Aya (77), Louise (56), Kyo (26, whose
paternal grandmother is Ann); Haru (72), Yuko (40); Kazuko (71), Sylvia (38); Margaret (65), Irene (36); S.[12] (65), Midori (27); May (64), Eiko
(44); Evelyn (64), Joanne (32); Esther (56), Janice (30); Yoshiko (55), Naomi (25). The ages of the mothers interviewed ranged from 55 to 82. The
daughters' ages ranged from 25 to 44.

As was stated in chapter 2, the categories of Issei, Nisei, and Sansei
have been used to construct monolithic images of Japanese Canadians. Due to the overdetermined nature of these terms and the ways in
which they have been used to homogenize Japanese Canadian identities through essentialized characteristics and cultural ascriptions, I do
not identify the women I interviewed by these terms. As pointed out by
some of the women, these terms can signify relationships to immigration, settlement in Canada, and to generations of Japanese Canadians.
However, they can erase the complexity of these relations. For example,
the term 'Issei' is used for anyone born in Japan who immigrated to Canada. Yet some of the Issei may have immigrated with children and thus
two generations may be categorized under the one term. One woman
in my study, Evelyn, was 64 when interviewed and is viewed as a Nisei
woman. Her paternal grandfather, however, lived and worked in the
United States prior to his move to Canada. Her maternal grandparents
also lived in Canada. But given that both of her parents were born in
Japan, they are identified as Issei and, as a result, she is identified by
some as Nisei. Another woman interviewed, Yoshiko, had a great-uncle
who lived in British Columbia and died before the Internment. Yet she
is described as Nisei. The term Issei, then, might refer to two generations of Japanese Canadians and not just one immigrating generation.
Indeed, some of the women commented that they feel they do not quite
fit into a generational category. Esther reported to me that someone had
told her she was 'almost like a Sansei.'[13] She explained that she was the
youngest child and her older sister was like a mother to her. She felt the
siblings in her family actually constituted two different generations. In

cases where two people from differently designated generations have children, for example an Issei and a Nisei, the children may be identified as Sansei or Nisei-Sansei or 'two and a half.' While these categories have served as a way of identifying Japanese Canadians in relation to the Internment and each other, the terms can erase heterogeneous histories and identities.

In the pre-Internment community, some Japanese Canadians were middle class.[14] Yet all of the families of the women who were incarcerated lost a great deal materially through the confiscation of their property, possessions, and savings; most felt that their opportunities for education were affected, as was their ability to work for any form of payment during and after the Internment. The women interviewed who were interned are not a monolithic group in terms of class and currently some of them have acquired a middle-class economic position.[15] Class is gendered, however, and women's class position is often contingent on the earning power of a partner. Some of the women interviewed lived with male partners, while others were widowed or divorced. All of the women had worked in paid labour and, at the time of their interviews, eight of the eleven women were still working, three were retired, and all of them were engaged in unpaid labour, which variously included domestic work, childcare, and involvement in community organizations. Class is also affected by processes of racialization and most of the women interned stated that their education was negatively affected by the Internment; their schooling was delayed or ended. For most of the women, continuing education after the Internment was impossible or their opportunities were limited. Therefore the cultural capital of education that informs class position, which includes where one is schooled and how, was affected for each woman.

As for their daughters, if education were the determining class factor, they might all be designated as middle class. All had completed some post-secondary education at the time of the interview; a few had completed graduate degrees. However, as Canadian research on pay inequity indicates, even women with higher education and experience equivalent to men are often paid less than those men.[16] Audrey Kobayashi points out that 'Japanese-Canadian men earn higher average salaries than Japanese-Canadian women,' and while she suggests that 'subtle problems of discrimination remain for Japanese-Canadian women,' she also emphasizes that more research is needed to understand these gendered differences in remuneration for paid labour.[17] Some of the women interviewed lived with their parents or a parent, and were financially supported, in part, by them. All were employed at least part-time. Some of them were full-time students. Some lived with male partners; others lived alone or with their parent(s). Two of the daughters interviewed had children.

As I stated in the introduction, this book does not claim to represent the experiences of all women who were expelled from BC or daughters whose mothers were expelled. In fact, this study does not claim to exhaustively represent the experiences of the women interviewed. This is not a reconstruction of their life histories; rather, the approach undertaken here aspires to uncover some of the subordinated knowledges of the women in relation to their histories of the Internment. The number of women interviewed reflects my desire to record multiple memories from each woman in order to illustrate the effects of the Internment across the generations and across time. This involved not only uncovering what women remember of their experiences of the Internment but also what knowledges their daughters remember receiving from their mothers and where these knowledges are contested. While ultimately the social analysis of the women's testimonies is mine, it is informed by the knowledge they each imparted to me.

Most of the analysis in the book is applied to the testimonies of women interviewed. However, I am in accord with Roger Simon and Claudia Eppert on the question of the responsibility of the witness to historical violence to attend to 'ethical and epistemological responsibilities' through a certain 'allegiance with structures of evidence and theorization.'[18] Hence in addition to interviews, I use and analyse documents from the Library and Archives Canada (LAC), especially those compiled by the BCSC,[19] and have been informed by theory as outlined in the Introduction. However, while there exists the notion that government or written documents are more accurate or objective than testimonial accounts, and some depictions of the Internment are based solely on these written sources and are devoid of any interviews with survivors, I consider written government documents to be mediated texts written by the architects and administrators of the Internment who wrote from positions of power. As suggested in chapter 1 and in the analysis of the government documents that follow, 'historical documents cannot reveal the plenitude of the past. In effect and in fact documents may well silence and even erase the full truth of what-happened-then.'[20]

This book focuses on how some women re-member and struggle against the forgetting of the Internment; it does not analyse the ways in which men reconstruct their memories of the Internment or how these memories are handed down to sons of families who were incarcerated. Yoshiko, a woman I interviewed, expressed this limitation of my work well when she stated, 'I really feel badly that more men and young men are not part of the discussion or not part of the discourse of making a whole picture.'[21] The position of Japanese Canadian men in relation to the Internment requires critical examination. In addition, research must be undertaken in order to understand the relationship to the Internment of our family members who are not Japanese Canadian. How do they understand their relationships to the Internment given their different subject positions and their witnessing of our memories of the Internment and our daily experiences as racialized women? Analysis is also needed on the relationship to the Internment of people of Japanese ancestry in Canada whose families immigrated in the post-war period and who were not, therefore, in Canada during the Internment.

Testimony and Knowledge Production

In this section, I discuss some of the issues critical to witnessing testimonies of Internment survivors. Given the context of the racialized, gendered, and classed silence–speech binary as discussed in chapter 2, is my choice of oral testimony as the primary methodology a reification of the speaking subject? The response to this question is contradictory as national violence can never be entirely 'spoken' or represented. Shoshana Felman argues that testimony is instructive to our understanding of historical violence and it has 'become a crucial mode of our relation to events of the times.'[22] Testimony is an important form of transmission of the Internment history, one that has been undertheorized in the Internment literature.[23]

The testimonies gathered for this book are understood as representations of the Internment and are used to analyse some of the effects of the Internment on the women interviewed. This is not a conventional historical use of testimonies as repositories of fact or as reflections of 'life histories.'[24] Rather than describing details about women's experiences of the Internment, my book focuses on and analyses the recurring themes suggested by them. The 'discursive practice' of testifying, witnessing, and interpreting testimonies must not be used therefore to depict these narratives as 'a totalizable account of … events.'[25]

The women's testimonies are used to understand what is remembered about how the Internment was produced and what it produced for them. The testimonies are analysed as constructed representations, constituted and negotiated by complex subjects interpellated through systems of domination and subordination. They are viewed as a 'genre of cultural production' and as 'sites through which subject, community, and struggle are signified and mediated.'[26] Also of interest is how they might be 'read, understood, and located institutionally.'[27]

History and Memory

The dependability of memory and the use of oral testimony in historical writing have been debated in the scholarly literature.[28] According to Joanna Bornat, since the 1990s the use of oral testimonies to 'expose gaps in knowledge'[29] and to fill in the facts has shifted to an analysis of '[i]ssues of difference, subjectivity and identity.'[30] Paul Thompson situates the preoccupation of historians with the facts of oral histories or the 'life story method' as occurring before the 1970s when the debates regarding 'whether or not people were telling "the truth"'[31] were especially lively. More recently, Thompson argues, historians are concerned with 'not only what people say and whether it was true, but how they remember it …'[32]

Re-membering, however, is not an unmediated process. As Roger Simon points out, 'memory [like history] is an extremely selective cultural artefact that can also be a prop of power and authority.'[33] In witnessing testimonies that reconstruct painful historical events, one must be aware that these testimonies are also traumatic cultural artefacts. Dori Laub contests a positivist use of survivors' testimonies and points to the limitations of looking for errors and omissions (considered important by historians) in the reading of these testimonies instead of attempting to understand what is important to the testifier and looking for the layers of meaning he or she conveys. He gives as an example of the criticism historians made of a 'factual' error in the testimony given by a survivor of the Holocaust and how they subsequently dismissed the entire testimony because of this error.[34] As witnesses to testimonies of historical violence, we must examine our own processes of knowledge production and what we consider to be the facts and the truth. When the survivor names the 'fact of the occurrence,'[35] the occurrence itself may be 'inconceivable' to the witness; the limits of our own knowledge or social privilege affect what we can and are willing to know. Hence, as Laub argues, testimonies must be heard with an awareness of our relationship to the inconceivability of historical violence. Perhaps in this way, their contests to existing frameworks of knowability may offer other forms of 'historical truth';[36] in the very least, the proposal that there is much we cannot know about historical violence underscores that factual representation does not bring closure to its legacy. Rather than focusing on compiling and judging the worth of the facts gleaned from the interviews for this book, it is the 'fact of the occurrence' of the Internment and the women's representations of it that are examined.

Women's testimonies of the Internment disrupt clear delineations between past and present; their memories are a testament to how survivors and their children live in multiple time spaces. The past overlaps with the present both in the generation and construction of memory and in the materiality of our day-to-day lives. Walter Benjamin suggests that the 'past can be seized only as an image which flashes up at the instant when it can be recognized.'[37] In my discussion of their memories, I am imposing a chronology that does not reflect the ways in which 'flashes' of memory were generated in the women's interviews. I am thus mediating the representation of their testimonies, not only through my interpretations but also in presenting a linear order of time, in imposing a chronology on the memories of the interview subjects.

Benjamin also discusses how articulating the past is about 'seiz[ing] hold of a memory as it flashes up at a moment of danger,' and he underlines that the oppressed are not safe from the threat that their memories can be used as a 'tool of the ruling classes.'[38] The moments of danger for the women I interviewed were both the moments when they experienced the violations of the Internment and racism as well as the moments of re-membering and articulating those violations. Re-membering the Internment and expressing these flashes of memory are still not safe activities for people living within the nation that incarcerated them and where the Internment and the extent of the harm done to them is largely forgotten in the national imaginary. The danger or harm, therefore, not only existed in the past but can also be relived through re-membering and disclosing. As I discuss below, as witnesses and interpreters of testimonies, our own positions of social dominance (gender, class, ethnicity, ability, sexuality, et cetera) make the interview and interpretation process one of risk for those who testify because of these unequal relations of power.

The interview process for this book was replete with moments that were not only verbal but also gestural and pensive; there were emotions that were lost in the translation from interview to transcript. These non-verbal expressions conveyed a sense of the effects and affects of this history, forms of embodiment that are pertinent to how we think about the transmission of this history to other family members and to children. This dialogic process is not one of passive information exchange. Testimony affects both the teller and witness through its telling; its revelations may trigger memories in both people present because the process can draw on experiences and preconceptions both people bring to the interview. For example, I knew some of the women from other contexts and brought these insights to the interview process. The fact that some of the women I interviewed knew of my literary writing or my participation in different community organizations may have influenced their interview process as well.

Women who were adults in the 1940s have different relationships to the Internment than do the children who were incarcerated at that time. The women interviewed ranged in age from three to twenty-nine years when they were expelled from the West Coast. What a twenty-nine-year-old woman went through during this period is different from the experience of a three year-old. Birth order and gender also affected the responsibilities held by female children. This is not to say that all children's experiences were easier than those of adults; it is these kinds of generalities that lead to totalizing accounts of the Internment. Rather, being conscious of the survivors' ages helps us to contextualize what they re-member and how they describe their memories.

Survivors and Traumatic Memory

S.'s statement in the epigraph to this chapter underlines that the Internment was composed of traumatic experiences, experiences that affect what is remembered and how it is remembered. The act of testifying itself can be one of traumatic re-membering, which can also affect what is remembered and disclosed.[39] Two of the women interviewed spoke directly to this issue. When I asked May if she had to report to the Royal Canadian Mounted Police (RCMP) upon her arrival in Toronto after leaving the Slocan camp, she responded:

> I had to report to the RCMP, I think when I got here. But I don't know if I had to report after that. If I did, I've put it out of my mind. And I'm sure, Mona, I'm sure there are things I've put out of my mind because I didn't want to remember them. I'm very sure. But I think that pertains to both my experiences with Japanese or outside the Japanese community. I think

there have been things that I've decided to forget. Partly it's a survival mechanism, I think.[40]

Yoshiko was five when she was forced to leave her home in Vancouver. She reported that she cannot remember her life prior to her incarceration in the Slocan camp and she has no memory of her parents packing their possessions in preparation to leave their home. She stated:

Do you know that I can't remember those times. Very interesting. Total blank. And I often consider that as being protected, overly protected, that such a terrible thing happened. I can't remember, I can't remember anything about traumatic times with my mother or my father during that time. Wow. Interesting. Can't.[41]

Forgetting on the part of Japanese Canadians, then, can be evidence of the violence they endured, as remembering the Internment can invoke an engagement with trauma, the effect of violence.

Psychology attempts to understand the trauma experienced by survivors of violence through diagnostic tools under the umbrella term post-traumatic stress disorder (PTSD). Various scholars use this psychological concept to help them understand the testimonies of survivors of the Holocaust and of other traumatic histories.[42] It is troubling, however, when such 'trauma' is analysed in isolation from an analysis of the psychology of the instigators of the trauma and the social processes that were used to produce the trauma. Through individualized diagnoses of PTSD, survivors – those who have already been greatly pathologized by the victimizer as the target of violence – risk being repathologized when their behaviours are construed as 'disorders.' Indeed, some of the psychological literature on trauma presumes the clients or patients are liberal subjects, which leads to their behaviours being scrutinized according to this model of rationality and autonomy.

Chalsa Loo has applied an understanding of PTSD in her analysis of the psychological effects of the Internment on Japanese Americans. According to Loo,

PTSD is an anxiety disorder that involved a constellation of symptoms ... The traumata commonly involve either serious threat to one's life or physical integrity; serious threat of harm to one's children, spouse, or other close relatives or friends; sudden destruction of one's home or community; or witnessing another person who has been seriously injured or killed.[43]

As is clear from the interviews presented in the following chapters, many of the traumata itemized by Loo are applicable to Japanese Canadians during and after the Internment. Importantly, the essay by Loo proposes 'group treatment' for Japanese American survivors. She gives the examples of 'pilgrimages' to the sites of incarceration, 'days of remembrance' that commemorate important dates in the Internment history, and 'house meetings' where participants can gather together to express their feelings about the Internment as 'appropriate recovery interventions' experienced by survivors during the redress campaign.[44] While the term 'treatment' also conveys a notion of pathology, the practices of remembrance initiated by survivors of the Internments and their families in the United States and Canada are important to supporting those who experienced these processes and the transmission and acquisition of knowledge about their histories. Examples of commemorative practices were described by some of the women interviewed and are discussed in chapters 7 and 8.

Survivors live with their memories and negotiate the risks involved in their revelation. They reconstruct their memories within and in response to already existing discourses, including those of the Internment. In an interview situation, they may protect themselves and the interviewer from the trauma of the events they have witnessed. This protective mechanism may not be grasped by the interviewer and she or he may diminish the harms that are, in different ways, being communicated. As well, it may be challenging or difficult to hear or read these testimonies if we occupy dominant social positions, such as those assigned through racial, class, or gender categories, or if we come from families who were interned or have other histories of trauma. Thus, subject position and the very notion of who is the subject inform the interpretation of survivors' testimonies.

In this book, I do not undertake an evidentiary search for trauma in the testimonies of the women interviewed. Neither do I scrutinize how the testimonies were delivered in order to garner conclusions about trauma or the psychology of the women testifying. Rather, I wish to focus on what women disclose about the effects of the Internment, about what it produced for them.

The Use of Memory in Contesting Domination

Remembrance is a practice of potential 'insurgency'[45] and contestation. This book questions homogeneous representations of the Internment and of Japanese Canadians, and it challenges the hegemony of a national selective memory and a collective forgetting. Memory is not just about individual remembrance. As the women reveal, their memories of the Internment are informed by their connections to others who were interned. My notion of 'memory of community' is derived from women's memories that reveal the destruction of communities and the wrenching apart of families and friends. While the term community may homogenize the identities of those deemed within it, it is used in this book to explain a collectivity who share a history of Internment. Hence its focus is not an essentialized notion of ethnicity or race as a determining factor of community but rather a community or communities that share a history of subordination, which included its members being racialized. It is used to capture a part of the discourse of remembrance used by those Japanese Canadians who remember communities destroyed in the 1940s and struggle to reconstruct social formations, in part, so that they can remember and articulate their histories together. This is not memory based on nostalgia for a fixed notion of the past but rather it re-members the moments of ruptures in and the destruction of families and communities. This notion of community contests the national imaginary of Canada as a seamlessly unified community of equal citizens.

I also argue that memories are connected to place. As Francesca Cappelletto states, 'the visual-spatial component appears to be crucial in the formation of a narrative [of memory].'[46] In my work, I underline that the places of the Internment are remembered by survivors and also affect their memories, not merely as 'locations' but as a mnemonic emplacement that continues to produce the identities of survivors and their non-interned children up to the present day. Women's memories question national narratives of closure that neatly relegate the Internment and other violences to the past. Moreover, in witnessing these testimonies, we can begin to understand what the telling of a memory in its complex articulations 'reveals about how the past affects the present.'[47]

Re-membering the Places of the Internment

It has largely been left to the survivors and their children to re-member the Internment; their naming of Internment sites resists a collective national forgetting of the 'other' meanings of these places. One such commemorative example is located in New Denver, BC, where the Kyowakai Society has established the Nikkei Internment Memorial

Centre. The Centre was officially opened on 23 July 1994, and it includes a museum and an 'original internment shack.'[48] New Denver was one of the camp sites and was controlled by the federal government until 1957.[49] At that time, the camp administrators 'agreed to give the shacks to the remaining Japanese Canadians.'[50] Most Kyowakai Society members were in their seventies and eighties at the time the Centre opened, and there were approximately thirty Nikkei people, most of whom had been incarcerated in New Denver, living there at the time.[51]

Marking the places of incarceration with such commemorative structures, even through less visible signs, has not been an easy feat. Roy Miki and Cassandra Kobayashi describe how the Greater Vancouver Japanese Canadian Citizens Association (GVJCCA) became 'embattled' with the board of directors of the Pacific National Exhibition (PNE) when a plaque funded by the federal government was to be installed at the entrance to the exhibition grounds marking it as a site of incarceration. The PNE is the location of Hastings Park, the first incarceration site for 8,000 people before they were sent to other sites outside of Vancouver.[52] According to Miki and Kobayashi, in 1987, 'Some directors did not want the public to know about the PNE's wartime use, and others even argued that the uprooting was justified as a security measure.'[53] The GVJCCA organized a protest and the Vancouver City Council decided that the plaque would be installed at the entrance of the grounds, 'on land beyond the jurisdiction of the PNE Board.'[54] The plaque was finally installed on 1 April 1989, a year after the redress settlement.

In the United States, the Manzanar commemorative site, near Independence, California, was officially opened in the summer of 1998. Manzanar is the only internment camp site to have been designated a National Park by the U.S. Congress.[55] The opposition to the visible commemoration of Manzanar as a site of incarceration was evident in the violence directed at the site's superintendent. He reported receiving 'five arson threats at the park and endur[ing] such verbal abuse and threats of violence that he has unlisted phone numbers.'[56] The responses to these efforts of Japanese Canadians and Japanese Americans to re-member the places of incarceration through public signifying practices illustrate how power and violence are used to actively produce and maintain the forgetting of the Internment in the present and confirm that remembering the Internment is not just about relations of power in the past. Yet even though Manzanar is not usually on California maps or in its guidebooks, over 80,000 people visit the site every year.[57] Collective struggles to re-map the places of the Internment against a cartography of forgetting must be seen as critical acts for generations of the Internment.

The act of contesting a nation's forgetting is also demonstrated individually by those who remember their own incarcerations. Louise was a child when she, her mother, and three siblings were moved to the Tashme camp. In our interview, she told me that in the 1950s, when she was in the ninth or tenth grade, she read a magazine article on Tashme.[58] It was the first time she had ever seen published material on the Internment. The article contained a map of Tashme and explained the origin of the place name. As she recalled, '[T]here were three Mounties involved and it was Taylor, Shane – I think it was – and Mead. So they took the two letters of each and that's how Tashme was named.'[59] Louise remembered telling someone about her discovery and his response had been, 'Oh no, that's not it.' 'But,' she emphasized, 'I remember distinctly, I still remember [it] from that article.' She also said that she wanted to 'track this [article] down for Kyo's [her daughter] and [her other] kids' sake.'

Despite two errors of 'fact'[60] – errors that may have been in the original article – Louise's disclosure of the memory of the importance of reading about Tashme and discovering the significance of its name was vivid and revelatory. If we were to focus on the errors in her testimony rather than on what was remarkably accurate over forty years later, we would negate the layers of meaning in her words and her own estimation of what information was important to pass on to her children and me.

Louise has had to live with her memory of the origin of the name of Tashme being contested. While it is unclear just what in her testimony was being challenged by its recipient, it is her memory of that challenge to her attempt to articulate the 'inconceivable' that is revealed. Those who were incarcerated had to confront challenges to their remembering and face many forms of forgetting when they left the places of incarceration.

Louise's story also illustrates how survivors learn about the internal operations of the government and their officials – the mechanisms of national violence – years after their actual incarcerations. This is a process that began with their expulsion in the 1940s and continues to this day. For some people, material on the Internment has been largely inaccessible because of their class positions, the lack of material in Japanese, or other reasons. And, as was mentioned in chapter 1, the experience of viewing representations of the Internment through various media may be traumatizing and extremely painful for survivors and their families. For example, Michi Weglyn experienced the traumatizing effects of reading government documents and other material on the Internment in the United States when she was writing *Years of Infamy: The Untold Story of America's Concentration Camps*.[61] Historian Alice Yang Murray reports that Weglyn spent seven years conducting research for her book and '[s]ometimes the revelations literally made her sick for days.'[62]

The Canadian federal government records that were kept on Japanese Canadians during the 1940s are largely inaccessible to most people. The records are located at the Library and Archives Canada (LAC) in Ottawa. To use them, one must learn and apply the LAC's procedures, which can be time consuming.[63] Archival research at the LAC can be an intimidating process, and those who use their materials either live in Ottawa or have the time and the financial resources to stay there. In addition, some of the federal government records remain restricted and application must be made to view them.[64] The application, however, does not guarantee access if an archivist determines that viewing the document or documents in question breaches the Privacy Act. Thus, even in a post-redress context, there are survivors who have not had ready or easy access to information about their own incarcerations or to discourses that are oppositional to those publicly presented by the government in the 1940s.

Conclusion: Responsible Witnessing

Gayatri Chakravorty Spivak recommends that we attend to the 'transaction between the speaker and listener.'[65] The social conditions of our listening inform what is heard and not heard, what is remembered and forgotten. The difficulties in re-membering and describing the Internment by survivors and their children are emblematic of its profound social, material, and psychological effects, and the pain invoked through re-membering.

In understanding how survivors negotiate painful and difficult memories through testimony, Roger Simon and Claudia Eppert refer to the 'excess' that marks 'something beyond the limits of what can be spoken through available discourses for articulating incomprehensible violence and human loss.'[66] This concept could be used to understand that, as argued in chapter 1 and in this chapter, there are reasons for which the Internment cannot be entirely named nor exhaustively known. Rather than seeking to access the 'excess,' to fill in what we consider to be 'silence,' we might understand what is 'unspeakable' as an effect of the Internment itself. As witnesses to testimonies of historical trauma, it is incumbent upon us to 'situate the said within the relational encounter marking it as something beyond the merely "said."'[67] In this way we come closer to witnessing how women negotiate the naming, the not naming, or the impossibility of naming the Internment.

Naming national violence is a risky act while living in the nation where it occurred and continues to occur and where our speech and representations are continually mediated through relations of power. Despite these risks, the responsibility for naming this violence has more often than not been assigned to the survivors themselves. For survivors, then, re-membering is a difficult negotiation and an act of resistance that is enmeshed with and informed by the hegemony of national forgetting.

Sara Ahmed recommends that we *'learn to hear what is impossible,'* which is only possible if 'we respond to a pain that we cannot claim as our own ... in such a way that the testimony is not taken away from others, as if it were about our feelings, or our ability to feel the feelings of others.'[68] As we witness these testimonies of the survivors of the Internment, to which 'image ... flash[ing] up at the instant' can we attend? Which conforms to a narrative that is part of a familiar collective forgetting that passes as knowing? Is our reading influenced by how we are, yet do not want to feel implicated in 'their' history? If we do not feel implicated, why is this so? And what of their stories will we forget when we are asked to re-member?

4 Cartographies of Violence: Creating Carceral Spaces and Expelling Japanese Canadians from the Nation

What was at issue was not whether the prison environment was too harsh or too aseptic, too primitive or too efficient, but its very materiality as an instrument and vector of power.

Michel Foucault, *Discipline and Punish*[1]

The men are dragged violently into the trains. Father can be seen. He is being pushed onto the train ... I see his mouth opening; he shouts to his friends, waves his clenched fist. But the words are lost in all the noise. Mother holds my hand tightly.

Shizuye Takashima, *A Child in Prison Camp*[2]

The Colonial Technologies of Expulsion, Forced Displacement, and Spatial Segregation

In his theorizing of the contemporary use of the 'camp' to detain 'illegal' immigrants and others, Giorgio Agamben draws our attention to the proliferation of such sites that he describes as 'space[s] devoid of law,'[3] and where there is a 'state of exception' or the 'force of law without law.'[4] As he writes, '[W]e must admit that we find ourselves virtually in the presence of a camp every time such a structure is created.'[5] While I agree with him that such sites – for example, all of the carceral sites of the Internment – must be viewed for the real purposes for which they are created, I underline that Canadians (and pre-Confederation settlers) have been present in the places from which Indigenous peoples have been expelled and in the presence of those places in which they have been confined and incarcerated before and since the founding of the nation, and furthermore that these sites are foundational to our identities as Canadians and our unmarked identities as settlers. As Sunera Thobani states in her critique of Agamben's theorization of the camp,

> Agamben's Eurocentric focus, like that of many other theorists, does not allow him to recognize that colonialism (which predated his analysis of the concentration camp as the paramount site of exception) has been central to the development of western forms of sovereignty as racialized forms of power through the institution of the law within modernity. Nor does it allow him to recognize that quintessential zone of exception, the reserve, which long proceeded the concentration camp and has endured far longer, indeed, by a number of centuries.[6]

The practices of expulsion and forced displacement, and the use of space to detain and control racialized groups are not new and have been practised for centuries against Indigenous peoples on their territories named by settlers as Canada. I begin this chapter, therefore, by acknowledging that unmapping Canada to find the cartography of the Internment requires acknowledging another map that has been rendered invisible – that of Indigenous nations on whose territories Canada was founded. The unmapping of Canada that this book advocates, therefore, begins by recognizing the making of Canada through colonialism and the use of colonial technologies against Indigenous peoples by the settler nation of Canada. Hence, the unmapping of the sites of the Internment must recognize the colonial cartographies of violence through which Canada was founded and the expulsion and forced displacement of Indigenous peoples.[7]

The technologies[8] or practices used against Indigenous peoples and authorized by the use of settler-state law, including the Indian Act,[9] such as expulsion, forced displacement, incarceration, segregation, dispossession, separation, and destruction of families and communities, denigration of languages other than English and French, the role of the Christian churches in destroying traditional spiritual practices and numerous other methods have been implemented and practised for centuries. Settler control of Indigenous nations established techniques that could be adapted for the policing of immigrants and the eventual formulation and administration of the Internment. While the settler practices used against Indigenous peoples were clearly intended as acts of genocide and the practices of the Internment were initially intended to achieve the expulsion of all Japanese Canadians from Canada, they must be seen as relational. Colonial technologies are foundational to the making of Canada and the 'spatial organization of domination.'[10] Although I would not conflate the processes of colonialism and the Internment, I would stress that it is essential to see them as linked.

The technologies of expulsion and forced displacement that were used against Indigenous peoples and Japanese Canadians and the use of space to create differential entitlements to power are, I argue, Canadian technologies of white settler nation-building. Honed through colonization and the establishment of reserves for status Indians, the technologies of expulsion and forced displacement created carceral spaces that settlers used to signify racial and Indigenous difference in relation to white bourgeois areas. This technique of expelling and displacing the first inhabitants from their territories materially and symbolically made the nation of Canada. In the 1940s the technologies of expulsion and displacement, authorized through the War Measures Act, were implemented against Japanese Canadians through the establishment of the 100-mile coastal radius. This Act was used to remove them from the BC coastal area, enforce their incarceration in different sites from British Columbia to central Canada, and eventually force their dispersal to destinations east of the province.

Hence, the distracting periodizing signpost that directs us to look at the war with Japan as the ultimate cause of the Internment also promotes Canada's innocence. The Internment, I argue, is not only connected to Canada's war with Japan but also is an extension of the efforts of white settlers to secure the territories taken from Indigenous peoples.[11] Rather than conceptualizing the Internment as being related solely to the war in the Pacific, I would suggest that our temporal and geographic gaze be adjusted to see it as reflecting the battle for white bourgeois settler supremacy that was variously and differently waged against Indigenous peoples, people of Japanese ancestry, and other racialized and marginalized groups living *in* Canada. The history of anti-Asian immigration legislation in Canada and juridical and social disentitlements to citizenship were also part of the process that led to the Internment.

A 'contrapuntal'[12] understanding of histories of subordination that illustrates how these histories interlock with each other in the building of a settler nation requires acknowledging that, prior to the 1940s, Indigenous peoples were living in carceral spaces of exclusion and marginalization, that is, places such as reserves and residential schools, and Canada itself. More research is clearly needed to connect the seemingly disparate and separate marginal and carceral spaces in Canada in order to unmap in greater detail how Indigenous identities, the identities of racialized and white settlers, and social differences are relationally constructed and surveillance and control secured.[13] In writing this book, my goal is to illustrate the historically and Canadian-specific use of spatial segregation and incarceration, the 'particularities of place,'[14] and show how these are connected to the production of identities as revealed by the Japanese Canadian women I interviewed.

The expulsion of Japanese Canadians from the restricted area occurred shortly after the finalization of the building of the reserve system in British Columbia.[15] The colonial and racial construction of the nation becomes even clearer when we unmap the first sites considered by the federal government for the incarceration of Japanese Canadians – residential schools and reserves across the country inhabited by Indigenous peoples.[16] Hence, in imagining the Canadian settler nation and its citizens, state officials also relationally imagined those who were considered extraneous to both. Their colonial and racial imagination conceptualized that Indigenous peoples could share carceral and Indigenous spaces with a group constructed as racially foreign, or that Japanese Canadians could be used to again displace Indigenous peoples through their own forced displacement.[17] In addition, the use of the permit system to control and monitor the movement of Japanese Canadians between internment sites and during the dispersal is reminiscent of the pass system developed to restrict and control the movement of Indigenous peoples.[18] The use of forced displacement and the spatialization of exclusion as tools of nation-building deployed against Japanese Canadians were simultaneously used again against Indigenous peoples. In Canada, the federal government used the War Measures Act to expel Japanese Canadians from the West Coast and the members of the Stoney Point reserve from their land in southern Ontario;[19] the United States used Executive Order 9066 to expel 120,000 Japanese Americans from the West Coast and to remove the Aleuts from their land in Alaska.[20] While the reason for the expulsion of Indigenous communities given by settler governments was because their territories were needed for 'military installations,'[21] and thus their existence was constructed as standing in the way of securing the nation, and the reason given for Japanese Canadians' expulsion was because they were deemed a threat to national security, these examples of the application of Canadian and U.S. law clarify against whom emergency legislation was applied for wholesale expulsion during the state-defined emergency of the 1940s and whose lives were heralded as in need of protection. Clearly, the settler state drew on colonial technologies in its construction of relational spaces and relational subjects.

Hence my unmapping must begin by acknowledging that the Canadian nation has been forged through the removal of Indigenous peoples from their territories and the enforcement of their racialized segregation, practices that were foundational to the creation of racial categorization as practised in Canada. The history of racialization for Japanese Canadians must therefore acknowledge the pre-establishment of the racial categories of 'Indian' and 'white' that were violently procured and maintained through the practices of colonialism both past and present. Moreover, as Japanese Canadians, we must examine our own positions as racialized 'settlers'[22] in relation to Indigenous peoples; we must examine the current practices of a settler and 'racial state'[23] that divides and positions us relationally, practices in which we participate and from which we differently benefit. I return to a discussion of these practices in chapters 9 and 10.

Spatializing the Narrative of the Internment

Politicians and citizens who supported the expulsion of Japanese Canadians established the zones of racial exclusion by legislating the 100-mile restricted area and creating numerous carceral sites. They argued that the expulsion of Japanese Canadians was necessary to the security of Canadians. Such an argument obscures the social relations and the racial violence of the expulsion and has been soundly debunked by Ann Sunahara and others. For years, however, this argument of national security masked who was actually being threatened and by whom. While Japanese Canadians committed no violence against Canada, violence was done to them by the Canadian government and others participating in the Internment causing long-term effects. These effects are difficult to see, and hence to name, unless we actually visualize and render visible the material spaces to which people were forced to move and the people who were moved into those spaces. With this cartography in mind, we can conceptualize the social relations and subjects produced through these spaces.

This chapter traces the spatial configurations of the Internment and how these spaces are remembered by the eleven women I interviewed who were incarcerated in them during the 1940s. An analysis of the production of these sites demonstrates how they were used to physically and socially divide families and communities and, at the same time, obfuscate the harms and effects caused by these divisions.

Once expelled, power was then disseminated spatially through 'multiple separations, individualizing distributions, and organization in depth of surveillance and control.'[24] The creation of the Internment as a multiply spatialized incarceration hinders our very ability to see these spaces as carceral and so facilitates our forgetting of the effects the Internment produced. As such, this chapter illustrates how carceral spaces were constructed relationally, producing relational subjects. The women's testimonies provide a verbal unmapping of the places of incarceration and illustrate some of the ways in which the very heterogeneity of these material and social spaces affect what is remembered and named.

In this chapter through to and including chapter 7, I focus on the spatial production of the Internment and some of what the Internment produced for the women I interviewed. I am aware of the fissures in the maps I have drawn from the women's descriptions and welcome further description and analysis of the places touched upon in these chapters. As Rob Shields states: 'Place-images, and our views of them, are produced historically, and are actively contested. There is no whole picture that can be "filled in" since the perception and filling of a gap lead to the awareness of other gaps.'[25]

The temporal limitations imposed by the liberal historical narrative relegate the violence of the Internment to the past. 'Spatializing the historical narrative'[26] enables us to conceptualize history as not solely about a linear march through time (see chapter 1) but also about space. By tracing the production of the places of incarceration and dispersal, we develop a picture of effects procured in each site. What this spatial analysis renders visible is how discourses of power are both produced through and produce these sites. Edward Soja refers to spatial analysis as an 'interpretive geography,' a way of recognizing 'spatiality as simultaneously ... a social product (or outcome) and a shaping force (or medium) in social life.'[27] This methodological approach enables an understanding of how social domination can actually be disguised and normalized. Keeping in mind that over 22,000 people were removed from their homes on the Canadian West Coast and incarcerated in different and separate locations, we can begin to understand how spaces organize different forms of surveillance and how 'discipline proceeds from the distribution of individuals in space.'[28] Understanding that spaces and subjects are produced in relation to each other underlines the importance of Edward Said's notion of analysing histories as contrapuntal through their intertwining and overlapping. What I emphasize, therefore, are the ways in which the material spaces of incarceration and the discourses produced through them impinge upon the memory and representation of them. The identities of subjects were made through these relational spaces. Both Japanese Canadians and white Canadians were relationally made through spatial expulsion, the establishment of carceral sites in six Canadian provinces, and the dispersal of Japanese Canadians. The ability of white bourgeois subjects to displace people based on the perceived 'race' of those they wished to expel served to secure their own whiteness and spaces of entitlement. Power necessarily enforced and normalized this social and spatial arrangement. The violence of these processes and their exclusionary discourses and practices, including racism, sexism, heteronormativity, economic exploitation, and ableism, were compounded and obscured by spatial separations and segregation.

Audrey Kobayashi uses a spatial analysis to describe the imposed 'placelessness' of Japanese Canadians. Kobayashi situates the denial of geographic rights, a 'right to place,' within the hands of the Canadian state, wherein concentrated power is used to control space. She names racism as the 'mechanism through which the power to deny geographic rights is released, and the ideological channel through which the contest of spatial control is negotiated.'[29] Kobayashi enumerates three ways, all of which were applied to Japanese Canadians, in which geographic rights can be denied or limited:

> one, *exclusion*, by which certain groups are denied spatial access to designated places, either entire countries or parts of countries; two, *restriction* of the freedom of movement from one place to another, or of the presence of designated persons in specific places and times; three, *expulsion*, whereby designated groups are removed from a place and subsequently excluded and restricted.[30]

As Kobayashi states, 'spatial discrimination' was imposed upon Japanese Canadians, particularly between the years 1941 and 1949. However, she emphasizes that the spatial exclusions that transpired during this period were but a 'logical extension' of a fifty-year history in which geographic rights were denied through a 'social context of racism.'[31]

As Kobayashi contends, spatial designations for Japanese Canadians occurred long before they were removed from the West Coast. Social exclusions in British Columbia were made through the law and thus were legal. For example, Indigenous peoples and Asian Canadians could not vote in municipal, provincial, and federal elections. Banned from the voting lists, they were by default excluded from holding public office and from becoming lawyers, pharmacists, architects, and chartered accountants.[32] A white citizenry strove to eliminate the sea changes that were occurring as Japanese Canadians became more economically able to move into other areas of Vancouver and the province and began organizing to fight for the vote and the rights of citizenship.[33] As Kobayashi states: 'The dominant notion that Asians should keep their place both geographically in ethnic ghettos and socially became stronger as Japanese-Canadian citizens attempted to secure a place beyond these realms.'[34] What better way to mark a racialized community that was striving to attain entitlement to the rights of nation than to further enunciate their difference through spatial confinement and imprisonment?

The Second World War presented an opportunity to ascribe to people of Japanese ancestry the mark of disloyalty and thus the pretext for their removal from the coastal area, away from the space claimed by white bourgeois citizens. Dispossessing Japanese Canadians of property and other possessions, and discounting the citizenship of even those who were born in Canada, were moves that normalized their disentitlement to the Canadian nation; hence, their statelessness easily identified them as belonging to the nation of the 'enemy.' White bourgeois men, such as those described in chapter 1, easily imagined and rationalized that Japanese Canadians should live in restricted spaces of incarceration and servitude. Japanese Canadians were thus barred from the 100-mile restricted coastal area and from the imagined white collective space of the Canadian nation.

Creating a Nationless People

Canada's entry into the Second World War provided the pretext for placing greater and greater spatial restrictions on all people of Japanese ancestry living in the country. The Canadian federal cabinet used the War Measures Act to authorize the wholesale expulsion of Japanese Canadians.[35] More than forty Orders-in-Council were applied to 'persons of the Japanese race' regarding detention, incarceration, movement, dispossession, housing, employment, dispersal, loyalty, citizenship and other matters.[36] Orders in Council issued by the federal government clearly specified where and when they could travel. For example, on 8 December 1941, all fishing boats were impounded and the waters were declared out of bounds. Order-in-Council P.C. 365, issued on 16 January 1942, designated the 100-mile 'protected area' from the Pacific Ocean to the Cascade Mountains and from the Yukon to the U.S. border.[37] Order-in-Council P.C.1486, issued on 24 February 1942, allowed the minister of justice to control the movements of all people of Japanese ancestry in these 'protected areas.'[38]

A dusk-to-dawn curfew imposed on all people of Japanese descent on 28 February 1942 limited their access to public places and to one another, thus curtailing their ability to gather in groups and to work outside of daylight hours.[39] Community infrastructures supporting communication and intracommunal relations were hastily dismantled and rendered illegal by the federal government. Japanese-language schools and the three vernacular newspapers published in Vancouver were closed.[40] Community gatherings were forbidden and churches were not permitted to hold services, except in the case of funerals.[41] Curfews and prohibitions placed upon communal gatherings were the first steps towards spatially separating friends and family members in separate carceral sites in far-flung regions.

Haru, who lived in Vancouver in what she called a 'Japanese community,' was forced to leave her home with her family when she was eighteen. When describing the curfew, she underlined the spatial limitations invoked through the law. From dusk to dawn Japanese Canadians became prisoners in their own homes.

> *Haru*: We had a curfew. You heard about the curfew? We couldn't go out after ten o'clock …, the Chinese could go but they all wore badges.
> *MO*: What did the badge say?
> *Haru*: They're not Japanese.[42]

Haru also situated herself in relation to Chinese Canadians. Historically banned from the rights of Canadian citizenship, both Japanese Canadians and Chinese Canadians tried to prove their loyalty to Canada. The badge worn by Chinese Canadians that identified them as 'Chinese' was an attempt to secure their safety in and access to public space after the curfew. While marking an association with China, one of the allied countries during the war, the badge also marked their own racial exclusion from Canadian citizenship. However, this self-marking procured spatial access that socially divided them from Japanese Canadians.

Haru also situated herself in relation to Italian Canadians and German Canadians, contextualizing the war's chronology and the fact that Canada was at war with several countries. She wondered why the treatment of other groups at war with Canada was different: 'But I couldn't understand because the war was with Italy and Germany, too. And yet they never went through that. Japan was the last to get into the war.'

Sunahara has pointed out that while German Canadian and Italian Canadian leaders of organizations were detained, the federal government 'resisted demands in 1940 by the Great War Veterans Association to intern all German and Italian aliens.'[43] However, 597 Italian Canadian men were interned at the Petawawa prisoner-of-war camp.[44] Franca Iacovetta has described the closing down of the Casa d'Italia (explained by her as the 'centre of fascist activity' in Toronto) by the Canadian government and the internment of 200 Italian Canadian men.[45] The RCMP also monitored the Italian Canadian community in Toronto and some people 'stopped speaking Italian and anglicized their names.'[46] According to Reg Whitaker and Gregory S. Kealey, '847 pro-Germans were interned (out of a potential population base of more than a half-million), with most released by late 1944 or early 1945.'[47] Twelve women of German descent were incarcerated in Kingston Penitentiary.[48]

Haru's testimony drew my attention to the differential treatment of these three Canadian groups, linked to the Axis powers during the war. Race and ethnicity as perceived within Canada and their penalties or privileges were therefore differently lived by differently racialized and ethnicized people during the 1940s. Race, ethnicity, and whiteness had to be re-imagined by the federal government and its officials in determining the status and fate of each racialized or ethnicized group in relation to who was wanted in the nation and the notion of who was a Canadian citizen. As differences were imagined and discursively operationalized, racialized and ethnicized communities were placed within a relational hierarchy in Canada, allowing most Italian Canadians and German Canadians to maintain spatial toeholds of varying sizes on the nation. All Japanese Canadians (both citizens and Japanese nationals), however, were racialized as one group and one enemy, and, as a group, they were expelled from their homes.

S. was 12 when her family was forced to leave Vancouver. She told me that they lived in a predominantly white area of the city and had close associations with white neighbours and Japanese Canadians, most of the latter living 'downtown.' When I asked her what she remembered about her parents being told to leave Vancouver, she began by describing how she learned about the government's actions. She then discussed the curfew and the support her family extended to their friends to ensure a way of getting together during the early days of upheaval and uncertainty:

> I'm not sure exactly how it happened. I know there was a great deal of talk. Friends would come over. And we would hear all the news of what's happening downtown and I can't remember the exact time that they were told or how it affected them. Well, I know they were quite upset at the time. But it always involved other friends who were going through worse circumstances than ours ... We had more people staying over at our house because we lived far away from the downtown area. They would come to visit us and they'd stay beyond the curfew time. So, we'd have people staying at our house. Just to get back home the next day.[49]

Evelyn, who was eleven, remembered that her first encounter with the notion of war was when England declared war on Germany. She bought 'war savings stamps' and 'bugged' her parents for the 25 cents to purchase them. When Canada declared war on Japan, there was a 'rush of activity.' She remembered that the curfew was imposed and one of her neighbours 'got caught' for being outside after dusk.[50]

May lived with the stress of fearing punishment for breaking the curfew. At the time, she was thirteen and lived in a predominantly white neighbourhood. She recalled one occasion when she was late one night: 'I remember seeing a policeman and being just slightly panicked, wondering, well, like was I going to go to jail or what was going to happen.' However, because she was 'in the middle' of a group of neighbourhood white children, 'he just simply turned a blind eye. Because he was a neighbourhood policeman.'[51]

The fear of being caught outside after the curfew was also expressed by Shizuye Takashima who lived in Vancouver and recalled hurrying home with her sister after seeing a movie. Takashima's book, *A Child in Prison Camp*, conveys the profound anxieties she observed and felt as a child and the day-by-day erosion of their lives as the restrictions were imposed. In this instance, a man threatened to call the police when he saw the two young girls and told them to 'Get off *our* streets!'[52] Takashima described how their worried mother greeted them and, in explaining their tardiness, her sister stated, 'I'm sorry. The film was longer than I thought. It was so great we forgot about the curfew.'[53]

Dispossession

Part of the process of creating a 'placeless' and hence 'nationless' people was to dispossess them. While Japanese Canadians were already excluded from many of the rights of citizenship prior to the Internment, the processes of dispossession and displacement from their homes authorized by the War Measures Act stripped them of any effective legal recourse and ensured the continued abrogation of their claim to rights well into the future. It also meant they would not have homes to return to if they were ever able to return to BC, and that they would have great difficulty in contesting their disentitlement to the rights of citizenship. Ownership of property is one of the defining criterion of the liberal subject;[54] those who dispossessed Japanese Canadians and claimed their property ensured their own security of place in the nation. This confiscation of property denied Japanese Canadians the material and symbolic right of owning a piece of the settler nation and sealed their fate in 1942 as landless, propertyless, and homeless. Thus, dispossession and dis-place-ment go hand-in-hand in the legislation that aimed to control Japanese Canadians, both spatially and socially, evict them from the Canadian nation, and deny their citizenship. Some of this legislation and how it was experienced by particular women is outlined in this section.

White citizens, as was mentioned in chapter 1, were appointed by the federal government to oversee the expulsion of Japanese Canadians from British Columbia. Order-in-Council P.C. 288 established a three-man Japanese Fishing Vessels Disposal Committee under the Department of Fisheries that was responsible for the disposal of fishers' boats.[55] On 8 December 1941, 1,200 fishing boats were impounded and placed under the control of this committee.[56] All of the men whose boats were confiscated were Canadian citizens.[57] On 4 March 1942, Order-in-Council P.C. 1665 was proclaimed and gave to the British Columbia Security Commission (BCSC) the right to

[r]equire by order any person of the Japanese race, in any protected area in British Columbia, to remain at his place of residence or to leave his place of residence and to proceed to any other place within or without the protected area at such time and in such manner as the Commission may prescribe in such order, or to order the detention of any such person, and any such order may be enforced by any person nominated by the Commission to do so.[58]

P.C. 1665 then enabled the establishment of the Custodian of Enemy Property in Vancouver, the responsibility for which came under the Department of the Secretary of State. All Japanese Canadian property, including 'Real Estate, personal effects, business and farms,'[59] was placed under the 'control and management'[60] of the Custodian and later sold without the permission of its owners.

Motor vehicles, radios, and cameras were confiscated by the Custodian. Families were allowed to take only 150 pounds of baggage per adult and 75 pounds per child over twelve with a maximum allowance of 1,000 pounds per family, which meant they had to leave behind possessions that were often looted or destroyed. Thus dispossession began well before the issuance of Order-in-Council P.C. 469 on 19 January 1943, which allowed the Custodian to liquidate all property under his control.

As Sunahara revealed, among the beneficiaries of this confiscated property were veterans of the Second World War. On 23 June 1943, 769 farms owned by Japanese Canadians and $43,000 worth of income accrued after the owners were expelled were given to the Veterans' Land Act Board.[61] While the farms were slated for use by veterans,[62] no Japanese Canadian veteran was included in this reward for patriotism.[63] The dispossession of Japanese Canadians thus enabled other citizens to own and belong to the nation, in this instance as reward for military service. Furthermore, there were racial limits to the rewards for participating in nationalism and proving one's loyalty to Canada through military service; despite their service, Japanese Canadian veterans of the First World War were incarcerated and dispossessed. My grandmother lost her home and farm acreage in the Fraser Valley when it was confiscated by the Custodian, and my father, as described in the preface, and his younger brother Robert, both veterans of the Second World War, were not rewarded with farms. In fact, my father never again saw the home he and his brothers bought for my grandmother; rather, along with all Japanese Canadians, my father was legally prevented from returning 'home' or to the 'restricted area' of the West Coast until 1949.

The women interviewed reminded me that gender and a women's relationship to property must be considered when discussing the dispossession of Japanese Canadians. Relationships to property are gendered and gender affects what people report as their losses. As many women did not own titles to boats or property, they sometimes did not report these items as being lost or confiscated even if these possessions were owned by fathers or partners; as such, gender and the often subordinate position of women in relation to familial property and the invisibility of their labour in procuring that property is also connected to class in these memories and constructions of ownership.[64] As Peter Nunoda revealed, in 1931 approximately two-thirds of Japanese Canadians were working class, 18 per cent of whom were designated as 'unskilled.'[65] Many of these people did not own property.[66] Not owning property is always constructed in relation to those who do and this relationship affects the ways in which people talk about the material losses they suffered. There is always a consciousness that other people might have lost more, in material terms, especially on the part of those who owned little in the pre-Internment period. Given a context wherein the focus of dispossession has largely rested on the material tangibility of loss as opposed to potentiality (for example, future income), those who did not possess according to these criteria may also tend to minimize their losses.[67] Clearly, much of material value was lost in the massive confiscation of everything other than the 'one bag' that most people were allowed to take with them. A study conducted by Price Waterhouse of Vancouver published in 1986 estimated the total loss for the community at $48 million in 1948 dollars, or $443 million in 1986 dollars.[68] Importantly, this study did include a calculation of the income that was lost. However, the researchers deemed it inappropriate to include a figure for 'lost education' or 'non-pecuniary' losses. Also, the accounting firm did not estimate those losses attributable to the 'dispersal.' What the women reported as *their* losses, however, were losses often less tangible than property, hence these 'effects' have not been counted.

Haru recalled that 'what little furniture we had, we had to sell it for next to nothing.' Kazuko, who was seventeen when her family was forced to move, remarked that they were allowed to carry one bag per person:

> The Mounties came and said that we're going, 'Here's a notice.' And we opened the notice and it said, 'You have to leave this place in twenty-four hours. And just one baggage to a person.' So we didn't have much time at all. Because this wasn't expected.[69]

Kazuko, however, was also conscious of the position of her parents and added: 'So that was, mostly for my parents, that was really sad. You know, everything, you lost.'

These 'adult' reports are to be contrasted to that of a woman who was a child at the time of the expulsion. Margaret, who lived in Richmond, was forced to move to Manitoba when she was twelve. When I asked her about leaving her home she told me all she could remember was that they were supposed to leave their dog:

> The only thing that we, the kids, remember was our dog. We couldn't take our dog. So we had to give our dog away. Of course, our dog came back the day before we left. So we did end up bringing it to Manitoba. We didn't know what else to do.[70]

Some of the women who were children at the time of the expulsion situate themselves within a childhood memory, less encumbered by what they report as the hardships of their elders. Yet when they did discuss their elders' losses, there was often a profound grief, reflective of the enormity of the loss. This age-specific self-situated experience may not be understood by those who hear these testimonies. We may expect the adult to report what an adult might have experienced over fifty years ago. We might not recognize that memories from childhood and the language in which they are expressed may be different from those of adults, nor do we see that some parents might have attempted to shield children from their own struggles and pain.

The ability to take something cherished with her was an important memory for Margaret. Yet, when she described her family's losses, she articulated them in relation to those who were older, who lost 'their' possessions. This ability to situate the self relationally to others is a theme to which I will return throughout this chapter and chapter 7. As Margaret states:

> We were only allowed to take one baggage each. So, my grandmother had a lot of heirloom things. The government said, 'You have to move, you have to leave everything. It'll only be a matter of a year and a half, two years tops. Leave everything and you're only allowed one baggage.' We had this woodshed which locked. So my grandmother put everything in there, locked it up, hoping, you know, within a couple of years to come back and claim it all. But when my brother went back after the war, they had smashed in the windows, taken, smashed everything that they could smash and took whatever was valuable. So, we had nothing left. I think that was the hardest part for my grandmother. 'Cause it was all family things that she had left. That was very hard for her. Well, that's war. Yeah.

I think a lot of people went through that, anyways, you know. It's not just us.

It is important to notice here that Margaret described her grandmother's losses as 'family things.' They symbolize a relationship to others. As well, she situated herself within a context of 'war' where others also suffered losses.

The relationships conveyed here spanned time and space, connecting people across national boundaries through history and family. Yoshiko, who was only five when she was forced to move from Vancouver, could not remember leaving the city.[71] She knew her parents owned a car and that 'very few people at that time owned cars.' The way their losses have manifested themselves for her is through her knowledge that they no longer have things that she remembered being a part of her familial surroundings before they were forced to move from Vancouver. The evidence of these possessions is materialized through the photographs they have retained from this period. She stated: 'We have pictures of us, our home in Vancouver before we moved. You know, those shelves of dolls, Japanese dolls? And things on the walls. We don't have any of that.'

S., who was twelve at the time her family was forced to leave Vancouver, described the process of dispossession in this way: 'We always thought we would go back. So, I can remember my mother packing boxes, which we left with the neighbours, thinking we would claim them. All our good Japanese things. And things we just didn't want to take.' In contrast to Yoshiko's experience, however, S.'s family did eventually retrieve the possessions they had entrusted to their neighbour.

Esther, who was three years of age at the time, did not remember the home she left in New Westminster. Her parents lived in a float house and had not bought any property. As she said, 'Perhaps it was just as well they didn't. Because it was confiscated anyways, right?' In contrast to Yoshiko's family, Esther's did not own a car. She reported that her 'father had a fishing boat. And my two oldest brothers had a fishing boat.' Her family left their other possessions in the float house and asked a neighbouring 'Polish man' to look after them.[72]

Evelyn, who was eleven at the time, recalled her father trying to reassure the children that leaving Vancouver would be 'like a holiday.' Her father's business contact bought his boat from him. Evelyn described this loss of her father's boat in relation to the loss sustained by other fishers: 'Yes. We were lucky. You see most of the people's boats were confiscated. But they bought my father's boat.' But she also told me that they had to sell their furniture to the neighbour 'for next to nothing.' She remembered one possession, in particular, that was very difficult to give up – her father's violin. Evelyn underscored this by saying, 'He did seem sad. He, I think, gave it to the neighbour's daughter.'

May recalled that the day the *hakujin* auctioneer sold all of their household goods was the day they also moved into the Hastings Park incarceration site. May's father had died just before Canada's declaration of war against Japan. She was fourteen when she, her mother, and sister were moved to Hastings Park in June 1942. She described how they were dispossessed and moved to their first site of incarceration, all in one day:

> So I finished my school year in June and then we sold all our furniture and stuff. By then my father was dead, you see. So there was a Japanese man, maybe there was more than one, who together with a, I think he was an auctioneer, a *hakujin* auctioneer. And they would come around, we got word that there were these people available who would come and give you a price for everything in your house and they just simply came and moved it out on a certain day. And on that day then we went into Hastings Park, so that we could be moved out from there. It was the Manning Pool. And by this time my mother was very sick. She was extremely sick. She had done some housework after my dad died because she needed some money.

In May's family, dispossession included the theft of money from a private insurance plan that her father had paid for by skipping lunches. Upon his death, a white lawyer had approached her mother and she asked his advice on what to do with the insurance policy money. This is what happened:

> When the evacuation notice came, mother went to talk to [the lawyer] and he had said, 'They're going to tell you to use your own money up, you know, before you can go on welfare. So maybe if I hold this, because you are certainly going to need some monies over and above welfare.' So this is what we did, we went out and bought things like blankets and things that would be needed for warmth, and we spent some of that money. But then we left the rest of the money with him. Unfortunately what we did not know was that he was an alcoholic. And so he never seemed to have the money to send us after we got in the camps. Those were some of the

kinds of things that feel bad to me. Heck, if that was going to happen, why didn't Daddy just go and eat lunch, you know. I mean he would have been better off to have eaten it, you know.

Connecting the Places of the Internment

When we think of the Internment of Japanese Canadians, we may think of the camps in the interior of British Columbia. The other places of incarceration are largely forgotten when the Internment is reduced to 'camps' alone.[73] The geographic and social distinctions among the Internment sites and the camps are effaced through the unitary word 'camp.' This collapsing of spaces in the collective memory of the Internment is part of the production of its forgetting. Spatially conflating the incarceration and displacement of over 22,000 people to the (sometimes) admitted sites of amorphous camps is a function of the denial of the spatial scope of the incarcerations and dispersal. Like the rendition of the Internment as a temporal moment, a 'sad chapter' or 'page' of past Canadian history, the singularity of space obfuscates the extent and materiality of the violence that destroyed communal and familial relations through incarceration and dispersal. What is also obscured through such monolithic representations are the ways in which different spaces produced heterogeneous gendered subjects.

We may not be aware, therefore, of the differences between the camps, their topographies, and the ways in which divisions were created within and between each site. For example, a BCSC report described the Sandon camp as being located 'high in the hills north-west of Kaslo and east of New Denver,' and could be 'reached by a narrow, winding, steeply graded road ... difficult to negotiate in the winter.'[74] The annual snowfall for Sandon was twenty feet and the town had two to three hours a day of sunlight in the winter.[75] When I visited this site near the middle of October 1992 as part of an organized community tour, the town and environs were snow-covered. The bus driver for the tour admitted that driving on the sole access road was risky. A participant on the tour who had been incarcerated in Sandon told me it was referred to as the 'hell hole.'

There were other carceral sites: Hastings Park in Vancouver (which for many was the first place of incarceration); the five so-called self-support camps; the various road camps to which men were sent (seventeen at the Yellow-Blue River Highway Project that traversed the border of BC and Alberta, seven at the Hope-Princeton Highway Project in

BC, seven at the Revelstoke-Sicamous Highway Project in BC, and six at the Schreiber-Jackfish Highway Project in Ontario)[76] and that were operated by the Department of Mines and Resources; the prisoner-of-war (POW) camps in Angler and Petawawa, Ontario, and Kananaskis-Seebe, Alberta, operated by the Department of National Defence to which some of the men were sent; Neys Hostel in northern Ontario; and other hostels in Saskatchewan, Manitoba, Quebec, and southern Ontario. There were the sites of forced labour on sugar beet and other farms on the Prairies and in Ontario. There were domestic service and other jobs that women and men were forced to accept 'east of the Rockies' in Quebec, Ontario, and Manitoba in the face of unemployment in the camps, destitution, or the threat of deportation to Japan when the repatriation survey was conducted.[77] There were industrial projects in Ontario and in Westwold and Taylor Lake, BC.[78] The most geographically distant site was Japan, the country from which Canada did not accept some visiting Japanese Canadians in the 1940s and the country to which 3,964 people were forced to move through the coercive signing of the repatriation survey.[79]

The RCMP and the BC Provincial Police enforced the policies of the BCSC. As people were moved to different carceral sites, 'permanent detachments' of the RCMP were set up at each of them.[80] '[T]he movement of all individual Japanese was controlled through a system of Permits rigorously enforced,'[81] issued by the RCMP or the BC Provincial Police. Road blocks were established at the 'necessary places.'[82] The BCSC underlined that 'it is not deemed desirable that the Japanese shall be permitted to wander at will throughout the country.'[83]

The remoteness of most of the Internment sites made the conditions of each site less visible to the politicians who envisioned and ordered the expulsions. Thus they protected *themselves* from witnessing the actions they had legislated and the harmful effects they caused.[84] The distribution of Japanese Canadians across multiple sites and provinces divided people into smaller groupings that were less visible than one large group of 22,000 people and ensured that any attempts to organize resistance could be contained. Importantly, as I will demonstrate, the spatial separations allowed the federal government to make relational identities for the incarceration sites themselves and relational site-specific identities for the subjects interned. This physical and discursive relational mapping obfuscated the carceral nature of the places of the Internment.

In addition, the use of euphemistic language at that time (as discussed in chapter 1) distanced the government and its administrators from the effects of their actions and left a semantic legacy with which we continue to struggle. For example, Lieutenant-Colonel of National Defence R.H. Webb's phraseology from his letter written in 1942, quoted in chapter 1, and his use of the term 'family system' to describe the BC interior camps obfuscates the fact that many men were forced to work and live outside of the camps, away from their families. His terminology suggests a particular notion of family that excludes the non-nuclear family and other forms of intimate relationships, including a network of relatives, lovers, and friends. It renders invisible the many women, men, and children who were 'missing' and 'missed' in the different sites, as they were separated over time and space, some never to be reunited. The word 'family' itself was a euphemism used by the government and its administrators to (mis)identify sites such as sugar beet farms and the 'self-support' camps as places where families were kept together. Hence the violence of forced separations, the destruction of families, and their effects were forgotten.

Families, however, as they were constituted in the Japanese Canadian community, were forever changed or destroyed in moving to these sites. For example, Evelyn was moved to Lillooet, a 'self-support' camp, and was separated from her maternal grandparents who were moved to the Lemon Creek camp. Aya, who was married at the time, was moved to Greenwood and Tashme and reported that her mother and brothers were moved to a sugar beet farm in Manitoba.

The women I interviewed saw and articulated their connections to different places and the people incarcerated therein. Haru, who was incarcerated in a BC interior camp, reported to me that she knew that life in the 'self-support' camps was difficult because one of her relatives had lived there. Yet it is this very awareness of the hardships inherent in each place that affects a survivor's ability to name her own experience as uniquely difficult. This memory of entire communities being expelled and how one constructs oneself in relationship to them is something that I refer to as 'memory of community.'

Women were moved from place to place, sometimes from camp to camp, camp to farm, farm to domestic service, and all combinations of overseen movement and control to places unknown, and often separated from partners and various family members and friends in this continual displacement. All of this occurred after the initial traumatic removal from their homes. Although historians of the Internment have struggled to name the processes of expulsion, the term 'second uprooting'[85] used to describe what is sometimes referred to as the 'dispersal' from the interior camps does not quite capture the number of movements that transpired after 1941.

Each description of each place gave me but a glimpse of life differently lived by each woman and the material and psychological challenges of those places. Each departure, including the one from 'home,' to unknown confinement and restriction, from familiar geography to changing landscapes and climates, was a leaving of cherished people and all the people who had surrounded them, a weeding through again of ever-diminishing possessions, and was replete with the accumulation of loss.

Racializing Masculinity: Road Camps and Prisoner-of-War Camps

Racializing discourses depicted Japanese Canadian men as Other in relation to a normative white bourgeois masculinity. The government mobilized a particular notion of racialized masculinity to produce the road camps through Order-in-Council P.C. 1271 issued on 13 February 1942. Men who were not Canadian citizens were the first to be expelled from the restricted area. This first expulsion of men who were Japanese nationals, as well as the creation of the POW camps as a site for men who were Japanese nationals and Canadian citizens, depended upon the heightened image of a demonized and racialized masculinity, that of the 'enemy' or 'alien,' constructed to legitimate their incarceration. The spectre of the 'disloyal Japanese' had to be made tangible to white Canadians on a continual basis, and the notion of disloyalty was discursively used to defend the construction of the incarceration sites. Ironically, at the same time that these men were constructed as the enemy and a threat to national security, the federal, British Columbia, Alberta, and Ontario governments assigned many of them to highway construction and other projects that were critical to securing spatial access for their citizens and to serving the interests of a capitalist economy in the building of the nation.

The classic notion of Jeremy Bentham's panopticon, described by Foucault as being built around a 'tower' in which the guard is able to 'see constantly and to recognize [prisoners] immediately,'[86] was a fitting description of the surveillance used at the Angler POW camp with its guard towers and barbed wire. In addition, Japanese Canadian men incarcerated there had to wear uniforms with red circles sewn onto the back that 'provided a target for camp guards.'[87] This use of the red symbol, a 'spectacle of identity,'[88] connoted the national identity of the Japanese 'enemy.' Hence, the BCSC masculinized and racialized the 750 men incarcerated in the Petawawa and Angler POW camps as 'those Japanese known to be dangerous, or to have the slightest subversive tendencies and, therefore, considered to be a potential menace.'[89] These places were the farthest in distance from the 100-mile restricted area.

The demonization of Japanese Canadian men and their spatial separation were critical to the government's legitimization of the Internment and forwarded its notion that Japanese men were inherently dangerous and essentially different from white men. In using the POW camps, the government also created another category of people it called 'internees,' and it then used this distinction to categorize other sites of incarceration as other (less severe) than 'internment.'[90] As Sunahara has demonstrated, the government was also careful in describing those born in Canada (even though they were in POW camps) as 'not interned,' since only 'aliens' could be legally interned according to the Geneva Convention.[91] The POW camps were used to produce notions of racialized men who were non-citizens and a threat to the nation while disguising their Canadian citizenship status.

Despite the lack of guard towers in other incarceration sites, all Japanese Canadians in these places were not free to leave and were monitored and controlled through site-specific techniques. What Foucault called a 'panoptic system' – in which those who monitor and discipline demonstrate 'a certain power, and for that reason ... also act as the vehicle for transmitting a wider power'[92] – was actualized across the sites of incarceration. Through P.C. 1271, 1,700 male Japanese nationals were eventually moved to road-camp sites, two-thirds of whom were married and had on average two or three children.[93] Men who were Canadian-born and able-bodied were soon to follow, with a total of 2,150 being sent to road camps in Ontario and in British Columbia.[94] Many of the men sent to the BC interior camps were forced to do hard labour outside the camp, sometimes returning on the weekends.[95]

Approximately 2,900 men were removed from their families in 1942. Over 7,000 women, fifteen years of age and older, were moved to various incarceration sites. Over 8,000 children under the age of fifteen (approximately 3,500 girls and 4,600 boys) had to be cared for in these sites.[96] As is shown in the next section, males over the age of thirteen were separated from women and children in the Hastings Park site. It was thus assumed by the government that women would care for the children, those who were not 'able-bodied,' and the elderly not only in Hastings Park but also in the camps to which they were eventually sent. The gendered presumption – the women must provide this care – was mobilized by the white officials and administrators and material-ized through the separation of men from the sites in which these activ-ities took place. While the government, at times, might have rendered women invisible – as in the case of a 1942 government report where 'women and children were listed in the same category'[97] – gender was always critical in the operationalization of the Internment. Although some of the Internment literature alludes to the patriarchal practices of Japanese, Japanese Canadian, or Japanese American men (see chapter 2), there has been little analysis of how male-domination and gender-specific roles were promulgated through the actions of the white politicians, public servants, Internment administrators, and other par-ticipants in this process.

It is important to also note that a category of physical ability and its correlates 'not able-bodied' and 'physically unfit'[98] were reinforced through the Internment, and forged through governmental discourses and spatial separations. In this process, some of the men who were sent to the BC interior camps were deemed not able to undertake the hard, physical labour required in the road camps and thus were character-ized as 'not able-bodied.' While many of the men and women deemed not able by the government had, in fact, been very able in their jobs and related responsibilities before the expulsion, their relegation to the in-terior camps reinforced their new identities as 'not able-bodied.' Hence, these gendered divisions of work and space that were enforced through spatial separations also assigned hegemonic notions of ability, further marking bodies already pathologized through racial exclusion within a spatially distinguishable hierarchical grid of identity categories.[99] Separating men who could not labour in the road camps for reasons of physical capability discursively emasculated them by designating them 'dependants' in this spatialized hierarchical arrangement.

Just as the removal of men constructed Japanese Canadians in rela-tion to a white hegemonic able-bodied masculinity, so too did it produce a white hegemonic able-bodied femininity. The separation of racial-ized women from their partners, lovers, children, parents, siblings, ex-tended family, friends, and neighbours and their forced removal from their homes relationally constructed the privilege of white families and communities who were assured of their entitlement to occupy the coastal area and their homes. While the removal of many Japanese Can-adian men from their families ensured that the women would assume the childcare functions prescribed in hegemonic white male-dominated family structures, Japanese Canadian women's gendered subject position was not unitarily similar to that of white women. White women, although differently located in terms of their own class and ethnicized positions, benefited from the bolstering of whiteness secured by the racial exclusions of the Internment.[100] How the Internment reinforced hierarchical arrangements among women will be further demonstrated in chapters 5 and 6.

As has been documented by Sunahara and others, many of the men forced into POW camps were those who protested their separation from their families through the expulsion process.[101] In particular, the Nisei Mass Evacuation Group (NMEG) is cited as an example of resistance to the governmental order calling for the break-up of families.[102] While the resistance of these men to the expulsion and separation of their families is undeniably significant and must be recognized, it is important to note that their actions are often the sole examples of 'resistance' signalled in Internment narratives. As Nunoda has pointed out, little is known about the Nisei Mass Evacuation Women's Group, formed in April 1942 to support the interned men and 'resist evacuation';[103] indeed, there is little mention in the literature or in community commemorative representations of women's individual and organized 'resistance.' For example, the actions of Mrs Tanaka-Goto, who refused the orders to leave her home in 1942 and who was incarcerated in Oakalla prison before being sent to the Greenwood camp, have largely remained unacknowledged.[104] Other than Muriel Kitagawa (chapter 2), very few women (and men for that matter) have been represented by Japanese Canadians as resisting during the Internment.

Hastings Park

When the Order-in-Council to remove Japanese Canadians was enacted, the first communities to be expelled were those in 'outlying' coastal areas.[105] Many of the people who did not live in Vancouver at the time of the expulsion were first incarcerated on the grounds of Hastings Park in the Pacific National Exhibition buildings: the women and children were placed in the Livestock Building and the men were kept in the Forum Building. Conceptualized by the BCSC as a place to hold at least 4,000 people at a time, Hasting Park was used to confine 8,000 people in total who were sent there before they were moved to other carceral sites.[106] The buildings of the Pacific National Exhibition, ordinarily used to display livestock and agricultural and manufacturing products, were expropriated by the Department of National Defence and quickly emptied of their usual exhibits. Sunahara describes Hastings Park as 'a holding pen for human beings ... converted from animal to human shelter in only seven days ... the ever-present stink of animals and the maggots and the dirt ... encrusted the buildings in Hastings Park.'[107] Sunahara's description must be contrasted to a BCSC report that describes it as '[a]t all times ... kept scrupulously clean.'[108] The report also states, 'Many valuable lessons in food values were learned by the Japanese during their stay in Hastings Park and while they were there every effort was made to educate them to the correct standard of proper diet. Sanitary and laundry conveniences and all the more simple accoutrements of *modern civilization* were installed.'[109] The notion of modern Western 'civilization' was critical to the construction of the Internment. Just as in the colonial project, in which the colonized must be shown to be 'uncivilized' and 'backward,' white officials continually referred to the need to 'civilize' or 'Canadianize' Japanese Canadians. Spatially segregating Japanese Canadians in livestock buildings and other uninhabitable environments created the uncivilized spaces needed as proof of 'Japanese backwardness.' In this way, white administrators created colonies to be conquered 'within' their nation; colonies that were in isolated and largely inaccessible spaces to which they could travel and from which they could leave, and over which they ultimately maintained control.

The construction of Japanese Canadians as disloyal hinged upon the Orientalist notion of their Otherness, and this difference was discursively repeated in the attempt to justify the unjustifiable actions volleyed against them. Meyda Yeğenoğlu delineates how temporality is used to legitimate the violence of colonialism by rendering the colonial project as one which seeks to modernize and raise to the 'advanced' moment of the colonist the 'backward' and 'primitive' Other.[110] I would extend her analysis to spatial as well as temporal constructions of domination and superiority, and specifically those spatial exclusions experienced by Japanese Canadians during the Internment. Separation from family and destruction of community were continually legitimized by the state and citizenry in the goal of 'civilizing' them. Confining Japanese Canadians to dehumanized spaces secured the liberal humanness of the white subjects outside of these spaces and those who inhabited them not by force but by 'choice.' In seeking to obscure the violence of incarceration and forced displacement, the white subject secured for itself the notion of being 'civilized,' and the continual repetition of the civilizing/Canadianizing discourse was essential to occluding the violence. To quote Yeğenoğlu, 'the dissimulation of the violence' was secured in the guise of 'dissemination of the benefits of modernity to uncivilized cultures.'[111]

Kazuko's comments in her interview shed light on what was deemed to be 'modern civilization' by the BCSC. They also reveal what 'valuable lessons in food values' were imparted:

> The first place where we went was Hastings Park, with lots of other people. You know, you just sleep on the floor and ... the sugar was rationed, so even when you got porridge, the sugar was not even a teaspoonful. And milk didn't even cover the porridge. Porridge was like a paste. You know, because it was so many people to cook for. And then also we had to help with the dishes afterwards, which is natural. But the meals were, oh gosh, I'm telling you, were like, you wouldn't even feed it to a dog. It was just terrible. So we were very happy to get out of there.

Haru, who was also forced to move from Vancouver, described her memories of Hastings Park in this way:

> The men were taken first to Hastings Park. My father and my mother, then even in Hastings Park we couldn't stay together. The men were all in one building and the women and children were in another building. That was an experience. And then once you're there, it's like a prison. There was a gate, you couldn't go out. You had to get a special permit to go into Vancouver if you wanted to go and do some business. And so our lives were: you slept in a horse building or manufacturer's building where they had bunks. And they gave you blankets that you could put a rope on to make a partition. And it was very hard because there were hundreds of people there and you didn't know who they were. They came from all over Vancouver and Vancouver Island. They were total strangers. Regardless of how hot, how rainy, we had to go to another building to stand in line for hours to get our food, for breakfasts, lunch, and supper. And we all got a tin plate. I can remember that it was so hot one day. By the time you got there, you just thought you were going to pass out, just to get your supper.

Haru began her description of the horror of Hastings Park by describing how boys over the age of thirteen and men, including her father, were 'taken' and separated from the women in this first site of incarceration. According to Sunahara, married men 'were prohibited from entering the building housing their wives and young children.'[112]

Muriel Kitagawa's writings provide an account of women contesting the treatment of Japanese Canadians incarcerated in Hastings Park. As someone who was not incarcerated there, she was differently situated in relation to the violence taking place in that site. It was through someone she knew who worked at Hastings Park that she learned of one woman's protest to a white nurse after finding maggots in the Livestock Building. According to Kitagawa, the nurse responded, 'Well, there's worms in the garden aren't there?'[113]

Kitagawa's friends, Eiko and Fumi, publicly challenged this nurse, who was known to call people 'filthy Japs.'[114] Eiko also protested the actions of a white RCMP officer who hit women when they congregated at the entrance of their 'cage' to find out what was happening to the men who were refusing to go to the road camp in Schreiber, Ontario. As Kitagawa reports, Eiko 'raked him with fighting words.'[115]

Forrest La Violette, who witnessed the conditions in Hastings Park, described how the anger of those confined 'became converted into demands upon the Security Commission for improvement.'[116] Some of these demands were articulated in a petition dated 19 June 1942, which was addressed to the representative of the International Red Cross in Montreal and written by a group confined in Hastings Park. This petition included the following demands:

> the emancipation from unnecessary restrictions, the rights of the democratic nation, freedom of speech ... sympathetic understanding of an oppressed people, differential treatment for Japanese nationals and Canadian citizens, appointment of a medical officer for Hastings Park, and the return from work camps of the husbands of expectant mothers.[117]

In contrast to Kitagawa, in describing the attempts of some Japanese Canadians to organize and protest in Hastings Park, La Violette demeaned their demands and compared them to Japanese Americans who had been labelled as exhibiting a 'demandatory psychology' by the American internment-camp administrators.[118]

Haru emphasized the fact that 'there were hundreds of people and you didn't know who they were.' May also felt isolated when she was confined in Hastings Park with her mother and sister. She knew none of the other people there, and her sense of isolation was reinforced by a memory shared by her sister-in-law decades later at the funeral of her mother-in-law. May's sister-in-law (whom she did not know during the Internment) confessed this recollection to her:

> She said, 'You know, May, I've been meaning to tell you because I think I've had a little bit of a guilty conscience. When you were in Hastings Park, I remember you and your sister and your mother sitting in the shade of a building in the afternoons. And you would be sitting there listening to a portable record player. We used to run past you and call [you] names.' I don't remember that particular incident, except that I knew that we were out of sync.

May said that hearing about this incident reinforced her sense 'that it was not just me ... internally feeling out of place ... I must have looked out of place.' The expulsion resulted in the ejection of Japanese Canadians from their places of home and nation. But being 'out of place' was a material and social condition to which they would be subjected for years to come.

May's sharing of her sister-in-law's memory years after their detention in Hastings Park illustrates that memories of the Internment and the displacements, and reflections upon these memories, are continually being built across time and space. Survivors may encounter people they knew or with whom they shared a space of incarceration and in whose presence they have not been since that time because of the dispersal policy and its effects. These reunions for some survivors are ongoing, particularly for those who renegotiate Japanese Canadian spaces, and thus some of the gaps in memories of community may be filled in through these encounters that are taking place more than sixty years after the Internment. How do people live with the anticipation and materialization of such meetings, I wonder, filled as they may be with narratives of years together and separated, evoking memories of why and how they were separated and the pain of those evocations? And by contrast, how do they wrestle with the absences of those who are missing, never to be seen again?

Conclusion

In the designation of Hastings Park in Vancouver as the first place of incarceration for 8,000 people, a prison to detain only Japanese Canadians was temporarily constructed within the 100-mile restricted zone. Women and children were placed in the Livestock Building on the site of the Pacific National Exhibition; the racialized space and the racial-ized subjects within were highly visible in the most inhabited city of British Columbia. By choosing this animal and uncivilized habitat, the BCSC then deemed those in it uncivilized. This spatial and racial construction was relationally used to secure the civility and spatial entitlements of the white residents of Vancouver. The confinement of men and of boys over thirteen years of age to the Forum Building and their separation from mothers, partners, sisters, and children normal-ized white masculinity by pathologizing the racialized male. This age and gendered distinction marked these male children as necessitating spatial exclusion and disentitled them from living with their mothers and other female community members. This determination of the age of thirteen was linked to a construction of an Orientalized heterosexuality and masculinity, delimiting spatial contact and heterosexual sexual re-lations between males and females by imposing upon all males around the age of puberty and older physical separation from females. Hence the construction of the 'enemy' entailed the interlocking of a racialized masculinity and a racialized heterosexuality. Gendered and age-specific restrictions and removals of racialized men from their families, spatially and socially disentitled them from living with their partners and fami-lies and in their communities. This action bolstered and normalized a white bourgeois heteronormativity by entitling white subjects to 'fam-ily,' heterosexual sexual relations, and 'community,' which reinforced white masculine and heterosexual hegemony.[119] Moreover, by separat-ing partners and determining if or when they would be reunited, the federal government controlled for years relationships, including sexual ones, and the spaces in which relating and sexuality could be expressed.

Japanese Canadian male and female identities were re-made spatial-ly through the Internment, and as well white and heterosexual identi-ties were relationally constructed through discourses that entrenched and normalized the practices of entitlement through the creation of social and spatial disentitlement for racialized Others. The Nisei Mass Evacuation Group (NMEG) called attention to the fact that Japanese Canadians were 'British subjects by birth' and to the inherent contra-dictions between the 'civil rights of any ordinary Canadian' and the practices to which Japanese Canadians were being subjected. In a letter to the chairman of the BCSC, members of the NMEG made it clear just how well they understood that being able to live in a family was sup-posed to be a right of Canadian citizenship and a right that Japanese Canadians were being denied,

... we think it totally unnecessary that our last remaining freedom should be taken from us – the freedom to live with our families. We were taught in our Canadian schools that we should always cherish freedom and do our utmost for the protection of women and children. We can now fully appreciate what that meant. We were also taught in our churches that the unity of family is sacred and must be regarded as a God-given human right and should be cherished as life itself.[120]

Hence, the NMEG and others mentioned above named these processes of relational subject formation between Japanese Canadians and their white incarcerators in their many acts of resistance. In naming the liberal principles upon which Canadian citizenship was supposed to be based, they made it clear they were well aware that their entitlement to these principles had been negated because they were constructed as an enemy 'race.' Moreover, their appeals to liberal values and to those who constructed themselves as liberal subjects went unaddressed and the men of the NMEG were eventually sent as far from the West Coast as possible, to POW camps. The women, from whom they were spatially separated, were left to care for the children, the elders, and those deemed not able-bodied.

5 Gendering the Subjects of the Internment: The Interior Camps of British Columbia

Each person that went through the war years has their own experience so, you know, they could write their own experience.

Aya, interview[1]

Audrey Kobayashi argues that race and gender differences were 'taken-for-granted facts in the 1940s.' As she states, 'It was "natural" to think that women and "orientals" should not be considered to have the same rights as white men, and the law reflected this attitude both implicitly and explicitly.'[2] She further argues that Asian women were given little attention by the Canadian state and 'their fates follow[ed] those of their husbands and fathers.'[3]

While I agree with Kobayashi that the government positioned Asians and women as subordinate to white men prior to and during the 1940s, I argue that the Canadian state mobilized race *and* gender discourses through the Internment, positioning women in relation to but differently from men. The Internment was accomplished through the interlocking of discourses of domination, including gender, race, class, sexuality, age, and ability. Gender was a critical tool that was used by the state and citizens to socially and spatially separate Japanese Canadians, and gendered notions of 'Japanese' and of 'Canadian' men and women were promulgated to normalize and rationalize their actions.

Male domination is continually reinscribed and contested through different processes. Women's experiences of the Internment were differently constructed – socially and spatially – from those of men. A feminist interlocking analysis of the Internment illustrates that all women interned did not have the same experience. Additionally, Japanese Canadian femininity was being conceptualized differently yet in relation to that of white women. As was argued in chapters 2 and 4, the inclination to see Japanese Canadian women within a patriarchal relationship of stasis with 'Japanese' men only elides the fact that white men produced and implemented gendered racial differences through the Internment. It is through an examination of these interlocking and relational processes that we can see how the discourses of the Internment were also interpellating mechanisms of both gender and race.

In this chapter and in chapters 6 and 7 that follow, Japanese Canadian women re-member the places of the Internment and describe the material carceral sites and who was in them. Their memories illustrate that heterogeneous relational subjects were produced through the discourses and places of the Internment.

In-between Places: Transportation to the Sites of Incarceration and Forced Labour

On 30 September 1942, the Hastings Park site was closed.[4] The 8,000 men, women, and children who had been incarcerated there had been moved to desolate and separate carceral sites along with 14,000 other people. This chapter focuses on women's descriptions of the British Columbia interior detention camps. Each place of incarceration presented different spatial arrangements and different encounters with white people. Women's testimonies reveal some of the conditions under which they were held and some of the effects of living in these carceral sites.

Before they arrived at the incarceration sites, people experienced the 'in-between' places through which they moved while being transported from one carceral site to another. In the spring and summer of 1942, Japanese Canadians boarded 'special trains' in Vancouver.[5] Their homes were vacated and trains were filled. They were categorized according to their destinations; gender, class, age, ability, and citizenship status were used to determine who went where and, thus, which train one boarded and with whom one travelled. For example, the trains that were headed for the Yellow-Blue River Highway Project road camps and Ontario POW camps transported some of the eldest men who were not naturalized citizens, while some of the youngest men, born in Canada, were headed for other road camps in BC and Ontario and for the Ontario POW camps.[6] The trains were distinguishable as they were 'old ... sometimes overdue for retirement,' and importantly, as Ann Sunahara reminds us, 'while the trains left Vancouver fully loaded, they returned empty.'[7]

Many women had to travel alone with children, separated from the support of friends and partners. Responsibility for the care of children was part of the gendering process they experienced. S., whose family was moved three times before they were finally moved to Toronto during the dispersal, described the process of transportation from their home in Vancouver to Tashme:

MO: What year did you actually have to leave Vancouver?
S: 1942. And it was late in the year, I think. We were later.
MO: And how did you travel?
S: By train. We went by train and then by truck. Tashme was fourteen miles from Hope, so we travelled by truck. And that was a very primitive way of getting up there. But it was a very primitive place, too, that we were going to live in, so. It was quite an experience.[8]

Evelyn reported that because she was a child, she had to rely on what was told to her by the adults. She stated, 'The news filtered down to us, as kids. So they may have known things that we were not told.' She learned that 'people were going to this place and this place' but it 'didn't make sense to us.' She first learned people were being moved to Hastings Park by hearing that 'people were coming in from all over the place to Vancouver to [the] Park.' Her association with the 'Park' was that it was used for fairs and she remembered asking, 'What are they doing there? Is the [Exhibition] in town?' The reply was that 'people are being moved out.' She described what she did with this information: 'We used to run down to the railroad; right behind the Japanese Language School were the rails. So we used to run down there and wave at people going out to Greenwood or wherever they were going.'[9] Evelyn revealed how her young self had processed this fact and what she did with the information that people were being 'moved out.' She also provided the devastating detail that the people being moved via Vancouver had to pass through the Powell Street area, the home and centre of social activities of many who were expelled and the heart of the Vancouver Japanese Canadian community.

When I asked Margaret how she and her family were moved from Vancouver to a sugar beet farm on the prairies, she emphasized that she was only twelve at the time. She stated, 'It didn't really affect us the way it did our parents. Because our parents had to leave everything behind and go to, god knows where. Whereas for [the children], it's great, we're going on a train. We're going across Canada. Isn't that exciting?' Later in the interview, however, Margaret remembered being on the train that took her to Manitoba:

> I don't even like to think of that train trip cause it took four or five days to come from Vancouver to Winnipeg. And it's cramped quarters, I mean there's nowhere you could lie down. You had to sit up on those cane seats all the way for four days. That was really, I thought it was really hard. And it was in the summer, we came, so it was really hot and uncomfortable.[10]

The Camps of the BC Interior: Greenwood, Rosebery, Tashme, Slocan, New Denver

The ten interior camps of British Columbia were located in Greenwood, Kaslo, Sandon, New Denver, Rosebery, Tashme, and the Slocan area (consisting of the four camps of Slocan City, Bay Farm, Lemon Creek, and Popoff). Eight of the women I interviewed were moved to interior camps. May, Yoshiko, and Ann were incarcerated in Slocan City, also referred to as Slocan. S. was incarcerated in Tashme and New Denver.[11] Kazuko was incarcerated in Rosebery. Aya and her daughter, Louise, were incarcerated in Greenwood and Tashme and were later moved to Manitoba. Haru has requested that I not name the camp in which she was forced to live.

The BCSC set up offices in six camp towns (Kaslo, Sandon, Greenwood, Slocan City, New Denver, and Tashme), each with its own supervisor and assistant supervisor. A general supervisor was the 'overseer' of all of the camps, except for Tashme, which was assigned its own general supervisor due to 'its remoteness from the others.'[12] These offices hired some Japanese Canadians to do clerical work. The treasury and welfare departments had 'managers in the field.'[13]

The BCSC used the labour of Japanese Canadian men to build the shacks of the camps; however, they worked under the supervision of 'white foremen.'[14] While some of the existing buildings in the ghost towns were used as housing, the BCSC-designed shacks were sixteen feet by sixteen feet, separated into two rooms and a communal room with a wood stove to be shared by a minimum of four people; larger shacks were sixteen feet by twenty-four feet, divided into four rooms and a communal room with a wood stove to be shared by a minimum of eight people. Those who did not meet the minimum number of people, shared with another family.[15] The shacks were made from green wood and tarpaper; the wood shrank as it dried and air and dust easily swept through the gaping cracks. Bunk beds were built for sleeping. Three shacks shared one outdoor privy.[16] There were no sewage or water connections to the shacks. Occupants had to build tables and chairs using the green wood; all other supplies and food were to be paid for by Japanese Canadians.[17] The cost for food and clothing, sold by local shopkeepers, was higher than what they had paid in their home communities.[18]

As Sunahara has demonstrated, Japanese Canadians were required to contribute to the payment of their own incarceration from the sale of their property confiscated by the Custodian. This policy, as outlined by the Department of Labour, read, 'a family must live on its own assets down to $260 (1,000 yen)[19] for each adult and $50 for each child.' Therefore, any savings or money acquired from the sale of their property had to be used to pay for food or other necessities until it was whittled down to these amounts. In the language of a paternalistic banker, the department stated the limit was to serve 'for postwar contingencies.'[20] In other words, after paying for their own incarcerations, they were then expected to pay for the 'contingencies' of their release with whatever money remained. In fact, as May and others reported, some families would not have even started out with these amounts, given that they received little or nothing for the sale of their belongings.

People with no savings were given the provincial relief rates according to the number of people in the family. A family of three, for example, received $29 per month. Approximately 26 per cent of the people in the camps received the relief payments at the outset, but after two years of incarceration and the depletion of their accounts with the Custodian, the rate of those receiving relief rose to 46 per cent.[21] To administer these policies and practices, a welfare department was set up within the BCSC.[22] One of the members of the BCSC Advisory Council, Dr G. Lyall Hodgins, was appointed as its welfare and medical advisor and therefore held a position of responsibility for the expulsion, as well as the 'health and welfare' of Japanese Canadians, two positions of administrative power that suggest a conflict of interest.[23] This new department created solely as a result of the expulsion of Japanese Canadians assured even more jobs in an expanding bureaucracy of control. A general supervisor was maintained in Vancouver at the BCSC head office and was responsible for welfare policies; a field supervisor set up welfare departments in each interior camp and supervised the staff;

and a welfare manager was placed in each camp where some Japanese Canadians were hired as social workers.[24] Hence, the control and monitoring of the camps was not only the responsibility of the RCMP, the BC Provincial Police, and the Internment administrators but also of the new welfare administration. This forced welfare scheme resulted from the forced impoverishment of the incarcerated. It also produced new identities for Japanese Canadians as they were described as 'on welfare' and 'maintained' by the government. This relationally constructed the enactors and administrators of the Internment as benevolent benefactors. As the BCSC stated of its welfare practices, '[C]lose attention was given to all the aspects of welfare and various [welfare] branches were set up to deal with the general and individual well-being of the Japanese who had become *the charges* of the Commission.'[25]

Given this context of incarceration and forced impoverishment, many Japanese Canadians had no choice but to try to find paid work in the camps, and if this was not possible, they had to move to sugar beet farms or domestic service or other positions in waged labour. The use of the term forced labour is not unwarranted here, as it indicates that there was no choice but to work in view of the need to support oneself and one's family members, and to replenish in some way one's diminishing funds being held by the Custodian. However, even many of those who secured work at the rate of 22.5 cents to 40 cents an hour for general labourers and for $40 to $75 per month as 'inside' employees of the BCSC found it impossible not to deplete their confiscated funds.[26] These differential pay scales also served to divide those who were incarcerated as they competed for the few jobs available and had to deal with the contradictions inherent in working for the incarcerators.

On 5 February 1943, Order-in-Council P.C. 946 dissolved the BCSC and vested in the federal minister of labour the power to 'provide for the welfare, placement, control of movement and discipline of persons of the Japanese race in Canada.'[27] In this move, the federal government created an expanded national structure that would deal with the administration of the Internment.[28] Under the authority of the minister and deputy minister of labour, a Japanese Division was created and a Commissioner of Japanese Placement was appointed. The first commissioner, George Collins, was responsible for the Japanese Division and established the head office in Vancouver. This bureaucracy took over the supervision of the ten interior camps as well as five placement offices that were established outside of British Columbia. Both the minister of labour and the commissioner were given responsibility for determining 'the localities in which persons of the Japanese race shall be placed or may reside' and for prohibiting 'any movement or specific residence of a Japanese [*sic*], or to prescribe the terms of such movement or residence, in any part of Canada.'[29] They could also prevent Japanese Canadians from 'associating or communicating with any person.'[30]

In September 1943, the Japanese Division denied relief payments to all single men considered to be employable, thus forcing them to accept work outside of BC.[31] To further force men and women to take employment outside of BC, in February 1944, all 'able, single people, numbering about 125' working for the Japanese Division were fired.[32]

Protests were organized across the carceral sites during the entire period of incarceration. While detailing all of these protests is beyond the scope of this book, I will mention a few instances to show that people did organize in the carceral sites. For example, strikes occurred in the road camps to protest the ongoing separations of families and the working conditions. Some of the protestors were then sent to POW camps.[33] In each camp, people organized and sent petitions as well as individual letters to the federal government. In 1943, petitions were sent to the Department of Labour, the Protecting Power (for Japanese Nationals), and the International Red Cross regarding the inadequate maintenance rates and the medical services, clothing allowances, housing, fuel, and lighting that were 'unsatisfactory and unhealthy.'[34] In 1943, the federal government struck a royal commission to investigate these claims and concluded unanimously that 'the provisions made for the welfare of the Japanese ... are, as a war-time measure, reasonably fair and adequate.'[35] In its report, the commission stated that the 'newly constructed housing was SUPERIOR' to their pre-war homes.[36] Given that members of the commission had not visited their pre-war homes, it is not clear how they made this deduction. However, their conclusion reiterated the notion that Japanese Canadians moved from degenerate spaces and thus were inferior, relationally constructing the Japanese Division and its shacks as 'SUPERIOR.' The commission also deemed the policy to refuse maintenance payments to people who were considered 'employable' as 'fair and necessary.'[37]

Greenwood

In a BCSC report, Greenwood was described as a 'once prosperous mining town,' 'nine miles north of the international boundary in central British Columbia.'[38] The former mining towns used by the BCSC were also referred to as 'ghost towns,' an encoded word in the lexicon of survivors. In 1942, 1,777 Japanese Canadians were moved to Greenwood. There was a 'white population' of 150 there at that time.

Aya was twenty-three when she was forced to leave her home in Steveston. She was pregnant and had three young children; they were sent to Greenwood, which was to be the first of five moves. Between 1942 and 1946, she and her children were moved four times; during the dispersal she was moved to the prairie city where she currently resides. Aya was born in Steveston, a predominantly Japanese Canadian community, and had lived there all of her life until the expulsion. Up to that time, all of her friends were Japanese Canadian. She described her displacement to Greenwood in this way:

> I was married. And I had my two eldest daughters and my son was still a baby when we had to evacuate from Steveston ... But the men couldn't go because they all, you know, went to road camps. And so I left my husband who went to Hastings Park and then with my kids and with the neighbours we all went to Greenwood ... I hadn't heard from my husband for quite a long time, over two months after I went to Greenwood. And I was wondering what happened to him ... And then I finally got a letter from him, from the internment camp. Angler. I wasn't too sure why he was sent there. And after the war, when we got together, he told me ... So we were separated four years. So we both had a hard time.[39]

Aya was also separated from her mother and brothers who were sent to Manitoba to work on a sugar beet farm.

Ann, like Aya, had children at the time of the expulsion from her home on the West Coast. At the time of their interviews, Ann was eighty-two and Aya was seventy-seven. They both bore children while in the camps. Hence, the camps were the birthplaces for a cohort of Japanese Canadians, spaces that link both mother and child and subsequent generations to contradictory origins of life and great loss.

Approximately 2,500 children were born during the Internment.[40] The experience of giving birth is a profoundly gendered one. Moreover, experiencing the pain of labour in such a desolate setting, forcibly removed from partners and from extended familial and communal support, was a violation that is barely fathomable even in its description here. And for those who trace their places of birth and those of family members back to these sites, there is the constant contestation of the normalcy of these birthplace names in a nation where their other meanings are forgotten.

Aya's narrative of displacement included her spatializing of absences as well as the gendered embodiments of giving birth, caring for her children, and living with the constant fear of the unknown. She described giving birth to the baby in Greenwood: 'I was the first one to have a baby in Greenwood ... I was in the hospital for six days, so they sent two girls to look after my kids.' When I interviewed Louise, Aya's daughter, she described what she remembered of her mother giving birth. She was three years old when they were moved to Greenwood: 'My younger sister was born there ... I remember when my mother was in the hospital, a couple of nuns would come by. I don't know if someone in the apartment looked after us but I just remember the nuns coming to wash us up and everything else.'[41] Prior to their expulsion, Louise's grandmother had cared for her and her siblings while her mother worked at the cannery in Steveston. Her grandmother, however, was separated from them and moved by the BCSC to a sugar beet farm in Manitoba.

The Greenwood camp appears to be unique in that there were a substantial number of people who had been moved from one community – Steveston – to this site. Some of Aya's neighbours and friends, therefore, were also incarcerated there. Yet after two years, Aya was forced to leave them and move again. She explained the reasons given for this second expulsion:

And then after two years the Security Commission, they called it ... Well they informed us that they wouldn't have internees' families – they called us internees' families because our husbands were interned [in the Angler or Petawawa POW camps] – in Greenwood. So they sent us to Tashme. And I was there until the war ended.

Thus, even between the BC camps, identities of social difference were spatially imposed, creating different categories of those incarcerated. Places therefore were used to denote hierarchical social differences, with Tashme marking the identities of some of the wives of those men incarcerated in the POW camps. Hence the identities of the POW camps and those of the men within them were used to produce the identities and spatial positioning of some of the wives of these men.

Aya's daughter Louise explained to me that she has 'happy memories' of the Internment because she was 'so young and didn't understand anything ... you ask questions and that but you don't hear the sadness or what [my parents] had to go through.' In Greenwood, the 'apartment,' as she mentioned above, another spatial euphemism, was in fact one room that she shared with her mother and her three siblings. The women cooked and fed their families in a communal kitchen downstairs. She also remembered being cared for by other Japanese Canadian women in Greenwood, for example, in the communal women's bath to which she and her sister would sometimes go without their mother. She stated, 'There were always women in there taking baths who would help us. They would either wash our faces or scrub our backs. They would always be there to help.'

The baths constructed by Japanese Canadians in the camps are demonstrative of their organizing to share the limited resources of water and wood to provide a communal facility. They may have also served as a practical form of remembering Japanese bathhouses or *ofuro* and of resisting the pressure to relinquish their connections to Japanese culture.[42] However, not all Japanese Canadians would have experienced this practice of communal bathing in their BC home communities.[43] As Louise suggested, bathing in the gender-segregated bathhouse was an experience shared by women and girls, and offered them the chance to gather away from the eyes of the camp administrators.[44]

Caring for children in these desolate environs posed numerous problems for the women, however. Despite Louise's comment that hers are 'happy memories,' she also alluded to what must have been hardships for her mother. For example, her younger brother nearly drowned, and she emphasized that her mother 'must have had it very, very rough with four young kids and being by herself.' While the lake offered a place for the children to swim and create identities as children, the camp environs posed difficult challenges for mothers.

Louise's mother sewed all of their clothing, and although she does not remember being able to take any toys with her to Greenwood, she remembered her mother took her sewing machine and her trunk, which was packed with all their 'life things.' Louise stated, 'I remember the old sewing machine and this trunk. And to this day, she still has the two of them.' Later in the interview Louise told me that her mother 'still has her wedding gown and the wedding pictures ... they were all in that trunk that she insisted be brought with her every time we moved.'

When I asked Louise about her father, she put his absence within the context of who else was 'missing' from the Greenwood and Tashme camps. Her grandmother, who had cared for her when they had lived in Steveston, had to resort to sending 'care' packages from the sugar beet farm to which she had been sent. It is evident from Louise's testimony that her mother tried to maintain communication with her husband and her own mother. Although Louise's mother told them where their father was and how he was doing, Louise was greatly affected by his absence:

> [My father] spent the rest of the war years in Angler. So my mom was left with the four kids in Greenwood ... I can't even remember my father before that. After he left, the memory of him was sort of erased. All we saw were his pictures. We didn't know where he was. He was gone, he wasn't with us right there.

Louise's memories of the camp give us a glimpse into how children's lives were gendered and how these practices of gendering were forged through the sites of incarceration and through separation from fathers and older male family members.

Tashme

A BCSC report noted that Tashme was 'situated on a ranch ... leased for the duration of the war,' '14 miles south-east of the village of Hope ... situated on the scenic Cariboo highway, a beautiful three hours drive from the city of Vancouver.' The road from Hope to Tashme was but a 'rough, narrow mountain trail,' and, as the report suggests, became a work site for Japanese Canadians whose forced labour upgraded it into 'part of the Hope-Princeton Highway.'[45] Despite the government's travelogue description, Tashme was clearly a carceral site. The report was ominously clear about its purpose:

> [T]he valley in which Tashme nestles is about one mile wide and about 15 miles long, surrounded by precipitous mountain slopes closing in at each end into very narrow and easily guarded entrances. A better place could hardly have been found to house a large number of Japanese evacuees.[46]

Another government report lauded the efforts of the RCMP in maintaining the 'security' of the camps. It underscored the fact that '[t]he settlements are situated in mountainous valleys from which the only outlets are by a few roads. On these roads the Royal Canadian Mounted Police established road blocks at which special guards check all passersby.'[47] Although some might contest the naming of the means of confining Japanese Canadians as incarceration, there is no doubt that the government ensured that there was no means of escape from these sites.

Tashme and its buildings were constructed solely for the purpose of incarcerating Japanese Canadians, which meant that there were very few white people living in the area other than those who were sent there to monitor Japanese Canadians and to work for the BCSC. The government report does not even list white residents in the area. In 1942, 2,636 Japanese Canadians were moved to the Tashme camp.

Louise reported there were no activities organized for children of her age in Tashme; however, she remembered the older boys playing baseball and having Boy Scout rallies and an annual jamboree. The Tashme Boy Scout troop was organized by Shige Yoshida and, by the time the camp was closed, included over 200 members. This troop was the largest in the British Commonwealth during this period. Catherine Lang describes Yoshida's effort as offering the boys 'a bridge to the white man's world, a way of installing pride in themselves and a means of demonstrating loyalty to king and country.'[48] Through activities such as scouting, boys and men (the latter were numerically fewer given the gendered separations of the Internment) were able to demonstrate their masculinity and loyalty to the Commonwealth, to other Japanese Canadians, and to camp administrators while at the same time being denied 'a bridge to the white man's world' by virtue of being in Tashme. Louise's comments indicated that she felt very young children and girls did not have the same level of activity. Practices of gender were therefore relationally constructed in Tashme. The visibility of scouting activities affirmed discourses of Western masculinity and their attachments to British nationalist discourses of empire at the same time as they contested the discourses of disloyalty to Canada used to incarcerate them. This activity also indicates that some men and boys attempted to use Tashme to forge their own identities and, in making these identities, they also marked Tashme as a *place* where scouting and the largest scout troop in the Commonwealth were located. Although this 'resistance' to being identified as an enemy and a foreigner that was assigned to them by the state ultimately served the nation through its appeal to the discourses of nationalism and imperialism that scouting in the Commonwealth supported, it was another indication that Japanese Canadians knew and could demonstrate that the identities given to them by the state and its reason for their incarceration were bogus.

Louise also remembered that she first encountered the Catholic Church in Greenwood and that she had to 'cross herself' during its services. The nuns were white women. She noted that in Tashme there was a United Church. Her comments emphasized that each camp was associated with a specific Christian denomination and, in being moved from Greenwood because of her new identity as 'internee's daughter,' she was moved from the place of Catholicism to the place of Protestantism. Her comments further illustrate that children were indoctrinated into Christian rituals and teachings without choice. While some may construct the churches' participation in the Internment as benevolent and humanitarian, clearly their goal was to proselytize to a captive group and their mission was one of moral regulation.

The federal government used the argument that education was a provincial responsibility in its initial decision not to fund schools in the interior camps.[49] It later agreed to provide elementary school education; however, it took up to a year for students to resume their schooling.[50] The Roman Catholic, United, and Anglican churches eventually funded eight high schools for approximately 1,000 students.[51]

Louise pointed out that the superintendents of the schools in Tashme were 'the whites,' yet her teachers were 'all Japanese.' She also recalled that the white RCMP officers had a station in Tashme and the 'whites' lived across the river in a 'separate area by themselves.' Her comments suggest that race was marked spatially even within the Internment sites; in Tashme, white people maintained their social distance from Japanese Canadians and social difference, including the marking of race, was delineated spatially.

S. lived in a white area of Vancouver before she was moved to Tashme. She was approximately twelve years old when she was moved from her home. In the interview, she referred to Tashme as one of the places that 'wasn't a ghost town,' thus distinguishing its identity relationally. After four years in Tashme, she was moved to New Denver, and in 1948, three years after the end of the war with Japan, she was moved to Toronto. S. remembered that some of her family's *hakujin* Vancouver friends visited them while they were in Tashme. On their second visit, they were stopped at the entrance by the RCMP and forbidden entry. She explained that 'anybody coming in or going out would have to stop there at the Mounties' office.' She also indicated that white officials monitored the boundary between Tashme and the 'outside world' and noted that the RCMP was a dominant presence in the Internment site: 'You couldn't come into Tashme unless you went past the Mounties' office. So you would see them all the time.' S. described this failed visit by her friends as a 'reminder that we were, what do you call it, not in prison, but there was a control factor there.'

S.'s struggle to name the spatial confinement of Tashme reflects the semantic legacy of the Internment. It was 'not a prison' in the sense of what she knew, and it is this spatial differentiation that the government used to define its methods as 'not incarceration' and the BC camps as 'not concentration camps.' In addition to lacking a language to name what perhaps cannot be named, S.'s description of Tashme is in relation to the other camps, which were ghost towns. Her selection of words also indicated the care that was taken in making semantic differentiations acknowledging the specificity of the sites. Given this example of careful re-membering, it is troubling that survivors' struggles to contextually name their experiences as 'not' that which conforms to a common-sense notion of a particular place or experience (for example, not 'prison') can be used to dispute that Japanese Canadians were incarcerated and used to interpret Japanese Canadians as being accepting or passive in the face of that indefinable place and experience. Clearly, her description and that of the RCMP at the only gate of exit from the camp indicate the carceral nature of Tashme.

S. reported that white people from Vancouver and the Okanagan visited her family, and she described these visits and her letter writing as keeping 'in touch with the outside world.' Thus the space of Tashme is clearly defined as a separate and insular site removed from the 'outside' inhabited by white people. At times the white visitors were allowed to enter the confines of Tashme, and yet, even in the moments when they were denied entry, they were always allowed to return to the 'outside world.' The 'inside' and non-freedom of Tashme was intrinsically connected to the 'outside' in the making of the freedom and privileges of that 'outside.' The racialized space of the camps and the denial that they were prisons by naming them relocation centres was necessarily a relational process that constructed white people as those who did not live in the camps and Japanese Canadians as those who could not leave when the visit was over. Of course, for these white 'visitors,' what constituted the 'outside' for S. was actually their 'inside.' The relegation of racialized spaces, such as reserves and the Internment camps, to the separated exteriority of white bourgeois existence secured white respectability in the face of these impoverished sites, and obscuring this relational construction secured the notion of white selves as being autonomous. How did the white people who visited and worked in those sites of incarceration understand themselves in relation to them? While some might consider these visits to be acts of charity or compassion, I would suggest that we also consider the power relations of charity and compassion and their production of a liberal subject who is redeemed through the discourses of charity and compassion.[52] As Sherene Razack argues, white people's ability to enter and leave marginalized, racialized zones with their own sense of selves unscathed is a process of subject-making that reproduces notions of white superiority and entitlement.[53] I would argue that these camp visits were exemplary moments of whiteness being reconstituted through violence done to racialized others. Part of this violence was the non-freedom of Japanese Canadians in relation to the freedom of white bourgeois Canadians. Hence the relative autonomy of the white liberal subject was made in relation to the non-autonomy of Japanese Canadians.

While she admits there may have been a lot happening in the camp of which she was unaware, what S. knew conveyed a sense of hardship. She described the shack they shared with another family as having 'single walls, covered with tarpaper.' 'Summers were extremely hot and the winters were extremely cold.' At an altitude of 2,410 feet, the temperatures in Tashme ranged from 95 degrees Fahrenheit in summer to as low as minus 10 degrees in winter. Water taps were outside of the houses and people filled pails with water and carried them into the houses. She emphasized that 'people survived in these conditions,' alluding to the fact that such conditions challenged one's ability to stay alive.

S.'s two sisters worked in the camp and her brother worked in an off-site sawmill, returning only on the weekends. S. felt that her education was greatly affected by the Internment. She missed a half year of schooling because it took so long to organize classes. She explained that Japanese Canadian teachers would be transferred to other camps and male Japanese Canadian teachers, in particular, would disappear overnight:

> We started out with some teachers and they vanished overnight ... the single men were not allowed to stay in the ghost towns. If they were over eighteen, they were supposed to be in [a road] camp or elsewhere and I think they all moved east or something happened. But we lost the teachers that we started out with and we had different teachers from then on.

S. managed to complete grade seven in a few months and was able to enter grade eight. She was aware of differences between Japanese Canadian students and white students, which she made clear in her comment that her brother, who took high school correspondence courses because there were no high school classes offered when they first moved to Tashme, had to pay 'about three or four times the amount that was paid by others.'[54] When S. began high school in Tashme, a year later, classroom space in the camp was at a premium and she had to go to school six evenings per week, from 4 p.m. to 6 p.m. and from 7 p.m. to 9 p.m.

In 1943, Ottawa began serious consideration of the deportation of Japanese Canadians to Japan.[55] Some senior civil servants viewed this as a means of getting the provinces to accept Japanese Canadians within their borders by suggesting that the 'disloyal' were being sent to Japan.[56] This approach was a modification of the one put forward by BC Member of Parliament Ian Mackenzie who had lobbied for the deportation of all Japanese Canadians as early as April 1942.[57] The federal government thus began to consider the two-pronged program of permanent dispersal and deportation.

On 12 March 1945 a notice 'To All Persons of Japanese Racial Origin' was issued by T.B. Pickersgill, commissioner of Japanese Placement. This announcement concretized the government's final ultimatum that 'Japanese Canadians who want to remain in Canada should ... re-establish themselves East of the Rockies as the best evidence of their intentions to co-operate with the Government policy of dispersal.'[58] Though the consequences were not explicit, the warning was ominous: 'Failure to accept employment east of the Rockies may be regarded ... as lack of co-operation with the Canadian Government,' and those refusing to relocate would 'seriously prejudice their own future.'[59] The federal government provided only train fare, an allowance to pay for food during travel, and a grant of $35 per adult, $60 for a married couple, $12 for each child.[60]

Simultaneously, the notice for 'repatriation' was issued. In contrast to the meagre assistance offered to those choosing dispersal, the conditions of deportation appeared to be more substantial in monetary terms. All transportation costs to Japan were covered by the federal government. People who signed in the affirmative to leave Canada could continue to work in British Columbia until they were deported. In addition, they were guaranteed the proceeds of the sale of their property or promised, if they did not own property, a grant of $200 per adult and $50 per child.[61] The terms of the government policy were thus weighed in favour of the deportation option.

From February 1945 to August 1945, the repatriation survey was conducted. S. was moved to New Denver in 1946 because her family agreed to move east of BC in response to the repatriation survey. They had to leave Tashme 'because people came from the other ghost towns ... [Those] who were going to go back to Japan were gathered together in Tashme.' When S. described her move to New Denver in 1946, she told me that members of her family had already been separated – her sister and brother had been moved to Ontario and her other brother was living near Kamloops, BC. It is important to note that the displacement of S. took place after the end of the war with Japan, and the incarceration in the camps continued years beyond armistice. It was not until 1948 that S. was moved to Ontario. Incarceration and dispersal were far-reaching processes across time and geographic space.

Slocan

A BCSC report described Slocan City as an 'abandoned mining town,' 'situated in the West Kootenays at the foot of Slocan Lake.'[62] The area known by the government as 'Slocan Extension' included the camps of Slocan City, Lemon Creek, Bay Farm, and Popoff. In 1942, there were 4,814 Japanese Canadians in the Slocan Extension sites. The report also stated that Slocan was used as a 'transfer point' for the New Denver, Rosebery, and Sandon camps. There were 350 'white people' in Slocan and its adjacent areas.

Yoshiko grew up in the Powell Street area of Vancouver and was approximately three years old when she was moved to Slocan. She had met few white people in Vancouver. She remembered swimming in the 'terribly dangerous' lake in Slocan and then warming herself by a fire that the older children would make after their swim. Despite her 'wonderful' memories of being with other children and swimming, she also described a 'white guy [who] would come around and tell us to put the fires out.' The white man wore 'a straw fedora and a suit with a bow tie and he had a cane ... He was officious but he must have been somebody official.' When I asked her how she felt when this happened, she replied:

> Oh god, that was terrible. It was like complete silence. Absolute silence. And I remember as he walked away, one of the older boys, you know, swore, muttered. When I look back on it now, it must have been really terrible, I mean as young people, to not be able to say anything, you know. And he was just a little man ... And he walked away so pompously. And, [we felt] just a whole lot of resentment. I mean, a terrific amount of resent-

ment. Because he was white? I don't think so. It was because this guy told a bunch of kids to put out a fire. It was around the evening, dusk, so you're cold when you come out of the water. I mean, it's ice cold water. So, you're always shivering around the fire, trying to get warm. And the guy says, 'Put it out. Put it out.' You know, of course, anybody's going to resent it. It just so happened he was white, so I mean you connect these things, you know, somewhere somehow. Subconsciously you connect it. So I'm sure there was a lot of resentment from the older kids. I was just astounded. And I remember thinking, 'Who the hell are you?' [I was] more angry than questioning because I was cold ... So, when you consider those are your first impressions ...[63]

This embodied memory of trying to make identities communally as children and young people and identify a place for those identities in Slocan also reveals that children were highly monitored and disciplined. Authority was inscribed in the bodies of the white people working in the camps. The question 'Who the hell are you?' indicates that the official did not need to identify himself when monitoring Japanese Canadians or disciplining them. Whiteness itself was the identity of authority and power. Such anonymity in the Internment process continues into the present day as few of the white administrators and participants are named in the literature.

A racial hierarchy was also spatially constituted in the Slocan camp. At one point, Yoshiko was taken to the hospital. She described the hospital as being 'at the very end of town in the area where the white people lived ... I guess they were the police commissioners. I remember white people living there.' She then told me another memory she had of being in the 'white area' of the camp with a group of children younger than herself and being confronted by a group of white children. She told me, 'I can remember saying, "If you leave us alone, I'll give you a chocolate bar or give you something."' She then told the younger kids to run home after 'fast-talking [her] way out of a situation.' The next day, this same group of white children came to look for her. She stated, 'I don't know where they got the nerve to come to our neighbourhood, but there they were at the bottom of the tenement building.' With the support of Yoshiko's brothers and their friends, she was able to tell them to 'go home.'

Among the group of white children was a girl who was in Yoshiko's kindergarten class. She was the only white girl in the class and Yoshiko remembered that she was chosen to play the role of Mary in their Christmas play. Yoshiko wanted to be Mary or an angel but had to play the part of a shepherd. Her mother has a photograph of the play's cast in her album. Yoshiko described what she remembered the most about the photograph: 'There's Mary, the only white girl in the class ... I often think about that.' Even within the racialized space of the classroom, white supremacy had to be maintained and performed: the part of 'the' woman in the nativity scene was assigned to the only white girl in the class. Not only were Japanese Canadian girls educated through the religious ideology that the camp schools and churches proselytized, but they were also a captive audience for the performance of the pre-eminent model of white Christian femininity to which they were compared. The symbolism is interesting here: when 'the' women's part was taken by a white woman, the racialized women were assigned those roles usually given to men.

In addition, the speaking of Japanese was policed. Yoshiko, who spoke little English upon arriving in Slocan, studied Japanese 'secretly' in a class organized by elders. She told me there was a sense of illegality in speaking and learning Japanese in the camp. She has a strong memory of yelling out of the window of the Japanese-language class 'hurry-up' in Japanese, warning another student not to be late. She was then 'hit over the head with a pointer and told not to yell those things [in Japanese] out the window' by the teacher. Clearly, children were also disciplined by Japanese Canadian elders. Yoshiko attributed this reaction to the pressure the adults were under to speak English:

> Of course, a kid, which school are they going to want to go to? Go to these missionaries who are very kind and sweet and you sing songs [or to a place where there is] this urgency to remember your language. The tension I'm sure that they were under. When you look back on it, it must have been really hard. I certainly was not that interested, which I really regret now.

Yoshiko's father was removed from the family for two years and forced to work in a BC road camp. He was later allowed to join them in Slocan and worked for the storekeeper who was a Doukhobor. When I asked her what positions other white people held in the camp, she listed the missionaries and the RCMP, explaining:

> They were all people of authority, you know. To this day I still have problems with this authority business, you know, coming from white people. That's how I grew up. Everybody who had any authority were all white.

And you didn't see them very often. Only when there were things to be done, things to be told, that kind of stuff. Except I must say the missionaries were very kind. But you just knew, you know, that they had more than you did. I mean, they were always the boss of things. You know, they led things ... That was my recollection of white people or my only contact with them.

From Louise's and Yoshiko's descriptions, we get a sense of the ways in which race and gender were spatialized and mapped out in the BC camps. White people, who appeared as figures of discipline, 'when there were things to be told,' clearly inhabited different spaces even within the camp. The micro details of the ways in which Japanese Canadians were excluded were reflective of the macro ways in which the nation secured spaces for its white citizens. Japanese Canadians were reminded of their tenuous position in the nation and even within the camp by the white people who lived in the area and by those who worked to maintain the incarceration sites. The fear and insecurity that these exclusions and constant surveillance produced for the people incarcerated were some of the effects of the practices of the Internment. Yoshiko's words strongly conveyed this sense of exclusion:

What happened in Slocan I think was just an indicator of what would happen in the future ... I remember that time very vividly. You know, telling the little ones to go home fast and being really scared that this person who was the same age as me, I don't know what they were going to do to me ... But the fact that this girl and her friends could say 'What are you doing here?' and had authority and the right to be there. I didn't feel as if I did have the right to be there at all and that I was invading somebody else's property and having to run home being scared. I don't know where that came from. But it was there and everybody accepted that. You know, it was just a part of that scenario.

Despite what Yoshiko had described earlier on as some memories of 'good times' in Slocan, her testimony was rife with recollections of exclusion and pain. She was aware that her father was 'very unhappy' while they were there. She contextualized her family's situation in relation to a community that experienced the Internment in different ways. When she mentioned her father's return to her family, she did so within the context of the other men who were 'missing.' Due to the NMEG protests and those of other men in the road camps, the official policy of the BCSC was changed in July 1942 to allow married men to work on constructing the interior camps and later join their partners.[64] However, those who moved to the interior camps had to find work in order to support their families. As Yoshiko explained, 'A lot of other men were not with their families. Or a lot of them were working in the bush and coming back on weekends.' She described her interactions with adults as mainly with women because 'there weren't too many men around all the time.' She also stated that hers was one family that did not go to Hastings Park but rather went straight from Vancouver to Slocan. When she described her own emergency visit to the Slocan hospital, she remembered that one of her classmates was hospitalized and she thought that she had died. She remembered that 'it was so scary' and the women were 'weeping and wailing.'

The move to Slocan separated Yoshiko's family from her great-aunt who was white. She described this relative as a 'German' woman who was married to her great-uncle. She was the only white person with whom her family had close contact prior to the Internment. Yoshiko's great-uncle died before the Internment. This is what she knew of what happened to her great-aunt and her great-aunt's children: '[My great-uncle's] family wasn't interned. The oldest son disappeared. He could pass as white. So he disappeared. And nobody knows where he went ... The daughter was quite a wild one, according to my dad. She disappeared also.'

A 1942 BCSC report outlined the policy on people who were married to 'Occidentals.' Interestingly, the report focused upon 'Japanese women' married to white men and the children of 'such mixed marriages,' although there were Japanese Canadian men who were married to white partners.[65] One could speculate that this focus on Japanese Canadian women being married to white men was a way of occluding the fact that Japanese Canadian men were partnered with white women. This omission may have been a paternalistic proprietary gesture of white men seeking to discursively 'keep white women to themselves.' Publicly disclosing this information may have countered the image of the 'alien' Japanese man that was so critical to the justification of the Internment. Under the heading 'Eurasians,' the BCSC stated that there were approximately 100 such cases.[66] On 11 April 1942, permits were issued to these individuals, 'exempting them from all rules and regulations applicable to Japanese.' The section of the report concluded: 'The fact of their racial origin was to be disregarded and they were to be recognized as Canadians in the full sense of the word.'[67]

The exact number of children who were allowed to stay in the restricted area within BC is difficult to deduce. A 1944 government report indicated that 'fifty-two children of registered Eurasians and Intermarried Japanese who were listed on their father's record have been removed from our files, being of part-blood only.'[68] It added that these children were not 'compelled' to register. Another reference to 'blood' occurred in the same report, where two people were described as exempt from registration because they were 'only quarter-blood Japanese.' In 1943, it was reported that there were seventy-four people who were 'exempt from regulations in prohibited area,' but a reason for this is not given.[69] A later report in August 1945 actually lists the category of 'Intermarriage inside Area,' listing the number as twenty-eight.[70] The October 1946 report gives the number as thirty.[71] The 'intermarriage' category included people married to other racialized people, as it was reported that 'one Japanese girl married a Canadian Born Chinese.'[72] It is also of note that at least one Japanese Canadian, gender unspecified, married a white partner during the Internment. A 1943 report indicated that an individual married an 'Occidental' while in Lemon Creek and moved to Vancouver.[73]

This Canadian policy can be contrasted to the U.S. policy that incarcerated all Japanese Americans married to white people. Elena Tajima Creef examines the work of white artist Estelle Peck Ishigo, whom she describes as one of many 'interracial spouses unwilling to break up their families, follow[ing] her husband Arthur Shigeharu Ishigo into relocation.'[74] Ishigo has become known through her art depicting life in the Heart Mountain internment camp and through the book she wrote about her life there.[75] Creef observes that although Ishigo mentions that there were other white family members in Heart Mountain, no studies of the Internment have tabulated 'the numbers of [C]aucasians held in the camps who refused separation from Japanese and Japanese American family members.'[76]

While biological notions of race functioned in the language of blood, it is clear from government reports that 'race' itself was socially constructed, a shifting signifier dependent upon different political, legal, and social discourses, mobilized to produce hierarchical notions of the 'Canadian' citizen. Heterosexuality codified through marriage to a white person allowed one to stay within the restricted zone or legally escape from the site of incarceration. Marriage to a 'Canadian-born Chinese' gave one Japanese Canadian a reprieve from leaving the coastal area. The Chinese Canadian would nevertheless be differently situated from the white Canadian. It would be assumed that Chinese Canadians no longer had to wear badges of identity given that Japanese Canadians were no longer in the restricted area. How did Chinese Canadians negotiate their spatial toehold in the nation? How did the Japanese Canadian spouses in each case negotiate their claims to citizenship as their bodies were marked by the codes of race in spaces which were supposed to be devoid of their existence? Some of the offspring from such unions were considered Canadian citizens, exempt from the restriction placed on other children deemed as of the 'Japanese race.' As we shall see in chapter 7, not all children of 'mixed' relationships were allowed to stay in the coastal area. And while people married to 'Occidentals' appear to have been precluded from the official regulations applied to other Japanese Canadians and secured a material privilege in relation to those incarcerated, they each would have suffered the consequences of being separated from families and friends. The geographic and social separations imposed upon a community of interlinking family and friendship relations resulted in ruptures such as occurred in Yoshiko's family. That the nation 'disappeared' these family members, separating them from those incarcerated and the incarcerated from them, is another effect of the Internment.

Women and Yoshiko's older brothers took care of her in Slocan, and she felt 'secure that everybody was looking after everybody else.' Just as Louise had recounted about Greenwood, Yoshiko also remembered being bathed by women in the communal bathhouse. Yet while her testimony conveys that some people cared for each other, it also demonstrates her awareness of the tensions that incarceration created for women. She remembered women arguing in the communal kitchen and commented, 'I think the people who had a hard time were the people who had to look after the kids in small, crowded apartments, having to share kitchen space.'

Yoshiko situated herself as the child she was with some 'wonderful memories' of playing with other children in relation to this memory she had of leaving Slocan. She emphasized that hers is a 'kid's point of view.' In this re-membering of people gathering together before they left Slocan, however, her evocation of the pain and the losses for herself and others is strikingly apparent:

We had a big huge picnic in the ballpark. Windy, windy day. And over the PA they were playing 'Auld Lang Syne.' And when you play something over the PA on a windy day, you know, how the wind crackles it and everybody started crying ... It strikes me. I think it strikes me because it was such a sad, sad time ... And to this day [when] I hear that song, it's like, oh my god, it's not a happy song. I was just six but I can remember how sad everybody was. And everybody was just weeping, weeping. And the sound of that song over the P.A. that was crackling in the wind ... it was so filled with pathos.

May was the eldest daughter of a family headed by women when she was moved to Slocan at the age of fourteen. Like S., May grew up in a predominantly white area of Vancouver. Between 1942 and 1945, she was moved from Vancouver to Hastings Park to Slocan, and then to Toronto. Her mother and sister were moved to New Denver after she left for Toronto. She described the 'evacuation' as a 'difficult time' for her and felt the Internment had a negative effect on her education. She missed a year of school because the high schools were not set up. As she stated, 'The government did not think it necessary to build high schools.' Anxious to support her family, May applied to teach the elementary school children, having responded hopefully to a notice soliciting Japanese Canadians with at least grade ten to apply to teach. She emphasized, 'And I was fourteen!' She was encouraged by Hide Hyodo, who was involved in the hiring of teachers, to wait until high school classes became available.[77] She went to the Anglican church-sponsored school because she was Protestant and she was taught at this school by missionaries. She reported that all of the missionaries in Slocan were white women. Her mother, who had been raised as a Christian in Japan, encouraged her to join the United Church while they were in Slocan, and to do so she 'had to walk up a road a considerable way because the United Church was up in Lemon Creek.' May, therefore, reinforced her identity as a Protestant by walking to another camp to reach the United Church. Unlike Louise, who has good memories of bathing communally with the women of Tashme, May described her experience in Slocan in this way:

> I had trouble feeling at home in the ghost town. I really did. I took part in church plays and taught Sunday school. I had some good friends. But there are very few people from the camps that I stay in touch with. It was really culture shock to go there. It was difficult for me. The communal bathhouses, I never got used to that.[78]

In her description of a woman with whom they shared a shack in Slocan, there is a sense of the spatial restrictions and how her life was lived in relation to the other occupants of the shack:

> We could not get a house with just three people. You had to have seven to eight people. The other family ... had five people ... They eventually asked if they could put a partition down the middle and we would have our own stoves, rather than the communal kitchen in the middle and the bedroom on the side ... we said you can move it farther over because you have more people. No, they cut it in half. And I used to have a terrible time lighting the fire in the morning ... [The mother of that family] eventually would tiptoe over in the morning and make my fire for me. I know it doesn't sound like a lot but it was just a godsend ... She was a very, very kind person and I owe her a lot.

Private space did not exist in the carceral sites, despite people's efforts to make their shacks into something that resembled homes. While the woman in the next room lent support, May's description indicates that one's movements were always known to others. And the shacks were always accessible to the white administrators; their knock on the door could signify another displacement for the family inside or the removal of a family member or an inspection by the welfare department or another regulatory body. The right to privacy was denied to Japanese Canadians and was a further signifier of their incarceration. The very construction and design of these spaces by the BCSC rendered them carceral in relation to the architecture of the white bourgeois home where privacy, especially for men, was a right that was spatially affirmed.[79]

May conveyed a sense of the interminability of the Internment; they were left in an unknown area with no idea of how long they would be confined. She stated, 'You have to understand that nobody knew when the war would end. It could have gone on for ages and ages.' She thought the move from home would be temporary; it is this hope of returning home that coexisted with the trauma of homelessness and an indeterminate future. She added, 'When you're in a camp like that and you've been moved out of your home, you think [in] awhile you'll be able to go back. We left things in a neighbour's attic, for goodness' sake, thinking we'd be back.'

Order-in-Council P.C. 3213, passed in April 1942, empowered the BCSC to enter into agreements with provincial governments regarding the placement of Japanese Canadians in employment. The federal and provincial governments received numerous requests for 'couples,' 'housemen,' 'houseboys,' and 'housegirls' to work in domestic service.[80] In 1944, the United Church missionaries in Lemon Creek referred May to a 'housegirl' job in Toronto. She departed from Slocan, leaving her mother and sister behind. Her mother and sister were later moved to New Denver, as had happened to S., after they agreed to move east of BC through the repatriation survey. May described the process of separating people in this way:

> The people who were going to stay here in Canada were shipped from Slocan to New Denver ... They started to pool them together ... [and] they decided to have the one kind of people in one place and one kind of people in another place.

Thus the BC camps continued to serve the purpose of spatially mapping and creating identities and notions of gradations of disloyalty and loyalty. Those who opted to move to Japan were constructed as different and disloyal in relation to those who agreed to move out of BC.

While in New Denver, May's sister was required to have surgery. The camp administrators allowed her to travel to a hospital in Vancouver, but she was not allowed to remain there for the course of her treatment. This meant she had to travel back and forth from New Denver to Vancouver for four separate surgeries. Despite the fact that May's sister agreed to move out of BC and was moved temporarily to New Denver with those who would be tentatively allowed to remain in Canada, she was not permitted to stay in Vancouver to convalesce between surgeries. The 100-mile restricted area was meticulously enforced to keep out the child racialized as 'Japanese.'

Ann was twenty-eight when she was moved to Hastings Park from Vancouver Island. Pregnant and with two small children, she was separated for six months from her husband. She was then sent to Slocan City and, from this camp, she was sent to a 'hostel' in southern Ontario, then to Chatham, and eventually to Toronto. Housing was not ready when Ann, who was in one of the first groups to be removed, arrived in Slocan in February 1942. She was forced to live in a tent. The use of tents in the interior camps was referred to as the 'erection of tent communities' in a government report; 1,000 U.S. Army tents were used and they measured sixteen feet by sixteen feet.[81] Ann described their living conditions in this way:

We were living in tents and it was freezing then ... And then in the after-noon it got so hot that there was no place you could cool off ... You know, it's in the mountains, and when the sun comes over the mountain, it's hot and then it goes down quick and you freeze. Even in the summer.[82]

In Slocan City, the temperatures ranged from ninety degrees Fahrenheit in the summer to twenty degrees below zero in the winter with an average rainfall of ten inches.[83] As in the case of S., the weather and the extremes of temperature in a mountainous climate, even in the time span of one day, are written on Ann's memory, the embodiment of the elements faced by her and her children with only a tent as shelter.

Ann lived in the tent for three or four months. She then had to move to a quarantined area of Slocan because her children contracted the measles. The body and its gendered relationship to space are vividly re-membered through Ann's testimony: her pregnancy and living in a tent, her children's illness and her responsibility to care for them and being quarantined in a separate area of the camp, her understanding of how hard it was for women to raise children in such spatial confine-ment. While describing her quarantine with her two children, Ann stat-ed that their food was brought to them by the camp staff. Her daughter Mayumi, who was present for the interview, suddenly intervened and exclaimed, 'Mom, you make it sound like a hotel.'[84] This one action uttered by Ann was commented upon by Mayumi, while she did not comment on the description of the conditions of living in a tent, which is a place different from a hotel (as was the quarantined location).

The interpretation of Internment testimonies by children of survivors will be examined more closely in chapter 8. What I wish to signal here is that survivors' attempts to create normalcy in testimonies of Intern-ment are sometimes misconstrued as acceptance of the harms done to them. As we have seen in the case of S., some people lived in the incar-ceration sites for seven years and longer. Her comment that Tashme was a 'primitive' place resists the construction of Japanese Canadians as uncivilized. What has been addressed infrequently in the critical lit-erature to date and what requires further investigation and analysis is how people tried to support themselves, their families, and com-munities within the camps, and how they worked to make places more habitable. In the case of women caring for children, the challenges in negotiating the effects of the expulsion (for example, separation from partners, families, friends, support systems, poverty, limited food sup-plies, restricted Japanese language practice) must have been enormous

and were met with individual and different responses. For some, attempting to salvage what they could from their 'lives before' generated
activities that seemed incongruous with the fact that they were being
physically detained and meticulously policed. For example, Ann reported that some women gathered together once a week to share cooking knowledge, 'a kind of cooking class.' Women organizing in this
way to share the value of food flew in the face of the BCSC's claims that
Japanese Canadians were not aware of proper 'food values.' Ann also
reported that she gardened. Gardening in the camps was a means of
providing food for the family, given the lack of food supplies and the
little money with which to purchase them. It was also a way in which
people attempted to deal with the dehumanization of incarceration
by creating health-supporting, aesthetically-pleasing elements in their
everyday struggles to survive.

Men and boys, as stated earlier and as Ann confirmed, worked
together in scouts and in baseball leagues. However, if we focus on
these acts of reconstitution of self, family, and community that were
initiated by Japanese Canadians themselves and were sometimes reported as the 'good' aspects of their experiences without seeing the
carceral places in which they occurred, without seeing who and what
was missing from those places and what those places secured, then the
violence of these experiences is forgotten.

When Ann described to me where she lived after she came out of
quarantine, she described her lodging in relation to that of others. A
shack housing two families was usually divided into three sections,
each family inhabiting one room separated by a shared kitchen. She
added that she did not have to share a shack with another family because, by that time, her husband had joined her and their three children
and she was pregnant again: 'I think those were the worst places. You
know when you have kids. We were lucky, we had [a place] to ourselves. Plus it was right at the edge of [Slocan]. So there's no neighbours
behind you or on the side of you.'

Ann pointed out frequently in her interview that she felt other people
suffered greater hardship. Early in her interview, she told me that her
father was a veteran of the First World War and this 'past' fact is part
of her re-membering of the Internment. When I asked her if there were
mainly women and children in Slocan, she told me, 'Yes. And the men
that were there were veterans of the World War I and that.' Her statement jogged my own memory, so focused was I on a 'different' war,
at times so chronologically driven I forgot how the present is ever so

saturated with the meanings and material effects of the past. I remembered that her father was a veteran of the First World War and I asked her what happened to her parents when she was moved to Slocan. Ann's daughter told me her grandfather had died by this point. Ann responded by telling me her mother was 'with the older group there. She had a sort of special ... because she was a veteran's widow.' The fact that her grandmother was also in the same camp as her mother was news to Ann's daughter. Ann stated, 'Yes, she was in the same place as we were ... She had one room. They were lucky to have a room to themselves. And so were we to have a house to ourselves. Rather than share, the shared kitchens. I think that's the worst thing ... and especially if you have children.'

According to Toyo Takata, single men and widows without families were housed in bunkhouses usually shared by two or three people, 'divided into cubbyhole-quarters,'[85] with a common room and a wood stove in the middle. These shacks were neither spacious nor differently designed from the other shacks. Ann's testimony, however, confirmed that divisions were created in the camps, socially and spatially, and people had to deal with these seeming hierarchical arrangements knowing that every Japanese Canadian faced hardship. Some people with four or more children were allowed to live in the pre-existing 'ghost town' shacks without sharing this space. Her mother was allowed to live in one room by herself because she was a veteran's widow. In these spatial separations from others, the right to privacy may have appeared to be secured by some and not by others. Ann's testimony conveys her awareness of her mother's and her own spatial locations that had social consequences, including a sense of privilege relative to other people in Slocan. The one room becomes loaded with the weight of privilege in Ann's re-membering of the many who shared one-room spaces and her acknowledgment of the hardship of those who had children in them. But the implications of her mother's incarceration and all of the male veterans in Slocan, 'loyal' families of First World War soldiers whose incarceration Ann re-membered, are also witnessed in her words even as she attempted to minimize their traumatic effect.

Ann's critical comments, filled with a sense of irony, conveyed her analysis of relations of power. When I asked her whether there was a store in Slocan, she responded by describing a Doukhobor family that owned property in the area. She mentioned in particular a woman from that family whom she saw again 'years later in Vancouver.' Ann discovered that the woman now lived in Shaughnessy Heights, on 'the better part of Dunbar.'[86] Ann's reflections suggested to me that she knew that people profited from the expulsion and incarceration of Japanese Canadians; this profit went beyond a temporal notion of the Second World War, producing future spatial and economic entitlements.

Mary Louise Pratt uses the term 'contact zones' to describe 'social spaces where disparate cultures meet, clash, and grapple with each other, often in highly asymmetrical relations of domination and subordination ...'[87] In expelling Japanese Canadians from their West Coast homes, the federal government established their new zones of contact, not only with white administrators but also with white residents of various ethnicities in the areas to which they were moved. While the Doukhobors as a group were marginalized within Canada – their very existence in the ghost town areas marked this exclusion – it is necessary to acknowledge the 'spatial and temporal copresence of subjects previously separated by geographic and historical disjunctures, and whose trajectories now intersect[ed].'[88] It is important to recognize the hierarchical arrangement of subordinated communities within these marginalized spaces, and that individuals within each community are not identically socially located. Sunahara writes that the 'Doukhobors helped by selling produce and other goods to the Japanese at lower prices than those charged by town merchants,'[89] and, while this may have been the case, the relationship between these two marginalized groups was more complex than that of one simply 'helping' the other. For example, Tamiko Haraga, who was incarcerated in Greenwood, reported, 'Doukhobors owned most of the farms in the Grand Forks area.' She and her younger sister worked on one of these farms in order to support their family.[90]

David Suzuki, who was incarcerated in Slocan, responded with a friend to the copresence of a Doukhobor farmer who sold vegetables in the Slocan camp by taunting him with what he described as a '"bad word" in Russian.'[91] The accomplice to the act had taught him the word and he admitted that they did not know 'what it meant.'[92] The farmer initially ignored them, but as they continued to say the word the farmer 'picked up the knife he used to cut the tops off the vegetables, shouted something at ...[them] and climbed off the wagon.'[93] Suzuki explained his reaction in this way, 'I guess the shot of adrenaline from fear is why little boys do such things, but I did not enjoy being terrified for my life ... I was absolutely convinced he was going to kill us.'[94] Some Japanese Canadians may have responded to the copresence of Doukhobors and other people in the contact zones, including other Japanese Canadians, by using techniques to try to resist being constructed as inferior.[95] Attempts to contest one's own oppression and make oneself feel superior by demeaning others did not undermine the relations of power that constructed them and their incarceration. The relations of power situated the dominant subject in this instance as the one who had the knife and who could leave the camp; the subjects with lesser power had to remain in the camp. In addition, even though the meaning of the word uttered was not known to Suzuki, Russian as a language, though marginalized in the Canadian nation, at the same time held a certain currency in the contact zone of the Slocan camp.[96]

Ann's and David Suzuki's comments point towards the necessity of a contrapuntal critique that analyses how hierarchical relations are produced and observed even when they are forged in seemingly inevitable or conciliatory circumstances. Spatialized social relations between white bourgeois subjects and others also explain more generally why subordinated groups inhabiting marginalized spaces may identify each other as the only source of power while more powerful beneficiaries are safely distanced from these contact zones. In the case of the Internment, the white people who moved to work in the sites of incarceration were spatially and socially differently located from the white working-class and poor who resided in those areas prior to the Internment because the former could leave them if they chose to do so. However, discourses of power, including the power of whiteness, differently benefited the various white participants in and witnesses to the Internment.

In the camps, people had different encounters with white administrators. Yoshiko reported, 'You didn't see them very often.' Especially for the children and younger adults, contact with the white staff and administrators may have been minimal, except, as Yoshiko says, when 'there were things to be done, things to be told,' and when they were reprimanded and disciplined. Furthermore, Japanese Canadians had little or no contact during the Internment with the politicians or most other Canadian citizens who also benefited from their incarceration. The people who profited financially from the Internment whom Japanese Canadians met were those who lived in or close to the areas used for incarceration, their employers, and salespeople. However, the buyers of houses, companies, farms, fishing boats, and other properties were spared contact with those Japanese Canadians whose losses produced their short- and long-term gains. This distance from Japanese Canadians was further ensured by not allowing them to return to the

West Coast until 1949. Moreover, the use of the War Measures Act to target racialized groups secured the social superiority and protection of whiteness as an identity in Canada, a collective benefit of the Internment that did not require any contact with Japanese Canadians.

Most of the people who had lived in Ann's community on Vancouver Island were moved to Tashme. She lost contact with them during her incarceration in Slocan. She stated that she wouldn't have been able to 'write very much anyway because all the mail at that time was censored.'

Ann's memory of the Internment was also informed by what she learned from those who were in Japan when the war broke out and were not allowed by the Canadian government to return to Canada. She described them as being 'caught' in Japan. Her memory was further informed by knowing people who were forced to go to Japan as a result of the repatriation survey. Some of these people were relatives. She described their experience as 'miserable. They had a pretty hard time when they went to Japan.'

Rosebery

The BCSC report detailing the camps barely mentions Rosebery; instead, it focuses on New Denver City. Rosebery was included as part of the 'New Denver Evacuation Area,' sixteen miles north of New Denver City.[97] Rosebery, however, was a distinct incarceration site, inhabited by the 219 adults and 137 children who arrived there on 3 June 1943.[98]

Kazuko described growing up in Haney and living in a community where most of her friends were Japanese Canadian and where 'everybody was very close to each other and friendly.' She remembered her school days there as being 'very happy.'[99] Kazuko was eighteen when she was removed from her home and sent to Hastings Park. From Hastings Park, she recalled being moved to Neys Hostel in northern Ontario and then to Rosebery.[100] When I asked her if other people from Haney were moved to Rosebery, she replied, 'No, we were all scattered.' Her description of Rosebery was constructed in relation to the camp in New Denver. She reported that there were few organized activities in Rosebery as compared to what she knew of the activities organized by people incarcerated in New Denver. She described Rosebery as being on the outskirts of New Denver and 'there was nothing' there.

Kazuko found there were few people her age in Rosebery; the children were generally older or much younger. In contrast to the reports made by Louise and Yoshiko, who had positive memories of being cared for by older women in the communal bathhouses, Kazuko 'dreaded going' to the bathhouse. She explained that 'it was really a fight because a lot of people use a lot of water and if you use more water, well, then the other person doesn't have any hot water. And so that was quite a trouble. So that part we didn't enjoy at all.'

A major concern for Kazuko, as a young woman, was the worry about money, contributing financially to her family, and not being able to find employment in the camp. She reported that while some people found work in the government office, 'the majority couldn't get a job.' For her and her family, 'it was very, very hard living.'

Kazuko's testimony suggested that competition over jobs, resources, and other necessities divided Japanese Canadians. The 'nothing there' of Rosebery is described in relation to New Denver, which she imagined as having more resources and more people her own age. Kirsten Emiko McAllister enumerates these other divisive effects produced through the Internment: '[T]he separation of family members, the depressing, impoverished conditions in the camps and on beet farms, the "repatriation" program and so on, led to painful schisms, breaches of trust and unresolveable conflicts within families and amongst groups within the community.'[101]

More than once in her interview, however, Kazuko indicated that her family was 'lucky' as compared to those whose families were separated. Despite the financial difficulties her family experienced during the Internment, she realized that men who contributed to the family income were usually removed from the family in doing so. She stated, 'Actually, the men had to separate from the family. But fortunately we were very lucky. Somehow we were all together, most of the time, the evacuation time.' Yet she made it clear that the Internment deeply affected their lives when she said, 'But it wasn't really a life at all, all those years.'

Another example of Kazuko's 'memory of community' and the relational construction of her memory occurred when I asked how she met her husband. Instead of answering this question, she told me that he had been incarcerated in a POW camp:

He was in an internment camp[102] and he was treated terribly. They were whipped around, all over ... he said he worked for seven cents an hour. And oh, they really, they were just watching you and the minute you just light a cigarette or anything ... they got a whipping ... He had a terrible time. I think he had a worse time than I did.

This knowledge of her husband's experience in a prisoner-of-war camp impinges upon how Kazuko re-members her experience of Rosebery, as does her knowledge that others were separated throughout this period. The pain and trauma of her husband's experience was disclosed to her after her own incarceration in Rosebery, knowledge that was shared when they began their relationship in Toronto after the dispersal. The very displacement of these two people has continually displaced memories, just as the piecing together of fragmented geographies is always incomplete though connected, riddled with the fissures of the 'missing' and the spaces both haunted and haunting. These 'past' ruptures of relationships and communities continue to leak into the present. Our memories, as Japanese Canadians with a history of Internment, suffer from the weight of incompletion, reminded as we are in the momentary 'image' flashing 'up at the instant' of meeting one of the missing or someone who notes we or our loved ones were/ are missed.

In the totality of the Internment, Kazuko situated herself relationally to others who suffered and lost differently than she. Later in my interview with her, I asked her about the repatriation survey and it triggered the memory of her oldest brother, with whom she had lost contact when they were separated during the Internment. Re-membering the spatial configurations of their separation and her brother's decision to go to Japan, invoked this memory of her loss:

> Oh, I forgot to tell you ... I had a big brother, too, that was born in Japan. But he didn't come with us. He went on his own. Yes ... And then he went to Tashme but he got married in New Denver. And then when we had a choice of going to Japan or coming here, well, he chose to go to Japan. So ever since that we haven't got in touch with him ... We don't know whether he's dead or alive ... We tried everything.

How to keep the threads together, how to re-member everyone who was lost, how to forget/not forget one's own losses and re-member other's losses too?

In reconstructing the spatial differences, sites of exile spread across a nation, Kazuko re-membered her brother's exile from nation, from family, from her. She re-membered she hasn't seen him since her family was allowed to attend his wedding in New Denver and, in her urgent telling of nearly forgetting, I felt she was reminding me that I must re-member him and include him in her story. Efforts to find him across the borders dividing 'enemy' nation from Canadian nation, across the boundaries that restrained and excluded Japanese Canadians within a nation through legislative restrictions, censorship of mail, continued displacement, and economic hardship, proved futile. She described this interminable separation in this way: 'We don't know how he, what he's doing or if he's not living ... It's a terrible feeling, you know ... we really feel bad about that ... But it's too late now. We think that he is gone anyways.'

Another BC Camp

Haru grew up in Vancouver in a 'Japanese community.' Most of her friends were 'Chinese and Japanese' students at Strathcona High School. She had Japanese Canadian friends with whom she went to a Japanese-language school after her day at high school and with whom she socialized on the weekends. Socializing with *hakujin* friends ended at 3:30 p.m., when classes were over.

Haru was nineteen when she was moved from Vancouver to a BC interior camp.[103] She reconstructed her memory of the camp in relation to how she perceived the experience of her younger siblings. She felt that her sister 'had the greatest time. She was so young.' She reported that this younger sister was allowed to go to camp activities because her younger brother would 'chaperone.' Being the eldest, she 'didn't have a chaperone' and wasn't allowed to socialize in the same way. She thus re-membered her time in the camp as being more difficult than that of her siblings.

Like Ann, Haru reported that some of the women got together to cook in the camp. She said that some of the families had 'older sisters who had worked in the *hakujin* housework' and they knew 'how to make cakes.' Her mother, however, 'didn't have time to cook anything fancy or learn how.'

After she was moved to the camp, Haru was unable to continue her high school education. Instead, she went to a sewing school whose teacher was a Japanese Canadian woman. Two of her classmates were moved from their families in different incarceration sites to attend the sewing school. She added, 'I had my family there.' Haru also volunteered in the camp, assisting a friend who taught kindergarten. In this way, she created an identity for herself as a teaching assistant. She had often been asked to assist teachers and take over classes at her high school in Vancouver. However, the limitations to her 'freedom' to become a teacher were exacted through the Internment. Haru told me, 'I really, really wanted to become a teacher when I was going to high school. I really enjoyed it ... But then I couldn't further my studies.'

Haru was also conscious of the other sites of incarceration and she mentioned to me that she knew that living in the 'self-support' camps was difficult because her cousin went to a 'self-support' camp. Her cousin's husband was moved to a POW camp, referred to by Haru as a 'concentration camp.' Her cousin lived in the 'self-support' camp with her father and brother. Even though Haru was aware that a criterion of living in the 'self-support' camps was 'if you had money,' she stated that 'there was no money coming in' for her cousin's family and 'so they had to work. They really worked hard, working on other people's farms and seasonal things.' Haru's memory also revealed that her cousin was not moved to the Tashme camp, the site of many 'internees' families,' as was described by Aya, illustrating how different hierarchies were maintained and cultivated by the government throughout the camp system. Having savings allowed some people to move to the 'self-support' camps, as they were able to share the costs of the leasing of the land (and the rent for their own incarcerations); however, as Haru suggests, their savings were depleted through this process. Also, the myth that the 'self-support' camps allowed families to remain together is contested by the fact that Haru's cousin was separated from her husband and the extended family that included Haru.

Haru 'was getting very unhappy' in the camp. Competition for the limited jobs in the camp created divisions among people. Haru had worked at a fruit and vegetable store in Vancouver and had hoped to get a job in the camp store. When all job opportunities failed, she decided she had to leave her family in order to contribute to it financially. She took a job as a domestic worker in northern Ontario. She said, 'There were a lot of domestic jobs coming out of the ghost towns, to come out east, you know.'

Like S., Haru kept in touch with the 'missing' through correspondence. She stated, 'It was the only way to keep in touch because we were scattered all over. I used to write to a lot of boys and girls that went to work somewhere else.' She has kept photographs of people she knew and her children have said to her, 'My gosh, Mom, you've got so many boyfriends.' She has explained to them that these photographs of men were 'not actually boyfriends. But if they were going to leave for the road camp or other places, they gave you snaps and signed in our autograph books.'

Haru reported that her letters were 'all censored' during the war. All of the correspondence of Japanese Canadians was read by staff of the Directorate of Censorship, which came under the responsibility of the Department of National War Services.[104] Even in the 'private' space of letters, the only means of communicating with the absent family members and friends, the government controlled what was conveyed through censorship. Not only were the spaces of incarceration policed, but so too were the attempts to create and maintain intimate relational spaces across the boundaries of incarceration.

Letters held in the government records of the Library and Archives Canada written by Japanese Canadians can be categorized in two ways: one, those written directly to the government, and two, those that were censored by the government.[105] I make use of letters from the first category in this book. The second category – a record of the experience of women, men, and children written in their own words – comes to us as a result of the extensive processes of surveillance mobilized during the 1940s, including the practice of state censorship, and the ways in which people's lives were subjected to scrutiny with extreme attention paid to minutiae. As compared to the letters written in 1942 by Kitagawa to her brother, the censored letters in the archives were never received intact by the addressees.[106] It is only through the government's copies of the originals and their deletions that we have a record of what was originally written in this correspondence. This property, still held by an institution of the Canadian government, is another part of the legacy of violence committed against Japanese Canadians. Most of the addressees never knew nor will ever know the contents of these censored letters in their entirety, while the public has access to those letters that are still in the possession of the Canadian government. Dispossession, therefore, did not begin or end with the confiscation of property put into place by the Custodian of Enemy Property in the 1940s.

Women and men wrote directly to the government to protest various elements of its policies. On 26 December 1942, a woman incarcerated in Tashme wrote to the Consul General of Spain[107] in Montreal requesting that her husband be released from a prisoner-of-war camp. In the letter, she outlined the steps she took in trying to secure the release of her husband and also explained her own situation as a woman living in Tashme:

On the very moment when learning of [my husband's] apprehension ... I consulted and requested ... the Barrister of Vancouver, B.C., for his every effort in obtaining my husband's release, but his effort was futile. There were sixteen men in this group including my husband at the time of apprehension at Slocan, B.C. Later I learned that nine of these men have [been] released from the internment. Question is why not my husband also? I am a mother of three infant child ... after breast operation, I am always in state of poor health.[108]

At least two letters were sent to the Spanish consulate from another woman in Tashme asking for her husband's release from a POW camp. On 4 May 1943, she wrote that she had three children, aged one, three, and four. She was suffering from neuralgia and she stated, "I feel uneasy for [my husband's] future life in Ontario and also my Tashme life without my husband.'[109]

In another letter, a woman wrote on 18 October 1944 that she had been separated from her husband since the early part of 1942. She had two children, eleven and twelve years of age. She was writing to request that her husband be released so that he might look for a job in Ontario. It was her hope that she might join him in Ontario and she expressed that she felt 'discouraged and lonely.'[110] Her concern for her children was articulated in her hope that in Ontario they would 'obtain a higher standard of education than what they are receiving here.'[111] Two months later, the woman, who was very ill, again tried to secure the release of her husband and asked that he be sent to Tashme before she was hospitalized. On this occasion, she addressed her letter to the Minister of Justice, Louis St Laurent. Her letter framed the ability to live as a family as a right of democracy and she argued that her children should have the right and the privilege of a 'sound guardianship of their parents.'[112] She added, 'in the name of democracy, I sincerely believe this may become true to them.'[113] As was seen in the case of the NMEG, this woman also asserted that preventing her to live with her family was a breach of democracy.

One woman in New Denver wrote to the Spanish Consul requesting the release of her son from a POW camp. In this letter, the woman revealed that she was responsible for taking care of her two children and her ailing husband, father-in-law, and mother-in-law. Her father-in-law was bedridden due to paralysis. In requesting the release of her son, she stated, 'Sometimes I feel it is almost too much to look after the two children and my father[-in-law] and mother-in-law.'[114]

A woman in the Lemon Creek camp requested that the government release her husband from a POW camp because she was due to give birth. Her letter indicates that the Internment and her separation from her husband profoundly affected her. She wrote, "When I look past through the nine months [of pregnancy], it wonders me that I am the same person yet, there were times when I felt like doing away with myself.'[115] She added, 'Usually to happy married people [having a baby is] a great event but not so ... with my beloved in a far off internment camp.'[116] She concluded that she was dreading giving birth in Lemon Creek.

In a letter to the Canadian delegate for the Red Cross, another woman in Lemon Creek asked why a previous letter was not answered. The correspondent had tried to get an interview with the delegate when he visited Lemon Creek but was not allowed to see him. She stated that her husband and two sons were interned in a POW camp and they had written several times requesting their release. In her letter, the woman described how the repatriation survey was being used to coerce people who were in difficult situations to sign to go to Japan. She stated that she agreed to go to Japan in order to allow her son to be temporarily released from Lemon Creek to do seasonal work in Vernon. Her son needed to earn money to pay for his high school entrance fees. She explained how difficult this decision was for her because she 'did not know definitely what [her] husband would do.'[117] If she had not agreed to go to Japan in the government survey, her son would not have been able to leave Lemon Creek to take employment in BC. She explained, 'Because he was not able to go I signed for repatriation ... thinking it was the only way to let my son have his necessary high school education. This is the only reason I signed the form.'[118] She ended the letter by asking for the release of her husband and sons, explaining that 'our separation for four years have been very unhappy years, and our only wish now is for family reunion.'[119]

The final letter to be described was written to the minister of external affairs by a man incarcerated in Rosebery. This letter furthers an understanding of the numerous separations occurring among the people separated across several carceral sites. The writer asked for the release of his brother from a POW camp and proposed that the brother could then take care of his own child, aged two. The brother's wife had been moved away from her child and placed in the New Denver sanatorium. The writer explained that he was taking care of his brother's older child but could not take the younger one because his wife was going to have a baby. The two-year-old was kept in the Hastings Park Hospital with her mother until the mother was moved to New Denver. The mother of the children was then moved to the St Joseph's Oriental Hospital in Vancouver awaiting an operation. The brother explained that he was concerned for the welfare of the child because the staff of the New Denver sanatorium 'wishes to have her placed in a foster home.'[120] He asked that the minister grant the release of his brother to New Denver 'where he can keep his family intact.'[121]

The welfare manager at New Denver, a white woman, would not support the request to release the children's father. In her letter to her supervisor she stated that a foster home had been found for the younger child in one of the camps and, as soon as it was approved by the Children's Aid Society in Vancouver, the child would be moved from the sanatorium. She did not think that the father could 'give the proper care to two small children,' and the children 'will most probably receive better care in the foster-home in which Worker intends to place her.'[122] She added that the worker would make monthly visits to the foster home. George Collins, the Commissioner of Japanese Placement for the Japanese Division, refused to give permission to release the father from the POW camp.[123] What is clear from this correspondence is that not only were the parents separated from each other and their children, but the two siblings were to be separated in different camps. In these multiple separations orchestrated through state processes, adults and children were heavily monitored, separated, and moved about when deemed appropriate by white officials. Interestingly, the Japanese Canadian child was to be sent to a foster home in another camp, not to a white family, and a Children's Aid worker from Vancouver was assigned to make monthly trips to the camp to report on the child and family. This underlines that there was also another arm of the social welfare system that had access to the camps – Children's Aid workers in Vancouver – for the purposes of monitoring Japanese Canadians. Not only was this one family markedly affected and divided through the Internment, but also the separations were supported by the people who enacted the practices of surveillance and who ultimately benefited financially through employment during the Internment. Furthermore, it must be emphasized that it was white officials who considered it inappropriate that a man care for his children, and instead assigned care of his children to a 'foster home.'

While these letters are just a few of the many held by the Library and Archives Canada, they are powerful reminders of how women and men contested the power imposed upon them, in this case the removal of men to prisoner-of-war camps. Also witnessed was one woman's reason for agreeing to go to Japan in the repatriation survey. Only if she said 'yes' would the administration allow her son to work in a paid position in BC. All of the people who brought these appeals forward were Japanese nationals and therefore categorized as Issei. Their testimonial letters stand in sharp contrast to the images of silent, passive Issei – a characterization especially assigned to Issei women – so commonly found in the Internment literature and critiques of it (see chapter 2).

Conclusion

Gender was a pivotal discourse in deciding who went where and who did what during the Internment. However, gender was not mobilized autonomously from other discourses of domination. Discourses of gender, race, class, sexuality, and disability, among others, interlocked and produced the subjection of the Internment and the subjects of the Internment. These discourses were used to create relational subjects through relational incarceration sites. Each carceral space functioned to identify each subject and both space and subject position (for example, gender, age, parent, child) came to bear both on their activities in the camps and their memories of the Internment. Relational hierarchies were formed between and within camp sites.

The sites of the interior camps were remembered as being overwhelmingly female with men who were there on a continuous basis being described as elders or deemed by the government not 'able-bodied.' 'Able-bodied' men (husbands, fathers, siblings, teachers) came and went, and 'disappeared.' These separations and disappearances were part of the violence done to Japanese Canadians; living with the unknown every day, including the uncertainty of when and if one would see a loved one or who would leave next, was part of the trauma of the Internment process. Methods of surveillance and discipline were embodied in the different white subjects enumerated in the women's testimonies. From the RCMP officers posted at the gates of the camps to the man in the fedora, and the child in the school play, white people embodied 'authority' in these camp sites. Ironically, the children who asked Yoshiko 'What are you doing here?' – a question that Japanese Canadians must have themselves asked numerous times – also confirmed their security, their right to place, and the right to police those interned. Whiteness was reconstituted as power through the entitlements to occupy and own space even within the camp sites themselves. Hence Japanese Canadians could be continually ejected from whatever spaces were deemed the 'property' of the white people who monitored them, and time and time again their 'right to be there' or their 'right to be' was questioned.

While the camp sites do not resemble the panopticon conceptualized by Bentham with its central guard tower, panoptic power circulated throughout the carceral sites through different bodies and different spatial arrangements. Each camp site had different topographies and features, which were used by those interned to carve out different identities and resistance to their inability to leave these sites. While the wooded terrain of some of the sites might suggest less surveillance than the POW camps or those used in the United States, it in fact provided a natural cover for acts of violence that were not witnessed or that were impossible to report.

It is clear from each woman's testimony that the relations of power were met by individual and collective struggle in each camp mentioned. For example, men and boys could demonstrate their loyalty to Canada through their scouting activities. As I witnessed women's memories of their activities within the spaces of incarceration and found women's correspondence in the Library and Archives Canada, I began to understand how resistance and our notion of resistance are informed by hierarchical hegemonies. For example, a woman who is pregnant and/or caring for children has different constraints placed upon her abilities to act as compared to a man without these responsibilities. Not being incarcerated, as was the case for Muriel Kitagawa (who was given a permit to move to Toronto), placed a person in a different position from someone who was imprisoned in the camps.

In trying to care for their children, women struggled in many ways with the power imposed through spatial and social limitations. It was not only through speech or writing, however, that women negotiated the conditions of the Internment; women like Aya, for example, took Japanese food staples with them as part of their poundage allotment. Aya also took her sewing machine so that she could make clothing for her children. While these acts by women become normalized and therefore rendered invisible – part of what women do to take care of children – they were means to resist the dehumanized conditions of incarceration. Surviving these conditions, as S. reminds us, was challenging, and women who undertook the task of ensuring their children's survival in the camps demonstrated exemplary instances of resistance to the destructiveness of the Internment.

6 Economies of the Carceral: The 'Self-Support' Camps, Sugar Beet Farms, and Domestic Work

As was shown in chapter 5, discourses of gender were integral to the implementation of the Internment and the construction of the subjects interned. Separating men from women and moving Japanese Canadians to different carceral places, each with its own physical and social characteristics, enabled the production of relational yet separate genders. It also enabled different discourses of threat and containment, suggesting that the men in POW camps wearing their red-circle uniforms were the most subversive, and that the women, elders, children, and the not able-bodied persons in the camps were 'maintained' and 'dependent' on the government. Spatial segregation enabled the production of relational gendered identities, and the specific identities of the carceral places were used to identify Japanese Canadians.

In this chapter, examples are given of discourses of social class and how they enabled the production of carceral sites in the forms of 'self-support' camps, the sugar beet farms, and paid domestic work. These places and discourses also produced the subjects incarcerated therein and therefore result in their having specific memories of the Internment.

A spatial analysis illustrates not only how the sites of incarceration were relationally structured but also that they depended upon and produced interlocking discourses of domination. When Japanese Canadians were moved to particular places, their bodies took on particular meanings. Japanese Canadian women, although homogenized as one race through racial discourses and one gender through gender discourses, were also divided by the government, which used class divisions and the creation of different relational gendered identities of working and non-working women that were enforced spatially. The government used 'valences of Otherness' (such as citizenship, class, race, gender, ability) to create these identities in relational sites, and none of these valences were 'independently articulated.'[1] Hence each woman's identity was formed in relation to the other's, both within and between carceral places.

'Self-Support' Camps

In the 'self-support' camps, the government mobilized the class divisions within the Japanese Canadian community by setting up a distinct category of people who were expected to support themselves by living on their savings for an indefinite period. Fourteen hundred people were sent to Christina Lake, Bridge River, Lillooet, McGillivray Falls, and Minto City, where they leased land and lived under government restrictions.[2] A BCSC report states that the 'self-support' areas were created as separate sites from the interior camps 'as it was felt that the presence of these families in the *maintenance* towns might create a disturbing influence by giving rise to class distinction.'[3] Approximately 300 other people who also leased the land for their own incarceration were moved to Taylor Lake and Westwold.[4] The latter were described by the BCSC as 'not desiring to be placed in the interior housing projects and thereby become entirely dependent on the Commission for support.'[5] Hence the people in the 'self-support' camps were constructed in relation to those in the BC interior camps. Those incarcerated in the interior camps were constructed as 'dependent' and 'maintained,' while those who were in the 'self-support' areas were 'enterprising'[6] and not 'entirely dependent.' While the material criterion for movement to these places of incarceration appears to have been access to money, the term 'self-support' conceals the fact that people living in these camps were also racialized, monitored, restricted in their movements, and subjected to hardship. A full-time white 'supervisor' was responsible for the 'inspection and checking of their activities' in the 'self-support projects.'[7]

Evelyn was eleven when she was moved from Vancouver to Lillooet. She described her father's actions when he went to the government office to register the family for an Alberta sugar beet farm destination. At the office, he asked the officials, 'What about our children's education?' Evelyn reported that he was told, '"Jap" kids don't need education.' This infuriated her father and 'he raised a huge kerfuffle,' overturning a table. The RCMP head officer called her father into his office and told him there was another 'choice,' and that was 'self-support' in Lillooet. According to Evelyn, her father was told he would have to 'build [their] home, and take all his supplies and limited luggage.'[8]

According to Ann Sunahara, some people who were moved to the 'self-support' camps leased 'special' trains.[9] In contrast to Margaret (see chapter 5), Evelyn did not remember her train trip as difficult. Although they both had memories of a certain 'excitement' which they attributed to being children and protected from some of the details of the expulsion by their elders, there were qualitative differences in their experiences attributable in part to their class positions. For example, Evelyn remembered stopping en route to Lillooet and being able to stay at a hotel and have breakfast there. This contrasts with Margaret's story of sitting on the cane seat of a train for four days during her move to Manitoba. Nevertheless, in the case of the people who were forced to move to 'self-support' sites, class privilege did not protect them from racial and spatial exclusions during the Internment, including the mass expulsion from the coastal area and the exclusionary practices encountered at their places of incarceration. However, class differences were used by the BCSC to produce different yet relational racialized, carceral spaces. Therefore, class was also produced by and embedded in the places of the Internment and thus is operational in the ways that people describe and remember the places of incarceration. People forced to move to 'self-support' camps may be reluctant to name the hardships they encountered within those places due to their understanding of how class situated them within the hierarchy of carceral spaces.

Evelyn's father built their shack prior to their arrival at the 'self-support' camp. Japanese Canadians were not allowed to go into the town of Lillooet 'across the river,' but had to live in East Lillooet. As Evelyn stated, 'We discovered that we were not allowed to go into town, that we were the enemy, I suppose.' Evelyn admitted that the 'house,' as it was described by the government, was in fact more like a 'hut.' When they arrived, the door wasn't securely hinged to the door frame, and they awoke 'in the middle of the night, looking out of this half-closed door, seeing the cows' heads looking down at us.' She added that 'lots of wild cows' roamed the property to which they were restricted. This land was leased from a white owner who lived on a midsection of the property. Evelyn also reported that RCMP officers were a visible presence and an 'RCMP town' was located nearby.

While Evelyn pointed out that for her, being in Lillooet was not a 'big distressful situation,' she also stated, after describing their exclusion from the town of Lillooet, 'I guess it was not pleasant.' She quickly added that even though they were not allowed within the town itself, the owners of the three general stores came to East Lillooet to take orders for supplies. 'I think it was a boost in their economy,' she emphasized. She later told me that there was an epidemic of stomach problems in the camp, and this was attributed to their water supply. The closest hospital was in Lytton, fifty miles from Lillooet. As a result of the epidemic, people organized to demand cleaner drinking water and the town of Lillooet eventually agreed to truck water into the camp for a fee.

Japanese Canadian children were not permitted to attend the school in the town of Lillooet. While the elementary school was being built in East Lillooet (the funding for it was provided by those incarcerated there), Evelyn took classes in a tent. High school students had to take correspondence courses if they wished to continue their education, and Evelyn took some of these courses for subjects like typing that were not part of the basic matriculation curriculum. When Japanese Canadian children were finally allowed to attend the high school in Lillooet, the trip to and from school took four hours on foot. One of Evelyn's teachers was a white man from Saskatchewan. She recalled him telling the Japanese Canadian students, 'You're such nice kids. I can't get over it. The only way I knew about you people was through a comic strip ... yellow skin and great big teeth.' While living close to an established white community distinguished the Lillooet incarceration site from some of the 'ghost town' camps, Evelyn's descriptions of the exclusions they encountered are indicative of their experiences of racism there.

In order to avoid the daily four-hour walk, Evelyn accepted a job as a live-in babysitter and dishwasher for a white family in Lillooet. This meant that she saw her family only on the weekends. 'I just detested that winter walk home,' she emphasized, and reported that 'other girls' were also doing domestic work while attending high school. Although Japanese Canadians were not allowed to live within the town's boundaries, they could temporarily enter white spaces as labourers. Again, Evelyn demonstrated how the incarceration benefited the white townspeople. She saw the direct result when Japanese Canadians were finally allowed to attend the Lillooet high school. '[T]hat gave them more money to develop the schools. Even in Lillooet there weren't enough students to have grades eleven and twelve. So by our coming, they were allowed to have grade eleven and twelve,' and the higher-grade white students no longer had to move to Vancouver. Evelyn's experience also illustrates that child labour was utilized during the Internment, something rarely written about in Internment narratives, except sometimes in the context of children working on the sugar beet farms, and only in passing. This labour situation also renders a different conception of the Lillooet incarceration site from that conferred by the term 'self-support.' In fact, unable to survive on past savings alone, some children and adults had to work in order to pay for their incarceration in Lillooet or to enable their schooling in town. The BCSC itself emphasized that some people in the 'self-support' camps would have to work, including those moved to Taylor Lake and Westwold, 'places where they would be able to earn a living.'[10]

Evelyn pointed out the 'irony' that there is now a bridge over the Fraser River directly linking East Lillooet and the town of Lillooet. At the time of the Internment, the only existing bridge crossed the river at a point distant from both the town and East Lillooet, therefore necessitating the four-hour trek to school. Evelyn emphasized, however, that her family 'was lucky' and did receive some material support from her father's former business contacts. This assistance came in the form of food at Christmas.

As suggested by Evelyn's account, people incarcerated in East Lillooet laboured in different ways to support themselves. Evelyn's example complicates an Internment discourse constituting those who lived in the 'self-support' camps as all alike and privileged. The term self-support not only masked the reality that these sites were carceral but also obfuscated the fact that people in the 'non-self-support' camps were required to support themselves financially as much as possible.

The fact that Evelyn's parents had access to funds did not, however, prevent the BCSC from separating her mother from her own parents. Evelyn's maternal grandparents were incarcerated in an interior camp. The notion that the 'self-support' camps kept families or communities together[11] is a misconception that is further problematized in chapter 7. The government's definition of family used to describe these places of incarceration drew upon a patriarchal notion of family in which the man is the head of the household. The 'self-support' sites did differ from the BC interior camps; men were allowed to live in the former as long as they could financially support themselves, unlike many of the men who had no savings and were removed from their families because they had to work outside of the detention camp sites.[12] What the government set in place with the claim that families were intact because the male 'head' of the family was present was a reinforcement of a Western-informed patriarchy and the notion of the nuclear family. This hegemonic notion of family, however, denied how families were constituted by Japanese Canadians; their construction of family went beyond connections of blood relations to include extended family members and valued friends. The governmental discourse of 'keeping families together' was therefore another linguistic masking of the violence that destroyed families and communities.

The Internment separated and thus profoundly affected members of Evelyn's family. Because her maternal grandparents were sent to an interior camp, she did not see them until they were reunited in Vancouver after the restrictions were lifted in 1949. When I asked her what it was like to see her grandparents after so many years, she responded by telling me about her grandmother. 'She'd go for a walk [in Vancouver] and she'd be knocking on doors asking, "Oh, are my children here? Are my children here?" She was looking for her children.' Reunion with her family did not change the absences created by years of separated incarceration for Evelyn's grandmother. Carrying the memory of her children after they had been separated from her, displaced to sites unseen that she could only imagine, she continued to look for her children even after she was reunited with them in Vancouver. Displaced from her home and her family, she is re-displaced to what was formerly the place of home, but can never be home in the same way, given the people who are missing from that space and the spaces of missing she carries within her. She enacts and re-enacts the memory, making visible the embodied trauma of her losses by knocking on doors in the spaces delineated as private Vancouver homes, in the formerly restricted area from which she had been forced to move. Displacement and incarceration were practices normalized by the government as necessary for Japanese Canadians, while Evelyn's grandmother lived the continuing legacy of the Canadian government's and citizens' violence. Whose actions and speech are forgotten and whose silence is invisible here?

This search for her children enacted by Evelyn's grandmother is a gendered and raced experience. Her continual search for her children as a Japanese Canadian woman, mother, and grandmother makes visible the effects of the violence and how its legacy seeps into the lives of individuals and families interned years beyond the initial destruction of their communities on the West Coast. The incarceration and dispersal carved up families and communities, remapping the national landscape with carceral spaces appearing and disappearing along with the people within them.

Before the expulsion, Chemainus Elementary School, Division 2, 1941. Private Collection of Sally Saeko Eguchi Oikawa.

Building A, section of the Women's Dormitory (formerly the Livestock Building), Hastings Park, Vancouver, BC. Japanese Canadian National Museum, Alex Eastwood Collection, 94/69.3.20.

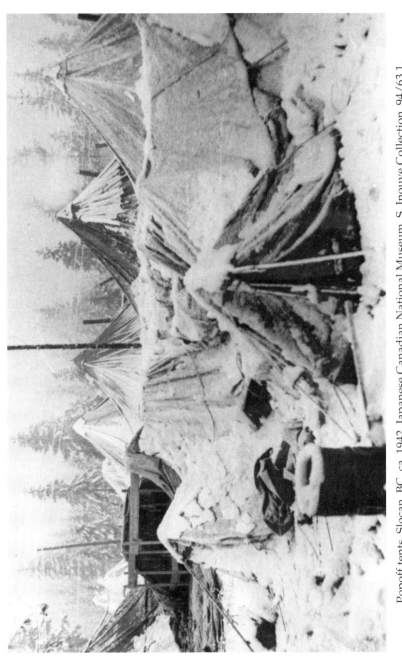

Popoff tents, Slocan, BC, ca. 1942. Japanese Canadian National Museum, S. Inouye Collection, 94/63.1.

Tashme, BC, overview, ca. 1943. Japanese Canadian National Museum,
John W. Duggan Collection, 94/60.15.

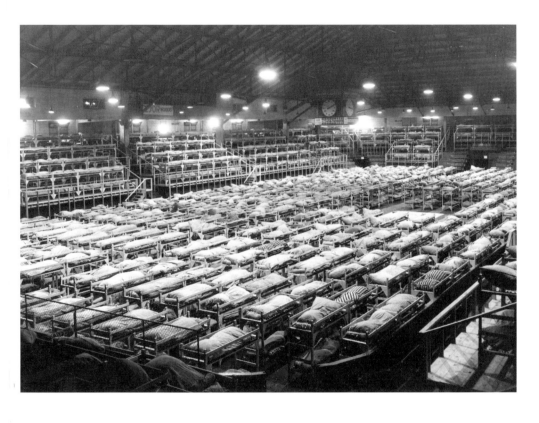

Building K, Men's Dormitory (formerly Forum), Hastings Park, Vancouver, BC. Japanese Canadian National Museum, Alex Eastwood Collection, 94/69.3.18.

Catholic high school class, Slocan City, BC, 1944–5. Japanese Canadian National Museum, Mary Ohara Collection, 95/100.1.006.

Repatriation of Japanese Canadians, Greenwood, BC, ca. 1945. Japanese Canadian National Museum, Mary Ohara Collection, 94/60.26.

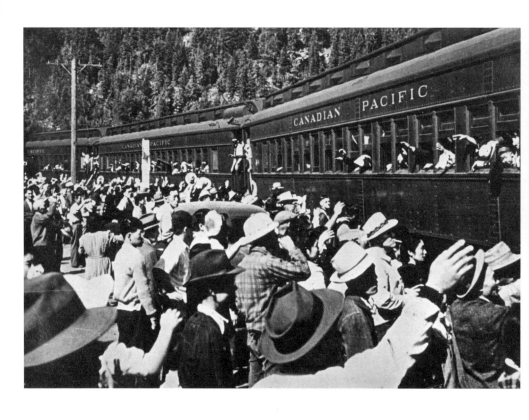

Repatriation, Slocan [?], BC, 1946. Japanese Canadian National Museum, Mary Ohara Collection, 95/141.1.008.

Sugar Beet Farm Incarcerations

Driven by a policy of administering the Internment at minimal cost, the government's construction of carceral sites hinged upon using the labour of Japanese Canadians. In this way, labour shortages caused by the absence of men fighting in the war could be alleviated and Japanese Canadians could further contribute towards funding their own incarcerations by purchasing necessities for their families or sending money to separated relatives.

Due to a 'serious labour shortage,' the BCSC negotiated with the provincial governments of Alberta and Manitoba and the beet grower associations to move Japanese Canadians to work on sugar beet farms.[13] Order-in-Council P.C. 3213 of April 1942 empowered the BCSC to enter into agreements with provincial governments regarding the placement of Japanese Canadians in employment. The provinces requested that most of the workers be Canadian-born.[14] In May 1942 an agreement was signed with Alberta and in June with Manitoba, in which it was stated that 'the Japanese [sic] would remain in agriculture and would be removed after the end of the war if the Province so requested.'[15] A total of 2,588 people were moved to southern Alberta to work on sugar beet farms, and another 1,053 were moved to Manitoba.[16] In its report, the BCSC stated that 'family groups' were sent to work on these sugar beet farms, because the 'preservation of the family group appealed to the Japanese.'[17] It was added that men from these families were 'recall[ed] from Camp' and moved to 'their newly reunited families' in the Prairie provinces.[18] The sugar beet farmers preferred families with as many adult male members as possible, as they considered these individuals to be the most productive in the back-breaking work of planting, harvesting, and processing beet crops. Therefore, some men were allowed to remain with their families in these carceral places and 'due regard ... [was] given to the number of workers in each family.'[19] However, women and children also laboured on the farms in Alberta and Manitoba to which they were sent.

As stated above, the government's notion of the family was different from that held by the people incarcerated. The promise to keep families together, in fact, acted as a coercive technique to get people to move to the sugar beet farms. The sugar beet industry needed as many adult farm workers as possible to replace those who were in the military or who had secured better-paying jobs. This need for adult workers resulted in some Japanese Canadians being able to include extended family members in their 'family group' when they were moved to sugar beet farms.[20] In 1944, it was reported that Japanese Canadians provided up to 50 per cent of the labour in the growing and harvesting of beets in Alberta and Manitoba and had 'provided at least $750,000 worth of necessary labour.'[21]

The Ontario government agreed to temporarily allow Japanese Canadians from British Columbia to work in designated placements on 18 March 1942. As a result, 350 men were sent without their families to work in Ontario on sugar beet farms.[22] One of the earliest and most prominent beneficiaries of the Ontario government policy to accept Japanese Canadian workers on a temporary basis was Ontario Premier Mitchell F. Hepburn, who had hired sixteen men to work on his 'Bannockburn' farm in St Thomas by July 1942.[23] His description of the workers as being of 'all classes' emphasized that discourses of class differentiated some men from others while reducing them simultaneously as one 'race' and as farm workers. Hepburn also mentioned that his crop 'would have been greatly diminished' without their labour.[24] On 11 April 1942, Premier Hepburn stated in the provincial legislature that 'on conclusion of the war, the Federal authorities will remove the Japanese from Ontario.'[25]

As is clear from the insistence that all single able-bodied men work in road camps (see chapter 4), the federal and provincial governments needed to fill shortages created by men enlisted in the Canadian military. Men in the interior camps were also sent to work on projects such as logging. The road camps were actually envisioned as but one 'step in evacuation,' and further 'steps' were construed in relation to work and the sending of 'family groups' from the camps to forced work projects 'wherever they may engage in available industry.'[26] In 1942, the government stated its 'primary principle' was to ensure 'all available man power and woman power be utilized.'[27] It added that it would constantly endeavour to 'relocate as many as possible in other parts of the Dominion,' to alleviate the 'country's labour shortage' and 'make them financially *independent of the Government assistance.*'[28] Hence, Japanese Canadians served as a captive labour force whose movement was determined by the federal and provincial governments. The fact that Japanese Canadians were considered as cheap or unpaid labour in addition to being racialized was made evident when the BCSC was dissolved in 1943 and its 'responsibilities and powers reverted to the Minister of Labour.'[29]

Employment outside of British Columbia did not constitute freedom.

In Manitoba, Japanese Canadians were paid according to the tonnage produced by the farm and earned approximately 25 to 30 cents per hour. Mrs Shizuko Miki stated that her family worked thirty acres, ten acres to each person.[30] The rate paid to 'white' employees was much higher, $3.00 to $4.00 per hour.[31] Japanese Canadians were required to work from dawn to nightfall in back-breaking work. Women were equally expected to undertake the gruelling labour of seeding, cultivating, and harvesting the beet crop.

According to Mas Nagamori, who had to assist in the construction of shacks on Manitoba beet farms, they were built in 'the middle of nowhere,' far from potable water.[32] The shacks were 'poor and inadequate and ill-equipped to withstand the cold winter months.'[33] The eight members of the Matsuo family lived in a shack measuring sixteen by twenty feet. They used sand to filter their drinking water from the Red River.[34] Most Japanese Canadians were scattered across different farms and were therefore isolated from one another. Some protested their living and working conditions on the sugar beet farms. For example, in Ritchot, Manitoba, on 2 October 1942, sixteen Japanese Canadians from the Kusano and Oka families staged a strike on the farm of Mr Schindel.[35] To end the strike, the Manitoba Sugar Company agreed to winterize their homes and give them a bonus.[36]

On 5 February 1943, Order-in-Council P.C. 946 was passed to broaden the government's ability to control Japanese Canadians. All Japanese Canadians were monitored by the RCMP and could not travel or change jobs except by special permit. Forced to carry their registration cards at all times, they were subjected to routine searches and lived with the threat of removal to a POW camp or a penitentiary for any infraction of the numerous laws that regulated their daily lives. As Shelly Ikebuchi Ketchell states, '[D]espite the illusions of freedom … what made these sites carceral was a combination of state, media and civic mediation.'[37] For example, the state controlled the hiring and firing of Japanese Canadians sent to private farms and companies, and the media expanded this system of control and surveillance through its reporting of news related to Japanese Canadians.[38]

Although one of the main reasons for the Internment was economic – to confiscate the property of Japanese Canadians and to rid the province of British Columbia of Japanese Canadian economic competitors – it was not the only reason, as is demonstrated by discourses of race and racism. This is apparent in the contradiction that despite labour shortages in British Columbia, including those in the industries they were forced to leave, federal policy insisted that any jobs outside of the camp system be secured in other provinces. Clearly, the dispossession process rendered all Japanese Canadians expelled from the coast homeless and, for the most part, destitute. The only means for them to secure any money was through their labour. Work itself was not a choice but a necessity for anyone who could secure it. The road camps and the sugar beet farms were places of coerced labour that benefited the nation, a wartime capitalist economy, and individual owners of farms and industry.

There is another contradiction in the fact that Japanese Canadians were labelled as disloyal and a threat to the nation, while at the same time their labour contributed to the success of Canada's war effort and hence the making of the Canadian nation. Lisa Lowe calls the contradictory positioning of Asians in the United States a 'double front' produced and managed by a 'racialized and gendered anti-Asian discourse.' As she states, the 'double front' is posed as the 'Asian threat and encroachment: on the one hand, as external rivals in overseas imperial war and global economy and, on the other, as a needed labour force for the domestic economy.'[39] In the war launched against Japanese Canadians through the Internment, the 'double front' served to control people within each site of incarceration, both through accusations that they were the enemy and through the work they had to perform to survive and enact their loyalty. While their labour was needed to support the war effort and the Canadian economy, this need was obscured by discourses presenting work on the sugar beet farms, in road camps, and in paid domestic service as lessening their 'dependence' upon the government. The racialized spaces of the Internment also depended, therefore, upon class constructions of the poor as degenerate and in need of moral reform through work. White bourgeois citizens could operationalize the interlocking discourses of class, gender, and race and produce themselves as 'respectable,' independent, and hard-working Canadian citizens; their denial of *their* dependence upon Japanese Canadians' labour is part of the process of forgetting white citizens' roles in the Internment.

As was discussed in chapter 1, the very names of these places – 'road camps' and 'sugar beet projects' – actually mask their primary function as sites of incarceration. In their interviews, women who were sent to the beet farms had some difficulty in naming these sites as internment. I discuss below the limitations of language and the relational identities of place that constrain survivors' abilities to describe their experiences as internment or incarceration. Two of the women interviewed were moved to Manitoba farms with some of their family members. Esther was three when she was moved and Margaret was fourteen.

Esther explained that her male kin owned three boats when they lived in New Westminster, BC, and her father was able to sell them 'before they were seized' by the government. She described her understanding of their move to Manitoba in this way: '[My father] sold the three boats and we weren't interned anywhere. Apparently, there was another option. The option was go to work in the sugar beet fields in Manitoba or Alberta.'[40] As I discussed in chapter 4, a gendered designation of property – the boats belonged to the men – was also indicated by some of the other women and their daughters when they described the loss of family possessions.

When I asked Esther whether she had to work on the farm, she replied that she was too young to work. But her mother had to work: weeding and picking in the beet fields, caring for the children, and cooking for the family. When I asked whether her sisters worked in the field, she replied, 'Yes. Everybody worked. Everybody worked in the fields. It was hard work. Yes. It's amazing. I don't know how they adjusted … And though seven years, I guess, in a person's life isn't very long, it must have been a long time for them.' Esther situated herself in a family of seven children where she, being the youngest, was taken care of by her parents and older siblings. She minimized the time she lived in Manitoba as a child compared to the seven years endured by the adults and older children in her family, toiling daily in arduous work.

While the government considered that the earnings from the beet season were sufficient for families to 'carry them through to next season'[41] and sustain them during the winter, members of Esther's family had to continue to work to support the family during this period. During the winter, Esther's older sister took in sewing and her brothers worked in Ontario in the pulp mills.

Racism was encountered by her older brother, who quit school at the age of fourteen because he 'ran into so much discrimination.' This same brother kept up his subscription to the *Vancouver Sun* while they were in Manitoba. To resist against his inability to attend the white school, her brother devoured the contents of the Vancouver newspaper. It was her family's ability to keep abreast of government policies, perhaps in part through this newspaper, which Esther linked to her father's informed decision to move the family back to Vancouver when the restrictions to live within the 100-mile coastal area were finally lifted in 1949.

Esther reported that the Red River flooded twice while they were living in Manitoba. Their home was flooded and they had to move to higher ground. She emphasized that it was other family members who had to deal with the difficulties they encountered, and 'somebody always looked after those kinds of things because of where I was in the family.'

As in previous testimonies, Esther re-membered the people separated from her family. She spoke about the losses experienced by her parents and cherished the possessions she inherited from them, photographs carried from British Columbia to Manitoba and back again. From Esther's testimony, one can deduce that her parents had strong connections to the Japanese Canadian community when they lived in New Westminster. She explained, 'In those days, they used to take a lot of pictures. I think it had to do with wanting to send photographs back to Japan. And in those photographs, you see gatherings of people standing on the steps of the Japanese-Language School and the Buddhist Church, and those kinds of important functions that they had.'[42] Esther's parents had also served as *baishaku-nin*, or go-betweens, introducing single men and women to each other. Among the photos carried to Manitoba were those of couples they had brought together. Of all the possessions they decided to carry with them, her parents chose these photographs. In this way the photographs became deeply symbolic of both the memory and the loss of community, relationships, and the esteemed roles her parents had played within that community. The cherishing of these photographs, part of a mnemonic record, was a form of resistance to the material dispossession which had occurred on so many levels. To this day, Esther continues to 'carry' these 'old photographs' with her each time she moves 'from house to house.'

This relation-filled community must be contrasted to the 'desolate place' in Manitoba to which they were sent, where three or four other Japanese Canadian families were hired to work on the sugar beet farms. Esther reported, however, that her family connected with other 'ethnic families' in this area who were of German and Ukrainian descent. Esther's comments suggested that they re-constituted their family in relation to other ethnicized people.

Another way in which Esther's mother tried to maintain connections to family members while in Manitoba was by sending packages of food and clothing to her family in Japan. Esther's older sister was designated the addresser of the parcels, and she could easily recount the names of all the addressees. While all parcels and letters were subjected to censorship during the war, only some arrived at their destinations. After the war, they received photographs of children wearing their clothing, confirming the receipt of their gifts.

Another possession that Esther's mother carried with her were the ashes of her daughter who had drowned when they lived in New Westminster. In contrast to the boats that she described as belonging to the male members of the family, Esther clearly identified the ownership of these ashes and their care to her mother. As Esther explained, 'My mother, being Buddhist, took this little box of ashes. It was in a box, all wrapped up in a cloth. And that box of ashes went from New Westminster to Manitoba.' While in Manitoba, another of Esther's sisters died from what was diagnosed as cancer. Esther stated, 'That was very sad ... And again, there are funeral pictures. She was only fourteen.' Esther described how her mother carried both boxes of her sisters' ashes back to New Westminster when they returned there in 1949: 'They carried all of that. It's interesting. So that those children would not be left in Manitoba. That's how strong the family, you know, the group was.' Esther then shared with me a memory she had of visiting her sister's high school after her sister had died and the discovery she made there:

> I always remember this sister that died ... I remember going upstairs and seeing this book on a stand and I looked at it and opened it up and it was a gift from my father and mother to the school in memory of my sister. And it was this great big dictionary ... And they had made this donation. But, holy smokes, wow, you know, in those days, to make a donation like that. And so I thought, wow, that was pretty nice.

Even in telling me of this memory, Esther recreated a constellation of family members who formed a part of her memoryscape, symbolic witnesses to this moment of re-membering. Her parents had not told her of this donation; however, she thought she had told her sister about it. She also added that she was not sure whether she had told her daughter about this gift. She explained why she thought her parents had not told her about their gift in her sister's memory in this way: 'People just never talked about a lot of things. And it was probably just to avoid the hurt.' Yet the symbolism of the dictionary, full as it is of words and the possibilities for communication, speaks enormously of the loss of a child and the parents' determination to make that loss visible in a white Canadian school. Even though their male child had been excluded from school and they themselves were in this rural setting because of their expulsion from the Canadian nation and the rights of citizenship, their gift speaks of a resistance to this exclusion and their awareness of the importance of the English language as a symbol of Canadian citizenship, marking the terrain of non-belonging with the presence of their loss. This loss would be marked for future classes of predominantly white students, saying 'We were here,' forever begging the questions *Why?* and *How?*: articulations from two parents, marked as Issei threats to Canada who were forced to give up everything to work on sugar beet farms, and who were hardly silent.

At the beginning of her interview, Esther stated, 'We weren't interned anywhere.' This delineation of being sent to the sugar beet farms of Manitoba as 'not internment' is also something that arose in Margaret's interview. From my exchanges with them (and for other reasons previously discussed), I realized that my own use of the term 'Internment' was read as exclusion by the two women who had been incarcerated on sugar beet farms. When I uttered this word in my interviews with women, I failed to tell them that I was using this overarching term to describe the forced removals of all Japanese Canadians from the West Coast and their subsequent incarcerations in various sites. My terminology was challenged by Margaret when I asked her how the Internment had affected her. She responded, 'Well, we never went to ghost towns, so I don't know what it's like. We came directly to Manitoba, so it wasn't like internment at all.'[43] Margaret also told me she had gone on a tour of the BC interior camps and had been asked by other participants, 'Where are you from?' 'Nowhere,' she replied, 'I never was in the ghost towns.' She was then asked: 'What made you come on this trip?' And while attending a conference on the Internment, she failed to meet anyone else who had been sent to work on sugar beet farms in Alberta or Manitoba. Margaret's comments underlined for me that the term 'Internment' is understood by some survivors as the incarcerations in the BC camps only. Importantly, Margaret constructs herself in relation to the identity of the 'ghost towns.' If the 'ghost towns' were Internment (and this is its reductive representation in some popular media; see chapter 4, note 73), then she concludes that she was not interned, and was 'nowhere.' Furthermore, the discursive dominance of the ghost town camps as the signifier of the Internment in the efforts made to represent and commemorate this history may, in fact, reproduce exclusions for the people who were incarcerated elsewhere. Hence, we must be aware of the importance of the places of the Internment in the fashioning of people's identities and memories, and the constraints of language and power that regulate survivors' naming of their experiences.

Margaret names her own experience as 'not internment' to differentiate it from the BC interior camps. The spatialization of the carceral sites, and the liberal discourses we have inherited to describe them inform the ways in which we can speak and cannot speak about the Internment. Margaret added: 'We came directly to Manitoba, so it wasn't like internment at all ... I mean there was freedom ... *as long as we worked on the fields*' (emphasis added). Margaret's description here invites us to 'reconsider the meaning of freedom'[44] and 'the nonautononomy of the field of action.'[45] If we only attend to the word 'freedom' without recognizing the limitation that was placed on her freedom through the qualification 'as long as we worked on the fields,' we do not see the placement of the beet fields in the carceral scheme of the Internment. The field is both literal and symbolic here. The discourse of equating the farm space with freedom is spatially produced through Margaret's comparison of the farm to the camps or what she calls the 'ghost towns.' The notion of the sugar beet farms or the Prairies as a 'free' place may also be influenced by a settler discourse where Canada is imagined as an empty space,[46] where the sprawling farmlands offer the subject the liberal promise of freedom and equal rights through hard work. However, the material place of the sugar beet field for those Japanese Canadians who were sent there operated within a panoptic field of power, less visible perhaps than was visible in the camps, but inscribed in the bodies of those for whom they toiled and the numerous persons in various fields who controlled their lives and movements.

As S. had struggled to name what the Tashme camp was to her – it did not resemble the common-sense notion of the space of prison as she knew it – so Margaret was careful to delineate the difference between the BC interior camps and the farm to which she was sent, concluding that the latter could not spatially be 'internment.' She was careful to explain, 'We were never in ghost towns, so we have no idea what life was like there. Our situation is a bit different, I think.'

Margaret also situated herself in relation to people of her mother's age. She stated:

> Anybody our age, we didn't really think it was too bad because we weren't old enough to appreciate what we had or how tough life was after the war started, being evacuated. So, I can't say that I had any really hard feelings except, of course, when we went to Winnipeg and were discriminated against.

Both age and position in the family structure influenced the ways in which women re-membered the camps, forced labour, and dispersal. These in addition to the discourses of class, race, and gender are some of the factors that influenced what women re-membered about the Internment and how they described it.

It is clear from Margaret's complete testimony that what she earlier denoted as 'freedom' was extremely oppressive and restrictive and was relationally constructed to the 'not freedom' of her elders. Her father had died when she was two and her family was headed by two women, her mother and paternal grandmother. She described arriving in Manitoba, where they had to stay in an 'animal shelter. The women had no privacy. It was just one big room. So, it must have been very hard for women.' From this central building, her family was moved to what she described as a 'two-room shack with a dirt floor.' 'That was the last straw, I think, for a lot of women,' she added.

Margaret explained that they were only able to move to a prefabricated 'house' after her 'outspoken' brother complained about their living conditions to the government. However, the 'prefab' wasn't much bigger than the shack, although it was divided into five rooms instead of two. She described it in this way:

> You only had room to walk into these rooms. And because there were seven of us, there was my mother and my grandmother, you know, it was very difficult ... And the winters there are very cold ... And we had to get water from the well. And the well would freeze in the winter because it was so cold.

Margaret's description of their living conditions must be contrasted with that given by a government report that described the 'Japanese families' as 'very fearful of the rigours' of winter, but concluded that 'housing is adequate and no hardships from the weather will be experienced.'[47] Once again government rhetoric obfuscated the harsh conditions people were forced to endure. The Manitoba winters were severe, and the coldest temperature recorded in the area during their first year was in January 1943 at minus 34 degrees Fahrenheit.[48]

Margaret walked a mile to school and was not able to see the roads in the winter blizzards. In the summer, after school, she worked on the farm. The children weeded the beet fields and, during the harvest, they cleaned the beets, cut off the tops, and put them on a machine. 'It was back-breaking work, because you're always bending down,' she stated.[49] She also emphasized that the entire family had to work in the field: 'In the prairies it was really hot. It was rough because even my grandmother was out in the field working ... the families who went to the farms really had to work hard.'

Margaret's family knew no one when they were moved to Manitoba. Two other Japanese Canadian families were later moved to the same area. Despite the fact that they lived 'east of the Rockies,' Margaret's family was asked to sign the repatriation survey. They decided to continue to live east of British Columbia rather than be deported to Japan. Her grandmother's brother, however, signed to go to Japan and was deported with his wife and their youngest daughter who was a year older than Margaret. Her young second cousin became ill in Japan. Margaret explained, 'Life was so rough down there that she died within a couple of years.' Margaret situated herself within this extended family and commented that 'women who had families and little, little children especially found it very hard. It was a pretty bad time for everybody, I think.' She concluded, 'It was a tragic time.'

The awareness of how much was lost by the first generation resonated through all of the interviews. Discourses of race, gender, class, physical ability, age, and others, and the different responsibilities and hardships accorded through them were conveyed by these testimonies. Margaret, for example, told me that her paternal grandmother's family owned 'a lot of property,' property that was lost. She stated, 'I think it was very hard for her ... And then having to come out east when she had nothing. She didn't even have her own place. She had nothing to call her own or her family history or anything.' Margaret added that she knew it was difficult for both her grandmother and her mother and concluded, 'They really had no place to call their own. I think that was the hardest part.' Just as Margaret had earlier described her grandmother's loss of 'family things' as a monumental loss, here she characterized the many displacements as producing the loss of 'history.' Margaret situated herself relationally to these elder women and stated, 'So, I can't see the kids suffering, not the kids so much as the parents.'

Margaret's analysis of the impact of the Internment upon her mother and grandmother emphasized the 'placelessness'[50] experienced by Japanese Canadians; their sense of place was destroyed by the Internment. As May stated in chapter 4, the displacements to various sites of incarceration left her feeling 'out of place.' Families and communities were thus forced out of place in Canada.

Margaret's family lived on the sugar beet farm for two years. Her brother was then given a permit to take a job in Winnipeg and moved the family into the city. 'He felt we shouldn't live in those conditions,' she stated. As she describes below, their exclusions from white spaces continued in this displacement to the city, as did all the other restrictions legislated by the federal government.

Neys Hostel

To facilitate the process of dispersal from all of the carceral sites, 'hostels' were set up by the federal government in Moose Jaw, Saskatchewan; Transcona, Manitoba; Neys, Hearst, Summerville, and Fingal, Ontario; and Farnham, Quebec.[51] These hostels were significant places, marking what was for many the last time they lived in a space inhabited by a number of Japanese Canadians. As had been the case in all of the racialized places of incarceration, the conditions in the hostels were wretched and were a source of painful memories.

According to Joseph Fry, Neys was established in 1941 as an internment camp for German POWs sent from Germany to be incarcerated in Canada; located on the north shore of Lake Superior, it proved to be what Fry calls a 'formidable POW camp' due to the 'inhospitable wilderness beyond the barbed wire fences and guard towers.'[52] In April 1946, the 'POW camp' became a 'hostel' for several hundred Japanese Canadians forced to move from British Columbia to Ontario. Through this discursive 'conversion,' what was and remained an untransformed place of incarceration for Japanese Canadians was linguistically translated from a 'POW camp' into a 'hostel.'

Two women I interviewed had been moved to Neys Hostel. Yoshiko described it as 'that camp by Lake Superior. That was a dreadful place.' For Yoshiko, Neys was 'the worst of the journey. [A] terrible place ... That was the camp where you were placed before they could find some place for you to go ... Dreadful, dreadful place.'[53] In turn, Kazuko described Neys as being comparable to Hastings Park. She characterized her experience in this way: 'When it's lunch time, you just hold your plate and march. It was just like a prison, I'm telling you. You couldn't go anywhere. You just stayed in the one place all the time. They wouldn't let you go out.'[54]

Kazuko here chooses the word 'prison' to delineate the space of Neys. The architecture of the prisoner-of-war-camp-turned-hostel is semantically linked to the notion of prison, with its four walls, compared to the BC camps, road camps, and the sugar beet farms *sans* walls. Place and our knowledge of other places and their identities and specific histories, then, affect memories and the metaphors and language used to represent them. What is clear from Kazuko's recollection is that for her it was a prison, and the 'marching' to line up for food connotes a militaristically enforced environment.

Leaving these hostels entailed grappling with the idea of being separated from other Japanese Canadians, perhaps forever, in the scattered cities and towns to which they were headed. The federal government's dispersal policy, as was articulated by Prime Minister Mackenzie King (see chapter 1), required that Japanese Canadians 'settle ... more or less evenly throughout Canada ... [and] do not present themselves as an unassimilable bloc or colony,'[55] and this separation was enforced for years after the end of the war.[56]

After the Internment, Japanese Canadians had to negotiate the white spaces in which they had to work, many without extended family or a community with whom they could name the harms done to them. They also had to deal with the racism they encountered as they moved to unknown places, individually confronting white people's racism and their forgetting of the Internment.

From the hostels, people were forcibly dispersed to different towns and cities. By the end of 1944, the federal government had also established 'Japanese Division Placement Offices' in Lethbridge, Winnipeg, Fort William, Toronto, and Montreal. In 1946, placement offices were set up in Moose Jaw and Ottawa.[57] The cartography of these offices illustrates the federal government's mapping of forced dispersal and ensured the continued separation of people who were dispersed from the carceral sites.

Domestic Labour during the Internment and the Dispersal

Women's unpaid labour during the Internment and dispersal variously included giving birth, childcare, cooking with few supplies, and other forms of domestic work. Some women were hired to do domestic service. Five of the eleven women I interviewed – May, Evelyn, Haru, S., and Kazuko – engaged in domestic service for families other than their own after they were expelled from their BC homes. Margaret's sister moved to Winnipeg in the winter to do domestic work, leaving her family on the sugar beet farm. Margaret explained, '[My sister] had to live with the white families in order to do this.'

In this section, I provide some examples of the spatial constitution of domestic work and how it was a process of constructing racialized gender relations. I consider the places of domestic work to be carceral. Women and men who undertook these positions did so under duress and were monitored by the regional placement offices set up by the federal government, which also established their wages and work placements. Domestic service was not a new occupation for Japanese Canadians, however. Both women and men were engaged in domestic service prior to their expulsion from BC.[58] Aya worked in domestic service before her marriage, and May's mother worked for the family of a white owner of a major BC corporation after the death of her second husband. Haru's mother worked as a 'nurse, maid, and cook' in Victoria before they moved to Vancouver.

Some women were hired by camp personnel and the RCMP. Yoshiko reported that, in Slocan, her 'girlfriend's mother cleaned house for the Mounted Police in another section of town.' She explained that this section of town housed the white people, and when she went with her friend to take something to her mother at her workplace, she saw 'a little girl in the house about our age. And we never saw her around. So there must have been another way to educate non-Japanese.' Even in the racialized space of the camps, a white space was carved out and kept pristine, in part, through the work of Japanese Canadian women. In this way, the white enforcers could continue to live separately and reassert a white community and its superior entitlements in the face of the reality of the racialized camp inhabited by people torn from their own homes. Their privilege and respectability were relationally secured through their proximity to the camps and the interned and even more closely through contact with the domestic servants engaged to maintain their homes as 'clean and civilized.'[59]

Through its enforced work placements, the government continued the Canadian practice of maintaining racialized women and men in the lowest job categories, while treating them as outsiders to the nation and disentitling them to the rights of citizenship.[60] The very language of the dispersal reflects how white Canadians continued to re-narrate Japanese Canadian citizens who were formerly residents of the BC West Coast as 'foreigners.' For example, when a ban was placed on Japanese Canadian residency in Toronto, Mayor R.H. Saunders referred to this change as a halting of 'further immigration.'[61] Their dispossession and placelessness enabled the continuing production of Japanese Canadians as foreign intruders at the mercy of the white 'in place' citizen.

Through government reports of the Internment, we see how the forced dispersal of Japanese Canadians from British Columbia came to be tied to the enforced performance of loyalty and independence. The terminology of 'self-support' was not just used to describe people in the 'self-support' camps. As the government coerced more and more people into taking jobs 'east of the Rockies,' those who were earning an income were called 'self-supporting' individuals, and this distinction was used to negatively construct people who were not being paid for their labour – for example, mothers in the camps – as dependent on the government. The government used the argument that work would ensure the independence of those unemployed in order to legitimize the forced dispersal. In this way, the government constructed itself as the paternal benefactor releasing its charges to 'freedom,' once again producing a forgetting of the violence of dispossession and imposed placelessness. Moreover, those who took up employment in eastern locations were also constituted as more 'Canadian' than those who remained in the BC camps. As a BCSC report stated: 'Only the very young and extremely Canadianized succumbed to the persuasion to accept employment east of the Rockies.'[62] In this way, discourses of liberalism interlocked with those of capitalism to produce work as 'freedom' and part of the performance of loyalty. However, the attainment of citizenship is always indeterminate for racialized subjects in a white-dominated nation, and the threat of the mark of 'disloyalty' continued to follow Japanese Canadians as they were dispersed across the country.

The movement of women into domestic work positions in Ontario and Quebec began as early as 1942, when 100 women were reported as receiving 'special permits' to leave British Columbia to work in private homes and institutions.[63] In the fall of 1942, more women were moved to Winnipeg and placed by the Young Women's Christian Association in domestic service positions for employers who were 'influential Winnipegers.'[64] In stating that women 'chose' to move to take up domestic positions (see chapter 1), government officials obfuscated the material circumstances that necessitated their moving to eastern provinces and also the threat of deportation for those who did not move after the repatriation survey was administered in 1945.[65]

The liberal discourse of 'choice' renders invisible the government's own gendering processes through the segregation of incarceration. With many men removed from the places inhabited by women and children, women were largely responsible for childcare and unpaid domestic work, and were not eligible for the nominally paid domestic service work designed for women with no dependents. Paradoxically, the women upon whom over 5,000 incarcerated children depended[66] (and upon whom the government depended for their care) were in turn characterized as 'dependent' and 'less Canadianized' by the government.

What is also forgotten in the discourse of 'choice' is the violence of forced dispersal to domestic labour positions and the separation of young women and men from their families and friends. A BCSC report made light of these separations, stating, 'The Jews did not face the Red Sea with greater trepidation than the first small group of Japanese domestics who entrained for London, Ontario.'[67] The discourse of women 'choosing' to take jobs in domestic service also obfuscates that labour shortages determined the eligibility of some Japanese Canadian women and men for entrance to white spaces, in this case, white homes, even when they were excluded from becoming permanent residents of the cities or towns in which these homes were situated. This was true in the case of Evelyn, who laboured in a white Lillooet home while being excluded from living with her own family in the same town. Another example of this prohibition on residency was the Alberta provincial government's agreement with the federal government that people would be removed as 'soon as the emergency ceases' or 'six months after the end of the war if the province so requested.'[68] The right to again expel Japanese Canadians, this time held by Alberta, was therefore legally guaranteed while white employers could benefit from their ability to hire and fire them at their will. In this way, Japanese Canadians served as a captive reserve army of labour who supported the Canadian economy during the Internment while being ideologically cast as dependents and a threat to Canada.

Forced to move from homes of their own, Japanese Canadians were hired to clean the houses of white employers. Racialized gendering constructed labourers in particular ways, and it is important to note that in the area of domestic service, both Japanese Canadian women and men were deemed to be appropriate workers. Historically, this has been the case for racialized men whose work options were extremely limited and who thus were compelled to take jobs in a feminized work sector.[69] In order to legitimate the forced movement of men to disparate, carceral places (POW camps, farms, road camps, the white family home, etc.) and the work imposed upon them in these places, racial, classed, and gendering discourses had to be simultaneously mobilized. Thus, Japanese Canadian men were gendered in relation to and rendered subordinate to white men through processes of incarceration, displacement, and work. In the case of domestic work, racializing and feminizing Japanese Canadian men was part of a discursive process of constituting a masculinity in relation to white bourgeois heterosexual men and women for whom they were allowed to work. In being allowed to enter white spaces, men and women were re-subjected to racialized, classed, gendered, and sexualized discourses that positioned white employers as dominant and in control.

There is evidence, however, that the federal government particularly targeted the women in the camps, exerting pressure on them to accept domestic service positions in response to the flood of requests received by the Department of Labour and by individual politicians.[70] As women were dispersed from the camps and sugar beet farms, domestic service was one area in which they were pressured to seek employment. Accepting a paid domestic position, as in all of the Internment-related (dis)placements described as 'chosen,' was largely coerced in a situation where financial need was desperate. And when the repatriation survey was imposed, there was only one option outside of being deported to Japan, which was to find work east of British Columbia.[71]

In discussing the critical definitional role of domestic service, Eric J. Hobsbawm argues that '[t]he widest definition of the middle class or those who aspired to imitate them was that of keeping domestic servants.'[72] White bourgeois employers constituted themselves in relation to their racialized employees. Through the hiring of racialized women to do domestic work, a white female employer reproduces white bourgeois femininity, allowing her time to 'choose' her activities and not be sullied by domestic labour. Even in the cases where the white female employer still had to undertake some of the domestic work and childcare functions, the fact that at least one servant was engaged met a certain minimum for white women desiring 'membership in the "respectable" class.'[73] It was not only married white women and men who sought the services of Japanese Canadian domestic workers, but also single white women who wrote to the government expressing their need for such assistance. One woman, in particular, argued that she should not have to pay '$30 a month for domestic help, when she knew of families who had employed "Japanese maids" at the same wage.'[74]

It was through domestic work that May moved to Toronto in 1945 at the age of seventeen. The United Church missionaries in Lemon Creek referred her to her first 'housegirl' position in Toronto. When I asked her about how she felt leaving Slocan, she recalled that she was 'quite excited ... I was worried, actually, about my mother and sister because my mother still was not well. But I felt on the one hand I was breaking out.'[75] The domestic service job to which she was sent was a live-in position with a Jewish family.

Sunahara has suggested that Jewish Canadians were 'the first to employ Japanese Canadians and the first to rent to them in Winnipeg' and 'elsewhere' because they identified with Japanese Canadians and wished to assist them.[76] However, this assistance too was forged through unequal relations of power. Although Jews of European ancestry have a tenuous relationship to whiteness,[77] their ability to hire Japanese Canadians as domestic workers reflected their class position. Hiring people who are racialized can also be a process of whitening oneself as the discourses of race interlock with class in the making of the bourgeois subject. All employers who hired Japanese Canadians during the Internment and dispersal came to know themselves through an unequal racialized, gendered, and classed work relationship, a relationship that was enmeshed with the processes of the Internment.

During the day, May went to high school. Every weekday after school, she cleaned her employers' home until 8 p.m. and then studied for the next day's classes. She worked all day Saturday and most of the day on Sunday until late afternoon, and then went to church at night. She worked 'seven days a week for three dollars a week.' She also undertook childcare at night for the employers' child. She worked at this home for one year.

Two weeks after beginning school in Toronto, May was called to the principal's office and was told she had to leave the school. The reason given was that she did not have a 'tax-paying family living in Toronto.' She was told she would therefore have to be a 'fee-paying student.' This, of course, meant that she could not continue her education because she could not afford the fees. This announcement 'just devastated me,' she emphasized. May reported that a school trustee eventually assisted her in contesting this decision and she was allowed to attend the high school without paying fees. Yet her encounter with this additional exclusionary practice gives a sense of some of the difficulties Japanese Canadians encountered upon moving to Toronto and how they continued to be monitored by the authorities and excluded from 'public' spaces.

May began teachers' college, but after two months she had to leave for financial reasons. In order to support her mother and her sister who were still in New Denver, she obtained a full-time job and continued to do domestic work. Japanese Canadians were therefore still held responsible for financially supporting the continuing internment of their families even after the war was over. May hoped to return to teachers' college one day because she wanted to be a teacher. She told me, 'I wanted to go to school more' and 'one of my great regrets' was not completing college. May changed domestic jobs during this period, looking for better positions, doing 'a lot of home-hopping.' She took live-in jobs because 'it's all I could afford. The jobs were paying me around seventeen dollars a week.' She stated, 'It was such a mixed-up time of my life: trying to get a job, save up, go to school, finding I couldn't go to school, and then having to find another job again.' May struggled to earn a living, working at an office and continuing her live-in domestic work. She sent money to her mother and sister in New Denver and eventually financially supported their move to Toronto.

When her ailing mother was moved to Toronto, a Japanese Canadian woman helped her to acquire a job in a laundry. May stated, 'My poor mother hadn't worked in years and years. It must have been horrendous for her.' May explained that she and her husband had difficulty supporting their families when they were moved to Toronto and her mother was 'determined to try' to contribute financially.

May described what it was like to be in Toronto when the atomic bomb was dropped on the cities of Hiroshima and Nagasaki by the United States. She attended a church service where the minister condemned the bombing. She described her reaction in this way:

> In August the Bomb had fallen in Japan. And VJ Day had been declared. I didn't know whether to feel good or awful. I was still feeling very unsure of my position, coming from the camps where I know we were not liked by the 'outside' somewhere. And coming and hearing a United Church Minister stand up for the people that looked like me who had been bombed, I didn't know whether everybody felt that way or what.

May also used the metaphor of the 'outside,' as had S. earlier, to denote a space 'where we were not liked.' Being thrust into this 'outside,' yet still 'outsiders' to it, was the social position of Japanese Canadians, living an unsettled uncertainty that continued over numerous years and displacements.

Married women in the 1940s were not allowed to work for the government. As a result of this policy, May was fired from her clerical job when she married in the 1950s. Her disapproval of this practice was known by some of her co-workers, and within a year of her dismissal she spoke on a panel for the civil service association expressing her criticism of this discrimination against women. 'I really do like speaking up, and I have sometimes very definite opinions,' she emphasized.

May moved with her husband to BC to help his parents with a business they were trying to establish with other Japanese Canadians. Displacement continued as people tried to make a living after the incarcerations; some moved back to BC after the restrictions were lifted in 1949 to try to rebuild their lives and families. The plans to rebuild a life were again disrupted for May and her family when there was a fire that destroyed their place of work. After this loss, May's family moved back to Toronto.

S. and her brother also moved to Toronto by taking domestic service positions. S.'s brother moved first and worked as a 'schoolboy' while attending school. She described his employers as 'inviting' her to join him in this employment. She moved to Toronto where she looked after the employers' child while completing grade thirteen. She underlined that she was able to 'do well in those grade thirteen exams, which was really something.'[78] S. eventually moved away from Toronto and currently resides in a town on the Prairies.

Haru also took a job in domestic service in northern Ontario. She recounted to me that '[t]here were a lot of domestic jobs coming out of the ghost towns, to come east.'[79] She had friends who had taken jobs in St Thomas at Alma College where they did domestic labour in order to get an education at the college. Haru was married in northern Ontario and described being there at the end of the war with Japan. She remarked: 'Til then, we were "Japs." You know what I mean? We kept to ourselves. There were more Europeans [in the town]: Italians and Ukrainians, Polish, Swedish, so they were good to us ... All our neighbours were *hakujin*.' She recalled being out for a walk with her partner and their baby when the armistice with Japan was announced and described this memory vividly: 'Everybody went wild. Even though I felt funny, we weren't scared.' Haru later moved to Toronto with her husband.

Although Kazuko was very anxious to leave Rosebery, it was difficult for her to leave the friends she had made. She left the camp by herself to take a job in southern Ontario. She wanted to 'get out of' Rosebery and found a domestic service position in the classified ads of the newspaper. When she arrived at the train station, there was no one to meet her. 'That was a terrible experience for me,' she stated, 'coming in the dark and not knowing where I was.' It was around 2 a.m. when her employers finally came to pick her up.

Kazuko worked as a housekeeper in the home of a white doctor and his wife, who was a nurse. There were other Japanese Canadians employed by the same family. As she stated, 'There was a chauffeur, he was Japanese. And also they had another maid there who was Japanese.' Kazuko described having to work 'long hours,' fifteen hours a day. The doctor would arrive home late and he and his wife would have cocktails and dinner. Kazuko lived with the family and did the cooking and cleaning; there were four children in the household who later attended private school in Toronto: the two girls went to Bishop Strachan and the boys went to Upper Canada College.

In the privatized space of the middle-class home, paid domestic work is a critical social process in the construction of class, gender, and racial difference. There has been little analysis of the position of Japanese Canadian women and men in paid domestic work. Very little work has been done to examine who the employers of these workers and workers in other industries were and the benefits these employers accrued from their labour. While Kazuko's labour was used to socially reproduce the family for whom she worked, her own family was separated and displaced through the Internment.

Although some women reported developing an attachment to their employers through domestic service placements, these employers played a critical role in ensuring the dispersal and separation of Japanese Canadians. Abigail Bakan and Daiva Stasiulis state that employers of domestic workers who refer to them as 'family' members 'mask their actual subordinate status and position in their employer's household.'[80] The irony of these false family formations for Japanese Canadians was that they had to leave their own families and sources of emotional support to take up work that supported white families.

Kazuko's family was moved to Toronto and she went to visit them once a week on her day off. This separation from her family continued for ten years while she worked for the doctor's family. Government regulations did not permit her to join them until she could secure a job in Toronto. Although other Japanese Canadians moved into the area in which she lived, their separation was ensured by distance; 'the houses were too far [apart] to visit.' Kazuko was willing to do anything in order to be closer to her family. Eventually, the Japanese Canadian woman with whom she worked put her in touch with her father who was working in Toronto at a factory. After securing a job offer at the factory, Kazuko was allowed to move. Her former employer later moved to Toronto to live in a seniors' apartment. Kazuko once again did domestic work for her and continued to do so until her employer died. By this time, Kazuko was sixty-seven. She had retired from this paid domestic position just four years before I interviewed her.

When her family moved from the sugar beet farm to Winnipeg, Margaret's sister had to work in domestic service. She explained, 'That was about the only thing my sister or any Japanese girls were able to do, was housekeeping.' Her brother went to work in a logging camp. Margaret also talked about other women who worked as domestics after leaving the 'ghost towns.' Every Sunday, her family would invite some of these women for dinner on their one day off. She explained:

> They had no family. They came out on their own. So they used to come to our place ... It was being together with other ... their own kind. So, it was just something we did. Every Sunday. They came, so it was a gay time. For us and for them, you know, they really enjoyed coming to our place.

Margaret's family organized a social space in Winnipeg to welcome other Japanese Canadians forcibly dispersed from various places of incarceration. Reconstituting community in this way provided a site of resistance in the face of continuing exclusions. An example of this exclusion was noted by Margaret who described how the white residents on the street where they rented their first house circulated a petition, 'saying they didn't want any "Jap" living there.' This action was later 'confessed' to Margaret's family by their neighbour.

Margaret also noted that they were stared at on buses and were not admitted to any restaurants, except for one 'Chinese restaurant.' No restaurants would serve them, including other restaurants owned by Chinese Canadians. There was only one bowling alley that would allow Japanese Canadians to be patrons, a Jewish-owned business. 'So, of course, they got a lot of business for years because they were the only ones who accepted us,' she explained. She continued to eat at that same restaurant whenever she visited Winnipeg and regretted that it had recently closed. Margaret concluded, 'My feeling is Winnipeg was kind of rough for the older generation.'

Displacement Continues

The War Measures Act, scheduled to expire on 1 January 1946, was used to enact the National Emergency Transitional Powers Act.[81] The Act allowed the government to continue Japanese Canadians' 'suspension of civil rights' until 31 March 1949, three and a half years beyond the end of the war.[82] On 15 December 1945, the Cabinet passed an Order-in-Council that allowed them to deport 'all Japanese aliens who had signed for repatriation or who had been interned at Angler; all naturalized Japanese Canadians who had not revoked their repatriation requests before 2 September 1945; all Nisei who did not revoke their repatriation requests before their actual deportation; and the wives and minor children of the above three classes.'[83]

Despite a protest launched against the deportation of Japanese Canadians after the coerced signings of the repatriation survey, 3,965 people were deported to Japan.[84] As Sunahara has demonstrated, most of those who went to Japan felt they had no other choice.[85] In addition, those who had partners or children in Japan had to leave Canada in order to be reunited with them. Dispossessed and impoverished, people knew they would face economic hardship in both Canada and Japan. They also knew they would have to continue to contend with racism wherever they were dispersed if they remained in Canada. As one man answered when asked why he was going to Japan, 'The white people hate us and we have no other place to go.'[86]

As the forced dispersal ensued on the heels of incarceration, Japanese Canadians appeared across the country, isolated in cities and towns. The geographic separations, a 'tactic of ... anti-concentration,'[87] were initiated and sustained by the federal government's dispersal policy. For example in Toronto, the placement officer for dispersed Japanese Canadians between 1942 to 1949, George Ernest Trueman, ensured that no 'Little Tokyos' (as he described them) would be permitted.[88] In March 1945, he reported that he had assured Toronto's mayor that Japanese Canadians lived on at least 134 different streets in Toronto.[89] In Winnipeg, organizing by Japanese Canadians was illegal, although the Mannisei (Manitoba Nisei) was organized before 1947 by meeting secretly in a Chinese restaurant 'where they would not be noticed by the RCMP.'[90]

In 1946, four years after her expulsion from her home, Aya finally rejoined her husband, her mother, and her brothers in the town to which her mother and brothers had been sent to work on a sugar beet farm. She recounted that the government was 'scatter[ing] everybody out there. But I said I wanted to go to Manitoba, where my mother was.'[91] Her husband found work on a farm and they later moved to northern Manitoba when her husband and brothers were employed in construction. When these jobs 'slowed down,' her mother and brothers moved to Winnipeg. Aya's final move was in 1954, to the city in which she now resides. She moved in order to be closer to her children who, as they had completed high school, needed to move to a city in order to further their education or find work.

Aya's husband developed a heart condition that she attributed to his working too hard in construction. After they moved, Aya and her daughters supported the family. Aya worked in a factory she described as owned by Jewish people. She made a distinction between the jobs Japanese Canadian women of her age were able to obtain and those acquired by younger women who had more education: 'So the women, they all went into the sewing factories. And the younger girls ... they went to business college and got secretary work. But people like myself and around that age, we all went to sewing factories.' She described Manitoba as a place where Japanese Canadians were scattered, living among people who were Ukrainian, German, Italian, and Jewish.

Louise, Aya's daughter, remembered her mother arguing with government officials in Tashme about the destination to which they were to be sent. The Department of Labour administrators wanted to send them to Moose Jaw, but her mother insisted they would go to join Louise's grandmother. When they moved to Manitoba, Louise saw her father again for the first time in four years. She described her feeling that her father 'was actually a stranger ... it took a while to get familiar with my dad. But once we were [together] we just became a normal family.' It was only upon reuniting with her husband that her mother found out why he had been incarcerated in the Angler prisoner of war camp. Louise recalled her father 'always tell[ing] a story about' his imprisonment:

> My father was sent on a road gang to Ontario, to mend roads and all that ... My mother was pregnant when we left Steveston. When she was going to have her baby, she sent word to my father that the baby was due and my father hopped on a train, and he said to one of the fellows working with him that he was going to his wife in Greenwood and to let the Mounties know because actually you're supposed to get a pass from them. And he didn't. He just went on the train and the fellow he was working with forgot to tell the Mounties. So he was caught on the train without a pass. So, they immediately shipped him to Angler in northern Ontario. So he spent the rest of the war years up in Angler. So my mom was left with the four kids in Greenwood.[92]

Louise's recounting of her father's story raises the question 'how many years did others have to wait to find out what had happened to their family members and friends?' As Kazuko indicated in her interview, quoted in chapter 5, some people never found out what happened to family members. Louise's testimony also indicates that people attempted to rejoin their families in different ways and were prevented from doing so during the Internment. The rigorously enforced permit system and the punishment for travel without it, as revealed by Louise, illustrates that surveillance of Japanese Canadians was a national process enforced across the country. Her testimony also demonstrates that the familial space is one where memories of the Internment are handed down to children, something I will examine further in chapter 8.

There were other Japanese Canadians in the town to which Louise's family moved, but they all eventually moved to Winnipeg, leaving her family alone. She stated, 'After that we sort of lost all contact with Japanese people. So when I was growing up I lost my Japanese [language].' Her grandmother moved to Winnipeg when Louise was in grade six or seven and they 'travelled a lot to Winnipeg' to see her. Her older sister moved to Winnipeg to continue her schooling after high school and lived with their grandmother. Louise followed, after deciding to attend business college in Winnipeg. Her parents moved to Winnipeg shortly thereafter. In Winnipeg, Louise found it 'awkward' being with other Japanese Canadians because, as she stated, 'I hadn't associated with Japanese people.' She eventually moved to Toronto, while her mother remained in Winnipeg.

Ann's family stayed in a 'hostel' in southern Ontario before being moved to Chatham. The first job held by her husband was on a dairy farm. A month later he moved to a job at a meat rendering plant because the farm work did not allow him to see his family. The milking times took him away at the hours when his children were at home. Ann's family later moved to Toronto, where both she and her husband worked until their retirement.[93]

Esther's family moved back to British Columbia after the restrictions were lifted in 1949. As she stated, 'All he [her father] wanted to do was to go back.' Esther's experience differs from that of most Japanese Canadians in that her family returned to the home they had been forced to abandon. They moved back to the float house on which they had lived prior to the expulsion. A Polish Canadian man from a neighbouring float house had watched over their possessions and they were intact. Esther recalled that 'Japanese dolls that somebody had given me ... were still there.' She described how pansies her brother had planted before their expulsion had reseeded and were blooming and 'he was shocked when he saw those flowers. He broke down and cried.'

After the restrictions were lifted, Evelyn moved to Vancouver to attend school. Her family later left Lillooet to return to the coast. She found that her maternal grandparents were 'older' when she saw them. 'They left at the prime of their lives.' She also saw that it was a 'struggle' for her father to tell his own father that he could not fish and be a buyer of fish in the same way as he had been before the Internment. Her grandfather, however, refused to quit and tried to fish, encouraging one of his sons to fish with him. Evelyn described her father's return to fishing in relation to her knowing that so many men whose boats were confiscated never returned to earning a living from fishing. Her father's employer, who had bought his boat before they were removed from the coast, assisted her father in building another boat after their return to Vancouver. While Evelyn was careful to acknowledge that her family received assistance in returning to British Columbia, her testimony illustrates that the white people who 'assisted' may have also bought Japanese Canadians' possessions at nominal prices and were witnesses to their expulsion and dispossession.

From Neys, Yoshiko's family was moved twice to two different towns in northern Ontario. As an adult, she later moved to British Columbia. Her mother still resides in the northern Ontario town to which they were sent after being incarcerated in Slocan.

While white middle-class women who were engaged in paid labour during the Second World War were encouraged to 'return to the home' to allow for full employment of returning white veterans in the post-war period,[94] racialized working-class and poor women, including Japanese Canadian women, continued to work out of necessity in jobs such as domestic service. The shortage of domestic workers, a situation that was constantly brought to the attention of politicians by white bourgeois citizens, continued well into the post-war period.[95] Even though people were being dispersed into white communities, paid labour positions continued to demarcate separate and racialized spaces for Japanese Canadians, reproducing the notion of their 'foreignness' at the same time as profit was acquired from their labour.

Conclusion

As Japanese Canadians were dispersed, their homes and community spaces in British Columbia were taken over by new occupants. The normalization of this process, authorized by Canadian law – the over 22,000 Japanese Canadians removed from their homes and the people, predominantly white, who occupied their former homes, farms, schools, churches, logging camps and who used their cars, equipment, boats, radios, musical instruments, and so on – is part of what has been forgotten about the Internment. Similarly, the appearances of dispersed Japanese Canadians in towns and cities across Canada and the uses of their labour through this process have been normalized and the reasons for their dispersal largely forgotten.

The identities of Japanese Canadians were manipulated through an orchestrated set of dis-placements and a discursive masking on the part of the state and participating citizens. In referencing the analysis of Hannah Arendt, Sherene Razack states, 'Camps are places where the rules of the world cease to apply.'[96] In the Canadian context of the Internment, the administrators set up conditions where they claimed to grant certain rights of the white bourgeois world (for example, schools and churches) to Japanese Canadians. However, these 'rights' were technologies of discipline and control, ensuring that the hegemony of the Canadian 'rulers' was enforced through numerous mechanisms and bodies of enforcement. Many could not attend school and never resumed their education; many had to visibly adopt Protestantism or Catholicism in order to receive schooling. In the case of the Canadian Internment, the insistence by the federal government that Japanese Canadians were not 'interned,' necessarily produced a host of euphemisms to describe what was, in fact, incarceration and the inability to leave the places to which they were sent without permission (and, literally, permits). People's efforts to create identities different from those assigned to them by the state, and their organizing to demand schooling and other necessities, are forms of resistance that may not have necessarily undermined the hegemonies of the white bourgeois world. However, their acts of resistance contributed to identifying the specific place in which they were incarcerated and should not be used to deny the fact of the material limits to their abilities to live and resist and the legal elimination of their freedom. Moreover, space was effectively used to divide people socially and physically. The past or common-sense notions of place identities, like 'ghost towns' or 'sugar beet farms' or 'prisons,' and the relational geographies of the Internment seep into survivors' narratives and affect the ways in which they describe and re-member their own experiences of incarceration. These past identities of place may also be used mistakenly by witnesses to survivor testimonies to interpret their descriptions of the places of the Internment as not incarceration or their acceptance of incarceration. The hegemonies that construct them and us, as I have argued, can therefore affect our reading of their testimonies.

Not only were Japanese Canadians relationally made through these places and social processes but so too were notions of Canada and its citizens. In using the War Measures Act to target and expel Japanese Canadians, and the members of the Stoney Point reserve, the Canadian settler nation used racial and colonial technologies to implement the law and ensure white settlers' right to place. As Sherene Razack argues, '[R]ace thinking becomes embedded in law and bureaucracy so that the suspension of rights appears not as a violence but as the law itself.'[97] In being expelled from their homes, Japanese Canadians were constituted as of the 'Japanese race' and not as Canadian citizens, and hence whiteness as a signifier of citizenship was bolstered as definitional. In protesting the separations of their families, men moved to POW camps decried their loss of this right held by Canadian citizens; those who denied them the right reasserted their own entitlement to live with their families. In being dispossessed, those in the BC interior camps – predominantly women, elders, the 'not able-bodied,' and children – were constructed as charges of the state, despite their work in paid and unpaid labour; the dispossessors then became their benefactors. Those who the government promised would live in families if they moved to 'self-support' camps and sugar beet farms, were constructed as freely 'self-supporting' or 'working,' when, in fact, family members were 'missing' from these sites, and those who moved to them worked under coercive conditions and were restricted by the same laws and methods of policing as those who were held in other sites. Paradoxically, while class divisions produced the places of the 'self-support' camps, the Internment materially minimized or erased the middle-class position of those who lived in them due to their payment over the years for their own incarcerations. Faced with no income or deportation, single Japanese Canadian women and men were coerced into entering white spaces through domestic service; their presence in these spaces did not reflect their autonomy but rather was used to bolster the autonomy of the employers and the 'spatial articulation of superiority.'[98] Japanese Canadians could not freely move from any of these places during the period of the Internment. Neither could they freely move to the restricted area until 1 April 1949. A 'carceral continuum'[99] thus structured their lives even as they left their carceral sites.

Japanese Canadians had to contend with dispossession and shifting placelessness and had to attempt to reconstitute identities in white areas with family members missing, and without friends and communities, that is, without social support. Expelled from their homes *in* Canada, they were scattered to towns and cities across the country where they continued to contend with racism because they were constructed as foreigners and, even after the end of the war, the enemy. The late Thomas Shoyama described this process in these words,

> We remember, despite the assurances of the BC Security Commission who were trying to 'relocate' us across the country, how many hostile environments, how many hostile critics we had to meet. And the psychic scars of all that, I am sure, have been very, very long-lasting, very, very deep.[100]

Racialized discourses inevitably re-immigrantized Japanese Canadians as 'immigrants' or 'refugees' from Japan or Asia (another technology of forgetting the Canadian places from which they were forced to move) – people who must prove themselves worthy to remain in Canada through work. They were allowed to conditionally provide labour for white citizens who, in turn, were entitled to discipline and monitor them. Dispersing Japanese Canadians from their carceral sites without financial and social means of support inculcated discourses that were used to redeem the nation and its citizens. For example, the discourse of indebtedness: Japanese Canadians should feel indebted to the federal government for allowing them to stay in Canada and to the people who allowed them to work for them, rent their accommodations, or who showed them any charity or kindness along the way. As Saidiya Hartman states of the position of African Americans supposedly emancipated from slavery, 'to be free was to be a debtor – that is, obliged and duty-bound to others.'[101] A relationship of indebtedness creates another kind of emotional and psychological bondage to people and the nation; this relationship serves to forget who, in fact, benefited from the Internment. The social relations and discourses of indebtedness bestow power upon those to whom Japanese Canadians may feel indebted or those who feel they should be indebted to them. Some of these relations are manifested in Japanese Canadians labouring for them, or in the ways in which they are represented (or represent themselves) as solely kind benefactors in Internment narratives, erasing the relations of power that construct benevolence. The nation itself continues to benefit from the Internment of Japanese Canadians in the ways in which it redeems itself through its construction of them as a now unified 'model minority,' reducing their complex and heterogeneous forms of surviv-al and resistance to a visible, redemptive stereotype. This allows the nation to render invisible and thus forget the innumerable effects and subjects forged through the Internment.

The women interviewed unmap some of the effects of national vio-lence and how racial, gendered, and classed segregations and incar-cerations were used to geographically and socially divide and separate families and communities. In ending this chapter, I articulate a false sense of closure in describing where women resided after their expul-sion from their homes in British Columbia. Much remains untold, and much of what happened during the Internment is untellable. The read-er may have questions about the details missing from my description of the places of incarceration. However, survivors too live with the gaps in what is known about the Internment and its complex construction, part of its lasting effects. The unknown and the unknowable, perhaps most apparent in the haunting absence of people whose fates we know not, are effects of the Internment, effects lived by the generations that fol-lowed. I will now attempt to re-member some of the subjects forgotten.

7 The Known and Unknown: Subjects Lost, Subjects Re-membered

All along the tracks, wherever they could, crowds of *nihonjin* lined up to wave goodbye to those going to work camps, to Schreiber and to beet fields, ghost towns and other places. They waved to us and we waved to them, whoever they were. Some we knew, some we didn't, but weren't we all in the same boat – forced to move out of the restricted area? I hated the thought of leaving Eiko behind, so I blew her a gentle kiss.

Muriel Kitagawa, *This Is My Own*[1]

The discussion of the places of incarceration ends where we began, in the province of British Columbia. Banishing Japanese Canadians from the restricted area of British Columbia required the government to account for every Japanese Canadian within that geographic area. As was shown in previous chapters, expulsion also involved constructing different and relational identity categories for those interned. Therefore, all of the women interviewed were discursively and spatially constructed in relation to one another, as well as to those I mention below.

Loss is constituted in innumerable ways for those interned. Homes, farms, possessions, automobiles, fishing boats, et cetera were the tangible losses sustained during the Internment. The less visible, yet perhaps even more painful losses were the missing and missed, as people were separated by great symbolic and geographic distances. Each woman volunteered information about the people from whom they were separated during the 1940s when I asked questions about their experiences. Their careful reconstruction of relationships important to them that were forever changed and, in some cases, forever lost are thus critical to understanding both the short- and long-term effects of the Intern-

ment. People died during the Internment; their deaths are forever tied
to those carceral places.

In this chapter, I re-member some of the unknown subjects of the
Internment and problematize other Internment subjects. I discuss examples of the expulsion of children to Assiniboia, Saskatchewan, and
the confinement of children and adults in the Essondale Mental Hospital in Vancouver. The discussion concludes by raising questions about
the notions of the subject and family re-membered and reproduced by
witnesses to the Internment, and how we interpret testimonies of re-
membering subjects.

Expelling Children from British Columbia

The majority of females expelled from the coastal area were children.
The 1941 Census indicates that 50 per cent of the females who were removed from the coast and 39 per cent of the males were children under
the age of twenty.[2] Children thus also had to be construed as 'enemies'
in order for the government to justify separating them from their families and removing them from the restricted areas. As was discussed in
chapter 4, male children over thirteen were separated from all females
in Hastings Park. This racialized masculinity and heterosexuality de-
marcated by age and by physical separation from Japanese Canadian
women, as well as white men and women, reinforced the notion of
all Japanese Canadian males, regardless of their age, as a 'threat' to
Canada. It was not solely male children, however, who were constituted as the enemy requiring banishment; female children were also
moved to a separate geographic location, far from Japanese Canadian
adults.

A clear example of the government's exhaustive effort to erase the
presence of any Japanese Canadian in the 100-hundred mile restricted
area in 1942 was the removal of eighteen children, described as 'orphans,' from the Oriental Home in Victoria to Assiniboia, Saskatchewan. The Oriental Home was maintained by the Women's Missionary
Society of the United Church of Canada. On 20 March 1942, the United
Church reported that 'fifteen Japanese girls of various ages' lived there.
The oldest was sixteen and the youngest was 'just a few years old.' In
addition, 'four Eurasian children, all of whom are Japanese,' were listed. Despite the government's description of the children as 'orphans,'
some of the children, in fact, had one living parent.[3] In a letter to one
of the BCSC commissioners, Hugh Keenleyside, assistant undersecre-
tary of state for the Department of External Affairs reported: 'They are

under supervision in an established home and could not possibly be any danger to public security even if the older ones were anxious to assist the enemy.'[4] Although Keenleyside had argued against their removal, he still constructed the 'older' girls as potentially 'disloyal.' Mrs Scurrah of Victoria, who was a member of the BCSC Advisory Board, did not agree with Keenleyside's recommendation to leave the girls in Victoria, and the removal of the children was authorized.[5] The decision to remove the children demonstrates the power held by the BCSC Advisory Board, which was composed of people who were not elected by the citizens of Canada, in determining the fate of Japanese Canadians.

The Board of Home Missions and the Women's Missionary Society of the United Church were opposed to the BCSC's original plan to send the children to 'a camp.' As Reverend George Dorey, associate director of the United Church, stated, 'To move nineteen children of various ages, all of whom are girls, and to put them in a camp is to my mind unthinkable on the part of the Government, and I think that unless reasons of extreme urgency dictate another course, we should try to be *humane.*'[6] Dorey then argued that the children should be sent 'in a body' to 'a school home' in Assiniboia, Saskatchewan, operated by the Women's Missionary Society. He asked Keenleyside whether the persons 'in charge of these children' from the Women's Missionary Society could accompany them. The BCSC accepted the United Church proposal and nineteen children were moved from the Oriental Home in Victoria on 7 May 1942.[7]

As was illustrated in chapter 1, the adjective 'humane' was applied to numerous actions mobilized against Japanese Canadians in the 1940s by their agents. Calling the movement of children to Assiniboia 'humane' is arguable. Most assuredly, moving the children to 'a camp' would have been 'unthinkable'; moving the children to Saskatchewan and separating them from any Japanese Canadians other than those with whom they moved, including the living parents with whom some may have had contact, was also unconscionable.[8] Moving the children to Assiniboia also extended the monitoring of Japanese Canadians to another provincial jurisdiction, giving the people inhabiting this area the responsibility of supervision and control. The extension and expansion of the places of incarceration engaged more and more people in the processes of policing and surveillance. In the case of the Oriental Home, the movement of the children reconfirmed the role of the Christian churches in the Internment and in the forced movements of children, and also provided work for their employees.

While the government's official policy was not to remove 'Eurasian' children from the restricted area, the four Eurasian girls living in the Home were moved from Victoria to Assiniboia. It is also of note that Dorey racially constructed these girls as 'Japanese,' even though the government's official policy stated that children with one white parent were allowed to remain in the coastal area and were therefore 'Canadians' (see chapter 5). The legal relationship of these children to whiteness was rendered non-existent, and so was their citizenship.

What happened to the children who were moved and to their parents is unknown to this author. Although their forced displacement from Victoria to Assiniboia was described as 'humane' by the United Church official, and although the Assiniboia United Church space was different from that of a camp, all of these places were carceral, involving civic and state processes of discipline and control. If camps were unthinkable for these children, why were they thinkable for other children and adults? How would the women who experienced this incarceration as children describe the Assiniboia site, and what memories do they have of separation and loss?

As was seen in women's reports of 'missing' family members in the previous chapters, it is clear that the government's notion of 'family' was not the same as that of those who were incarcerated. Keeping children with mothers and/or fathers was not a priority. The removal of racialized children from their families is a technology of colonialism practised on Indigenous peoples, for example, in the forced displacement of their children to residential schools and continuing with their forced adoptions. It is a strategy that has defined Canadian colonialism and a technology of white settler control of Indigenous communities and their territories.[9] The practice of controlling the composition of the family has been applied to racialized immigrants through immigration policies and practices.[10] As Enakshi Dua argues, 'Canadian state managers have acted to destroy, prevent, or disrupt the ability of people of colour to participate in family relations.'[11]

The war in the Pacific presented the federal government with the opportunity to destroy a complex arrangement of Japanese Canadian families, kinship networks, friendships, and communities that had extended into the white spaces of British Columbia. This destruction was integral to controlling this racialized group. In order to justify the separation of family members, the government had to construct Japanese Canadian family formations as foreign and in need of reform.

As I have shown, Japanese Canadians protested these separations through actions and direct correspondence with government officials.

The government demeaned these protestations by describing the desire to remain with family members as an intrinsic manifestation of being 'Japanese.' For example, a BCSC report described the people remaining in Steveston in this way: 'The remainder of the community wished to be evacuated in large groups. They were almost *tribal* in their intense desire to remain together and they are now resettled in one of our interior towns, Greenwood.'[12] The same report states that 'it is undeniably a *Japanese characteristic* that the men-folk will not leave their families unless given reasonable assurance that they will be cared for.'[13]

The Orientalist construction of the essentialized Asian family as one where people are tied to each other and their Asian origins through an unwavering loyalty has historically been used to further the notion of Asians as Other, unable to conform to the demands of a liberal democracy, and thus undeserving of the rights of the liberal subject.[14] It is also part of the Orientalist discourse mobilized to imagine and construct Asians as being outside of the nation. This imaginary was materialized through the expulsions, incarcerations, and dispersal and the discourses produced for their justification.

Government officials also ridiculed young women's reluctance to leave their families to take up domestic service positions in other provinces. A 1944 Department of Labour report outlined what were seen as the 'causes' for the refusal of some Japanese Canadians to move east. The report described parents as reluctant to 'let their sons and daughters go east away from home before marriage, especially the girls who are brought up to shun independent action.'[15] This construction of Japanese Canadian women was in relation to an implied norm for white bourgeois women, founded upon the notion of the liberal subject as 'free' and 'independent.'[16] What was, in fact, a forced separation of women from families and communities was masked by an essentialist and Orientalist discourse constructing the Japanese as 'backward' and 'different' from 'Canadians.' Meyda Yeğenoğlu reminds us that the result of such binary constructions of racialized subjects and Western subjects is 'not only the identification of what is Western with what is universal, but also the creation of an essentialist typology in which the distinction between East and West is conceived of as constitutively contrary and profoundly different.'[17] The construction of Japanese Canadian families' 'difference' was then used to justify the spatial separations as a means of inculcating 'civilization.' The Japanese Canadian family itself became another material and symbolic space to be scrutinized and controlled.

Re-membering the Deceased and Institutionalized

I remember my mother telling me about her memories of funerals in Slocan. She described the night-time burning of the bodies of those who had died in the camp and how mourners later went to the cremation site to retrieve the bones. Perhaps, as in the case of Esther's mother, the ashes became a part of what people carried with them, honouring those lost by creating spaces of remembrance in the limited luggage they were allowed and in the subsequent places to which they were moved. The people who died during the Internment are some of the 'missing' family and community members whose passing is forever linked to the places of incarceration.

All of the women I interviewed 'lost' people they knew. Most of them witnessed the death of a family member or knew someone who had died during the Internment. From the beginning of the expulsion until 31 October 1946, a total of 717 people died – 570 adults and 147 children.[18] While this figure included those who lived outside of the restricted BC coastal area before the Internment, the majority of people counted would have been in the various incarceration sites. Due to the spatial separations between family members, people were not always allowed to see their dying relatives or attend their funerals. Forrest La Violette, who visited the camps to undertake his research, reported that 'several sons were unable to visit dying parents.'[19]

May speculated that her father's health immediately before Canada declared war with Japan may have been negatively affected by the exclusionary processes in force in Vancouver. Her father had been a translator who worked for the Canadian government after Canada declared war on Germany in 1939. May believed that her father had been hired to censor letters sent from Canada to Japan. He was fired very suddenly one day, and May still had the notice of termination from the government in her possession. He received the notice of termination 'shortly before he died.' May stated: 'I would also suspect it was quite a blow to him. And having a bad heart, I would not be surprised, knowing what we know about emotional involvement in physical health, that that would have been something that would have, perhaps not hastened so much, but didn't help his health.'[20] Her father was in his sixties when he died. S. emphasized that the Internment affected the health of both of her parents and reported that her father died in the camp.

Donna Nagata's work on the cross-generational effects of the incarceration of Japanese Americans investigated the effects the Internment had on health as perceived by the children of those incarcerated. She found that Sansei 'saw the internment as contributing to health problems and even premature deaths in their parents.'[21] Nagata's study included Sansei whose parents were not incarcerated. As most Japanese Americans living in Hawai'i at the time of the Internment were not incarcerated,[22] Nagata was able to compare Sansei with interned and non-interned parents.

Out of a sample of over 700 people, Nagata found that '41% of the Sansei who had a father in camp reported that their father died before the age of 60 compared with only 19% of those from the group in which a father had not been interned.' Five per cent of the Sansei reported their mothers had died: 'Fifty-eight per cent of the deceased mothers in both groups died before the age of 60 ... mothers who were interned did not differ from non-interned mothers in their age of death.' Nagata concludes, 'The findings are suggestive that fathers, in particular, may have been at risk for an early death following the internment.'[23]

It would be erroneous to conclude from Nagata's findings that the Internment was psychologically or physically more difficult for Nisei men who were incarcerated than Nisei women. However, Nagata's work is valuable in raising the question of the Internment's and racism's effects on health, and it points out the need for an examination of its long-term effects. Her work also illuminates that these perceived effects are noted by the children of families who were interned.

As was stated in chapters 5 and 6, people who needed to be hospitalized for physical illness or injury during the Internment had to travel to institutions at other incarceration sites, or in rare cases, they were sent to Vancouver. These medical emergencies resulted in further separation from family and support systems, as was seen in the case of the woman who was separated from her children when she was sent from the hospital in Hastings Park to the one in New Denver. The rigorous maintenance of the 100-mile restricted zone forced those requiring follow-up procedures at the Vancouver hospital to make several trips despite their illnesses and disabilities. May's sister, who was sent to Vancouver for separate surgeries, had to return to New Denver between each operation.

The hospital is an epitomic space for signifying pathology, associated as it is with disease and contagion. In March 1942, there were 105 people described as 'TB patients' in the Hastings Park hospital who were to be sent to the 'new hospital' at New Denver.[24] A BCSC report indicates that even though Hastings Park is in Vancouver, it was deemed necessary to establish a separate hospital within the Hastings Park incarceration site. According to a former staff nurse in the Hastings Park hospital, 'The hospital unit was located in the poultry section of the livestock buildings.'[25] She added that Japanese Canadian patients were transferred from all the hospitals in Vancouver, including the Oriental Hospital in east Vancouver, to the Hastings Park hospital. Acutely ill patients were transferred to Vancouver General Hospital but returned to Hastings Park for recuperative care.[26] Pregnant women in Hastings Park went to Vancouver General for delivery and immediate post-partum care. In describing ailing children in Hastings Park, the staff nurse stated, 'Children suffering communicable diseases were cared for by families and isolated as much as possible in the *main residential area* under the supervision of a public health nurse.'[27] Ken Adachi noted that '[h]ospitals were either constructed or refurbished in Tashme, Greenwood, Slocan and Sandon, and a 100-bed tuberculosis sanitorium was built in New Denver.'[28]

The extreme effort to remove every last Japanese Canadian from the coast and to keep them separated from white people is also illustrated by the construction of hospitals in different camps. The hospitals also provided jobs for white medical staff; the bureaucratic control in these isolated places extended from the government to social workers, doctors, and nurses. Hospitalization itself often resulted in further penalty and isolation for the ill or injured. The woman who was moved from Vancouver to the New Denver hospital mentioned in chapter 5 was separated from both of her children, and the foster home found for her younger daughter was not in New Denver.

While some might argue that the hospitals built were closer to some of the camps than Vancouver was, I would suggest that the hospitals established in the incarceration sites were not built out of regard for the people incarcerated but were a way of rigorously ensuring the absence of Japanese Canadians from the restricted area. These hospitals firmly established their inability to leave the camp sites and reinforced the notion that the camps were degenerate and contained spaces of disease or diseased people. Given the concern for the cost of the Internment, the costs involved in establishing five different hospitals in the incarceration sites seems curious. This construction of Japanese Canadians as potential disease carriers was also demonstrated through the practice of mandatory testing for venereal disease conducted for each person who moved out of BC to the eastern provinces.[29]

An exception to the removal of all hospitalized patients from the 100-mile restricted zone took place at the Essondale Mental Hospital. In March 1943, there were fifteen Japanese Canadians – eight men, two women, and five children – in this hospital.[30] In June 1943, there were nineteen (twelve adults and seven children),[31] and in October 1945, there were fifty-eight (fifty-six adults and two children).[32] From these statistics, it seems that a unique movement of Japanese Canadians back into the restricted area entailed an incarceration of another kind – the institutionalization of psychiatrized individuals. There is also an indication that individuals were moved from this hospital to other places, most demonstrably in the case of children.

These institutionalized people who remained in the Vancouver area may not have been expelled to the interior camps for financial reasons (how much would it have cost to build another Essondale at one of the camp sites?), yet I suspect that the psychiatric institution itself served to bolster the sense of 'respectability' and the relational construction of 'sanity' for the people living within Vancouver. While removing Japanese Canadians from the coastal area achieved white spatial dominance and created racialized spaces of incarceration for those expelled, the psychiatric hospital also served to create a population different from those incarcerated in other places. This difference could be legitimated through what Michel Foucault refers to as the 'scientificity'[33] of a medicalizing discourse. The mythology of respectability for the 'sane' could be derived from knowing that racialized Others were diagnosed as mentally ill and from the discursive masking of this process: 'making the place of confinement look like a hospital.'[34]

Essondale functioned as another place of relational subject constitution and discipline for Japanese Canadians, both those incarcerated within it and those at other sites. Many would have known of its connotations as a 'mental hospital,' and the threat of being sent there would have held incredible disciplinary power. It is interesting that statistics according to gender were not given in some of the later reports. But from the reports prior to 1943, it is evident that women outnumbered men in the hospital. While men were sent to the POW camps as a way of promoting the myth of a racialized, demonized manhood, I would propose that Essondale may well have served the purpose of offering another place for the punishment, disciplining, and pathologizing of women. Some of the patients were eventually banished even from this small institutionalized area of BC to which they had been confined. There were patients from the hospital who were deported to Japan, an event that T.B. Pickersgill, the second commissioner of Japanese Placement for the Department of Labour, later described as 'merely one of the many trivial details' in the history of the Japanese Division.[35] Some patients were deported as late as 1946, after the end of the war with Japan.[36]

I do not know the reasons for these confinements, but I suspect that people were pathologized in many ways, including through racialized diagnoses. In 1973, Michiko Sakata described meeting a man at what she describes as a BC 'government mental institution.' When Sakata met him, he had been in the hospital for thirty-two years; he was probably one of the patients listed in the government's statistics from the reports cited earlier. This is how she re-membered him:

> He was arrested in 1941 and committed to the hospital for not carrying his registration card identifying him as a person of Japanese origin. On my regular visits, I tried to talk to him in Japanese, but he said, 'Don't speak Japanese. They are watching us.' I tried to talk to him in English, but he could not speak English ... On one of my visits in 1976, I was told that he had stopped eating and had died.[37]

Re-membering Families, Communities, and Cherished Relationships

In contrast to the notion of the nuclear family that was operationalized during the Internment by the state, both through practices that ensured that Japanese Canadians were disentitled to live as families and by limiting who was defined as a family member, women re-membered other family forms. Three of the women I interviewed – Aya, Margaret, and May – lived in family arrangements headed by women before and during the Internment.[38] In addition, S.'s father died while she was in a BC camp, leaving her mother as sole parent. While it can be argued that many women in the camps were 'single' parents during the period of incarceration, that is, largely responsible for the parenting of their children due to the absence of men from these sites,[39] the structures of families were varied and some women lived prior to, during, and after the Internment without a male partner.[40] Although women growing up in situations similar to that of Aya, May, and Margaret may have been statistically few, their experiences contest the notion of homogeneous Japanese Canadian families.

May, who was fourteen when she was expelled from Vancouver, described her pivotal role in her family. The family was headed by a woman before and during the time they were living in Slocan. Her mother, who had been married in Japan and came from a 'fairly wealthy' family, divorced her first husband after arriving in Canada because he was a 'gambler.' May stated: 'So she ended up going to a minister in Vancouver, which must have been horrendous for her, and he suggested she go to the Oriental Home in Victoria.' The information that 'the Oriental Home was for women, mostly, and girls,' was added by May, although she was aware that there were boys there as well. May's mother was later sent from the Home to work as a maid in a 'wealthy home.' Her mother eventually remarried, and May was born in Victoria. They moved to Vancouver when May was three. In October 1941, when May was thirteen, her father (her mother's second husband) died. Their family – a mother and two daughters, of which May was the oldest – supported one another during and after the Internment.

Even though they lived in Vancouver, May's family was moved to Hastings Park, or what she referred to as the 'Manning Pool,' before being sent to an interior camp. Her mother's condition was described by her in these words: 'She was extremely sick. She had done some housework after my dad died because she needed some money.' Her mother was diagnosed as having Addison's disease. May began taking care of the family at this time. She described her role in this way: 'At the age of thirteen, when my dad died, I stopped being a kid ... From that point on I simply looked after everything that was happening.'

Another memory May shared with me was one concerning her stepbrother, her father's nephew who was adopted by her parents upon the death of her uncle. May said she had felt close to this stepbrother as a child. He was considerably older, in his thirties during the Internment, and a 'playboy' who tried to borrow money from her mother while they were in Slocan. He had no dependants, was living at another camp, and made no effort to support May's mother or family financially. May explained that due to the cost of medicine for her mother's condition, food, and other expenses, 'I couldn't afford this man in my life. I simply could not afford him.' She became estranged from him as a result, although her sister maintained contact with him after they moved to Toronto.

It was also May who decided that they would move east when they were forced to make a decision because of the repatriation survey. May stated: 'Later on when we had to decide whether we were staying in

Canada or going back, you know the repatriation thing, [my mother] really left it up to me as to whether we wanted to stay or go.' As was described in chapter 6, in order to financially support her mother and sister, May left Slocan at the age of seventeen and moved to Toronto in 1945 to undertake domestic work while attending high school.

May has kept the many letters she wrote to the government after she moved to Toronto. She tried to bring to the government's attention the difficulties of supporting her mother, her sister, and herself on 'seventeen dollars a week.' In her interview, she described what it was like to be responsible for her mother's and sister's welfare: 'I think that was part of it, was knowing I had to do it myself. It seemed to me a lot of other kids my age seemed to have an older brother or mother or dad that was doing this. I didn't have that ... It was a tough time.'

May's history complicates the notion of 'family' and the roles that women played during the Internment. She took over many decision-making responsibilities and financial support for a woman-led family. Many men may have financially assisted their parents, partners, and children during their incarcerations and separations, but in May's case, the only male in her family did not contribute in this way.

Margaret's father died when she was two. She was raised by her mother and paternal grandmother. Her paternal grandfather had lived with them but had moved back to Japan before the Internment. Her grandmother remained with her mother. Margaret described this as her grandparents' 'separation' and her grandmother 'stayed with our family right to the end.'[41] Margaret, therefore, was parented by two women.

In 1941, Margaret was eleven years old. When I asked whether her mother made the decision to go to the sugar beet farm, she replied: 'To tell you the truth, my grandmother was the strongest person. She was the one who held the family together when my father died ... She. was a ... really tough lady.' Seven members of her family were moved to Manitoba. Margaret, however, had an older brother who assumed a great deal of responsibility for the family. Both he and her older sister left the family in order to work to support them through the winter months. It was through their efforts that they eventually moved to Winnipeg.

Other women also told me that it was the women in their families who made the crucial decision necessitated by the repatriation survey. Ann, who was in Slocan and whose husband was not with her when the survey was imposed upon her, reported: 'Well, my husband said he decided to go to Japan, and I said no. And I didn't. In the end, he didn't.'[42] When her daughter, Mayumi, asked her mother: 'How did you work that out, who was staying and who was going?' Ann answered: 'We couldn't write very much because all the mail at that time was censored.' Mayumi pursued her question: 'So how did he know you weren't going [to Japan]?'[43] Ann laughed when she replied: 'Because he knew me.'

Esther also remembered that her mother made the decision not to move to Japan. They were living on a sugar beet farm in Manitoba when they were ordered to sign the survey. Esther recalled 'my older brothers and sister talking about that. And I think they discussed it. But my mother would have nothing to do with it. So I don't think it went beyond just a quick discussion ... So my family just carried on.'[44]

These examples make it clear that families were also female-headed and extended beyond relations of a closed parent-child system or nuclear formation. In describing sugar beet farms and 'self-support' camps as places where families were kept together because men were there, the state's discourse of family reinforced the notion that when a man who is the head of the household is present, the family is complete. Thus, what the federal government reproduced is the normalization of patriarchy, the hegemony of heterosexual relations, and male (head-of-the-house) domination.

As Dua has demonstrated, the control of the construction of racialized families has been critical to Canadian nation-building and '[b]y practising alternative familial and gender practices, people of colour pose a threat to the moral order that underlay the racialized imperialist nation.'[45] While the family as a social structure is used to support patriarchy and class inequality by reproducing labour for capital exploitation, uncovering women's roles in different Japanese Canadian families underscores the heterogeneity of family formations, and this fact can be used to contest the notion of a patriarchal nuclear family that was imposed upon Japanese Canadians during the Internment and dispersal. The testimonies of the women interviewed also illustrate the ways in which the family served as a place of remembrance and support in dealing with the racism that they experienced.

According to each woman interviewed, there were family members from whom they were separated during and after the Internment. The euphemism of 'family' used by the government erased the fact that they had destroyed families. One of the innumerable effects of the Internment was the destruction of networks of related people and people to whom one could relate (including those who were able to relate to the experiences of the Internment), and the imposition of an isolated singularity, brutally reinforced by the removal of family from community, partners from partners, lovers from lovers, children from family, mothers from sons ... and all justified through discourses that demeaned and racialized a subjecthood connected to others. As Foucault suggests, 'multiple separations, individualizing distributions' result from and produce 'surveillance and control.'[46] The separation and destruction of Japanese Canadian families and communities, therefore, was violence that marked and controlled them and produced a racialized subject separated from others similarly racialized with whom they shared a history of Internment and without whom they could not communally re-member it.

This violent and strictly policed pressure to annihilate a subjecthood connected to other Japanese Canadians was differently lived by each person. However, it was rigorously enforced through numerous, deliberate separations, the processes of dispersal, and the many forms of policing that followed them wherever they moved. The divisions that were inculcated through the discourses and practices of the Internment, differently socially and geographically locating 'individual' subjects, also served to ensure that some would inevitably be critical of and alienated from others interned. As Thomas Shoyama suggested, 'I think the worst aspect of the whole experience was the way in which it split and rendered divisions within our community ... I know people found themselves in deep disagreement even with members of their own family as to how we should react.'[47] These social and physical divisions that continued through the forced dispersal served the government's purpose to disable and render illegal community organizing for many years. Living under surveillance and enforced discipline for so long, including the forces of policing that continued in the dispersal sites, instituted forms of self-discipline and self-regulation, processes that merit further investigation and analysis. An example of this can be found in an editorial from a 1945 Hamilton YWCA newsletter written by a survivor, warning people that 'gabbing out aloud in Japanese ... gathering around in large groups out in the streets' would be commented on 'unfavourably.'[48] The plea to speak English only was reflective of the Anglo-Christian orientation of the newsletter and the real repercussions for speaking Japanese in public places.

It is in light of this violence of separating and dividing Japanese Canadians and the ways it was represented by government officials that I urge caution in how we construct 'family' in Internment narratives. I would hope that the different family forms, inclusive of all the people cherished, can be remembered as an echo of the possibilities of social formations that do not aspire to a singularity and autonomy but instead seek to remember each other.

For some of the women interviewed, it is an accomplishment to live with cherished family members or to be in contact with family and non-related extended family members after years of physical separation. The ongoing maintenance of family connections may be as much an effect of the Internment as are ongoing familial separations, divisions, and alienations for others. Some of the latter are described in the next chapter in relation to daughters who were linguistically separated from their grandparents and Japanese-speaking relations. An example of the former was reported by Aya, who told me that much of her time is spent travelling to see her children in different parts of the country. During and after the dispersal, some of her children moved to different regions of the country. She proudly told me about her ten grandchildren and one great-grandchild, most of whom she is now separated from by great distances. Her commitment to maintaining these connections was expressed by her travel itinerary for visiting family members in the year following our interview, the seventy-eighth year of her life. In the spring, she planned to travel to help her daughter in BC, cooking for her while she and her family harvest crops. She would then travel to Toronto to see her other daughter, Louise, and her grandchildren. In the year of our interview she had also visited a granddaughter in Calgary and attended the graduations of other grandchildren. 'The years seem so short,' she exclaimed.[49] Ann also told me of her fifteen grandchildren and three great-grandchildren, the oldest thirty years and the youngest seven months.

S. credited her mother in particular, for supporting her close-knit family: 'Our mother ... carried on and never gave up.'[50] Her mother, who wrote haiku and played the koto, was asked to teach Japanese-language classes before the Internment, but this dream remained unfulfilled due to the expulsion. When a family member celebrates an accomplishment, they remember her by saying, 'Mom would have been proud of us.'

Through a discussion of some of the places of Internment, I have shown that these places were relationally constituted. To acknowledge that space is used to construct and justify domination is to recognize that different places assist in constituting and denying the rights of citizenship. To understand how women negotiated these spatial separations and how they describe them is to see that the Internment produced gaping holes, the 'spaces of missing' in families and in communities. The tactic of spatially separating people was the sine qua non of the Internment, and I have illustrated that displacement was used to destroy communities, families, and people's very selves. People, however, resisted, contested, and negotiated the violence of the Internment in various ways, and I now turn my attention to one means of expressing resistance that I feel has been overlooked in the analysis of women's testimonies.

Resisting the Hegemony of the Autonomous Subject

Representations of Japanese Canadians as unequivocally 'silent,' 'passive,' and exhibiting a *'shikata ga nai* attitude' continue to subjugate those who were interned. I consider these representations to be mechanisms used for ongoing surveillance of Japanese Canadians who were interned that simultaneously draw our attention away from scrutinizing the power that produces survivors and their testimonies, and our interpretation of their testimonies.

In an essay based on interviews with women she identifies as Issei and Nisei American, Malve Von Hassel analyses the dynamics of Issei women's self-presentation and the ways in which their testimonies are interpreted by their daughters. What is revealing in Von Hassel's interpretation of Issei women's testimonies is how she reduces particular phrasings to a demonstration of their 'submission and acceptance.' This conclusion is reached, for example, in her reading of a woman's statement describing the loss of their family dry-cleaning business: 'There was a chance to claim losses but though we submitted our claim in writing, nothing ever came of it. But that's all right – it wasn't only us. Everyone got taken, not just us. No one is upset about it. It was okay, because that was the war.'[51]

While one might be drawn to analyse the words that led Von Hassel to conclude that this woman was passive and submissive, what strikes me in these comments are the phrases 'it wasn't only us. Everyone got taken, not just us.' This recognition of others is a referent to family and community, that is, the Japanese American community incarcerated and destroyed. There is an implicit understanding that many people suffered as a result of the expulsion, and there is also an examination of the testifier's position in relation to others. The understanding that people who survived the Internment and dispossession carry this memory of community and also position themselves within a community of memory is critical to developing a deeper analysis for the processes of witnessing and interpreting oral testimonies.

While Von Hassel argues for a more complex reading of Issei women's self-expression, her work links the themes of silence, femininity, and submission to Japanese cultural origins. As well as critiquing Von Hassel's reiteration of racialized and gendered representations of Japanese American women, I would argue that the notion of the autonomous subject informs many interpretations of testimonies of Internment survivors and the survivor is judged according to the weight of this presumption. If we read women's testimonies according to the standard of an autonomous, rational subject (the symbolic liberal subject discussed in the introduction and chapter 1), we will be disinclined to see the complexity of negotiation in their words and lean towards reading their insistence on relationality and the fact that they situate themselves within a relational field of loss as non-autonomous and therefore suspect.

I have indicated throughout chapters 3 to 7 that women constructed their memories and themselves in relation to other people, both family members and community members. This re-membering of the Internment and dispersal, constructed relationally, is what is referred to as 'memory of community.' The following examples illustrate that the women interviewed for this book situate themselves within a community re-membered. Their testimonies have wordings similar, although not identical, to the testimony used by Von Hassel.

When Kazuko described how her family was told by the RCMP that they had to move from their home, she stated:

> We opened the notice and it said, 'You have to leave this place in twenty-four hours. Just one baggage per person.' So we didn't have much time at all. Because this wasn't expected. The main thing for which we were lucky – because, actually, the men had to separate from the family – we were lucky because we were all together most of the time, the evacuation time.[52]

Another example can be found when Margaret recalled that her grandmother lost her 'family things' when they were forced to leave Richmond:

> My grandmother had a lot of heirloom things, so when the government

said, 'You have to move, you have to leave everything, it'll only be a matter of year and a half, two years tops. Leave everything and you're only allowed one baggage.' So we had this woodshed which locked, so my grandmother put everything in there, locked it up, hoping you know, within a
couple of years to come back and claim it all. But when my brother went
back after the war, they had smashed in the windows, taken, smashed
everything that they could smash and took whatever was valuable. So,
we had nothing left. I think that was the hardest part for my grandmother.
'Cause it was all family things that she had left. That was very hard for her.
Well, that's war. Yeah. *I think a lot of people went through that, anyways, you
know. It's not just us.* (emphasis added)

Lastly, here is an example from Aya's testimony:

But I think it's not only me. It's all the other people too. There's so many
who experienced different hardships. Even in the sugar beet farms, if they
had a family, small kids you know, and they're not used to the cold climate. I'm sure they had a, you know, a hard time too. So I guess, wherever
you were shipped out to, you know, I'm sure they all went through different hardships.

Kim Lacy Rogers has concluded that two narrative forms arose out
of her interviews with African American men and women who had
been active in the civil rights movement. She describes these two forms
as the trauma narrative and the narrative of redemption. Using Judith
Herman's work on post-traumatic stress disorder, Rogers describes
trauma narratives as those 'encoded in the form of vivid sensations and
images.' She adds that these narratives give 'an otherworldly quality to
appalling scenes of violence and terror.'[53] Rogers states that redemption narratives frequently follow the trauma narratives; the former emphasize 'physical rescue or preservation from evil, or ... the redemptive
aspects of relationships that save the narrator from fear, isolation, or
emotional collapse in the face of violence or death.'[54]

I prefer to see testimonies of historical trauma as more complex negotiations of violence than the dichotomy proposed by Rogers. The
expression of trauma is not discretely separate from the different narrative voices expressed through testimony. What is defined by Von Hassel in the example above as 'submission and acceptance' is a narrative
so steeped with the trauma of loss that it articulates, within the moment
of testifying, a reconstitution of others' losses as well. In this way, sur-

vivors are in fact recognizing and implicitly naming their losses within an understanding of a community's losses.

The phrasings used in testimonies are part of a larger negotiation of the painful memories of loss and violation. What is of interest to me in the interpretation of testimonies of Internment survivors, is how such interrelated and complex constructions of traumatic histories are simplistically reduced and essentialized as being reflective of 'passivity and acceptance' or 'translated' as evidence of a *shikata ga nai* attitude. Such reductive interpretations and representations of testimonies are riddled with Orientalist assumptions of Japanese Canadian/American subjectivity, and are also reflective of a Western subject claiming to 'know' the Other.

Nagata has also commented on descriptions of the Internment where Japanese Americans compare themselves to other people who were incarcerated. She calls this 'phenomenon' 'the denial of personal disadvantage' and elaborates on the concept in this way:

> Individuals who have been disadvantaged or victimized often rely on social comparisons with others to assess their status ... (i.e., downward comparisons), [which] can help victims believe that their situation could have been worse, reduce other-blame for the circumstances, and maintain a sense of justice. Research suggests that stigmatized individuals are especially likely to compare themselves with others who share a common fate within their own group. Such in-group comparisons can play a vital role in protecting the self-esteem of the stigmatized individual.[55]

Nagata's use of psychological discourse to explain why the testifier may compare the self to others in a testimony emphasizes the 'individual' and his/her behaviour. While I do not reject the analysis that esteeming the self is critical in surviving violence, what concerns me in Nagata's analysis is the way in which the survivor is isolated through the ontological construction of the 'individual.' The survivor is thus viewed as the 'autonomous' narrator, and her/his attempts to 'esteem' others who are 'victimized' are reduced to her/his own need to protect 'self-esteem' and the self. A greater understanding of the violence of the Internment is needed, but not one that is only individualized and that further isolates the subject interned from others.

Meyda Yeğenoğlu states, 'Understanding power as a productive and formative process requires a questioning of the presumptions of the paradigms which conceive of the subject in terms of the primacy of mind.'[56] The mind re-members and negotiates the violence of the Internment in different ways, but what also is re-membered and is integrally linked to the cognitive and psychological are the social and spatial, the subject's own social and material placement and the placing of those with whom one underwent the violence and who experienced it differently. As women re-membered the effects of the Internment, they described their own social locations and the subject positions of gender, class, age, et cetera that positioned them differently in relation to others. What might appear to be a minimization of their own losses, therefore, is often in fact a careful tracing of how subject positions affected their own experiences of the Internment.

Some might consider these testimonies as demonstrative of a 'Japanese' or Asian subjectivity tied to family or community, and hence culturalize them as not Western or modern. Rather than focus on how the survivors' testimonies reflect a subject not in keeping with what is presumed to be the norm, I would like to attend to what is considered the norm and how the norm is contested by them. For example, what processes are at work to produce the forgetting of our interrelatedness and how our own social positions are procured in relation to the dominant and subordinate positions of others? Interrogating our own subject positions in relation to those of the survivors may also enable us to hear them in different ways and to ask questions of the discourses that continue to subjugate Japanese Canadians through comparisons to a normative, dominant figure of a 'Canadian' (by way of the imputed lack of their: 'voice,' 'resistance,'... or by their excess of 'reserve,' 'silence'...). Despite their separations from one another and the annihilation of some of their relationships, the women I interviewed keep these relationships alive within a mnemonic record. I read these articulations of the interrelatedness of lives and loss as resistance to both the violence of the Internment and the hegemonic notion of the autonomous subject that, by its very definition, must forget her/his attachments to others. Embodying the self within this memory of community marks the grief for the absence of all those not present and continues to produce their embodiment. It underscores the connection of the testifying self to others. These statements evoking a 'memory of community' reveal in many ways the magnitude of the violence of the Internment through re-membering the numbers of people affected; even within the description of how the Internment affected one's self, there is a recognition of the wider context of violence against subjugated communities and not always just Japanese Canadian/American ones. Lawrence Langer's description of survivors of the Holocaust as being 'pursued not only by their own earlier traumatic moments but by the traumas of others too'[57] has implications for interpretations of memories of historical violence, and hence the relational reconstruction of memories of the Internment. Furthermore, women's abilities to carefully trace their losses in relation to those who they believe lost more (parents, people who were in different places, people whose fathers were not with them, et cetera), invite us to consider our own connectedness to the histories and subordination of others. While some may read complex negotiations of self in relation to others' experiences of the Internment as 'submission' and 'acceptance,' I read them as resistance to the very notion of the autonomous subject that forgets its connections to the subjugation of others, a notion that enables domination and forgets complicity.

Conclusion

Government officials located every Japanese Canadian within the 100-mile restricted coastal area, even going to great lengths to move children and those in hospitals to other locations. An exception to this removal from the coastal area were the people confined in the Essondale Hospital. This hospital, however, represented another kind of incarceration and, as Sakata's testimony cited above suggests, it continued to serve as a place of confinement and exile decades after Japanese Canadians were allowed to return to the West Coast in 1949.

Over 22,000 people were forcibly moved and re-moved during the Internment. Relationships, families, and communities were ruptured and destroyed. With each individual move, families were affected and changed. While some people were forcibly dispersed away from their families, others missing from families had either died or were one of the 4,000 people deported to Japan.[58] In order to justify their actions, discourses were mobilized by the government that demeaned Japanese Canadian family formations, equating the need to be with family and community with 'backwardness,' proof of an essentialized and racialized 'Japaneseness.'

The women interviewed emphasized that they played different roles in supporting family members and friends, some of them giving birth to children, caring for children, working at paid and unpaid labour in the camps and other carceral places, and in the places to which they were dispersed. All of the women I interviewed who were not young children at the time of the Internment made critical decisions that involved profound changes in the social organization of their families. They struggled to maintain contact with other cherished family members despite displacement, and even agreed to move away from loved ones in order to support them.

During the dispersal relationships between Japanese Canadians continued to be monitored. The RCMP submitted monthly reports concerning the political and social activities of Japanese Canadians in each divisional area.[59] Threats of further imprisonment or deportation followed Japanese Canadians and deterred socializing and organizing. Separating Japanese Canadians from networks of support and people with whom they shared a history of Internment enforced an individuality different from that held by the white bourgeois subject. Race was used to mark the Japanese Canadian 'individual,' relative to the unmarked whiteness of those with whom it was legal to communicate and for whom it was imperative to work. Hence, autonomy and the ability to be 'free' (and being racially unmarked is part of what constitutes freedom) was socially produced in relation to the non-autonomy of others. As Hartman asks, 'What does autonomy mean in the context of coercion, hunger, and uncertainty?'[60] Being destitute and homeless, both outcomes of federal Internment policies, could be criminalized by the state. For example, in August 1945, after the war with Japan was over, an Issei man was arrested in Toronto on a vagrancy charge.[61] His crime, as described by the arresting officer, was that he 'had only the clothes that he wore, nothing to eat, no money, no place of abode and had lost his National Registration and Japanese Registration cards.'[62] He was asked to sign the repatriation survey and agree to go to Japan. At his court appearance he was sentenced to three months definite and three months indefinite jail terms in the Guelph Reformatory.[63] When the Toronto Placement Officer, George Trueman, learned of the arrest he demonstrated relief in knowing that the man, after completing his jail sentence, would be returned to British Columbia and from there sent to Japan. He described him as 'lazy, improvident and non-co-operative.'[64]

Much will remain unknown about the experiences of over 22,000 people during and after the Internment. My father, who in 1942 was a salesperson for Furuya, a Japanese Canadian trading company, travelled in the BC interior prior to and during the expulsion. Some of his customers reported to him that during this period of upheaval, women were sexually assaulted by white men in positions of authority.[65] My father wanted this fact to be known and he shared it with me in one of many conversations regarding the Internment. *The extent of the unknown can never be known, but we must resist forgetting.*

The destructive processes of the Internment necessitated the reconstruction of selves, families, and communities. As people left the sites of incarceration through forced dispersals, the reconstituted familial space became one of the only places for sharing memories of the Internment.

8 'It Is Part of My Inheritance': Handing Down Memory of the Internment

Time heals the details, but time cannot heal the fundamental wrong. My children will not remember the first violence of feeling, the intense bitterness I felt, but they will know that a house was lost through injustice.

Muriel Kitagawa, *This Is My Own*[1]

It is part of my inheritance, as its effects are my children's inheritance and theirs. And it will just go on.

Mayumi, interview[2]

In 2009, a CBC Radio host introduced his interview with me as follows: he stated that our discussion was about the effects of the Internment on the children of Japanese Canadians who were interned over seventy years ago. Given that the expulsion began in 1942 and Japanese Canadians were not allowed to return to the West Coast until 1949, and that the dispersal continued past this date, the seventy years cited was an overstatement. Nevertheless, it is the notion that the Internment was a finite process, occurring in one particular year and ending in another without affecting those incarcerated and subsequent generations beyond those years that this chapter seeks to disrupt. As I have argued throughout this book, the effects of the Internment cannot be fully acknowledged if we only attend to it as one event of the linear past. History reduced to temporality masks the consequences and effects of national violence. In this chapter and the next, the interviews of the daughters will be used to analyse the transmission of the history of the Internment and some of its long-term effects across generations.

I look at Japanese Canadian spaces in which the history of the Internment is passed down to daughters, the 'familial space'[3] and Japanese Canadian community spaces. Both daughters and mothers use these spaces to represent, communicate, understand, and analyse the history of the Internment and its legacy in their lives. In establishing representational spaces in families and Japanese Canadian communities, some survivors and their children attempt to resist the effects of the Internment.

The first section of this chapter presents the notion of cross-generational transmission of historical trauma, as it is used in the psychological literature on children of Holocaust survivors. I will then examine how this concept of transmission is utilized by Donna K. Nagata in her study on Japanese American Sansei.[4]

In the second section, I will investigate how women 'hand down,' acquire, and negotiate their memories of the Internment in families and Japanese Canadian community spaces. The chapter ends with a summary of the some of the effects of the Internment as articulated by the daughters interviewed.

Cross-Generational Transmission of Memories of the Internment

Yael Danieli defines 'intergenerational transmission' in relation to families of Holocaust survivors as 'behaviors of survivors' offspring (children born after the war) which are dynamically assumed to have their origins either in symbolic relationship to their parents' Holocaust experiences or to be shaped by Holocaust-related pathogenic behaviors.'[5]

Danieli's definition focuses on the pathogenesis of 'intergenerational transmission.' As in the literature on the Internment, the adjective 'silent' is also used in relation to Holocaust survivors to describe the gaps in knowledge experienced by their children.[6] The double bind of the deleterious effects of an excess of 'silence' or 'speech' is exemplified by Martin Bergmann's and Milton Jucovy's statement: 'There is ... the difficulty of determining which has a more salutary effect and which a more traumatic one: the endless account of tribulations or the silence practised by many about the traumatic past.'[7] This statement begs the questions: How much speech is too much? How little is too little? How does a survivor negotiate memories of violence within a nation where the management of these memories is relegated to that survivor alone?

However, Danieli extends the notion of what she calls the 'conspiracy of silence' beyond the parent–child dyad and situates it as existing 'between survivors, their children, and society,' a result of 'pervasive

negative societal reactions and attitudes, such as indifference, avoid-
ance, repression, and denial of their Holocaust experiences that most
survivors encountered after the war.'[8] She also raises questions about
the psychological response of 'experts' by interrogating the diagnoses
of psychologists and researchers in relation to Holocaust survivors.
Namely, she mentions the 'pervasiveness of *bystander guilt*' as accounting for experts' 'overuse, stereotypical attribution, and reductionist
misinterpretation of concepts such as "survivor guilt"' and its application to behaviours exhibited by survivors.[9] I would further analyse the
notion of 'bystander guilt' by problematizing the witness' position of
power in relation to the survivor. Perhaps a notion such as 'bystander
complicity' would enable a more complex understanding of the dynamics of witnessing behaviours exhibited by survivors. This would
include a social analysis of the position of so-called bystanders to historical violence. Nevertheless, Danieli's emphasis on the psychological
response to survivors opens up avenues of interrogation that go beyond the closed space of parent–child relations.

Donna Nagata used the research on children of Holocaust survivors in her survey of over 700 non-interned Sansei in the United States,
which included over forty in-depth interviews. Nagata used this research and its finding that '[t]he legacy of the Holocaust continues to
have an impact on survivors and their children' in order to illustrate
that 'the Internment continues to affect ... Japanese Americans and their
children.'[10] She cautions, however, that an overemphasis on the psychiatric literature may lead to 'blaming the victim' by 'labelling survivors
and their children as permanently impaired socially and emotionally.'[11]
One of Nagata's major contributions to the literature on the Internment
of Japanese Americans is her conclusion that 'the repercussions of the
incarceration extended far beyond the date [of the closing of the internment camps]. Individuals, families, and whole communities felt the
economic, social, and psychological ramifications for years to come.'[12]
Using her sample of over 700 Sansei, Nagata underlines the reality that
'the vast majority of Sansei feel that the incarceration has affected their
lives in significant ways.'[13]

Nagata's work, however, maintains the closed space of parent–child
relations as the site of scrutiny. She uses the trope of silence to describe
the difficulties in speaking about the Internment. She does, however,
assign responsibility for this 'silence' to the survivors *and* their children in her statement, 'Rather than seeking explanations for the silences solely within the Nisei or Sansei generation, the findings suggest

that the interactional pattern between the generations best accounts for the lack of communication.'[14] Importantly, Nagata emphasizes that it is not only parents who may not have imparted details about their internment but it is also the 'social context [that] has contributed to the Sansei's lack of information.'[15]

While Nagata concludes that silence is a 'major long-term effect of the internment,'[16] her work, in fact, complicates the notion of what constitutes silence in relation to the transmission of knowledge. In quantitative detail, she provides information on how Sansei learned of the Internment, stating that many found out about it from their interned parent(s), that they were a certain age when they were told, and so on. She also notes differences in how Sansei who had no parents interned (especially those who lived in Hawai'i; see chapter 1 for a discussion of Japanese Americans in Hawai'i), who had one parent interned, or who had two parents interned reported intergenerational communications of the incarceration, and how Sansei in different areas of the United States reported this communication. Contrary to the popular notion of survivors being silent about the Internment, 'close to half of both the Two-Parent [interned] and One-Parent [interned] Sansei' in Nagata's study reported 'first learning of the internment by talking with their parents.'[17] She adds, 'Half ... of the interviewees who had a parent interned reported their age of first memory [of learning about the Internment] to be before junior high school.'[18] Nagata's findings are invaluable in providing information on how specific knowledges of the Internment have been conveyed to the non-interned members of this generation. Her examination of the geographical locations of the Sansei respondents also suggests the connection between place and its relationship to knowledge production.

Creating Representational Spaces for the 'Handing Down' of Knowledge of the Internment

The familial space is a place of transmission of national and family narratives. Racialized and other marginalized people may try to establish representational space within families for describing and analysing oppression and developing strategies to combat it. For Japanese Canadians with an Internment history, it can be the first and only place where this history is transmitted.

The concept of transmission or 'handing down' of knowledge is useful in examining the long-term effects of the Internment across generations. In contrast to the work on psychological transmission, however, I seek to understand how knowledge of the Internment is socially constructed in different spaces and how these spaces enable or disable the production of this knowledge. I wish to analyse some of the ways in which survivors pass down knowledge of the Internment and how this subjugated knowledge that has been marginalized, disqualified, or forgotten in white spaces can be used by survivors and their daughters to contest domination.

In this section, I examine familial and Japanese Canadian community spaces as sites of production of remembrance of the Internment for daughters of families who were interned. A spatial analysis traces where the discourses and histories of the Internment can actually be spoken and also where they are actively denied and forgotten. While this and the next chapter give some examples of the effects of the Internment as articulated by daughters of families who were interned, more research is needed to describe and analyse the long-term effects of the Internment as lived by children of the Internment.

Handing Down Memories of the Internment in the Familial Space

How are memories of the Internment handed down to children and how do different spaces enable or disable this transmission? Survivors have to manage the memories of the harms they witnessed and experienced; their families are often the primary witnesses to their memories. The family is also a space for negotiating the violence of systems of domination, including 'everyday racism,'[19] sexism, heterosexism, ableism, and economic and work relations.[20] Therefore, the family setting can provide a critical representational space for re-membering the Internment, and can be a 'counterspace'[21] to the other spaces inhabited by survivors and their families in which there is a resounding silence about the Internment and other forms of violence. In the dyadic construction of the family consisting of parents and children only, the parents alone are held accountable for managing and communicating their knowledge of the Internment appropriately. Holding survivors alone accountable for communicating their memories denies the importance of communal support, and as a result, the exclusionary hegemony of an autonomous familial space is recreated.

In chapters 3 to 7, women described what and who they had lost. In this chapter, women report other losses of material, historical, and personal value. Haru recounted that her parents owned little, but they did have second-hand furniture, which would now be 'nice antiques.'[22] Haru's description led me to wonder, as she did, where those antiques are now. In this way, the 'antiques' for Haru symbolize what she cannot hand down to her children. Instead, this furniture became the inheritance of people who benefited from her family's expulsion.

May explained the processes of dispossession in this illuminating way:

> I think most people, certainly a lot of people, left things behind they really felt they would retrieve at some point. Otherwise you would have brought a lot more things. I really think they felt they'd be able to retrieve them, which, of course, most of us couldn't. So there are pieces of family history that are certainly lost. Where a lot of my friends here can say, 'Oh I have my mother's plate or I have a wedding gift of my mom and dad's,' you know, these things. They're simply in your memory. They're locked in your memory. And they're not there for you to be able to have or to hold onto or pass on. And so those are some of the things that are hard to put up with.[23]

Whether 'antiques,' 'Japanese dolls,' 'boats,' 'houses,' 'farms,' or other items, these possessions symbolize what has become heritable for others through Japanese Canadian dispossession. The normalization of this dispossession – not to question how one becomes entitled to own what belonged to others or how we benefit from others being dispossessed – leads one ultimately to questions of who is entitled to pass down and inherit Canada, and how this intrinsically colonial inheritance is acquired.

What mnemonic record is handed down to daughters and how does this transmission occur? Mayumi, Ann's daughter, was born in 1953 in Toronto. She learned about the incarceration of her parents in this way:

> I think I was about twelve or thirteen. But I'm not positive. It just seems something that I've always known, but didn't ... I've always sensed that, maybe from [family] pictures that I've seen, but I can't remember a particular moment where it suddenly all fell into place. I do remember being totally grossed out because the picture I had in my mind of it was somebody knocking on the door and handing them a duffle bag and saying, 'That's all you can bring. You can fill a duffle bag and you have twenty-four hours.' And I might have got that from my aunt or from my father, not from my mom.

In her testimony, Mayumi raises four aspects that I will continue to explore in this chapter. First, she raises the connection between memory and place, and the importance of imagining where people were when they heard the 'knock on the door,' were given the order to leave in twenty-four hours, and were told where they would be sent. Second, she mentions the use of photographs as being linked to her accumulation of knowledge and the shaping of her own memory. Third, she underlines that it was not from her mother that she learned about the 'knock on the door,' but from her aunt or her father. Hence, access to different family members may impart different knowledges of the Internment. Fourth, there is the 'it' that stands in for what cannot be named, that I have reductively collapsed under the inadequate term 'Internment,' a gap in our language reminding us of the difficulties in naming. These four elements – the importance of place in memory and knowledge production; the critical function of photographs and other forms of representation in constructing knowledge of the Internment; the importance of family, extended family, and community in remembrance and in accumulating knowledge and analysis; and the struggle to know what cannot be exhaustively known and name what cannot be named – will be examined throughout this chapter.

Midori, who was born in a Prairie province in 1968, is S.'s daughter. Like Mayumi, she also described her accumulation of knowledge about the Internment as 'gradual' and told to her in the form of 'stories' recounted by both her mother and father: 'I don't remember a point where all of a sudden we were told about this thing ... My dad tells us more stories than my mom.'[24]

Yuko, who was born in Toronto in 1955, is Haru's daughter. The Internment was never 'something that was ever discussed' with her mother or father. She never had a conversation with her father about it before his death.[25] However, she later recounted that her parents had taken their family to Vancouver when she was in grade six. Her memory of this visit was described in relation to the places they had visited, 'they took us to Gastown and the places where they grew up, and then told us about Hastings Park. But I don't remember the details of the conversation.' She also remembered hearing her parents talk during the redress struggle about 'Vancouver and going to Hastings Park.' She explained, 'It was like I heard about it, but I didn't really listen.' It was only after Yuko went on a community-organized tour of the BC camps that she 'talked a little bit' with her mother about the Internment.[26]

Born in 1969 in the northern Ontario town to which her mother was forced to move, Naomi, Yoshiko's daughter, associated being in Vancouver with her first awareness of the Internment. When she was a year old, members of her family moved from Ontario to rural BC and then later to Vancouver, and it was in this city that her mother became involved in a Japanese-Canadian community project. She did not recall knowing about the Internment as a young child or prior to their move to Vancouver. 'That was the same time we became aware of it as something in my mother's life,' she stated.[27] Naomi also commented that she could not remember her mother talking about having to move, but she could remember her describing 'what it was like to be a kid in the camp.' This comment is of note, because Yoshiko had reported in her interview that she could not remember anything about her move from Vancouver. The gap in memory remarked upon by Yoshiko is handed down to Naomi, although Naomi may not be aware that it is lack of memory that accounts for it. Naomi also connected her development of awareness of the Internment with Vancouver and in relation to the Japanese Canadian community and her mother's involvement in that community.

Eiko experienced the continuing displacement of her family as her parents moved to British Columbia to assist her grandparents in setting up a business. Born in Toronto in 1951, Eiko moved at the age of four and lived in BC for approximately four years. She explained, 'After the war, grandpa, my dad's dad – you know, none of the property or anything was ever returned – decided to ... start a [business] ... and he needed my dad's help.'[28] She described learning about the Internment 'incidentally' from both of her parents and never as a 'conscious "sit down and we're going to teach you this because you need to know it."'

Kyo, Louise's daughter and the granddaughter of Aya and Ann, was born in Toronto in 1970. She attributed her first awareness of the Internment to the discussions in her family regarding redress. She was a teenager at the time and remembered being at her grandparents' home where family members were discussing compensation. She stated, 'I think I just listened. And I picked up a lot of things from just listening.'[29] This accumulation of knowledge about the Internment came for her 'in bits and pieces as they talked about it more and more in terms of what the government was doing.' Within a family that included grandparents, Kyo became aware of the incarceration of these family members.

Kyo emphasized that her mother told stories about 'camp' that contrasted to stories of her earlier history: 'At one point they were living in a house with running water and electricity on the West Coast; my grandfather had a car and a boat. And suddenly they were in these shacks without [electricity].' This shift from a home to a shack raised the question for Kyo, 'Who decided this?' In both Yuko's and Kyo's situations, the redress movement was a pivotal moment in their hearing or attending to information about the Internment within their families. This political mobilization, therefore, influenced and supported the ability to speak about the incarcerations within familial settings. Working on a community project in Vancouver supported Naomi's mother in speaking about the Internment, and being on a community tour enhanced Yuko's ability to speak to her mother about her history.

Sylvia first learned about the 'events' of the Internment from her cousin, with whom she was very close. Born in 1958, Sylvia grew up in Toronto. She knew 'a little bit about it as a child.'[30] She added, 'Not that my parents volunteered very much information about it or spoke about it at all.' When she was a teenager, she began to ask her mother and father questions. But she recalled 'they'd say they couldn't remember and they wouldn't give many details.' She also added that her mother was 'more reluctant to talk about it than my father.' Sylvia stated that her cousin was pivotal in helping her develop an understanding of the injustice of the Internment. She described coming to the awareness that 'it was wrong' as a gradual process. Sylvia was also told about the Internment by her cousin's mother and 'to some extent' her own mother.

Janice, Esther's daughter, was born in 1965 and grew up in Vancouver. In describing how she acquired knowledge about the Internment, she stated: 'I always had a sense that I always knew. It was never a secret in our family ... It was just part of their lives.'[31] The description she gave to me of how she learned about her family being moved to a sugar beet farm constructed her family as including all of her mother's sisters and brothers who attended their Sunday 'family dinners.' She added that she had always known her family had lived in Manitoba, and, at their dinners, relatives would refer to being 'in the beet fields' and 'they'd always talk about people they knew, and some of the people were from [Manitoba].' Janice remembered the emphasis in the conversations was on returning to Vancouver, 'when we moved back.' As in the case of Kyo and Sylvia, family for Janice includes people outside of the dyadic construction of parents and children. Her aunts and uncles each conveyed information about working on the Manitoba farm. Janice's mother was an active participant in these conversations, and her father, who is white, was also present when these discussions occurred.

Joanne, Evelyn's daughter, was born in 1963. She also reported that accumulating knowledge of her mother's incarceration in Lillooet was a gradual process. 'I don't think there was a point of shock or realization,' she stated, 'I think the knowledge was always integrated. But the meaning of it and the weight of the meaning grew with time.'[32] Joanne also talked about her extended family gathering at her grandmother's home, and it was in this place that her elders were able to talk about their incarceration in Lillooet.

Joanne's uncle talked about her grandmother's Japanese dolls and regretted that 'they're all gone now.' He also told her, 'We had lots of boats.' When she asked him whether he missed fishing, he replied, 'There's nothing like being out in the boat and bringing in fish, the smell of the sea, out there in the ocean. We'd dry fish and cook it.' Joanne's aunt sometimes expressed 'great sadness and loss.'

Irene was born in Toronto in 1959. Many members of her family talked to her about the Internment. She stated, 'It was discussed and references were made to it throughout my life. It didn't occur to anyone in my family to hide it from us. This was their life as they grew up ... [It didn't occur] to my Nisei aunts and uncles to hide it from us.'[33] Place is also an important element in Irene's understanding of the Internment. Her mother 'made references only to ghost towns,' even though she had been incarcerated on a sugar beet farm. Irene's father, however, was incarcerated in a BC interior camp. 'It wasn't until I was in my teens that I realized people went to different places. I think [my mother] made references to ghost towns because that was the general experience of Japanese Canadians.' She recalled her mother discussing this with her more than her father, but she heard her aunts' descriptions of some of her father's experiences when they gathered together for monthly family meetings. The memories Irene inherited, however, are predominantly those of her father's family in the 'ghost towns.' While her mother, Margaret, spoke about the Internment, her own memories of the sugar beet farms were not conveyed until Irene was older. Just as the places of the BC interior camps had affected Margaret's description of her own experience relative to the camps, so too did it appear to affect the knowledge of the Internment passed down to her daughter. The interior camps became emblematic of the Internment in their familial narratives.

Irene described family members as being 'very open. Almost pleased to be asked.' An aunt asked her uncle why he hadn't told her some information about his childhood that he had disclosed to Irene. He replied, 'No one has ever asked me.' Irene concluded, 'There's all this information that no one ever asked him. It's too bad.' According to Margaret, her son did not ask as many questions as Irene did. 'I guess he's heard everything there is to hear,' she surmised. This suggests that siblings may have different knowledge of their parents' histories. Since gendered-divisions of labour and socializing occur within particular spaces, siblings may not have the same access to a person and the space in which histories of the Internment are told.

The family in these testimonies includes members outside of the dyadic relationship of parent and child. Families had to be reconstituted after years of separation and dispersal, and it appears that for these women, the family was one social form in which they were able to resist the total destruction of historical, communal interconnections. These familial spaces, where many family members gather, may provide support for the discussion of memories of the Internment, and are thus sites of knowledge production for children. Children in contact with only their parent[s], therefore, have fewer opportunities to learn about their family's history of incarceration.

Naomi, who lives in Vancouver, described 'having to buy a plane ticket to [a northern Ontario airport] and then having to get on a bus, which took three hours' to reach her grandmother's home. Although she visited her grandmother in the summer when she was a child, she could not stay for long visits. A recent trip to see her grandmother concretized Naomi's feelings that she expressed in this way:

> It really made me angry that she lives there. I was making the connection to that being a part of this internment process. And I thought, I'm all pissed off that I have to [travel so far] and then I thought my grandmother lives there and has lived there for over fifty years ... I would not want to live there ... my grandmother could be here, living with us and having more of a natural relationship with me and my mother and this whole city ...

Naomi's description of the long journey she must undertake from Vancouver to see her grandmother in the place to which she was sent after her incarceration in Slocan, retraces the geography of her grandmother's expulsion. While her own mother finally returned to Vancouver, her grandmother could not make this additional journey. Geography is critical to Naomi's own memory of her family's history of internment and the place of her grandmother's current residence signifies her spatial exclusion and the separation of family members that the Internment promoted.

Naomi's grandmother has a few Japanese Canadian friends, people who were also forced to move to this northern town, but her absence from her daughter and granddaughter is marked by the long distance separating their homes. Naomi believes the reason she can't speak Japanese is 'a direct result of all of this' and 'that's one thing that I'm really upset about.'

While Naomi is able to speak with her grandmother in English, she raised the point of language, also underlined by other women. As a result of the lack of the Japanese language, some of the daughters were unable to speak with their grandparents. Not only do geographic distances impede communication with family members, but so do linguistic differences. The dismantling of the West Coast Japanese Canadian communities through the expulsion and dispersal entailed the destruction of their infrastructures, including institutions such as Japanese-language schools and community religious and spiritual centres, the Buddhist ones in particular. Additionally, the demonization of any cultural associations with Japan was clearly part of the process of constructing Japanese Canadians as the enemy, and was also part of the mechanism of surveillance through their dispersal. How could one learn or maintain the Japanese language without a language teacher, school, or a community with whom one could speak, in places where English speakers constituted Japanese speakers as disloyal to Canada? Given this context, it is not surprising that none of the non-incarcerated daughters I interviewed learned Japanese as children.[34]

Some parents I interviewed felt that their children hold them responsible for this language loss. In her interview quoted in chapter 5, Yoshiko noted that she felt she had to study Japanese under clandestine conditions in the Slocan camp. While she can still 'converse to a certain degree' in Japanese, Yoshiko feels her children are 'so angry ... that I haven't retained the language.' In northern Ontario, 'it was not the thing to do ... I'm sure [my parents] must have struggled ... in bringing up their children,' she explained. 'I don't have any occasion to speak it,' she emphasized, describing the geographical distance between her and her mother. She understands her children's anger and has told them, 'We were schooled out and educated out of [our] own culture, to be assimilated.'[35]

Some might hold parents alone responsible for the lack of Japanese language transmission. This obscures the relations of power impinging upon survivors who had to contend with racism in the places to which they were sent. A liberal discourse might construct these parents as 'choosing' not to speak Japanese; however, we have seen how the discourse of choice negates the material and social constraints on choice. Forced to move from Steveston, where she could speak Japanese with her family and within a community, Aya explained that, living in Winnipeg, she learned English: 'I feel more comfortable in Japanese ... Well, the kids all spoke English, so to converse with them I had to [speak English].'[36]

In one family, the acquisition and practice of English and the disuse of Japanese mark the paths of dispersal and continuing separation of family members years beyond the end of the Internment. As a result, the loss of the Japanese language was reported by Mayumi as an effect of the Internment. Mayumi's mother, Ann, and her father 'only spoke Japanese to each other' when she was a child. She had known her maternal grandmother who spoke some English. Mayumi added,

> I don't speak Japanese. And I think it's a very common trait for my generation. I think it was done so we could assimilate and not appear to be anything but Canadian. But also probably because [language classes] weren't as readily available. But all my other friends went to after school classes for whatever language they happened to speak [in the home].

Ann told me that her mother, Mayumi's grandmother, learned to speak English 'after,' which I took to mean after they were forced to leave the West Coast. Ann thenceforth spoke primarily in English with her. Kyo reported that she can converse with her grandmother, Ann, in English, but that she wasn't able to communicate with her grandfather on a 'critical level' due to her own lack of the Japanese language.

Irene's parents asked her whether she wanted to take Japanese-language classes when she was a child, and she declined. She stated that her maternal grandmother spoke 'quite a bit of English,' but in their later years both of her grandmothers spoke more frequently in their first language and she couldn't communicate with them.

Sylvia never knew her paternal grandparents. Her grandmother died before she was born. She knows her grandfather only from photographs of him holding her when she was a baby. He had lived with her parents and her, and died when she was very young. Her maternal grandparents lived with her uncle in Toronto. 'I didn't know them well because they didn't speak any English. And I, of course, didn't speak any Japanese,' she stated. Although she said that she loved her grandmother, who was especially affectionate towards her, she emphasized that their relationship was 'quite limited.' She added, 'We never had conversations. And she died when I was maybe in my early teens.' Her grandfather lived to be a 102 years, and she spent time with him, but she 'didn't talk to him, didn't really converse.' Sylvia was aware of the intellectual and artistic world inhabited by her grandfather, a world to which she did not have linguistic access:

> Even after the war, he was still in touch with other Japanese Canadians and he wrote haiku poetry. He'd meet in this little rundown house every Sunday afternoon with his poetry group. And they'd read and write and they, in fact, published a book. And I can't read it ... But he had all of those contacts ...

There were social limitations imposed upon families dispersed into white communities. Establishing Japanese-language schools and sending children to these schools was another negotiation families had to make in a country that had incarcerated them based on their construction as foreigners. As was shown in chapter 6, women met with racism in the white areas to which they were moved. In chapter 9, some of their daughters' experiences of racism are described. One of the ways in which Asian children and adults are racially attacked, mentioned by many of the women interviewed, is through the ways in which white people demean Asian languages and approach us with racist and defiling mockeries in schoolyards and other places. Everyday racism, used as a means of disciplining racialized people, can influence our decisions about whether or not to learn or speak a language associated with us.

The 1951 Canadian Census described the 'impressive drop' in number of people of 'Japanese origins' unable to speak English or French from 12.4 per cent in 1941 to 7.5 per cent in 1951.[37] Reducing such a 'drop' to assimilation obscures the processes through which the English or French language become the sign of normality and other processes that ensured their dominant practice. While many of the daughters interviewed had family members from whom they could learn about the Internment, this communication most often occurred in English. Some of the daughters clearly attributed this loss of a language and the lack of or the inability to develop intimate relationships with family members and others who spoke Japanese as their predominant language, especially those of the Issei generation, to the Internment, part of its long-term effect in their lives.

With the loss of language came the loss of linguistic connection to

relatives living in Japan. This book does not undertake an analysis of
the complex relationships that survivors and their children have with
Japan and their relatives there. It is evident that the Internment
and the repatriation survey also produced conflicted relationships with
the people and the nation of Japan. The deportations produced the loss
of thousands of people[38] and the resulting social differences among
Japanese Canadians: those who were deported to Japan and remained
there, those who returned to Canada after their deportation, and
those who were dispersed within Canada. These differences continue
to be lived by the surviving subjects of those policies and subsequent
generations.

Living with Histories and Memories of the Internment

The familial space, as some of the women have suggested, is also one
where memories of the Internment must be managed by survivors.
The following examples illustrate how different women communicate
the experience of expulsion, incarceration, displacement, and dispossession. Rather than being categorically silent about the Internment,
they live with their memories and decide which memories to hand
down.

   Daughters described the content of memories of the Internment in
varying ways. Mayumi reported that she still doesn't 'really understand what happened,' that she can't 'get a picture of it.' She attributed
this gap in her knowledge to her mother's description, which Mayumi
pictured as a 'resort,' drawn from her mother's words that 'they had
a whole house to [them]selves.' But she knew from a 'gut reaction'
that 'somehow Japanese were second class.' Mayumi's niece, Kyo, also
raised the same issue in relation to her grandmother Ann's reference
to being able to live in a 'house' in the camp because they had children
and to her description of herself as 'lucky.' But she also stated that Ann
described having to live in a horse stall with her young children and
that 'they' took her grandfather away.

   When relatives speak the details of the Internment and situate themselves within a 'memory of community,' images are conveyed of loss
and hardship, along with what may appear as a contradictory minimization of these wrongs. This reflects a complex process of negotiating
how to impart information and select the memories and appropriate
means to represent them to younger family members. For example,

Kyo's grandmother, Ann, handed down some of her knowledge of the Internment, but chose not to disclose the pain or her affective response. In addition, Kyo commented that her mother was able to talk to her about the 'historical point of view ... But I don't think we've ever dealt with the emotional side.'

The 'emotional side,' however, may be expressed by other family members. Kyo stated that her great-aunt is 'really bitter' about the death of her brother in Japan. He was in Japan at the outbreak of the war and was not allowed to return to Canada. Yet she has noticed that her grandmother 'never talks' about his death. Children who have access to many family members may therefore acquire different forms of knowledge about the Internment. All adults have to decide whether or not to disclose to children, regardless of their age, the details and hardships of the Internment, and the responsibilities of living day-to-day with these negotiations may be more heavily felt by parents. They may be less likely, therefore, to share the 'emotional side' with their children than other relatives might be.

Access to her mother's sister gave Joanne insight into how another family member viewed her incarceration in Lillooet. Joanne described her mother's account of Lillooet as a 'positive construction,' whereas her aunt refers to being incarcerated as the 'ruin of her life.' Janice remarked that she has not heard her family members say the word 'racism.' Irene stated that family members described the Internment 'more on a human level than the political issues.' She explained this by saying she thought her family was 'not political at all.' However, Yoshiko's father sometimes talked about the 'political conditions,' and said 'what a shame' the people he had known in Vancouver 'weren't able to go to university' because they all had 'that potential' in the pre-Internment period. Yet her parents never talked about the 'things that they lost.' Midori's parents told her stories, but 'they wouldn't always say exactly what the story was about.' By contrast, S., Midori's mother, explained how she and her husband conveyed this history to their children:

> They may not thoroughly understand what it was all about, but they did know what we went through ... We never tried to ... bring it up as a point of education or anything you should learn because we went through this. That's not the way we use it. As a matter of information, we tell them. What they do with that information is up to them. But it's more from what they can observe themselves. And they know what we have been through.

S.'s explanation suggests that knowledge acquisition for children of survivors also involves decision-making on their part. They can find out more about the Internment and then 'do' something with the information.

Despite Janice's recollection of the many ways in which her family's experiences of being moved to work on a sugar beet farm have been conveyed to her by different family members, her mother, Esther, speculated that Janice 'might tell you that it was something that just never really was discussed.'[39] The dissonances between how women who were interned felt they were conveying or not conveying information about the Internment, and how their daughters felt they had received or not received information are processes more complex than the word 'silence' might suggest. That Japanese Canadians feel responsible and are held solely responsible for this re-membering and speaking, especially by non-Japanese Canadians, obscures relations of power and the effects of the Internment, for those interned, their children, and for other persons whose 'not knowing' is an effect of the forgetting of the Internment. It also ignores the fact that survivors live and struggle with the limits of what they know and remember, and what they feel they can impart to their children about the complex experiences of expulsion, incarceration, forced labour, deportation, and dispersal.

The age of a child is a factor in some parents' decisions whether or not to describe the details of the Internment or their analyses of them to their children. This age-appropriate transmission of knowledge is not unique to the issue of the Internment. However, given the pain that is inherently embedded within these 'stories,' parents who wish to manage their children's exposure to the traumatic details must deliberate about what to tell them and how they should be told. Joanne said her mother's family 'didn't talk about it in terms of injustice'; however, 'those sorts of stories came later,' when she was older. One of Ann's grandchildren interviewed her for a project, yet she felt the younger ones 'are not at the age to ask [questions] yet.' 'I think that, at one time or another, they should be told what happened,' she emphasized.[40]

The familial space is therefore one of pedagogical strategy in relation to how the history of Internment is communicated. What is not conveyed in the portrayal of Japanese Canadians as being silent about the Internment is how difficult it is to re-member and speak about it because it necessitates controlling the 'images flashing up in the moment,' especially when speaking to children. What children describe as the gaps in their understanding of the Internment, the silences sometimes equated with 'no speech,' is integrally linked to this negotiation. While survivors must continually manage their own memories and knowledge of the Internment within the family, in deciding to hand down their knowledge they must consciously decide how and what they will reveal. Some of the gaps (for example, not expressing one's feelings about certain events, not giving details of certain events, or emphasizing the 'good' times) can be attempts to avoid handing down the pain and grief. The gaps may also reflect the lack of memory or knowledge of specific details for the reasons suggested in chapter 3. In addition, the language of the Internment, coined in the 1940s, including government euphemisms, may continue to inform what words survivors do and do not articulate. Survivors have been burdened with the daunting task of transmitting their knowledge of the Internment. Therefore the work of parent survivors in the familial space is one of enormous importance and struggle that requires support.

Children also struggle with asking about the Internment within the familial space. Yuko described the Internment as 'almost like a taboo subject in some ways.' She explained the dynamic with her mother, 'It's funny because I don't press it and she doesn't offer.' Naomi explained what was required for her to ask her grandmother about her experience:

> To this day, I haven't talked to [my grandmother] about it ... This is not something that you just lightly [ask about]. It's not a casual issue ... I'm sure that I could talk to her about it. But I feel I have to learn a little bit more first and be aware of a lot more things before I feel confident and comfortable in doing that.

With an awareness that conversations regarding the Internment may affect their family members, some daughters take great care when they initiate these discussions. Just as parents develop strategies to cope with the memories they live with, children also develop strategies for living with the memories shared and not shared in their own families.

Just as the effects induced by the Internment inform the abilities of survivors to communicate this experience to others, its effects also inform our interpretations of these testimonies. The psychological notion of 'secondary victimization'[41] may be useful in acknowledging how survivors' children hear and read testimonial accounts and representations of the Internment. It is troubling, however, when a term like 'vicarious traumatization'[42] is applied indiscriminately to witnesses to accounts of violence; the notion that people are traumatized by witnessing accounts of violence should be problematized to address how we are differently positioned socially in relation to the violence we are witnessing. For example, children of those who were interned are differently socially located from those who do not come from families who were interned.

Children of people interned may respond to what is communicated to them about the Internment by trying to fill in the gaps in their knowledge of their families' histories and the Internment by writing what Roger Simon and Wendy Armitage-Simon describe as 'shadow texts.' The 'shadow texts' are the 'secondary narratives constructed in response to the unresolved questions a primary narrative elicits.'[43] As I argue below, the gaps in knowledge themselves are effects of the Internment. Children and descendants of people interned live with what becomes internalized as *their* gaps in knowledge and *their* inability to fill in all of the blanks in a cartography of violence, 'since the perception and filling of a gap lead to the awareness of other gaps.'[44] As I illustrate in the next chapter, some daughters create representational spaces for the production of these shadow texts in efforts to fill in their own gaps in knowledge and to analyse the Internment and its effects.

Visualizing the Places of the Internment through Photographs

Methods that assist in visualizing and imagining the places of incarceration are used by some of the children of survivors in order to learn about the Interment.[45] Marita Sturken refers to such methods and the objects, images, and representations used as 'technologies of memory' that are not passive 'vessels of memory,' but are 'objects through which memories are shared, produced, and given meaning.'[46] She emphasizes that technologies of memory are 'inevitably implicated in power dynamics ... [and] are also practices that people enact upon themselves.'[47]

Joanne, like Mayumi, talked about using photographs to visualize the family's life before, during, and after the Internment. Stories of moving from place to place and the different landscapes and conditions conveyed hardship and toil. Joanne stated: 'Through ... different uncles and aunts at family gatherings, different stories [were told] when we would be asking about the photos. Mom would talk about having to go to school in a tent.' The photos at her grandmother's house were a vital visual aid. She remembered looking at the photos when she was a child and seeing her mother's life in Vancouver; the photos conveyed 'a sense of beautiful clothes, house, different activities, like going shopping and running freely around Powell Street.' On the other hand, the photographs from Lillooet and her mother's description of it conveyed a 'sense of the tent schoolhouses, having to pick tomatoes ... While it was adventuresome, there's this sense of a desolate landscape.'

Like Joanne and Mayumi, Janice and Kyo also stated that photographs enhanced their understanding of the Internment. As did Joanne, Janice situated her understanding of the hardship of the beet farms by comparing the photos her mother has kept from her parents' duties as *baishakunin* (matchmakers) to the photos taken on the sugar beet farms. 'You have the real working photos of them in the fields. And then you have these really beautiful glamorous studio wedding portraits of all these people we don't really know. You can see my grandpa and grandma in [all of these photos].'[48] The photographs were always accessible to Janice and served as a continual technology of memory, commemorating Janice's grandparents and documenting the shifts in place and living conditions. She recounted, 'I remember always looking at those, and my mom never put them away. You could always pull them out and look through them all the time. So I always knew that they'd lived there [in Manitoba] and moved back.' Janice's mother, Esther, offered to show me family photographs at the end of her interview (although time precluded this), reinforcing how photographs are used in their family to enhance knowledge production.

Kyo actually showed me a family photograph during her interview. While talking about her paternal grandmother, Ann, she used the photograph to describe what had happened to the various members of the family as a result of the Internment, the separations of family members and the death of her grandmother's brother who was in Japan during the war. Like Joanne and Janice, by using this technology of memory, Kyo was able to imagine a pre-Internment familial space. Through information provided by her grandmother and other family members, she understood why her grandmother's sisters now live in two different Canadian cities; from putting together the pieces, she gained an understanding that these separations were the direct result of the Internment. The knowledge she had acquired to date included the fact that her great-uncle had died and her great-aunt was 'really bitter' about his death. This 'bitterness' was related to the fact that her great-grandfather was a Canadian veteran of the First World War and despite this act of loyalty to Canada, their family had been interned, dispossessed, and separated. Kyo used the photograph to understand the effects of the Internment on her family and to transmit this knowledge visually to me. In this way, she enacted an embodiment of the memories handed down to her and used the photograph as the 'substitute for the body' of all those represented through its image, using this technology to analyse 'institutions and practices' promulgated through the Internment.[49]

Yoshiko, who was incarcerated in Slocan, spoke about the importance of photographs in her continuing development of knowledge about the Internment. She knew that her family had been dispossessed of items, such as Japanese dolls: she saw them in the photographs, but they had lost the dolls during the expulsion. These photographs were located in their home. While she described her parents as 'never talking' about the Internment, she stated that when she was older, she and her siblings would ask questions about 'the things in the pictures and then they would talk about people ... It was wonderful, everybody becomes alive through the pictures. So that was where we got most of our information about people.' As I stated in chapter 3, survivors, as well as being involved in a process of knowledge transmission, are also engaged in acquiring knowledge from various sources, and this production of knowledge and its transmission are constantly shifting and are not fixed as the trope of silence suggests.

Photographs, therefore, were an important resource used by survivors and their daughters to convey and discern the changes in place and social position that occurred from a pre-Internment period to the years of incarceration and dispersal. Yet given the government's policy of confiscating cameras at the outset of the expulsion,[50] many people may not have photographs as documentation of their places of incarceration and dispersal. Many photographs from the pre-Internment period, including those taken of relatives in Japan, were also lost in the forced movement from the coast. Photographs depicting the history particular to one's own family, therefore, may not be available as a technology of memory. This lack of family photos is yet another loss.

The Critical Function of Representation in Acquiring Knowledge of the Internment

Representation is critical in providing another means of handing down the knowledge of the Internment. In addition to memories, other representational forms, such as photographs, communicate this history to children of survivors. Yoshiko's daughter, Naomi, mentioned the importance of 'trying to get some images' of the Internment and watching films about the Holocaust to try to imagine what 'prison camps' were like. She also remembered seeing a picture from a book on the Internment depicting a 'group of women' in a camp. She concluded from the picture that the interior camps were 'where there were lots of women and children.' She connected this image to her knowledge that her mother's father was separated from the family and sent to a road camp. The memory of the group photograph of the women, in conjunction with the information that her grandfather was separated from his family, was used by her to imagine who was separated and where they were sent.

Both Joanne and Kyo specifically mentioned the use of the book *A Child in Prison Camp,* by Shizuye Takashima, in expanding their comprehension of their mothers' histories. Joanne stated that her mother gave that book and others to her and her siblings: 'I knew those books were about ... what she and her family went through ... Takashima's book was another way for us ... to imagine Lillooet.' Kyo compared Takashima's description of 'taking a walk to the river to get water,' to her mother's account of 'going with her sister to fetch water' in the camp. Kyo's maternal grandmother, Aya, also mentioned the importance of books in teaching children about the Internment. She thought they would not know about it unless 'we tell them the history of what we went through and reading the books.' While she reported that her grandchildren asked her about the Internment, she qualified what she thought was really possible for them to know by adding, 'You have to experience it, or otherwise it doesn't click in your mind.'

Irene went to her public school library 'week after week' to 'try to figure out who [she] was.' In grades five and six, she took out books on Japan and then realized that 'Japan ... is over here and maybe it's a part of me, but not really.' Her comments underline that the gaps in knowledge about the Internment are evident in institutions such as the school when books on the Internment are not available. Yet her weekly search speaks of the desire to acquire more knowledge about her history in Canada.

Janice's first exposure to a book on the Internment was one about the U.S. incarcerations. She later became aware of a Canadian book, but wanted to use visual representations in a school project and therefore she used the U.S. book because of its photographs. Her preference for the photographic imagery in the U.S. book illustrates that people attend to information in different ways. If visual representation is useful to learning about the Internment, then perhaps it should be recognized as a technology that is different but as valuable as speech or text in the transmission of this history to subsequent generations.

The difficulties in reading or viewing representations of the Internment, however, were speculated upon by Eiko. She stated, 'I haven't done a lot of reading. One always wonders psychologically if I'm just in this perpetual state of denial. I don't think so, but I do wonder why I haven't gotten more into [reading] ... It's hard to figure it all out.' As I argued earlier, reading or viewing representations of the Internment exposes survivors and their children to traumatic material intrinsically connected to their identities. Thus, supports should be made available to Japanese Canadian survivors and their families so that these sightings of the places, policies, experiences, and discourses of Internment do not have to be engaged in alone.

While all of the women who mentioned the importance of photographs used them as an adjunct to their conversations in familial spaces, other children of families who were incarcerated may have limited access to this representation or may feel they cannot discuss it with family members. It is evident, however, from the use of photographs in the production of knowledge of the Internment, that imagining the places of incarceration enhances a daughter's understandings of what that experience meant for family members. Other forms of representation, including written texts, visual, sound, and performative media are also important in supporting survivors and their children in the handing down of this history. This cultural production on the Internment would include community-based projects, multimedia artistic representation, and academic research. We cannot trust, however, that critical representations will be supported by publishing houses or government funding sources and must develop strategies to ensure that representational work is produced by people who understand that this work itself produces effects, including notions of Japanese Canadians, and affects them.

We must also identify, translate, and keep in print critical texts, such as Ann Sunahara's book *The Politics of Racism*,[51] find ways to access restricted documents at the LAC, and make documents housed in various archives more accessible to survivors and their descendants. In addition, we must find ways of supporting community projects that resist the forgetting of the Internment. Projects such as the Nikkei Internment Memorial Centre, which marks the site of New Denver as one where Japanese Canadians were incarcerated and still live as a result of the Internment, are important geographic reminders and necessary to a practice of commemoration. Discussions about the politics and practices of commemoration must also be engaged. However, on a terrain where Japanese Canadians' expulsion, incarceration, and dispersal have been materially and discursively obscured, we need to think about how to re-member and mark these carceral places for ourselves and future generations. Much representational work is ongoing within families. May's mother began to write her own history, and now her daughter Eiko 'is really after [her] to get [her] story down.' These individual projects may never be acknowledged publicly, but they inspire us to think of different ways in which we might create representational spaces through which to pass on our knowledge.

Although those who were interned have been variously described as silent about the Internment, we have, in fact, depended upon their speech, inviting survivors to speak at special commemorative events and educational functions, or to be interviewed in projects such as this one. Alice Yang Murray has suggested that mobilizations of survivors' memories were critical to the redress movement in the United States;[52] survivors' memories were also critical to the initiation and execution of the Canadian redress struggle.[53] This dependence upon embodied transmission of the history was reinforced by Eiko, who asked me, 'What happens when the last internment camp survivor dies?' The process of handing down the history will therefore change in subsequent generations.

Most survivors rarely have the public venues to critique representations of themselves and the Internment. May shared with me some of her own criticism of this representation. Her mother had been very active in a community organization about which a book was written, yet her mother was not even mentioned in the book. May felt this omission 'hurt her.' While May emphasized, 'I don't think it was malice ... I think it was simply an oversight,' she then speculated, 'I also think that if it were a man who had done this [work in the organization], the oversight wouldn't have taken place.' May's comment reminds us that patriarchy affects representation, in both senses of the word.

In acknowledging attempts by Sansei and Yonsei to represent the Internment, May impressed upon me that she 'resent[ed] third- and fourth-generation persons writing about [her] experience and saying we were like slaves.' Her comment indicates the need to construct herself in opposition to such representations authored by Sansei and Yonsei. There have, however, been survivors who have described their treatment as a form of slavery;[54] those who were in the forced labour sites draw upon different discourses to depict their experiences. May offered this explanation, 'What happened was completely contrary to what the bigoted politicians aimed for when they moved us out. In the larger picture, they certainly didn't get rid of us or put us down.'[55] I take May's comments as a challenge to understand the impact of our representational work upon survivors; we must begin by examining our own social locations in relation to our efforts to re-member. With her expression of protest against objectifying portrayals of Japanese Canadians, May is also conscious of what the government's aims were – to 'get rid of us' and 'put us down.'

Concomitant with one's desire to produce representational work on the Internment, therefore, is one's responsibility to consider its effects for Japanese Canadians, survivors in particular. As Kirsten Emiko McAllister states, we must work towards 'critical cultural production' that is 'self-reflexive' and creates the 'capacity to discern and critique not only the efficacy of various actions, but the implications of its own epistemological framework.'[56] As is evident by some of the critiques raised regarding the representation of the Internment and Japanese Canadians, I find some of this representation troubling. Yet I also view the continuing production of work by Japanese Canadians as part of a commemorative practice,[57] reflecting our efforts to bear witness to this history and our desire to bring this knowledge to others into the present and future.

I would also suggest that non-Japanese Canadians similarly interrogate their relationship to the Internment and to the people they claim to be re-presenting. Lacunae in the works authored by many of them are analyses of their own social positions or those of their families or forebears in relation to the Internment. This lack of analysis of the writing subject's position sidesteps important questions of their relationships to the people interned. 'Why are you writing about Japanese Canadians? Do you consider the effects of your representation on Japanese Canadians?' are questions I would ask. The academic response to the novel *Obasan* illustrates that many non-Japanese Canadians are writing about us and generating critical commentaries about our work at the same time as problematic images of Japanese Canadians are being produced and being received uncritically by their audiences. I know that some Japanese Canadians may disagree with my analysis or conclusions, but given that I live and work in relation to their communities, I live the consequences of my work in a different way from those who have little or no contact with Japanese Canadians.

Returning to the Places of Home and of Incarceration

Returning to British Columbia and viewing both the home sites from which Japanese Canadian communities were forcibly moved and the places of incarceration is another way in which daughters reported acquiring more knowledge about the Internment. Survivors who visit these places with their children imbue 'empty' or 'differently' occupied spaces with meaning derived from their experiences and their memories of community. In this way, 'places and spaces are actualized and endowed with meaning'[58] by survivors and their families, and they resist the erasure of their history and the normalization of space as it is presently configured. '[I]n generating [these] antithetical place-myths,'[59] Japanese Canadians contest the 'place-myths' that forget the Internment and Canada's history of racism.

While a young child such as Yuko, as described above, did not fully understand the significance held by her parents for these places of home and incarceration, returning to see them is an embodied means of communicating part of an Internment history to family members. The places themselves and their use in relation to Japanese Canadians can then become etched in the memory of survivors' children and are available to them to use in developing knowledge of the Internment despite the other meanings associated with these places that render them benign.

When Midori was in high school, her parents took her to their former homes in British Columbia. She described her memory of her mother's reaction in this way, 'I remember driving down the street where my mom used to live. Her house was still standing. She was really excited.' Years later, she accompanied her parents to the sites where they were incarcerated. When they visited Tashme, her mother tried to figure out where the houses had been. She reconfigured the 'empty' space through her recollections: 'I think it must have been over there. There were some barns there.' She was able to reconstruct where her family had lived in relation to the barns, and was then able to describe the locations of other buildings occupied by particular people. Midori concluded from this trip with her parents, 'You go there and stories come out.'

'Going back' to British Columbia was something that Kazuko did with her son-in-law, who is white. 'It was very nice of him to take me,' she stated. She had not returned to the province since she left Rosebery. The Internment history is not only handed down to children of survivors, it can also be transmitted to non-Japanese Canadian partners, relatives, and friends. In this way, survivors can affect how the nation is imagined by non-Japanese Canadians, widening the possibilities for re-membering and for re-imagining.

Eiko's aunt, her father's sister, took her to the farm they had owned. She explained that it is now worth 'ten million [dollars] U.S.' and is a 'prime property.' Mayumi, her partner, and their children accompanied Ann to British Columbia where they saw the memorial dedicated to Japanese Canadian veterans in Stanley Park and read Ann's father's name engraved on it. Naomi, who lives in Vancouver, has become aware that Powell Street is now differently organized than it was when her grandmother lived there. 'There was an amazing community here ... which you could never imagine just going down to Powell Street now. That just disappeared, you know, that's gone,'[60] she emphasized. The desire to view the places of her parents' and grandparents' incarcerations was expressed by Kyo, who stated that 'it would be really interesting to go back to the interior of BC and see how I would react to that.' She wondered how she would identify the sites and what remained of their former use, 'I think they have little plaques saying things, but I don't know if they've actually, you know, kept a shack.' This return to British Columbia and carceral sites in other provinces in order to *place* the Internment was envisioned by some women as something they will continue to do with their own children. Sylvia told me she planned to take her child to British Columbia when she is older in order to explain to her what happened to her family during the Internment.

The importance of returning to the place of her father's incarceration is recounted by Midge Ayukawa:

> For 50 years, I had been obsessed by a need to see where my father had been in the spring of 1942. In the months and years that followed, after our family was whole again, we lived in Lemon Creek, in an ex-German POW camp in Neys, Ontario, and in Hamilton ... finally in September this year ... Our aim was to find Thunder River – and I finally had!
>
> I closed my eyes and silently spoke to my father. 'Papa, I am here at the Thunder River road camp site. It's beautiful – but it must have been so cold, so full of snow when you first came here! *Taihen – data – desho!*' ... How worried my father must have been about my mother, my brothers and yes, me, his only daughter whom he doted upon. How can we ever forget or dismiss the existence of such camps? The least we can do is to erect some landmark, so that others who felt the way I did can at least locate the sites. One 80-plus-year-old woman whom I recently interviewed regretfully told

me of a recent trip on the Yellowhead Highway when she searched in vain for the location of Lempriere where her husband had been sent. How well I could understand her feelings![61]

Survivors employ different strategies in coping with the difficulties that the re-sighting of the Internment places may invoke, including decisions not to return to these sites. Their children may witness their decisions, for example, not to return to visit British Columbia or go to the vicinity or location of an incarceration site. When Janice was 'really young,' she noticed that one member of her extended family could not go 'by the barns' whenever they went to the Pacific National Exhibition. Janice's aunt explained to her that her relative couldn't stand to go near the barns 'because she was in the barns.' As a child, Janice 'couldn't quite figure out why' her relative had been 'in the barns.' As she accumulated more knowledge about where her family members were incarcerated, she learned that this woman was put in the barns in Hastings Park and 'it was so horrible ... because ... their father was actually taken right away. He was sent to a work camp.' She compared this experience to her mother's family, where her grandmother and grandfather were together and were with their children on the sugar beet farm. In this way, Janice demonstrated that *she* developed a memory of community that made the connections between the different places, how they were different yet related, and that the places affect what story is told. Importantly, seeing the spatialization of the Internment and the connections between all the places and the people interned assists us in understanding the Internment's effects.

In addition to the painful memories generated by revisiting the incarceration sites,[62] survivors and their descendants must deal with the racialization and racism that may occur when their physical presence in these places raises questions about the processes of their historical erasure. Although Kyo expressed the desire to see the places where her parents had been incarcerated, she described her first visit to British Columbia as one where she experienced racism. In the early 1990s, she travelled from Toronto to meet for the first time her white ex-boyfriend's family who lived in British Columbia. After his family picked her up at the airport, his grandmother kept repeating remarks about the '"Japs" bombing ...' in the car ride to the family home where she was to meet her boyfriend. Kyo had to deal with the racism of the situation herself, as no one else in the car challenged the woman's statements. Her comment that 'I'm sort of angry at myself that I didn't say anything' illustrates how racialized people feel responsible for challenging racist assaults while experiencing the shock and trauma of those remarks. She described her feelings about visiting British Columbia in this way, 'As beautiful as the West Coast may be ... I think a lot of those racist, overt racist attitudes still exist out there.'

Japanese Canadian Community Spaces

In thinking about Japanese Canadian communities and the Internment, I hold many memories of the people who have inspired me to re-member in different ways. One memory is of my mother with whom I attended a bazaar at the Toronto Buddhist Church. In the lively setting of the dining hall, we were seated at a long crowded table and my mother began to speak to the woman beside her. I had the sense that I was witnessing another reunion between my mother and someone she had not seen in a very long time. I later discovered that the woman seated next to her had been her Japanese-language teacher prior to her incarceration in Slocan. She told me she had not seen her since she was a child. As I witnessed this and as I have witnessed other reunions be-tween my parents and the people from 'before,' I have been struck by their significance. It has become important to me to find ways where I, too, would be challenged to re-member and be part of a commu-nity of memory. Japanese Canadian community spaces can therefore be critical to a commemorative practice. As the example of my mother illustrates, survivors who enter diverse Japanese Canadian spaces con-tinue to build upon their own knowledge of the Internment through encounters with other survivors, some of whom they have not seen since they were moved from their homes on the West Coast or from the incarceration sites. Although the conversations held in community spaces may not always impart to witnessing children specific informa-tion about the Internment, just being in the presence of these reunions has conveyed to me how extensive my parents' and grandparents' fa-milial and communal relationships were before the expulsion and that these relationships were disrupted, changed, or ended through the Internment.

Hence, one of the effects of the Internment articulated by some of the daughters interviewed was that of being spatially separated from other Japanese Canadians. In addition to being separated from her grand-mother, as was explained by Naomi above, she described this effect of the Internment and dispersal, 'There's no Japantown, like there's Chinatown. I have no connection to that sense of community.' Mayumi grew up in Toronto; she reported, 'I didn't know any Japanese people.' Despite living in Vancouver and Toronto, respectively, the two cities with the largest number of Japanese Canadians,[63] Naomi and Mayumi demonstrated a lack of connection to Japanese Canadians outside of their families. Yuko also described growing up in Toronto without a community of Japanese Canadians: 'I think it [the internment] affected the way I was raised. I think it affected the whole community. I think it was as a result of the internment that they all spread out. And they tried more than anything to be like the mainstream Canadian.' Midori, who grew up in a Prairie province, explained her sense of isolation from other Japanese Canadians as an outcome of the Internment, and she compared her own experience to others whose geographies of childhood and family were differently forged:

I'm fairly sure the connection to the Japanese Canadian community wouldn't have come so late in my life. I think a lot of Sansei are really isolated when they're young. I've met some people who grew up in North Vancouver or whatever and same sort of story, you know, they didn't really have that much connection to the community. Although, that really depends on the family. Some people took their kids to JC community events and they would get to know people. Or they have a lot of relatives and that's how they were involved.

Therefore, as Midori suggests, Japanese Canadian spaces can be important in resisting the effects of the Internment. As in the example of my mother above, it is in these spaces where survivors meet people who knew them from before or during the Internment and with whom they can speak about this history while adding to their own knowledge of the other person's experiences since their last encounter. Louise reported that when she meets people for the first time in a community setting, she asks: '"Where were you during the internment?" and things like that ... You find out where they were and whether they knew so and so.'[64] These 'reunions' are sometimes formalized through dinners organized by people who were incarcerated in particular places. In this way, survivors create their own places for commemoration and being together. The dinners in Toronto are usually held at the Japanese Canadian Cultural Centre. Kazuko has attended one reunion and met people from her home town whom she had not seen since before her forced move to Hastings Park. She told me it was difficult to recognize some of her former neighbours and friends because 'most of them have grey hair now and some of them have lost a lot of weight ... But most of them you recognize.' She added it is 'quite expensive' to attend these dinners.[65] Their cost may therefore be prohibitive to some people.

Living in Vancouver is a critical site of learning about the Internment for Midori. She adds to her knowledge in talking with friends whose parents were interned and through activities such as the Powell Street Festival, an annual event held in Vancouver's Oppenheimer Park.[66] Midori has witnessed people 'who come back' to British Columbia at the festival site and 'meet up with their old friends in the park.' For Midori, these meetings generate discussions about 'the internment.' One of Midori's friends met her parents while they were visiting Vancouver, and through this meeting Midori realized that her parents knew people in her friend's family. This friend is one with whom she can discuss her history. Midori emphasized, however, that she learns the most about the Internment from her parents.

Midori witnesses her parents and family members re-member family and communal relationships each time they discuss people they knew. At one family gathering, they watched a film containing shots of people taken during the Internment, and her parents and other family members verbally sketched out the familial relationships of each person they identified. She described witnessing their memory of community in this way:

What I always find interesting about my parents' generation is they know all these Japanese Canadians and their families. It's so different from most of the people I know my age who know some people. But they know who the parents were, all the brothers and sisters. Who they married. The brothers and sisters [of the partners]. You know, it's just like this huge network of families ... It's just incredible to listen. I don't know how they remember all the names ... I should pay more attention because it'll be lost.

Like Midori, I too have witnessed this phenomenal reconstruction of a network of relationships, rendered in seconds before my eyes. I once remarked to my friend Toshi Oikawa that I wished that I could remember all the interfamilial connections in the ways in which my Nisei family members and friends demonstrate to me regularly. She responded, 'We can remember because we knew each other before, when we were all together.'[67] Although some of these reconstructions may not even mention the incarcerations, they convey an idea of what was, the will to re-member what was, and the connections between people.

In her book *Bittersweet Passage*, Maryka Omatsu describes how being in Japanese-Canadian community spaces during the redress struggle actively engaged her with these memories of pre-Internment communities. She was often asked if she 'was related to such and such a person.' On occasion, people would tell her an 'unknown story about [her] father or [her] family.'[68] These spaces for re-membering are therefore critical to supporting speech about the Internment and the people interned. Descendants of survivors who enter these representational spaces created by our elders, as well as those we create ourselves, may have opportunities to learn more about the Internment and explore our own relationships to that history.

Japanese Canadian community spaces are not always ones where everyone feels supported, however. As Kirsten Emiko McAllister reminds us, the concept of 'community' is useful as long as we recognize that communities are 'not necessarily or primarily organized around undermining the relations of subordination in which its members are situated.'[69] When Naomi first moved to Vancouver, it was difficult for her to participate in some of the community events, and she felt excluded by some community members. Even though she has lived in Vancouver all of her life, Janice did not attend the Powell Street Festival until the 1990s. She appreciates that the festival is 'coming from certain traditions, but it's transforming and creating something entirely new.' Japanese Canadian community spaces are not therefore unitarily exclusionary or inclusionary. The same community space may have multiple and different meanings for each participant.

Returning to British Columbia offers generations of the Internment opportunities to see pre-Internment homes, if they are still standing, and some of the incarceration sites. Different Japanese Canadian individuals and organizations have formalized commemorative visits to the camp sites in the BC interior to provide survivors, their families, and others with an opportunity to re-member and learn about the Internment.[70] Yuko stated that going on a tour enabled her to speak with her mother about her experiences. Irene participated in one tour and described it in this way: 'Hearing the stories of the people as we passed through the different internment camps, hearing it from the people who experienced it, was something.' The tour may also impress upon subsequent generations how spatial separations through incarceration and dispersal shifted the configurations of their families. On the tour, Irene met some of her father's relatives for the first time and learned about him from speaking with them: 'It was great to connect with people who knew his family or lived down the street from his family in [the camp] and hear some of their stories about the family or just about living [there] and that whole experience.' Her mother, however, emphasized the spatial differences in the Internment process in commenting that visiting only the BC camp sites presents a limited view.

My aunt, Kiyoko (married to my uncle Norman Oikawa) and I participated in a tour in 1992. Something she said when we were standing at the site of Tashme, the camp where this aunt, my paternal grandmother, and my uncles were incarcerated, has stayed with me. She remarked that the children who want to know more about the Internment should participate in the community tours, adding, 'We can't tell you everything ourselves, but when you see where we were, you will find out more about what it was like for us.'[71]

Other means of understanding the spatial and social impact of the Internment have become formalized through individual and community effort. While these contributions are too numerous to mention here, they have included tours of the Powell Street area conducted by Audrey Kobayashi, whose descriptions of the 1941 locations of businesses and community organizations gave a stark lesson on what was dismantled and lost in the 1942 expulsion.[72]

These efforts to build an understanding of the Internment and of the importance of communal spaces are not just a reflection of present-day efforts, however. Haru reminded me of this in her interview when she told me her husband decided he wanted one of their daughters to go to Washington to attend a Japanese American Conference in the 1960s. Their daughter, who was a teenager at the time, asked her father, 'What do I want to go there for?' Nevertheless, she attended the conference. Its importance for her was remembered in this way by Haru: 'She was so impressed ... She just raved.' When I interviewed Yuko, she too mentioned the conference as an important event for her sister, contextualizing it in this way: 'my oldest sister went ... And I'm really sorry that I didn't go. I wasn't ready, obviously, to go.'

Interrogating the Notion of *A* Japanese Canadian Community

While women have reported the ability to learn about the Internment in community spaces, these spaces are not intrinsically liberatory. To paraphrase McAllister's insight about the use of the term 'community,' what if the communal projects we organize were 'primarily organized around undermining the relations of subordination in which its members are situated'?[73] In Japanese Canadian community organizing, therefore, we would have to look at where our positions of dominance (for example, class, gender, ability, sexuality, English language facility, age, etc.) are used to dominate or exclude others.

Despite the use of the term 'community,' all of the women traced differences between Japanese Canadians, both in their descriptions of different experiences of incarceration and in how they saw themselves, some using different identifiers while critiquing them. For example, Yuko participated in the development of anti-discrimination policies in her workplace as well as other social justice projects. She stated, 'I don't represent all Japanese Canadian women. I try ... to not have people [make] a generalization about *all* Japanese Canadians are like this or *all* Japanese Canadian women are like this.'

Midori also argued against the homogeneous construction of Japanese Canadians. Referring to the Japanese Canadian communities in Vancouver, she said, 'It's not something that you can generalize.' She pointed out that the Vancouver communities are made up of those whose families were interned, those whose families have immigrated to Canada in the post-Internment period, and those who have immigrated more recently: 'Trying to classify that as a unified group is pretty difficult.' In expressing her alienation from some activities in the Japanese Canadian community in Vancouver, Naomi emphasized that she constitutes herself as Japanese Canadian through her connections to her Japanese Canadian family and friends. She felt that the Japanese Canadian community has 'a lot of different parts ... we are a part of that as well.'

Janice told me that she plans to have children with her white male partner and thinks they 'won't look Asian at all ... [but] they're going to identify with being JC.' Janice added that her children might be questioned about this identification, but for her, identity is about how you understand yourself in relation to your familial and communal history:

> How I perceive myself to be Japanese Canadian isn't how I look, because that isn't my defining thing to the outside world. It's ... your values, how you treat your family, your relationships with people. I know for my kids too that's what their cultural identity is going to be. It's not going to be [from] taking *odori* and learning to do flower arranging ... It's going to be the fact that they know who all their cousins are. They'll know about their aunts and uncles. They'll know about their grandparents, and they'll know everything that's happened to our family. The idea of people identifying with who they are is knowing who you actually are.

Sylvia, whose partner is white, also wondered how her daughter will be racially constructed by others but is clear about how she wants her to see herself. When she was a child, racist and sexist constructions of Japanese Canadian women produced the feeling that she did not look 'right' because she 'didn't look white.' In thinking about her child, she stated, 'She doesn't look all that Japanese' but 'I don't want her to think that she's white.' She added, 'I want her to be aware of her ancestry, and I want her to socialize with other Japanese Canadians,' and concluded, 'I want her to be very aware of who she is.'

Effects of the Internment for Non-Interned Daughters

More work must be done to analyse the long-term effects of the Internment for subsequent generations. Losses such as growing up geographically and/or linguistically separated from grandparents and other family members and a community with whom one shares a history of the Internment were noted in this chapter. The lack of acquisition of the Japanese language was emphasized as a barrier to knowing elder Japanese Canadians and relatives whose dominant or only language was Japanese.

The return to British Columbia to view home and community sites is emblematic of the need to see the effects of the expulsion, the 'before' of our parents' and grandparents' lives compared to the 'after' of the incarceration sites. As I have argued throughout the book, the geography of the Internment and the dispersal affect memories of those experiences. This connection to place is also handed down to children of those interned through the place names of home and carceral sites, and the encoded spatial lexicon that includes the words Hastings Park, camp, hostels, self-support, sugar beet farms, and others. The discourses of the Internment themselves, therefore, are an effect of the Internment that includes government euphemisms still in use today. Our inability to describe 'it,' due in part to this euphemistic language and the spatial differences between the sites, is also an effect.

Many women mentioned the loss of property and possessions, a material reminder that others had benefited from their families' dispossession. The return to view places of home also exemplifies the material losses sustained, but at the same time the erasure of the losses. Dispossession has become normalized through ownership, regardless of its means, through property rights entrenched by a settler system of law that also legally authorized the dispossession of Indigenous peoples.[74]

Thus a Japanese Canadian woman standing on Powell Street or before the home once owned by her parents or grandparents re-members the subjects of the Internment, including herself, while these subjects have been largely erased from these places and the memories of the current occupants.

Mayumi speculated that her extended family tries to counter these past losses or those that might be impending in the future by holding onto possessions: 'I think a common thread for my whole family is that we're pack rats.' When I asked her what the connection was between this family trait and the Internment, she replied, 'from losing stuff.' Moreover, the Internment itself has become a material and symbolic inheritance for Mayumi that she hands down to her children as they will to theirs, evidenced in the quote in the epigraph that began this chapter, 'It is part of my inheritance, as its effects are my children's inheritance and theirs. And it will just go on.'

In regards to the issue of partner choice, Yuko stated, 'I really felt like nobody would ever want to go out with me because I was Japanese and I was different.' Of all 'ethnocultural' groups, in 2006 Japanese Canadians had the highest proportion of 'mixed' marriages and 'mixed' common law unions in Canada.[75] Kyo described her own and her family members' choices of partners in this way:

> Most of my father's brothers and sisters, by marrying white people, are trying to assimilate into the culture. And the same for me, that I'm not attracted to Asian men … In terms of dating they have always been white men and is that something in terms of assimilating into the culture and wanting to be accepted? If my boyfriend's white, then people have to accept me on one level? Am I attracted to my boyfriend because he has this power in society?

By contrast, Yuko explained to me that her father told her, 'we weren't to go out with anyone who was non-Japanese.' Histories of the Internment may inform different positions taken by survivors and their children regarding relationships. While geographic separation affected Japanese Canadians' ability to meet each other, Kyo's testimony raises questions about the social construction of desire and partner 'choice.'

Research is needed on the psychological effects of the Internment on those interned and subsequent generations. As I argued in chapter 3, the psychological cannot be separated from social causes and processes. Examples of some of the psychological and social pressures exerted by a gendered and racial capitalist state and culture were articulated by the women interviewed and are further explored in the next chapter. Sylvia connected the social to the psychological in this way: 'I just think of my own family and I think that we are sometimes really lacking in self-confidence. I really do trace that in large part to the internment experience even though none of us cousins experienced the events of the internment because we're all too young ... We always felt that we were peripheral in this society and that we had to explain ourselves all the time and became very sensitive about who we were.' Eiko connected the Internment to her sense of self by underlining key points:

> Our family was raised having to prove that we're as good as they ['mainstream' Canadians] are or better ...Yet I think it backfired in that what it did for me was instill in me a sense of low self-esteem as opposed to feeling that I'm worthy of being who I am, always concerned about what it looks like to other people. Actually, now if I think about it, I always felt as an outsider. But yeah, absolutely, I think it had a major impact on our lives.[76]

Midori emphasized the effects of the Internment and dispersal and growing up separated from other Japanese Canadians in this way:

> Instead of always trying to not be Japanese, you would be a little more secure with the fact that you have your family's history... If you were surrounded by more people who are like you (you know how you think of yourself as different?) that part of the history in terms of dispersement, the dispersal of the community, I think is a pretty big thing ... Growing up in a mainly white community, I think has really affected me.

This consciousness of the significance of the racial geography of Canada and its effects was echoed in almost identical wording by Kyo who grew up in a different region of the country: 'growing up in a mainly white community here, I think has really affected me.'

Conclusion

In this chapter, I have described some of the processes through which family members convey knowledge of the Internment to their daughters. I have looked at some of the ways this knowledge is transmitted through familial and Japanese Canadian community spaces. It must be emphasized that these spaces are not discrete and separate but are interconnected and overlapping.

While some have constituted survivors as categorically 'silent' about their incarcerations, I suggest that we problematize that construction and acknowledge that Japanese Canadians struggle both to acquire knowledge about the Internment and to communicate this knowledge to others. The daughters interviewed expressed knowledge of the Internment, knowledge that develops over time, and their understanding of the effects of the Internment in their own families and lives. Through their imagined reconstitution of communal and familial relationships, a reconstruction that is, in part, traced spatially by visualizing the Internment sites, they traced their families' cartographies of the Internment and the importance of familial and communal connections lost and re-made.

The delineation of the parent–child relationship as solely responsible for knowledge transmission of the Internment obscures the critical interrelationship of various spaces in the formation of knowledge. The spatial isolation of survivors as the only conveyors of knowledge of the Internment, therefore, is part of the way in which collective responsibility for the Internment is continually forgotten. The inclination towards situating the responsibility for re-membering and forgetting the Internment solely in the parent–child relationship is also part of the process of producing a collective forgetting. The continual resituating of the causes of children's lack of knowledge about the Internment as due to the silence of their parents, rather than in the processes of forgetting the violence of nation-building, also serves as a technology of Othering and a means of extending surveillance of survivors' behaviour to include their children, and thus to what is construed as 'the Japanese Canadian family.' In discursively constituting the space of the dyadic parent–child relationship as 'silent,' we rely upon a notion of family that re-inscribes the hegemony of a nuclear family form. Hence, in situating the responsibilities for silence *and* speech in relation to the Internment within families of those who were incarcerated, we discursively repeat the process of separating survivors and their children from a larger familial context and community, a process seen in this and previous chapters as part of the long-term effect produced through the Internment itself.

This relegation of knowledge production on the Internment to a particular dyadic relationship also illustrates that space is critical to an analysis of transmission of this knowledge. Situating the cause of not knowing about the Internment within the parent–child relationship occludes how power operates in other places and impinges upon the ability to know and to name. This spatial isolation forgets other social spaces shared with non-Japanese Canadians who are silent about the Internment. Imagining the familial space of silence bolsters the notion of a binarily imagined space where subjects speak freely. The liberal notion of 'freedom' works in concert with that of 'equality,' implying that all spaces are equal; some people just 'choose' to be silent within them. If speaking is relegated merely to choice, then one need not examine the relations of power that impede speech in the service of producing dominant narratives. Silence and speech, and the variations in between, therefore, should not be relegated to the siting of the survivor alone, but recognized as a spatially and socially constructed process negotiated multidirectionally between survivors, their families, their communities, and other social spaces.

Not one of the women I interviewed used the term 'silent' to describe her mother in relation to the conveying of memories of the Internment. Just as their mothers took care in describing their experiences of incarceration, each daughter was careful in explaining how she acquired knowledge of her mother's incarceration. Their careful tracing of their own gaps in knowledge and understanding might be used to re-signify that which some identify as the 'silence' of our parent(s). The term silence itself might then be understood as another effect of the Internment, both in identifying the difficulties in speaking about the Internment, and as another Internment euphemism forged through relations of power, including the power that non-Japanese Canadians, non-interned children of survivors, and others hold in representing and speaking for those who were interned. The word silence signifies that which cannot be named because language fails them and us, as children of survivors, and because we live in the country where our parents were incarcerated; what cannot be named is the extent of the violence of the Internment and that this violence and its effects were critical in the making of the Canadian nation and ourselves as citizens of the nation.

My examination of how daughters acquire knowledge about the Internment underlines the critical connection between space and memory. Returning to the places of 'home' and of incarceration assisted in the re-membering of experiences that were lived in each place. As Francesca Cappelletto states, 'Places are the trigger and, at the same time, the setting of the memory.'[77] Moreover, those places continue to make identities of the non-interned generations of the Internment through their mnemonic connections to the places of their families' and friends' incarcerations and the ways in which survivors place them in relation to those sites. For example, while many survivors ask each other 'Where were you?' as in Margaret's example in chapter 6, their non-interned children are also asked by survivors and their families, 'Where were your parents?' Thus, the places of the Internment continue to place and identify Japanese Canadians in relation to it and to a community of memory.

All of the daughters I interviewed reported feeling profoundly affected by their families' histories of the Internment. Their testimonies reveal that part of the long-term effect of the Internment is the very constitution of places in white communities to which Japanese Canadians were forced to move and who occupies those places. In addition, they have underlined another effect of the Internment and the dispersal, a loss of a historical memory of community, a memory that my friend Toshi reminded me was clearly connected to place and to Japanese Canadians' placement within a web of communal relations. Through the processes of the Internment and forced dispersal, survivors and subsequent generations were forced to be a different kind of subject, one who is geographically separated from and socially pressured to lose connections to other Japanese Canadians who have a history of the Internment. While non-interned children have sought to retrieve this memory and resist the violence of these processes in many ways, including through efforts to re-member the Internment, this retrieval and resistance can never re-place the relationships and people destroyed in the 1940s and after. The enforced individualization of us as subjects may be reflected in the ways in which we might judge our interned relatives' memories or lack of memories, rather than seeing our own loss of memory as a product of a violent process of enforced forgetting of the subjects we were forced to leave and of the histories that compel us to be the forgetting subjects.

Moreover, the daughters' testimonies contest Tomoko Makabe's statement, 'For the Canadian Sansei the internment seemed to have had little bearing on their upbringing ... Generally, they seemed unaware of the enduring effects of the internment or its significance on the individual as well as the group.'[78] However, Makabe's own citing of the work of many Sansei artists and academics who have represented the Internment in art and writing and whose cultural production utilizing imagery and discourses related to the Internment contradicts her own conclusion.[79] I would argue that the work generated by children of survivors utilizing Internment discourses attests to the profound effects of the Internment on these cultural producers. Furthermore, in contrast to Makabe's conclusion that the Sansei 'do not perceive discrimination as a problem and thus do not conceive their ethnic background as having ever been an obstacle,'[80] all of the daughters I interviewed reported that they had experienced racism. These racist incidents occurred in different places, from British Columbia to Ontario, and will be discussed in the next chapter.

The gaps in our knowledge of the Internment, as children of survivors, are also one of its ongoing effects. The need to fill in these gaps, to know the Internment history, I would argue is resistance to the effects of the Internment, something that will be explored further in the next chapter. In this way, people with an enduring knowledge of national violence create representational spaces for describing and analysing racial oppression and its production and effects in Canada.

9 'Crushing the White Wall with Our Names': Re-membering the Internment in White Spaces

We will come like autumn shedding sleep
a sky about to open with rage,
thunder on high rocks.
I crush the white wall/with my name.

Janice Mirikitani, 'Generations of Women'[1]

In this chapter, I examine how women resist the institutionalization of forgetting of the Internment in what I call the white space of the school. I focus on their experience of schooling up to the time of their interviews in the mid-1990s and I analyse some of their educational experiences. The chapter also includes descriptions of the daughters' experiences of racism during childhood and up to the time of their interviews. I then examine what knowledge is produced through 'mnemonic encounters'[2] between these witnesses to the Internment and non-Japanese Canadians. I will do this by first looking at how women used educational institutions to produce knowledge about the Internment. Second, I will illustrate how women experienced and contested the racism that targeted them in other white spaces. In these examples of resistance to forgetting the Internment and resistance to racism, we see that generations of the Internment are simultaneously rendered both visible and invisible.

Contesting the Forgetting of the Internment in the White Space of School

In her study of the effects of the Internment on the children of those interned, Donna Nagata mentions that the lack of curricular attention to the 'injustice of internment' in schools contributed to the paucity of information provided to the Sansei.[3] The women I interviewed confronted the forgetting of the Internment in school, a white-dominated space[4] where racialized students regularly endured racist attacks. These schools were described by some mothers and daughters as sites of racism. Women also took note of the 'silence' of teachers and curriculum on the history of the Internment and other marginalized histories. The ways in which women struggled to produce knowledge that fundamentally challenges how the nation of Canada is imagined[5] in the educational system are evidence of their insurgent knowledge and resistance to forgetting.

After being moved to Winnipeg, Margaret attended high school in the late 1940s. She reported, 'There were times when I really hated to go to school,' due to fights with other children because 'we were Japanese.'[6] I asked Louise, who went to public school in northern Ontario in the 1950s, whether she was ever taught about the Internment in school and she replied, 'No. Never. Never. No.'[7]

As I stated in chapter 3, public access to government records on the Internment was restricted until the 1970s, and some of the records continue to be restricted at the time of the writing of this book. Lack of accessibility to these records contributed to the national forgetting of the Internment, as the documentary evidence of the reasons for and practices of the Internment lay buried in government vaults or were destroyed. In addition, all survivors had to attend to immediate material needs, and thus researching and representing their own histories would have entailed resources and time that few could have afforded. As we saw in the last chapter, people continued to produce knowledge of the Internment in various forms in families and other spaces. Despite the racism encountered in schools, this space was and is used by survivors and their children to contest the ways in which the Internment is forgotten in the educational system.

Eight of the daughters interviewed reported completing projects on the Internment during their years of schooling. Four of these women undertook this work in university. All of them initiated this research on their own as special topics not part of the regular curriculum. Only two women reported being taught about the Internment in a school setting.

Two survivors used their university studies to find out more about the government's policies during the Internment. Esther undertook research at a university and discovered that 'Japanese Canadians only got the vote in 1949.' 'I never knew that ... It's not very long ago, is it?' she added.[8] Yoshiko also did research on the Internment for a university course. Both women's testimonies indicated that survivors continue to accumulate knowledge on the Internment years after the events. Haru reminded me, however, that many people from her generation were unable to continue their education after they were expelled from British Columbia. 'My husband and I didn't even go to university,' she stated. 'It was a big accomplishment when our children wanted to go to.'[9] Although Japanese Canadians as a group have been noted for their level of education, in 1986 only 3 per cent over 75 years of age had acquired some university education.[10] University education, therefore, has not been accessible to all Japanese Canadians, and as we shall see, university courses or their professors have not necessarily supported a critical understanding of the Internment.

The daughters interviewed went to elementary and high schools between the 1950s and 1990s. Some of them attended university in the 1990s. Most of the women had white teachers during their public school and post-secondary education.[11] Most of the daughters reported the school as a site where they experienced racism.

Mayumi, who went to school in Toronto in the late 1950s and early 1960s, reported she was taught by white teachers only. There were no other Japanese Canadian children in her elementary school. There was only one other Japanese Canadian student in her senior public school. 'The only other Japanese people I knew were my relatives,' she added. Mayumi was never taught about the Internment, although she speculated that 'it is now [taught] in school ... It wasn't then, not at all.'[12]

Before I interviewed Yuko, her mother Haru had described to me the social context of her daughter's public school education. She said: 'My daughter was the only Japanese in that school.' She also compared her family's working-class economic position to her daughter's middle-class classmates who were 'children of young executives, vets, and middle-class families' and who could afford to participate in different social activities. She repeated that her daughter's classmates were children of 'young vets that came back from the war, who were involved in war.'

In these brief comments, Haru contextualized her daughter's and her own social position in relation to those of the students and their parents. Her description illustrated to me her awareness that the classroom is a place through which discourses of race, class, and nationalism are mobilized. Her testimony conveyed that her daughter was constructed as 'different' from the other students. Haru also indicated that being a child of a veteran of the Second World War was an identity that was known and displayed in the classroom. This remark made me aware that her daughter could have been targeted by the 'disloyalty' discourse, as the badge of 'loyalty' would have been the much-lauded mark of the white veteran's children, serving to obscure Yuko's family's history of incarceration and their own years of service as labourers for Canada before, during, and after the war. Evoked through her repetition of the word 'vets' was a concern for her daughter, as the highly masculinized sign of the white war hero was emblematically displayed through the bodies of their children in the school that Yuko had attended daily. Haru stated, 'I remember she was accepted as who she was as another student, but socially I don't think she was fully accepted.' Haru's comments suggest that she had to negotiate the knowledge she had of her own history and social difference from these parents in relation to the histories of her daughter's classmates and her care of Yuko.

Yuko, who is two years younger than Mayumi, reported there were no other Japanese Canadian families in her neighbourhood, and that it was not until high school that another Japanese Canadian family moved into the area. She had found out recently that one of her classmates from high school is a 'Native' person, but in this educational setting he had not openly identified as Native. There were no other racialized students in elementary or high school and all of her teachers were white.

Yuko recalled that a much younger child had directed racist words at her and she felt really hurt by this.[13] She didn't remember experiencing racism when she was in public school, but then remarked that she may have rationalized how she was treated by explaining to herself it was due to her small size. As she stated, 'I always used to be labelled a "China doll" because I was so tiny.'[14] Racialized constructions are always about racialized gendering. In this case the 'doll,' being the heightened sign of femininity and sexuality, is racialized by the determination of the originary as China (standing in for all of Asia). The white Orientalist gaze mobilizes the punning notion of the feminine figurine of China and distinguishes itself as objectifier of *the woman, who herself remembers and names the naming*.

Yuko also noted that a couple of teachers in high school described her as Japanese and even asked what being Japanese was like for her. It was at high school that she began to discuss her experiences of racism with her friends. She remembered their reply: '[We] don't see you as being Japanese. We just treat you the same and don't see you as being any different.' In her sharing of her hurt from racism with her white friends, it is notable that they constructed themselves as not racist through being friends with her and in denying the differences that mark her and un-mark themselves. Yuko remembered that the Internment was not on the school curriculum. She said, 'We were never taught about the intern-ment. We were never taught about the Canadian Indians ... We were taught about European history, American history, and never taught about any ethnic group. It was really from a Eurocentric perspective.' Within the context of discussing racism, Yuko recounted that she had applied for a bursary after graduation from high school and had to at-tend an interview. Most applicants' interviews lasted an hour; hers was fifteen minutes. She remembered the questions revolved around her 'being Japanese.' 'I thought that was very odd,' she added. She further noted: 'Now, in hindsight, I can see that it was probably racism and dis-crimination, and they had just gone through the motions to be polite. They had no intention of awarding me any kind of bursary.'

Sylvia, who is a few years younger than Yuko, also went to school in Toronto. She and her cousins were the only Japanese Canadians at their public school. In elementary school, there were no other Asian Cana-dian students and when she reached grade six or seven, there was one Black student in her class. All the other students were white. At high school there were one or two other Japanese Canadian students. Sylvia had 'very, very, strong, vivid memories' of racism at school. 'That was very hurtful and I dealt with it by myself,' she stated. Sylvia had to deal with both racism and the class divisions she and her working-class family encountered in the middle-class neighbourhood in which they lived. She was never taught about the Internment at school, 'not in high school, not in university either.'[15]

Irene, who attended school in Toronto in the 1960s and 1970s, report-ed there were only two other Japanese Canadian families in her area who had children attending her school. She experienced racism 'most-ly from people who didn't know me very well, acquaintances ... just knew me to see me across the school yard.'[16] The racism was uttered in the form of 'rhymes' and other kinds of speech. She explained that her friends were supportive of her and she hadn't felt that she was 'differ-ent' until people said these things to her. She also described her primary school teachers as 'patronizing' in their request that she perform *odori*, a traditional form of Japanese dancing, and go from one class to another dressed in a kimono for show-and-tell. Her realization, she said, that these teachers had been 'treating me as an object or curiosity,' as a 'cul-tural sort of exhibit,' came years later when she was an adult.

When I asked Irene whether she was ever taught about the Internment in public school or college, she replied, 'No. No. Never. No, it was never mentioned.' She added, 'I don't know how much Canadian history I ever learned to begin with. I don't think I learned anything about World War II anyways. So, the opportunity wasn't there to learn about the internment.' Within this context of discussing curriculum, she emphasized her own role as pedagogue, 'I must have mentioned it to people as a kid. I'm sure a lot of people were surprised.' This is a role she continues to this day, 'talking to adults.'

Midori, who went to school in a Prairie province in the 1970s and 1980s, thought she may have studied the Internment in school. She remembered doing a project on it in junior high. This, however, was not her initial exposure to representations of the Internment; she recalled, 'knowing about it, some of it, a bit before that.' She chose to work on this project because she was 'interested and knew a little bit about it and wanted, by doing a project, to find out more of the details.' She stated, 'It could have been about anything, really. So it wasn't taken as something that you shouldn't talk about. It was just like anybody's project.'[17]

Joanne went to public school in British Columbia in the 1960s and 1970s. She recalled being taught by only one teacher who was not white and this was at the high school level. She described the racism experienced by her and the few other classmates of colour. Her mother switched her to a more middle-class school, but the white boys at that school also called her racist names. Although some of the other women interviewed reported being the target of racist attacks by both male and female children and adults, Joanne emphasized that the perpetrators in her school were male: 'It was always the boys in class who would say horrible things … or would call me names.'[18]

Joanne was never taught about the Internment in public school or university. In high school there was a section on the Second World War in social studies. She remembered, 'I was given another project to work independently on, which is interesting.' In this instance, Joanne remembered curricular practices that racialized her. The mnemonic encounter between the Japanese Canadian student and the white teacher resulted in the student's 'removal' from the lesson. That the teacher was also negotiating the mnemonic differences suggested by the study of the Second World War for different students is apparent here. Yet the solution offered, to exclude one student and continue with the lesson, assumed that all the other children were uniformly included and addressed in its undertaking. As Lisa Lowe points out, the 'history' lessons on the Second World War instantiate a nationalist narrative that 'recognizes, recruits, and incorporates male subjects, while "feminizing" and silencing the students who do not conform to that notion of patriotic subjectivity.'[19] It is also a pedagogical moment that re-en-figures the 'Asian as "enemy."'[20] In this case, the teacher's conscious removal of Joanne from the lesson signified the choice to continue with the narrative of dominance. The strategy of removing one child from the textual encounter with the set curriculum does not change the rela-tions of domination embedded therein and also continues to mark the 'difference' of the excluded child. The unifying address witnessed in this pedagogical moment – how *we*, as Canadians, view the Second World War – is about imagining a hegemonic whiteness in relation to nation, while the view of Others is relegated to the margins and rein-scribes their 'difference.'

Janice went to school in Vancouver in the 1970s and 1980s. She lived in a 'very all-white neighbourhood.' In her elementary school, there was one 'Black girl,' one Native 'Indian boy' and 'maybe two Asian kids.'[21] There was only one time where she was in the same class as an-other Asian person; he was Chinese Canadian. All of her teachers were white, with the exception of one teacher in high school.

From an early age, Janice was aware she was living in an 'anti-Asian' province. She deduced this from the racial slurs she heard directed at Chinese Canadians, which she remembered as pre-dating her memo-ries of racist language directed at her and other Japanese Canadians. She shared this profound insight into how she came to understand that racism directed at other people was intrinsically connected to the Internment: 'I knew that somehow the racism directed at other racial groups had something to do with what happened to us.'

Janice remembered being called a racist word by a white male class-mate when she was in grade four. In her vivid memory of that incident, she was able to describe the appearance of the student and even recalled his name. She situated herself, however, in relation to her friends of co-lour by stating that 'a lot of time people can't tell I'm Asian' (because of her mixed ancestry), and in high school she witnessed the racism targeted at her friends who 'were always' experiencing these attacks.

In the early 1980s, in grade twelve, Janice 'chose to do' a multimedia project on the Internment for her social studies class. She recalled, 'It was a free-for-all kind of choose whatever topic you want to do.' Her aunt was pivotal in helping her to research the project and 'copied all these photos out of books.' 'It was easy for me because I was really familiar with the material,' she concluded.

Here, Janice emphasized that she was already very familiar with some of the history of the Internment and worked with her aunt to present this knowledge to her classmates and teacher. Years later, when Janice met former classmates, some of them remarked, '[We] remember that presentation you did.' Janice described this reaction as reflecting what before her presentation had been a 'huge gap in their learning' and, she noted, 'That's the first time they'd ever known anything about it ... there was nothing in any history book about internment.' As do many other Japanese Canadians who contest the forgetting of the Internment in white spaces, Janice did the pedagogical work not undertaken by white people themselves. Her lesson occurred in Vancouver in the 1980s. Whose silence is reflected in this space of school? It was certainly not Janice or her family who were silent. Rather they had instilled her with a 'familiarity' with their history and supported her in its representation. Who were the other students in this classroom, and how was this 'gap' in their learning about part of the history of Vancouver and Canada (and the places 'inherited' by some of them from their parents) produced? The strength it takes to generate this insurgent knowledge is underscored by Janice's marking it as 'the first time I'd ever really had to publicly talk about it.'

Naomi went to school in northern British Columbia in the 1970s. Her family members were the only Asians in the town where they resided. Although there were a few white children in the school, most of her schoolmates were Indigenous and she learned to communicate with them in their traditional language. She described growing up in a context where there was 'a lot of racism' directed at Indigenous peoples. She constructed her own experience of racism spatially as she described visiting her father, who is white and who lived in the white area, and being verbally assaulted with racist language by white people there who thought she was 'Native.' Her mother, however, lived in the area identified as 'Native,' and it was there that Naomi was the target of anti-Japanese racism. Naomi answered my question about how she came to know herself as 'Japanese Canadian' by telling me a schoolmate had called her by an anti-Japanese word in the school yard when she was in grade three: 'I didn't understand what [the word] meant really. I knew it was bad, but that's the extent of it.'[22]

Naomi recounted that she was 'crossing those boundaries all the time' between the white area where she was called by anti-Native racist epithets, 'And then going to school and being called [anti-Japanese racist words] by the Native kids.' Naomi's description illustrated that her construction by others was contingent upon the place she inhabited or entered, and the histories and systems of domination constructing these places. She identified the instigator of anti-Japanese racism as occupying a higher class position than most Indigenous people. She further analysed his social position in this way:

> It gets quite complex when you look at who this person is in the community [who was calling me by racist names]. He was a very, sort of, white-looking Native person[23] ... and you know who these slurs came from ... it fits in with how racism works. The poorer darker-skinned Native kids got it too, you know, they got the brunt of that kind of stuff as well. And they weren't the ones who would call me [by racist names].

White supremacy, male and class domination, and colonialism or the desire to be dominant in relation to these systems and discourses of power, as suggested by Naomi's testimony, created a hierarchy within racialized Indigenous and white settler spaces, mobilized through attacks on differently racialized, classed, and gendered people. Although Naomi's mother moved to northern BC to work in solidarity with Indigenous peoples, she and her daughter were socially situated differently from them. Just as the boy described held multiple subject positions, Naomi and her mother, a survivor of the Internment, were racialized settlers[24] on Indigenous territory, but as the only Japanese Canadian women. Therefore, as Japanese Canadians were dispersed across the country and as some returned to British Columbia after 1949, contact zones with Indigenous peoples and with white and racialized settlers were forged anew. As I argued in chapter 5, interlocking discourses of domination position people inhabiting marginalized spaces relationally. They also serve to divide them and thus inhibit their organizing together.

Naomi was able to talk to her mother about incidents of racism and, although she did not recall the content of these conversations, she knew her mother supported her and told her that any racist language used against her was wrong. She did not, however, remember specifically discussing the anti-Japanese language or the history of those words in Canada.

Naomi's family moved to Vancouver and she attended a school where there were many Asian Canadian children. However, there were no other Japanese Canadians in her class. Naomi was perceived by some to be a Native person and she remarked that the other children 'didn't like me because I was [thought to be] Native.' This mistaken identity was reinforced by the teacher, who told Naomi to sit beside the lone Indigenous student in the class who was ostracized by everyone. Naomi's testimony provides an unmapping of colonialism, race, and whiteness at the micro level of a classroom and the deliberate mapping on the part of the white teacher that reflected macro processes of a settler nation. She recalled one day she was asked 'What are you?' by the students. She replied she was Japanese and white, and the response was 'We can be your friend now, you're not Native.' 'It was really disturbing to me,' she concluded. She learned that 'the Native kids ... in this city were always ostracized.'

Naomi's testimony points towards questions of complicity, including the complicities of being able to 'cross the boundaries' of Indigenous and racialized spaces (and hence enter and leave them) through class, gender, settler, or white privilege, and of our residing on Indigenous territories, mapped as Canada. While Sherene Razack warns, 'We still cannot speak out loud about the complexities of racial identities without risking that the oppressive contours of racism will be denied,'[25] it is my hope that the complexities of Indigenous and racialized settler subject formations in Canada can be better understood through our efforts to analyse the ways in which these formations are constructed and lived. Japanese Canadians, therefore, must critically examine our historical and social relationships to the processes of colonialism and our own social and material locations as settlers on Indigenous territories.

Naomi's analysis of her own identity formation lays bare the interlocking discourses of domination constructing relational identities through relational spaces. The same racialized person can move through different spaces and find her/himself positioned differently according to the racial perception of those inhabiting these spaces and the racial histories that divide them. People who are of mixed ancestral backgrounds,[26] as is Naomi, may find themselves on the boundaries of fixed racial categories; the desire on the part of others to fix her racial identity and hence their own (including the identity of whiteness), was evidenced in the racism she experienced. The pinnacle of whiteness inscribed through white supremacy, however, will never be attained by the racialized body. Moreover, if we do not see how we are relationally constructed through these social hierarchies, we cannot hope to undermine their constructions.

Within these educational settings, which included a school in Vancouver – a city from which Japanese Canadians were expelled in the

1940s – Naomi was never taught about the Internment. In high school, students were allowed to 'choose topics,' and she chose to work on the topic of Japan. She wrote something about the Internment because 'that came up in the project,' but 'nothing in depth.' Even though there were many racialized students present, the school still remained a white-dominated space of forgetting the Internment.

Kyo, who went to school in Toronto from the mid-1970s to the 1990s, was the only person other than Midori to report being taught about the Internment in public school. There were no Japanese Canadians in her elementary school, but there were members of one Korean Canadian family attending classes. She reported experiencing racism as well as verbal abuse from other schoolchildren. She was taught by only one person of colour, and that was in high school. Kyo described the lesson on the Internment as lasting only 'ten minutes' in a grade nine Canadian history class.[27] She recalled being shown a film and the teacher 'talked briefly about it in terms of World War II, in that context.' She stated, 'at that point, I didn't really know that much about it either, just that my grandfather's boat had been taken away, had been confiscated.' She told the teacher during the film, 'That happened to my grandfather.' The teacher replied, 'Oh, that's interesting.' But then 'After the film, the teacher discussed the film and said, "That happened to Kyo's grandfather."' When I asked her how she felt after seeing the film, Kyo replied: 'I don't even remember what the film was. I probably [felt] angry but also maybe a little embarrassed, too. You know, being in this whole class of white people.'

Kyo's example reminds us that the 'risky stories'[28] of racialized students can become the example used by a teacher or other students. Disclosing these stories can be even more risky given the teacher's power and the power of whiteness in the classroom. The very bodies of racialized students become the ground on which a national collective forgetting and the students' forgetting are pedagogically displayed. The lone student is constructed as the object of the lesson. She is given more responsibility for knowing the story, and for telling it according to the teacher's rules. White students are normalized through the focus upon the racialized student. The analysis of the historical production of whiteness as dominance, produced in part through the Internment, is not taught in this curriculum. The white participants and witnesses who benefited from the Internment and did not contest it are not discussed. As white students listen to Kyo's history, the fact that the Internment is also their history is masked through the process of re-making Japanese Canadians once again the sole object of scrutiny.

Eiko, who went to school in Toronto in the 1950s and 1960s, replied, 'No. Not in high school, not anything' when I asked her whether she was ever taught about the Internment. She remembered, however, 'learning about World War II though. And not quite knowing how to feel.'[29] She compared the feeling to that which she had recently experienced when a fellow classmate was criticizing a well-known Japanese Canadian man and kept looking at her during his comments. Her response to these pedagogical moments that call attention to her body in the classroom was to ask, 'Why are *you* uncomfortable with this history? ... Why are *you* uncomfortable?'

The desire to create a representational space for analysing the social significance of the Internment continued for some of the women in post-secondary institutions. Four of the women conducted research for projects on the Internment at university. The only woman who reported that the Internment was mentioned in a university course lecture was Kyo. This occurred in an Ontario university in a women's studies course when the students studied the novel *Obasan*. When I asked her what it was like to study the novel in that context, she replied,

> For the first time you're reading about experiences that you can really identify with ... I'd read articles for that class that I could identify with in [terms of] gender. It was really interesting to be able to identify with a woman on a racial level, too, in terms of experiences. Not just racial, but cultural level.

The reading of *Obasan* gave Kyo the opportunity to address issues of gender and racialization in a women's studies course, and particularly the position of Japanese Canadian women within Canada. Yet, as we saw in chapter 2, 'critical' interpretations of this novel do not necessarily undermine stereotypical representations of Japanese Canadian women.[30]

Janice reported that at her university in British Columbia, all of her professors were white except for one woman. Her first-year Canadian history textbook included a paragraph about the Internment in the section discussing the Second World War. 'A whole paragraph!' she emphasized. Joanne reported that she had conducted research on the Internment for a university geography course, thus contesting the disciplinary boundaries that might relegate the study of the Internment to the discipline of history.

Sylvia did research on the Internment when she was working on a bachelor's degree. This was for a 'gender course' in sociology and the students chose to 'do a research paper on anything [they] wanted.' The Internment 'wasn't part of the formal course curriculum,' she emphasized.

Yuko wrote a paper on the Internment in a sociology course at an Ontario university. She emphasized that the Internment 'wasn't part of the curriculum' and the paper could have been on 'any topic.' She described herself as 'naive' in the selection of the topic, which was 'the psychological and sociological implications of the internment during the Second World War.' She read through all of the newspapers on microfilm to 'dig' for information because 'there wasn't a whole lot of information around about the internment.' Her father was 'really reluctant to give [her] any information' for her project. She was pleased that she received a 'good grade on the paper.'

Naomi completed a project on the Internment while she attended a university in BC. 'It wasn't part of the curriculum. No one else had to do it ... That was the one and only time that I've actually done research and pursued that in any depth,' she stated. She used 'well-known' books as her secondary sources; in addition, her literature search included empirical research produced by Japanese Canadians, which she retrieved through a Japanese Canadian community library. Naomi described the response of her white professor, a 'British woman,' in this way:

> The professor criticiz[ed] me for being too political and for coming to the conclusion that I did. [She commented] that I wasn't being fair to the Canadian government. I read it now and I just get really angry ... This is racism. This is terrible ... The one time that I pursued this and came to a clear conclusion that what happened to Japanese Canadians was to appease the fears of the white racists in BC, the professor flipped out. She really did not like to hear that in a paper; that was not acceptable. That was in university ... That was only in 1990!

Naomi concluded: 'It's pretty frightening that this happens and a lot of people don't realize this is what it is like ... There's a lot of resistance to this stuff. Just talking to you I'm realizing how non-existent it has been. And ... just the silence around it.'

In this commentary, Naomi identified what she confronts in school as a 'resistance' to the articulation of her subjugated knowledge of the

Internment and the knowledge produced by scholars and community members. She also noted that her interventions challenged the silence of the university on this topic. Naomi's experience, which took place not that long ago and after the publication of Sunahara's and Adachi's critical texts, also points out how even after one federal government acknowledged the injustice of the expulsions and incarcerations of Japanese Canadians, the identification of racism as one cause of the Internment was penalized in a university course. Importantly, a familial witness to the Internment's legacy was challenged and even disciplined for bearing witness through research and scholarship. Naomi's experience helps to illustrate that it has been difficult to write and research about the Internment and racism in educational institutions, particularly as Japanese Canadians, and it was not often considered an important topic to teach. Japanese Canadians' ability to critique the Canadian nation through representation of the Internment is always therefore mediated through relations of power.

Naomi's school experiences led her to develop strategies for dealing with the racism in school and the racial order that shaped her education. She acknowledged the support she has received from her mother and sister with whom she can discuss events in their daily lives. She credited her mother for sharing 'insights' with her gleaned from her life experience. She added, 'I feel really, really lucky that I've had that because I know a lot of people of colour that are going to university with me don't have that [support].' She, along with other students, formed a group for students of colour 'to try and be a support system for each other and also try and change the kind of institutionalized racism and white supremacy that we felt was going on.' She also kept lists of racial incidents that occurred in the classroom and has addressed some of her concerns to the university administration. She added, 'It was very empowering. Nothing happened, but it was still empowering.'

In this section, we have seen that the schools in various geographic locations can be a space of violence for racialized children. The fact that children are taught from a very early age the 'sticks and stones' adage of racist language as benign and merely words is part of the process of the forgetting of racial violence. As Mari Matsuda and others argue, racist speech is made up of 'words that wound'[31] and can be a form of 'spirit murder.'[32] That women can remember particular incidents of racism with such clarity and describe and even name the perpetrators decades after the incident is indicative of how it has been cognitively and emotionally mnemonically inscribed. Midori, for example, was regularly assailed with anti-Japanese and anti-Chinese language by a white boy in grade nine. She referred to this experience as 'traumatizing ... because I still think about it now.' These testimonies describing racism are reflective of its psychological impact and the 'trauma of racism.'[33]

The institutionalization of the forgetting of violence perpetrated upon certain communities is promulgated through curricula that do not teach that oppression has occurred and is occurring. In speaking about the curriculum in the United States, Donald Nakanishi states that 'although the bulk of the literature on the Internment appeared during the twenty-year period following the war, very little found its way to American textbooks or the mass media.'[34] Although the Canadian context differs in that very little literature was generated on the Canadian incarcerations in the period immediately following the Internment, there are now many interdisciplinary representations with which to engage through the curriculum.[35]

Esther pointed out to me that many Japanese Canadian teachers are committed to curriculum development on the Internment, including a Japanese Canadian educators' group in British Columbia. Curriculum development should ideally be undertaken in collaboration with other subordinated communities in order to develop pedagogical strategies that take into account the relational nature of oppression and histories. While it may be argued that the Internment of Japanese Canadians is now taught in some elementary and high schools and universities in Canada, in my experience, very few university students that I taught between 1996 and 2009 in Toronto, Winnipeg, and Ottawa knew about this history, and those who did had scant knowledge of its occurrence.[36] In addition, while there are more racialized teachers than there were in the years that the women discussed, the numbers are still lacking.[37] The school as a site of knowledge production, therefore, cannot be relied upon for support in developing a critical understanding of the Internment or other histories of violence. Children, however, carry the dissonance of the history of Canada, which includes the Internment, inherited from familial and community spaces, and what is represented in schools, and thereby take note of curricular amnesia. That the women chose to intellectually and creatively engage with the legacy of the Internment in an environment where this history was suppressed indicates a prior epistemic acquisition of it. Women had to 'know' something about the incarcerations in order to even conceptualize and propose it as a subject of research. The seeds of that knowing were

282 Cartographies of Violence

planted in the familial space or the Japanese Canadian community, in contrast to schools where their subjugated knowledge met with a barren silence or even hostility.

To see the daughter of the survivor as the only source of representation of the Internment, therefore (as was shown in Stan Yogi's esteeming of the speaking Sansei in chapter 2), obscures how knowledge and memory are derived from survivors themselves. This limited view forgets that knowledge is imparted within the family and/or Japanese Canadian community and that the daughter brings her knowledge of and from those spaces into representational work, transforming absence into presence. It also occludes how access to different spaces is socially constituted and that spaces are arranged in a hierarchy, with work done in 'respectable' white educational institutions, like the university, often recognized as more intellectually valuable than cultural production independently produced. As Haru suggested, education is a class-related activity and a university education is, for the most part, accessible only to middle-class students.

We must, therefore, rethink the simplistic binary constitution of the child of a survivor as 'speaking' and the parent survivor as 'silent' and recognize the complex negotiations of re-membering from differently located spaces and subject positions. In this way, perhaps we will begin to dismantle the reification of the autonomous subject and acknowledge the ways in which our knowledge of violence and oppression, *and* our resistance to domination, depend upon our connectedness to communities who remember.

The fact that women accomplished projects on the Internment within these institutions is a testament to their determination and a reflection of their profound desire to articulate and represent the Internment and its legacy. Women could see the intellectual and political significance of the Internment across various disciplines, including sociology, geography, and women's studies. The curricular consignment of the Internment to the discipline of history and the study of the Second World War is therefore a function of disciplinary containment. Envisioning projects across disciplines enables us to question the ways in which knowledge of racial violence is contained in intellectual production; the testimonies of survivors and their descendants can also contest the temporal relegation of the Internment as a past and therefore 'forgettable' historical event. In addition, by identifying all of the subjects of the Internment, we might be able to demonstrate that this history has shaped not only Japanese Canadians but also all Canadians.

All of the women who worked on these projects did them within the curricular framework of being able to 'choose any topic' and where they alone were 'marked' for acquiring this knowledge. Some were rewarded institutionally for completing these projects by achieving good grades, yet most had little material support from their instructors. What would it be like for students to be supported intellectually for undertaking the difficult work of examining their histories of racism and other forms of oppression, and not just simply be 'allowed' to attempt this work? Yuko's feeling, for example, that she was perhaps 'naive' to undertake the study of the 'psychological and sociological' effects of the Internment reflects the ways in which the inheritor of the Internment history is left to internalize what is unknowable about this history as a personal limitation rather than evidence of its complexity and necessary 'forgetability' within spaces where hegemonic narratives and subjects of the nation are upheld. Instead, we might see in these examples that the gaps in knowledge about the Internment demonstrated by survivors, their children, and subsequent generations are, in actuality, part of its ongoing effects. We might also see their need to describe, analyse, and represent the Internment as resistance to its effects, an ongoing process of wanting to understand and fill in the gaps of a legacy in progress. We might also see the social and political limitations of the institutions in which this work is attempted, limitations that are also ongoing effects of the Internment and the institutionalized processes of racial formation and the forgetting of that formation. That the effects of the Internment are still under-explored in the Canadian theoretical literature underscores that Yuko's work was groundbreaking, as it foreshadowed the concerns of her own generation and subsequent ones. How many more works on the Internment might exist if these women and other Japanese Canadians had received institutional support for their projects?

In writing this section, I have come to hear myself through many of the stories told to me by women who attended schools in various places 'after the Internment.' I also acknowledge the many 'silences' I have encountered within educational institutions, only ever attending two classes as a student where the Internment was a part of the curriculum – a class at the graduate level where *Obasan* was taught and another graduate course taught by a visiting white historian from the United States. Any attention given to the Internment in other courses I have attended has been the result of work I have done. Like Naomi, I have been challenged for undertaking this work at a university, not by professors, however, but by fellow students at the graduate level. The statements made by two individuals stand out: a white feminist stated that the government was 'protecting' Japanese Canadians by expelling them from the West Coast (one might ask how mass expulsion, dispossession, incarceration, and the destruction of families and communities could be considered 'protection'); and a white male teacher at a private boys' school who refused to believe that Prime Minister Mackenzie King opined of the dropping of the atomic bomb on Japan, 'It is fortunate that the use of the bomb should have been upon the Japanese rather than upon the white races of Europe,'[38] even though I showed him documentation of this statement.

The lack of curricular attention to subordinated histories is part of the social construction of what I have named the collective national forgetting of the Internment, and it is a forgetting that can be furiously defended when confronted by remembering, as is witnessed by both my testimony and Naomi's. But it is also pedagogically questionable to include a lesson on the Internment, for example, only because there is a Japanese Canadian student in the classroom (determined as 'the' subject of that history) and to position that student as the object of the lesson. Through this singularization of the subject of the Internment, we continue to deny that the Internment and other histories of violence are constitutive of everyone's history within the classroom, part of the making of the Canadian nation and its citizens. In regards to teaching children historical traumatic texts, Roger Simon and Wendy Armitage-Simon suggest, however,

> If teachers have little background information about a historical event and its context, and have neither resolved the questions such stories elicit nor found a way to live with the unknowability of many of the questions they raise, perhaps they should not incorporate these stories in their curriculum.[39]

Mere inclusion of the Internment or any other representation of violence in the curriculum is insufficient and even potentially damaging. As Simon and Armitage-Simon note, 'risky stories' of 'violence, cruelty, destructiveness and suffering'[40] can profoundly affect the children exposed to them. However, while some analyses of the effects of representations of violence upon children and adults show concern for those children whose view of the world as 'meaningful and orderly'[41] may be challenged in learning about histories of violence and suffering, I would suggest that this view of the world, when it is posited as universal, must itself be problematized. This would inevitably entail examining what constitutes 'meaning' and 'order,' whose world view is represented as 'meaningful and orderly,' and how we are each differently socially situated in relation to this view of the world. How do positions of dominance construct our own complicities in a world imagined to be 'meaningful and orderly,' when for many it is disordered by social oppression? Some students may come from backgrounds similar to those whose world views shape the definitions of 'meaning' and 'order' in disciplines such as psychology; other students may in fact find support from the skilled presentation of representations of the violences of history. This may also support them in writing the shadow texts of their histories and thus may be meaningful to them as, for example, was the case in Naomi's report in chapter 8 of learning about the Holocaust.

In learning from the women I interviewed and in re-membering my own experiences and those of friends and colleagues, it is evident that racism occurs in schools, targeting racialized students. Violence is mobilized through various means and various bodies, and these practices are more probable than unlikely. In response, students may mobilize contesting discourses, and the work that these women have done within schools is evidence of a resistance to racial violence and the forgetting of racial violence.

Mnemonic Encounters and the 'Confessional'

Kyo described an encounter she had with a white woman working for the Ontario Progressive Conservative party in an election. As the woman began to defend her party's policies, Kyo retorted that these policies discriminated against poor people, women, and people of colour. When she was asked about her position on racism, the woman replied, 'Racism doesn't exist.' When Kyo informed her that she was called racist words while walking on the street, the woman denied her experience by saying 'That doesn't happen.' Kyo replied, 'It doesn't exist for you.' The woman then added, 'Your people are so respected in our community.' When Kyo reminded her of the events of the 1940s, the woman replied, 'Well, except for that incident. I forgot about that.' Kyo explained her strategy, 'Making [racism] political is a way for me to survive, a way to resist.'

This example emphasizes the ways in which women mobilize their memories of the Internment and racism in encounters with white spaces of forgetting. In these mnemonic encounters, the forgetting of racial violence is reiterated, producing the myth of Canada as a nation of racial equality. Bearing witness to the Internment is not just about remembering it as the past but also about how this history informs the struggles of women in the present.

Japanese Canadians encounter the forgetting of the Internment in different ways. Another kind of mnemonic encounter occurs when white people 'confess' their 'ignorance' of the Internment to Japanese Canadians.[42] In this confessional encounter, Japanese Canadians are expected to act as the pedagogical witness for the 'ignorant' confessor. Although there were white witnesses to and beneficiaries of the Internment, it is doubtful that they are called upon to remember the Internment in this way. These encounters can be invasive when they re-enfigure the autonomous subject who constitutes himself as free to ask anything, assuming permission without invitation, breaking the boundaries of the bodily and psychological space of survivors. This expectation that others speak for our benefit might be contrasted to Naomi's understanding of her own position of power when she stated that she had to do her own work before asking her grandmother about her experience of the Internment (chapter 8). These confessional encounters are also an effect of the silences of white people, and reveal who is held accountable for speaking. Not only do some white people confess their not knowing about the Internment to Japanese Canadians, but as Margaret revealed in chapter 6, some also confess their acts of racism to them. Eiko told me her mother had recently been approached by a white woman who 'confessed' something she had done to a Japanese Canadian man just after the Internment: 'Years later, she confessed all this to my mother, whom she didn't even know.' While I have been arguing for the importance of memory in constructing knowledge of the Internment and its subjects, I do not think it is Japanese Canadians' responsibility to act as the confessional for a nation's forgetting or to give absolution to those who confess their actions or ignorance.

Whenever the Internment entered public discourse through the media or other avenues, people approached Louise by saying, 'We didn't know this happened to the Japanese people ... Did it happen to you? And were you affected?' These confessional encounters were especially frequent during the redress struggle. While Louise will respond to some questions when asked, she stated, 'It's not something I bring up.' Demands to meet the needs of confessors/interrogators once again demonstrate that relations of power construct memory and forgetting. Holding Japanese Canadians alone accountable for remembering and speaking about the Internment itself absolves non-Japanese Canadians of the responsibility for knowing what is also their history. Feeling entitled to ask others to speak for our benefit (education, information, et cetera) and their choosing either not to speak or when they do, what they choose to speak of in these 'risky' spaces is very much connected to power and the epistemic violence hovering beneath the surface of these mnemonic encounters. Negotiating whether to disclose memories in these encounters and if disclosed, which memories to share, is also about 'how and where women see dominance.'[43]

Gendered Racism in White Spaces

The women interviewed experienced gendered racism in the post-Internment period and reported that they continued to experience racism when they were interviewed in the 1990s. While I cannot detail the many instances that all women cited, I have included some of them in this section. These examples illustrate that women who were interned continued to experience racism 'after' the Internment and so, too, did their daughters. I do not claim, however, that the anti-Japanese racism in the 1940s produced the same effects as racism mobilized in later years. Clearly one of the effects of racism in the 1940s was the Internment itself. Discourses of domination, including racism, are not static. They shift over time, and as I have argued throughout the book, are place specific. In this respect, David Goldberg's concept of 'racisms'[44] is useful in conveying the historically and geographically specific mobilizations of racial domination. Racial discourses used in relation to Japanese Canadians, however, continue to draw upon earlier discourses. For example, many of the racial epithets used against women in the 1940s were used against these same women and their daughters again in the 1990s. These epithets and the assumptions on which they are based must therefore be part of the mnemonic record handed down by some white people to their children. Moreover, racism continues to be used to control the bodies of Japanese Canadians through the operationalization of discourses of assimilation and exclusion, the determination of what bodies are appropriate where, and what should be done to people that are seen as being in the wrong place. Hegemonic notions of the nation and citizenship still produce the nation as variously exclusive, and Japanese Canadian women can and do name and contest these exclusions. What is important in this section is how the racism targeting Japanese Canadian women in white spaces continues to position them as outside of the Canadian nation and how women name their lived cartographies of racism and use their understandings of their histories of Internment in analysing and contesting these exclusionary practices.

While the focus in this section is on the daughters' experiences of racism as children and adults, the women interned also reported that they experienced racism during and after the dispersal period. After her incarceration, Evelyn felt that people in her British Columbia environment reacted to her 'mixed marriage' as a 'novelty.' However, the novelty was not always well received. She gave the example of going to the bank to withdraw money from her joint family account using her married name. The staff, she reported, 'looked at me as if they doubted I was that person.' She added, 'But then I wouldn't be thinking of it as discrimination. Maybe I was naive.'[45] Evelyn questioned her own perceptions at the time, and yet her experience illustrates clearly that the boundaries of whiteness and racialized people's relationship to it are policed.

Evelyn then gave examples of racism in her town, underlining the problems in the school system. She described the situation of South Asian Canadian students and their experiences of racism in the schools as 'horrifying.' 'It's removing their dignity, removing their self-confidence as students,' she explained. Due to her outrage at the situation, she became involved in instigating 'an anti-discrimination policy' within the schools.

Ann told me she had experienced a lot of racism from white people when she was growing up in British Columbia. After she left Slocan and moved to Ontario she was worried that her son would experience racism at a rural school close to the farm on which they were working. Her family moved from the farm to Chatham.[46] In 1942, the Chatham town council had demanded of the Ontario Premier that Japanese Canadians not be allowed to live in the town and that 'no Japanese [sic] are permitted to settle in Kent County permanently ... after the termination of the present war.'[47] The federal government met the Chatham town council's request by forcing Japanese Canadians sent to work in the Canada Dominion Sugar Refinery to live outside of the town.[48] The federal government eventually set up a placement office in Chatham to administer the dispersal of people in that area. The placement office was established in a town where residents had actively organized to keep them out.

In setting up a placement office in Chatham, the federal government created a new contact zone, not only between Japanese Canadians and whites but also between Japanese Canadians and Black Canadians. The Black residents of Chatham trace their communities back to at least 1790 when slaves were brought to that area by white settlers. Peggy Bristow states that in 1790, '[Sally Ainse] is said to have brought at least one slave and possibly more' to the Chatham area.[49] The area was later a destination for fugitive slaves from the United States.[50] Black Canadians' places in Chatham are the result of a long history of slavery and racist exclusion; the racist exclusions of the Internment and dispersal placed Ann's family in Chatham. When I asked Ann whether she experienced racism in Chatham, she reported that her son was 'picked on' at a Chatham school by some Black students and this resulted in a fight. She said her son defended himself and the students' actions did not reoccur.

As in the case of Naomi above, racialized individuals (and in this category, I would include Japanese Canadians), can also target those differently racialized through language and actions. Acknowledging these moments of racial tension between racialized groups is important in understanding the power of white supremacy as it mediates the relationships between differently racialized groups. In this moment of contact between Black Canadians and Japanese Canadians, racism not only produced their racialized identities but also positioned them against each other and served to divide them. The racial discourses used in their racialized contact zones must be viewed in relation to the white Canadian nation promoting and promoted by these discourses. Although unmapping zones of contact between Indigenous and racialized peoples and between racialized peoples is beyond the scope of this book, the memories of the existence of these zones importantly contests the historical erasure of narratives and examples of our communities' existence and copresence in Canada, and points towards the need for analysis of the social divisions instilled, and the alliances that developed in the different racialized and settler spaces in which we have lived and worked.

One of the daughters described her mother being targeted by racism. Janice witnessed her mother ask a 'big, burly' white man seated behind them at a hockey game to stop disturbing people. He replied using racist language and made the comment, 'Why don't you just go back to where you came from.' Her mother stood up and said, among other things, 'I'll have you know, I was born in this country.' Janice's memory of the man's response was that he shrunk into his seat. Janice, however, said she felt uncomfortable with this confrontation because it was a very public exchange. Women continually negotiate their responses to racism and consider the risks entailed in challenging it in the different places in which they work and live. Children of Internment survivors, therefore, may feel ambivalent or judgmental about their parents' not speaking *and* speaking about racism.

Sylvia was aware of her father's 'very strong feelings about racism' and had seen him verbally assaulted by white people. Due to the dispersal, her father was isolated and had few Japanese Canadian friends with whom he could speak about his incarceration in a POW camp and the racism he experienced. Subjugated knowledges of the Internment are conveyed in many ways, and Sylvia's father's protests against the racism directed at him was one way in which he conveyed his understanding of the Internment. By situating the lack of discussion about the harms of the Internment and racism within a white community where such speaking was disallowed, Sylvia emphasized that support is necessary to speak about the Internment and its violations. She concluded that for her, 'one of the damages, one of the wounds' of the Internment and of racism was not being able to talk about it and when the injustice of the Internment is denied by non-Japanese Canadians.

Joanne described a vivid memory she had of a white boy who verbally abused her with racist language. His mother owned a major company in their town. Joanne stated that she did not wish to describe racist incidents to her parents when she was a child because she felt these incidents were 'too shameful' and 'too embarrassing.' She also considered her mother's feelings when she decided not to disclose these experiences, 'I couldn't relay something so cruel that might hurt her ... So I took it upon myself.' Sylvia also emphasized that she did not tell her parents when she was called anti-Japanese names at school because she 'thought it would hurt them.' Like the example of Kyo and her encounter with racism in British Columbia, these two women dealt with racist incidents alone. Ideally, children should be able to tell their parents when they experience racism. However, Joanne's and Sylvia's reluctance and reasons for not telling their parents about their experiences of racism might be instructive in informing our understanding of why parents might not wish to discuss the harms and their feelings about the Internment with their children.

Irene stated that 'racist words' were used against her in Toronto and that these took various anti-Asian forms. She gave this example, 'A white European gentleman passed me in the street and said something derogatory about Koreans and how we should all go back to our country.' She also noted that one of her childhood friends always referred to her as 'her Japanese Canadian friend,' which she found offensive because it was in contrast to those she named as simply her 'friends.' She added, 'It's how she views the world, in specific categories,' and these categories marked her in this relationship.

Sylvia visited St Catharines, Ontario, and as she was driving into town, a white man passing in his car yelled out an anti-Chinese racist word. Both Irene's and Sylvia's reports of being the targets of anti-Asian hate language illustrate that Asian Canadians are 'imagined outside the political community'[51] and imagined to be essentially the same. As McAllister states, this non-differentiated sign of *the Asian* 'becomes a flexible image that can be loaded with changing national anxieties.'[52] Getting the Asian 'origin' wrong (i.e., we are not Chinese) is not the point. Instead, we must examine the origins of practices that legitimize and normalize the marking out of spaces of white entitlement and monopoly: the repetitive exclusion of Asians, Indigenous peoples, and other racialized groups discursively and materially reinforced by violence in the form of hate speech and attacks.

Sylvia also underlined that racism cannot be separated from sexism in analysing incidents where our bodies are marked for exclusion. She pointed out that racism seeks to diminish women of colour. She saw this when she and other Asian women were referred to as 'girls' and not 'real' women: 'I'd be in situations where a white woman my age would be calling me "dear" or refer to me as a "girl."' Laura Hyun Yi Kang also sees in the infantilization of Asian women or the 'emphasis on [their] youth' as echoing 'both patriarchal and colonial representational modes of reducing these women as subjects.'[53] In this 'national fantasy,'[54] Asian women are seen as subordinate to white people. Sylvia recounted that her cousins were asked whether they were the 'nannies' of their own mixed-ancestry children while walking in their neighbourhoods. The children were perceived to be white, and the relationship between an Asian woman and a white child was immediately construed to be that of worker and white employer.

Kyo did not enjoy travelling with her white male partner to towns or rural areas in Ontario. She remarked, 'It's really obvious when people stare at us ... I don't know whether they're staring at me or they're staring at us because we're an interracial couple.' Her comment that 'the way [my partner] experiences [a rural area] and the way I experience it are two different things' indicates that the same place is experienced differently, contingent upon how one's body is perceived in relation to that place. Women often talked about their experience of racism in relation to the places they inhabited or visited. Incidents of racism in these various places indicate that white people must continually mark the space as white in order to recreate the myth of white entitlement to ownership. Indigenous and racialized peoples in Canada are routinely seen as out of place and are reminded of what is imagined as their rightful place.[55]

In 1995, in Vancouver, Midori saw the wall of the spectacular ocean walkway in Kitsilano spray-painted with the words 'Japs Go Home.' She analysed the racist slogan in this way: 'That's the same as fifty years ago when it was "Japs Go Home." You're born in Canada. It's incongruous. Or when people say things to you on the street ...Vancouver is starting to feel to me like there's so much aggression in the city. And there's still so much of it that it's scary.' Glenn Deer's research asserts that '[r]acialized tensions over space in Vancouver and Richmond' between Asian Canadians and white Canadians in the 1990s were prevalent.[56] While Midori and the other women interviewed reported being subjected to racism throughout their lives, Midori's accounts of being 'sporadically' the target of racist language while walking in public places in the 1990s also gives lie to the mythology of large Canadian cities being 'multicultural' havens and of Vancouver as being a safe city for Asian Canadians. The street is the contact zone where 'white claims to spatial primacy'[57] marked Midori's body as not belonging and her self as not a rightful citizen of Canada. She also described the risk involved in naming incidents of racism: 'You don't want to risk sometimes saying, "I think I was being treated that way because I'm Asian." When it's not blatant, you don't know for sure. But I think there's a bit of a backlash because there are so many Asians in Vancouver.'

May indicated that she is reminded of the 1940s and her incarceration when she encounters racism and draws upon her experience in analysing it: 'When you've gone through, knowing the evacuation and all of that happened ... it scared me, for instance, when that young Chinese man was beaten to death in Detroit ... he was killed by mistake ... [the killers] were protesting against Japanese cars ...'[58]

Midori emphasized that she felt that she experienced racism in her everyday life more than sexism. 'I felt more effects from being Japanese

Canadian than from being a woman ... you know, in the Western world, it's blonde hair and, and big eyes and you know, those kind of things are supposed to be what you're aiming for. So, you know, when you're Asian, there's not much you can do about that.' Processes of racialization are also gendered, however, as in the model of womanhood offered to Midori as the norm, a norm from which she is excluded.

Sylvia explained some of the effects of gendered racism on her: 'We lived with that for all of our lives as children and as adults. I feel like I'm just coming to terms with it ... So, you know, all of that accumulates and it's very destructive.' Yuko underlined that gender, racialization, and geographic location all affected the way she was treated by others: 'Being Japanese. Being a woman. Where you grew up.' She added, 'It's hard to separate because it's all one, being a Japanese Canadian woman.'

Irene concluded that the history of the Internment taught her that 'one of the first things I formulated in my mind as a child was that I was not allowed to be racist. I could not justify being racist, because of internment.' However, she underlined that not all Japanese Canadians may have learned this lesson from their history. 'I came across another Japanese Canadian who said something racist and I thought "How could you say that?" Your family has gone through this situation. You have absolutely no right to judge somebody on their colour, their culture, their ethnicity because of that.' Irene's insights underline the contradiction of racialized people who engage in racist behaviour, as also seen above in relation to the experiences of Naomi, and Ann's son. The contradiction of racialized men enacting racism is explained by Sherene Razack in this way:

> The terms and conditions of membership in a white nation include that men of colour must forget the racial violence that is done to them ... Joining the nation ... also requires that men actively perform a hegemonic masculinity in service of the nation. This masculine ideal includes engaging in acts of racial domination. The ideal man is one who is superior to both women and racial minorities. For racial minority men, joining the nation requires, then, both forgetting racial violence and engaging in racial violence.[59]

In engaging in racism, the racialized subject becomes complicit in the web of white supremacy while simultaneously living with the devastating consequences of its power. Just as the forgetting of the Internment produces white subjects disconnected from histories of racial violence, racism between racialized groups requires forgetting their own histories of racial violence or perhaps remembering only their own and forgetting its connections to other histories of violence. This raises the following questions: By what means do Japanese Canadians attempt to join the nation? Does it require forgetting our history of the Internment and racial violence? Does it require remembering only the history of the Internment and forgetting its connection to other histories of colonial and racial violence? How do we secure our spatial toeholds in the settler nation? How are we complicit in the hegemonies of citizen constitution and settler nation-building?

Naomi recounted that she and her mother discussed the racism they experienced, but she added:

> We talk about [racism] a lot with each other and with my sister. It's ironic that we talk about issues like racism and how she experiences that in her work and how I experience it at school ... but we don't specifically talk about the internment. It's this whole idea that it's past. *But that's the root of it.* That's a really fundamental part of my mother's history and my grandmother's history and my history. And yet it's unspoken. Whereas these other things, they're happening in our lives now so ... that's what we talk about.

Naomi traces her own experiences of racism to the Internment, 'the root,' 'fundamental' to the lives of her grandmother, mother, and sister, and to her own life. In this way, she traces a history of racial exclusion by connecting the racism she experiences to that which led to the Internment. As a result, she contests the relegation of the Internment to the past because it shaped who they are and how they understand the racism they continue to experience. Hence, conversations or activities engaged in by survivors that do not specifically speak to the Internment may, in fact, be conveying their subjugated knowledge of this history in different ways. Importantly, the knowledge survivors acquired about the processes of racism and racial exclusion can be used, as illustrated by Yoshiko, to support their children's struggles.

Mayumi told me that she had submitted a complaint to the Human Rights Commission about the racism she had experienced. She was able to discuss the complaint with her mother Ann before it was launched and described Ann's response as '[i]f you think it's wrong, then you have to do whatever you think is right.' From taking responsibility in making the decision in response to the federal government's 'repatriation' scheme in 1945 – a decision that affected her family and subsequent generations – to this moment of support for her daughter, we see the everyday negotiations a survivor of the Internment made in relation to a history of racism. A cross-generational history of struggle and resistance to racism has been underexplored in relation to Japanese Canadians. Ann's, Mayumi's, and Naomi's testimonies contest the masculinized notion of resistance (see chapter 2) and also illustrate that women such as Ann and Yoshiko enable and support the fight against racism undertaken by their children.

Resisting with Other Subordinated Communities

Just as the denial of the ability to live as families during the Internment produced different responses, the destruction of their communities in the 1940s resulted in people reconfiguring their notions of community, which included trying to establish Japanese Canadian communities or being alienated from other Japanese Canadians. May explained that she was separated from all of her Vancouver friends and felt that others who were incarcerated 'seemed to have a friend,' while she had to start at 'square one ... That felt really unfair somehow, that everybody else had a community.' This isolation resulted in what May called a 'disorientation,' going 'back and forth' between spending time with Japanese Canadians and white Canadians, but 'not being anywhere.' May's feeling of disorientation was experienced spatially in social dissonances that resulted from crossing the boundaries between Japanese Canadian spaces and white spaces even after the Internment and redress struggle.

While all of the women interviewed made reference to the term 'Japanese Canadian community,' both in referring to collectivities past and present, some of the women interviewed described the Internment in relation to the struggles of other subordinated groups. Hence their reconfigured community included these groups. May used her understanding of her experience of the Internment to criticize the position of a Canadian church and some of its members on homosexuality. Some of the church members told her they knew individual gay people and yet they 'were down on these people as a *group* of people.' She wondered, 'Does that mean they know me but they would still be down on my people?' Aware that Japanese Canadians are accused of passivity – of not resisting – during the Internment, Esther made a comparison of their situation to how women have historically struggled against male domination and concluded, 'We [women] are still fighting for change.' Hence being subordinated should not be confused with accepting subordination.

However, comparing the position of Japanese Canadians to other subordinated groups, does not mean that their positions of subordination are identical nor does it erase their positions of privilege. As non-interned daughters of Internment survivors, we are socially situated differently from our interned relatives by not having been interned, despite the racism and effects of the Internment that we continue to differently live. Sylvia situated herself in relation to the privilege she experiences as a middle-class woman while still being subjected to racism. She stated that she has options that working-class people of colour do not have in dealing with the racism they experience.

Some of the women emphasized that the history of the Internment led them to work for social justice. Many worked in unpaid capacities for community organizations. For instance, Evelyn explained that because she has been affected by her history, her 'attitude to the society would be affected.' She stated that she will not tolerate injustice or discrimination and that her children will be affected by witnessing the stands that she takes. Eiko saw her involvement in social justice issues as reflective of what her own parents had done with their analyses of their own experiences of the Internment. She told me her parents were volunteering for a community organization on the day that I interviewed her, and remarked, '[My] involvement in social justice ... comes as a direct result of an experience that's not even mine to claim, that sort of by osmosis is mine.' She added: 'I also think that in terms of very basic human rights, just to be on the side of the disabled, to be on the side of women, I know that's all shaped in me, wheelchair or not, woman or not, to fight for people of colour who live in situations of racism ... and, and.'

Joanne proposed an image of community that she has built in relationship with other people. For her, resisting domination is about 'actually changing the space of the violations against people ... [to present meaningful] possibilities for loving and living and producing.' Naomi, Janice, Joanne, Eiko, Kyo, and others suggested that it was critical to organize with other subordinated communities to fight racism and other systems of domination. In so doing, we may be able to trace how systems and spaces of domination position us relationally, and we may be able to examine the ways in which we variously experience and enact domination.

'Japanese Canadians' and the Canadian Nation

The women interviewed discussed the historical language of their naming, the term 'Japanese Canadian.' This term is another effect of the Internment, linked as it is to the identity used by the Canadian state to describe those who were allowed to remain in Canada and those who were dispersed.[60] Wendy Brown warns of the problems of 'politicized identity' and of 'identity politics' with 'its defensive closure on identity, its insistence on the fixity of position.'[61] Clearly, I am complicit in reproducing the notion of a 'Japanese Canadian' identity, as my decision to use the term 'Japanese Canadian' has taken discursive precedence throughout this book. However, Brown's identification of these identities as based on 'a past of injury' does not adequately address the dichotomy of past and present as a function of liberal discourses that deny the sediments of the past in the present, and the present and ongoing interpellations of racialized identity and exclusionary notions of citizenship with which racialized subjects must continue to contend. The challenge for Japanese Canadians is to critically assess these identifiers and why they are important to ourselves and others. How do the terms 'Japanese' or 'Japanese Canadian' or 'Canadian' (their use or non-use) situate us in relation to citizenship and Canada?

Women's negotiations of their own identities as named by others and themselves indicate the problems they have with discourses of racialized identity and normalized citizenship and the challenges their self-identifications have endured. For example, Sylvia explained that she and her cousins have been questioned since childhood about their relationship to Canadian citizenship:

> Someone meets you and the old situation, they immediately say 'Where do you come from?' and we'd defensively say, 'We were born here' and were denying our Japanese ancestry at the same time. But we wanted to make a point that we weren't immigrants. I can recall a number of incidents where even people I knew and liked would ask me where I came from and would assume that I was an immigrant even though they knew better.

In her statement, Sylvia points out the trap of constituting oneself as 'Canadian' in response to the familiar interrogation because she must then differentiate her own identity from identities demeaned by others in the genealogy of her subjecthood and reify the identities of 'Japanese' and 'immigrant' as different from 'Canadian.'

Irene has found that her self-identification is questioned by white people in two ways. First: 'Why doesn't she call herself a "Canadian?"' And second: When she does call herself 'Canadian,' the interrogator insists that she must be 'from' somewhere else and must disclose this. From an early age, Irene felt her resistance against people who sought an originary country with their racializing questions, 'Are you Korean? Are you Chinese? Are you from Taiwan?' was best expressed by her response 'I am Canadian.' Yet her interrogators would predictably not accept this and would 'go back far enough in the family history to find out' the where. 'That turned me off saying "I'm Canadian!" ... But I'm not Japanese. That's not what I am. I'm Japanese Canadian,' she concluded.

Naomi, however, admitted that calling herself 'Japanese Canadian' makes her uncomfortable. 'It doesn't feel as real or natural ... as saying ... Sansei or Asian or mixed.' For Naomi, Canada or Canadian does not 'reflect' who she is. Rather, these words – Canadian, American, Western – convey to her the notions of 'consumption ... exploitation ... monoculture.'

Some of the women I interviewed used the term 'Japanese' as a self-identifier or identifier of people with whom they share a history of Internment. The term Sansei or Yonsei is also mobilized in different ways. Irene stated that she only uses the term Sansei when she is with Japanese Canadians and Japanese Americans. Although I have been critical of the ways in which the generational designations of 'Issei,' 'Nisei,' and 'Sansei' have been used to produce totalizing images of each generation, I do see the use of these terms as a technology of memory that is encoded to situate us in relation to histories of immigration and the Internment.[62] They can serve as a linguistic mapping of living the effects of national violence and a form of enunciated resistance to the demonization of our historical connections to the Japanese language.

In her critique of the normalization of the process called 'assimilation,' Yoshiko suggested that the term actually disguises what is an inherently racist imperative. She stated, 'I know people say it's not racism, but to me it is. It's the arrogance of one particular culture or group of people over another.' 'There are so many different cultures or ethnic groups in Canada,' she stated. 'You come out of it without really a claim to any ... particular group or specific culture. You're this individual person.'[63] Yoshiko's analysis challenges the processes of racialization and ethnocentrism inherent to the assimilation discourse, and the processes that serve to Other cultures and groups in the process of producing an unmarked, autonomous, 'individual' citizen.

Conclusion

The women's descriptions of their schooling in three different regions of Canada emphasize the isolation that each one experienced in terms of knowing that she was alone or nearly alone in being racialized within these institutional spaces. The fact that many could name themselves as the only racialized person in the class or could name the only other racialized person in the class or school indicates that their schools were largely attended by white students who were taught mostly by white teachers. Naomi was an exception in that she went to primary school with other racialized students; whiteness still regulated the relationships among the racialized, however, in a complex web where divisions were produced between racialized settlers and Indigenous peoples. The women's isolation is also underlined in their memories of trying to address the forgetting of the Internment in schools, the ways in which they were singled out by anti-Japanese and anti-Asian racist acts and language, and their efforts to deal with racism at school and in other white spaces. This isolation from other Japanese Canadians and growing up in 'white communities,' as women described them, is an effect of the Internment and dispersal policies of the federal government. Spatially separating Japanese Canadians through the dispersal resulted in individualized racialized families and subjects who, while allowed to remain in Canada, had to contend with ongoing racism on their own. In classrooms in different regions of Canada, the daughters interviewed were variously confronted with gendered, racist, and middle-class speech and behaviours that were initiated by dominant subjects or those seeking to be dominant. Their descriptions of objectification, exoticization, and being targeted by racism attest to the ways in which the white social order, in part solidified during the Internment, continued to be constructed in relation to their bodies long after the sites of the Internment were closed. Based on this racial schema, their visibility as Japanese Canadians in white landscapes made them easy to see and hence to scrutinize, at the same time as they and their histories of Internment were rendered invisible. Racialization continued to be a technology of surveillance and control, part of the carceral continuum of their present.

In her oft-cited description of her social position in the United States, Mitsuye Yamada, a survivor of the U.S. Internment, described her 'invisibility' as an 'unnatural disaster.'[64] In this chapter we saw the genealogy of visibility/invisibility in the historically specific case of Japanese Canadian women, where the process through which their racialized visibility was produced simultaneously to their invisibility as citizen-subjects who also had a 'Canadian' history. Their visibility and invisibility are witnessed through their experiences of racism in three different regions of Canada while their and Canada's histories of the Internment were forgotten.

Traise Yamamoto describes the 'Asian American as an invisible subject who is nevertheless highly visible as a racially marked object … the differing levels of Asian American in/visibility will have as their complement the subject visibility/racial invisibility of the dominant white subject'[65] At the same time that the Internment was forgotten in various white spaces and by the white people in them, Asian origins were continuously imagined and remembered by white people in their encounters with Japanese Canadian women. The imagining of the nation and its proper citizens as white necessitates this forgetting of the Internment, an act that renders Japanese Canadians' histories invisible; racist speech marks their visibility and reinscribes the violence forgotten. While discourses of race shift over time and are different from those that were mobilized in the 1940s, there were constant reminders for the women interviewed that their place in Canada was still questionable and re-placeable in the imaginations of those who rendered them as perpetual foreigners. Hence the sediments of the 1940s anti-Japanese racism lived on in specific racial epithets and a discourse that enfigured white people as legitimate citizens entitled to name the racialized as not belonging in Canada. As Deer argues, 'the vestigial elements of the older warning signals of the "yellow peril" racializations continue to haunt us in the symbolic economy.'[66]

While the outcomes of the racism experienced by the daughters were not the same as what was produced for their mothers through the Internment, the move to minimize the racism experienced by the daughters interviewed and those who report experiencing racism in the present functions as a liberal narrative of progress (it is better than it was) and a re-individuating process of subject formation (it is random and you are singular in its reception), which serve as an attempt to silence any action taken to disclose it or to fight it. Thus the binary of visibility/invisibility is reiterated through the visible claim of racism as occurring in Canada and the dismissal of the claim, rendering it and racism invisible. The histories of racism lived by Japanese Canadian women and men must be further investigated. A disclosure offered by one of the daughters who knew that her brother was beaten by white male schoolmates, demonstrates that white supremacy is enforced through different modalities of violence. More recently, Hijin Park has exposed numbers of sexual assaults and murders where East Asian women were specifically targeted. These women were citizens of or visiting students in Canada and the United States between 2000 and 2005.[67] The forgetting of the racial component in these crimes reflects the way in which 'race' has been rendered insignificant by each nation-state,[68] hence reproducing the myth of the United States and Canada and the people who reside within them as free of the tarnish of racism and, in this case, anti-Asian racism.

Concomitant to this production of the myth of racism as not existing in Canada, the history of the effects of the Internment must be forgotten or contained. Even when the Internment is a seemingly allowed part of the narration of Canada's history, it must necessarily be controlled, so that the moral of the story is that racism in Canada is a thing of the past. But racism is very present for racialized people in Canada. The forgetting of who has been and must be removed or excluded in producing Canada is a reiterative memory formation for white subjects. Moreover, part of the ongoing production of forgetting requires that Japanese Canadians also forget their histories of Internment or remember it in ways that are 'disciplined.'[69] Thus the forgetting of the Internment must also be institutionalized, for example, through the silence and silencing practices of the educational system witnessed by the daughters. This occurred concretely in the lack of curriculum on the Internment or the ways in which its acknowledgment by the institution and its teachers was contained by disciplinary and temporal contexts of the study of the Second World War or variously inhibited by a lack of support, exclusion, or penalty.

Women, however, resisted the forgetting of the Internment in schools and in other white-dominated spaces. As is demonstrated in this chapter, in re-membering the Internment, Japanese Canadian women also remember the nation as one in which they and their families have struggled against racism. These histories of struggle illustrate not only the racialized marking of the Japanese Canadian/Asian Canadian subject within the nation-state but also reveal the cracks in the mythology of the nation as an always stable entity. As is stated by Kang, 'A solid "presence" of nationality can be conceived only through the virulent marking out of various alien-others for exclusion and repression but these very gestures of negation ... can reveal the uncertainty and instability of that very national identity.'[70] Homi Bhabha also contends that 'the racist gaze' enunciated through 'racist stereotypes, statements, jokes, myths' reveals the 'narcissism and paranoia' of the figure of domination. It is through these representational admissions that the figure of domination loses its 'representational authority' by revealing the 'phobic myth of the undifferentiated whole white body.'[71] Yet it must be emphasized that the racist violence unleashed through these repetitive processes of re-stabilization of the national identity and hegemonic subject produce harms of enormous consequence for racialized peoples. In the mnemonic encounter with a forgetting of the Internment, and a denial of racism in the past and present, women resist through re-membering in distinct and diverse ways. In resisting through the spaces of forgetting, I argue in the next chapter that women's subjugated knowledge of the Internment can be mobilized to raise questions about nation, citizenship, and the subject.

10 Conclusion: Re-membering the Subjects of the 'Internment'

It shouldn't have happened in the first place. And so it shouldn't happen again ... that would be a mistake not to tell future generations what happened. And I hope that they will learn from what's gone on and this evacuation that we went through.

S., interview[1]

Through ... remembering ... re-composition, new forms of subjectivity and community are thought and signified.

Lisa Lowe, Immigrant Acts[2]

In 2002 at a university function, I was introduced to a white woman described as a progressive activist who said she wanted to meet me because of my research on the Internment. In a lowered voice, she said, 'I am determined to find evidence that the internment of Japanese Canadians was justified.' In this confessional moment, the Internment was clearly not a past and finished event but continued to shape our encounter and our different investments in its telling.

Rita Dhamoon and Yasmeen Abu-Laban argue that 'it has been by now well established by historians that the Othering of Japanese-Canadians in the name of the "security and defence of Canada" in the 1940s had more to do with a re-nationalization project than the "necessities of war."'[3] While I agree with Dhamoon and Abu-Laban that the Internment was and is a 're-nationalization project,' the contention that this analysis is well established does not account for the ongoing contests over its meaning faced by Japanese Canadians, not only in individual encounters with forgetting but also in national ones, such as the one with the Canadian War Museum (see chapter 2). Grace Eiko Thomson, past president of the National Association of Japanese Canadians, argues that some Internment histories have been 'written by others who never experienced these events but interpret this history,' and are '(*mis*)interpreted,' and 'prejudicial language' is still used by 'those in possession of power, in exhibits, or as entries on plaques designating our history at heritage sites, and in various publications and media which use our lives as subject matter'; therefore, Thomson calls for a vigorous examination of representations of the Internment.[4]

The Internment and its representation continue to construct and affect Japanese Canadians who were incarcerated and the generations that have followed. As I have argued, the Internment continues to produce subjects, and the nation of Canada, through the very positions we take in relation to it and in the ways we construct Japanese Canadians and constitute ourselves through this process.

Furthermore, in looking over the body of research and writing on the Internment, I conclude that those who were interned continue to be scrutinized through the use of their selves and their histories. I know that I am complicit in this process, asking women to expose their selves to my interpretation and inevitably to the judgment of readers. The discourses of the Internment, including this book itself, continue to construct Japanese Canadians and, relationally, also construct us as witnesses. Moreover, I find it notable that the subjects who established and enforced the Internment and the participants in and witnesses to it have been less written about and hence less scrutinized. This is a material imbalance in scholarly and cultural production that I would suggest has everything to do with an imbalance in power, which includes the power of whiteness.

Interestingly, in some of the accounts authored by Japanese Canadians, white participants and witnesses are remembered. Two women interviewed by me remembered that their white neighbours, one described as a 'Polish man,' did look after their possessions until they could be retrieved after years of incarceration. While these gestures were appreciated by the women interviewed, they were also aware that they had to leave, while their neighbours remained. This illustrates that the web of power, which includes the power of whiteness, assigned to these neighbours benefits and rights even while they may have been attempting to resist the total dispossession of those who trusted them with their possessions. Except for Indigenous peoples who were themselves in carceral spaces in British Columbia and across Canada, being able to remain or be in the restricted area was a right that was protected relationally to the denial of rights to Japanese Canadians. While some people may have not agreed with the federal policies, the lack of organized protest on the part of these witnesses raises questions about silent complicity with these policies,[5] and responsibility for witnessing and benefiting from violences past and present.

Re-membering the 'Internment'

I contrast the 2002 encounter described above with the ongoing practices of witnessing histories of the Internment and their effects engaged in by survivors and their descendants. On one such occasion, a man told me his partner had recurring nightmares about being sexually assaulted because her mother was sexually assaulted during the Internment. This handing down of a memory of violence that took place during the Internment reveals an example of the effects of the violence committed through the context of the Internment, for both mother and daughter. It is some of these effects of the Internment that I wished to unmap in this book, at the same time as I know the impossibility of naming, let alone addressing most of its effects.

Acts of remembrance can also be acts of resistance, and the burden of remembering the Internment falls heavily upon those who were interned and their families. While the interviews for the book were conducted fifteen years ago, I am constantly reminded of their relevance and the contribution of the women who participated in the research for this book as I work with other Japanese Canadians who were interned and their descendants. Most research thus far on the Internment has not analysed what the Internment produced in the lives of Japanese Canadians and for Canada as a nation. As Thomson suggested in her quote in the introduction, little has been represented about Japanese Canadians' lives in the post-Internment period. This book attempts to address some of the effects of the Internment and how they were re-membered and understood soon after the redress settlement.

As I argued in chapter 3, the women interviewed would have continued to acquire knowledge on the processes of the Internment and its effects both for themselves and others interned. The Internment as a social and political process of subject formation did not therefore end in 1949 when the legal restrictions upon their movements were finally lifted. It is an ongoing process for those interned and their families. Sadly, one of the women passed on the year after I interviewed her. Her passing underlines the finite nature of recording survivor Internment testimonies and the important gift of knowledge that she and all of the women interviewed extended to me.

I know that others will continue to re-member and analyse in their own ways and perhaps respond to the ways in which I have re-membered and analysed. This work is produced in relation to the women I have interviewed and to the many people through whose work and example I have found inspiration and hope. It is offered in the desire that we remember we are each connected to the history of the Internment and to the histories of other people with whom we share national and transnational spaces, and that within *our* imagined communities we will seek creative possibilities for challenging domination in all its forms.

Kirsten Emiko McAllister suggests that 'collective forms of remembering play a vital role in rebuilding and transforming the communities of historically persecuted groups.'[6] Supportive community environments for this engagement must be developed, both for parents and for children of all ages who may not have elder family members or peers with whom they can discuss these histories. Pedagogical strategies that address the challenges in communicating with children about the Internment and other histories of violence must also be developed.

That so many survivors have worked on our behalf in transmitting knowledge of the Internment to us are pedagogical acts that must not go unnoticed. It must also be recognized that the work necessarily engages psychological processes of remembering traumatic events, and it is my hope that we can develop non-pathologizing forms of support for those who are called upon to remember. Most Internment survivors' memories, however, will not be represented publicly or be known by those outside of their families (and maybe not even by them). Recent efforts by Japanese Canadian community groups illustrate the need for the generations of the Internment to continue to record and analyse the histories of the Internment in Canada.[7] The participation of children and grandchildren of survivors in organizing these communal spaces of remembrance attests to the need of non-interned children to fill in the gaps of the history of the Internment and understand its effects in their own lives.

Some might ask, 'What about the "positive" memories of the Internment?' I would suggest that 'positive' memories are due to social practices of resisting. How people organized to make 'positive memories' and to survive the years of living in carceral places is a subject that still requires critical examination. As I have argued, people were differently, socially positioned during the Internment according to class background, gender, ability, age, citizenship, facility with the English language, et cetera. They were also differently spatially located, another factor that affected their experiences and memories of the Internment. Ultimately, I would ask how our own subject positions, and a liberal and multicultural discourse that renders racial violence as of the past, inform the inclination to yearn for a redemptive narrative that minimizes the violence, and sees Japanese Canadians as unidimensionally and unilaterally successful. Furthermore, judging those who have suffered from violence for not expressing 'pain' (or what *we* consider to be pain) raises the question, 'Why is this expression required as evidence of violence?' As Sara Ahmed argues,

> The reduction of judgements about what is bad or wrong to experiences of hurt, pain or suffering would be deeply problematic. For the claim would allow violence to be sustained in the event that the other claimed not to suffer, or that I claimed the other did not suffer. We must remember that some forms of violence remain concealed *as* violence, as effects of social norms that are hidden from view. Given this, violence itself could be justified on the grounds of the absence of consciously-felt suffering.[8]

Wendy Brown argues that an identity forged through violation may 'resubjugate itself through its investment in its own pain, through its refusal to make itself in the present, memory is the house of this activity and this refusal.' Brown, however, does not advocate forgetting and argues that 'erased histories and historical invisibility are themselves such integral elements of the pain inscribed in most subjugated identities that the counsel of forgetting ... seems inappropriate if not cruel.'[9] Survivors are differently socially located in this practice of re-membering the Internment than are their children. Non-Japanese Canadians are differently located than Japanese Canadians. I would hope that the interned and non-interned generations can continue to organize Japanese Canadian spaces of remembrance. In addition, inspired by the survivors I interviewed, and their ability to locate themselves socially and relationally, I ask of my generation and the ones that follow how we might re-member relationally and organize in non-colonizing ways, 'remembering that serves to illuminate and transform the present.'[10] That is, re-member in a way that acknowledges all of the histories and places through which we are constituted, our places of penalty (for example, of racialization and racism) *and* our places of privilege (for example, living on Indigenous territories and variously positions of class, gender, ability, sexuality, et cetera). In placing ourselves in this way, we might be able to re-member in relation to and with others (including other subordinated groups), not with the goal of negating or forgetting 'a' particular history that has shaped us but to see its relational and historical continuities and complicities, resituating ourselves as relational subjects of the Internment and subjects of relational Canadian and global histories. In this way we might be able to see what was suggested by the women's interviews – the extent of the violence – and the ways in which violences and complicities can be obscured.

Against Forgetting the Subjects of the 'Internment': The Redress Agreement

The 1988 redress settlement between the National Association of Japanese Canadians (NAJC) and the federal government was the result of years of negotiation and strategy within Japanese Canadian communities. Part of the settlement included a token payment of $21,000 to each survivor who was alive at the time the settlement was signed on 22 September 1988.[11] It also included $12 million for the rebuilding of Japanese Canadian communities and $12 million for the establishment of a Race Relations Foundation[12] in commemoration of all those interned, an amount which was matched by the federal government.[13] Throughout the redress struggle, the NAJC fought for the elimination of the War Measures Act.[14]

McAllister argues that in fighting for redress, Japanese Canadians 'realized that it was politically necessary to write themselves into the nation's public sphere.'[15] Clearly, the redress movement drew on notions of individual rights and equality, and in attempting to 'write themselves' into a narrative that the nation would hear they appealed to the discourses of liberalism and hence laid claim to being entitled to the 'equality' of the liberal subject. However, the processes of the redress movement involved complex political theorizing, consensus-building activities, the sharing of memories, and practices of commemoration, which situated many subjects in discourses of subjecthood that require further analysis.

Japanese Canadians live the contradictory positions of being officially acknowledged for the injustice of the Internment by a federal govern-

ment and at the same time being aware of the harms of the Internment
that will never be addressed while still living with their effects. Given
that the women interviewed for this project spoke to me within a de-
cade after redress, their critiques of the settlement are informative as
to how some survivors and their children viewed this action by the
federal government soon after the 1988 agreement was signed. Rather
than the closure that some might suggest redress signifies, just as the
Internment lives on in our memories and in its material and social effects, the effects of the process of redress are ongoing and are informed
by and inform the memories of Japanese Canadians and other citizens.
As McAllister states, '[T]he redress movement in itself was not capable
of resolving the violations of the past nor issues and concerns that faced
the contemporary community.'[16] Hence, to attribute to redress a closure
to or healing of the Internment legacy reinscribes the liberal narrative
of progress, a familiar trope in the narrativization of the Japanese Canadian subject.

In writing about the redress settlement in the United States, Marita
Sturken asks, 'Can we really say that, in the case of the United States, an
apology and the payment of twenty thousand dollars to survivors was
a gesture that absolved the act? Doesn't this allow for the placement of
a very small price on the losses generated by the camps? ... if the mere
mention of the camps by an American president or former president
constitutes atonement, as is often noted in the media, then the price
to assuage guilt is small indeed.'[17] Roy Miki characterizes redress as an
'event that redeemed the nation' and a 'gift to the official history of the
nation.'[18] In concluding with the testimonies of women regarding the
redress settlement, I realize that their words may be read in many ways,
including the judgment of them as 'ungrateful' (of which critical racialized Canadians are sometimes accused), or even, in view of Sturken's
critique, that they have settled for too little. Your readings and mine,
I would argue, are ongoing moments in the construction of Japanese
Canadians and reflect the imagined position of Japanese Canadians
at the moment of our reading. In making women's critiques visible, I
wish to acknowledge their ambivalence and careful remembrance of
the subjects of the Internment, subjects who cannot be neatly contained
by the discourse of the resolved 'redressed subject.'[19] My intent in this
section is to render visible the subordinated knowledges of the women
interviewed in order to illustrate their awareness of the subjects not
redressed by this important yet incomplete process. I also wish to argue
against the forgetting of the Internment and its effects in order to con-

tinue to problematize notions of the Canadian nation, citizenship, and the subject.

The struggle against the forgetting of the harms and effects of the Internment was cogently expressed when I asked the women I interviewed about their impressions of the redress settlement. As I showed in chapter 8, the activities of the redress movement supported the discussion of the Internment within some families and in some Japanese Canadian community spaces. But despite a federal government's acknowledgment and public declaration of the injustice of the Internment, women's testimonies indicate that re-membering the Internment in other places was still met with forgetting and sometimes hostility, even post-redress.

Many of the women, such as Aya, expressed appreciation for the work that was done by Japanese Canadians who participated in the redress movement.[20] Evelyn hoped that one direct effect of redress would be a change in the education curriculum, a change in what is taught as Canadian history. Without redress, she felt her history would not have been recognized as 'history.'[21] Therefore the redress settlement was viewed by her as affecting education for all children and adults, promoting an epistemological shift in how they view the history of Canada. The memories of Japanese Canadians could be used to make a public collective memory, enabling them to enter 'into history.'[22] Her comment also suggests that in order to have a history in Canada, the federal government must recognize it as history. Yet what is recognized by the federal government and incorporated into a national narrative may, as we saw in chapters 1 and 2, result in reproducing the notion of Canada as a nation where equality reigns, relegating racism to the past. As Lisa Lowe argues, the eventual inclusion of some racialized peoples as citizens necessitates a disavowal of the history attesting to their historical exclusion.[23] In the case of Japanese Canadians, this disavowal occurs through a masking of the residual effects of the Internment not only in the lives of those incarcerated and in subsequent generations but also in the making of the nation and its citizens. In addition, narratives of the Internment and redress, when evoked by the Canadian state, are moments that reinstate notions of a moral nation and citizens.

Margaret insisted that the monetary component was an essential contribution of the redress settlement. She was conscious that some people were critical of this part of the agreement with the government, but maintained, 'I'm not like some people saying, "I don't want to touch that money."' She also re-membered other Japanese Canadians who died before the settlement was negotiated and emphasized, 'there were a lot of people who worked towards that end.'[24] Kazuko raised the issue of the redress settlement and stated, 'It didn't take the place of everything we lost but it's something ... We had an apology from the prime minister, but that doesn't cover everything.' She explained that her father died before the settlement, and he had 'lost everything ... the ten acres, the berry farm, the chickens, the horses.' 'We have lost an awful lot,' she emphasized.[25] Kazuko's daughter, Sylvia, remembered her father as she discussed the redress settlement: 'It's a very small sum of money. And the money obviously doesn't repair all of the hurts and the loss of property, et cetera.' She also underlined that the amount of $21,000 only went to those who were alive at the time the agreement was signed with the government: 'My father died before the settlement. A number of relatives had died.' In her view, the settlement did not erase 'the lasting wounds that even people in my generation feel.'[26] Evelyn defined redress as a 'major contribution to Canadians.' She added, 'It would never, never be able to compensate for all that they have robbed. But financial compensation is a recognition of the wrong they have done to Japanese Canadians.'

Irene expressed her concern about how Japanese Canadians were constructed after the redress agreement: 'Winning redress has marked Japanese Canadians as somehow special, somehow privileged. I think people saw us as being middle and upper-middle class to begin with.'[27] Midori remarked that she was happy for her parents, but thought the 'hard part for a lot of people was that most of the Issei who really deserved it weren't around to receive it.'[28] Louise also expressed regret that her father had not lived to see redress accomplished and that her father-in-law had not lived to receive the acknowledgment. She also pointed out the elders' losses of property and rights, but thought the settlement was good in acknowledging that the government 'had done wrong.'[29]

Haru, too, regretted that her husband 'wasn't here to see that day.' While other women stated that the Issei faced the greatest hardship during the Internment, Haru felt that the Nisei had the most difficult experiences during and after the incarcerations: 'They went through the war, they all had to start with nothing. My husband came out with one little canvas bag. So did I. Everybody did.'[30] Ann expressed her view on the redress settlement in this way:

I guess nobody gains by [redress], do they? At least I don't think so. I guess for most, a lot of us, it came too late. Like my husband didn't have much time to enjoy it. I guess the monetary thing is the least of it, isn't it? No matter how much of an apology we get, it'll never make up for those lost years. But the thought that is there says something, doesn't it?[31]

Mayumi, Ann's daughter, also emphasized that her father was personally committed to the redress struggle and knew that a negotiated agreement had been reached, but he died a few weeks before the cheque from the federal government arrived. 'After everything he had been through and I know how he felt about it. But it never arrived,' she stated. Her mother's cheque had arrived before her father's death. Mayumi also found it 'interesting that [the government] did that at all' and acknowledged 'how much work it took to get there.' However, she concluded: 'But that doesn't make it over. It doesn't make it okay.'[32] Eiko's mother and father 'gave a lot of the [redress money] away.' She explained, 'They carefully went through their whole history and thought of all those places, people that had helped' and added, 'I really admired my parents for doing that. And they're not well-off.'[33]

S. recalled how the Internment changed her 'daily existence' and affected her education. She stated that it was 'an experience that turned out – essential in someone's eyes – but not good for the Japanese. I think we lost a great deal, and in a sense, if you were able to go back and think of all the small things that made the difference, then that's what we lost.' In each of these instances, women again used their memories of community to situate themselves within a network of relationships remembered: those who did not live to see the redress settlement or receive the token compensation, those who worked on the redress campaign, and those to whom we pass on the responsibility to continue to remember the losses sustained.

Many of the women I interviewed saw redress as a warning that 'it should not happen again.' For example, Evelyn concluded, 'One hopes that the government having had to [make redress] would think twice the next time.' Kazuko expressed the fear that her daughter and others could be treated in the same way and emphasized: 'I just hope it won't happen again.' The mnemonic record carried by the generations of the Internment informs a present knowledge that despite the redress settlement 'it' could happen again, as Evelyn and Kazuko suggest. Living with the fear of the 'knock on the door,' a fear held for themselves and other racialized Canadians, is also an effect of the Internment. However, this fear should not be reduced to a psychological paranoia; rather it is informed by the racism women still experienced and observed others experiencing. This insight was expressed by Janice, who stated,

> It's a real unnerving, insidious feeling that everything can just be taken away from you and that the government has so much power, that people have so much power to shape what government does. Knowing how all the things that happened before the internment – my uncle used to talk about that too – the racism. That's just engrained in my experience and who I am and how I see the world. So I'm very freaked out when I see [racism]. I sense a potential rise in fascism or something.[34]

Kyo expressed her feeling that her knowledge of her parents' incarcerations has impressed upon her 'how easily things can be pulled from under you with legal authority. And that's scary.'[35]

Because the women were interviewed in the mid-1990s, before the attack on the World Trade Center in New York, I do not address the effects of emergency legislation[36] in Canada post-September 11, 2001, and the forms of policing of immigrants and racialized people that have ensued.[37] This carceral continuum must necessarily draw upon colonial, internment, and other discourses that have historically rendered Indigenous peoples and racialized groups outside of or marginal to the Canadian nation and have been relationally constitutive of the notions of 'national security' and 'freedom.' Further critical writing on the Internment is needed, including writing that would contribute to an analysis of the ongoing use of the law to detain and incarcerate those deemed a threat to national security and the production of carceral sites nationally and internationally.[38]

The women interviewed remembered the nation as one where unjust incarceration, dispossession, and dispersal of citizens occurred, and they could also imagine unjust expulsion and incarceration as a present and future possibility. As many of them reported, racism in Canada did not stop with the signing of the redress agreement. Racial profiling and racism continue to be technologies of physical and symbolic expulsion in the present. The women's prediction that 'it' might occur again also suggests a notion of Canada different from 'a society that ensures equality and justice for all, regardless of race or ethnic origin'[39] – reiterated within the written text of the redress agreement itself. 'It' may take different forms, but the present policing of Muslim and Arab

Canadians by the Canadian state, and the ongoing policing of and assaults on Indigenous peoples and Black Canadians are evidence of the
continuing production of a settler and racial state.[40]

Sturken argues that in order to fully acknowledge the memory of the
Internment we must ask questions about the meaning of the national
myth of the moral nation.[41] While the 'redressed' Japanese Canadian
subject has been written into Canadian history and is used, as Roy Miki
suggests, to redeem the Canadian nation, the ongoing subjugation of
Indigenous peoples and racialized citizens through colonialism and
racism has not ended nor been redressed. While Canada is purported
to be a multicultural society and hence accepting of multiple cultures,[42]
racism and processes of racialization continue to produce the hegemony of whiteness. As Hijin Park argues in relation to the construction
of Asian Canadians, 'histories of the fear of Asian migration and more
recently the threat of Asian capital are a constant and enduring part
of the Canadian imaginary ... the discourse of Asian foreignness and
invasion reinvents itself in familiar and yet novel ways. The threat of
Asian invasion, bodily, culturally, economically and politically, must
also be managed and regulated.'[43] In the mnemonic encounters with
people who imagine the nation and its citizens as white, Asian Canadian women are assailed with questions about our supposed other origins. We are imagined as outside of the Canadian nation. As Japanese
Canadian women who have lived through or inherited the history of
Internment, we negotiate the relations of power in our lives and confront the 'orienting' of our selves – the images of racialized, sexualized
Asian women – that situate us as gendered and raced subjects outside
of the Canadian nation. Each of us develops various strategies for resisting these disorienting processes and the systems of domination that
produce them.

However, in order to appear moral and benevolent, the Canadian nation needs some Japanese Canadians, including the grateful redressed
Japanese Canadian, especially those who are seen to have 'made it' in
hegemonic economic or social terms, to fulfil the function of redemption
as well as the proof of multiculturalism.[44] The liberal subject needs to
claim that some racialized subjects have achieved equality (even if this
is not quite the case) in order to appear liberal. Hence some Japanese
Canadian men and women are called upon to fulfil this public role.

Laura Hyun Yi Kang suggests we rethink the position of the Asian
female; she is not '(merely) an abjected or desired body,' but is also

used to constitute a national identity. Asian Canadian women thus can use their subordinated knowledge to 'calibrate ... the membership criteria of the nation-state.'[45] Japanese Canadian women's memories of the Internment and our historical relationships to the Canadian nation can therefore be mobilized in this calibration of citizenship. If we know that racism and other forms of oppression exist in Canada, how do we contest the claim that Canada ensures 'equality and justice for all'? If we understand that our visibility and invisibility, our speech and our 'silence' (imposed or self-chosen) are used to serve the self-redeeming narrative of the moral Canadian nation, and also to divide us from other subordinated people, how do we contest this use of our selves? I hope that this book will serve to raise these questions and address some of the mechanisms that construct the multiple subjects of the Internment in order to honour the memory of those who were interned.

The Subjects of the 'Internment'

The federal government created a web of relational carceral spaces and subjects interned therein. The expulsion, incarceration, dispossession, forced labour, dispersal, and deportation of Japanese Canadians, racially marked as the enemy of Canada (though most were Canadian citizens), were destructive processes procuring long-term effects. The women who were interned testify to the effects, carefully unmapping Canada's cartographies of violence. Daughters inherit and unmap these cartographies in relation to those they currently inhabit to connect past racial exclusions to those they live in the present.

The analysis of the spatial construction of the Internment has included discussion of what these places produced and continue to produce across generations of Japanese Canadians, and suggests what was produced for white citizens of Canada. Part of the legacy of loss experienced through the Internment were the separations of people and the changes in and destruction of families, relationships, communities, and the self that was expelled from and moved to definitional places. There are numerous other ways in which the Internment touched each person's life, and the effects of the Internment for survivors can never be claimed to be known by those of us who did not undergo these experiences of incarceration and dispersal. My work is an attempt to resist the forgetting of this history and some of its effects, my way of witnessing a profound familial and communal legacy.

In analysing the memories of Japanese Canadian women who were forged as subjects of the Internment, I have raised questions about the symbolic liberal subject simultaneously constructed in relation to them. I have illustrated examples of the relational construction of freedom and non-freedom, and how liberal discourses can be used to forget this relational construct. I have also given examples of the racial limits to notions of autonomy and equality. By using a discourse of rights in this book in order to illustrate moments of the relational construction of rights and denial of rights, I am underlining the limits of this liberal discourse. Yet, the liberal construct of equality continues to mediate all of our relationships and our relationships with the state, a construct that necessarily positions white bourgeois subjects as those with whom racialized peoples in Canada are struggling to be equal to and from whom we must necessarily always fall racially short.[46] This discourse of rights also divides us from Indigenous peoples because it positions us as aspiring to acquire the rights of settlers as we bid for equality 'within the laws, economy, and institutions of the colonial settler state.'[47]

The women interviewed live with the memory of their individual, familial, and communal losses. Their testimonies demonstrate the historical and social relationality of the subject. All the women who were incarcerated invoked the memory of their parent(s) and situated themselves relationally to them in comparing their own losses. Many reported their parents' and older siblings' losses as greater. All of them talked about the Internment within a memory of community, and in reconstructing their memories of the Internment, they construct themselves as connected to others. Through the handing down of this knowledge of the Internment, daughters may learn from different memory sources, embodiments of community and relationships that reconfigure their own subjecthoods relationally in the negotiations with the meanings of this history. It is this memory of a community connected through the Internment and a memory resisting forgetting that challenges us to struggle against constructing ourselves as autonomous from the struggles of others.

The representation of Canada as a moral and benevolent country, nationally and internationally, necessitates a forgetting of the violence done within the nation. When violence occurs, its representation must be contained. The forgetting of the subjects of the Internment and its long-term effects was not only a process of the past. It must be continually reiterated through the containment of what is admitted and remembered. What and who is remembered, and what is forgotten, are therefore reflective of social relations of power. The discourse of the silent Internment survivor is part of this process of forgetting, and I have interrogated its raced and gendered insinuations, and raised questions about whose silences are scrutinized and whose silences are forgotten. Survivors of the Internment and their children can offer memories to counter the forgetting of the long-term effects the Internment produced. While memory is not intrinsically counter-hegemonic, the memories of the women I interviewed have revealed subjugated knowledges that raise questions regarding the numerous subjects of the Internment.

Through the Internment, white bourgeois subjects mapped out spaces of dispersed exclusion for Japanese Canadians and simultaneously spaces of entitlement for themselves. Japanese Canadians were made in relation to other Canadian citizens through the use of the War Measure Act and the legalization of incarceration and segregation for people based on a racial category yet who committed no crime, the confiscation of their property, and the destruction of their families and communities. They were then relationally made through the Mackenzie King government's policy of forced dispersal and assimilation. Each place of incarceration and dispersal was part of a chain in a carceral continuum. This was a relational process of subject constitution and emplacement forged through state policies and practices, and the microprocesses of contacts with administrators, police, employers, Christian church members, welfare workers, and so on. These processes and the discourses producing and produced by them, including ongoing representations of the Internment and redress, continue to inform notions of Japanese Canadians and Canadian citizenship. Despite the histories uncovered thus far, there are fragments of histories that remain uncovered and may never be recovered: in the cracks of walls of old buildings in British Columbia, under soil in now vanished incarceration sites, in the files in the LAC, in the memories and forgetting of survivors and witnesses. Differently located than survivors, yet also produced, in part, by the Internment, I have tried to analyse some of its effects and reveal some of its other differently located subjects.

The spatial configurations of the Internment, its violence and relations of power, were processes legitimized through Canadian law. Women's testimonies begin to unmap the long-term effects of the Internment. The daughters of women interned testify to the effects of the Internment in their own lives. The past is in their present through living its material, social, and psychological effects and the witnessing of a parent's speech/speechlessness, rage, grief, humour in relation to events and places that we cannot really imagine nor describe. While the Internment is construed as of the past, racism is still present, and the settler and racial state continue to position Japanese Canadians in relation to Indigenous, racialized, and white people. We continue to live with the Internment through haunting absences and presences: a sense of great loss, yet the inability to name it, language fails us, our words are challenged by the euphemisms (part of our inheritance), euphemisms still repeated that undermine the claim to harms anew. Access to government documents that were not destroyed by Internment participants may not be available until the generations to come, if the crumbling papers survive the test of time. Hence we must remember to pass on the knowledge to those who might be able to read the written record (although incomplete), the record kept on those to whom this reading was denied.

The women interned constituted themselves in relation to family members and communities through their re-membering of the Internment. Their narratives reconstruct the subject as one who struggled to maintain connections to others interned even if only through re-membering them, despite the government's concerted efforts to destroy these connections. They presented a subject who remembers the self in relation to others. Their testimonies forge memoryscapes integrally linked to the places of their incarcerations simultaneously remembered in relation to the places where other family members and friends were incarcerated. Their memories unmap the terrain of loss and effect, offering a remembrance of violence iterated by politicians and citizens in numerous places. Women's remembrance of the violence of expulsion, forced separation, dispossession, homelessness, and loss of family members and communities also refigures their selves relationally to multi-various carceral places and the social relations producing materialized divisions. The heterogeneity of the carceral places produce specific memories of landscape and social relations simultaneous to the memory of places unseen yet always remembered. It is this very awareness of the hardships inherent in each place and how people were differently located within them (according to age, class background, gender, physical ability, parenting responsibilities, religious affiliation, immigrant/citizenship status, language spoken, et cetera) that affects the ability of women who were interned to name their own experiences as uniquely difficult. This memory of entire communities destroyed and how one constructs oneself in relationship to remembering them impinge upon how women describe their own experiences of racism, loss, and hardship.

In lieu of more complex readings of testimonies generated by Japanese Canadians, what often occurs is an Orientalist scrutinizing of the testifier, a search for their flaws of social or cultural difference. Better to focus on *their* silences than on the unutterable, the loud incongruencies their/our embodiedness in different spaces signify, their confrontations with national spaces and citizens devoid of the memory of the Internment and other histories of violence in Canada. The normalized erasure of people, communities, and their histories differently affects the ability of us *all* to admit the extent of the violence and to name it.

The gestures to remember the loss of others and others' losses, sometimes problematically interpreted by researchers and writers as demonstrative of passivity or an attitude of *shikata ga nai* are, in fact, revelatory of the extent of the violence.[48] These articulations of the interrelatedness of places of the Internment and the memory of the losses produced through displacement and separation in many ways continue to contest the erasure of communities. The ability of women who were incarcerated to locate their losses spatially and relationally instructs us to think further about how we are all implicated in the enforced scattering of Japanese Canadians and the 'scattered hegemonies'[49] of nation-building and citizen constitution.

It is hoped that we can widen our understanding of resistance in our commemorative practices to include more complex notions of how women, men, and children struggled during and after the Internment. Re-membering the places of the Internment and the people who were forced into them can be used to contest a forgetting of the colonial, racial, and national violence used to map Canada, and to re-member it as a place where there are many people who have been and are in constant struggle against domination and who daily live its effects. Re-membering our 'embodiment, relationality, difference'[50] through the history of Internment and other histories of violence in Canada may offer us and subsequent generations support for imagining and enacting resistance. The memories of the Internment we inherit and pass on offer possibilities for unsettling hegemonic notions of nation, citizenship, and the subject. 'Disidentification'[51] with these hegemonies may be a starting point for re-imagining ourselves, our communities, and for developing new forms of remembrance and political engagement.

Notes

Preface

1 Toni Morrison, 'The Site of Memory,' in *Out There: Marginalization and Contemporary Cultures*, ed. Russell Ferguson, Martha Gever, Trinh T. Minh-ha, and Cornel West (New York: New Museum of Contemporary Art and Cambridge, MA: The MIT Press, 1990), 302.
2 For descriptions and analyses of the redress movement and settlement, see Roy Miki and Cassandra Kobayashi, *Justice in Our Time: The Japanese Canadian Redress Settlement* (Vancouver: Talonbooks and Winnipeg: National Association of Japanese Canadians, 1991); Roy Miki, *Redress: Inside the Japanese Canadian Call for Justice* (Vancouver: Raincoast Books, 2004); Audrey Kobayashi, 'The Japanese-Canadian Redress Settlement and Its Implications for "Race Relations,"' *Canadian Ethnic Studies* 24, no. 1 (1992), 1–19; Maryka Omatsu, *Bittersweet Passage: Redress and the Japanese Canadian Experience* (Toronto: Between the Lines, 1992); Adhoc Committee for Japanese Canadian Redress, *Japanese Canadian Redress: The Toronto Story* (Toronto: Adhoc Committee for Japanese Canadian Redress, 2000); National Association of Japanese Canadians, *The Case for Redress* (Toronto: National Association for Japanese Canadians, n.d). The redress settlement and movement will be further discussed in the introduction and in chapter 10.
3 I use this term as a composite metonym for the processes of incarcerating Japanese Canadians in the 1940s and underline that the term is a contested one. For example, Ann Sunahara points out its specialized legal use and states that the government was careful not to use the term 'internment' for Canadian-born men who were incarcerated in prisoner-of-war (POW) camps because 'internment under the Geneva Convention is a legal act

applicable only to aliens.' Instead, they were described as 'detained at the pleasure of the Minister of Justice [Louis St Laurent].' See *The Politics of Racism: The Uprooting of Japanese Canadians during the Second World War* (Toronto: James Lorimer, 1981), 66. She also emphasizes that, rather than utilize the government's term 'detention,' Nisei (second generation) men who were incarcerated in POW camps continue to refer to their incarceration as 'internment.' Rather than conform to the logic and arguments of the Canadian state of the 1940s, I would like to suggest that the actions of detaining Japanese Canadians and their treatment as aliens, despite their Canadian citizenship, were contrary to the terms of the Geneva Convention. The Department of Labour itself described the 'internment' of 'chiefly Canadian born' in the Internment (POW) camps and 'half [of the men interned] were Canadian-born Japanese.' See Canada, Department of Labour, *Report of the Department of Labour on the Administration of Japanese Affairs in Canada, 1942–1944* (Ottawa: Department of Labour 1944), 28 (hereafter *Administration*). Although the term 'internment' is used specifically in relation to the men incarcerated in the POW camps in its report, its admission here indicates that they did 'intern' Canadian citizens. Roy Miki and Cassandra Kobayashi lend a more general use to this term in describing how some Japanese Canadians encapsulate the multiple processes of expulsion from the BC coast, 'their uprooting and dispossession as internment' (*Justice in Our Time*, 24). Also note that lawyer Maryka Omatsu uses the term 'internment camp survivors' in her book *Bittersweet Passage* (102). I adopt its application from current community discourses used by some survivors and their children who struggle to name these processes in opposition to the government euphemism describing the events as the 'evacuation,' and I emphasize its deleterious and life-changing effects by capitalizing the 'i.'

4 Prime Minister Brian Mulroney to Sally Saeko Eguchi Oikawa, 'Acknowledgment/Reconnaissance,' n.d. Private collection of Mona Oikawa.

5 The term 'Japanese Canadian' is used to describe the people who were expelled and their descendants. For an analysis of the term Japanese Canadian, see Roy Miki who argues that the term was formulated by the state and is a 'reproduction of "Japanese race" in the more benign face of "Japanese Canadian" – the preferential term of those identified as such' and is emblematic of a 'desire as "outsiders" to enter the nation's family as "Canadian."' *Broken Entries: Race, Subjectivity, Writing* (Toronto: The Mercury Press, 1998), 194.

6 Audrey Kobayashi states that for 'most Japanese Canadians' the term 'survivor' means 'someone who lived through the dispossession of the 1940s.' See 'A Demographic Profile of Japanese Canadians and Social Implications

for the Future' (Canada: Secretary of State, September 1989), mimeograph, 21. I use it to emphasize the process of living through the expulsion, incarceration, and dispersal, and living with the memories of these actions and violations. This inadequate term is chosen over other words used in the literature, for example, 'internee,' to denote how the subject of the Internment is situated in different times and spaces through a continuing relationship to national violence.

7 Issei is translated as first generation, Nisei is second, Sansei is third, Yonsei is fourth, and Gosei is fifth.

8 For examples of visual representations that mobilize the 'silence' metaphor, see for example, Anne Wheeler's film, *The War between Us* (Atlantic Films/Troika Films, Canada, 1995); and the photographic exhibit by Andrew Danson, *Face Kao*, exhibited at The Photo Passage, Harbourfront, Toronto, March–May 1996. It is interesting to note that in separate interviews held after the redress struggle, both Wheeler and Danson invoked the uninterrogated metaphor of 'silence' in describing Japanese Canadians. In an interview with Vicki Gabereau, Wheeler commented that Japanese Canadians who were incarcerated 'have been very quiet about their past' (*Gabereau*, CBC Radio, 7 December 1995). Danson disclosed in an interview with Deidre Hanna that he was married to a Japanese Canadian woman, stating that 'I asked my wife's family and was met with a wall of silence. The silence was significant' (Deidre Hanna, 'Andrew Danson's Face Kao Shows Canada's Lack of Honour,' *NOW*, 21–27 March 1996, 60). The Danson photographs warrant analysis that cannot be attempted here.

9 See Lisa Lowe's analysis, in which she writes, 'the American soldier, who has in every way submitted to the nation, is the quintessential citizen and therefore the ideal representative of the nation, yet the American of Asian descent remains the symbolic "alien," the metonym for Asia who by definition cannot be imagined as sharing in America' and the contradictions this raises for Asian American and other soldiers of colour. Lisa Lowe, *Immigrant Acts: On Asian American Cultural Politics* (Durham, NC: Duke University Press, 1996), 6. For a description of Japanese Canadian men's participation in the Canadian military, see Roy Ito, *We Went to War: The Story of the Japanese Canadians Who Served during the First and Second World Wars* (Stittsville, ON: Canada's Wings, 1984).

10 According to Ito, the British Army paid less than the Canadian Army (*We Went to War*, 170). Although thirty-two Nisei (most who lived outside of BC) managed to enlist in the Canadian Army in regular service before 1945, my father and 115 other Nisei men were not allowed to join the ranks of the Canadian Army until January 1945 (ibid., 195).

11 I use the term 'white' to describe what Sherene Razack calls the 'colour of domination.' She states further that using the 'language of colour' emphasizes 'the physicality of the encounter between powerful and powerless groups and ... the importance of the visible in colonial encounters – who and what is seen and not seen.' See *Looking White People in the Eye: Gender, Race, and Culture in Courtrooms and Classrooms* (Toronto: University of Toronto Press, 1998), 11. Contrary to convention in a society where whiteness is unmarked due to its dominance, I use the term with the intent to 'mark' the subject of racial dominance at the same time as I often discursively leave unmarked the Japanese Canadian subject.

12 I use the term 'national violence' to indicate that this violence was perpetrated to further nation-building. See the introduction and chapter 1.

13 Mona Oikawa, '"Driven to Scatter Far and Wide": The Forced Resettlement of Japanese Canadians to Southern Ontario, 1944–1949' (MA thesis, University of Toronto, 1986).

14 'For Shizu' was first published in *Fireweed* 28 (Spring 1989), 19.

15 Mona Oikawa, 'For Shizu,' trans. Deirdre Tanaka and Yusuke Tanaka, *Nikkei Voice* 10, no. 1 (1996), 14. I am grateful to Deirdre and Yusuke for their translation.

16 I am using Roger I. Simon and Claudia Eppert's definition (informed by Cathy Caruth) of 'historical trauma': 'human-initiated, catastrophic events which, when witnessed, often evoke a specific set of experiential dynamics. Most importantly, historically traumatic events simultaneously summon forgetting and remembrance.' Simon and Eppert, 'Remembering Obligation: Pedagogy and the Witnessing of Testimony of Historical Trauma,' *Canadian Journal of Education* 22, no. 2 (1997), 176. See also King-Kok Cheung who refers to '[h]istorical trauma (most notably the internment of Japanese Americans during World War II) resulting from the unjust conflation of racial, cultural, and political affinities,' in *Articulate Silences: Hisaye Yamamoto, Maxine Hong Kingston, Joy Kogawa* (Ithaca, NY: Cornell University Press, 1993), 18n24.

17 I hyphenate the word 'remember' to emphasize the embodiment of memory and also the embodiment of those remembered.

Introduction

1 Canada, *Statutes of Canada*, 1914, 5 Geo.V, c. 2. For a description of the use of the War Measures Act during the First and Second World Wars, see Ann Gomer Sunahara, 'Legislative Roots of Injustice,' in *In Justice: Canada, Minorities, and Human Rights*, ed. Roy Miki and Scott McFarlane (Winnipeg: National Association of Japanese Canadians, 1996), 7–22.

2 For a more detailed description of the political and historical context of the Internment see, the fine histories authored by Ann Gomer Sunahara, *The Politics of Racism: The Uprooting of Japanese Canadians during the Second World War* (Toronto: James Lorimer, 1981) and Ken Adachi, *The Enemy That Never Was: A History of the Japanese Canadians* (Toronto: McClelland and Stewart, 1976).

3 For descriptions of the incarceration of Japanese Americans, see, for example, Roger Daniels, *Concentration Camps: North America. Japanese in the United States and Canada During World War II* (Malabar, FL: Robert E. Krieger, 1981); and Michi Weglyn, *Years of Infamy: The Untold Story of America's Concentration Camps* (New York: William Morrow, 1976).

4 Sunahara, *The Politics of Racism*, 105.

5 Mona Oikawa, '"Driven to Scatter Far and Wide": The Forced Resettlement of Japanese Canadians to Southern Ontario, 1944–1949' (MA thesis, University of Toronto, 1986), 48.

6 Ibid., 68. In addition, forty-two people were deported in 1942 and sixty-one were deported in 1943. See Canada, Department of Labour, *Report of the Department of Labour on the Administration of Japanese Affairs in Canada, 1942–1944* (Ottawa: Department of labour, 1944), 28–9 (hereafter *Administration*).

7 Oikawa, '"Driven to Scatter Far and Wide,"' appendix 1, 107.

8 Adachi, *The Enemy That Never Was*, 346. All subsequent references from *The Enemy That Never Was* are cited from the 1976 edition unless otherwise specified.

9 Grace Eiko Thomson, 'National Association of Japanese Canadians President's Report: JC Community Loses a Good Friend,' *Nikkei Voice* 22, no. 2 (2008), 10.

10 Arthur K. Miki, *The Japanese Canadian Redress Legacy: A Community Revitalized* (Winnipeg: National Association of Japanese Canadians, 2003), 13.

11 Brian Mulroney quoted in Roy Miki and Cassandra Kobayashi, *Justice in Our Time: The Japanese Canadian Redress Settlement* (Vancouver: Talonbooks and Winnipeg, MB: National Association of Japanese Canadians, 1991), 143. (See pp. 143–4 for the text of the prime minister's speech. For the terms of the agreement, see pp. 138–9.)

12 Kirsten Emiko McAllister, 'Captivating Debris: Unearthing a World War Two Internment Camp,' *Cultural Values* 5, no. 1 (2001), 97.

13 Ibid., 98; emphasis in original.

14 Roy Miki, *Redress: Inside the Japanese Canadian Call for Justice* (Vancouver: Raincoast Books, 2004), 233.

15 Sunahara, *The Politics of Racism*, 3.

16 Ibid.

17 R. Miki, *Redress*, 260.

18 Annette Kuhn and Kirsten Emiko McAllister, 'Introduction,' in *Locating Memory: Photographic Acts*, ed. Annette Kuhn and Kirsten Emiko McAllister (New York: Berghahn Books, 2006), 4. See also McAllister's use of the term in 'Photographs of a Japanese Canadian Internment Camp: Mourning Loss and Invoking a Future,' *Visual Studies* 21, no. 2 (2006): 133–56 and 'Remembering Political Violence: The Nikkei Interment Memorial Centre' (PhD diss., Carleton University, 2000).

19 Peter Li, *Race and Ethnic Relations in Canada*, 2nd ed. (Don Mills: Oxford University Press, 1999), 7; Robert Miles, 'Apropos the Idea of "Race"... Again,' in *Theories of Race and Racism*, ed. Les Back and John Solomos (London: Routledge, 2000).

20 Ruth Frankenberg defines 'whiteness' as a 'location of structural advantage, of race privilege ... a "standpoint," a place from which white people look at ourselves, at others, and at society [note omitted] ... a set of cultural practices that are usually unmarked and unnamed' in her *White Women, Race Matters: The Social Construction of Whiteness* (Minneapolis: University of Minnesota Press, 1993).

21 Michel Foucault, *Power/Knowledge: Selected Interviews and Other Writings, 1972–1977*, ed. Colin Gordon, trans. Colin Gordon, Leo Marshall, John Mepham, and Kate Soper (New York: Pantheon Books, 1980), 98; emphasis in original.

22 Michel Foucault, *'Society Must be Defended': Lectures at the Collège de France 1975–1976*, ed. Mauro Bertani and Alessandro Fontana, trans. David Macey (New York: Picador, 2003), 29.

23 Michael Foucault, *The History of Sexuality*, vol. 1, trans. Robert Hurley (New York: Vintage Books, 1990), 100.

24 Mary Louise Fellows and Sherene Razack, 'The Race to Innocence: Confronting Hierarchical Relations among Women,' *The Journal of Gender, Race and Justice* 1, no. 2 (1998), 335–52.

25 An exception is Peter Ward's study, *White Canada Forever: Popular Attitudes and Public Policy toward Orientals in British Columbia*, 3rd ed. (Montreal: McGill-Queen's University Press, 2002). However, Ward reifies the notion of race rather than examining how race and whiteness are socially constructed, for example, when he states, 'In 1901 the two races clashed once more when striking whites condemned the Japanese ...' (121). For studies in the historical and social construction of whiteness, see, for example, Barbara Heron, *Desire for Development: Whiteness, Gender, and the Helping Imperative* (Waterloo, ON: Wilfrid Laurier University Press, 2007); Adele Perry, *On the Edge of Empire: Gender, Race, and the Making of British Columbia,*

1849–1871 (Toronto: University of Toronto Press, 2001); and Vron Ware, *Beyond the Pale: White Women, Racism and History* (London: Verso, 1992).

26 Sunera Thobani, *Exalted Subjects: Studies in the Making of Race and Nation in Canada* (Toronto: University of Toronto Press, 2007), 7.

27 For a description of some of the Orders-in-Council, see chapter 4. See also Sunahara, *The Politics of Racism*, and Adachi, *The Enemy That Never Was*.

28 Foucault, *Power/Knowledge*, 84.

29 Ian McKay, 'Canada as a Long Liberal Revolution: On Writing the History of Actually Existing Canadian Liberalisms, 1840s–1940s,' in *Liberalism and Hegemony: Debating the Canadian Liberal Revolution*, ed. Jean-François Constant and Michel Ducharme (Toronto: University of Toronto Press, 2009), 401.

30 Sunahara, *The Politics of Racism*, 4.

31 Saidiya V. Hartman, *Scenes of Subjection: Terror, Slavery, and Self-Making in Nineteenth-Century America* (New York: Oxford University Press, 1997), 122.

32 Thobani, *Exalted Subjects*, 7.

33 Ibid., 9.

34 I use the pronoun 'he' in recognition that by the characteristics of its definition the liberal subject is 'coded male.' See Adele Perry, 'Women, Racialized People, and the Making of the Liberal Order,' in *Liberalism and Hegemony: Debating the Canadian Liberal Revolution*, ed. Jean-François Constant and Michel Ducharme (Toronto: University of Toronto Press, 2009), 277.

35 Wendy Brown, *States of Injury: Power and Freedom in Late Modernity* (Princeton, NJ: Princeton University Press, 1995), 56; emphasis in original.

36 Ernest Renan, 'What is a Nation?' in *Nation and Narration*, ed. Homi K. Bhabha (London: Routledge, 1990), 11.

37 Marita Sturken, *Tangled Memories: The Vietnam War, the AIDS Epidemic, and the Politics of Remembering* (Berkeley: University of California Press, 1997), 5.

38 Audrey Kobayashi, 'The Historical Context for Japanese-Canadian Uprooting,' in *Social Change and Space: Indigenous Nations and Ethnic Communities in Canada and Finland*, ed. Ludger Müller-Wille (Montreal: Northern Studies Program, McGill University, 1989), 69–82, and 'Racism and Law in Canada: A Geographical Perspective,' *Urban Geography* 11, no. 5 (1990), 447–73.

39 Kirsten Emiko McAllister, *Terrain of Memory: A Japanese Canadian Memorial Project* (Vancouver: UBC Press, 2010).

40 Adachi, *The Enemy That Never Was*; Manitoba Japanese Canadian Citi-

zens' Association, *The History of Japanese Canadians in Manitoba* (Winnipeg: Manitoba Japanese Canadian Citizens' Association, 1996); Takeo Ujo Nakano, with Leatrice Nakano, *Within the Barbed Wire Fence: A Japanese Man's Account of His Internment in Canada* (Toronto: University of Toronto Press, 1980); Robert K. Okazaki, *The Nisei Mass Evacuation Group and P.O.W. Camp 101, Angler Ontario*, trans. Jean M. Okazaki and Curtis T. Okazaki (Scarborough, ON: Self-Published, 1996); Yon Shimizu, *The Exiles: An Archival History of the World War II Japanese Road Camps in British Columbia and Ontario* (Wallaceburg, ON: Shimizu Consulting and Publishing, 1993); and Sunahara, *The Politics of Racism*.

41 Kathryn Woodward explains 'subject position' in this way, '... language and culture give meaning to our experiences of ourselves and where we adopt an identity. Discourses, whatever sets of meaning they construct, can only be effective if they recruit subjects. Subjects are thus subjected to the discourse and must themselves take it up as individuals who so position themselves. The positions which we take up and identify with constitute our identities.' See 'Concepts of Identity and Difference,' in *Identity and Difference*, ed. Kathryn Woodward (Thousand Oaks, CA: Sage in Association with the Open University, 1997), 39.

42 For an explanation and application of interlocking analysis, see Sherene H. Razack, *Looking White People in the Eye: Gender, Race, and Culture in Courtrooms and Classrooms* (Toronto: University of Toronto Press, 1998). Razack argues that interlocking analysis is different from intersectional analysis. As she states, 'Interlocking systems need one another, and in tracing the complex ways in which they help to secure one another, we learn how women are produced into positions that exist symbiotically but hierarchically' (13). Razack's notion of interlocking analysis is used in this book. For an explanation and analysis of intersectional theory, see Daiva Stasiulis, 'Feminist Intersectional Theorizing,' in *Inequality in Canada: A Reader on the Intersections of Gender, Race, and Class*, ed. Valerie Zawilski and Cynthia Levine-Rasky (Don Mills: Oxford University Press, 2005), 36–62.

43 Caroline Knowles, *Race and Social Analysis* (Thousand Oaks, CA: Sage Publications, 2003), 80.

44 Doreen Massey, *Space, Place, and Gender* (Minneapolis: University of Minnesota Press, 1994), 120.

45 Edward Soja, *Postmodern Geographies: The Reassertion of Space in Critical Social Theory* (London: Verso, 1989), 11.

46 For a discussion of material and symbolic space, see R.J. Johnston et al., eds., *The Dictionary of Human Geography* (Oxford: Blackwell Publishers, 2000), 769.

47 Massey, *Space, Place, and Gender*, 22.
48 Radhika Mohanram, *Black Body: Women, Colonialism, and Space* (Minneapolis: University of Minnesota Press, 1999), 3.
49 Richard Phillips, *Mapping Men and Empire: A Geography of Adventure* (New York: Routledge, 1997), 143.
50 Fellows and Razack, 'The Race to Innocence,' 352.
51 Kathleen Kirby, 'Re: Mapping Subjectivity: Cartographic Vision and the Limits of Politics,' in *Body Space: Destabilising Geographies of Gender and Sexuality*, ed. Nancy Duncan (New York: Routledge, 1996), 49.
52 Michel Foucault, *Discipline and Punish: The Birth of the Prison*, trans. Alan Sheridan (New York: Vintage Books, 1995), 299.
53 Nicholas Blomley, 'Law, Property, and the Geography of Violence: The Frontier, the Survey, and the Grid,' *The Annals of the Association of American Geographers* 93, no. 1 (2003), 123.
54 Foucault, *The History of Sexuality*, vol. 1, 95.
55 Phillips, *Mapping Men and Empire*, 143.
56 Brown, *States of Injury*, 3. See also Foucault's statement, 'I do not think that there is anything that is functionally – by its very nature – absolutely liberating.' See 'Space, Knowledge, and Power,' in *The Foucault Reader*, ed. Paul Rabinow (New York: Pantheon Books, 1984), 245.
57 Foucault, *Power/Knowledge*, 86.
58 Tomoko Makabe and Ronald Takaki both use the term 'community of memory.' Makabe attributes the term to Robert N. Bellah and defines it as 'a community that people do not choose but are born into, where people inherit a commitment to historical ties through the community and commonly shared experiences,' *The Canadian Sansei* (Toronto: University of Toronto Press, 1998), 91. While Takaki does not define his use of this term, he does use it to describe members of a community who are 'recovering roots deep within [the United States] and the homelands of their ancestors,' in *Strangers from a Different Shore: A History of Asian Americans* (New York: Penguin, 1989), 488. My use of the term 'memory of community' is meant to emphasize that a person re-members the self in relationship to other subordinated people.
59 Foucault defines subjugated knowledge as 'a whole set of knowledges that have been disqualified ... which owes its force only to the harshness with which it is opposed by everything surrounding it ... it is through the re-appearance of this knowledge, of these local popular knowledges, these disqualified knowledges, that criticism performs its work.' *Power/Knowledge*, 82.

1 The Forgetting Subjects and the Subjects Forgotten

1 Canada, Department of Labour, Deputy Minister of Labour, *Report on Mission to England to Confer with the British Authorities on the Subject of Immigration to Canada from the Orient and Immigration from India in Particular*, by W.L. Mackenzie King, No. 36a (Ottawa: S.E. Dawson, 1908), 7.
2 British Columbia Premier John Oliver to Prime Minister Mackenzie King, 21 January 1927, quoted in W. Peter Ward, *White Canada Forever: Popular Attitudes and Public Policy toward Orientals in British Columbia*, 3rd ed. (Montreal: McGill-Queen's University Press, 2001), 138.
3 Canada, Department of Labour, *Report of the Department of Labour on the Re-Establishment of the Japanese in Canada, 1944–1946* (Ottawa: Department of Labour, 1947), 24 (hereafter *Re-Establishment*). The Department of Labour became responsible for the administration of the Internment in February 1943. See Ann Sunahara, *The Politics of Racism: The Uprooting of Japanese Canadians during the Second World War* (Toronto: James Lorimer, 1981), 83.
4 Kirsten Emiko McAllister, 'Remembering Political Violence: The Nikkei Internment Memorial Centre' (PhD diss., Carleton University, 2000), 33. See also Pamela Sugiman's argument that the Internment was political violence in 'Passing Time, Moving Memories: Interpreting Wartime Narratives of Japanese Canadian Women,' *Histoire Sociale/Social History* 37, no. 73 (2004), 51–79.
5 McAllister, 'Remembering Political Violence,' 131.
6 The term 'national' violence is also used by Sunera Thobani to describe 'malevolent expressions' of the rites and rituals that have 'inducted individuals into the national political communities,' *Exalted Subjects: Studies in the Making of Race and Nation in Canada* (Toronto: University of Toronto Press, 2007), 79. See my use of the term in 'Cartographies of Violence: Women, Memory and the Subjects of the "Internment,"' *Canadian Journal of Law and Society* 15, no. 2 (December 2000), 42.
7 David Theo Goldberg, *Racist Culture: Philosophy and the Politics of Meaning* (Oxford: Blackwell Publishers, 1993), 59.
8 Ibid., 60.
9 Allen Feldman, *Formations of Violence: The Narrative of the Body and Political Terror in Northern Ireland* (Chicago: University of Chicago Press, 1991), 5. I would like to thank Kirsten Emiko McAllister for informing me of Feldman's work.
10 Goldberg, *Racist Culture*, 8.
11 Feldman, *Formations of Violence*, 2.
12 Ibid., 2–3.

13 Foucault, *Power/Knowledge: Selected Interviews and Other Writings, 1972–1977*, ed. Colin Gordon, trans. Colin Gordon, Leo Marshall, John Mepham, and Kate Soper (New York: Pantheon Books, 1980), 72.

14 Canada, Dominion Bureau of Statistics, *Eighth Census of Canada, 1941*, vol. 3 (Ottawa: Edmond Cloutier, 1946), 164.

15 Ibid.

16 The BCSC was formed on 4 March 1942 and was under the authority of the Department of Labour. The BCSC Chairman was Austin C. Taylor, an industrialist from BC, and the two Assistant Commissioners were F.J. Mead, an RCMP officer, and John Shirras, an officer with the BC Provincial Police. An Advisory Board of twenty people from 'all walks of life' in BC was struck to advise the Commission. Canada, British Columbia Security Commission, *Removal of Japanese from Protected Areas: Report of the British Columbia Security Commission* (Vancouver: BCSC, 1942), 4 (hereafter *Removal*). According to Ken Adachi, ten days after the Commission was established, it began to move 'some 2,500 people, mainly fishermen and their families living along the upper coastline,' *The Enemy That Never Was: A History of the Japanese Canadians* (Toronto: McClelland and Stewart, 1976), 218.

17 LAC, Records of the British Columbia Security Commission, RG 36/27, vol. 1, file 17, 'Japanese Movement – Pacific Coast (Period ending October 31, 1942),' 1.

18 Ibid.

19 Canada, Department of Labour, *Re-Establishment*, 15, 25.

20 Sunahara, *The Politics of Racism*.

21 Inderpal Grewal and Caren Kaplan, '*Warrior Marks*: Global Womanism's Neo-Colonial Discourse in a Multicultural Context,' *Camera Obscura* 39 (September 1996), 10.

22 Canada, BCSC, *Removal*; Canada, Department of Labour, *Report of the Department of Labour on the Administration of Japanese Affairs in Canada, 1942-1944* (Ottawa: Department of Labour, 1944) (hereafter *Administration*); Canada, Department of Labour, *Re-Establishment*. The latter two reports have been reprinted in Roger Daniels, ed., *Two Reports on Japanese Canadians in World War II* (New York: Arno Press, 1978). All three reports are found in LAC, RG 36/27, vol. 41, file 2505, part 1.

23 Foucault uses the term carceral to describe places where people are punished, disciplined, and monitored: 'The "carceral" with its many diffuse or compact forms, its institutions of supervision or constraint, of discreet surveillance and insistent coercion,' *Discipline and Punish: The Birth of the Prison*, trans. Alan Sheridan (New York: Vintage Books, 1995), 299.

24 LAC, Records of the Department of External Affairs, RG 25, G 2, Accession
     83-84/259, Box 210, file 3464-AD-40, F. Charpentier to G. Glazebrook, 18
     August 1944. See also Roy Miki, *Redress: Inside the Japanese Canadian Call for
     Justice* (Vancouver: Raincoast Books, 2004) where he describes the National
     Film Board's *Of Japanese Descent* and the narrator's pronouncement, 'It
     should be made clear … that Japanese in these towns are not living in
     internment camps' (141).
25 LAC, Records of the Department of Labour, RG 27, vol. 645, file 23-2-3-7-1,
     part 6, E.C. Anderson to Department of Internal Affairs, 22 March 1948.
     See comments regarding Anderson's letter in the same file, Pammett to
     MacKinnon, 30 March 1949.
26 LAC, RG 27, vol. 645, file 23-2-3-7-1, part 6, Booth to Anderson, 12 April
     1948; emphasis added. C.V. Booth worked as Director of Education and
     Women's Projects for the Japanese Division in Vancouver. For more about
     her role, see Mona Oikawa, '"Driven to Scatter Far and Wide": The Forced
     Resettlement of Japanese Canadians to Southern Ontario, 1944–1949' (MA
     thesis, University of Toronto, 1986), chapter 2.
27 Ann Sunahara, 'Legislative Roots of Injustice,' in *In Justice: Canada, Minori-
     ties, and Human Rights*, ed. Roy Miki and Scott McFarlane (Winnipeg:
     National Association of Japanese Canadians, 1996), 7. See also Ken Adachi,
     The Enemy That Never Was, 220.
28 Ken Adachi, *The Enemy That Never Was*, 267, note omitted.
29 Sunahara, *The Politics of Racism*, 132.
30 Goldberg, *Racist Culture*, 1.
31 Canada, Department of Labour, *Administration*, 5.
32 In his book, *The Canadian Japanese and World War II: A Sociological and
     Psychological Account* (Toronto: University of Toronto Press, 1948), La
     Violette does not examine his social position as a researcher in relation
     to Japanese Canadians. The project raises questions about the methods
     and protocols used. Similar research projects conducted in the U.S.
     camps, the most prominent by Dorothy Swaine Thomas and Richard S.
     Nishimoto, have been criticized for their research conduct. See Dorothy
     Swaine Thomas and Richard S. Nishimoto, *The Spoilage: Japanese American
     Evacuation and Resettlement* (Berkeley: University of California Press,
     1946). For a critical evaluation of Thomas' and Nishimoto's project, see
     Yuji Ichioka, ed., *Views from Within: The Japanese American Evacuation and
     Resettlement Study* (Los Angeles: UCLA Asian American Studies Center,
     1989).
33 La Violette, *The Canadian Japanese and World War II*, 63. La Violette's
     statement clearly contradicts the government's own self-congratulatory
     remarks on the speed with which the expulsion occurred.

34 Ibid., 64. In contrast, Roy Miki reveals that '[d]uring the years of the re-dress movement, many reporters and researchers were taken aback when they learned that Japanese Canadians were treated more harshly than the Japanese Americans who were incarcerated during the same period.' He summarized the differences between Canadian and U.S. govern-ment policies in this way, 'American properties were not confiscated and liquidated; families were moved together; the costs of their internment were born by the U.S. government ... the U.S. did not enact policies of deportation and forced dispersal ... By December 1944 ... the U.S. lifted the exclusion orders,' *Redress*, 87–8. While the federal policies of Canada and the United States were different, it behooves us to be cautious in comparing the effects of these policies. The discourse of comparison may support a liberal discourse utilized by nations to suppress criticism of intranational oppression.

35 Canada, BCSC, *Removal*, 17; emphasis added.

36 LAC, RG 27, vol. 640, file 23-2-2-4, 'Japanese Division-Administration Ad-visory Board Meetings and Recommendations,' A. MacNamara to George Pearson, 6 April 1942; emphasis added.

37 Ibid.

38 LAC, RG 36/27, vol. 22, file 800, 'Slocan: General 1942–1943, 1945–1948,' R.H. Webb to Austin Taylor, 29 March 1942, 2; emphasis added.

39 LAC, RG 36/27, vol. 22, file 800, 'Slocan: General 1942–1943, 1945–1948,' A. Taylor to A. MacNamara, 29 March 1942, 1. For a description of Taylor, see Sunahara, *The Politics of Racism*, 53.

40 Sunahara, *The Politics of Racism*, 105. See as well where Sunahara states that the government was reluctant to intern more men in prisoner-of-war camps in June 1942 because this would be 'more costly than confining them in road camps' (71).

41 See Saidiya Hartman's argument that 'the texture of freedom is laden with the vestiges of slavery, and abstract equality is utterly enmeshed in the narrative of black subjection,' *Scenes of Subjection: Terror, Slavery, and Self-Making in Nineteenth-Century America* (New York: Oxford University Press, 1997), 116.

42 Canada, Department of Labour, *Re-Establishment*, 24. For another example, see Canada, Department of Labour, *Administration*, where, in reference to people being moved to 'self-supporting projects,' it states that 'a number of Japanese on the Coast moved out voluntarily to various parts of the interior' (34). In the same report the Department of Labour states, 'In 1942 the pioneers were several hundred young Japanese Canadian men who went to Schreiber road camps ... Approximately 100 young women ven-tured east in 1942 for domestic and nursing service' (40).

43 Sunahara, *The Politics of Racism*, 119.
44 Mary Louise Fellows and Sherene Razack, 'The Race to Innocence: Confronting Hierarchical Relations Among Women,' *Journal of Gender, Race and Justice* 1, no. 2 (1998), 352.
45 Report by T.G. Norris quoted in Ken Adachi, *The Enemy That Never Was*, 53.
46 Meyda Yeğenoğlu, *Colonial Fantasies: Towards a Feminist Reading of Orientalism* (Cambridge: Cambridge University Press, 1998), 5.
47 Canada, BCSC, *Removal*, 17.
48 Foucault, *Discipline and Punish*, 29.
49 Ibid., 90.
50 Canada, BCSC, *Removal*, 17.
51 Ibid., 16.
52 Comparisons indicating that the Canadian government resembled the German National Socialist state were actively suppressed by Canadian officials. See, for example, how F. Charpentier, the Chief Censor of Publications at the Directorate of Censorship, condemned a publication comparing the treatment of Japanese Canadians to that of Jews in Germany for being 'against the successful prosecution of the war.' According to Charpentier, '[T]he real parallel should be drawn between our treatment of the Japs and the Jap treatment of the Canadians.' LAC, RG 25, G 2, accession 83-84/259, box 201, file 3464-AD-40, F. Charpentier to T.A. Stone, 19 January 1944.
53 See Eva Mackey, who argues that Canadian nationalism creates a 'national innocence' that 'elides the way the Canadian nation can victimize internal "others" on the basis of race, culture, gender or class' in *The House of Difference: Cultural Politics and National Identity in Canada* (Toronto: University of Toronto Press, 2005), 12.
54 For example, Prime Minister Jean Chrétien's 1998 statement regarding the RCMP's use of pepper spray against protesters against the 1997 Asia-Pacific (APEC) summit held in Vancouver: 'Instead of picking up a baseball bat or something else, they are now trying to use more civilized methods.' See Editorial, 'Chrétien's Quips Inspire No Confidence,' *Toronto Star*, 21 October 1998, A20. See also Thobani's analysis of the 'master narrative of the nation,' in which its nationals are 'presented (for the most part) as responsible citizens, compassionate, caring, and committed to the values of diversity and multiculturalism,' in her *Exalted Subjects*, 4, notes omitted.
55 Oikawa, '"Driven to Scatter Far and Wide."'
56 See my analysis of this speech in ibid., 37–9.
57 Canada, House of Commons, *Debates*, 4 August 1944, 5915.

58 The repatriation survey is described by Sunahara as having two objectives: 'to repatriate or deport as many Japanese Canadians as possible,
and to disperse the rest across Canada ... selecting Japan would be considered "disloyal," while the loyalty of those selecting Canada was to be
further tested by a loyalty commission.' A loyalty commission was never
established by the federal government. Sunahara, *The Politics of Racism*,
118.

59 Canada, House of Common's, *Debates*, 4 August 1944, 5917.

60 Ibid.

61 Canada, BCSC, *Removal*, 2.

62 Foucault, *Discipline and Punish*, 129.

63 In *The Canadian Japanese and World War II*, La Violette states: 'No forceful
or sustained opposition had been directed towards the mode of property
disposal, travel restrictions, or the many regulations which handicapped
the Japanese in their resettlement into normal community life.' He adds
that 'Occidentals' 'picked up the protests' of Japanese Canadians on the
issue of deportation (247). See also Ward, *White Canada Forever*, who names
the groups comprising an 'anti-Japanese movement, including the Provincial Council of Women, the Vancouver Real Estate Exchange, the North
Burnaby Liberal Association, The National Union of Machinists, Fitters
and Helpers (Victoria Local Number 2), and others.' Ward adds, 'Not only
did these organizations represent major interest groups in the province,
but their influence cut across most social, economic, and political bounds
in west coast society ... If there were some provincial whites who did not
share prevailing attitudes, they remained largely silent in the face of the
consensus' (159). Werner Cohn, in his 'Persecution of Japanese Canadians
and the Political Left in British Columbia, December 1941–March 1942,'
BC Studies, 68 (1985–1986), 3–22, reveals that in addition to the Liberal and
Conservative Parties, pro-Communist writers for *The Fisherman*, published
in BC, and the BC Cooperative Commonwealth Federation (CCF) supported the expulsion in 1941–1942.

64 Barbara Heron, *Desire for Development: Whiteness, Gender, and the Helping
Imperative* (Waterloo, ON: Wilfrid Laurier University Press, 2007), 6–7.

65 See Sherene Razack's analysis of Asian and African women who are seen
as 'bodies to be saved by benevolent and more civilized Europeans' in
*Looking White People in the Eye: Gender, Race, and Culture in Courtrooms and
Classrooms* (Toronto: University of Toronto Press, 1998), 7, and her analysis
of the imperialist role of women in the west in relation to Muslim women
in 'Modern Women as Imperialists: Geopolitics, Culture Clash, and Gender after 9/11,' in *Casting Out: The Eviction of Muslims from Western Law*

and Politics (Toronto: University of Toronto Press, 2008), 83–106. See also Heron, *Desire for Development*.

66 Oikawa, '"Driven to Scatter Far and Wide,"' 85–6. See also Ken Adachi's description of Canadian Christian churches' support for the expulsion and dispersal policies in *The Enemy That Never Was*, 219.

67 For an analysis of the effects of the imposition of Christianity in these communities, see, for example, Taiaiake Alfred, *Wasáse: Indigenous Pathways of Action and Freedom* (Peterborough, ON: Broadview Press, 2005) and Kim Anderson, *A Recognition of Being: Reconstructing Native Womanhood* (Toronto: Second Story Press, 2000). For an analysis of the effects of forced removal of Indigenous children from their families, see, for example, Bonita Lawrence, *'Real' Indians and Others: Mixed-Blood Urban Native Peoples and Indigenous Nationhood* (Vancouver: UBC Press, 2004); Janet Campbell Hale, *Bloodlines: Odyssey of a Native Daughter* (New York: Random House, 1993); Patricia Monture-Angus, *Thunder in My Soul* (Halifax: Fernwood, 199), 59, 88. For a description and analysis of the residential school system, see, for example, Roland David Chrisjohn, Sherri Lynn Young, and Michael Maraun, *The Circle Game: Shadows and Substance in the Indian Residential School Experience* (Penticton, BC: Theytus Books, 1997); Suzanne Fournier and Ernie Crey, *Stolen from Our Embrace: The Abduction of First Nations Children and the Restoration of Aboriginal Communities* (Vancouver: Douglas and McIntyre, 1997); Lenore Keeshig-Tobias, 'Of Hating, Hurting and Coming to Terms with the English Language,' *Canadian Journal of Native Education* 27, no. 1 (2003), 89–100; Diane Million, 'Telling Secrets: Sex, Power and Narratives in Indian Residential School Histories,' *Canadian Woman Studies* 20, no. 2 (2000), 92–104; J.R. Miller, *Shingwauk's Vision: A History of Native Residential Schools* (Toronto: University of Toronto Press, 1996).

68 Frank Moritsugu and the Ghost Town Teachers, *Teaching in Canadian Exile: A History of the Schools for Japanese-Canadian Children in British Columbia Detention Camps during the Second World War* (Toronto: The Ghost Town Teachers Historical Society, 2001), 124.

69 La Violette, *The Canadian Japanese and World War II*, 113n22. See also Stephanie D. Bangarth, 'Religious Organizations and the "Relocation" of Persons of Japanese Ancestry in North America: Evaluating Advocacy,' *American Review of Canadian Studies* 34, no. 3 (2004), 511–40.

70 Moritsugu and the Ghost Town Teachers, *Teaching in Canadian Exile*, 121; italics in original. Hakujin may be translated as 'white person.'

71 La Violette, *The Canadian Japanese and World War II*, 114. For a description of Japanese Canadian Buddhist organizing during the expulsion, see

Terry Watada, *Bukkyo Tozen: A History of Jodo Shinshu Buddhism in Canada 1905–1995* (Toronto: HpF Press and Toronto Buddhist Church, 1996).

72 On the relational construction of colonizer and colonized, see Franz Fanon, *Black Skin, White Masks*, trans. Charles Lam Markmann (New York: Grove Press, 1967); Edward W. Said, *Culture and Imperialism* (New York: Vintage Books, 1994); Linda Tuhiwai Smith, *Decolonizing Methodologies: Research and Indigenous Peoples* (London: Zed Books, 1999).

73 H.F. Angus, preface to La Violette, *The Canadian Japanese and World War II*, vi.

74 Oikawa, '"Driven to Scatter Far and Wide,"' 69–70. Trueman had worked for the Young Men's Christian Association (YMCA) in Japan from 1909 to 1931.

75 In February 1943, the Department of Labour replaced the BCSC with the Japanese Division. For a description of this process, see chapter 5.

76 Moritsugu and the Ghost Town Teachers, *Teaching in Canadian Exile*, 79.

77 For example, Fraudena Eaton, associate director of the National Selective Service in charge of the Women's Division, was invited by the Department of Labour to consult on the dispersal of Japanese Canadians. Oikawa, '"Driven to Scatter Far and Wide,"' 52.

78 Heron, *Desire for Development*, 28.

79 Edward Said in his *Orientalism* (New York: Random House, 1979) defines Orientalism as 'a Western style for dominating, restructuring, and having authority over the Orient' (3). He explains further that 'Orientalism depends for its strategy on this flexible *positional* superiority, which puts the Westerner in a whole series of possible relationships with the Orient without ever losing him the relative upper hand' (7); emphasis in original. Lisa Lowe in her *Critical Terrains: French and British Orientalisms* (Ithaca, NY: Cornell University Press, 1996) points to the necessity of geographically and historically situating the discourses and practices of Orientalism. I use the term to address the production of Japanese Canadians and Asian Canadians as Orientalized subjects in Canada.

80 Ken Adachi, *The Enemy That Never Was*, 257.

81 See Kay Komori's and Leslie Komori's efforts to 'map memory' of the Lemon Creek camp in John Endo Greenaway, 'Mapping Memory/Reflecting on History: Lemon Creek Map Project and Broken Only at Sky,' *The Bulletin* 81, no. 9 (2009), 2, and Leslie Komori, 'In Her Own Words,' *The Bulletin* 81, no. 9 (2009), 3, 23.

82 Joseph Fry, 'Omoide Garden, Neys, Ontario' (unpublished manuscript, n.d.). I would like to thank Joseph for sharing his work with me.

83 Pearson quoted in Adachi, *The Enemy That Never Was*, 366.
84 Prime Minister Mulroney to Sally Oikawa, 'Acknowledgment/Reconnaissance,' n.d. Private collection of Mona Oikawa.
85 Ian McKay, 'The Liberal Order Framework: A Prospectus for a Reconnaissance of Canadian History,' *Canadian Historical Review* 81, no. 4 (2000), 630.
86 Ibid.
87 Ken Adachi, *The Enemy That Never Was*, 251–2.
88 Roger Daniels, 'The Conference Keynote Address: Relocation, Redress, and the Report – A Historical Appraisal,' in *Japanese Americans: From Relocation to Redress*, rev. ed., ed. Roger Daniels, Sandra C. Taylor, and Harry H.L. Kitano (Seattle: University of Washington Press, 1991), 6. See also Roger Daniels, *Concentration Camps, North America: Japanese in the United States and Canada during World War II* (Malabar, FL: R.E. Krieger, 1981).
89 Daniels, 'The Conference Keynote Address,' 6.
90 Lubomyr Luciuk states that the Canadian government used the War Measures Act between 1914 and 1920 to incarcerate 5,441 Canadians of Ukrainian descent; over 80,000 others were categorized as 'enemy aliens' and had to report regularly to the North West Mounted Police. In his description of what he delineates as the 'first national internment,' Luciuk states, 'the term "concentration camp" was officially and widely used at the time' to describe the places where they were incarcerated. See *In Fear of the Barbed Wire Fence: Canada's First National Internment Operations and the Ukrainian Canadians, 1914–1920* (Kingston, ON: Kashtan Press, 2001), 63n7. The government's suppression of this term during and after the 1940s in relation to the Internment of Japanese Canadians reflects an interesting and deliberate shift in state discourse.
91 Raymond Okamura, 'The American Concentration Camps: A Cover-Up through Euphemistic Terminology,' *Journal of Ethnic Studies* 10, no. 3 (1982), 95. Okamura points out that language used by the U.S. government to describe their practices of expelling and incarcerating Japanese Americans were euphemisms deliberately chosen to obfuscate 'embarrassing or horrible truths.' Okamura charges that writers continue to undermine our abilities to conceptualize the atrocities committed by the U.S. government by continuing to use these terms.
92 Audrey Kobayashi, 'Review of *Mutual Hostages: Canadians and Japanese during the Second World War*, by Patricia Roy, J.L. Granatstein, Masako Iino, and Hiroko Takamura,' *B.C. Studies* 96 (1992–1993), 118; emphasis in the original.
93 For an analysis of the term 'repatriation,' see Roy Miki, 'Introduction: The Life and Times of Muriel Kitagawa,' *This Is My Own: Letters to Wes and*

Other Writings on Japanese Canadians, 1941–1948, by Muriel Kitagawa, ed.
Roy Miki (Vancouver: Talonbooks, 1985), 47. See also Roy Miki and Cas-
sandra Kobayashi's analysis of the term 'self-supporting community' in
Justice in Our Time: The Japanese Canadian Redress Settlement (Vancouver:
Talonbooks and Winnipeg: National Association of Japanese Canadians,
1991), 41.

94 Ken Adachi, *The Enemy That Never Was*; Audrey Kobayashi, 'The His-
torical Context for Japanese-Canadian Uprooting,' in *Social Change and
Space: Indigenous Nations and Ethnic Communities in Canada and Finland*, ed.
Ludger Müller-Wille (Montreal: Northern Studies Program, McGill Uni-
versity, 1989), 69–82; Patricia Roy, *The Oriental Question: Consolidating a
White Man's Province, 1914–1941* (Vancouver: UBC Press, 2003); Sunahara,
The Politics of Racism; and Ward, *White Canada Forever*.

95 A. Kobayashi, 'The Historical Context for Japanese-Canadian Uprooting.'

96 See Sunahara's description of police and military officers who argued
that Japanese Canadians did not pose a threat to the nation's security. For
example, in 1941, Assistant Commander of the Royal Canadian Mounted
Police (RCMP) Frederick John Mead stated, 'No fear of sabotage need be
expected from the Japanese in Canada.' *The Politics of Racism*, 23.

97 Bain Attwood, 'Unsettling Pasts: Reconciliation and History in Settler
Australia,' *Postcolonial Studies* 8, no. 3 (2005), 243–59.

98 Sunahara, *The Politics of Racism*, xi.

99 Sunahara does state, 'Although outwardly they appear to have recovered,
Japanese Canadians still carry the scars of their wartime experience,' in
The Politics of Racism, 166.

100 Thirty-three years before Sunahara, La Violette made a similar claim in
The Canadian Japanese and World War II, 145.

101 Michael Omi and Howard Winant define 'racial formation' as the 'process
by which social, economic and political forces determine the context and
importance of racial categories, and by which they are in turn shaped by
racial meaning.' *Racial Formation in the United States: From the 1960s to the
1980s* (New York: Routledge, 1991), 61.

102 La Violette, *The Canadian Japanese and World War II*, 43.

103 Patricia Roy, J.L. Granatstein, Masako Iino, and Hiroko Takamura, *Mutual
Hostages: Canadians and Japanese during the Second World War* (Toronto:
University of Toronto Press, 1990), x.

104 Roger Daniels, afterword to Ken Adachi, *The Enemy That Never Was: A
History of the Japanese Canadians* (Toronto: McClelland and Stewart, 1991),
371.

105 David J. O'Brien and Stephan S. Fugita, *The Japanese American Experience*

(Bloomington and Indianapolis: Indiana University Press, 1991), 48. Ac-cording to O'Brien and Fugita, 1,037 Japanese Americans, of whom 912 were U.S. citizens, were sent to the mainland and interned (49). In *Cane Fires: The Anti-Japanese Movement in Hawaii, 1865–1945* (Philadelphia: Temple University Press, 1991), Gary Okihiro writes, '1,400, or less than 1 per cent, of the territory's Japanese were interned' (ix). Ronald Takaki reveals that Japanese Americans in the U.S. military defended other citi-zens in the Japanese attack on Pearl Harbor. In *Strangers from a Different Shore* (New York: Penguin, 1989), he writes, 'During the morning of the attack, two thousand Nisei serving in the U.S. Army stationed in Ha-waii fought to defend Pearl Harbor against enemy planes' (384; see also 385–6).

106 O'Brien and Fugita, *The Japanese American Experience*. The population of Hawai'i in 1940 was 423,330 people. See U.S. Bureau of the Cen-sus, *Population Hawaii 1940*, prepared under the supervision of Leon E. Truesdell, Chief Statistician for Population (Washington, DC: 1942), retrieved 23 December 2007 from www2.census.gov/prod2/decennial/ documents/19900609ch04.pdf.

107 Sunahara, *The Politics of Racism*, 164–5.

108 Ibid., xi.

109 Julian Henriques, 'Social Psychology and the Politics of Racism,' in Julian Henriques et al., *Changing the Subject: Psychology, Social Regulation and Subjectivity* (London: Methuen, 1984), 80.

110 Goldberg, *Racist Culture*; see esp. chap. 7.

111 Henry F. Angus, preface to La Violette, *The Canadian Japanese and World War II*. Henry F. Angus was a professor at the University of British Co-lumbia in the 1940s. He served on the Standing Committee on Orientals in 1940 whose mandate was to 'advise the federal government on Asian matters' (Sunahara, *The Politics of Racism*, 15). He later moved to Ottawa to work as a special assistant to the Department of External Affairs (ibid., 31).

112 Jean Burnet and Howard Palmer, introduction to Ken Adachi, *The Enemy That Never Was*, n.p.

113 Roy et al., *Mutual Hostages*, ix.

114 Ibid., xi.

115 Compare J.L. Granatstein's and Gregory A. Johnson's statement that their analysis is a 'realist critique of the received version.' See 'The Evacuation of the Japanese Canadians, 1942,' in *On Guard for Thee: War, Ethnicity, and the Canadian State, 1939–1945*, ed. Norman Hillmer, Bohdan Kordan, and Lubomyr Luciuk (Ottawa: Minster of Supply and Services Canada, 1988),

101–29. Their contention that historians must treat history as a science is another indication of their positivist approach.

116 In 1982, a year after the publication of Sunahara's *The Politics of Racism*, Canadian historian W. Peter Ward described the book as 'contentious and superficial.' Ward also uses the term 'evacuation' in his *The Japanese in Canada* (Ottawa: Canadian Historical Association, 1982), 21.

117 Sherene H. Razack, *Casting Out: The Eviction of Muslims from Western Law and Politics* (Toronto: University of Toronto Press, 2008), 160.

118 Audrey Kobayashi, Review of *Mutual Hostages*, 120; emphasis in the original. See also Maryka Omatsu's critique of *Mutual Hostages* in her book *Bittersweet Passage: Redress and the Japanese Canadian Experience* (Toronto: Between the Lines, 1992), 167–8.

119 I adapt Henri Lefebvre's term 'representational spaces,' which he defines as '[r]edolent with imaginary and symbolic elements, they have their source in history – in the history of a people as well as in the history of each individual belonging to that people' to describe symbolic and material spaces that Japanese Canadians have developed in which to represent their histories of the Internment. See *The Production of Space*, trans. Donald Nicholson-Smith (Malden, MA: Blackwell, 1991), 41.

120 Roy et al., *Mutual Hostages*, xi.

121 Lisa Lowe, *Immigrant Acts: On Asian American Cultural Politics* (Durham, NC: Duke University Press, 1996), 63.

122 Sunahara, *The Politics of Racism*, 8.

123 Roy et al., *Mutual Hostages*, x.

124 Yuji Ichioka, 'The Meaning of Loyalty: The Case of Kazumaro Buddy Uno,' *Amerasia Journal* 23, no. 3 (1997), 56.

125 Roy et al., *Mutual Hostages*, xii.

126 Joan W. Scott, 'Experience,' in *Feminists Theorize the Political*, ed. Judith Butler and Joan W. Scott (New York: Routledge, 1992), 25.

127 Roy et al., *Mutual Hostages*, 214.

128 Audrey Kobayashi, 'Review of *Mutual Hostages*,' 120; emphasis in the original.

129 Roy et al., *Mutual Hostages*, ix.

130 Ibid., 218.

131 La Violette, *The Canadian Japanese and World War II*, 98. Spain was the neutral power assigned to oversee Canada's compliance with the Geneva Convention and so acted as the Protecting Power for 'Japanese' interests in Canada and the United States. Only Japanese Nationals were covered by this agreement with Spain. Information from Canada, Department of Labour, *Administration*, 30.

132 Ken Adachi, *The Enemy That Never Was*, 225.
133 Ibid., 355.
134 May [pseud.], interview by author, 24 March 1992.
135 La Violette, *The Canadian Japanese and World War II*, 106.
136 Sunahara, *The Politics of Racism*, 1.
137 Ken Adachi, *The Enemy That Never Was*, 356. Roy Miki also uses this term
     in *Redress*: 'After the Bird Commission … They [Japanese Canadians]
     shied away from political controversy and chose to assume the role of a
     model minority' (231).
138 For analyses of the Model Minority ascription, see Dana Y. Takagi, *The
     Retreat from Race: Asian-American Admissions and Racial Politics* (New Bruns-
     wick, NJ: Rutgers University Press, 1992), 58, and Lowe, *Immigrant Acts*, 67.
139 Donald T. Nakanishi, 'Surviving Democracy's "Mistake": Japanese
     Americans and the Enduring Legacy of Executive Order 9066,' *American
     Journal* 19, no. 1 (1993), 23.
140 Kyo Maclear, 'The Myth of the "Model Minority": Re-thinking the Educa-
     tion of Asian Canadians,' *Our Schools/Our Selves* 5, no. 3 (1994), 71. See
     also Sherene Razack's critique of the Model Minority construct in 'The
     Perils of Talking about Culture: Schooling Research on South and East
     Asian Students,' *Race, Gender and Class* 2, no. 3 (1995), 76–7.
141 Sunahara, *The Politics of Racism*, 167, and Ken Adachi, *The Enemy That
     Never Was*, 361–2.
142 Sunahara, *The Politics of Racism*, 167.
143 For an example of a recent book commenting on the 'success' of Japanese
     Canadians after the internment, see Mary Taylor, 'The Japanese-Canadian
     Community Today,' in *A Black Mark: The Japanese Canadians in World War
     II* (Ottawa: Oberon Press, 2004), 195–201.
144 Here I emphasize that we have differently experienced these subordinat-
     ing processes and assaults on our selves as Japanese Canadians. While
     some might argue that 'Japanese food,' for example, is more accepted
     now than in the past, this acceptance does not necessarily signal the end
     of white supremacy or racism. See chapter 9 in this volume, for example.
     bell hooks' concept of 'eating the other' is useful in understanding how
     cultural practices developed by racialized people are appropriated by
     and consumed for the benefit of dominant groups. See 'Eating the Other,'
     in *Black Looks: Race and Representation* (Toronto: Between the Lines, 1992),
     21–39.
145 See Roy Miki's analysis in *Redress* that '"Japanese Canadians" were now
     reborn as model "citizens," whose rapid upward social mobility in the
     aftermath of the mass uprooting demonstrated their loyalty to the nation'
     (310).

146 For example, based on the 2001 Census, Colin Lindsay concluded that
     'Canadians of Japanese origin are about as likely as other Canadians to
     have incomes that fall below Statistics Canada's Low-income Cut-offs.'
     He added that '48% of unattached adults of Japanese origin had low
     incomes, compared with 38% of those in the overall population.' Colin
     Lindsay, 'Profiles of Ethnic Communities in Canada: The Japanese Com-
     munity in Canada' (Ottawa: Statistics Canada, 2007), 16, retrieved 26 July
     2010 from http://dsp-psd.pwgsc.gc.ca.ezproxy.library.yorku.ca/
     collection_2007/statcan/89-621-X/89-621-XIE2007013.pdf. In the 2006
     Census, 46.4 per cent of unattached Japanese Canadians were consid-
     ered below the low-income cut-off (39.4 per cent male and 51.5 per
     cent female). Canada, Statistics Canada, Statistics Canada, 'Population
     Groups (28), Age Groups (8), Sex (3) and Selected Demographic, Cul-
     tural, Labour Force, Educational and Income Characteristics (309), for
     the Total Population of Canada, Provinces, Territories, Census Metro-
     politan Areas and Census Agglomerations, 2006 Census – 20% Sample
     Data' (Ottawa: Statistics Canada, 2006) retrieved 25 September 2010
     from http://www12.statcan.gc.ca/census-recensement/2006/dp-pd/
     tbt/Rp-eng.cfm?TABID=1&LANG=E&APATH=3&DETAIL=0&DIM=0
     &FL=A&FREE=0&GC=0&GK=0&GRP=1&PID=97615&PRID=0&PTY
     PE=88971,97154&S=0&SHOWALL=0&SUB=0&Temporal=2006&THE
     ME=80&VID=0&VNAMEE=&VNAMEF.

147 An exception is Thomas K. Shoyama who was economic advisor to Pre-
     miers T.C. Douglas and W.S. Lloyd in Saskatchewan. Shoyama served the
     federal government as deputy minister of energy, mines and resources
     from 1973 to 1974 and as deputy minister of finance from 1975 to 1979.
     According to the Department of Finance Canada, 'One of his major re-
     sponsibilities was introducing a national version of the medicare system
     he had helped develop in Saskatchewan' (retrieved 21 January 2010 from
     www.fin.gc.ca/comment/ShoyamaBio-eng.asp). It must be noted, how-
     ever, that Shoyama was not an elected government representative. The
     first Japanese Canadian elected to serve in the parliament of Canada was
     Bev Oda who was elected as a Conservative Party member in 2004. She
     was the first Japanese Canadian to serve in a federal government when
     the Conservative Party formed a minority government in 2006. Oda was
     born in Thunder Bay; her parents met in Fort Williams after their expul-
     sion from BC.

148 At the '20th Anniversary of the Japanese Canadian Redress Settlement
     Celebration and Conference,' 20 September 2008, in Vancouver, BC,
     writer Hiromi Goto commented that she does not write about the Intern-
     ment because her parents immigrated to Canada from Japan in the 1960s.

149 Elena Tajima Creef, 'Re/Orientations: The Politics of Japanese American Representation' (PhD diss., University of California, Santa Cruz, 1994), 65.
150 Evelyn [pseud.], interview by author, 26 August 1995.

2 The Silencing Continues

1 Audrey Kobayashi, 'Birds of Passage or Squawking Ducks: Writing Across Generations of Japanese-Canadian Literature,' in *Writing Across Worlds: Literature and Migration*, ed. Russell King, John Connell, and Paul White (London: Routledge, 1995), 227.
2 Roy Miki, 'Asiancy: Making Space for Asian Canadian Writing,' in *Broken Entries: Race, Subjectivity, Writing* (Toronto: The Mercury Press, 1998), 116–17; emphasis in original.
3 Michel Foucault, *'Society Must be Defended': Lectures at the Collège de France 1975–1976*, ed. Mauro Bertani and Alessandro Fontana, trans. David Macey (New York: Picador, 2003), 29.
4 R. Miki, 'Asiancy,' 117.
5 Lisa Lowe, *Immigrant Acts: On Asian American Cultural Politics* (Durham, NC: Duke University Press, 1996), 4.
6 Laura Hyun Yi Kang, 'Compositional Subjects: Enfiguring Asian/American Women' (PhD diss., University of California, Santa Cruz, 1995), 85.
7 Ibid., 36.
8 Ibid., 94.
9 Keibo Oiwa, *Stone Voices: Wartime Writings of Japanese Canadian Issei* (Montreal: Véhicule Press, 1991); Janice Mirikitani, *Shedding Silence* (Berkeley, CA: Celestial Arts, 1987); Roger W. Axford, *Too Long Silent: Japanese Americans Speak Out* (Lincoln, NB: Media Publishing and Marketing, 1986). By citing these sources, I am not indicating that these authors view silence in the same way. Rather, it is my intent to illustrate the predominance of this theme or its metaphorical usage in the titles of Japanese Canadian/American-specific writings. For an analysis of silence in Joy Kogawa's *Obasan* (Toronto: Penguin Books, 1983), see King-Kok Cheung, *Articulate Silences: Hisaye Yamamoto, Maxine Hong Kingston, Joy Kogawa* (Ithaca, NY: Cornell University Press, 1993), and Smaro Kamboureli, 'The Body in Joy Kogawa's *Obasan*: Race, Gender, Sexuality,' in *Scandalous Bodies: Diasporic Literatures in English Canada* (Don Mills, ON: Oxford University Press, 2000), 178–221.
10 Although Shizuye Takashima's book, *A Child in Prison Camp* (Montreal: Tundra, 1971) was published before *Obasan*, Takashima's account was

categorized as belonging to the genre of autobiographical writing and therefore as non-fiction. It also was identified as a book for children and received numerous awards, including the Choice Book Medal of the Toronto Children's Book Centre.

11 R. Miki, 'Asiancy,' 114.

12 Kogawa, *Obasan*, 32.

13 Ibid.

14 Shirley Geok-Lin Lim, 'Japanese American Women's Life Stories: Maternality in Monica Sone's *Nisei Daughter* and Joy Kogawa's *Obasan*,' *Feminist Studies* 16, no. 2 (1990), 291.

15 Roy Miki and Cassandra Kobayashi, *Justice in Our Time: The Japanese Canadian Redress Settlement* (Vancouver: Talonbooks and Winnipeg: National Association of Japanese Canadians, 1991), 37.

16 Cheung, *Articulate Silences*, 1.

17 Ibid., 2.

18 Ibid., 8.

19 I have chosen not to reproduce translations of these concepts as it is the fact that translation can occur unreflexively, reproducing a position of Western authority in relation to Japanese Canadians that I am trying to draw attention to here.

20 See, for example, the description of the Nisei as inheriting these qualities from the Issei in Ken Adachi, *The Enemy That Never Was: A History of the Japanese Canadians* (Toronto: McClelland and Stewart, 1976): 'Enryo ... gaman ... and, perhaps most significantly, the shikata-ga-nai syndrome (it can't be helped), along with an innate respect for authority, helped to shape their acquiescence to evacuation and enabled them to overcome, at least outwardly, the traumatic events and to carry on with the task of resettlement' (355–6).

21 Rey Chow, *Writing Diaspora: Tactics of Intervention in Contemporary Cultural Studies* (Bloomington: Indiana University Press, 1993), 45.

22 Frank Davey, 'This Land That Is Like Every Land: *Obasan*,' in *Post-National Arguments: The Politics of the Anglophone-Canadian Novel since 1967* (Toronto: University of Toronto Press, 1993), 104.

23 Ibid.

24 Ibid., 103.

25 Ibid.

26 Ibid.

27 Audrey Kobayashi, 'Birds of Passage or Squawking Ducks,' 216.

28 Kang, 'Compositional Subjects,' 217.

29 Kirsten McAllister and Scott McFarlane, 'Reflections on *The Pool*: Interning

Japanese Canadian History,' *The Bulletin* 34, no. 12 (1992), 25. See also Mc-Farlane's argument that some of the 'language of internment' constructs Japanese Canadians as 'feminized, innocent, naïve children,' in 'Covering *Obasan* and the Narrative of Internment,' in *Privileging Positions: The Sites of Asian American Studies*, ed. Gary Y. Okihiro, Marilyn Alquizola, Dorothy Fujita Rony, and K. Scott Wong (Pullman, WA: Washington State University Press, 1995), 408.

30 Davey, 'This Land That Is Like Every Land,' 103.

31 Ibid., 104.

32 Wendy Brown, *States of Injury: Power and Freedom in Late Modernity* (Princeton, NJ: Princeton University Press, 1995), 42.

33 For a discussion of how the West and Western feminists reinforce notions of Western superiority in their depictions of racialized women's oppression, see Sherene H. Razack, *Looking White People in the Eye: Gender, Race, and Culture in Courtrooms and Classrooms* (Toronto: University of Toronto Press, 1998), 5–6, and 'Modern Women as Imperialists: Geopolitics, Culture Class, and Gender after 9/11,' in *Casting Out: The Eviction of Muslims from Western Law and Politics* (Toronto: University of Toronto Press 2008), 83–106.

34 Davey, 'This Land That Is Like Every Land,' 105.

35 Ibid., 104.

36 Kerri Sakamoto, *The Electrical Field* (Toronto: Alfred A. Knopf, 1998).

37 Kitigawa's papers under discussion here were edited and published in Muriel Kitagawa, *This Is My Own: Letters to Wes and Other Writings on Japanese Canadians, 1941–1948*, ed. Roy Miki (Vancouver: Talonbooks, 1985).

38 I would like to thank Roy Miki for discussing this point with me.

39 R. Miki and C. Kobayashi, *Justice in Our Time*, 150.

40 Muriel Kitagawa, 'This is My Own, My Native Land!' in *This Is My Own*, ed. R. Miki, 288.

41 Weiner cited in R. Miki and C. Kobayashi, *Justice in Our Time*, 151. See Scott Toguri McFarlane's comment that 'both Ed Broadbent and Gerry Weiner quoted from the novel *Obasan* after a negotiated settlement was reached between the NAJC and the federal government,' in 'Covering *Obasan*,' 402.

42 Editorial, 'We Are the Israelites on the Move,' *Toronto Star*, 20 November 1997, A28. Although the agreement to establish a 'Race Relations Foundation' was part of the 1988 negotiated redress settlement with the federal government, it was not until October 1996 that the Foundation was proclaimed into law. See R. Miki and C. Kobayashi, *Justice in Our Time*, 138–9, for a description of the terms of the redress agreement, and Arthur Miki, *The Japanese Canadian Redress Legacy: A Community Revitalized* (Winnipeg:

National Association of Japanese Canadians, 2003), for a description of the
Canadian Race Relations Foundation and its activities.

43 Editorial, 'We Are the Israelites on the Move,' A28.

44 Ibid.

45 Gordon Hirabayashi, 'Review of *This Is My Own: Letters to Wes and Other
Writings on Japanese Canadians, 1941–1948,* by Muriel Kitagawa, edited by
Roy Miki,' *Canadian Ethnic Studies* 21, no. 3 (1989), 140.

46 Ibid.

47 Sucheng Chan, *Asian Americans: An Interpretive History* (Boston: Twayne,
1991), 136. Hirabayashi was one of three men (Fred Korematsu and Minoru Yasui were the others) who challenged the constitutionality of the
curfew and expulsion orders in the U.S. Supreme Court. Mitsuye Endo
legally challenged the War Relocation Authority's 'right to keep her under
custody.' Years after her incarceration, the Supreme Court ruled that Endo
be released 'unconditionally.' The charges against the men were upheld
(Chan, *Asian Americans*, 135–8). For an analysis of these cases, see Peter
Irons, *Justice at War: The Story of the Japanese American Internment Cases*
(New York: Oxford University Press, 1983). In the 1980s, a campaign was
organized to reverse the decisions in the cases of the three men. On 10
February 1986, Judge Voorhees vacated Hirabayashi's conviction for fail-
ing to report but did not overturn the curfew conviction. Upon appeal,
the charge of violating curfew was set aside. See Peter Irons, ed., *Justice
Delayed: The Record of the Japanese American Internment Cases* (Middleton,
CT: Wesleyan University Press, 1989) for a description of the appeals of
these convictions. For an interpretation of the Hirabayashi case by a child
of Internment survivors, see David Mura, *Where the Body Meets Memory*
(New York: Doubleday, 1996).

48 Gordon Hirabayashi quoted in Kandice Chuh, 'Transnationalism and Its
Pasts,' *Public Culture* 9 (1996), 101.

49 Due to the problematic representation of the Internment in the museum
exhibit, the NAJC has requested changes. This request was formally initiated in 2007. While the projection of a Japanese military flag on the floor in
front of the Internment exhibit has been removed, the NAJC continues to
wait for the Museum to address other problems with the exhibit. See Grace
Eiko Thomson, 'National Association of Japanese Canadians President's
Message July,' 25 June 2008, retrieved 15 February 2009 from www.najc.ca/
community-news/presidents-message-july/. In the article 'CWM Finally
Making Changes to JC Exhibit,' *Nikkei Voice* 24, no. 5 (June 2010), 2, it was
reported that '[m]odifications are expected to be completed by October
2010.' In the article by the NAJC, 'JCs Re-victimized, Canadians Misled,'

Nikkei Voice 24, no. 9 (November 2010), 3, it was reported that 'the need for more changes than originally anticipated would delay the revision until early 2011.' The exhibit as described in this chapter was viewed by the author on 17 August 2008 and was unchanged when again viewed on 16 June 2009. Also note that two paintings in the museum have been protested by the National Aboriginal Veterans' Association and the Congress of Aboriginal Peoples. See 'CAP and Native Veterans Call for Removal of "Offensive Paintings,"' *The First Perspective* 14, no. 9 (September 2005), 1.

50 The same photo is found in Kitagawa, *This Is My Own*, 175.

51 Canadian War Museum, *Forced Relocation. Un Déplacement Forcé* (Ottawa: Canadian War Museum, 2008).

52 For descriptions and analyses of the Nisei Mass Evacuation Group and the organizing against the dispossession, see Roy Miki, *Redress: Inside the Japanese Canadian Call for Justice* (Vancouver: Raincoast Books, 2004), chapters 3 to 6.

53 Canadian War Museum, 'Get Involved' (Ottawa, ON: Canadian War Museum, 2008), retrieved 1 November 2008 from http://www.ottawakiosk .com/cgi-bin/linkto.pl?url=/go/link.php?url=http://www.warmuseum .ca/.

54 While the NAJC has requested that the museum add a representation of Japanese Canadian men who served in the Canadian forces during the Second World War, this had not been accomplished when the exhibit was last viewed by this author. Even if this representation is added, it must be noted that millions of visitors have viewed the *Forced Relocation* panel without this representation; the museum first opened on 8 May 2005, and the 'one-millionth visitor arrived just one year and nine months later.' See J. Geurts, foreword to *Reflections/Réflections: On the Canadian War Museum/ Sur le Musée canadien de la guerre* (Ottawa: Canadian War Museum, 2007), 2. See also Roy Miki's critique of *Forced Relocation* and his analysis of the photograph of Mitsui: 'Stripped of his military affiliations, viewers remain unaware of the significance of his contribution to the country,' in 'Japanese Canadians in the National Museum,' *Nikkei Voice* 21, no. 5 (2007), 5.

55 See Roy Ito, *We Went to War: The Story of the Japanese Canadians Who Served during the First and Second World Wars* (Stittsville, ON: Canada's Wings, 1984).

56 See, for example, Calvin W. Ruck, *Canada's Black Battalion: No. 2 Construction, 1916–1920* (Dartmouth, NS: Society for Protection and Preservation of Black Culture in Nova Scotia, 1986); James W. Walker, 'Race and Recruitment in World War I: Enlistment of Visible Minorities in the Canadian Expeditionary Force,' *Canadian Historical Review* 70, no. 1 (1989),

1–26; Dennis McLaughlin and Leslie McLaughlin, *For My Country: Black Canadians on the Field of Honour* (Ottawa: Military Gender Integration and Employment Equity, Department of National Defence, 2004); Vivienne Poy, 'The Role Played by Chinese-Canadians in WWII – With Reference to the Life of Kam Len Douglas Sam' (paper presented at the annual meeting of the Association for Asian American Studies, Toronto, ON, 29 March 2001), retrieved 25 June 2009 from http://sen.parl.gc.ca/vpoy/english/ Special_Interests/speeches/Speech%20-%20AAAS%20,Toronto.htm. For the participation of Indigenous peoples in the Canadian military during the First and Second World Wars, see, for example, Fred Gaffen, *Forgotten Soldiers* (Penticton, BC: Theytus Books, 1985); Janice Summerby, *Native Soldiers, Foreign Battlefields* (Ottawa: Veterans Affairs Canada, 1993); L. James Dempsey, *Warriors of the King: Prairie Indians in World War I* (Regina, SK: University of Regina, Canadian Plains Research Center, 1999); P. Whitney Lackenbauer and Craig Leslie Mantle, eds. *Aboriginal Peoples and the Canadian Military: Historical Perspectives* (Kingston, ON: Canadian Defence Academy Press, 2007).

57 According to Roy Miki and Cassandra Kobayashi, in 1977, 'the National Japanese Canadian Citizens' Association (re-named the National Association of Japanese Canadians in 1980) … first established a Reparation Committee to investigate the question of redress' (*Justice in Our Time*, 64). Although the Bird Commission was struck by the federal government in 1947 to investigate the actions of the Custodian of Enemy Property's action and compensation for Japanese Canadians, Mr. Justice Bird who headed the commission ruled: 'I am satisfied … that the very onerous task … was competently performed, with due regard to the interest of the owners …' (Bird quoted in R. Miki, *Redress*, 117).

58 Linda Ohama, director, *Obāchan's Garden*, 94 min., National Film Board of Canada, Toronto, 2001.

59 Deborah L. Begoray, '*Obāchan's Garden*,' *Canadian Review of Materials* 8, no. 15 (2002), 2.

60 Rocio Davis, 'Locating Family: Asian Canadian Historical Revisioning in Linda Ohama's *Obaachan's [sic] Garden* and Ann Marie Fleming's *The Magical Life of Long Tack Sam*,' *Journal of Canadian Studies* 42, no. 1 (2008), 6.

61 Ibid., 7.

62 Ibid., 11.

63 Suhoken Kukai quoted in Audrey Kobayashi, 'Structured Feeling: Japanese-Canadian Poetry and Landscape,' in *A Few Acres of Snow: Literary and Artistic Images of Canada*, ed. Paul Simpson-Housley and Glenn Northcliffe (Toronto: Dundurn Press, 1992), 253.

64 Audrey Kobayashi, 'Birds of Passage or Squawking Ducks,' 217.
65 Michael Fukushima, director, *Minoru: Memory of Exile*, 18 min., National Film Board of Canada, Montreal, 1992; Ohama, *Obāchan's Garden*; Midi Onodera, director, *Displaced View*, 52 min., VHS/16mm, McCano Film Artists, New York, 1988.
66 Haruko Okano, *Come Spring: Journey of a Sansei* (Vancouver: Gallerie, 1992), 7.
67 Rea Tajiri, director, *History and Memory: For Akiko and Takashige*, 32 min., Women Make Movies, New York, 1991, VHS/DVD. For a critique of *History and Memory*, see Laura U. Marks, 'A Deleuzian Politics of Hybrid Cinema,' *Screen* 35, no. 3 (August 1994), 244–64.
68 Stan Yogi, 'Yearning for the Past: The Dynamics of Memory in Sansei Internment Poetry,' in *Memory and Cultural Politics: New Approaches to American Ethnic Literatures*, ed. Amritjit Singh, Joseph T. Skerritt Jr., and Robert E. Hogan (Boston: Northeastern University Press, 1996), 253.
69 Ibid., 158.
70 Ibid., 246.
71 Chow, *Writing Diaspora*, 34; emphasis in the original.
72 Razack, *Looking White People in the Eye*, 5.
73 Gayatri Chakravorty Spivak, 'Can the Subaltern Speak?' in *Marxism and the Interpretation of Culture*, ed. Cary Nelson and Lawrence Grossberg (Urbana, IL: University of Illinois Press, 1988), 271–313. See, in addition, both Alarcón's and Chow's analyses of the 'speaking subject': Norma Alarcón, 'The Theoretical Subject(s) of This Bridge Called My Back and Anglo-American Feminism,' in *Making Face, Making Soul: Creative and Critical Perspectives by Women of Color*, ed. Gloria Anzaldúa (San Francisco: Aunt Lute Foundation, 1990), 356–69; and Chow, *Writing Diaspora*.
74 Spivak, 'Can the Subaltern Speak?' 296.
75 Ibid.; emphasis in the original.
76 Masumi Hayashi was shot to death by her neighbour in Cleveland, Ohio, on 17 August 2006, after she had complained about his loud music. Hayashi was born on 3 September 1945 in the Gila River internment camp on the Gila River reservation in Arizona. To view some of her photography, go to www.masumimuseum.com (last accessed 31 March 2010).

3 Method, Memory, and the Subjects of the Internment

1 S. [pseud.], interview by author, 16 August 1995.
2 See, for example, Audrey Kobayashi, 'For the Sake of the Children: Japanese/Canadian Workers/Mothers,' in *Women, Work, and Place* ed. Audrey Kobayashi (Montreal: McGill-Queen's University Press, 1994), 44–72; To-

moko Makabe, *Picture Brides: Japanese Women in Canada* (Toronto: Multicultural History Society of Ontario, 1995); Midge Ayukawa, 'Good Wives and Wise Mothers: Japanese Picture Brides in Early Twentieth-Century British Columbia,' *B.C. Studies*, 105–106 (1995), 114; Midge Ayukawa, *Hiroshima Immigrants in Canada, 1891–1941* (Vancouver: UBC Press, 2008).

3 For example, see the work of Audrey Kobayashi, Cassandra Kobayashi, Leslie Komori, Kirsten Emiko McAllister, Cindy Mochizuki, Maryka Omatsu, Baco Ohama, Linda Ohama, Haruko Okano, Midi Onodera, Kerri Sakamoto, and Pamela Sugiman.

4 For an analysis of the construction of memories among three generations of women in one family, see Pamela Sugiman, '"A Million Hearts from Here": Japanese Canadian Mothers and Daughters and the Lessons of War,' *Journal of American Ethnic History* 26, no. 4 (2007): 50–68. See Donna K. Nagata, *Legacy of Injustice: Exploring the Cross-Generational Impact of the Japanese American Internment* (New York: Plenum Press, 1993) for an analysis of the psychological effects of the Internment in the United States on the children of interned parents.

5 Lisa Lowe, *Immigrant Acts: On Asian American Cultural Politics* (Durham, NC: Duke University Press, 1996), 79.

6 For a discussion of purposive strategy, see Kristin G. Esterberg, *Qualitative Methods in Social Research* (Boston: McGraw Hill, 2002), 93; and Janice L. Ristock and Joan Pennell, *Community Research as Empowerment: Feminist Links, Postmodern Interruptions* (Toronto: Oxford University Press, 1996), 74.

7 In consultation with the women interviewed, I have not included certain biographical data, particularly with regard to their current geographical residence and occupations. Given the small population of Japanese Canadians – 98,900 in 2006 (Canada, Statistics Canada, 'Ethnic origins, 2006 counts, for Canada, provinces and territories – 20% sample,' *Census 2006*, retrieved 23 January 2010 from www12.statcan.ca/census-recensement/2006/dp-pd/hlt/97-562/pages/page.cfm?Lang=E&Geo=PR&Code=01&Table=2&Data=Count&StartRec=1&Sort=3&Display=All) – details such as occupation may easily identify some women, particularly those who were incarcerated. Their places of birth, however, are presented as reported and also their sites of incarceration. One woman, however, requested that the site of her incarceration not be disclosed.

8 One interview was conducted in 1992; the woman interviewed was invited to make changes and add comments to her interview transcript in 1997. Her daughter was interviewed in 1995.

9 Many of the women interviewed negotiated requests to be interviewed with their mothers or daughters, work for which I am sincerely grateful.

Some women declined to participate and the deliberations involved in their decisions are also very much appreciated.

10 Esterberg, *Qualitative Methods in Social Research*, 87.
11 Each interview was transcribed verbatim by the author. Every woman was sent a copy of her interview transcript to review and invited to make changes and deletions where necessary. After I received the edited transcript, I made all of the changes requested. All the women were given a photocopy of the transcript with the changes they had requested. Each woman received the original audiotape of her interview and the copy used for transcription purposes.
12 The initial S. was self-selected.
13 Esther [pseud.], interview by author, 17 August 1995.
14 Peter Nunoda, 'A Community in Transition and Conflict: The Japanese Canadians, 1935–1951' (PhD diss., University of Manitoba, 1991).
15 Out of regard for the privacy of the families of the women interviewed, the complex issues of loss of familial possessions and property, and the limited educational opportunities for most of the women interviewed who were interned, I did not ask questions about their income.
16 Canada, Statistics Canada, 'Rising Education of Women and the Gender Earnings Gap,' *The Daily* (12 June 2007), retrieved 28 December 2007 from www.statcan.ca/Daily/English/070612/d070612b.htm.
17 Audrey Kobayashi, 'A Demographic Profile of Japanese Canadians and Social Implications for the Future' (Ottawa: Department of the Secretary of State, 1989), 48. In the 2006 Census, the average income for Japanese Canadians 15 years and older who were employed was $40,578 ($55,829 for men and $29,512 for women). Canada, Statistics Canada, 'Population Groups (28), Age Groups (8), Sex (3), and Selected Demographic, Cultural, Labour Force, Educational and Income Characteristics (309), for the total Population of Canada, Provinces, Territories, Census Metropolitan Aras and Census Agglomerations, 2006 Census – 20% Sample Data' (Ottawa: Statistics Canada, 2006), retrieved 25 September 2010 from *2006 Census*, www12.statcan.gc.ca/census-recensement/index-eng.cfm.
18 Roger Simon and Claudia Eppert, 'Remembering Obligation: Pedagogy and the Witnessing of Testimony of Historical Trauma,' *Canadian Journal of Education* 22, no. 2 (1997), 180–1.
19 Library and Archives Canada (hereafter LAC), Records of the British Columbia Security Commission, RG 36/27.
20 Miranda Johnson, 'Honest Acts and Dangerous Supplements: Indigenous Oral History and Historical Practice in Settler Societies,' *Postcolonial Studies* 8, no. 3 (2005), 270.

21 Yoshiko [pseud.], interview by author, 22 December 1994. All subsequent quotes by Yoshiko are taken from this interview.

22 Shoshana Felman, 'Education and Crisis, Or the Vicissitudes of Teaching,' in *Testimony: Crises of Witnessing in Literature, Psychoanalysis, and History*, by Shoshana Felman and Dori Laub (New York: Routledge, 1992), 5.

23 For important contributions, see Pamela Sugiman, 'Memories of Internment: Narrating Japanese Canadian Women's Life Stories,' *Canadian Journal of Sociology* 29, no. 3 (2004), 359–88; and Roy Miki, *Redress: Inside the Japanese Canadian Call for Justice* (Vancouver: Raincoast Books, 2004), 262–3.

24 For a survey and discussion of the debates on the use of oral history, see, for example, Paul Thompson, 'Pioneering the Life Story Method,' *International Journal of Social Research Methodology* 7, no. 1 (2004), 81–4; Joanna Bornat, 'Women's History and Oral History: Developments and Debates,' *Women's History Review* 16, no. 1 (2007), 19–39; Joan Sangster, 'Telling Our Stories: Feminist Debates and the Use of Oral History,' *Women's History Review* 3, no. 1 (1994), 5–28; Sherna Berger Gluck and Daphne Patai, eds., *Women's Words: The Feminist Practice of Oral History* (New York: Routledge, 1991).

25 Felman, 'Education and Crisis, Or the Vicissitudes of Teaching,' 5.

26 Lowe, *Immigrant Acts*, 156–7.

27 Chandra Talpade Mohanty quoted in ibid., 157. The issue of the testifying subject and the witness to testimony will be revisited in chapter 7.

28 For an important analysis of the use of oral testimony and the reliability of memory, see Lawrence Langer, *Holocaust Testimonies: The Ruins of Memory* (New Haven: Yale University Press, 1991).

29 Bornat, 'Women's History and Oral History,' 22.

30 Ibid., 34.

31 Thompson, 'Pioneering the Life Story Method,' 81.

32 Ibid., 81–2.

33 Roger Simon, 'The Pedagogy of Commemoration and Formation of Collective Memories,' *Educational Foundations* 8, no. 1 (1994), 9.

34 In the disputed testimony, the survivor described four chimneys having been blown up during the Auschwitz uprising; historians maintained that only one was destroyed. The survivor's testimony was hence discounted due to its 'inaccuracy.' Laub disagreed with the historians' dismissal of the entire account because of the factual error, because the 'number mattered less than the fact of the occurrence.' Dori Laub, 'Bearing Witness or the Vicissitudes of Listening,' in *Testimony: Crises of Witnessing in Literature, Psychoanalysis, and History*, by Shoshana Felman and Dori Laub (New York: Routledge, 1992), 60.

35 Laub, 'Bearing Witness or the Vicissitudes of Listening,' 60.
36 Ibid.
37 Walter Benjamin, *Illuminations*, ed. Hannah Arendt (New York: Harcourt, Brace and World, 1955), 257.
38 Ibid.
39 See Kirsten Emiko McAllister's careful argument that the 'term "traumatic" emphasizes the experience of the survivors ...' (33), and the trauma is a result of the destruction of 'their lifeworld' (132), in 'Remembering Political Violence: The Nikkei Internment Memorial Centre' (PhD diss., Carleton University, 2000).
40 May [pseud.], interview by author, 24 March 1992.
41 Yoshiku, interview.
42 For discussions of PTSD as applied to understanding historical trauma, see, for example, Cathy Caruth, ed., *Trauma: Explorations in Memory* (Baltimore: Johns Hopkins University Press, 1995); Cathy Caruth, *Unclaimed Experience: Trauma, Narrative, and History* (Baltimore: Johns Hopkins University Press, 1996); Judith Lewis Herman, *Trauma and Recovery* (New York: HarperCollins, 1992); Frank M. Ochberg, ed., *Post-Traumatic Therapy and Victims of Violence* (New York: Brunner/Mazel, 1988); Shoshana Felman and Dori Laub, *Testimony: Crises of Witnessing in Literature, Psychoanalysis, and History* (New York: Routledge, 1992); Dominick LaCapra, *Representing the Holocaust: History, Theory, Trauma* (Ithaca, NY: Cornell University Press, 1994); and Robert Jay Lifton, *The Broken Connection: On Death and the Continuity of Life* (New York: Simon and Schuster, 1979).
43 Chalsa Loo, 'An Integrative-Sequential Treatment Model for Posttraumatic Stress Disorder: A Case Study of the Japanese American Internment and Redress,' *Critical Psychology Review* 13, no. 2 (1993), 90. See also Donna K. Nagata's description of PTSD and its relationship to the Internment in *Legacy of Injustice: Exploring the Cross-Generational Impact of the Japanese American Internment* (New York: Plenum Press, 1993), 100.
44 Loo, 'An Integrative-Sequential Treatment Model,' 106. On 10 August 1988, President Ronald Reagan signed the Civil Liberties Act, which was the U.S. government's redress legislation for the internment of Japanese Americans. See, for example, Roger Daniels, Sandra C. Taylor, and Harry H.L. Kitano, eds., *Japanese Americans: From Relocation to Redress* (Seattle: University of Washington Press, 1991); Dorothy Fujita-Rony, '"Destructive Force": Aiko Herzig-Yoshinaga's Gendered Labor in the Japanese American Redress Movement,' *Frontiers* 24, no. 1 (2003), 38–60; Alice Yang Murray, *Historical Memories of the Japanese American Internment and the Struggle for Redress* (Stanford: Stanford University Press, 2008); Robert Sadamu

Shimabukuro, *Born in Seattle: The Campaign for Japanese American Redress* (Seattle: University of Washington Press, 2001); Yasuko I. Takezawa, *Breaking the Silence: Redress and Japanese American Ethnicity* (Ithaca, NY: Cornell University Press, 1995).

45 See Roger Simon's argument for 'insurgent commemoration,' which he defines as 'attempts to construct and engage representations that rub taken-for-granted history against the grain so as to revitalize and rearticulate what one sees as desirable and necessary for an open, just and life-sustaining future,' in 'Forms of Insurgency in the Production of Popular Memories: The Columbus Quincentary and the Pedagogy of Counter-Commemoration,' *Cultural Studies* 7, no. 1 (1993), 76. See also Roger I. Simon, Sharon Rosenberg, and Claudia Eppert, eds., *Between Hope and Despair: Pedagogy and the Remembrance of Historical Trauma* (Lanham, MD: Rowman and Littlefield, 2000).

46 Francesca Cappelletto, 'Long-Term Memory of Extreme Events: From Autobiography to History,' *Journal of the Royal Anthropological Institute* 9, no. 2 (2003), 254.

47 Marita Sturken, *Tangled Memories: The Vietnam War, the AIDS Epidemic, and the Politics of Remembering* (Berkeley: University of California Press, 1997), 2.

48 Norm Ibuki, 'Nikkei Centre, Breaking the Silence,' *The Bulletin* 36, no. 7 (1994), 13. See also, 'Nikkei Internment Memorial Centre opening in New Denver,' *The Bulletin* 36, no. 8 (1994), 17 (no author given). For a description of being incarcerated in New Denver, see Henry Shimizu, *Images of Internment: A Bitter-Sweet Memoir in Words and Images: Life in the New Denver Internment Camp, 1942–1946* (Victoria: Ti-Jean Press, 2008). For important analyses of the New Denver incarceration site, see McAllister, 'Remembering Political Violence' and 'Captivating Debris: Unearthing a World War Two Internment Camp,' *Cultural Values* 5, no. 1 (2001), 97–114, and *Terrain of Memory: A Japanese Canadian Memorial Project* (Vancouver: UBC Press, 2010); and Monika Kin Gagnon, 'Tender Research: Field Notes from the Nikkei Internment Memorial Centre,' *Canadian Journal of Communication* 31, no. 1 (2006), retrieved 2 January 2008 from www.cjc-online.ca/viewarticle.php?id=1743&layout=html. The term Nikkei can be translated as people of Japanese ancestry.

49 McAllister, 'Captivating Debris,' 102.

50 Ibid.

51 I was present for a groundbreaking ceremony for the Centre during a 1992 tour of the sites of incarceration and appreciate the generosity and work of the New Denver Kyowakai Society.

52 Chapter 4 will provide more of a description of Hastings Park.
53 Roy Miki and Cassandra Kobayashi, *Justice in Our Time: The Japanese Canadian Redress Settlement* (Vancouver: Talonbooks and Winnipeg: National Association of Japanese Canadians, 1991), 155.
54 Ibid.
55 For an account by a woman incarcerated in the Manzanar camp, see Jeanne Wakatsuki Houston and James D. Houston, *Farewell to Manzanar* (Boston: Houghton Mifflin, 1989). A description and photographs of Manzanar are found in John Armor and Peter Wright, *Manzanar* (New York: Vintage Books, 1989). *Manzanar* showcases photographs by Ansel Adams who was invited to take photographs of Manzanar in the fall of 1943. According to Armor and Wright, Adams was a friend of the second director of the Manzanar site. For a critique of Adams' Manzanar photographs, see Elena Tajima Creef, 'Re/Orientations: The Politics of Japanese American Representation' (PhD diss., University of California, Santa Cruz, 1994) and *Imagining Japanese America: The Visual Construction of Citizenship, Nation, and the Body* (New York: New York University Press, 2004), 18–37.
56 Kathleen Kenna, 'Land of the Free?' *Toronto Star*, 12 July 1998, E5. It is interesting to note that this article on the Manzanar site was facing a page in the newspaper with an article subtitled, 'Case of the "Asian Flu" More Like a Plague,' on the economic situation in Asia. In a literal sense, remembering the Internment is a process 'faced' with racial discourses, like those demonstrated through the association between Asians and contagion. I would like to thank Edward Oikawa for showing me these articles.
57 Ibid.
58 Louise [pseud.], interview by author, 11 July 1995.
59 See chapter 1 for a description of the origin of the name Tashme.
60 Shirras was the BCSC Commissioner whose first two initials were used (see chapter 1) and only Mead was an RCMP Officer (see chapter 1n16).
61 Michi Weglyn, *Years of Infamy: The Untold Story of America's Concentration Camps* (New York: William Morrow, 1976).
62 Murray, *Historical Memories of the Japanese American Internment and the Struggle for Redress*, 245. I would like to thank Dana Takagi for informing me of Murray's work. Frank Moritsugu, writing on the death of Weglyn in April 1999, noted that when *Years of Infamy* was published in 1976, 'Initial reaction included refusal from some bookstores to stock it.' See 'In 1976, Some Stores Refused to Sell Michi's Book,' *Nikkei Voice* 13, no. 4 (May 1999), 5.
63 It may be difficult for individuals to access government records collected

on them, their families, and communities due to the application of the Privacy Act. For example, when I applied to see individual case files from the Office of the Custodian of Enemy Property fonds (RG 117) for my father and mother, I was told that ordinarily without their permission (they are both deceased) I would have to wait twenty years after their deaths. My grandmother, who was alive at the time of my query, was able to access some of her and her children's information (including that of my mother) using the access to information process. However, after requesting permission to view my father's records, I was sent some photocopies of his documents and a letter that stated, 'Our preliminary investigation of this reel was ceased due to the time we had already expended without having successfully located Mr. Oikawa's name and, the additional time that would be required to examine the microfilm which contains approximately *3,000 documents*. Please be advised that microfilm reel C-9478 is *not open to the public* and therefore cannot be accessed through interlibrary loan,' Access to Information and Privacy Analyst, National Archives of Canada (NAC), letter to author, 13 July 1998, 2, emphasis added. (Note: The acronym NAC was later changed to LAC.) Correspondence received from a LAC Reference Archivist on 18 December 2009 confirms that these case files (RG117) 'are restricted and must be reviewed by our Access to Information and Privacy Division,' Reference Archivist, Reference Services, Library and Archives Canada to Mona Oikawa, 18 December 2009.

64 Current restrictions are a result of the Privacy Act. In comparing past national archives' access practices to more recent practices, Ann Sunahara states, 'The Access to Information Act and the Privacy Act did not come into force until 1983. Instead, there was a "gentlemen's convention" that documents would be made available after 30 years. But even then access was entirely at the discretion of the government of the day, who could impose restrictions on it,' quoted in Roy Miki, *Redress*, 233n3. For examples of restricted records pertaining to the Internment of Japanese Canadians, use the search engine of the LAC website www.collectionscanada.gc.ca/index-e.html.

65 Gayatri Chakravorty Spivak, 'Subaltern Talk: An Interview with the Editors (1993–94),' in *The Spivak Reader*, ed. Donna Landry and Gerald Maclean (New York: Routledge, 1996), 289.

66 Simon and Eppert, 'Remembering Obligation,' 182.

67 Ibid.

68 Sara Ahmed, *The Cultural Politics of Emotion* (New York: Routledge, 2004), 35; emphasis in original.

4 Cartographies of Violence

1 Michel Foucault, *Discipline and Punish: The Birth of the Prison*, trans. Alan Sheridan (New York: Vintage Books, 1995), 30–1; note omitted.
2 Shizuye Takashima, *A Child in Prison Camp* (Montreal: Tundra Books, 1971), n.p.
3 Giorgio Agamben, *State of Exception*, trans. Kevin Attell (Chicago: University of Chicago Press, 2003), 51.
4 Ibid., 39.
5 Giorgio Agamben, *Homo Sacer: Sovereign Power and Bare Life*, trans. Daniel Heller-Roazen (Stanford: Stanford University Press, 1998), 174.
6 Sunera Thobani, *Exalted Subjects: Studies in the Making of Race and Nation in Canada* (Toronto: University of Toronto Press, 2007), 37.
7 Bonita Lawrence, 'Rewriting Histories of the Land: Colonization and Indigenous Resistance in Eastern Canada,' in *Race, Space, and the Law: Unmapping a White Settler Society*, ed. Sherene H. Razack (Toronto: Between the Lines, 2002), 21–46.
8 The term 'technology' is borrowed from Foucault. See, for example, *Discipline and Punish*, 30.
9 Canada, *An Act to Amend and Consolidate the Laws Respecting Indians*, R.S.C. (1876), c. 18, ss. 1–100. This version of the Act was in effect during the Internment.
10 Saidiya V. Hartman, *Scenes of Subjection: Terror, Slavery, and Self-Making in Nineteenth-Century America* (New York: Oxford University Press, 1997), 69.
11 For an analysis of Canada as a 'settler society,' see, for example, Daiva Stasiulis and Nira Yuval-Davis, 'Introduction: Beyond Dichotomies – Gender, Race, Ethnicity and Class in Settler Societies,' in *Unsettling Settler Societies: Articulations of Gender, Race, Ethnicity and Class*, ed. David Stasiulis and Nira Yuval-Davis (Thousand Oaks, CA: Sage, 1995), 1–38. See also Bonita Lawrence, *'Real' Indians and Others: Mixed-Blood Urban Native Peoples and Indigenous Nationhood* (Vancouver: UBC Press, 2004), and 'Rewriting Histories of the Land.'
12 I am using Edward Said's notion of contrapuntal analysis here. As Said states in *Culture and Imperialism* (New York: Vintage Books, 1994), 'We must be able to think through and interpret together experiences that are discrepant, each with a particular agenda and pace of development, its own internal formations, its internal coherence and system of external relationships, all of them co-existing and interacting with others' (32).
13 For examples of theorizing the racialization of space in the production of

Canada, see Katherine McKittrick and Clyde Woods, eds., *Black Geographies and the Politics of Place* (Toronto: Between the Lines, 2007); Jennifer J. Nelson, *Razing Africville: A Geography of Racism* (Toronto: University of Toronto Press, 2008); Sherene H. Razack, ed., *Race, Space, and the Law: Unmapping a White Settler Society* (Toronto: Between the Lines, 2002); Cheryl Teelucksingh, ed., *Claiming Space: Racialization in Canadian Cities* (Waterloo, ON: Wilfrid Laurier University Press, 2006). For an example of the relational construction of Indigenous peoples and Chinese Canadians in British Columbia, see Renisa Mawani, *Colonial Proximities: Crossracial Encounters and Juridical Truths in British Columbia, 1871–1921* (Vancouver: UBC Press, 2009).

14 Lynn A. Staeheli, 'Place,' in *A Companion to Political Geography*, ed. John Agnew, Katharyne Mitchell, and Gerard Toal (Malden, MA: Blackwell, 2003), 160.

15 According to Richard Colebrook Harris, by the early 1900s, 'more than 1,500 small reserves [were] scattered' across British Columbia, in *Making Native Space: Colonialism, Resistance, and Reserves in British Columbia* (Vancouver: UBC Press, 2002), 265.

16 Mona Oikawa, 'Re-Mapping Histories Site by Site: Connecting the Internment of Japanese Canadians to the Colonization of Aboriginal Peoples in Canada,' in *Aboriginal Connections to Race, Environment and Traditions*, ed. Rick Riewe and Jill Oakes (Winnipeg: Aboriginal Issues Press, University of Manitoba, 2006), 17–26.

17 The federal government considered moving some Japanese Canadians to the Muncey Reserve in Ontario, for example. They also considered moving the children from residential schools and then moving Japanese Canadians into those schools. See Oikawa, 'Re-Mapping Histories Site by Site.' The U.S. government built two of the camps to incarcerate Japanese Americans on two different reservations. See Richard Drinnon, *Keeper of Concentration Camps: Dillon S. Myer and American Racism* (Berkeley: University of California Press, 1987), xxiii.

18 In citing historian F. Laurie Barron, Olive Patricia Dickason refers to the pass system as a 'form of selectively applied administrative tyranny,' in *Canada's First Nations: A History of Founding Peoples from Earliest Times*, 2nd ed. (Toronto: Oxford University Press, 1997), 289; note omitted. See also Lawrence, *'Real' Indians and Others*, 35. Shelly Ikebuchi Ketchell describes Japanese Canadians forced to work on sugar beet farms as requiring by the BCSC 'a permit to travel more than ten miles from where they lived, making social surveillance unproblematic, thus guaranteeing that Japanese Canadians were never outside of this civic gaze,' in 'Carceral Ambiva-

lence: Japanese Canadian "Internment" and the Sugar Beet Programme During WWII,' *Surveillance and Society* 7, no 1 (2009), 33.

19 Ann Sunahara, 'Legislative Roots of Injustice: The Abuse of Emergency Law in Canada: Is It Inevitable?' in *In Justice: Canada, Minorities, and Human Rights*, ed. Roy Miki and Scott McFarlane (Winnipeg: National Association of Japanese Canadians, 1996), 8.

20 Gerald D. Berreman describes the forced displacement of Aleuts and the military presence in the Aleutian village of Nikolski in a laudatory fashion, illustrating how the violence of expulsion is forgotten through a discourse of progress: 'More recent but effective acultural influences have been the presence of the military and other outside personnel in and around the village since 1957; a period of wartime removal to a good sized town and education outside increased communication with the outside world ... and greatly expanded the opportunities to acquire and use a cash income in and out of the village,' in 'Aleut Reference Group Alienation, Mobility, and Acculturation,' *American Anthropologist* 66, no. 2 (1964), 232. Chalsa Loo reports that the U.S. government offered $12,000 to each Aleut survivor as reparation for their forced displacement in 'An Integrative-Sequential Treatment Model for Posttraumatic Stress Disorder: A Case Study of the Japanese American Internment and Redress,' *Clinical Psychology Review* 13, no. 2 (1993), 100.

21 Sunahara, 'Legislative Roots of Injustice,' 18.

22 On this point, see Bonita Lawrence and Enakshi Dua, 'Decolonizing Antiracism,' *Social Justice* 32 (2005), 120–43, and Oikawa, 'Re-Mapping Histories Site by Site.'

23 David Goldberg, *The Racial State* (Malden, MA: Blackwell, 2002).

24 Foucault, *Discipline and Punish*, 198.

25 Rob Shields, *Places on the Margin: Alternative Geographies of Modernity* (London: Routledge, 1991), 18.

26 Edward Soja, *Postmodern Geographies: The Reassertion of Space in Critical Social Theory* (London: Verso, 1989), 1.

27 Ibid., 7.

28 Foucault, *Discipline and Punish*, 141.

29 Audrey Kobayashi, 'The Historical Context for Japanese-Canadian Uprooting,' in *Social Change and Space: Indigenous Nations and Ethnic Communities in Canada and Finland*, ed. Ludger Müller-Wille (Montreal: Northern Studies Program, McGill University, 1989), 70.

30 Ibid.; emphasis in the original.

31 Ibid.

32 National Association of Japanese Canadians, *The Case for Redress* (Toronto:

National Association of Japanese Canadians, n.d.), 2. See also Ken Adachi, *The Enemy That Never Was: A History of the Japanese Canadians* (Toronto: Mc-Clelland and Stewart, 1976), 52–3.

33 See Ken Adachi's description of the Japanese Canadian Citizens League's organizing drive and efforts to win the franchise in 1936, in *The Enemy That Never Was*, 160–4, and Roy Miki's analysis of their actions in *Redress: Inside the Japanese Canadian Call for Justice* (Vancouver: Raincoast Books, 2004), 30–7.

34 Audrey Kobayashi, 'The Historical Context,' 74. See also Forrest La Violette's description of Vancouver Alderman Halford Wilson's proposal in early 1941 (before the bombing of Pearl Harbor) that Japanese Canadians be segregated into a ghetto; La Violette states that the proposal was based on the claim that Chinese Canadians were moving into the 'newest' and 'most exclusive' areas of Vancouver. He further states, 'A by-law was drafted for the purpose of requiring Orientals to live in "their recognized localities."' See *The Canadian Japanese and World War II* (Toronto: University of Toronto Press, 1948), 27n51.

35 See note 1 in the introduction to this volume.

36 Audrey Kobayashi, 'Racism and Law in Canada: A Geographical Perspective,' *Urban Geography* 11, no. 5 (1990), 456.

37 Ken Adachi, *The Enemy That Never Was*, 209.

38 Ibid., 216.

39 Ibid., 232.

40 Ibid., 200.

41 Terry Watada, *Bukkyo Tozen: A History of Jodo Shinshu Buddhism in Canada* (Toronto: HpF Press and the Toronto Buddhist Church, 1996), 107.

42 Haru [pseud.], interview by author, 23 November 1995. All subsequent quotes by Haru are taken from this interview. See Wayson Choy's description of the relationship between Chinese Canadians and Japanese Canadians in Vancouver as the war in Asia began and 'the tin buttons pinned on our lapels that had the Chinese flag proudly stamped on them … I also had one that said: I AM CHINESE,' in *Jade Peony* (Vancouver: Douglas and McIntyre, 1995), 219. See also Sunahara, *The Politics of Racism: The Uprooting of Japanese Canadians during the Second World War* (Toronto: James Lorimer, 1981), 68, and Shelly Ikebuchi Ketchell's newspaper citation regarding Chinese Canadians in Manitoba who wore 'victory buttons' with the word 'Chinese … plainly on the button.' Ikebuchi Ketchell argues that the buttons indicate the 'ever-vigilant surveillance of Japanese Canadians,' in 'Carceral Ambivalence,' 30.

43 Sunahara, 'Legislative Roots of Injustice,' 17.

44 Maria De Angelis describes the incarceration of Italian Canadian men in 'Testimonies: Internment, Racism and Injustice in Canada,' in *In Justice*, ed. Miki and McFarlane, 25. She adds that men were also incarcerated at three other internment camps: one at St Helen's Island in Quebec and two in Fredericton, New Brunswick. She states that the total number of men incarcerated is unknown.

45 Franca Iacovetta, *Such Hardworking People: Italian Immigrants in Postwar Toronto* (Montreal: McGill-Queen's University Press, 1992), 143–4. For critical essays on the Internment of Italian Canadians, see Franca Iacovetta, Roberto Perin, and Angelo Principe, eds., *Enemies Within: Italian and Other Internees in Canada and Abroad* (Toronto: University of Toronto Press, 1999).

46 Iacovetta, *Such Hardworking People*, 144.

47 Reg Whitaker and Gregory S. Kealey, 'A War on Ethnicity? The RCMP and Internment,' in *Enemies Within: Italian and Other Internees in Canada and Abroad*, ed. Franca Iacovetta, Roberto Perin, and Angelo Principe (Toronto: University of Toronto Press, 2000), 137.

48 Michelle McBride, 'The Curious Case of Female Internees,' in *Enemies Within*, ed. Iacovetta, Perin, and Principe, 156.

49 S. [pseud.], interview by author, 16 August 1995. All subsequent quotes by S. are taken from this interview.

50 Evelyn [pseud.], interview by author, 26 August 1995. All subsequent quotes by Evelyn are taken from this interview.

51 May [pseud.], interview by author, 24 March 1992. All subsequent quotes by May are taken from this interview.

52 Takashima, *A Child in Prison Camp*, n.p.; emphasis added.

53 Ibid.

54 Ian McKay, 'Canada as a Long Liberal Revolution: On Writing the History of Actually Existing Canadian Liberalisms, 1840s–1940s,' in *Liberalism and Hegemony: Debating the Canadian Liberal Revolution*, ed. Jean-François Constant and Michel Ducharme (Toronto: Univeristy of Toronto Press, 2009), 376.

55 Canada, British Columbia Security Commission, *Removal of Japanese from Protected Areas: Report of the British Columbia Security Commission* (Vancouver: BCSC, 1942), 3. See also Ken Adachi, *The Enemy That Never Was*, 209.

56 NAJC, *The Case for Redress*, 2.

57 Sunahara, *The Politics of Racism*, 28.

58 Order-in-Council, P.C. 1665, 4 March 1942, quoted in Audrey Kobayashi, 'Racism and Law,' 457.

59 Canada, BCSC, *Removal*, 3. See also Ken Adachi, *The Enemy That Never Was*, 218. Often the names of white people involved in the Internment and

dispersal are not mentioned in the literature and are thus forgotten. The Custodian of Enemy Property was Glen McPherson (Miki, *Redress*, 142).

60 Ken Adachi, *The Enemy That Never Was*, 233.

61 See Sunahara, *The Politics of Racism*, 107–8, for a description of the legislative processes surrounding the confiscation of property through the Veterans' Land Act.

62 Sunahara, *The Politics of Racism*, 107.

63 Zennosuke Inouye, a veteran of the First World War, had purchased land in Surrey, British Columbia, on 20 September 1919 through the Soldier Settlement Act, 1910. Considered a 'soldier settler,' he was given special consideration by the federal government and was able to return to his property on 20 December 1948. Inouye was not given a house through this special consideration; he was merely allowed to keep the house that he owned before the expulsion. According to Peter Neary, Inouye 'was the only dispossessed Japanese-Canadian veteran to get his land back' ('Zennosuke Inouye's Land: A Canadian Veterans Affairs Dilemma,' *Canadian Historical Review* 85, no. 3 [September 2004], 446). Neary adds that Inouye's house was 'destroyed by fire on 19 February 1949. The building had been insured for only $300 by the custodian ...' (447, note omitted).

64 The description of men as owners of property is also reproduced in narratives of the Internment. For example, Roy Miki writes of Masue Tagashira who, with her husband, 'resettled outside the "protected area" in Revelstoke, and from there, for many years, her husband tried to prevent the sale of *his* assets' (*Redress*, 251; emphasis added).

65 Peter Nunoda, 'A Community in Transition and Conflict: The Japanese Canadians, 1935–1951' (PhD diss., University of Manitoba, 1991), 58.

66 Ibid., 59.

67 See Nunoda's discussion of the 1947 Co-operative Committee on Japanese Canadians' (CCJC) fight for compensation for losses sustained by Japanese Canadians. Nunoda contends that initially the CCJC advocated fighting for lost income as well as property losses. This demand was eventually dropped. Nunoda argues that by dropping the claim for lost income, 'the CCJC was already predisposed to ignoring a large segment of working class claims,' in 'A Community in Transition,' 287.

68 National Association of Japanese Canadians, *Economic Losses of Japanese Canadians after 1941* (Winnipeg: National Association of Japanese Canadians, 1985), 1.

69 Kazuko [pseud.], interview by author, 19 October 1995. All subsequent quotes by Kazuko are taken from this interview.

70 Margaret [pseud.], interview by author, 20 June 1995. All subsequent

quotes by Margaret are taken from this interview. I would suspect that few people were allowed to take their family pets with them and I believe this was permitted in Margaret's family's case because they were sent to a sugar beet farm.

71 Yoshiko [pseud.], interview by author, 22 December 1994. All subsequent quotes by Yoshiko are taken from this interview. See also chapter 3, where Yoshiko describes not being able to remember the pre-Internment period.

72 Esther [pseud.], interview by author, 17 August 1995. All subsequent quotes by Esther are taken from this interview.

73 See, for example, critic Christopher Hume's review of Andrew Danson's photographic exhibit *Face Kao: Portraits of Japanese Canadians Interned during World War II* in 'Facing the Enemy that Never Was,' *Toronto Star*, 11 April 1996, 66. Hume states, 'In 1941 … Pearl Harbor had just been attacked and if you were a Canadian of Japanese descent, you suddenly found yourself in a prison camp.' In addition, Hume states, '4,000 Japanese Canadians [were] forced into exile.' See also Lisa Rochon who states, 'Japanese-Canadians on the West Coast were placed in internment camps,' in 'Devoted to Driving "A Nail of Gold,"' *Globe and Mail*, 17 April 2010, R7.

74 Canada, BCSC, *Removal*, 20.

75 Watada, *Bukkyo Tozen*, 115.

76 Yon Shimizu, *The Exiles: An Archival History of the World War II Japanese Road Camps in British Columbia and Ontario* (Wallaceburg, ON: Shimizu Consulting and Publishing, 1993).

77 See, Oikawa, '"Driven to Scatter Far and Wide": The Forced Resettlement of Japanese Canadians to Southern Ontario, 1944–1949 (MA thesis, University of Toronto, 1986), chapter 2.

78 Canada, BCSC, *Removal*, 28.

79 Ibid., 68.

80 Ibid., 16.

81 Ibid., 7.

82 Ibid., 16.

83 Ibid.

84 For a discussion of the distantiated processes of expelling racialized people from the nation, see David Goldberg, *Racist Culture: Philosophy and the Politics of Meaning* (Oxford: Blackwell, 1993), 81, 98, 137.

85 Sunahara uses this term in *The Politics of Racism* to describe the specific events of 1946 and the pressure exerted by the government to force people to leave the camps at that time. She is not alone in the use of this term to describe the process of leaving the camps.

86 Foucault, *Discipline and Punish*, 200.

87 Ken Adachi, *The Enemy That Never Was*, photo caption, n.p.

88 Paul Gilroy, 'Diaspora and the Detours of Identity,' in *Identity and Difference*, ed. Kathryn Woodward (London: Sage in association with the Open University, 1997), 305.

89 Canada, BCSC, *Removal*, 2. The number cited is from Canada, Department of Labour, *Report of the Department of Labour on the Administration of Japanese Affairs in Canada, 1942–1946* (Ottawa: Department of Labour, 1944), 5. It is important to note that numbers may differ in different government reports. This reflects the constant movement of people between places at different moments of officials counting them.

90 According to Sunahara, 296 Issei men and 470 Nisei men were interned in prisoner-of-war camps. See *The Politics of Racism*, 70.

91 Sunahara, *The Politics of Racism*, 66. See note 3 in my preface for evidence that the government did refer to citizens as 'interned.'

92 Foucault, *Power/Knowledge: Selected Interviews and Other Writings, 1972–1977*, ed. Colin Gordon, trans. Colin Gordon, Leo Marshall, John Mepham, and Kate Soper (New York: Pantheon, 1980), 72.

93 Ken Adachi, *The Enemy That Never Was*, 232.

94 Canada, Department of Labour, *Administration*, 5.

95 See Yoshiko's comments about the men who left Slocan to work in logging camps and returned on the weekends, chapter 5 of this volume.

96 Numbers are calculated from the 1941 census. Canada, Dominion Bureau of Statistics, *Eighth Census of Canada 1941*, vol. 3 (Ottawa: Edmond Cloutier, 1946), 164.

97 The numbers show that 9,389 'males' and 14,091 'women and children' were accounted for. Note that the total was 23,480, sixteen of whom were citizens of the United States. LAC, Records of the British Columbia Security Commission, RG 36/27, vol.1, file 'Distribution of Japanese,' 'Memorandum Covering Japanese Movement Pacific Coast,' July 18, 1942.

98 Canada, Department of Labour, *Administration*, 18.

99 For an analysis of the relationship between space and constructions of disability, see Rob Kitchin, '"Out of Place," "Knowing One's Place": Space, Power and the Exclusion of Disabled People,' *Disability and Society* 13, no. 3 (1998), 343–56.

100 See Adele Perry's analysis of the historical construction of a white Canadian citizenry that functioned to consolidate the white identities of women from different class and ethnic backgrounds, *On the Edge of Em-*

pire: Gender, Race, and the Making of British Columbia, 1849–1871 (Toronto: University of Toronto Press, 2001).

101 See Sunahara, *The Politics of Racism*, especially 66–70. See also Takeo Ujo Nakano's account of being incarcerated at the Angler POW camp in Takeo Ujo Nakano, with Leatrice Nakano, *Within the Barbed Wire Fence* (Toronto: University of Toronto Press, 1980), and Robert K. Okazaki's *The Nisei Mass Evacuation Group and P.O.W. Camp '101'*, trans. Jean Okazaki and Curtis Okazaki (Scarborough, ON: Self-published, 1996).

102 See, for example, Okazaki, *The Nisei Mass Evacuation Group*; Sunahara's description of the NMEG in *The Politics of Racism*, 67–71; Roy Miki's description in *Broken Entries: Race, Subjectivity, Writing* (Toronto: The Mercury Press, 1998), 19–20, 190–1, and in *Redress*, 57–66.

103 Nunoda, 'A Community in Transition,' 98.

104 For a description of Tanaka-Goto, see Midge Ayukawa, 'Good Wives and Wise Mothers,' *B.C. Studies* 105–6 (1995), 116.

105 Canada, BCSC, *Removal*, 5.

106 Canada, Department of Labour, *Administration*, 5.

107 Sunahara, *The Politics of Racism*, 55.

108 Canada, BCSC, *Removal*, 8.

109 Ibid.; emphasis added.

110 Meyda Yeğenoğlu, *Colonial Fantasies: Towards a Feminist Reading of Orientalism* (Cambridge: Cambridge University Press, 1998), 96.

111 Ibid., 94.

112 Sunahara, *The Politics of Racism*, 57.

113 Muriel Kitagawa, *This Is My Own: Letters to Wes and Other Writings on Japanese Canadians, 1941–1948*, ed. Roy Miki (Vancouver: Talonbooks, 1985), 116.

114 Ibid.

115 Ibid.

116 La Violette, *The Canadian Japanese and World War II*, 65.

117 Ibid., 67.

118 Ibid., 65n23.

119 See Lisa Lowe, *Immigrant Acts: On Asian American Cultural Politics* (Durham, NC: Duke University Press, 1991), 11, for her analysis of Asian masculinity and its construction as 'different' from Anglo- and Euro-American white masculinity; and also David Eng's extension of Lowe's analysis in his argument that Asian masculinity is excluded from definitions of 'normative heterosexuality' in 'Out Here and Over There: Queerness and Diaspora in Asian American Studies,' *Social Text 52/53*, 15, nos. 3/4 (1997), 40.

120 NMEG to Austin Taylor, 15 April 1942, quoted in Okazaki, *The Nisei Mass Evacuation Group*, Appendices, A107.

5 Gendering the Subjects of the Internment

1 Aya [pseud.], interview by author, 26 August 1996.

2 Audrey Kobayashi, 'The Historical Context for Japanese-Canadian Uprooting,' in *Social Change and Space: Indigenous Nations and Ethnic Communities in Canada and Finland*, ed. Ludger Müller-Wille (Montreal: Northern Studies Program, McGill University, 1989), 76.

3 Ibid.

4 Canada, British Columbia Security Commission (BCSC), *Removal of Japanese from Protected Areas: Report of the British Columbia Security Commission* (Vancouver: BCSC, 1942), 8 (hereafter *Removal*).

5 Ann Gomer Sunahara, *The Politics of Racism: The Uprooting of Japanese Canadians During the Second World War* (Toronto: James Lorimer, 1981), 77.

6 Ibid.

7 Ibid.

8 S., [pseud.], interview with author, 16 August 1995. All subsequent quotes by S. are taken from this interview.

9 Evelyn [pseud.], interview with author, 26 August 1995. All subsequent quotes by Evelyn are taken from this interview.

10 Margaret [pseud.], interview with author, 20 June 1995. All subsequent quotes by Margaret are taken from this interview.

11 References to New Denver are sparse as the woman I interviewed who had been moved there was also incarcerated in Tashme, which was the focus of our discussion.

12 Canada, BCSC, *Removal*, 13.

13 Ibid.

14 Canada, Department of Labour, *Report of the Department of Labour on the Administration of Japanese Affairs in Canada, 1942–1944* (Ottawa: Department of Labour. 1944), 6 (hereafter *Administration*).

15 Sunahara, *The Politics of Racism*, 91.

16 Toyo Takata, *Nikkei Legacy: The Story of Japanese Canadians from Settlement to Today* (Toronto: NC Press, 1983), 132.

17 Sunahara, *The Politics of Racism*, 91.

18 Ken Adachi, *The Enemy That Never Was: A History of the Japanese Canadians* (Toronto: McClelland and Stewart, 1976), 259.

19 The conversion of this amount to Japanese currency is important to note. It would seem that this ensured a quick accounting of the books if people were deported to Japan.

20 Canada, Department of Labour, *Administration*, 20.

21 Ken Adachi, *The Enemy That Never Was*, 260.

22 Canada, BCSC, *Removal*, 13.
23 Canada, Department of Labour, *Administration*, p. 8.
24 Canada, BCSC, *Removal*, 14.
25 Ibid., 8; emphasis added.
26 Ken Adachi, *The Enemy That Never Was*, 260.
27 LAC, Records of the British Columbia Security Commission, RG 36/27, vol. 34, file 2202, Memorandum to the Cabinet Committee on Japanese Problems Re Orders-in-Council Relating to Persons of the Japanese Race, 11 December 1946.
28 Mona Oikawa, '"Driven to Scatter Far and Wide": The Forced Resettlement of Japanese Canadians to Southern Ontario, 1944–1949' (MA thesis, University of Toronto, 1986), 34.
29 Canada, Department of Labour, *Administration*, 32.
30 Forrest E. La Violette, 'Two Years of Japanese Evacuation in Canada,' *Far Eastern Survey* 13, no. 11 (1944), 97.
31 Canada, Department of Labour, *Administration*, 40.
32 La Violette, 'Two Years of Japanese Evacuation in Canada,' 98.
33 Canada, BCSC, *Removal*, 12.
34 Canada, Department of Labour, *Administration*, 21.
35 Ibid., 22.
36 Ibid., 23; uppercase letters in the original.
37 Ibid., 23.
38 Canada, BCSC, *Removal*, 20.
39 Aya [pseud.], interview with author, 26 August 1996. All subsequent quotes by Aya are taken from this interview.
40 Audrey Kobayashi, 'A Demographic Profile of Japanese Canadians and Social Implications for the Future' (Ottawa: Department of the Secretary of State, September 1989), mimeograph, 7.
41 Louise [pseud.], interview with author, 11 July 1995. All subsequent quotes by Louise are taken from this interview.
42 For a description of a Japanese American bathhouse in pre-Internment Seattle, see, Gail Dubrow with Donna Graves, *Sento at Sixth and Main: Preserving Landmarks of Japanese American Heritage* (Seattle: University of Washington Press, 2002), 92–103. According to these authors, 'One of the indirect effects of internment was that it marked the end of an era for Japanese bathhouses in the United States' (101).
43 According to Tsutae Sato, who was the principal of the Vancouver Japanese Language School before the Internment, there was a 'Japanese public bath' in the Powell Street area (Dubrow with Graves, *Sento at Sixth and Main*), 100.

44 See also, Joy Kogawa's description of the communal bath in Slocan in *Obasan* (Toronto: Penguin Books, 1983), 175–81.

45 Canada, BCSC, *Removal*, 25.

46 Ibid., 26.

47 Canada, Department of Labour, *Administration*, 11.

48 Catherine Lang, *O-Bon in Chimunesu: A Community Remembered* (Vancouver: Arsenal Pulp Press, 1996), 22. See Lang's description (22) of the way Yoshida was denied membership in the Chemainus white Boy Scout troop in the pre-Internment period. As a result, he took a correspondence course on scouting and formed his own troop in Chemainus in 1930, a troop that had 'the distinction of being comprised exclusively of Japanese Canadian boys.'

49 Adachi, *The Enemy That Never Was*, 264.

50 Ibid.

51 Ibid. For a description of education in the interior camps, see Frank Moritsugu with the Ghost Town Teachers Historical Society, *Teaching in Canadian Exile*; and Mary Ashworth, *The Forces which Shaped Them: A History of the Education of Minority Group Children in British Columbia* (Vancouver: New Star Books, 1979), 117–32.

52 See Sara Ahmed who states, 'The [subject] ... is also elevated into a position of power over others: the subject who gives to the other is the one who is 'behind' the possibility of overcoming pain ... generosity becomes a form of individual and possibly even national character, something "I" or "we" have, which is "shown" in how we are moved by others. The transformation of generosity into a character trait involves fetishism: it forgets the gifts made by others, as well as prior relations of debt accrued over time ... the West gives to others only insofar as it is forgotten what the West has already taken in its very *capacity* to give in the first place.' *The Cultural Politics of Emotion* (New York: Routledge, 2004), 22; emphasis in original. See also, Lauren Berlant, ed., *Compassion: The Culture and Politics of an Emotion* (New York: Routledge, 2004).

53 Sherene H. Razack, 'Gendered Racial Violence and Spatialized Justice: The Murder of Pamela George,' in Sherene H. Razack, ed., *Race, Space and the Law: Unmapping a White Settler Society* (Toronto: Between the Lines, 2002), 127.

54 According to Moritsugu et al., correspondence courses were $9 per course, approximately $56 for the entire school year: 'a heavy sum in those money-poor times when a ghost-town family was lucky to earn $54 a month with which to pay for food and clothing' (*Teaching in Canadian Exile*, 122).

55 Ann Sunahara, 'Deportation: The Final Solution to Canada's "Japanese Problem,"' in *Ethnicity, Power and Politics in Canada*, ed. Jorgen Dahlie and Tissa Fernando (Toronto: Methuen, 1981), 255.
56 Ibid., 256.
57 Ibid.
58 LAC, Records of the Department of Labour, RG 27, vol. 643, file 23-2-3-1, part 2, 'Notice to all Persons of Japanese Racial Origin now Resident in British Columbia,' II, 12 March 1945.
59 Ibid.
60 LAC, RG 27, vol. 643, file 23-2-3-1, part 2, 'Financial Assistance to Persons of Japanese Race Relocating East of Rockies,' February 1945.
61 Sunahara, *The Politics of Racism*, 12.
62 Canada, BCSC, *Removal*, 24.
63 Yoshiko [pseud.], interview with author, 22 December 1994. All subsequent quotes by Yoshiko are taken from this interview.
64 Sunahara, *The Politics of Racism*, 75.
65 Canada, BCSC, *Removal*, 7. More research is needed to further analyse the government's policy and its impact on those partnered with non-Japanese Canadians and on their children.
66 Note that in *The Enemy That Never Was* Ken Adachi states that '92 persons, representing Japanese married to whites and their children, were issued permits on April 11, 1942.' Adachi quotes his source as Canada, BCSC, *Removal* (415, table 7).
67 Canada, BCSC, *Removal*, 7.
68 LAC, RG 36/27, vol. 1, file 17, 'Distribution of Japanese,' 'Japanese Population in the Dominion of Canada as of February 29th, 1944,' 6.
69 LAC, Records of the Department of External Affairs, RG 25, vol. 2939, file 2997-40, part 1, 'Japanese Population in the Dominion of Canada as of June 30th, 1943,' 2.
70 LAC, RG 25, vol. 2939, file 2779-40, part 2, 'Japanese Population in the Dominion of Canada as of August 31st, 1945,' 2.
71 LAC, RG 25, vol. 2939, file 2779-40, part 2, 'Japanese Population in the Dominion of Canada as of October 31st, 1946,' 1.
72 LAC, RG 36/27, vol. 1, file 17, 'Distribution of Japanese,' 'Japanese Population in the Dominion of Canada as of October 31st, 1944,' 5.
73 LAC, RG 36/27, vol. 1, file 17, 'Distribution of Japanese,' 'Japanese Population in the Dominion of Canada as of November 30th, 1943,' 4.
74 Elena Tajima Creef, 'Re/Orientations: The Politics of Japanese American Representation' (PhD diss., University of California, Santa Cruz, 1994), 97.
75 Estelle Peck Ishigo, *Lone Heart Mountain* (Los Angeles: Communicart, 1989

[1972]). See also Stephen Okazaki's film depicting Ishigo, *Days of Waiting*, discussed in Creef, 'Re/Orientations,' 98–100.

76 Creef, 'Re/Orientations,' 113.

77 For a description of Hide Hyodo, see Sunahara, *The Politics of Racism*, 97. Also note that Hyodo was one of the members of a four-person delegation that appeared before the Special Committee on Elections and Franchise Acts of the House of Commons on 22 May 1936, lobbying for the vote for Japanese Canadians. Hyodo was the only woman delegate. See Ken Adachi, *The Enemy That Never Was*, 160–4.

78 May [pseud.], interview with author, 24 March 1992. All subsequent quotes by May are taken from this interview.

79 For a feminist critique of the white bourgeois notion of privacy, see Gillian Rose, *Feminism and Geography: The Limits of Geographical Knowledge* (Cambridge, UK: Polity Press, 1993), 126.

80 Oikawa, '"Driven to Scatter Far and Wide,"' 25–6, 30.

81 LAC, RG 36/27, vol. 1, file 17, 'Distribution of Japanese,' 'Memorandum Covering Japanese Movement Pacific Coast,' July 18, 1942, 2.

82 Ann [pseud.], interview with author, 1 November 1995. All subsequent quotes by Ann are taken from this interview.

83 Canada, BCSC, *Removal*, 24.

84 Mayumi [pseud.], interview with author, 1 November 1995. All subsequent quotes by Mayumi are taken from this interview.

85 Takata, *Nikkei Legacy*, 132.

86 Kay Anderson describes 'Shaughnessy' as 'Vancouver's British-origin neighbourhood,' emphasizing its elite spatial positioning in the city in *Vancouver's Chinatown: Racial Discourse in Canada, 1875–1980* (Montreal: McGill-Queen's University Press, 1991), 30. See also James Duncan, 'Elite Landscapes as Cultural (Re)productions: The Case of Shaughnessy Heights,' in *Inventing Places: Studies in Cultural Geography*, ed. Kay Anderson and Fay Gale (Melbourne: Longman Cheshire, 1992), 37–51.

87 Mary Louise Pratt, *Imperial Eyes: Travel Writing and Transculturation* (London: Routledge, 1992), 4.

88 Ibid.

89 Sunahara, *The Politics of Racism*, 91. In 1953, 104 Doukhobor children and some of their parents were incarcerated in the sanatorium in New Denver after their parents were arrested for protesting the government's decision to force their children to attend public schools. The children were not released until their parents agreed to send them to school. Some remained incarcerated in New Denver for as long as six years. Gregory J. Cran, *Negotiating Buck Naked: Doukhobors, Public Policy, and Conflict Resolution* (Vancouver: UBC Press, 2006), 94.

90 Tamiko Haraga, 'My Experiences during the Second World War,' *Nikkei Images: Japanese Canadian National Museum Newsletter* 7, no. 3 (2002), 19.

91 David Suzuki, *David Suzuki: The Autobiography* (Vancouver: Douglas & McIntyre, 2006), 20.

92 Ibid.

93 Ibid.

94 Ibid., 21. On the same page, Suzuki states, 'Years later, I apologized for the prank to an audience in the Doukhobor Centre in Castlegar and thanked the Doukhobor community for its support of Japanese Canadians during those trying years.'

95 I would like to thank Tod Duncan for discussing this point with me.

96 See Mia Stainsby's article, 'I Learned Russian and English and Lost Any Ability to Speak Japanese,' *The Vancouver Sun*, 3 January 1994, C4. Stainsby's parents were interned and she grew up in the Slocan area in the 'midst of a largely Doukhobor community.' She states that her parents speak 'broken English' and 'I've had very few conversations with them, ever, and I know little about who they are and where they came from.'

97 Canada, BCSC, *Removal*, 23.

98 LAC, RG 25, vol. 2937, file 2997-40, part 1, 'Japanese Population in the Dominion of Canada as of June 30, 1943,' 1.

99 Kazuko [pseud.], interview with author, 19 October 1995. All subsequent quotes by Kazuko are taken from this interview.

100 Sunahara states that hostels such as Neys were established around 1946 to facilitate the dispersal. See, Sunahara, *The Politics of Racism*, 140–1. Joseph Fry comments that Neys Hostel was used between the summer of 1946 and the summer of 1947, 'Omoide Garden, Neys, Ontario' (unpublished manuscript, n.d.). More work is needed on the use of these 'hostel' sites. The chronology of Kazuko's displacement is not of issue to me here. What is revelatory in her testimony are the multiple displacements suffered by her and what she re-members of them.

101 Kirsten Emiko McAllister, 'Remembering Political Violence: The Nikkei Internment Memorial Centre' (PhD diss., Carleton University, 2000), 82.

102 See chapter 4 for a discussion of the government's use of the term 'internment' to describe the POW camps.

103 Haru has requested that the name of the camp not be used. Haru [pseud.], interview with author, 23 November 1995. All subsequent quotes by Haru are taken from this interview.

104 Oikawa, '"Driven to Scatter Far and Wide,"' 45.

105 See Pamela Sugiman, 'Passing Time, Moving Memories: Interpreting Wartime Narratives of Japanese Canadian Women,' *Histoire Sociale/Social*

History 37, no. 73 (2004), 51–79, for a description and analysis of some of the censored letters.

106 Kitagawa corresponded with her brother, Wesley Fujiwara, between December 1941 and May 1942. See *This Is My Own: Letters to Wes and Other Writings on Japanese Canadians, 1941–1948*, ed. Roy Miki (Vancouver: Talonbooks, 1985), 67–151. According to Ken Adachi, censorship of the mail began in August 1942, *The Enemy That Never Was*, 267.

107 See chapter 1n131 for the role of Spain as the 'Protecting Power' for Japanese Nationals in Canada and the United States during the war with Japan. Ironically, while Japanese Nationals could appeal to Spain for assistance during the Internment, the majority (75 per cent) of those incarcerated were Canadian citizens and considered to be Canadian by international law and could therefore only appeal to Canada for assistance.

108 LAC, RG 25, G2, vol. 3005, file 3464-AC-40, 'Petition from Ten Japanese Women,' Correspondent to Pedro Schwartz, 26 December 1942. I have not disclosed the names of the correspondents whose letters are in the possession of the LAC.

109 LAC, RG 25, G2, vol. 3005, file 3464-AC-40, 'Petition from Ten Japanese Women,' Correspondent to Pedro Schwartz, 4 May 1943.

110 LAC, RG 25, G2, vol. 3005, file 3464-AC-40, 'Petition from Ten Japanese Women,' Correspondent to Daniel de Yturralde, 18 October 1944.

111 Ibid.

112 LAC, RG 25, G2, vol. 3005, file 3464-AC-40, 'Petition from Ten Japanese Women,' Correspondent to Louis St Laurent, 18 December 1944.

113 Ibid.

114 LAC, RG 25, G2, vol. 3005, file 3464-AC-40, 'Petition from Ten Japanese Women,' Correspondent to Fernando De Kobbe, 12 January 1942.

115 LAC, RG 25, G2, vol. 3005, file 3464-AC-40, 'Petition from Ten Japanese Women,' Correspondent to Pedro E. Schwartz, 28 January 1943.

116 Ibid.

117 LAC, RG 25, G2, vol. 3005, file 3464-AC-40, 'Petition from Ten Japanese Women,' Correspondent to Ernest L. Maag, 20 July 1945.

118 Ibid.

119 Ibid.

120 LAC, RG 25, G2, vol. 3005, file 3464-AC-40, 'Petition from Ten Japanese Women,' Correspondent to Minister of External Affairs, n.d.

121 Ibid.

122 LAC, RG 25, G2, vol. 3005, file 3464-AC-40, 'Petition from Ten Japanese Women,' Isabel G. Stott to Mr Swain, 21 May 1943.

123 LAC, RG 25, G2, vol. 3005, file 2464-AC-40, 'Petition from Ten Japanese Women,' George Collins to RCMP Constable R. Davidson, 25 May 1943.

6 Economies of the Carceral

1 Lisa Lowe, *Immigrant Acts: On Asian American Cultural Politics* (Durham, NC: Duke University Press, 1996), 57.
2 Ann Gomer Sunahara, *The Politics of Racism: The Uprooting of Japanese Canadians during the Second World War* (Toronto: James Lorimer, 1981), 65, 78.
3 Canada, British Columbia Security Commission, *Removal of Japanese from Protected Areas: Report of the British Columbia Security Commission* (Vancouver: BCSC, 1942), 11; emphasis added (hereafter *Removal*).
4 Ibid.
5 Ibid.
6 Canada, Department of Labour, *Report of the Department of Labour on the Administration of Japanese Affairs in Canada, 1942–1944* (Ottawa: Department of Labour, 1944), 6 (hereafter *Administration*).
7 LAC, Records of the British Columbia Security Commission, RG 36/27, vol. 1, file 17, 'Distribution of Japanese,' 'Japanese Movement – Pacific Coast' (Period ending October 31, 1942), 4.
8 Evelyn [pseud.], interview with author, 26 August 1995. All subsequent quotes by Evelyn are taken from this interview.
9 Sunahara, *The Politics of Racism*, 65.
10 Canada, BCSC, *Removal*, 11.
11 See Canada, BCSC, *Removal*, 'Numerous Japanese ... undertook to settle themselves, more or less on a community basis,' 11.
12 For example, A. MacNamara, associate deputy minister of labour, wrote, 'Single men in work camps will be required to assign at least $20.00 per month toward maintenance of their families in the interior towns.' LAC, Records of the Royal Canadian Mounted Police, RG 18, F-3, vol. 3564, file C-11-19-2-9, 'Proposed Policy-Japanese,' 16 November 1942, 1.
13 Canada, BCSC, *Removal*, 10.
14 Archives of Ontario (hereafter AO), Office of the Deputy Minister of Agriculture, RG 16, series 16-09, box 172, file 'Farm Service Force: Japanese, 1942–1943,' Memorandum in Connection with Family Settlement and General Japanese Evacuation Program, 18 June 1942.
15 Canada, Department of Labour, *Administration*, 6.
16 Canada, BCSC, *Removal*, 19.
17 Ibid., 10.

18 Ibid.

19 Ibid.

20 See Roy Miki's description of the relationships between people who moved with his family to Ste Agathe, Manitoba. This included his mother's closest friend. In *Redress: Inside the Japanese Canadian Call for Justice* (Vancouver: Raincoast Books, 2004), 6.

21 Canada, Department of Labour, *Administration*, 37.

22 Only men were sent to Ontario because the farmers there were 'not in a position to house families.' The farmers later 'gave these men credit for helping to save the Ontario sugar beet crop.' LAC, RG 36/27, vol. 1, file 17, 'Distribution of Japanese,' 'Japanese Movement – Pacific Coast' (Period ending October 31, 1942), 3. For a description of farm work in Ontario, see Stephanie Bangarth, 'The Long, Wet Summer of 1942: The Ontario Farm Service Force, Small-Town Ontario and the Nisei,' *Canadian Ethnic Studies* 37, no. 1 (2005), 40–62.

23 AO, Hepburn Papers, RG 3, box 325, file 1, A.V. Lyman to G. Pipher, 27 July 1942.

24 AO, Hepburn Papers, RG 3, box 218, file 'Japanese Help in Ontario,' Hepburn to G.E. Trueman, 25 September 1942.

25 AO, Library Collection, Govt Doc Leg D, Official Report of Debates (Hansard): Legislative Assembly of Ontario, microfilm, B32, Reel 13, 11 April 1942. See also, AO, Hepburn Papers, RG 3, box 325, file 2, Heenan to R.J. Warnock, 4 May 1942; and AO, Office of the Deputy Minister of Labour, RG 7, J-W, 11-1, vol. 29, Memorandum Respecting Proposed Agreement Between the Dominion Government and the Provincial Government of Ontario, 1 April 1942.

26 LAC, RG 36/27, vol. 1, file 17, 'Distribution of Japanese,' 'Japanese Movement – Pacific Coast' (Period ending October 31, 1942), 4.

27 Canada, BCSC, *Removal*, 11.

28 Ibid.; emphasis added.

29 Canada, Department of Labour, *Administration*, 8. The same report (8) states that the BCSC was dissolved and the Department of Labour given sole responsibility by Order-in-Council P.C. 946, 5 February 1943.

30 Manitoba Japanese Canadian Citizens' Association, *The History of Japanese Canadians in Manitoba* (Winnipeg: Manitoba Japanese Canadian Citizens' Association, 1996), 18.

31 Ibid., 19.

32 Ibid., 16.

33 Ibid.

34 Ibid., 20.

35 Ibid., 19.

36 Ibid., 16.

37 Shelly Ikebuchi Ketchell, 'Carceral Ambivalence: Japanese Canadian "Internment" and the Sugar Beet Programme During WWII,' *Surveillance and Society* 7, no. 1 (2009), 21.

38 Ibid.

39 Lowe, *Immigrant Acts*, 102.

40 Esther [pseud.], interview with author, 17 August 1995. All subsequent quotes by Esther are taken from this interview.

41 LAC, RG 36/27, vol.1, file 17, 'Distribution of Japanese,' 'Japanese Movement – Pacific Coast' (Period ending October 31, 1942), 2.

42 For descriptions of pre-Internment photographs, see Grace Eiko Thomson, 'Archival Photographs from Cumberland BC: With An Afterword,' *West Coast Line: A Journal of Contemporary Writing & Criticism* 38, no. 1 (2004), 57–89; and Grace Eiko Thomson, *Shashin: Japanese Canadian photography to 1942* (Burnaby, BC: Japanese Canadian National Museum, 2005).

43 Margaret [pseud.], interview with author, 20 June 1995. All subsequent quotes by Margaret are taken from this interview.

44 Saidiya Hartman, *Scenes of Subjection: Terror, Slavery, and Self-Making in Nineteenth-Century America* (New York: Oxford University Press, 1997), 10.

45 Ibid., 61.

46 See Ward Churchill, *Struggle for the Land: Native North American Resistance to Genocide, Ecocide and Colonization* (Winnipeg: Arbeiter Ring Press, 1999), and Dara Culhane, *The Pleasure of the Crown: Anthropology, Law and First Nations* (Burnaby, BC: Talonbooks, 1998) for a discussion of Terra Nullius or empty land, a concept that colonizers used to justify their theft of Indigenous territories.

47 LAC, RG 36/27, vol. 1, file 17, 'Distribution of Japanese,' 'Japanese Movement – Pacific Coast' (Period ending October 31, 1942), 2. Note that in another report, the BCSC stated, 'housing accommodation was extremely limited and quite unsatisfactory for year-around habitation of families with young children.' However, it concluded that it was up to Japanese Canadians to make 'every attempt to adjust themselves to their new environment' (BCSC, *Removal*, 10).

48 Canada, Department of Transport, Meteorological Division, *Monthly Record Observations in Canada and Newfoundland, January 1943* (Toronto: Department of Transport, Meteorological Division, 1943), 13.

49 Even the government acknowledged that the 'topping' of the beets was a 'very heavy job.' LAC, RG 36/27, vol. 1, file 17, 'Distribution of Japanese,' 'Japanese Movement – Pacific Coast' (Period ending October 31, 1942), 2.

50 Audrey Kobayashi, 'The Historical Context for Japanese-Canadian Uprooting,' in *Social Change and Space: Indigenous Nations and Ethnic Communities in Canada and Finland*, ed. Ludger Müller-Wille (Montreal: Northern
   Studies Program, McGill University, 1989), 70.
51 Sunahara, *The Politics of Racism*, 141.
52 Joseph Fry, 'Omoide Garden, Neys, Ontario' (unpublished manuscript,
   n.d.).
53 Yoshiko [pseud.], interview with author, 22 December 1994. All subsequent quotes by Yoshiko are taken from this interview.
54 Kazuko [pseud.], interview with author, 19 October 1995. All subsequent
   quotes by Kazuko are taken from this interview.
55 Canada, House of Common's, *Debates*, 4 August 1944, 5917.
56 Mona Oikawa, '"Driven to Scatter Far and Wide": The Forced Resettlement of Japanese Canadians to Southern Ontario, 1944–1949' (M.A. thesis,
   University of Toronto, 1986).
57 Canada, Department of Labour, *Report of the Department of Labour on the
   Re-Establishment of the Japanese in Canada, 1944–1946* (Ottawa: Department
   of Labour, 1947), 16.
58 Evelyn Nakano Glenn's groundbreaking work analyses the relationship
   of Japanese American women to paid domestic work in her *Issei, Nisei,
   War Bride: Three Generations of Japanese American Women in Domestic Service*
   (Philadelphia: Temple University Press, 1986). See also Valerie Matsumoto's
   findings regarding the pre-Internment community of Cortez, California, in
   which she writes that 'the majority of women did domestic work,' *Farming the Home Place: A Japanese American Community in California, 1919–1982*
   (Ithaca, NY: Cornell University Press, 1993), 83. For the Canadian context,
   see Oikawa, '"Driven to Scatter Far and Wide"' and the interview with Mrs
   Ellen Enomoto in the Special Collections and University Archives Division,
   University of British Columbia Library, UBC Aural History Transcripts,
   76–1, Mrs Ellen Enomoto, May 16, 1972, 7, for a description of her mother
   who did 'housework ... in English households' in Vancouver.
59 Sherene H. Razack, 'Race, Space and Prostitution: The Making of the Bourgeois Subject,' *Canadian Journal of Women and the Law* 10, no. 2 (1998), 363.
60 See, for example, Agnes Calliste, 'Race, Gender and Canadian Immigration Policy: Blacks from the Caribbean, 1900–1932', in *Gender and History in
   Canada*, ed. Joy Parr and Mark Rosenfeld (Toronto: Copp Clark Ltd, 1996),
   70–97; and Tania Das Gupta, *Racism and Paid Work* (Toronto: Garamond,
   1996).
61 LAC, Records of the Department of Labour, RG 27, vol. 644, file 23-2-3-7-1,
   part 2, D. MacTavish to A. H. Brown, 24 January 1945.

62 Canada, BCSC, *Removal*, 11.
63 LAC, RG 36/27, vol. 1, file 17, 'Distribution of Japanese,' 'Japanese Move-ment – Pacific Coast (Period ending October 31, 1942),' 4.
64 Sunahara, *The Politics of Racism*, 82.
65 See Oikawa, '"Driven to Scatter Far and Wide,"' chap. 2.
66 This figure is derived from the 1941 census, which lists 3,520 females in BC between the ages of one to fourteen years. There were 2,208 males between the ages of one to nine years. The census also lists 1,356 males between the ages of ten and fourteen, but it must be remembered that some males over the age of thirteen were incarcerated separately from their female relatives. Canada, Dominion Bureau of Statistics, *Eighth Census of Canada, 1941*, vol. 3 (Ottawa: Edmond Cloutier, 1946), 164.
67 Canada, BCSC, *Removal*, 11. The comparison with 'the Jews' is also inter-esting here.
68 Ken Adachi, *The Enemy That Never Was: A History of the Japanese Canadians* (Toronto: McClelland and Stewart, 1976), 281.
69 For example, Kay Anderson states, 'In the homes of the [BC] provincial elite, young Chinese men, in the absence of sufficient white women, helped with the menial activities of domestic life,' in *Vancouver's China-town: Racial Discourse in Canada, 1875–1980* (Montreal: McGill-Queen's University Press, 1991), 36. Research is needed in this area to determine whether domestic service jobs held by men differed in content or wages from those held by women.
70 Oikawa, '"Driven to Scatter Far and Wide,"' 54–8.
71 Ibid., 48.
72 Eric John Hobsbawm, *Industry and Empire: From 1750 to the Present Day* (Harmondsworth, UK: Penguin Books, 1990), 157.
73 Ibid., 161.
74 LAC, RG 27, vol. 645, file 23-2-3-7-1, part 3, I. Florence Meakins to the War-time Prices and Trade Board, 1 June 1945.
75 May [pseud.], interview with author, 24 March 1992. All subsequent quotes by May are taken from this interview.
76 Sunahara states, 'To the Jews who helped Japanese Canadians, what was happening in Canada and to the Jews in Europe were two sides of the same coin.' *The Politics of Racism*, 86; note omitted. See also Oikawa, '"Driven to Scatter Far and Wide,"' 46–7.
77 See Caren Kaplan, '"Beyond the Pale": Rearticulating U.S. Jewish White-ness,' in *Talking Visions: Multicultural Feminism in Transnational Age*, ed. Ella Shohat (New York: New Museum of Art, and Cambridge, MA: MIT Press, 1998), 369–90.

78 S. [pseud.], interview with author, 16 August 1995. All subsequent quotes by S. are taken from this interview.

79 Haru [pseud.], interview with author, 23 November 1995. All subsequent quotes by Haru are taken from this interview.

80 Abigail B. Bakan and Daiva Stasiulis, Introduction to *Not One of the Family: Foreign Domestic Workers in Canada*, ed. Abigail B. Bakan and Daiva Stasiulis (Toronto: University of Toronto Press, 1997), 11.

81 Canada, Statutes of Canada, 1945, Bill C-15, *National Emergency Transitional Powers Act*, 1st sess., 20th Parliament, 1945 (assented to 18 December 1945).

82 Audrey Kobayashi, 'Racism and Law in Canada: A Geographical Perspective,' *Urban Geography* 11, no. 5 (1990), 459.

83 Sunahara, *The Politics of Racism*, 127; note omitted.

84 Ibid., 143. Sunahara also describes the fight against deportation in chapter 7.

85 Ibid.

86 Quoted in Ken Adachi, *The Enemy That Never Was*, 317.

87 Michel Foucault, *Discipline and Punish: The Birth of the Prison*, trans. Alan Sheridan (New York: Vintage Books, 1995), 143.

88 LAC, Records of the Department of Labour, RG 27, vol. 644, file 23-2-3-7-1, part 2, G.Trueman to A. MacNamara, 12 March 1945. See also Oikawa, '"Driven to Scatter Far and Wide,"' 91.

89 LAC, RG 27, vol. 644, file 23-2-3-7-1, part 2, Trueman to MacNamara, 12 March 1945. See also Oikawa, '"Driven to Scatter Far and Wide,"' 92.

90 Roy Miki, *Redress*, 166.

91 Aya [pseud.], interview with author, 26 August 1996. All subsequent quotes by Aya are taken from this interview.

92 Louise [pseud.], interview with author, 11 July 1995. All subsequent quotes by Louise are taken from this interview.

93 Ann [pseud.], interview with author, 1 November 1995.

94 See Ruth Roach Pierson's description of the decrease in women's participation in paid employment in 1945 and 1946 in *'They're Still Women After All': The Second World War and Canadian Womanhood* (Toronto: McClelland and Stewart, 1986), 215.

95 Ibid., 83.

96 Sherene H. Razack, *Casting Out: The Eviction of Muslims from Western Law and Politics* (Toronto: University of Toronto Press, 2008), 7; note omitted.

97 Ibid., 9. See also, Audrey Kobayashi, 'Racism and Law in Canada.'

98 Hartman, *Scenes of Subjection*, 197.

99 Foucault, *Discipline and Punish*, 303.

100 Thomas Shoyama quoted in Kirsten Emiko McAllister, 'Remembering
Political Violence: The Nikkei Internment Memorial Centre' (PhD diss.,
Carleton University, 2000), 85. For a description of Shoyama, see chapter 1, note 147. Shoyama edited the newspaper *The New Canadian* (the
only Japanese Canadian newspaper allowed to publish in the 1940s and
subjected to government censorship) in the camp of Kaslo during the
Internment.

101 Hartman, *Scenes of Subjection*, 131; note omitted.

7 The Known and Unknown

1 Kitagawa, quoted in Roy Miki, 'Introduction: The Life and Times of
Muriel Kitagawa,' in *This Is My Own: Letters to Wes and Other Writings
on Japanese Canadians, 1941–1943*, ed. Roy Miki (Vancouver: Talonbooks,
1985), 1.

2 In the same report, people from the ages of twenty to thirty-four were
designated 'youths.' All of the women I have interviewed would have
been included in the government categories of 'children' or 'youths' in
the 1941 Census. Canada, Department of Labour, *Report of the Department
of Labour on the Administration of Japanese Affairs in Canada, 1942–1944* (Ottawa: Department of Labour, 1944), 2.

3 LAC, Records of the Department of External Affairs, RG 25, G2, vol. 2779,
file 773-G-40, letter from Reverend G. Dorey to Dr. H.L. Keenleyside, 20
March 1942.

4 LAC, RG 25, G2, vol. 2799, file 773-G-40, Keenleyside to Mead, 'Movement to a school home in Assiniboia of Japanese Girls in Oriental home in
Victoria – Proposals of United Church of Canada Board of Home Missions,' 21 March 1942.

5 LAC, RG 25, G2, vol. 2799, file 773-G-40. Mead to Keenleyside, 'Movement to a school home in Assiniboia of Japanese Girls in Oriental home
in Victoria – Proposals of United Church of Canada Board of Home Missions,' 27 March 1942.

6 Ibid.; emphasis added.

7 Although the file states that twenty girls were to be 'selected,' a later
BCSC report indicated that nineteen 'orphan children' were removed
(LAC, RG 25, vol. 2939, file 2997-40, part 1, 'Japanese Population, Location by Province as at March 27, 1943,' 3). This appears to match the total
of residents noted by Dorey. Note that an earlier memorandum reported
that '18 homeless children have been evacuated to a Mission School in
Assiniboia, Saskatchewan.' See LAC, Records of the Department of

Labour, RG/27, vol. 2, file 17, 'Distribution of Japanese,' 'Memorandum Covering Japanese Movement Pacific Coast, 9 June 1942,' 3.

8 In 1941, there were 105 people of Japanese ancestry in the entire province of Saskatchewan; Ken Adachi, *The Enemy That Never Was: A History of the Japanese Canadians* (Toronto: McClelland and Stewart, 1976), appendix 1, 'Immigration and Population,' 413.

9 For analyses of the effects of forced removal of Indigenous children from their families, see chapter 1, note 67.

10 See, for example, Agnes Calliste, 'Race, Gender and Canadian Immigration Policy: Blacks from the Caribbean, 1900–1932,' in *Gender and History in Canada*, ed. Joy Parr and Mark Rosenfeld (Toronto: Copp Clark, 1996), 70–97; Peter Li, *Destination Canada: Immigration Debates and Issues* (Toronto: Oxford University Press, 2002).

11 Enakshi Dua, 'Beyond Diversity: Exploring the Ways in which the Discourse of Race has Shaped the Institution of the Nuclear Family,' in *Inequality in Canada: A Reader on the Intersections of Gender, Race, and Class*, ed. Valerie Zawilski and Cynthia Levine-Rasky (Toronto: Oxford University Press, 2005), 110. See also Sunera Thobani, *Exalted Subjects: Studies in the Making of Race and Nation in Canada* (Toronto: University of Toronto Press, 2007), 129–31.

12 Canada, British Columbia Security Commission, *Removal of Japanese from Protected Areas: Report of the British Columbia Security Commission* (Vancouver: BCSC, 1942), 5; emphasis added (hereafter *Removal*).

13 Ibid., 13; emphasis added.

14 For an analysis of the essentializing discourse of Asian families in film, see Kirsten McAllister, 'Asians in Hollywood,' *Cineaction* 30 (1992), 11.

15 Department of Labour, *Administration*, 42.

16 Whether white bourgeois women attained this 'norm' is another question. It is the mobilization of discourses of 'independence' that is of interest to me here and how it services the notion of racialized others as being 'dependent' and 'Other.'

17 Meyda Yeğenoğlu, *Colonial Fantasies: Towards a Feminist Reading of Orientalism* (Cambridge: Cambridge University Press, 1998), 104.

18 LAC, RG 25, vol. 2939, file 2779-40, part 2, 'Japanese Population in the Dominion of Canada as of October 31, 1946,' 3.

19 Forrest E. La Violette, *The Canadian Japanese and World War II: A Sociological and Psychological Account* (Toronto: University of Toronto Press, 1948), 151.

20 May [pseud.], interview with author, 24 March 1992. All subsequent quotes by May are taken from this interview.

21 Donna Nagata, *Legacy of Injustice: Exploring the Cross-Generational Impact of the Japanese American Internment* (New York: Plenum Press, 1993), 141.
22 See chapter 1, note 105.
23 Nagata, *Legacy of Injustice*, 141.
24 LAC, Records of the British Columbia Security Commission, RG 36/27, vol. 1, file 17, 'Distribution of Japanese,' 'Japanese Movement – Pacific Coast (Period ending October 31, 1942),' 1.
25 Irene Smith, 'Hastings Park Hospital – Memories of Nurse Irene (nee Anderson) Smith,' *The Bulletin*, 38, no. 4 (April 1996), 24.
26 Ibid.
27 Ibid.; my emphasis. Smith also states that 'Japanese RNs' were 'paid on the scale set for internees rather than RN salary.' The 'Japanese doctors,' she adds, 'visited and ordered medication for their patients but prescriptions and treatments had to be approved by salaried medical staff.' Smith describes her work as a 'challenging and interesting experience.'
28 Ken Adachi, *The Enemy That Never Was*, 263.
29 T.B. Pickersgill, the second commissioner of Japanese Placement, reported, 'The practice had always been followed, in the relocation of people of Japanese origin to the Eastern provinces from BC, of having individuals given the blood test for venereal disease.' See LAC, Records of the Department of Labour, RG 27, vol. 643, file 23-2-3-1, part 2, T.B. Pickersgill to MacNamara, 3 June 1946.
30 LAC, RG 25, vol. 2939, file 2997-40, part 1, 'Japanese Population, Location by Province as at March 27, 1943,' 2.
31 LAC, RG 25, vol. 2939, file 2997-40, part 1, 'Japanese Population in the Dominion of Canada as of June 30th, 1943,' 2. Note that the gendered breakdown between men and women was not included in this and subsequent reports.
32 LAC, RG 25, vol. 2939, file 2779-40, part 2, 'Japanese Population in the Dominion of Canada as of August 31st, 1945,' 2.
33 Michel Foucault, 'Confinement, Psychiatry, Prison: A Dialogue with Michel Foucault, David Cooper, Jean-Pierre Faye, Marie-Odile Faye, and Marine Zecca,' in *Politics, Philosophy, Culture: Interviews and Other Writings, 1977–1984*, ed. Lawrence C. Kritzman, trans. Alan Sheridan and Others. (New York: Routledge, 1990), 180.
34 Ibid.
35 LAC, RG 36/27, vol. 32, file 1813, Memorandum of Suggested Revisions and Deletions in Draft Report of Activities of the Japanese Division, T.B. Pickersgill to A.H. Brown, 10 April 1946.
36 See Gabrielle Nishiguchi's '"Reducing the Numbers": The "Transporta-

tion" of the Canadian Japanese [1941–1947]' (MA thesis, Carleton University, 1993), 3, where she states that five sailings deporting people to Japan occurred between 31 May and 24 December 1946. Nishiguchi adds, 'Among the passengers were World War I veterans, stretcher cases, psychiatric patients, seniors, and families – including pregnant women, dependent children and babies. Over sixty-five per cent of them were Canadian citizens by naturalization or birth.'

37 Michiko Sakata quoted in Japanese Canadian Centennial Project, *A Dream of Riches* (Vancouver: Japanese Canadian Centennial Project, 1978), 3.

38 According to the 1941 Census, there were 6,150 Japanese Canadian women over the age of fourteen. Approximately 34 per cent were single (2,078 women). The remaining 60 per cent were married (3,712 women) and 6 per cent were widowed, divorced, separated, or did not state their status (360 women). Approximately 40 per cent of women over the age of fourteen were not married in 1941. Canada, Dominion Bureau of Statistics, *Eighth Census of Canada, 1941*, vol. 4 (Ottawa: Edmond Cloutier, 1946), 21. Note that my calculations differ from those of the Department of Labour, which reported that 58 per cent were single, 38 per cent were married, and 4 per cent were widowed, divorced, or separated (Department of Labour, *Administration*, 3).

39 More work is needed to examine how women parented within the sites of incarceration. As one of the women I interviewed suggested, women shared these responsibilities and young children were cared for by many adults and older children.

40 Roger Obata, 'recounted the devastating effects of uprooting and dispossession on his single mother,' to the Special Joint Committee of the Senate and the House of Commons on the Constitution in 1980. In Roy Miki, *Redress: Inside the Japanese Canadian Call for Justice* (Vancouver: Raincoast Books, 2004), 221. Obata later served as a member of the NAJC Negotiation Committee during the redress movement.

41 Margaret [pseud.], interview with author, 20 June 1995. All subsequent quotes by Margaret are taken from this interview.

42 Ann [pseud.], interview with author, 1 November 1995. All subsequent quotes by Ann are taken from this interview.

43 Mayumi [pseud.], interview with author, 1 November 1995. All subsequent quotes by Mayumi are taken from this interview.

44 Esther [pseud.], interview with author, 17 August 1995. All subsequent quotes by Esther are taken from this interview.

45 Dua, 'Beyond Diversity,' 119.

46 Michel Foucault, *Discipline and Punish: The Birth of the Prison*, trans. Alan Sheridan (New York: Vintage Books, 1995), 198–9.
47 Thomas Shoyama quoted in Kirsten Emiko McAllister, 'Remembering Political Violence: The Nikkei Internment Memorial Centre' (PhD diss., Carleton University, 2000), 85.
48 LAC, RG 27, vol. 645, file 23-2-3-7-1, part 3, *The Sophy-Ed*, 20 June 1945, 1.
49 Aya [pseud.], interview with author, 16 August 1995. All subsequent quotes by Aya are taken from this interview.
50 S. [pseud.], interview with author, 16 August 1995. All subsequent quotes by S. are taken from this interview.
51 Malve Von Hassel, 'Issei Women: Silences and Fields of Power,' *Feminist Studies* 19, no. 3 (1993), 252.
52 Kazuko [pseud.], interview with author, 19 October 1995. All subsequent quotes by Kazuko are taken from this interview.
53 Kim Lacy Rogers, 'Trauma Redeemed: The Narrative Construction of Social Violence,' in *Interactive Oral History Interviewing*, ed. Eva M. McMahan and Kim Lacy Rogers (Hillsdale, NJ: Lawrence Erlbaum Associates, 1994), 33.
54 Ibid.
55 Nagata, *Legacy of Injustice*, 155.
56 Yeğenoğlu, *Colonial Fantasies*, 113.
57 Lawrence Langer, *Holocaust Testimonies: The Ruins of Memory* (New Haven, CT: Yale University, 1991), 13.
58 An analysis of the deportation and its effects, including the reorganization of families in Japan and in Canada, requires further attention. For now, see Ann Sunahara's description of the repatriation survey and the policies of deportation in *The Politics of Racism: The Uprooting of Japanese Canadians During the Second World War* (Toronto: James Lorimer, 1981) and 'Deportation: The Final Solution to Canada's "Japanese Problem,"' in *Ethnicity, Power and Politics in Canada*, ed. Jorgen Dahlie and Tissa Fernando (Toronto: Methuen, 1981); see Gabrielle Nishiguchi's analysis in '"Reducing the Numbers": The "Transportation" of the Canadian Japanese (1941–1947)' (MA thesis, Carleton University, 1993) and Tatsuo Kage, *Nikkei Kanadajin no Tsuihou* (Tokyo: Akashi Shoten, 1998).
59 LAC, RG 27, vol. 640, file 23-2-6, part 3, Commissioner of the RCMP to MacNamara, 13 September 1946.
60 Hartman, *Scenes of Subjection*, 126.
61 LAC, RG 27, vol. 645, file 23-2-3-7-1, part 4, D.R.S. Murray to RCMP Commissioner, 25 August 1945.
62 Ibid.

63 Ibid. In the Ontario Reformatory system, judges were allowed to sentence convicted persons to 'imprisonment for a term of not less than three months and for an indeterminate period thereafter of not more than two years less one day,' Canada, Section 46, *The Criminal Code and Other Selected Statutes of Canada, with the Amendments Passed Up to the End of the Session of Parliament, Held in 1937, Incorporated Therein* (Ottawa: J.O. Patenaude, 1937).

64 LAC, RG 27, vol. 645, file 23-2-3-7-1, part 4, Trueman to Pammett, 13 September 1945.

65 Ernest Yoshio Oikawa, conversation with author, 1992. See also Muriel Kitagawa's description, 'And the horrors that some young girls have already faced ... outraged by men in uniform ... in the hospital ... hysterical. Oh we are fair prey for the wolves in democratic clothing. Can you wonder the men are afraid to leave us behind and won't go unless their women go with them?' Muriel Kitagawa, in *This Is My Own*, ed. Roy Miki, 91. See also Toyo Takata's statement regarding Hastings Park: 'A guard or two attempted to take physical liberties with the women,' in *Nikkei Legacy: The Story of Japanese Canadians from Settlement to Today* (Toronto: NC Press, 1983), 120.

8 'It Is Part of My Inheritance'

1 Muriel Kitagawa, *This Is My Own: Letters to Wes and Other Writings on Japanese Canadians, 1941–1948*, ed. Roy Miki (Vancouver: Talonbooks, 1985), 229.

2 Mayumi [pseud.], interview by author, 1 November 1995. All subsequent quotes by Mayumi are taken from this interview.

3 Rather than use the term 'home,' I use the term family space or 'familial' space, because of the history of expulsion and dispersal and the significance of 'home' for people expelled from their 'homes' in BC. For the concept of 'familial' space, see Henri Lefebvre, *The Production of Space*, trans. Donald Nicholson-Smith (Oxford: Blackwell, 1991), 232. For a feminist geographic critique of the term 'home,' see Doreen Massey, *Space, Place, and Gender* (Minneapolis: MN: University of Minnesota Press, 1994), chap. 7.

4 Donna Nagata, *Legacy of Injustice: Exploring the Cross-Generational Impact of the Japanese American Internment* (New York: Plenum Press, 1993). Nagata used the term Sansei to describe the third generation cohort she interviewed.

5 Yael Danieli, 'Treating Survivors and Children of Survivors of the Nazi

Holocaust,' in *Post-Traumatic Therapy and Victims of Violence*, ed. Frank M. Ochberg (New York: Brunner/Mazel, 1988), 280.

6 See, for example, Dan Bar-On who states, 'It was precisely this gap – between what was transmitted verbally and what was transmitted nonverbally – that most strongly influenced the next generation,' in *Fear and Hope: Three Generations of the Holocaust* (Cambridge, MA: Harvard University Press, 1995), 355.

7 Martin S. Bergmann and Milton E. Jucovy, prelude to *Generations of the Holocaust* (New York: Columbia University Press, 1990), 19–20.

8 Danieli, 'Treating Survivors and Children of Survivors of the Nazi Holocaust,' 279.

9 Ibid., 289; emphasis in original.

10 Nagata, *Legacy of Injustice*, xiv.

11 Ibid., 51.

12 Ibid., 17.

13 Ibid., ix.

14 Ibid., 101.

15 Ibid., 113.

16 Ibid., 102.

17 Ibid., 77.

18 Ibid., 76.

19 Essed states that 'everyday racism' is 'various types and expressions of racism experienced by ethnic groups in everyday contact with members of the more powerful (white) group. Everyday racism is, thus, racism from the point of view of people of color, defined by those who experience it.' Philomena Essed, *Everyday Racism: Reports from Women of Two Cultures* (Claremont, CA: Hunter House, 1990), 31.

20 How Japanese Canadian women negotiate male domination within the family is an area for further study. The issue of violence within Japanese Canadian families is also one that has received very little attention.

21 Rob Shields, *Places on the Margins: Alternative Geographies of Modernity* (London: Routledge, 1991), 53.

22 Haru [pseud.], interview by author, 23 November 1995. All subsequent quotes by Haru are taken from this interview.

23 May [pseud.], interview by author, 24 March 1992. All subsequent quotes by May are taken from this interview.

24 Midori [pseud.], interview by author, 24 August 1995. All subsequent quotes by Midori are taken from this interview.

25 Yuko [pseud.], interview by author, 6 November 1995. All subsequent quotes by Yuko are taken from this interview.

26 See Kirsten Emiko McAllister, 'Remembering Political Violence: The Nikkei Internment Memorial Centre' (PhD diss., Carleton University, 2000), 396-400, for a description and analysis of tours of the camps.
27 Naomi [pseud.], interview by author, 31 December 1994. All subsequent quotes by Naomi are taken from this interview.
28 Eiko [pseud.], interview by author, 30 November 1995. All subsequent quotes by Eiko are taken from this interview.
29 Kyo [pseud.], interview by author, 30 June 1995. All subsequent quotes by Kyo are taken from this interview.
30 Sylvia [pseud.], interview by author, 29 September 1996. All subsequent quotes by Sylvia are taken from this interview.
31 Janice [pseud.], interview by author, 23 August 1995. All subsequent quotes by Janice are taken from this interview.
32 Joanne [pseud.], interview by author, 31 October 1995. All subsequent quotes by Joanne are taken from this interview.
33 Irene [pseud.], interview by author, 16 June 1995. All subsequent quotes by Irene are taken from this interview.
34 One daughter later learned the language, and lived for a while in Japan to accomplish this goal.
35 Yoshiko [pseud.], interview by author, 22 December 1994. All subsequent quotes by Yoshiko are taken from this interview.
36 Aya [pseud.], interview by author, 26 August 1996. All subsequent quotes by Aya are taken from this interview.
37 Canada, Dominion Bureau of Statistics, *Ninth Census of Canada, 1951*, vol. 10 (Ottawa: Edmond Cloutier, 1956), 194. Also mentioned within this context of illustrating 'improvements in ability to speak official languages' were Indigenous peoples, for whom the percentages changed from 32.1 per cent who were unable to speak English or French in 1941 to 25.6 per cent in 1951. The 'population of Chinese origin' was reported at 24 per cent in 1941 who were not able to speak English or French and this dropped to 17 per cent in 1951.
38 See, Tatsuo Kage, *Nikkei Kanadajin no Tsuihou* (Tokyo: Akashi Shoten, 1998); and Gabrielle Nishiguchi, '"Reducing the Numbers": The "Transportation" of the Canadian Japanese (1941–1947)' (MA thesis, Carleton University, 1993).
39 Esther [pseud.], interview by author, 17 August 1995. All subsequent quotes from Esther are taken from this interview.
40 Ann [pseud.], interview by author, 1 November 1995. All subsequent quotes from Ann are taken from this interview.
41 McCann and Pearlman define 'secondary victimization' as when 'persons

close to the victim, such as family members, suffer signs and symptoms of traumatization similar to those of the victim,' in 'Vicarious Traumatization,' 135.

42 Ibid., 133.

43 Roger I. Simon and Wendy Armitage-Simon, 'Teaching Risky Stories: Remembering Mass Destruction through Children's Literature,' *English Quarterly* 28, no. 1 (1995), 30.

44 Shields, *Places on the Margin*, 18.

45 See Kirsten Emiko McAllister's articles on the use of photographs to analyse histories of Internment: 'A Story of Escape: Family Photographs From Japanese Canadian Internment Camps,' in *Locating Memory: Photographic Acts*, ed. Annette Kuhn and Kirsten Emiko McAllister (New York: Berghahn Books, 2006), 81–112; 'Photographs of a Japanese Canadian Internment Camp: Mourning Loss and Invoking a Future,' *Visual Studies* 21, no. 2 (2006), 133–56. See also her analysis of postcards sent and kept by people interned, in 'Held Captive: The Postcard and the Internment Camp,' *West Coast Line: A Journal of Contemporary Writing and Criticism* 35, no. 1 (2001), 20–40.

46 Marita Sturken, *Tangled Memories: The Vietnam War, the AIDS Epidemic, and the Politics of Remembering* (Berkeley: University of California Press, 1997), 9. Sturken uses Foucault's notion of 'technologies,' defined as 'social practices.'

47 Ibid., 10.

48 For an example of photographs taken in the pre-Internment period, see Grace Eiko Thomson, 'Archival Photographs from Cumberland BC: With an Afterword,' *West Coast Line: A Journal of Contemporary Writing & Criticism* 38, no. 1 (2004), 57–89; and *Shashin: Japanese Canadian Photography to 1942, Exhibition Catalogue* (Burnaby, BC: Japanese Canadian National Museum, 2005).

49 Sturken, *Tangled Memories*, 10.

50 Ken Adachi, *The Enemy That Never Was: A History of the Japanese Canadians* (Toronto: McClelland and Stewart, 1976), 209. See also Kirsten Emiko McAllister, 'A Story of Escape,' 83, for an analysis of photographs taken before and after the Internment and her finding that 'internees illicitly took hundreds of photographs with smuggled cameras.'

51 Because the book has gone out of print, Ann Sunahara has generously allowed the book to be posted online. Retrieved 22 July 2009 from www.japanesecanadianhistory.ca/Politics_of_Racism.pdf.

52 Alice Yang Murray, *Historical Memories of the Japanese American Internment and the Struggle for Redress* (Stanford: Stanford University Press, 2008).

53 Adhoc Committee for Japanese Canadian Redress, *Japanese Canadian Re-*

dress: The Toronto Story (Toronto: Adhoc Committee for Japanese Canadian Redress, 2000); Roy Miki, *Redress: Inside the Japanese Canadian Call for Justice* (Vancouver: Raincoast Books, 2004); Maryka Omatsu, *Bittersweet Passage: Redress and the Japanese Canadian Experience* (Toronto: Between the Lines, 1992).

54 See, for example, Elmer Oike's statement that when Japanese Canadians arrived in Manitoba, farmers picked the workers 'like slaves in the old slave markets.' Oike quoted in Manitoba Japanese Canadian Citizens' Association, *The History of Japanese Canadians in Manitoba* (Winnipeg: Manitoba Japanese Canadian Citizens' Association, 1996), 19.

55 May [pseud.], interview by author.

56 Kirsten Emiko McAllister, 'Cultural Production and Alternative Political Practices: Dialogic Cultural Forms and the Public Sphere in the Japanese Canadian Community' (MA thesis, Simon Fraser University, 1993), 66.

57 Roger Simon, 'The Pedagogy of Commemoration and Formation of Collective Memories,' *Educational Foundations* 8, no. 1 (1994), 10.

58 Shields, *Places on the Margin*, 60.

59 Ibid., 61. Shields' definition of a 'place-myth' (60) is a set of 'place-images.' The latter are 'various discrete meanings associated with real places or regions regardless of their character in reality.'

60 For a description of the Powell Street area and the groups that organized there in the 1970s, see Masumi Izumi, 'Reclaiming and Reinventing "Powell Street": Reconstruction of the Japanese Canadian Community in Post-World War II Vancouver,' in *Nikkei in the Pacific Northwest: Japanese Americans and Japanese Canadians in the Twentieth Century*, ed. Louis Fiset and Gail M. Nomura (Seattle: Center for the Study of the Pacific Northwest in association with University of Washington Press, 2005), 308–33. See also, Audrey Kobayashi, *Memories of Our Past: A Brief Walking Tour of Powell Street* (Vancouver: NRC Publishing, 1992).

61 Midge Ayukawa, 'A Sentimental Journey to Thunder River,' *The Bulletin* 34, no. 11 (1992), 13.

62 Other reasons for not returning to the places of home and incarceration include the prohibitive costs involved in travelling to British Columbia, Alberta, Saskatchewan, Manitoba, Ontario, and Quebec, especially with children. Some families would have to travel to more than one province and even to Japan, in order to retrace their processes of incarceration and expulsion.

63 In the 2006 Census, there were 19,010 people of Japanese ancestry living in the Greater Toronto area and 25,425 in the Greater Vancouver area. Canada, Statistics Canada, *Census 2006*, 'Visible Minority Population, By Census

Metropolitan Areas,' retrieved 23 January 2010 from www40.statcan.gc.ca/
l01/ind01/l3_30000_30007-eng.htm?hili_demo53.

64 Louise [pseud.], interview by author, 11 July 1994. All subsequent quotes
from Louise are taken from this interview.

65 Kazuko [pseud.], interview by author, 19 October 1995. All subsequent
quotes from Louise are taken from this interview.

66 For a description of the Powell Street Festival, see Susan Nishi, 'The
Neighbourhood and Local Heroes,' *Powell Street Festival* 5, no. 1 (February
1999), n.p. See also Tamio Wakayama's photographic representation and
textual description of the Powell Street Festival in *Kikyó: Coming Home to
Powell Street*, ed. Linda Uyehara Hoffman (Madeira Park, BC: Harbour
Publishing, 1992).

67 I would like to thank Toshi Oikawa for sharing her knowledge with me.

68 Maryka Omatsu, *Bittersweet Passage: Redress and the Japanese Canadian Experience* (Toronto: Between the Lines, 1992), 35.

69 McAllister, 'Cultural Production and Alternative Political Practices,' 44.

70 For a filmic representation of a bus tour to the Lemon Creek incarceration
site, see *With Our Own Eyes: A Trip to Lemon Creek*, directed by Ruby Truly
(Vancouver: Ruby Truly, 1993); for an analysis of the film, see McAllister,
'Cultural Production.'

71 I am indebted to my late aunt, Kiyoko Oikawa, for sharing her knowledge
with me.

72 Audrey Kobayashi, *Memories of Our Past: A Brief Walking Tour of Powell
Street* (Vancouver: NRC Publishing, 1992).

73 McAllister, 'Cultural Production,' 44.

74 See Constance Backhouse, *Colour-Coded: A Legal History of Racism in Cana-
da, 1900–1950* (Toronto: University of Toronto Press, 1999); Dara Culhane,
The Pleasure of the Crown: Anthropology, Law and First Nations (Burnaby, BC:
Talonbooks, 1998); Bonita Lawrence, *'Real' Indians and Others: Mixed-Blood
Urban Native Peoples and Indigenous Nationhood* (Vancouver: UBC Press,
2004); Patricia Monture-Angus, *Journeying Forward: Dreaming First Nations'
Independence* (Halifax: Fernwood, 1999); and Ila Bussidor and Üstün
Bilgen-Reinart, *Night Spirits: The Story of the Relocation of the Sayisi Dene*
(Winnipeg: University of Manitoba Press, 1997).

75 '74.7% of these pairings included a non-Japanese partner. The second and
third groups to be most likely involved in a mixed union were Latin Americans (47.0%) and Blacks (40.6%).' Canada, Statistics Canada, *Census 2006*,
'Canada's Ethnocultural Mosaic, 2006 Census: National Picture Mixed Unions Involving Visible Minorities on the Rise,' retrieved 10 February 2010
from www12.statcan.ca/census-recensement/2006/as-sa/97-562/p9-eng
.cfm.

76 See also David Suzuki's comment, '"To do well in Canada as a Japanese-Canadian," my father said, "you have to work 10 times harder, you must be able to get up and speak extemporaneously, and you must be able to dance."' See 'Lessons My Father Taught Me Are Worth Sharing,' retrieved 24 January 2010 from www.davidsuzuki.org/about_us/Dr_David_Suzuki/Article_Archives/weekly08270802.asp.

77 Francesca Cappelletto, 'Long-Term Memory of Extreme Events: From Autobiography to History,' *Journal of the Royal Anthropological Institute* 9, no. 2 (2003), 254.

78 Tomoko Makabe, *The Canadian Sansei* (Toronto: University of Toronto Press, 1998), 82. Makabe's respondents raise interesting issues and in fact contradict the uniformity rendered in her conclusions. Her book is deserving of more analysis than can be accomplished here. See Yuko Shibata's critique of the book in 'Snapshot of Japanese Canadians,' *International Examiner*, 31 May 2004, 8. See also McAllister's critique of the book in 'Remembering Political Violence,' and my critique in 'Cartographies of Violence: Women, Memory, and the Subject(s) of the "Internment"' (PhD diss., University of Toronto, 1999).

79 Examples include Norm Ibuki, Audrey Kobayashi, Cassandra Kobayashi, Bruce Kuwabara, Arthur Miki, Roy Miki, Maryka Omatsu, Terry Watada, and myself. Examples of other Sansei writers and cultural workers include David Fujino, Michael Fukushima, Jay Hirabayashi, Sally Ito, Bryce Kanbara, Leslie Komori, Kirsten Emiko McAllister, Scott Toguri McFarlane, Cindy Mochizuki, Mark Tadao Nakada, Peter Takaji Nunoda, Baco Ohama, Linda Ohama, Haruko Okano, Midi Onodera, Kerri Sakamoto, Gerry Shikatani, Kathy Shimizu, Rick Shiomi, Katherine Shozawa, Aiko Suzuki, and David Suzuki. See the bibliography to this book for references and also Aiko Suzuki's important directory of artists, *Japanese Canadians in the Arts: A Directory of Professionals* (Toronto: SAC/rist, 1994). In addition, see Aiko Suzuki, ed., *About Japanese Canadians, Resource Listings III*, revised by David Fujino (Toronto: Toronto Nikkei Archive and Resource Centre, 1996).

80 Makabe, *The Canadian Sansei*, 5.

9 'Crushing the White Wall with Our Names'

1 Janice Mirikitani, 'Generations of Women,' in *Shedding Silence* (Berkeley: Celestial Arts, 1987), 15.

2 Henri Lustiger-Thaler, 'Remembering Forgetfully,' in *Re-Situating Identities: The Politics of Race, Ethnicity, and Culture*, ed. Vered Amit-Talai and Caroline Knowles (Peterborough, ON: Broadview Press, 1996), 196.

3 Donna Nagata, *Legacy of Injustice: Exploring the Cross-Generational Impact of the Japanese American Internment* (New York: Plenum Press, 1993), 113.
4 See Carol Schick, who describes universities as a white space in her article 'Keeping the Ivory Tower White: Discourses of Racial Domination,' in *Inequality in Canada: A Reader on the Intersections of Gender, Race, and Class*, ed. Valerie Zawilski and Cynthia Levine-Rasky (Don Mills: Oxford University Press, 2005), 213.
5 Benedict Anderson, *Imagined Communities: Reflections on the Origin and Spread of Nationalism* (London: Verso, 1991).
6 Margaret [pseud.], interview by author, 20 June 1995. All subsequent quotes from Margaret are taken from this interview.
7 Louise [pseud.], interview by author, 11 July 1995. All subsequent quotes from Louise are taken from this interview.
8 Esther [pseud.], interview by author, 17 August 1995. All subsequent quotes from Esther are taken from this interview.
9 Haru [pseud.], interview by author, 23 November 1995. All subsequent quotes from Haru are taken from this interview.
10 From an analysis of 1986 Census data, Audrey Kobayashi concludes that 'close to half of Japanese Canadians under age 45 have some university education, and about one-quarter hold university degrees ... Canadians as a whole are about one-fifth having some university education, and about 10 percent holding a university degree.' In 'A Demographic Profile of Japanese Canadians and social Implications for the Future' (Canada, Department of the Secretary of State, 1989), mimeograph, 39. In 1996, 7.5 per cent of Japanese Canadians sixty-five years and over had received a bachelor's degree or higher. See Akemi Kikumura-Yano, *Encyclopedia of Japanese Descendants in the Americas: An Illustrated History of the Nikkei* (Walnut Creek, CA: AltaMira Press, 2002), 175. However, in 2001, while 10.4 per cent of Japanese Canadians sixty-five years and older held a bachelor's degree or higher, only 7.1 per cent were women of this age group, which was lower than the percentage of both women and men of this age group in 1996. See Colin Lindsay, 'Profiles of Ethnic Communities in Canada: The Japanese Community in Canada' (Canada: Statistics Canada, 2007), 13.
11 The gender of the teachers was not always reported.
12 Mayumi [pseud.], interview by author, 1 November 1995. All subsequent quotes from Mayumi are taken from this interview.
13 I have decided not to repeat most of the racist words used against the women because of the harm these words have inflicted upon the women testifying and also on other racialized people.
14 Yuko [pseud.], interview by author, 6 November 1995. All subsequent quotes from Yuko are taken from this interview.

15 Sylvia [pseud.], interview by author, 29 September 1996. All subsequent quotes from Sylvia are taken from this interview.
16 Irene [pseud.], interview by author, 16 June 1995. All subsequent quotes from Irene are taken from this interview.
17 Midori [pseud.], interview by author, 24 August 1995. All subsequent quotes from Midori are taken from this interview.
18 Joanne [pseud.], interview by author, 31 October 1995. All subsequent quotes from Joanne are taken from this interview.
19 Lisa Lowe, *Immigrant Acts: On Asian American Cultural Politics* (Durham, NC: Duke University Press, 1996), 55.
20 Ibid.
21 Janice [pseud.], interview by author, 23 August 1995. All subsequent quotes from Janice are taken from this interview.
22 Naomi [pseud.], interview by author, 31 December 1994. All subsequent quotes from Naomi are taken from this interview.
23 For an analysis of 'light-skin privilege' in relation to Native peoples, see Bonita Lawrence, *'Real' Indians and Others: Mixed-Blood Urban Native Peoples and Indigenous Nationhood* (Vancouver: University of British Columbia Press, 2004), especially 189.
24 See Mona Oikawa, 'Re-Mapping Histories Site by Site: Connecting the Internment of Japanese Canadians to the Colonization of Aboriginal Peoples in Canada,' in *Aboriginal Connections to Race, Environment and Traditions*, ed. Rick Riewe and Jill Oakes (Winnipeg: Aboriginal Issues Press, University of Manitoba, 2006), 17–26, and Bonita Lawrence and Enakshi Dua, 'Decolonizing Antiracism,' *Social Justice* 32 (2005): 120–43.
25 Sherene H. Razack, *Looking White People in the Eye: Gender, Race, and Culture in Courtrooms and Classrooms* (Toronto: University of Toronto Press, 1998), 167.
26 For theory on 'mixed race' as an identity, see Lawrence, *'Real' Indians and Others*; Minelle Mahtani, *Interrogating the Hyphen-Nation: Canadian Multicultural Policy and 'Mixed Race' Identities* (Toronto: Joint Centre of Excellence on Immigration and Settlement, 2004); Jayne O. Ifekwunigwe, ed. *'Mixed Race' Studies: A Reader* (London: Routledge, 2004).
27 Kyo [pseud.], interview by author, 30 June 1995. All subsequent quotes from Kyo are taken from this interview.
28 Roger I. Simon and Wendy Armitage-Simon, 'Teaching Risky Stories: Remembering Mass Destruction through Children's Literature,' *English Quarterly* 28, no. 1 (1995), 27.
29 Eiko [pseud.], interview by author, 30 Novembe 1995. All subsequent quotes from Eiko are taken from this interview.
30 While much literary criticism on *Obasan* has been generated by non-

Japanese Canadians, how survivors and their children respond to this text would be important to investigate. For two examples, see Roy Miki, 'Asiancy: Making Space for Asian Canadian Writing,' in *Broken Entries: Race, Subjectivity, Writing* (Toronto: The Mercury Press, 1998), 101–24; and Scott McFarlane, 'Covering *Obasan* and the Narratives of the Internment,' in *Privileging Positions: The Sites of Asian American Studies,* ed. Gary Y. Okihiro, Marilyn Alquizola, Dorothy Fujita Rony, and K. Scott Wong (Pullman, WA: Washington State University Press, 1995), 401–11.

31 Mari J. Matsuda, Charles R. Lawrence III, Richard Delgado, and Kimberlé Williams Crenshaw, *Words That Wound: Critical Race Theory, Assaultive Speech, and the First Amendment* (Boulder, CO: Westview Press, 1993).

32 Patricia Williams, quoted in ibid., 24.

33 Chalsa Loo, 'An Integrative-Sequential Treatment Model for Posttraumatic Stress Disorder: A Case Study of the Japanese American Internment and Redress,' *Clinical Psychology Review* 13, no. 2 (1993), 90.

34 Donald Nakanishi, 'Surviving Democracy's "Mistake": Japanese Americans and the Enduring Legacy of Executive Order 9066,' *Amerasia Journal* 19, no. 1 (1993), 16.

35 For an example of a curriculum resource guide funded by the BC Ministry of Education, see, *Internment and Redress: The Japanese Canadian Experience: A Resource Guide for Social Studies 11 Teachers* (Victoria: Queen's Printer for British Columbia, 2005).

36 See the report by the Canadian Federation of Students – Ontario that found 'Racialised students said that their history was erased, under-represented, or obscured by curriculum.' In *The Final Report of the Task Force on Campus Racism* (Toronto: Canadian Federation of Students-Ontario 2009), retrieved 22 April 2010 from http://fileserver.cfsadmin.org/file/noracism/3740e2f04018e5b4d7a821095cdab4381e964801.pdf, 13.

37 'A study of Toronto's [public school] teachers show only about 23 per cent are from visible minorities – yet seven in 10 high school students are not white … of the 1,000 teachers York [University] graduates each year, a little more than one in five are a visible minority.' Louise Brown, 'Today's Search for Tomorrow's Teachers: U of T Makes Pitch to Inner-City Middle Schoolers to Consider Leading Diverse Classrooms of the Future,' *Toronto Star*, 19 May 2008, A12.

38 King quoted in Ann Gomer Sunahara, *The Politics of Racism: The Uprooting of Japanese Canadians during the Second World War* (Toronto: James Lorimer, 1981), 15. See also Ken Adachi, *The Enemy That Never Was: A History of the Japanese Canadians* (Toronto: McClelland and Stewart, 1976), 367.

39 Simon and Armitage-Simon, 'Teaching Risky Stories,' 30.

40 Ibid., 27.

41 Lisa McCann and Laurie Anne Pearlman quote R. Janoff-Bulman in stating that 'victimizing life events' challenge 'the belief in a meaningful, orderly world.' See 'Vicarious Traumatization: A Framework for Understanding the Psychological Effects of Working with Victims,' *Journal of Traumatic Stress* 3, no. 1 (1990), 137. I would like to thank Claudia Lopez for providing me with this reference.

42 See Lustiger-Thaler's description in 'Remembering Forgetfully' of Jews who moved to Germany from other parts of Europe after the Holocaust and were placed in the position of 'playing "confessors" to German "sinners" through the good offices of the philosemitic state' (196). The Christian symbolism of this metaphor is also of interest here.

43 Trinh T. Minh-ha quoted in Meyda Yeğenoğlu, *Colonial Fantasies* (Cambridge: Cambridge University Press, 1998), 154n82.

44 David Goldberg, *Racist Culture: Philosophy and the Politics of Meaning* (Oxford: Blackwell, 1993), 97.

45 Evelyn [pseud.], interview by author, 26 August 1995. All subsequent quotes from Evelyn are taken from this interview.

46 Ann [pseud.], interview by author, 1 November 1995. All subsequent quotes from Ann are taken from this interview.

47 Archives of Ontario (AO), Hepburn Papers, RG 3, Box 325, file 1, W.M. Forman to Hepburn, 30 June 1942. See also AO, Hepburn Papers, RG 3, Box 325, file 2, R.A. Gaskin to Mr. Roberts, 23 May 1942, regarding 'unfavourable opposition' in the town of Aylmer.

48 AO, Office of the Deputy Minister of Labour, RG 7, J-W, 11-1, vol. 29, J.F. Marsh to A. MacNamara, 13 May 1942.

49 Peggy Bristow, '"Whatever You Raise in the Ground You Can Sell it In Chatham": Black Women in Buxton and Chatham, 1850–65,' in *We're Rooted Here and They Can't Pull Us Up: Essays in African Canadian Women's History*, ed. Peggy Bristow (Toronto: University of Toronto Press, 1994), 96.

50 Ibid. See also, Adrienne Shadd, 'Where are you *Really* from? Notes of an "Immigrant" from North Buxton, Ontario,' in *Talking about Identity: Encounters in Race, Ethnicity, and Language*, ed. Carl James and Adrienne Shadd (Toronto: Between the Lines, 2001), 13; and Rinaldo Walcott, *Black Like Who? Writing Black Canada*, second revised edition (Toronto: Insomniac Press, 2003), 34–5.

51 Kirsten McAllister, 'Asians in Hollywood,' Cine*action* 30 (1992), 13.

52 Ibid., 10.

53 Laura Hyun Yi Kang, 'Compositional Subjects: Enfiguring Asian/Ameri-

can Women,' (PhD diss.: University of California, Santa Cruz, 1995), 221.

54 Lauren Berlant, *The Anatomy of National Fantasy* (Chicago: University of Chicago Press, 1991).

55 See, for example, Himani Bannerji, *The Dark Side of the Nation: Essays on Multiculturalism, Nationalism and Gender* (Toronto: Canadian Scholars' Press, 2000); Amita Handa, *Of Silk Saris and Mini-Skirts: South Asian Girls Walk the Tightrope of Culture* (Toronto: Women's Press, 2003); Sherene H. Razack, ed. *Race, Space and the Law: Unmapping a White Settler Society* (Toronto: Between the Lines, 2002); Shadd, 'Where are you *Really* from?' 10–6.

56 Glen Deer, 'The New Yellow Peril: The Rhetorical Construction of Asian Canadian Identity and Cultural Anxiety in Richmond,' in *Claiming Space: Racialization in Canadian Cities*, ed. Cheryl Teelucksingh (Waterloo, ON: Wilfrid Laurier University Press, 2006), 21.

57 Ibid., 34.

58 May [pseud.], interview by author, 24 March 1992. All subsequent quotes by May are taken from this interview. The 'mistake' she is referring to is that the killers claimed they believed Vincent Chin was Japanese. For a filmic representation of the murder of Chin in 1982, see, Christine Choy and Renee Tajima (directors), *Who Killed Vincent Chin?* (New York: Film-makers Library, 1988); for a textual account, see Ronald Takaki, *Strangers from a Different Shore: A History of Asian Americans* (New York: Penguin, 1989), 481–4.

59 Sherene H. Razack, *Dark Threats and White Knights: The Somalia Affair, Peacekeeping, and the New Imperialism* (Toronto: University of Toronto Press, 2004), 90.

60 Roy Miki, *Broken Entries: Race, Subjectivity, Writing* (Toronto: The Mercury Press, 1998), 194.

61 Wendy Brown, *States of Injury: Power and Freedom in Late Modernity* (Princeton, NJ: Princeton University Press, 1995), 75.

62 See Pierre Nora, 'Between Memory and History: *Les Lieux de Mémoire,'* *Representations* 26 (Spring 1989), 19, for an analysis of the relationship of 'historical generation' to the construction of memory.

63 Yoshiko [pseud.], interview by author, 22 December 1994. All subsequent quotes by Yoshiko are taken from this interview.

64 Mitsuye Yamada, 'Invisibility is an Unnatural Disaster: Reflections of an Asian American Woman,' in *This Bridge Called My Back: Writings by Radical Women of Color*, ed. Cherríe Moraga and Gloria Anzaldúa (Watertown, MA: Persephone Press, 1981), 35–40.

65 Traise Yamamoto, *Masking Selves, Making Subjects: Japanese American Women, Identity, and the Body* (Berkeley: University of California Press, 1999), 67.

66 Deer, 'The New Yellow Peril,' 31; note omitted.

67 Hijin Park, 'Constituting "Asian Women": Canadian Gendered Orientalism and Multicultural Nationalism in an Age of "Asia Rising"' (PhD diss., University of Toronto, 2007), 159–63. Also see her 'Incorporating Ji-Won Park into the Canadian Nation: The Good Girl, the Monster and the Noble Savage,' in *Han Kŭt: Critical Art and Writing by Korean Canadian Women* by Korean Canadian Women's Anthology Collective (Toronto: Inanna Publications and Education, 2007), 77–93. See also the attacks against East Asian Canadian fishers in southern Ontario. In the Ontario Human Rights Commission report, 'Fishing Without Fear: Follow-Up Report on the Inquiry Into Assaults on Asian Canadian Anglers' (2009), one person testified that 'her friends had their bucket of fish turned over and a man swore at them and yelled repeatedly, "go back to China, go back to Japan." The man then pushed her friend's fishing rod out of his hand' (11), retrieved 21 July 2009 from www.ohrc.on.ca/en/resources/discussion_consultation/finalangler?page=finalangler-Contents.html. See also, Noor Javed, 'Attacks on Anglers Tied to Racism: Rights Commission Sees Racial Profiling in Verbal, Physical Assaults on Asian Canadian Fishermen,' *Toronto Star*, 14 May 2008, retrieved 21 July 2009 from www.thestar.com/News/Ontario/article/425178. See also Deer, 'The New Yellow Peril,' for a discussion of the racial construction of Asian Canadian fishers in Vancouver.

68 Park, 'Constituting "Asian Women,"' 161.

69 See Michel Foucault *Discipline and Punish: The Birth of the Prison*, trans. Alan Sheridan (New York: Vintage Books, 1995), where he states, 'A relation of surveillance, defined and regulated, is inscribed at the heart of the practice of teaching, not as an additional or adjacent part, but as a mechanism that is inherent to it and which increases its efficiency' (176).

70 Kang, 'Compositional Subjects,' 130. See also Bannerji's statement, '"Canada" as a nationalist project, is perceived to be a homogeneous, solid, and settled entity, though its history constantly belies this.' *The Dark Side of the Nation*, 73.

71 Homi Bhabha, *The Location of Culture* (London: Routledge, 1995), 91–2.

10 Conclusion

1 S. [pseud.], interview by author, 16 August 1995. All subsequent quotes by S. are taken from this interview.

2 Lisa Lowe, *Immigrant Acts: On Asian American Cultural Politics* (Durham, NC: Duke University Press), x.
3 Rita Dhamoon and Yasmeen Abu-Laban, 'Dangerous (Internal) Foreigners and Nation-Building: The Case of Canada,' *International Political Science Review* 30, no. 163 (2009), 171.
4 Grace Eiko Thomson, 'National Association of Japanese Canadians President's Message, July 2008,' retrieved 18 April 2010 from www.najc.ca/community-news/presidents-message-july/.
5 See Werner Cohn's critique of the BC provincial CCF for not opposing the expulsion of Japanese Canadians: 'One may argue that perhaps a determined opposition by one of the country's major parties – the largest one in the key province of British Columbia – could have forestalled government action,' in 'Persecution of Japanese Canadians and the Political Left in British Columbia, December 1941–March 1942,' *BC Studies*, no. 68 (1985–6), 22.
6 Kirsten Emiko McAllister, 'Remembering Political Violence: The Nikkei Internment Memorial Centre' (PhD diss., Carleton University, 2000), 26–7.
7 For example, in Toronto there is the Sedai: The Japanese Canadian Legacy Project, 'dedicated to collecting and preserving the stories of earlier generations of Canadians of Japanese ancestry for all future generations' (retrieved 21 July 2009 from www.sedai.ca). In Vancouver, a conference called Honouring Our People: Stories of the Internment was held on 26–7 September 2009. See John Endo Greenaway, 'Honouring Our People: Stories of the Internment,' *The Bulletin* (5 June 2009), retrieved 21 July 2009 from http://jccabulletin-geppo.ca/featured/honouring-our-people-stories-of-the-internment/.
8 Sara Ahmed, *The Cultural Politics of Emotion* (New York: Routledge, 2004), 193; emphasis in original.
9 Wendy Brown, *States of Injury: Power and Freedom in Late Modernity* (Princeton, NJ: Princeton University Press, 1995), 74.
10 bell hooks, *Yearning: Race, Gender, and Cultural Politics* (Toronto: Between the Lines, 1990), 147.
11 Those who received individual acknowledgment had to have been born before 1 April 1949, the date on which Japanese Canadians were allowed to return to the 100-mile coastal zone, four years after the end of the Second World War. See Roy Miki, *Redress: Inside the Japanese Canadian Call for Justice* (Vancouver: Raincoast Books, 2004), 9.
12 Audrey Kobayashi has described the foundation as 'potentially the most proactive move ever taken by a single government to overcome racism,' in 'Racism and Law in Canada: A Geographical Perspective,' *Urban Geog-*

raphy 11, no. 5 (1990), 462; note omitted. Kobayashi served on the NAJC Strategy Committee that negotiated the redress settlement.

13 Roy Miki and Cassandra Kobayashi, *Justice in Our Time: The Japanese Canadian Redress Settlement* (Vancouver: Talonbooks and Winnipeg: National Association of Japanese Canadians, 1991), 138. See this reference for other terms of the agreement. R. Miki and C. Kobayashi served on the NAJC Strategy Committee.

14 See Maryka Omatsu's statement that the War Measures Act was replaced by the 'son of the WMA, now the Emergency Procedures Act,' and her expression of disappointment at not achieving the elimination of the Act and changes to the Constitution to protect 'all Canada's minorities.' As she states, 'I feel sorrow that we do not leave behind a treasure of such strength and worth ... My expectations exceed our ability.' *Bittersweet Passage: Redress and the Japanese Canadian Experience* (Toronto: Between the Lines, 1992), 173. Omatsu served on the NAJC Strategy Committee.

15 McAllister quoted in Roy Miki, *Redress*, 322.

16 Kirsten Emiko McAllister, 'Cultural Production and Alternative Political Practices: Dialogic Cultural Forms and the Public Sphere in the Japanese Canadian Community' (MA thesis, Simon Fraser University, 1993), 174.

17 Marita Sturken, 'Absent Images of Memory: Remembering and Reenacting the Japanese Internment,' *Positions: East Asia Cultures Critique* 5, no. 3 (1997), 702.

18 Roy Miki, *Redress*, 325.

19 Ibid., 323.

20 Aya [pseud.], interview by author, 26 August 1996.

21 Evelyn [pseud], interview by author, 26 August 1995. All subsequent quotes by Evelyn are taken from this interview.

22 Francesca Cappelletto, 'Long-Term Memory of Extreme Events: From Autobiography to History,' *Journal of the Royal Anthropological Institute* 9, no. 2 (2003), 247.

23 Lowe, *Immigrant Acts*, 10.

24 Margaret [pseud.], interview by author, 20 June 1995.

25 Kazuko [pseud.], interview by author, 19 October 1995.

26 Sylvia [pseud.], interview by author, 29 September 1996.

27 Irene [pseud.], interview by author, 16 June 1995.

28 Midori [pseud.], interview by author, 24 August 1995.

29 Louise [pseud.], interview by author, 11 July 1995.

30 Haru [pseud.], interview by author, 23.November 1995.

31 Ann [pseud.], interview by author, 1 November 1995.

32 Mayumi [pseud.], interview by author, 1 November 1995.

33 Eiko [pseud.], interview by author, 30 November 1995.

34 Janice [pseud.], interview by author, 23 August 1995.

35 Kyo [pseud.], interview by author, 30 June 1995.

36 See, for example, Ronald J. Daniels, Patrick Macklem, and Kent Roach, eds., *The Security of Freedom: Essays on Canada's Anti-Terrorism Bill* (Toronto: University of Toronto Press, 2001); and Ken Roach, 'Better Late Than Never? The Canadian Review of the *Anti-Terrorism Act*.' *IRPP Choices* 13, no. 5 (2007), 1–40.

37 See, for example, Sherene H. Razack, *Casting Out: The Eviction of Muslims from Western Law and Politics* (Toronto: University of Toronto Press, 2008); Sunera Thobani, *Exalted Subjects: Studies in the Making of Race and Nation in Canada* (Toronto: University of Toronto Press, 2007); G. Rao, 'Inventing Enemies: Project Thread and Canadian "Security,"' *Canadian Dimension*, 38 (2004), 9–11; and Sujit Choudhry, 'Protecting Equality in the Face of Terror: Ethnic and Racial Profiling and s.15 of the *Charter*,' in *The Security of Freedom: Essays on Canada's Anti-Terrorism Bill*, ed. Ronald J. Daniels, Patrick Macklem, and Kent Roach (Toronto: University of Toronto Press, 2001), 367–82.

38 On this point, see, for example, Giorgio Agamben, *State of Exception*, trans. Kevin Attell (Chicago: University of Chicago Press, 2003); Paul Gilroy, *Between Camps: Nations, Cultures and the Allure of Race* (London: Routledge, 2000); and Razack, *Casting Out*.

39 Prime Minister Mulroney to Sally Oikawa, 'Acknowledgment/Reconnaissance,' n.d. Private collection of Mona Oikawa.

40 See Anna Pratt and Mariana Valverde, 'From Deserving Victims to "Masters of Confusion": Redefining Refugees in the 1990s,' *Canadian Journal of Sociology* 27, no. 2 (2002), 135–61; Razack, *Casting Out*; Carol Tator and Frances Henry, *Racial Profiling in Canada: Challenging the Myth of a Few Bad Apples* (Toronto: University of Toronto Press, 2006).

41 Sturken, 'Absent Images of Memory,' 704.

42 For critiques of multiculturalism, see Himani Bannerji, *The Dark Side of the Nation: Essays on Multiculturalism, Nationalism and Gender* (Toronto: Canadian Scholars' Press, 2000); Amita Handa, *Of Silk Saris and Mini-Skirts: South Asian Girls Walk the Tightrope of Culture* (Toronto: Women's Press, 2003); Gerald Kernerman, *Multicultural Nationalism: Civilizing Difference, Constituting Community* (Vancouver: UBC Press, 2005); Peter S. Li, 'The Multiculturalism Debate,' in *Race and Ethnic Relations in Canada*, ed. Peter S. Li, 2nd ed. (Don Mills: Oxford University Press, 1999), 148–77; and Eva Mackey, *The House of Difference: Cultural Politics and National Identity in Canada* (Toronto: University of Toronto Press, 2005).

43 Hijin Park, 'Constituting "Asian Women": Canadian Gendered Oriental-ism and Multicultural Nationalism in an Age of "Asia Rising"' (PhD diss., University of Toronto, 2007), 175–6.

44 Dhamoon and Abu-Laban, 'Dangerous (Internal) Foreigners and Nation-Building'; Park, 'Constituting "Asian Women."'

45 Laura Hyun Yi Kang, 'Compositional Subjects: Enfiguring Asian/American Women' (PhD diss., University of California, Santa Cruz, 1995), 134.

46 See Saidiya Hartman's argument that liberalism and the notion of equality in the United States further entrenched racial divisions between African Americans and white Americans by positing whiteness as humanity at the same time that racial divisions were obfuscated by the discourse of equality for all. *Scenes of Subjection: Terror, Slavery, and Self-Making in Nineteenth-Century America* (New York: Oxford University Press, 1997), 121.

47 Zainab Amadahy and Bonita Lawrence, 'Indigenous Peoples and Black People in Canada: Settlers or Allies?' in *Breaching the Colonial Contract: Anti-Colonialism in the U.S. and Canada*, ed. Arlo Kempf (Dordrecht, The Netherlands: Springer, 2009), 128.

48 For an analysis of the use of the term *shikata ga nai*, see, for example, chapter 1 in this volume.

49 Inderpal Grewal and Caren Kaplan, 'Introduction: Transnational Feminist Practices and Questions of Postmodernity,' in *Scattered Hegemonies: Postmodernity and Transnational Feminist Practices*, ed. Grewal and Kaplan (Minneapolis: University of Minnesota Press, 1994), 7.

50 Meyda Yeğenoğlu, *Colonial Fantasies: Towards a Feminist Reading of Orientalism* (Cambridge: Cambridge University Press, 1998), 8.

51 Lowe, *Immigrant Acts*, 103.

Bibliography

Archival Sources

Archives of Ontario

Archives of Ontario Library Collection, Govt Doc Leg D. Official Report of
    Debates (Hansard): Legislative Assembly of Ontario
Hepburn Papers
Office of the Deputy Minister of Agriculture
Office of the Deputy Minister of Labour

Japanese Canadian National Museum

Midge Ayukawa and Betty Andrews Collection
John W. Duggan Collection
Alex Eastwood Collection
Joe Hayaru Oyama Collection
S. Inouye Collection
Kariatsumari Collection
Mary Ohara Collection

Library and Archives Canada, Ottawa (LAC)

British Columbia Security Commission
Department of External Affairs
Department of Labour
Muriel Fujiwara Kitagawa Papers
Royal Canadian Mounted Police

University of British Columbia Library, Special Collections and University Archives Division

Aural History Transcripts: Mrs Ellen Enomoto

Secondary Sources

Adachi, Ken. *The Enemy That Never Was: A History of the Japanese Canadians.* Toronto: McClelland and Stewart, 1991.
– *The Enemy That Never Was: A History of the Japanese Canadians.* Toronto: McClelland and Stewart, 1976.
Adachi, Pat. *Road to the Pinnacle: Sequel to Asahi: A Legend in Baseball.* Toronto: Self-published, 2004.
– *Asahi: A Legend in Baseball.* Etobicoke, ON: Asahi Baseball Organization, 1992.
Adhoc Committee for Japanese Canadian Redress. *Japanese Canadian Redress: The Toronto Story.* Toronto: Adhoc Committee for Japanese Canadian Redress, 2000.
Agamben, Giorgio. *State of Exception.* Translated by Kevin Attell. Chicago: University of Chicago Press, 2003.
– *Homo Sacer: Sovereign Power and Bare Life.* Translated by Daniel Heller-Roazen. Palo Alto, CA: Stanford University Press, 1998.
Agnew, John, Katharyne Mitchell, and Gerard Toal, eds. *A Companion to Political Geography.* Malden, MA: Blackwell, 2003.
Ahmed, Sara. *The Cultural Politics of Emotion.* New York: Routledge, 2004.
Alarcón, Norma. 'The Theoretical Subject(s) of This Bridge Called My Back and Anglo-American Feminism.' In *Making Face, Making Soul: Creative and Critical Perspectives by Women of Color,* edited by Gloria Anzaldúa, 356–69. San Francisco: Aunt Lute Foundation, 1990.
Alfred, Taiaiake. *Wasáse: Indigenous Pathways of Action and Freedom.* Peterborough, ON: Broadview Press, 2005.
Alonso, Ana Maria. 'The Politics of Space, Time and Substance: State Formation, Nationalism and Ethnicity.' *Annual Review of Anthropology* 23 (1994): 379–405.
Amadahy, Zainab, and Bonita Lawrence. 'Indigenous Peoples and Black People in Canada: Settlers or Allies?' In *Breaching the Colonial Contract: Anti-Colonialism in the U.S. and Canada,* edited by Arlo Kempf, 105–34. Dordrecht, The Netherlands: Springer, 2009.
Anderson, Benedict. *Imagined Communities: Reflections on the Origin and Spread of Nationalism.* London: Verso, 1991.

Anderson, Kay. *Vancouver's Chinatown: Racial Discourse in Canada, 1875–1980.* Montreal: McGill-Queen's University Press, 1991.

Anderson, Kim. *A Recognition of Being: Reconstructing Native Womanhood.* Toronto: Second Story Press, 2000.

Angus, H.F. Preface to *The Canadian Japanese and World War II: A Sociological and Psychological Account,* by Forrest E. La Violette, i–vi. Toronto: University of Toronto Press, 1948.

Antze, Paul, and Michael Lambek, eds. *Tense Past: Cultural Essays in Trauma and Memory.* New York: Routledge, 1996.

Armor, John, and Peter Wright. *Manzanar.* New York: Vintage Books, 1989.

Ashworth, Mary. *The Forces which Shaped Them: A History of the Education of Minority Group Children in British Columbia.* Vancouver: New Star Books, 1979.

Attwood, Bain. 'Unsettling Pasts: Reconciliation and History in Settler Australia.' *Postcolonial Studies* 8, no. 3 (2005): 243–59.

Axford, Roger W. *Too Long Silent: Japanese Americans Speak Out.* Lincoln, NB: Media Publishing and Marketing, 1986.

Ayukawa, Midge. *Hiroshima Immigrants in Canada, 1891–1941.* Vancouver: UBC Press, 2008.

– 'From Japs to Japanese Canadians to Canadians.' *Journal of the West* 38, no. 3 (1999): 41–8.

– 'Good Wives and Wise Mothers: Japanese Picture Brides in Early Twentieth-Century British Columbia.' *BC Studies* 105–106 (1995): 103–18.

– 'A Sentimental Journey to Thunder River.' *The Bulletin* 34, no. 11 (1992): 13.

Backhouse, Constance. *Colour-Coded: A Legal History of Racism in Canada, 1900–1950.* Toronto: University of Toronto Press, 1999.

Bakan, Abigail B., and Daiva Stasiulis. Introduction to *Not One of the Family: Foreign Domestic Workers in Canada,* edited by Abigail B. Bakan and Daiva Stasiulis, 3–27. Toronto: University of Toronto Press, 1997.

Bangarth, Stephanie D. 'The Long, Wet Summer of 1942: The Ontario Farm Service Force, Small-town Ontario and the Nisei.' *Canadian Ethnic Studies* 37, no. 1 (2005): 40–62.

– 'Religious Organizations and the "Relocation" of Persons of Japanese Ancestry in North America: Evaluating Advocacy.' *The American Review of Canadian Studies* 34, no. 3 (2004): 511–40.

Bannerji, Himani. *The Dark Side of the Nation: Essays on Multiculturalism, Nationalism and Gender.* Toronto: Canadian Scholars' Press, 2000.

Bar-On, Dan. *Fear and Hope: Three Generations of the Holocaust.* Cambridge: Harvard University Press, 1995.

Begoray, Deborah L. 'Obachan's Garden.' *Canadian Review of Materials* 8, no. 15 (2002): 1–3.

Benjamin, Walter. *Illuminations*. Edited by Hannah Arendt. New York: Harcourt, Brace and World, 1968.

Bergmann, Martin S., and Milton E. Jucovy. Prelude to *Generations of the Holocaust*, edited by Bergmann and Jucovy, 3–29. New York: Columbia University Press, 1990.

Berlant, Lauren, ed. *Compassion: The Culture and Politics of an Emotion*. New York: Routledge, 2004.

– *The Anatomy of National Fantasy*. Chicago: University of Chicago Press, 1991.

Berreman, Gerald D. 'Aleut Reference Group Alienation, Mobility, and Acculturation.' *American Anthropologist* 66, no. 2 (1964): 231–50.

Bhabha, Homi K. *The Location of Culture*. London: Routledge, 1994.

– 'The Other Question.' *Screen* 24, no. 6 (1983): 18–36.

Blomley, Nicholas. 'Law, Property, and the Geography of Violence: The Frontier, the Survey, and the Grid.' *The Annals of the Association of American Geographers* 93, no. 1 (2003): 121–42.

Bornat, Joanna. 'Women's History and Oral History: Developments and Debates.' *Women's History Review* 16, no. 1 (2007): 19–39.

Boyarin, Jonathan. 'Space, Time, and the Politics of Memory.' In *Remapping Memory: The Politics of TimeSpace*, edited by Jonathan Boyarin, 1–37. Minneapolis: University of Minnesota Press, 1994.

– ed. *Remapping Memory: The Politics of TimeSpace*. Minneapolis: University of Minnesota Press, 1994.

– *Storm from Paradise: The Politics of Jewish Memory*. Minneapolis: University of Minnesota Press, 1992.

Breen, David, and Kenneth Coates. *Vancouver's Fair: An Administrative and Political History of the Pacific National Exhibition*. Vancouver: University of British Columbia Press, 1982.

Bristow, Peggy. '"Whatever You Raise in the Ground You Can Sell It in Chatham," Black Women in Buxton and Chatham, 1850–65.' In *We're Rooted Here and They Can't Pull Us Up: Essays in African Canadian Women's History*, edited by Peggy Bristow, 69–142. Toronto: University of Toronto Press, 1994.

Broadfoot, Barry. *Years of Sorrow, Years of Shame: The Story of Japanese Canadians in World War II*. Toronto: Doubleday, 1977.

Brown, Louise. 'Today's Search for Tomorrow's Teachers: U of T Makes Pitch to Inner-City Middle Schoolers to Consider Leading Diverse Classrooms of the Future.' *Toronto Star*, 19 May 2008, A1, A12.

Brown, Wendy. *States of Injury: Power and Freedom in Late Modernity*. Princeton, NJ: Princeton University Press, 1995.

Burnet, Jean, and Howard Palmer. Introduction to *The Enemy That Never Was:*

A History of the Japanese Canadians, by Ken Adachi. Toronto: McClelland and Stewart, 1976.

Burton, Antoinette. 'Who Needs the Nation? Interrogating "British" History.' *Journal of Historical Sociology* 10, no. 3 (1997): 227–48.

Burton, Jeffery F., Mary M. Farrell, Florence B. Lord, and Richard W. Lord. *Confinement and Ethnicity: An Overview of World War II Japanese American Relocation Sites*. Seattle: University of Washington Press, 2002.

Bussidor, Ila, and Üstün Bilgen-Reinart. *Night Spirits: The Story of the Relocation of the Sayisi Dene*. Winnipeg, MB: University of Manitoba Press, 1997.

Calliste, Agnes. 'Race, Gender and Canadian Immigration Policy: Blacks from the Caribbean, 1900–1932.' In *Gender and History in Canada*, edited by Joy Parr and Mark Rosenfeld, 70–97. Toronto: Copp Clark, 1996.

Canadian Federation of Students–Ontario. *The Final Report of the Task Force on Campus Racism*. Toronto: Canadian Federation of Students-Ontario, 2009. Retrieved 22 April 2010 from http://fileserver.cfsadmin.org/file/noracism/3740e2f04018e5b4d7a821095cdab4381e964801.pdf.

Canadian War Museum. 'Get Involved.' Retrieved 1 November 2008 from http://www.ottawakiosk.com/cgibin/linkto.pl?url=/go/link.php?url=http://www.warmuseum.ca/.

– *Forced Relocation. Un Déplacement Forcé*. Ottawa, ON: Canadian War Museum, 2008.

'CAP and Native Veterans Call for Removal of "Offensive Paintings."' *The First Perspective* 14, no. 9 (2005): 1.

Cappelletto, Francesca. 'Long-Term Memory of Extreme Events: From Autobiography to History.' *Journal of the Royal Anthropological Institute* 9, no. 2 (2003): 241–60.

Caruth, Cathy. *Unclaimed Experience: Trauma, Narrative, and History*. Baltimore: Johns Hopkins University Press, 1996.

– ed. *Trauma: Explorations in Memory*. Baltimore: Johns Hopkins University Press, 1995.

Chan, Sucheng. *Asian Americans: An Interpretive History*. Boston: Twayne Publishers, 1991.

Cheung, King-Kok. *Articulate Silences: Hisaye Yamamoto, Maxine Hong Kingston, Joy Kogawa*. Ithaca, NY: Cornell University Press, 1993.

Choudhry, Sujit. 'Protecting Equality in the Face of Terror: Ethnic and Racial Profiling and s.15 of the *Charter*.' In *The Security of Freedom: Essays on Canada's Anti-Terrorism Bill*, edited by Ronald J. Daniels, Patrick Macklem, and Kent Roach, 367–82. Toronto: University of Toronto Press, 2001.

Chow, Rey. *Writing Diaspora: Tactics of Intervention in Contemporary Cultural Studies*. Bloomington: Indiana University Press, 1993.

Choy, Christine, and Renee Tajima. Directors. *Who Killed Vincent Chin?* 87 min. Filmmakers Library, New York, 1988.

Choy, Wayson. *The Jade Peony*. Vancouver: Douglas and McIntyre, 1995.

Cohn, Werner. 'Persecution of Japanese Canadians and the Political Left in British Columbia, December 1941–March 1942.' *BC Studies* no. 68 (1985–6): 3–22.

Chrisjohn, Roland David, Sherri Lynn Young, and Michael Maraun. *The Circle Game: Shadows and Substance in the Indian Residential School Experience*. Penticton, BC: Theytus Books, 1997.

Chuh, Kandice. 'Transnationalism and Its Past.' *Public Culture* 9 (1996): 93–112.

Churchill, Ward. *Struggle for the Land: Native North American Resistance to Genocide, Ecocide and Colonization*. Winnipeg, MB: Arbeiter Ring Press, 1999.

Collins, Patricia Hill. *Black Feminist Thought: Knowledge, Consciousness, and the Politics of Empowerment*. New York: Routledge, 1991.

Cran, Gregory J. *Negotiating Buck Naked: Doukhobors, Public Policy, and Conflict Resolution*. Vancouver: UBC Press, 2006.

Creef, Elena Tajima. *Imaging Japanese America: The Visual Construction of Citizenship, Nation, and the Body*. New York: New York University Press, 2004.

– 'Re/Orientations: The Politics of Japanese American Representation.' PhD diss., University of California, Santa Cruz, 1994.

Culhane, Dara. *The Pleasure of the Crown: Anthropology, Law and First Nations*. Burnaby, BC: Talonbooks, 1998.

'CWM Finally Makes Changes to JC Exhibit.' *Nikkei Voice* 24, no. 5 (June 2010).

Danieli, Yael. 'Treating Survivors and Children of Survivors of the Nazi Holocaust.' In *Post-Traumatic Therapy and Victims of Violence*, edited by Frank M. Ochberg, 278–94. New York: Brunner/Mazel, 1988.

Daniels, Roger. 'Afterword.' *The Enemy That Never Was: A History of the Japanese Canadians*, by Ken Adachi. Toronto: McClelland and Stewart, 1991.

– 'The Conference Keynote Address: Relocation, Redress, and the Report – A Historical Appraisal.' In *Japanese Americans: From Relocation to Redress*. Revised ed. Edited by Roger Daniels, Sandra C. Taylor, and Harry H.L. Kitano, 3–11. Seattle: University of Washington Press, 1991.

– *Concentration Camps: North America. Japanese in the United States and Canada during World War II*. Malabar, FL: Robert E.Krieger, 1981.

– ed. *Two Reports on Japanese Canadians in World War II*. New York: Arno Press, 1978.

Daniels, Roger, Ken Adachi, and David Iwaasa, eds. *Two Monographs on Japanese Canadians*. New York: Arno Press, 1978.

Daniels, Roger, Sandra C. Taylor, and Harry H.L. Kitano, eds., *Japanese Americans: From Relocation to Redress*. Seattle: University of Washington Press, 1991.

Daniels, Ronald J., Patrick Macklem, and Kent Roach, eds. *The Security of Freedom: Essays on Canada's Anti-Terrorism Bill*. Toronto: University of Toronto Press, 2001.

Das Gupta, Tania. *Racism and Paid Work*. Toronto: Garamond, 1996.

Davey, Frank. 'This Land That Is Like Every Land: *Obasan*.' In *Post-National Arguments: The Politics of the Anglophone-Canadian Novel since 1967*, 100–12. Toronto: University of Toronto Press, 1993.

Davis, Rocio. 'Locating Family: Asian Canadian Historical Revisioning in Linda Ohama's *Obaachan's* [sic] *Garden* and Ann Marie Fleming's *The Magical Life of Long Tack Sam*.' *Journal of Canadian Studies* 42, no. 1 (2008): 1–22.

De Angelis, Maria. 'Testimonies: Internment, Racism and Injustice in Canada.' In *In Justice: Canada, Minorities, and Human Rights*, edited by Roy Miki and Scott McFarlane, 23–6. Winnipeg, MB: National Association of Japanese Canadians, 1996.

Deer, Glen. 'The New Yellow Peril: The Rhetorical Construction of Asian Canadian Identity and Cultural Anxiety in Richmond.' In *Claiming Space: Racialization in Canadian Cities*, edited by Cheryl Teelucksingh, 19–40. Waterloo, ON: Wilfrid Laurier University Press, 2006.

Dempsey, L. James. *Warriors of the King: Prairie Indians in World War I*. Regina, SK: University of Regina, Canadian Plains Research Center, 1999.

Dhamoon, Rita, and Yasmeen Abu-Laban. 'Dangerous (Internal) Foreigners and Nation-Building: The Case of Canada.' *International Political Science Review* 30, no. 163 (2009): 163–83.

Dickason, Olive Patricia. *Canada's First Nations: A History of Founding Peoples from Earliest Times*. 2nd ed. Don Mills, ON: Oxford University Press, 1997.

Di Matteo, Enzo. 'Tories Slam Book on Anti-Racist Schooling.' *Now*, 15–21 October 1998, 24.

Drinnon, Richard. *Keeper of Concentration Camps: Dillon S. Myer and American Racism*. Berkeley: University of California Press, 1987.

Dua, Enakshi. 'Beyond Diversity: Exploring the Ways in which the Discourse of Race has Shaped the Institution of the Nuclear Family.' In *Inequality in Canada: A Reader on the Intersections of Gender, Race, and Class*, edited by Valerie Zawilski and Cynthia Levine-Rasky, 105–25. Don Mills, ON: Oxford University Press, 2005.

Dubrow, Gail, with Donna Graves. *Sento at Sixth and Main: Preserving Landmarks of Japanese American Heritage*. Seattle: University of Washington Press, 2002.

Ducharme, Michel, and Jean-François Constant. 'Introduction: A Project of Rule Called Canada – The Liberal Order Framework and Historical Practice.' Translated by Alexander Macleod. In *Liberalism and Hegemony: Debating the Canadian Liberal Revolution*, edited by Jean-François Constant and Michel Ducharme, 3–32. Toronto: University of Toronto Press, 2009.

Duncan, James. 'Elite Landscapes as Cultural (Re)productions: The Case of Shaughnessy Heights.' In *Inventing Places: Studies in Cultural Geography*, edited by Kay Anderson and Fay Gale, 37–51. Melbourne: Longman Cheshire, 1992.

Eng, David L. 'Out Here and Over There: Queerness and Diaspora in Asian American Studies.' *Social Text* 52/53, 15, nos. 3/4 (1997): 29–50.

Essed, Philomena. *Understanding Everyday Racism*. Newbury Park, CA: Sage Publications, 1991.

– *Everyday Racism: Reports from Women of Two Cultures*. Claremont, CA: Hunter House, 1990.

Esterberg, Kristin G. *Qualitative Methods in Social Research*. Boston: McGraw Hill, 2002.

Fanon, Frantz. *Black Skin, White Masks*. Translated by Charles Lam Markmann. New York: Grove Press, 1967.

Farber, Michael. 'Two Different Worlds.' *Sports Illustrated* 88, no. 3 (January 26, 1998): 66–9.

Feldman, Allen. *Formations of Violence: The Narrative of the Body and Political Terror in Northern Ireland*. Chicago: University of Chicago Press, 1991.

Fellows, Mary Louise, and Sherene Razack. 'The Race to Innocence: Confronting Hierarchical Relations among Women.' *The Journal of Gender, Race and Justice* 1, no. 2 (1998): 335–52.

Felman, Shoshana. 'Forms of Judicial Blindness, or the Evidence of What Cannot Be Seen.' *Critical Inquiry* 23, no. 4 (1997): 738–88.

– 'Education and Crisis, Or the Vicissitudes of Teaching.' In *Testimony: Crises of Witnessing in Literature, Psychoanalysis, and History*, 1–56. New York: Routledge, 1992.

Figley, Charles R. *Trauma and Its Wake: The Study of Post-Traumatic Stress Disorder*. New York: Brunner/Mazel, 1985.

Foucault, Michel. *'Society Must be Defended': Lectures at the Collège de France 1975–1976*, edited by Mauro Bertani and Alessandro Fontana. Translated by David Macey. New York: Picador, 2003.

– *Discipline and Punish: The Birth of the Prison*. Translated by Alan Sheridan. New York: Vintage Books, 1995.

– *The History of Sexuality*. Vol. 1. Translated by Robert Hurley. New York: Vintage Books, 1990.

- 'Confinement, Psychiatry, Prison: A Dialogue with Michel Foucault, David Cooper, Jean-Pierre Faye, Marie-Odile Faye, and Marine Zecca.' In *Politics, Philosophy, Culture: Interviews and Other Writings, 1977–1984*, edited and with an introduction by Lawrence D. Kritzman, 178–210. Translated by Alan Sheridan and Others. New York: Routledge, 1990.
- 'Space, Knowledge, and Power.' In *The Foucault Reader*, edited by Paul Rabinow, 239–56. New York: Pantheon Books, 1984.
- *Power/Knowledge: Selected Interviews and Other Writings, 1972–1977*, edited by Colin Gordon. Translated by Colin Gordon, Leo Marshall, John Mepham, and Kate Soper. New York: Pantheon Books, 1980.

Fournier, Suzanne, and Ernie Crey. *Stolen from Our Embrace: The Abduction of First Nations Children and the Restoration of Aboriginal Communities*. Vancouver: Douglas and McIntyre, 1997.

Frankenberg, Ruth. *White Women, Race Matters: The Social Construction of Whiteness*. Minneapolis: University of Minnesota Press, 1993.

Fry, Joseph. 'Omoide Garden. Neys, Ontario.' Unpublished manuscript, n.d.

Fujita-Rony, Dorothy. '"Destructive Force": Aiko Herzig-Yoshinaga's Gendered Labor in the Japanese American Redress Movement.' *Frontiers* 24, no. 1 (2003): 38–60.

Fukushima, Michael. Director. *Minoru: Memory of Exile*. 18 min. National Film Board of Canada, Montreal, 1992.

Gaffen, Fred. *Forgotten Soldiers*. Penticton, BC: Theytus Books, 1985.

Gagnon, Monika Kin. 'Tender Research: Field Notes from the Nikkei Internment Memorial Centre.' *Canadian Journal of Communication* 31, no. 1 (2006): 215–25. Retrieved 2 January 2008 from http://www.cjc-online.ca/viewarticle.php?id=1743&layout=html.

Geiger-Adams, Andrea. 'Writing Racial Barriers into Law: Upholding BC's Denial of the Vote to Its Japanese Canadian Citizens, *Homma v. Cunningham*, 1902.' In *Nikkei in the Pacific Northwest: Japanese Americans and Japanese Canadians in the Twentieth Century*, edited by Louis Fiset and Gail M. Nomura, 20–43. Seattle: Center for the Study of the Pacific Northwest in association with University of Washington Press, 2005.

Geurts, J. Foreword to *Reflections/Réflections: On the Canadian War Museum/Sur le Musée canadien de la guerre*, 2–5. Ottawa: Canadian War Museum, 2007.

Gilroy, Paul. *Between Camps: Nations, Cultures and the Allure of Race*. London: Routledge, 2000. (Also known as *Against Race: Imagining Political Culture Beyond the Color Line*, Harvard University Press.)
- 'Diaspora and the Detours of Identity.' In *Identity and Difference*, edited by Kathryn Woodward, 300–46. London: Sage in association with the Open University, 1997.

Glenn, Evelyn Nakano. *Issei, Nisei, War Bride: Three Generations of Japanese American Women in Domestic Service*. Philadelphia: Temple University Press, 1986.

Gluck, Sherna Berger, and Daphne Patai, eds. *Women's Words: The Feminist Practice of Oral History*. New York: Routledge, 1991.

Goldberg, David Theo. *The Racial State*. Malden, MA: Blackwell Publishers, 2002.

– *Racist Culture: Philosophy and the Politics of Meaning*. Oxford: Blackwell Publishers, 1993.

Goto, Hiromi. *Chorus of Mushrooms*. Edmonton: NeWest Press, 1994.

Granatstein, J.L., and Gregory A. Johnson. 'The Evacuation of the Japanese Canadians, 1942: A Realist Critique of the Received Version.' In *On Guard for Thee: War, Ethnicity, and the Canadian State, 1939–1945*, edited by Norman Hillmer, Bohdan Kordan, and Lubomyr Luciuk, 101–29. Ottawa: Minister of Supply and Services Canada, 1988.

Greenaway, John Endo. 'Honouring Our People: Stories of the Internment.' *The Bulletin* 81, no. 6 (2009). Retrieved 21 July 2009 from http://jccabulletin-geppo.ca/featured/honouring-our-people-stories-of-the-internment.

– 'Mapping Memory/Reflecting on History: Lemon Creek Map Project and Broken Only at Sky.' *The Bulletin* 81, no. 9 (2009): 2.

Gresko, Jacqueline. 'Roman Catholic Sisters and Japanese Evacuees in British Columbia: A Research Note.' *Journal of the Canadian Church Historical Society* 38, no. 1 (1996): 123–6.

Grewal, Inderpal. 'Autobiographic Subjects and Diasporic Locations: *Meatless Days* and *Borderlands*.' In *Scattered Hegemonies: Postmodernity and Transnational Feminist Practices*, edited by Inderpal Grewal and Caren Kaplan, 231–54. Minneapolis: University of Minnesota Press, 1994.

Grewal, Inderpal, and Caren Kaplan. '*Warrior Marks*: Global Womanism's Neo-Colonial Discourse in a Multicultural Context.' *Camera Obscura* 39 (1996): 4–33.

– 'Introduction: Transnational Feminist Practices and Questions of Postmodernity.' In *Scattered Hegemonies: Postmodernity and Transnational Feminist Practices*, edited by Inderpal Grewal and Caren Kaplan, 1–33. Minneapolis: University of Minnesota Press, 1994.

– eds. *Scattered Hegemonies: Postmodernity and Transnational Feminist Practices*. Minneapolis: University of Minnesota Press, 1994.

Hale, Janet Campbell. *Bloodlines: Odyssey of a Native Daughter*. New York: HarperCollins, 1993.

Handa, Amita. *Of Silk Saris and Mini-Skirts: South Asian Girls Walk the Tightrope of Culture*. Toronto: Women's Press, 2003.

Hanna, Deirdre. 'Andrew Danson's Face Kao Shows Canada's Lack of Honour.' *Now*, 21–27 March 1996, 60.

Haraga, Tamiko. 'My Experiences during the Second World War.' *Nikkei Images: Japanese Canadian National Museum Newsletter* 7, no. 3 (2002): 18–19.

Harris, Richard Colebrook. *Making Native Space: Colonialism, Resistance, and Reserves in British Columbia*. Vancouver: UBC Press, 2002.

Hartman, Saidiya V. *Scenes of Subjection: Terror, Slavery, and Self-Making in Nineteenth-Century America*. New York: Oxford University Press, 1997.

Hashizume, William T. *Japanese Community in Mission: A Brief History 1904–1942*. Scarborough, ON: William T. Hashizume, 2003.

Henriques, Julian, Wendy Hollway, Cathy Urwin, Couze Venn, and Valerie Walkerdine. *Changing the Subject: Psychology, Social Regulation and Subjectivity*. London: Methuen, 1984.

Herman, Judith Lewis. *Trauma and Recovery*. New York: Basic Books, 1992.

Heron, Barbara. *Desire for Development: Whiteness, Gender, and the Helping Imperative*. Waterloo, ON: Wilfrid Laurier University Press, 2007.

Hirabayashi, Gordon. 'Review of *This Is My Own: Letters to Wes and Other Writings on Japanese Canadians, 1941–1948* by Muriel Kitagawa, edited by Roy Miki.' *Canadian Ethnic Studies* 21, no. 3 (1989): 139–41.

Hobsbawm, Eric John. *Industry and Empire: From 1750 to the Present Day*. Harmondsworth, UK: Penguin Books, 1990.

Hoffman, Linda Uyehara. 'A Long Strange Trip It's Been.' In *Bringing It Home*, edited by Brenda Lea Brown, 184–98. Vancouver: Arsenal Pulp Press, 1996.

hooks, bell. 'Eating the Other.' In *Black Looks: Race and Representation*, 21–39. Toronto: Between the Lines, 1992.

– *Yearning: Race, Gender, and Cultural Politics*. Toronto: Between the Lines, 1990.

Horiuchi, Carol Lynne. 'Dislocations and Relocations: The Built Environment of Japanese American Internment.' PhD diss., University of California, Santa Barbara, 2005.

Houston, Jeanne Wakatsuki, and James D. Houston. *Farewell to Manzanar*. Boston: Houghton Mifflin, 1973.

Hume, Christoper. 'Review of Andrew Danson's Photographic Exhibit *Face Kao: Portraits of Japanese Canadians Interned during World War II*.' *Toronto Star*, 11 April 1996, 66.

Iacovetta, Franca. *Such Hardworking People: Italian Immigrants in Postwar Toronto*. Montreal: McGill-Queen's University Press, 1992.

Iacovetta, Franca, Roberto Perin, and Angelo Principe, eds. *Enemies Within: Italian and Other Internees in Canada and Abroad*. Toronto: University of Toronto Press, 1999.

Ibuki, Norm. 'Nikkei Centre, Breaking the Silence.' *The Bulletin* 36, no. 7 (1994): 13–15.

Ichioka, Yuji. 'The Meaning of Loyalty: The Case of Kazumaro Buddy Uno.' *Amerasia Journal* 23, no. 3 (1997): 45–71.

– ed. *Views from Within: The Japanese American Evacuation and Resettlement Study*. Los Angeles: UCLA Asian American Studies Center, 1989.

Ichikawa, Akira. 'A Test of Religious Tolerance: Canadian Government and Jodo Shinshu Buddhism during the Pacific War, 1941–1945.' *Canadian Ethnic Studies* 26, no. 2 (1994): 46–69.

Ifekwunigwe, Jayne O., ed. *'Mixed Race' Studies: A Reader*. London: Routledge, 2004.

Ikebuchi Ketchell, Shelly. 'Carceral Ambivalence: Japanese Canadian "Internment" and the Sugar Beet Programme during WWII.' *Surveillance and Society* 7, no. 1 (2009): 21–35.

Internment and Redress: The Japanese Canadian Experience: A Resource Guide for Social Studies 11 Teachers. Victoria: Queen's Printer for British Columbia, 2005.

Irons, Peter, ed. *Justice Delayed: The Record of the Japanese American Internment Cases*. Middleton, CT: Wesleyan University Press, 1989.

– *Justice at War: The Story of the Japanese American Internment Cases*. New York: Oxford University Press, 1983.

Ishigo, Estelle Peck. *Lone Heart Mountain*. Los Angeles: Communicart, 1989 [1972].

Ito, Roy. *Stories of My People*. Hamilton, ON: S-20 and Nisei Veterans Association, 1994.

– *We Went to War: The Story of the Japanese Canadians Who Served during the First and Second World Wars*. Stittsville, ON: Canada's Wings, 1984.

Iwaasa, David B. 'The Mormons and their Japanese Neighbours.' *Alberta History* 53, no. 1 (2005): 7–22.

Iwama, Marilyn. 'Transgressive Sexualities in the Reconstruction of Japanese Canadian Communities.' *Canadian Literature* 159 (1998): 91–110.

Izumi, Masumi. 'Reclaiming and Reinventing "Powell Street": Reconstruction of the Japanese Canadian Community in Post-World War II Vancouver.' In *Nikkei in the Pacific Northwest: Japanese Americans and Japanese Canadians in the Twentieth Century*, edited by Louis Fiset and Gail M. Nomura, 308–33. Seattle, WA: Center for the Study of the Pacific Northwest in association with University of Washington Press, 2005.

– 'Lessons from History: Japanese Canadians and Civil Liberties in Canada.' *The Journal of American and Canadian Studies* 17 (1999): 1–24.

Jackson, Paul. 'The Enemy Within the Enemy Within: The Canadian Army and Internment Operations during the Second World War.' *Left History* 9, no. 2 (2004): 45–83.

Japanese Canadian Centennial Project. *A Dream of Riches*. Vancouver: The Japanese Canadian Centennial Project, 1978.

Javed, Noor. 'Attacks on Anglers Tied to Racism: Rights Commission Sees Racial Profiling in Verbal, Physical Assaults on Asian Canadian Fishermen.' *The Toronto Star*, 14 May 2008. Retrieved 21 July 2009 from http://www.thestar.com/News/Ontario/article/425178.

Johnston, R.J., et al., eds. *The Dictionary of Human Geography*. Oxford: Blackwell Publishers, 2000.

Kage, Tatsuo. *Nikkei Kanadajin no Tsuihou*. Tokyo: Akashi Shoten, 1998.

– 'Exiled Japanese Canadians.' Translated by Tatsuo Kage and edited by Kathleen Merken. Unpublished manuscript.

Kamboureli, Smaro. 'The Body in Joy Kogawa's *Obasan*: Race, Gender, Sexuality.' In *Scandalous Bodies: Diasporic Literatures in English Canada*, edited by Smaro Kamboureli, 178–221. Don Mills, ON: Oxford University Press, 2000.

Kanbara, Bryce, ed. *Shikata Ga Nai*. Art Exhibition Catalogue. Hamilton, ON: Hamilton Artists' Inc., 1989.

Kanbara, Tameo, Harry Yonekura, and Mits Sumiya. 'The Courage to Resist: Angler and The Nisei Mass Evacuation Group.' In *Homecoming '92 – Where the Heart Is*, edited by Randy Enomoto, with Tatsuo Kage and Victor Ujimoto, 19–27. Winnipeg, MB: National Association of Japanese Canadians, 1993.

Kang, Laura Hyun Yi. 'Compositional Subjects: Enfiguring Asian/American Women.' PhD diss., University of California, Santa Cruz, 1995.

Kaplan, Caren. '"Beyond the Pale": Rearticulating U.S. Jewish Whiteness.' In *Talking Visions: Multicultural Feminism in a Transnational Age*, ed. Ella Shohat, 369–90. New York: New Museum of Art and Cambridge, MA: MIT Press, 1998.

Kawano, Roland M. *Ministry to the Hopelessly Hopeless*. Scarborough, ON: The Japanese Canadian Christian Churches Historical Project, 1997.

Keeshig-Tobias, Lenore. 'Of Hating, Hurting and Coming to Terms with the English Language.' *Canadian Journal of Native Education* 27, no. 1 (2003): 89–100.

Kenna, Kathleen. 'Land of the Free?' *Toronto Star*, 12 July 1998, E5.

Kernerman, Gerald. *Multicultural Nationalism: Civilizing Difference, Constituting Community* Vancouver: UBC Press, 2005.

Kikumura-Yano, Akemi. *Encyclopedia of Japanese Descendants in the Americas: An Illustrated History of the Nikkei*. Walnut Creek, CA: AltaMira Press, 2002.

Kim, Elaine, and Norma Alarcón, eds. *Writing Self, Writing Nation*. Berkeley, CA: Third Woman Press, 1994.

Kirby, Kathleen. 'Re: Mapping Subjectivity: Cartographic Vision and the Limits of Politics.' In *Body Space: Destabilising Geographies of Gender and Sexuality*, edited by Nancy Duncan, 45–56. New York: Routledge, 1996.

Kitagawa, Muriel. *This is My Own: Letters to Wes and Other Writings on Japanese Canadians, 1941–1948*, edited by Roy Miki. Vancouver: Talonbooks, 1985.

Kitano, Harry H.L. *Japanese Americans: The Evolution of a Subculture*. 2nd ed. Englewood Cliffs, NJ: Prentice Hall, 1969.

Kitchin, Rob. '"Out of Place," "Knowing One's Place": Space, Power and the Exclusion of Disabled People.' *Disability and Society* 13, no. 3 (1998): 343–56.

Kiyooka, Roy. *Mothertalk: Life Stories of Mary Kiyoshi Kiyooka*, edited by Daphne Marlatt. Edmonton, AB: NeWest, 1997.

– *Pacific Windows: Collected Poems of Roy K. Kiyooka*, edited by Roy Miki. Burnaby, BC: Talonbooks, 1997.

Knight, Rolf, and Maya Koizumi. *A Man of Our Times: The Life-History of a Japanese-Canadian Fisherman*. Vancouver: New Star Books, 1976.

Knowles, Caroline. *Race and Social Analysis*. London: Sage Publications, 2003.

Kobayashi, Addie. *Exiles in Our Own Country: Japanese Canadians in Niagara*. Richmond Hill, ON: Nikkei Network of Niagara, 1998.

Kobayashi, Allan O. *The Okanagan Boy: Memories of 'The Good Times.'* Brampton, ON: Gprint, Self-published, 2008.

Kobayashi, Audrey. 'Birds of Passage or Squawking Ducks: Writing Across Generations of Japanese-Canadian Literature.' In *Writing Across Worlds: Literature and Migration*, edited by Russell King, John Connell, and Paul White, 216–28. London: Routledge, 1995.

– 'Coloring the Field: Gender, "Race," and the Politics of Fieldwork.' *Professional Geographer* 46, no. 1 (1994): 73–80.

– 'For the Sake of the Children: Japanese/Canadian Workers/Mothers.' In *Women, Work, and Place*, edited by Audrey Kobayashi, 45–72. Montreal: McGill-Queen's University Press, 1994.

– 'Review of *Mutual Hostages: Canadians and Japanese during the Second World War*, by Patricia Roy, J.L. Granatstein, Masako Iino, and Hiroko Takamura.' *BC Studies* 96 (1992–1993): 117–21.

– 'The Japanese-Canadian Redress Settlement and Its Implications for "Race Relations."' *Canadian Ethnic Studies* 24, no. 1 (1992): 1–19.

– *Memories of Our Past: A Brief Walking Tour of Powell Street*. Vancouver: NRC Publishing, 1992.

– 'Structured Feeling: Japanese Canadian Poetry and Landscape.' In *A Few Acres of Snow: Literary and Artistic Images of Canada*, edited by Paul Simpson-Housley and Glen Norcliffe, 243–57. Toronto: Dundurn Press, 1992.

- 'Racism and Law in Canada: A Geographical Perspective.' *Urban Geography* 11, no. 5 (1990): 447–73.
- 'The Historical Context for Japanese-Canadian Uprooting.' In *Social Change and Space: Indigenous Nations and Ethnic Communities in Canada and Finland*, edited by Ludger Müller-Wille, 69–82. Montreal: Northern Studies Program, McGill University, 1989.
- 'A Demographic Profile of Japanese Canadians and Social Implications for the Future.' Canada: Department of the Secretary of State, September 1989. Mimeograph.
- 'The Uprooting of Japanese Canadians After 1941.' *Tribune Juive* 5, no. 1 (1987): 28–35.
- 'Emigration from Kadeima, Japan, 1885–1950: An Analysis of Community and Landscape Change.' PhD diss., UCLA, Los Angeles, 1984.
Kogawa, Joy. *Itsuka*. Toronto: Penguin Books, 1992.
- *Obasan*. 1981. Reprint, Toronto: Penguin Books, 1983.
Komori, Leslie. 'In Her Own Words.' *The Bulletin* 81, no. 9 (2009): 3, 23.
Kuhn, Annett, and Kirsten Emiko McAllister. Introduction to *Locating Memory: Photographic Acts*, edited by Annette Kuhn and Kirsten Emiko McAllister, 1–15. New York: Berghahn Books, 2006.
- eds. *Locating Memory: Photographic Acts*. New York: Berghahn Books, 2006.
Kunimoto, Namiko. 'Intimate Archives: Japanese-Canadian Family Photography, 1939–1949.' *Art History* 27, no. 1 (2004): 129–55.
LaCapra, Dominick. *Representing the Holocaust: History, Theory, Trauma*. Ithaca, NY: Cornell University Press, 1994.
Lackenbauer, P. Whitney, and Craig Leslie Mantle, eds. *Aboriginal Peoples and the Canadian Military: Historical Perspectives*. Kingston, ON: Canadian Defence Academy Press, 2007.
Lang, Catherine. *O-Bon in Chimunesu: A Community Remembered*. Vancouver: Arsenal Pulp Press, 1996.
Langer, Lawrence L. *Admitting the Holocaust*. New York: Oxford University Press, 1995.
- *Holocaust Testimonies: The Ruins of Memory*. New Haven, CT: Yale University, 1991.
Laub, Dori. 'Bearing Witness or the Vicissitudes of Listening.' In *Testimony: Crises of Witnessing in Literature, Psychoanalysis, and History*, edited by Shoshana Felman and Dori Laub, 57–74. New York: Routledge, 1992.
La Violette, Forrest E. *The Canadian Japanese and World War II: A Sociological and Psychological Account*. Toronto: University of Toronto Press, 1948.
- 'Two Years of Japanese Evacuation in Canada.' *Far Eastern Survey* 13, no. 11 (1944): 93–100.

Lawrence, Bonita. *'Real' Indians and Others: Mixed-Blood Urban Native Peoples and Indigenous Nationhood*. Vancouver: UBC Press, 2004.
– 'Rewriting Histories of the Land: Colonization and Indigenous Resistance in Eastern Canada.' In *Race, Space and the Law: Unmapping a White Settler Society*, edited by Sherene H. Razack, 21–46. Toronto: Between the Lines, 2002.
Lawrence, Bonita, and Enakshi Dua. 'Decolonizing Antiracism.' *Social Justice* 32 (2005): 120–43.
Lefebvre, Henri. *The Production of Space*. Translated by Donald Nicholson-Smith. Oxford: Blackwell Publishers, 1991.
Li, Peter S. *Destination Canada: Immigration Debates and Issues*. Don Mills, ON: Oxford University Press, 2002.
– 'The Multiculturalism Debate.' In *Race and Ethnic Relations in Canada*, 2nd ed., edited by Peter S. Li, 148–77. Don Mills, ON: Oxford University Press, 1999.
– ed. *Race and Ethnic Relations in Canada*. 2nd ed. Don Mills, ON: Oxford University Press, 1999.
Lifton, Robert Jay. *The Broken Connection: On Death and the Continuity of Life*. New York: Simon and Schuster, 1979.
Lim, Shirley Geok-Lin. 'Japanese American Women's Life Stories: Maternality in Monica Sone's *Nisei Daughter* and Joy Kogawa's *Obasan*.' *Feminist Studies* 16, no. 2 (1990): 289–312.
Linden, R. Ruth. *Making Stories, Making Selves*. Columbus: Ohio State University Press, 1993.
Lindsey, Colin. 'Profiles of Ethnic Communities in Canada: The Japanese Community in Canada.' Canada: Statistics Canada, 2007. Retrieved 26 July 2009 from http://dsp-psd.pwgsc.gc.ca.ezproxy.library.yorku.ca/collection_2007/statcan/89-621-X/89-621-XIE2007013.pdf.
Liu, Lydia. 'The Female Body and Nationalist Discourse: *The Field of Life and Death* Revisited.' In *Scattered Hegemonies: Postmodernity and Transnational Feminist Practices*, edited by Inderpal Grewal and Caren Kaplan, 37–62. Minneapolis: University of Minnesota Press, 1994.
Loo, Chalsa M. 'An Integrative-Sequential Treatment Model for Posttraumatic Stress Disorder: A Case Study of the Japanese American Internment and Redress.' *Clinical Psychology Review* 13, no. 2 (1993): 89–117.
Loomba, Ania. *Colonialism/Postcolonialism*. London: Routledge, 1998.
Lowe, Lisa. *Immigrant Acts: On Asian American Cultural Politics*. Durham, NC: Duke University Press, 1996.
– *Critical Terrains: French and British Orientalisms*. Ithaca, NY: Cornell University Press, 1991.

Luciuk, Lubomyr. *In Fear of the Barbed Wire Fence: Canada's First National Internment Operations and the Ukrainian Canadians, 1914–1920*. Kingston, ON: Kashtan Press, 2001.

Lustiger-Thaler, Henri. 'Remembering Forgetfully.' In *Re-Situating Identities: The Politics of Race, Ethnicity, and Culture*, edited by Vered Amit-Talai and Caroline Knowles, 190–217. Peterborough, ON: Broadview Press, 1996.

Mackey, Eva. *The House of Difference: Cultural Politics and National Identity in Canada*. Toronto: University of Toronto Press, 2005.

Maclear, Kyo. *Beclouded Visions: Hiroshima-Nagasaki and the Art of Witness*. Albany, NY: State University of New York Press, 1999.

– 'Beclouded Visions: Hiroshima-Nagasaki and the Art of Witness.' MA thesis, University of Toronto, 1996.

– 'The Myth of the "Model Minority." Re-thinking the Education of Asian Canadians.' *Our Schools/Our Selves* 5, no. 3 (1994): 54–76.

– 'Not in So Many Words: Translating Silence Across "Difference."' *Fireweed* 44/45 (1994): 6–11.

Mahtani, Minelle. *Interrogating the Hyphen-Nation: Canadian Multicultural Policy and 'Mixed Race' Identities*. Toronto: Joint Centre of Excellence on Immigration and Settlement, 2004.

Makabe, Tomoko. *The Canadian Sansei*. Toronto: University of Toronto Press, 1998.

– 'Ethnic Group Identity: Canadian-Born Japanese in Metropolitan Toronto.' PhD diss., University of Toronto, 1976.

– *Picture Brides: Japanese Women in Canada*. Translated by Kathleen Chisato Merken. Toronto: Multicultural History Society of Ontario, 1995.

– *Shashinkon no Tsumatachi*. Tokyo: Mirai-sha, 1983.

Malkki, Lisa. 'National Geographic: The Rooting of Peoples and the Territorialization of National Identity Among Scholars and Refugees.' *Cultural Anthropology* 7, no. 1 (1992): 24–44.

Manitoba Japanese Canadian Citizens' Association. *The History of Japanese Canadians in Manitoba*. Winnipeg, MB: Manitoba Japanese Canadian Citizens' Association, 1996.

Marks, Laura U. 'A Deleuzian Politics of Hybrid Cinema.' *Screen* 35, no. 3 (1994): 244–64.

Mass, Amy Iwasaki. 'Psychological Effects of the Camps on Japanese Americans.' In *Japanese Americans: From Relocation to Redress*, edited by Roger Daniels, Sandra C. Taylor, and Harry H.L. Kitano, 159–62. Seattle: University of Washington Press, 1991.

Massey, Doreen. *Space, Place, and Gender*. Minneapolis: University of Minnesota Press, 1994.

Matsuda, Mari, Charles R. Lawrence III, Richard Delgado, and Kimberlè Williams Crenshaw, eds. *Words That Wound: Critical Race Theory, Assaultive Speech and the First Amendment*. Boulder, CO: Westview Press, 1993.

Matsumoto, Valerie J. *Farming the Home Place: A Japanese American Community in California, 1919–1982*. Ithaca, NY: Cornell University Press, 1993.

– 'Japanese American Women during World War II.' In *Unequal Sisters: A Multi-Cultural Reader in U.S. Women's History*, edited by Ellen Carol DuBois and Vicki L. Ruiz, 373–86. New York: Routledge, 1990.

– 'Reflections on Oral History: Research in a Japanese American Community.' In *Feminist Dilemmas in Fieldwork*, edited by Diane L. Wolf, 160–9. Boulder, CO: Westview Press, 1996.

Mawani, Renisa. *Colonial Proximities: Crossracial Encounters and Juridical Truths in British Columbia, 1871–1921*. Vancouver: UBC Press, 2009.

McAllister, Kirsten Emiko. *Terrain of Memory: A Japanese Canadian Memorial Project*. Vancouver: UBC Press, 2010.

– 'A Story of Escape: Family Photographs from Japanese Canadian Internment Camps.' In *Locating Memory: Photographic Acts*, edited by Annette Kuhn and Kirsten Emiko McAllister, 81–112. New York: Berghahn Books, 2006.

– 'Photographs of a Japanese Canadian Internment Camp: Mourning Loss and Invoking a Future.' *Visual Studies* 21, no. 2 (2006): 133–56.

– 'Captivating Debris: Unearthing a World War Two Internment Camp.' *Cultural Values* 5, no. 1 (2001): 97–114.

– 'Held Captive: The Postcard and the Internment Camp.' *West Coast Line: A Journal of Contemporary Writing and Criticism* 35, no. 1 (2001): 20–40.

– 'Remembering Political Violence: The Nikkei Internment Memorial Centre.' PhD diss., Carleton University, Ottawa, ON, 2000.

– 'Narrating Japanese Canadians In and Out of the Canadian Nation: A Critique of the Realist Forms of Representation.' *Canadian Journal of Communications* 21, no. 1 (1999): 79–103.

– 'Confronting Official History with Our Own Eyes: Video-Documentary in the Japanese Canadian Community.' *West Coast Line* 13/14 (1994): 66–84.

– 'Cultural Production and Alternative Political Practices: Dialogic Cultural Forms and the Public Sphere in the Japanese Canadian Community.' MA thesis, Simon Fraser University, 1993.

– 'Asians in Hollywood.' *Cineaction* 30 (1992): 8–13.

McAllister, Kirsten, and Scott McFarlane. 'Reflections on *The Pool*: Interning Japanese Canadian History.' *The Bulletin* 34, no. 12 (1992): 25.

McBride, Michelle. 'The Curious Case of Female Internees.' In *Enemies Within: Italian and Other Internees in Canada and Abroad*, edited by Franca Iacovetta, Roberto Perin, and Angelo Principe, 148–70. Toronto: University of Toronto Press, 2000.

McCann, I. Lisa, and Laurie Anne Pearlman. 'Vicarious Traumatization: A Framework for Understanding the Psychological Effects of Working with Victims.' *Journal of Traumatic Stress* 3, no. 1 (1990): 131–49.

McKittrick, Katherine, and Clyde Woods, eds. *Black Geographies and the Politics of Place*. Toronto: Between the Lines, 2007.

McClintock, Anne. *Imperial Leather: Race, Gender and Sexuality in the Colonial Context*. New York: Routledge.

McClintock, Anne, Aamir Mufti, and Ella Shohat, eds. *Dangerous Liaisons*. Minneapolis: University of Minnesota Press, 1997.

McFarlane, Scott. 'Covering *Obasan* and the Narrative of Internment.' In *Privileging Positions: The Sites of Asian American Studies*, edited by Gary Y. Okihiro, Marilyn Alquizola, Dorothy Fujita Rony, and K. Scott Wong, 401–11. Pullman: Washington State University Press, 1995.

McKay, Ian. 'Canada as a Long Liberal Revolution: On Writing the History of Actually Existing Canadian Liberalisms, 1840s–1940s.' In *Liberalism and Hegemony: Debating the Canadian Liberal Revolution*, edited by Jean-François Constant and Michel Ducharme, 347–452. Toronto: University of Toronto Press, 2009.

– 'The Liberal Order Framework: A Prospectus for a Reconnaissance of Canadian History.' *Canadian Historical Review* 81, no. 4 (2000): 617–45.

McLaughlin, Dennis, and Leslie McLaughlin. *For My Country: Black Canadians on the Field of Honour*. Ottawa: Military Gender Integration and Employment Equity, Department of National Defence, 2004.

Miki, Arthur K. *The Japanese Canadian Redress Legacy: A Community Revitalized*. Winnipeg, MB: National Association of Japanese Canadians, 2003.

Miki, Roy. 'Japanese Canadians in the National Museum.' *Nikkei Voice* 21, no. 5 (2007): 5, 10.

– *Redress: Inside the Japanese Canadian Call for Justice*. Vancouver: Raincoast Books, 2004.

– 'Asiancy: Making Space for Asian Canadian Writing.' In *Broken Entries: Race, Subjectivity, Writing*, 101–24. Toronto: The Mercury Press, 1998.

– *Broken Entries: Race, Subjectivity, Writing*. Toronto: The Mercury Press, 1998.

– *Random Access File*. Red Deer, AB: Red Deer College Press, 1995.

– *Saving Face*. Winnipeg, MB: Turnstone Press, 1991.

– 'Introduction: The Life and Times of Muriel Kitagawa.' In Muriel Kitagawa,

This Is My Own: Letters to Wes and Other Writings on Japanese Canadians 1941–1948, edited by Roy Miki, 1–64. Vancouver: Talonbooks, 1985.

Miki, Roy, and Cassandra Kobayashi. *Justice in Our Time: The Japanese Canadian Redress Settlement*. Vancouver: Talonbooks and Winnipeg, MB: National Association of Japanese Canadians, 1991.

Miki, Roy, and Scott McFarlane, eds. *In Justice: Canada, Minorities, and Human Rights*. Winnipeg, MB: National Association of Japanese Canadians, 1996.

Miles, Robert. 'Apropos the Idea of "Race"… Again.' In *Theories of Race and Racism: A Reader*, edited by Les Back and John Solomos, 125–43. London: Routledge, 2000.

Miller, J.R. *Shingwauk's Vision: A History of Native Residential Schools*. Toronto: University of Toronto Press, 1996.

Million, Diane. 'Telling Secrets: Sex, Power and Narratives in Indian Residential School Histories.' *Canadian Woman Studies* 20, no. 2 (2000): 92–104.

Mirikitani, Janice. *Shedding Silence*. Berkeley, CA: Celestial Arts, 1987.

Mochizuki, Cindy. 'Kanashibari, Shadow Archive.' MFA thesis, Simon Fraser University, 2000.

Mohanram, Radhika. *Black Body: Women, Colonialism, and Space*. Minneapolis: University of Minnesota Press, 1999.

Mohanty, Chandra Talpade. 'Under Western Eyes: Feminist Scholarship and Colonial Discourses.' In *Third World Women and the Politics of Feminism*, edited by Chandra Talpade Mohanty, Ann Russo, and Lourdes Torres, 51–80. Bloomington: Indiana University Press, 1991.

Monture-Angus, Patricia. *Journeying Forward: Dreaming First Nations' Independence*. Halifax: Fernwood, 1999.

– *Thunder in My Soul*. Halifax, NS: Fernwood, 1995.

Moritsugu, Frank. 'In 1976, Some Stores Refused to Sell Michi's Book.' *Nikkei Voice* 13, no. 4 (1999): 5.

Moritsugu, Frank, with the Ghost Town Teachers Historical Society. *Teaching in Canadian Exile: A History of the Schools for Japanese-Canadian Children in British Columbia Detention Camps during the Second World War*. Toronto: The Ghost-Town Teachers Historical Society, 2001.

Morrison, Toni. 'The Site of Memory.' In *Out There: Marginalization and Contemporary Cultures*, edited by Russell Ferguson, Martha Gever, Trinh T. Minh-ha, and Cornel West, 299–305. New York: The New Museum of Contemporary Art and Cambridge, MA: MIT Press, 1990.

– 'Unspeakable Things Unspoken: The Afro-American Presence in American Literature.' *Michigan Quarterly Review* 28, no. 1 (1989): 1–34.

Mufti, Aamir, and Ella Shohat. Introduction to *Dangerous Liaisons*, edited by Anne McClintock, Aamir Mufti, and Ella Shohat, 1–12. Minneapolis: University of Minnesota Press, 1997.

Mura, David. *Where the Body Meets Memory*. New York: Doubleday, 1996.

Murray, Alice Yang. *Historical Memories of the Japanese American Internment and the Struggle for Redress*. Palo Alto, CA: Stanford University Press, 2008.

– '"Silence, No More": The Japanese American Redress Movement, 1942–1992.' PhD diss., Stanford University, 1994.

Nagata, Donna K. 'The Japanese-American Internment: Perceptions of Moral Community, Fairness, and Redress.' *Journal of Social Issues* 46, no. 1 (1990): 133–46.

– *Legacy of Injustice: Exploring the Cross-Generational Impact of the Japanese American Internment*. New York: Plenum Press, 1993.

Nakada, Mark Tadao. *Ryukyu Rheology*. Calgary, AB: disOrientation Chapbooks, 1997.

Nakahara, Yoko Urata. 'Ethnic Identity among Japanese Canadians in Edmonton: The Case of Pre-World War II Immigrants and Their Descendants.' PhD diss., University of Alberta, Edmonton, AB, Spring 1991.

Nakanishi, Donald T. 'Surviving Democracy's "Mistake": Japanese Americans and the Enduring Legacy of Executive Order 9066.' *Amerasia Journal* 19, no. 1 (1993): 7–35.

Nakano, Mei. *Japanese American Women*. Berkeley, CA: Mina Press and San Francisco: National Japanese American Historical Society, 1990.

Nakano, Takeo Ujo, with Leatrice Nakano. *Within the Barbed Wire Fence*. Toronto: University of Toronto Press, 1980.

Nakayama, Gordon G. *Issei: Stories of Japanese Canadian Pioneers*. Toronto: NC Press, 1984.

National Association of Japanese Canadians. 'JCs Re-victimized, Canadians Misled.' *Nikkei Voice* 24, 9 (November 2010): 1, 3.

– *The Case for Redress*. Toronto: National Association for Japanese Canadians, n.d.

– *Economic Losses of Japanese Canadians after 1941*. Winnipeg, MB: National Association of Japanese Canadians, 1985.

Neary, Peter. 'Zennosuke Inouye's Land: A Canadian Veterans Affairs Dilemma.' *Canadian Historical Review* 85, no. 3 (2004): 423–50.

Nelson, Jennifer J. *Razing Africville: A Geography of Racism*. Toronto: University of Toronto Press, 2008.

'Nikkei Internment Memorial Centre opening in New Denver.' *The Bulletin* 36, no. 8 (1994): 17.

Nishi, Susan. 'The Neighbourhood and Local Heroes.' *Powell Street Festival* 5, no. 1 (1999), n.p.

Nishiguchi, Gabrielle. '"Reducing the Numbers": The "Transportation" of the Canadian Japanese (1941–1947).' MA thesis, Carleton University, 1993.

Nora, Pierre. 'Between Memory and History: *Les Lieux de Mémoire.'* *Representa-tions* 26 (1989): 7–25.

Nunoda, Peter. 'A Community in Transition and Conflict: The Japanese Cana-dians, 1935–1951.' PhD diss., University of Manitoba, 1991.

O'Brien, David J., and Stephan S. Fugita. *The Japanese American Experience.* Bloomington and Indianapolis: Indiana University Press, 1991.

Ochberg, Frank M., ed. *Post-Traumatic Therapy and Victims of Violence.* New York: Brunner/Mazel, 1988.

Ohama, Baco. *Red Poems of Rain and Voice.* Montreal: Self-published, 1995.

– *Chiraishi. Stories from the Garden.* Vancouver: Self-published, 1997.

Ohama, Linda. Director. *Obāchan's Garden.* 94 min. National Film Board of Canada, Toronto, 2001.

– Director. *The Last Harvest.* Harvest Productions, Vancouver, 1993. VHS.

Oikawa, Mona. 'Re-Mapping Histories Site by Site: Connecting the Intern-ment of Japanese Canadians to the Colonization of Aboriginal Peoples in Canada.' In *Aboriginal Connections to Race, Environment and Traditions,* edited by Rick Riewe and Jill Oakes, 17–26. Winnipeg, MB: Aboriginal Issues Press, University of Manitoba, 2006.

– 'Cartographies of Violence: Women, Memory and the Subject(s) of the "In-ternment."' In *Race, Space and the Law: Unmapping a White Settler Society,* edited by Sherene H. Razack, 72–98. Toronto: Between the Lines, 2002.

– 'Cartographies of Violence: Women, Memory and the Subjects of the "In-ternment."' *Canadian Journal of Law and Society* 15, no. 2 (2000): 39–69.

– 'Cartographies of Violence: Women, Memory, and the Subject(s) of the "In-ternment."' PhD diss., University of Toronto, 1999.

– 'For Shizu.' Translated by Deirdre Tanaka and Yusuke Tanaka. *Nikkei Voice* 10, no. 1 (1996): 14.

– 'For Shizu.' *Fireweed* 28 (1989): 19.

– '"Driven to Scatter Far and Wide": The Forced Resettlement of Japanese Ca-nadians to Southern Ontario, 1944–1949.' MA thesis, University of Toronto, 1986.

Oiwa, Keibo. *Stone Voices: Wartime Writings of Japanese Canadian Issei.* Montreal: Vehicule Press, 1991.

Okamura, Raymond Y. 'The American Concentration Camps: A Cover-Up Through Euphemistic Terminology.' *The Journal of Ethnic Studies* 10, no. 3 (1982): 95–109.

Okano, Haruko. *Come Spring: Journey of a Sansei.* Vancouver: Gallerie, 1992.

Okazaki, Robert K. *The Nisei Mass Evacuation Group and POW Camp 101 Angler, Ontario.* Translated by Jean M. Okazaki and Curtis T. Okazaki. Scarborough, ON: Self-published, 1996.

Okazaki, Stephen. Director. *Days of Waiting*. 74 min. Mouchette Films, United States, 1989. VHS/DVD.

Okihiro, Gary. *Cane Fires: The Anti-Japanese Movement in Hawaii, 1865–1945*. Philadelphia: Temple University Press, 1991.

Okihiro, Gary Y., and Joan Myers. *Whispered Silences: Japanese Americans and World War II*. Seattle: University of Washington Press, 1996.

Omatsu, Maryka. *Bittersweet Passage: Redress and the Japanese Canadian Experience*. Toronto: Between the Lines, 1992.

Omi, Michael, and Howard Winant. *Racial Formation in the United States: From the 1960s to the 1980s*. New York: Routledge, 1991.

Onodera, Midi. Director. *Displaced View*. 52 min. Mcano Film Artists Inc., Toronto, 1988. VHS.

Palmer, Howard. 'Commentary.' In *On Guard for Thee*, edited by Norman Hillmer, Bohdan Kordan, and Lubomyr Luciuk, 233–40. Ottawa: Ministry of Supply and Services, 1988.

Park, Hijin. 'Constituting "Asian Women": Canadian Gendered Orientalism and Multicultural Nationalism in an Age of "Asia Rising."' PhD diss., University of Toronto, 2007.

– 'Incorporating Ji-Won Park into the Canadian Nation: The Good Girl, the Monster, and the Noble Savage.' *Han Kŭt: Critical Art and Writing by Korean Canadian Women*, by Korean Canadian Women's Anthology Collective, 77–93. Toronto: Inanna Publications and Education, 2007.

Perry, Adele. 'Women, Racialized People, and the Making of the Liberal Order.' In *Liberalism and Hegemony: Debating the Canadian Liberal Revolution*, edited by Jean-François Constant and Michel Ducharme, 274–97. Toronto: University of Toronto Press, 2009.

– 'Whose Sisters and What Eyes?' In *Sisters or Strangers? Immigrant, Ethnic, and Racialized Women in Canadian History*, edited by Marlene Epp, Franca Iacovetta, and Frances Swyripa, 49–70. Toronto: University of Toronto Press, 2004.

– *On the Edge of Empire: Gender, Race, and the Making of British Columbia, 1849–1871*. Toronto: University of Toronto Press, 2001.

Phillips, Richard. *Mapping Men and Empire: A Geography of Adventure*. New York: Routledge, 1997.

Pierson, Ruth Roach. *'They're Still Women After All': The Second World War and Canadian Womanhood*. Toronto: McClelland and Stewart, 1986.

Poy, Vivienne. 'The Role Played by Chinese-Canadians in WWII – With Reference to the Life of Kam Len Douglas Sam.' Paper presented at the annual meeting of the Association for Asian American Studies, Toronto, ON, 29 March 2001. Retrieved 25 June 2009 from http://sen.parl.gc.ca/vpoy/

english/Special_Interests/speeches/Speech%20-%20AAAS%20,Toronto
.htm.

Pratt, Anna, and Mariana Valverde. 'From Deserving Victims to "Masters of Confusion": Redefining Refugees in the 1990s.' *Canadian Journal of Sociology* 27, no. 2 (2002): 135–61.

Pratt, Mary Louise. *Imperial Eyes: Travel Writing and Transculturation*. London: Routledge, 1992.

Rao, G. 'Inventing Enemies: Project Thread and Canadian "Security."' *Canadian Dimension* 38 (2004): 9–11.

Razack, Sherene H. *Casting Out: The Eviction of Muslims from Western Law and Politics*. Toronto: University of Toronto Press, 2008.

– *Dark Threats and White Knights: The Somalia Affair, Peacekeeping, and the New Imperialism*. Toronto: University of Toronto Press, 2004.

– 'Gendered Racial Violence and Spatialized Justice: The Murder of Pamela George.' In *Race, Space and the Law: Unmapping a White Settler Society*, edited by Sherene H. Razack, 121–56. Toronto: Between the Lines, 2002.

– 'Introduction: When Place Becomes Race.' In *Race, Space and the Law: Unmapping a White Settler Society*, edited by Sherene H. Razack, 72–98. Toronto: Between the Lines, 2002.

– ed. *Race, Space, and the Law: Unmapping a White Settler Society*. Toronto: Between the Lines, 2002.

– *Looking White People in the Eye: Gender, Race, and Culture in Courtrooms and Classrooms*. Toronto: University of Toronto Press, 1998.

– 'Race, Space and Prostitution: The Making of the Bourgeois Subject.' *Canadian Journal of Women and the Law* 10, no. 2 (1998): 338–76.

– 'The Perils of Talking About Culture: Schooling Research on South and East Asian Students.' *Race, Gender and Class* 2, no. 3 (1995): 67–82.

– 'What is to Be Gained by Looking White People in the Eye? Culture, Race, and Gender in Cases of Sexual Violence.' *Signs* 19, no. 4 (1994): 894–923.

– 'Collective Rights and Women: "The Cold Game of Equality Staring."' *The Journal of Human Justice* 4, no. 1 (1992): 1–11.

– *Canadian Feminism and the Law*. Toronto: Second Story Press, 1991.

Renan, Ernest. 'What is a Nation?' In *Nation and Narration*, edited by Homi K. Bhabha, 8–22. London: Routledge, 1990.

Ristock, Janice L., and Joan Pennell. *Community Research as Empowerment: Feminist Links, Postmodern Interruptions*. Don Mills, ON: Oxford University Press, 1996.

Roach, Ken. 'Better Late Than Never? The Canadian Review of the *Anti-terrorism Act*.' *IRPP Choices* 13, no. 5 (2007): 1–40.

Rochon, Lisa. 'Devoted to "Driving a Nail of Gold."' *Globe and Mail*, 17 April 2010, R7.

Rose, Gillian. *Feminism and Geography: The Limits of Geographical Knowledge.* Cambridge, UK: Polity Press, 1993.

Rogers, Kim Lacy. 'Trauma Redeemed: The Narrative Construction of Social Violence.' In *Interactive Oral History Interviewing*, edited by Eva M. McMahan and Kim Lacy Rogers, 31–46. Hillsdale, NJ: Lawrence Erlbaum Associates, 1994.

Roy, Patricia E. *The Oriental Question: Consolidating a White Man's Province, 1914–1941.* Vancouver: UBC Press, 2003.

Roy, Patricia, J.L. Granatstein, Masako Iino, and Hiroko Takamura. *Mutual Hostages: Canadians and Japanese during the Second World War.* Toronto: University of Toronto Press, 1990.

Ruck, Calvin W. *Canada's Black Battalion: No. 2 Construction, 1916–1920.* Dartmouth, NS: Society for Protection and Preservation of Black Culture in Nova Scotia, 1986.

Said, Edward. *Culture and Imperialism.* New York: Vintage Books, 1994.

– *Orientalism.* New York: Vintage Books, 1979.

Sakamoto, Kerri. 'Surviving History: Kerri Sakamoto interviewed by Pilar Cuder-Dominguez.' *The Journal of Commonwealth Literature* 41, no. 3 (2006): 137–43.

– *The Electrical Field.* Toronto: Alfred A. Knopf, 1998.

Sangster, Joan. 'Telling Our Stories: Feminist Debates and the Use of Oral History.' *Women's History Review* 3, no. 1 (1994): 5–28.

Schick, Carol. 'Keeping the Ivory Tower White: Discourses of Racial Domination.' In *Inequality in Canada: A Reader on the Intersections of Gender, Race, and Class*, edited by Valerie Zawilski and Cynthia Levine-Rasky, 208–20. Don Mills, ON: Oxford University Press, 2005.

Scott, Joan W. 'Experience.' In *Feminists Theorize the Political*, edited by Judith Butler and Joan W. Scott, 22–40. New York: Routledge, 1992.

Shadd, Adrienne. 'Where are you *Really* from? Notes of an "Immigrant" from North Buxton, Ontario.' *Talking about Identity: Encounters in Race, Ethnicity, and Language*, edited by Carl James and Adrienne Shadd, 10–16. Toronto: Between the Lines, 2001.

Shibata, Yuko. 'Snapshot of Japanese Canadians.' *International Examiner*, 31 May 2004, 8.

Shields, Rob. *Places on the Margin: Alternative Geographies of Modernity.* London: Routledge, 1991.

Shikatani, Gerry. *Selected Poems and Texts/Nineteen Seventy-Three.* Toronto: Aya Press, 1989.

Shikatani, Gerry, and David Aylward, eds. *Paper Doors*. Toronto: Coach House Press, 1981.

Shimabukuro, Robert Sadamu. *Born in Seattle: The Campaign for Japanese American Redress*. Seattle: University of Washington Press, 2001.

Shimizu, Henry. *Images of Internment. A Bitter-Sweet Memoir in Words and Images: Life in the New Denver Internment Camp, 1942–1946*. Victoria: Ti-Jean Press, 2008.

Shimizu, Yon. *The Exiles: An Archival History of the World War II Japanese Road Camps in British Columbia and Ontario*. Wallaceburg, ON: Shimizu Consulting and Publishing, 1993.

Shiomi, R.A. 'Crossing Borders.' *Canadian Theatre Review* 56 (1988): 16–19.

– *Yellow Fever*. Toronto: Playwrights Union of Canada, 1984.

Simon, Roger I. 'The Pedagogy of Commemoration and Formation of Collective Memories.' *Educational Foundations* 8, no. 1 (1994): 5–24.

– 'Forms of Insurgency in the Production of Popular Memories: The Columbus Quincentary and the Pedagogy of Counter-Commemoration.' *Cultural Studies* 7, no. 1 (1993): 73–88.

Simon, Roger I., Sharon Rosenberg, and Claudia Eppert, eds. *Between Hope and Despair: Pedagogy and the Representation of Historical Trauma*. Lanham, MD: Rowman and Littlefield, 2000.

Simon, Roger I., and Claudia Eppert. 'Remembering Obligation: Pedagogy and the Witnessing of Testimony of Historical Trauma.' *Canadian Journal of Education* 22, no. 2 (1997): 175–91.

Simon, Roger I., and Wendy Armitage-Simon. 'Teaching Risky Stories: Remembering Mass Destruction through Children's Literature.' *English Quarterly* 28, no. 1 (1995): 27–31.

Smith, Irene. 'Hastings Park Hospital – Memories of Nurse Irene (Nee Anderson) Smith.' *The Bulletin* 38, no. 4 (1996): 24.

Smith, Linda Tuhiwai. *Decolonizing Methodologies: Research and Indigenous Peoples*. London: Zed Books, 1999.

Soja, Edward W. *Postmodern Geographies: The Reassertion of Space in Critical Social Theory*. London: Verso, 1989.

Sone, Monica. *Nisei Daughter*. Seattle: University of Washington Press, 1982.

Spivak, Gayatri Chakravorty. 'Subaltern Talk. Interview with the Editors (1993–94).' In *The Spivak Reader*, edited by Donna Landry and Gerald Maclean, 287–308. New York: Routledge, 1996.

– 'Can the Subaltern Speak?' In *Marxism and the Interpretation of Culture*, edited by Cary Nelson and Lawrence Grossberg, 271–313. Urbana: University of Illinois Press, 1988.

Stacey, Judith. 'Can There Be a Feminist Ethnography?' In *Women's Words: The Feminist Practice of Oral History*, edited by Sherna Berger Gluck and Daphne Patai, 111–19. New York: Routledge, 1991.

Staeheli, Lynn A. 'Place.' In *A Companion to Political Geography*, edited by John Agnew, Katharyne Mitchell, and Gerard Toal, 158–70. Malden, MA: Blackwell, 2003.

Stainsby, Mia. 'I Learned Russian and English and Lost My Ability to Speak Japanese.' *The Vancouver Sun*, 3 January 1994, C4.

Stasiulis, Daiva. 'Feminist Intersectional Theorizing.' In *Inequality in Canada: A Reader on the Intersections of Gender, Race, and Class*, edited by Valerie Zawilski and Cynthia Levine-Rasky, 36–62. Don Mills, ON: Oxford University Press, 2005.

Stasiulus, Daiva, and Nira Yuval-Davis. 'Introduction: Beyond Dichotomies – Gender, Race, Ethnicity and Class in Settler Societies.' In *Unsettling Settler Societies*, edited by Daiva Stasiulus and Nira Yuval-Davis, 1–38. Thousand Oaks, CA: Sage Publications, 1995.

Stoler, Ann. *Race and the Education of Desire*. Durham, NC: Duke University Press, 1995.

Storr, Merl. 'The Sexual Reproduction of "Race": Bisexuality, History and Racialization.' In *The Bisexual Imaginary: Representation, Identity and Desire*, edited by Bi Academic Intervention, 73–89. London: Cassell, 1997.

Sturken, Marita. 'Absent Images of Memory: Remembering and Reenacting the Japanese Internment.' *Positions: East Asia Cultures Critique* 5, no. 3 (1997): 687–707.

– *Tangled Memories: The Vietnam War, the AIDS Epidemic, and the Politics of Remembering*. Berkeley: University of California Press, 1997.

Sugiman, Pamela. '"A Million Hearts from Here": Japanese Canadian Mothers and Daughters and the Lessons of War.' *Journal of American Ethnic History* 26, no. 4 (2007): 50–68.

– 'Memories of Internment: Narrating Japanese Canadian Women's Life Stories.' *Canadian Journal of Sociology* 29, no. 3 (2004): 359–88.

– 'Passing Time, Moving Memories: Interpreting Wartime Narratives of Japanese Canadian Women.' *Histoire Sociale/Social History* 37, no. 73 (2004): 51–79.

Summerby, Janice. *Native Soldiers, Foreign Battlefields*. Ottawa: Veterans Affairs Canada, 1993.

Sunahara, Ann Gomer. 'Legislative Roots of Injustice: The Abuse of Emergency Law in Canada: Is it Inevitable?' In *In Justice: Canada, Minorities, and Human Rights*, edited by Roy Miki and Scott McFarlane, 7–22. Winnipeg, MB: National Association of Japanese Canadians, 1996.

– *The Politics of Racism: The Uprooting of Japanese Canadians during the Second World War*. Toronto: James Lorimer, 1981.
– 'Deportation: The Final Solution to Canada's "Japanese Problem."' In *Ethnicity, Power and Politics in Canada*, edited by Jorgen Dahlie and Tissa Fernando, 255–78. Toronto: Methuen, 1981.

Suzuki, Aiko. *Lyra*. (Fibre Suspension Installation.) Commissioned by the Metropolitan Toronto Reference Library, 1981.

Suzuki, Aiko, ed. *About Japanese Canadians, Resource Listing III*, revised by David Fujino. Toronto: Toronto Nikkei Archive and Resource Centre, 1996.
– ed. *Japanese Canadians in the Arts: A Directory of Professionals*. Toronto: SAC/rist, 1994.

Suzuki, David. 'Lessons My Father Taught Me Are Worth Sharing.' Retrieved 24 January 2010 from www.davidsuzuki.org/about_us/Dr_David_Suzuki/Article_Archives/weekly08270802.asp.
– *David Suzuki: The Autobiography*. Vancouver: Douglas and McIntyre, 2006.
– *Metamorphosis*. Toronto: General, 1988.

Szasz, Eva. Director. *Cherished Memories and Lost Years*. Filmstrip, Filmstrip Notes, and Audiocassettes. Written and narrated by Toshi Oikawa and Nobuko Oikawa. National Film Board of Canada and National Museum of Man, Montreal, 1980.

Tajiri, Rea. Director. *History and Memory: For Akiko and Takashige*. 32 min. New York, Women Make Films, 1991. VHS/DVD.

Takagi, Dana Y. 'Maiden Voyage: Excursion into Sexuality and Identity Politics in Asian America.' In *Asian American Sexualities*, edited by Russell Leong, 21–35. New York: Routledge, 1996.
– *The Retreat from Race: Asian-American Admissions and Racial Politics*. New Brunswick, NJ: Rutgers University Press, 1992.
– 'Personality and History: Hostile Nisei Women.' In *Reflections on Shattered Windows*, edited by Gary Y. Okihiro, Shirley Hune, Arthur A. Hansen, John M. Liu, 184–92. Seattle: Washington State University Press, 1988.

Takaki, Ronald. *Strangers from a Different Shore: A History of Asian Americans*. New York: Penguin, 1989.

Takashima, Shizuye. *A Child in Prison Camp*. Montreal: Tundra Books, 1971.

Takata, Toyo. *Nikkei Legacy: The Story of Japanese Canadians from Settlement to Today*. Toronto: NC Press, 1983.

Takezawa, Yasuko I. *Breaking the Silence: Redress and Japanese American Ethnicity*. Ithaca, NY: Cornell University Press, 1995.

Tator, Carol, and Frances Henry. *Racial Profiling in Canada: Challenging the Myth of a Few Bad Apples*. Toronto: University of Toronto Press, 2006.

Taylor, Mary. 'The Japanese-Canadian Community Today.' *A Black Mark: The Japanese Canadians in World War II*, 195–201. Ottawa: Oberon Press, 2004.

Teelucksingh, Cheryl, ed. *Claiming Space: Racialization in Canadian Cities.* Waterloo, ON: Wilfrid Laurier University Press, 2006.

Terr, Lenore. *Unchained Memories.* New York: Basic Books, 1994.

Thobani, Sunera. *Exalted Subjects: Studies in the Making of Race and Nation in Canada.* Toronto: University of Toronto Press, 2007.

Thomas, Dorothy Swaine, and Richard S. Nishimoto. *The Spoilage: Japanese American Evacuation and Resettlement.* Berkeley: University of California Press, 1946.

Thompson, Paul. 'Pioneering the Life Story Method.' *International Journal of Social Research Methodology* 7, no. 1 (2004): 81–4.

Thomson, Grace Eiko. 'National Association of Japanese Canadians President's Report: JC Community Loses a Good Friend.' *Nikkei Voice* 22, no. 2 (2008): 10.

– 'National Association of Japanese Canadians President's Message July 2008.' 25 June 2008. Retrieved 15 February 2009 from http://www.najc.ca/community-news/presidents-message-july/.

– *Shashin: Japanese Canadian Photography to 1942.* Exhibition Catalogue. Burnaby, BC: Japanese Canadian National Museum, 2005.

– 'Archival Photographs From Cumberland BC: With an Afterword.' *West Coast Line: A Journal of Contemporary Writing & Criticism* 38, no. 1 (2004): 57–89.

Toronto Star. Editorial: 'Chrétien's Quips Inspire No Confidence.' 21 October 1998, A20.

– Editorial: '"We Are the Israelites on the Move."' 20 November 1997, A28.

Trinh, T. Min-ha. *Woman, Native, Other.* Bloomington: Indiana University Press, 1989.

Truly, Ruby. Director. *With Our Own Eyes: A Trip to Lemon Creek.* 35 min. Ruby Truly, Vancouver, 1993.

Uno, Kathleen S. 'The Death of "Good Wife, Wise Mother?"' In *Postwar Japan as History*, edited by Andrew Gordon, 293–322. Berkeley: University of California Press, 1993.

Von Hassel, Malve. 'Issei Women: Silences and Fields of Power.' *Feminist Studies* 19, no. 3 (1993): 549–69.

Wakayama, Tamio. *Kikyō: Coming Home to Powell Street*, oral histories edited by Linda Uyehara Hoffman. Madeira Park, BC: Harbour Publishing, 1992.

Walcott, Rinaldo. *Black Like Who? Writing Black Canada.* 2nd rev. ed. Toronto: Insomniac Press, 2003.

Walker, James W. 'Race and Recruitment in World War I: Enlistment of Visible
    Minorities in the Canadian Expeditionary Force.' *Canadian Historical Review*
    70, no. 1 (1989): 1–26.
Ward, W. Peter. *White Canada Forever: Popular Attitudes and Public Policy toward
    Orientals in British Columbia.* 3rd ed. Montreal: McGill-Queen's University
    Press, 2002.
– *The Japanese in Canada.* Ottawa: Canadian Historical Association, 1982.
Ware, Vron. *Beyond the Pale: White Women, Racism and History.* London: Verso,
    1992.
Watada, Terry. *Daruma Days.* Vancouver: Ronsdale Press, 1997.
– *Bukkyo Tozen: A History of Jodo Shinshu Buddhism in Canada, 1905–1995.*
    Toronto: HpF Press and the Toronto Buddhist Church, 1996.
Weedon, Chris. *Feminist Practice and Poststructuralist Theory.* Oxford: Basil
    Blackwell, 1987.
Weglyn, Michi. *Years of Infamy: The Untold Story of America's Concentration
    Camps.* New York: William Morrow, 1976.
Wheeler, Anne. Interview by Vicki Gabereau. CBC Radio, *The Vicki Gabereau
    Show,* 7 December 1995.
– Director. *The War Between Us.* 93 min. Atlantis Films/Troika Films, Canada,
    1995.
Whitaker, Reg, and Gregory S. Kealey. 'A War on Ethnicity? The RCMP and
    Internment.' In *Enemies Within: Italian and Other Internees in Canada and
    Abroad,* edited by Franca Iacovetta, Roberto Perin, and Angelo Principe,
    128–47. Toronto: University of Toronto Press, 2000.
White, Hayden. 'The Modernist Event.' In *The Persistence of History,* edited by
    Vivian Sobchack, 17–38. New York: Routledge, 1996.
Wiener, Nan, and Morley Gunderson. *Pay Equity: Issues, Options and Experi-
    ences.* Toronto: Butterworths, 1990.
Wong, Sau-ling Cynthia. *Reading Asian American Literature.* Princeton, NJ:
    Princeton University Press, 1993.
Woodward, Kathryn. 'Concepts of Identity and Difference.' In *Identity and Dif-
    ference,* edited by Kathryn Woodward, 8–61. London: Sage Publications in
    association with Open University, 1997.
Yamada, Mitsuye. *Desert Run: Poems and Stories.* Latham, NY: Kitchen Table,
    1988.
– 'Invisibility is an Unnatural Disaster: Reflections of an Asian American
    Woman.' In *This Bridge Called My Back: Writings by Radical Women of Color,*
    edited by Cherríe Moraga and Gloria Anzaldúa, 35–40. Watertown, MA:
    Persephone Press, 1981.
– *Camp Notes.* San Lorenzo, CA: Shameless Hussy Press, 1976.

Yamamoto, Hisaye. *Seventeen Syllables and Other Stories*. Latham, NY: Kitchen Table, 1988.

Yamamoto, Traise. *Masking Selves, Making Subjects: Japanese American Women, Identity, and the Body*. Berkeley: University of California Press, 1999.

Yeğenoğlu, Meyda. *Colonial Fantasies: Towards a Feminist Reading of Orientalism*. Cambridge: Cambridge University Press, 1998.

Yesaki, Mitsuo. *Steveston Cannery Row: An Illustrated History*. Vancouver: Peninsula Publishing, 2005.

– *Sutebusuton: A Japanese Village on the British Columbia Coast*. Vancouver: Peninsula Publishing, 2003.

– *Watari-dori = (Birds of Passage)*. Vancouver: Peninsula Publishing, 2005.

– *A Historical Guide to the Steveston Waterfront*. Vancouver: Self-published, n.d.

Yogi, Stan. 'Yearning for the Past: The Dynamics of Memory in Sansei Internment Poetry.' In *Memory and Cultural Politics*, edited by Amrijit Singh and Joseph T. Skerritt, 245–64. Boston: Northeastern University Press, 1996.

Yoneyama, Yutaka Harold. *An Evacuee's Memoir: An Account from the Writer's Own Recollection*. Toronto: Pro Familia Publishing, 2008.

Young, Charles, and Helen R.Y. Reid. *The Japanese Canadians*. Toronto: University of Toronto Press, 1938.

Government Sources

Canada. *An Act to Amend and Consolidate the Laws Respecting Indians*, R.S.C. (1876), c. 18, ss. 1–100.

Canada. British Columbia Security Commission. *Removal of Japanese from Protected Areas: Report of the British Columbia Security Commission*. Vancouver: BCSC, 1942.

Canada. Department of Labour. *Report of the Department of Labour on the Re-Establishment of the Japanese in Canada, 1944–1946*. Ottawa: Department of Labour, 1947.

– *Report of the Department of Labour on the Administration of Japanese Affairs in Canada, 1942–1944*. Ottawa: Department of Labour, 1944.

– Deputy Minister of Labour. *Report on Mission to England to Confer with the British Authorities on the Subject of Immigration to Canada from the Orient and Immigration from India in Particular*, by W.L. Mackenzie King, No. 36a. Ottawa: S.E. Dawson, 1908.

Canada. Department of Transport, Meteorological Division. *Monthly Record Observations in Canada and Newfoundland, January 1943*. Toronto: Department of Transport, Meteorological Division, 1943.

Canada. Dominion Bureau of Statistics. *Ninth Census of Canada, 1951*. Vol. 10. Ottawa: Edmond Cloutier, 1956.

– *Eighth Census of Canada, 1941*. Vol. 3. Ottawa: Edmond Cloutier, 1946.

Canada. House of Commons. *Debates*. Ottawa: Queen's Printer, 1944.

Canada. Statistics Canada. 'Study: Rising Education of Women and the Gender Earnings Gap.' *The Daily*, 12 June 2007. Retrieved 28 December 2007 from http://www.statcan.ca/Daily/English/070612/d070612b.htm.

– 'Canada's Ethnocultural Mosaic, 2006 Census: National PictureMixed Unions Involving Visible Minorities on the Rise.' Retrieved 10 February 2010 from http://www12.statcan.ca/census-recensement/2006/as-sa/97-562/p9-eng.cfm.

– 'Population Groups (28), Age Groups (8), Sex (3) and Selected Demographic, Cultural, Labour Force, Educational and Income Characteristics (309), for the Total Population of Canada, Provinces, Territories, Census Metropolitan Areas and Census Agglomerations, 2006 Census – 20% Sample Data.' Ottawa: Statistics Canada, 2006. Retrieved 25 September 2010 from http://www12.statcan.gc.ca/census-recensement/2006/dp-pd/tbt/Rp-eng.cfm?TABID=1&LANG=E&APATH=3&DETAIL=0&DIM=0&FL=A&FREE=0&GC=0&GK=0&GRP=1&PID=97615&PRID=0&PTYPE=88971,97154&S=0&SHOWALL=0&SUB=0&Temporal=2006&THEME=80&VID=0&VNAMEE=&VNAMEF.

– *Census 2006*. Ottawa: Statistics Canada, 2006.

– *Census 1991, Ethnic Origin*. Ottawa: Ministry of Industry, Science and Technology, 1993.

Canada. Statutes of Canada, 1914, 5 Geo.V, c. 2.

Canada. Statutes of Canada, 1945, Bill C-15, *National Emergency Transitional Powers Act*, 1st sess., 20th Parliament, 1945 (assented to 18 December 1945).

Ontario. Ontario Human Rights Commission. 'Fishing Without Fear: Follow-Up Report on the Inquiry into Assaults on Asian Canadian Anglers,' 2009. Retrieved 21 July 2009 from http://www.ohrc.on.ca/en/resources/discussion_consultation/finalangler?page=finalangler-Contents.html.

United States Bureau of the Census. *Population Hawaii. 1940*. Prepared under the supervision of Dr Leon E. Truesdell, Chief Statistician for Population. Washington, DC, 1942. Retrieved 23 December 2007 from http://www2.census.gov/prod2/decennial/documents/19900609ch04.pdf.

Index

100-mile radius restricted/exclusion zone: children expelled from, 204–7; detailed accounting of Japanese Canadians, 22; dismantling of Japanese Canadian community, 237; distribution of population, xix; mapping of material and social, 13; and medical care, 209–11; number forcibly removed, 3; Order-in-Council P.C. 365, 103; spatial configuration of Internment, 99–102; statistics of, 3–4; technology of expulsion, 97. *See also* British Columbia Security Commission (BCSC)

ability: categorization criterion, 126. *See also* categorization

Abu-Laban, Yasmeen, 303

academics and scholars: depiction of the subjects of Internment, 56; ethical research conduct, 332n32; euphemisms of Internment, 40–1; historian as rational, 45–7; interviewees' university experience, 268–9, 277, 278–80, 282; silences encountered, 283–4; statistics on Japanese Canadian education, 269

access to information, 93, 356–7nn63–64. *See also* Library and Archives Canada (LAC)

Adachi, Ken: 1991 afterword, 43; contribution of work of, 4–5, 44; on euphemisms, 39–40; on hospital construction, 210; on labelling Japanese Canadians as docile, 50, 51, 52, 345n20; on the work of BCSC, 331n16

administration of Internment. *See* British Columbia Security Commission (BCSC); Department of Labour (Canada); Japanese Division (Department of Labour)

Agamben, Giorgio, 95–6

age: categorization criterion, 126. *See also* categorization

Ahmed, Sara, 94, 369n52

Alberta: carceral sites in, 112–13, 115; expel Japanese Canadians after 'emergency,' 188; forced labour of sugar beet farm workers, 173–4. *See also* prisoner-of-war camps; road camps; sugar beet farms or projects

Aleuts, 98, 360n20. *See also* Indigenous and Native peoples

alien and aliens: carceral spaces become, 35–6; deportation of, 195 (*see also* repatriation survey); in First World War, 104; in freedom discourse, 30; in Geneva Convention, 116; and intermarriage category, 145; Japanese Canadians and Americans as, 321n3, 323n9; in national identity, 302; spectre of disloyal Japanese, 47–8, 115

Anderson, E.C., 25

Angler POW camp, Ontario, 113, 115–16, 132, 135, 196, *illustration pages. See also* prisoner-of-war camps

385n65. *See also* citizens and citizenship; liberalism; War Measures Act

Department of Labour (Canada): administration of Internment, 19, 23, 26, 174, 330n3, 337n75, 375n29; construction of Japanese Canadian women, 207; cost saving measures, 28; deportation of psychiatrized patients, 212; discourse of choice, 29; Education and Women's Projects, 36; expulsion so-called voluntary, 29, 333n42; Internment and Canadian unity, 20; lexicon of Internment, 24–5; petitions sent to, 131; requests for domestic labour, 189. *See also* British Columbia Security Commission (BCSC); Japanese Division (Department of Labour)

Department of Mines and Resources, 113

Department of National Defence, 113, 119

deportations: after war, 382n36; discourse of choice in, 29, 187, 189; euphemisms for, 24; financial arrangements for, 29, 140; government decision to order, 140, 195; long-term results of, 72, 73–4, 240, 242; numbers, 3–4, 22, 223, 325n6; and permanent dispersal, 140; for protection of white citizens, 19; of psychiatric patients, 211–12. *See also* repatriation survey and Co-operative Committee on Japanese Canadians (CCJC)

detention: use of term, 321n3

detention camps. *See* interior camps (BC)

Detention Island, 38

Dhamoon, Rita, 303

Directorate of Censorship, 24

discourse as concept, 7. *See also* language

disloyalty. *See* loyalty and disloyalty discourse

dispersal, 20, 24. *See also* repatriation survey

Displaced View (Onodera), 74

dispossession, 20, 106–12, 161–2; effect of Internment on non-interned daughters, 260–2. *See also* property stolen/lost; repatriation survey

domestic service placements. *See* employment

Dominion Sugar Refinery, 288, 375n22

Dorey, George, 205–6

Doukhobors, 143, 153–4, 371n89, 372n94, 372n96

Dua, Enakshi, 206, 215

economics of Internment: categories of camps and, 160; cost of correspondence courses, 369n54; critique of Japanese Canadians as benefiting from expulsions, 52–3; discourse of indebtedness, 201–2; Doukhobors and, 153–4; government welfare, deportation, and dispersal rates, 129, 131, 140, 333n40; impoverishment, 129–30; pay for own incarceration, 3, 28, 129, 190–1, 214; property stolen or nominally paid for, 43, 70, 111–12 (*see also* property stolen/lost); of self-support camps, 168–72, 170–1 (*see also* self-support camps or communities); single men supporting families, 374n12; sugar beet farms in, 173–6; in use of mining towns, 27–8; wages for domestic labour, 189; wages of health care workers, 382n27; wages paid for forced labour, 130, 190, 191; welfare administration, 130. *See also* employment; forced labour

education: Christian churches' role in, 35; correspondence courses, 139–40, 170, 369n54; and concept of model minority, 52–3; effect of redress on, 312; effect on employment, 196; forgetting the Internment in, 267–85; funding and responsibility of, 137; of Internment at university, 268–9, 278–81; Internment projects by daughters, 268, 272, 273–4, 277, 283; interviewees' experience of, 139–40, 148, 159–60, 177, 179–80; interviewees' university experience, 268–9, 277, 278–80, 282; of Japanese language, 143, 237, 239; missed opportunities, 241, 269; in *Obasan*, 60; protest letters mentioning, 163; racism in, 186, 288; self-support camps, 168–9, 170; as solution to racism, 44; statistics on Japanese Canadian education, 269; as technology of discipline, 199; tent schools, 244–5; transmitting knowledge of Internment,

discourse, 107; power of, 37, 44, 53–4, 304; production of, 8, 317, 326n25; race as marking Japanese Canadians, 224; and racialized hierarchies, 267–8, 269, 270, 272, 273, 274–6, 277, 278–9; reconstituted in visits to camps, 138–9; and space, 267, 392n4; use of term white, 7, 324n11. *See also* citizens and citizenship (white); colonialism; complicity; race, racism, and racialization; settler nation; witnesses

widows, 153

Wilson, Halford, 44

Winant, Howard, 339n101

Winnipeg: domestic work positions in, 187, 194; interviewee's school experiences, 268; Jewish Canadians, 190; organizing as illegal, 195

witnesses, 304–5, 335n63, 396n5; and bystander guilt, 228; collective forgetting, 55; in constructions of silence, 77–8; government and national project, 7–9; and history of Internment, 277; as participating in property confiscation and theft, 111–12; resistance and complicity, 34, 198; to survivor histories/testimonies, 77, 84, 85, 90, 93–4, 219, 228, 243, 244, 254, 256, 315; as unexamined, 304. *See also* complicity; white and whiteness

women, white middle-class: role in Internment, 36

Women's Missionary Society of the United Church, 204–5

women's organizations: Education and Women's Projects, 36; Japanese Division (Department of Labour), 36, 332n26, 337n77; Nisei Mass Evacuation Women's Group, 70, 118; support of expulsion, 61, 187

Woodward, Kathryn, 328n41

Yamada, Mitsuye, 300

Yamamoto, Traise, 300

yasashi, 62

Yasui, Minoru, 347n47

Years of Infamy (Weglyn), 93

Yeğenoğlu, Meyda, 30, 119–20, 207, 221–2

Yellow-Blue River Highway Project road camps, 112; categorization for, 126

Yogi, Stan, 74

Yonsei (fourth generation): definition of, 323n7; subject constitution by, 73–4; writing about Internment, 249

Yoshida, Shige, 136, 369n48

Young Men's Christian Association, 337n74

Young Women's Christian Association, 187

STUDIES IN GENDER AND HISTORY

General editors: Franca Iacovetta and Karen Dubinsky